Heart to Heart

Heart to Heart

The Spiritual Christology of Joseph Ratzinger

Peter John McGregor

☙PICKWICK *Publications* · Eugene, Oregon

HEART TO HEART
The Spiritual Christology of Joseph Ratzinger

Copyright © 2016 Peter John McGregor. All rights reserved. Except for brief quotations in critical publications or reviews, no part of this book may be reproduced in any manner without prior written permission from the publisher. Write: Permissions, Wipf and Stock Publishers, 199 W. 8th Ave., Suite 3, Eugene, OR 97401.

Pickwick Publications
An Imprint of Wipf and Stock Publishers
199 W. 8th Ave., Suite 3
Eugene, OR 97401

www.wipfandstock.com

PAPERBACK ISBN: 978-1-4982-2413-0
HARDCOVER ISBN: 978-1-4982-2415-4
EBOOK ISBN: 978-1-4982-2414-7

Cataloguing-in-Publication data:

Names: McGregor, Peter John.

Title: Heart to heart : the spiritual christology of Joseph Ratzinger / Peter John McGregor.

Description: Eugene, OR: Pickwick Publications, 2016 | Includes bibliographical references.

Identifiers: ISBN 978-1-4982-2413-0 (softcover) | ISBN 978-1-4982-2415-4 (hardcover) | ISBN 978-1-4982-2414-7 (ebook).

Subjects: LSCH: Benedict XVI, Pope, 1927– Jesus von Nazareth. | Jesus Christ—Person and offices.

Classification: LCC BX1378.6 .M33 2016

Manufactured in the U.S.A.   06/24/16

The Catholic Edition of the Revised Standard Version of the Bible, copyright 1965, 1966 by the Division of Christian Education of the National Council of the Churches of Christ in the United States of America. Used by permission. All rights reserved.

Contents

Preface | vii
Acknowledgments | ix
An Insight on the Way | xi
Abbreviations | xix

Theory
1. Doctor of Reconciliation | 3
2. Prolegomena to a Spiritual Christology | 35
3. The Spiritual Christology of *Behold the Pierced One*—Theory | 62

Theoria
4. Understanding *Jesus of Nazareth* | 101
5. The Spiritual Christology of *Jesus of Nazareth*—Method | 119
6. The Spiritual Christology of *Jesus of Nazareth*—Content | 151
7. Questions about Ratzinger's *Theoria* | 183

Evaluation
8. Assessing Ratzinger's Christological Theses | 201
9. Ratzinger and the Dyothelitism of St. Maximus the Confessor | 225
10. Human Freedom as the Terminus of Ratzinger's Spiritual Christology | 242
11. Ratzinger's Anthropology of the Heart | 279
12. The Symbolic Theology of the Father's Heart | 311
13. The Heart of Jesus in Christ and the Church | 324

Development
14. An Unfinished Symphony—Completing Ratzinger's Spiritual Christology | 339

The Last Homily | 373

Bibliography | 377
Index | 391

Preface

Who is Jesus? This simple question has led to the writing of many books. In surveying them one might feel like the writer of Ecclesiastes and say: "Of making many books [about Christ] there is no end, and much study is a weariness of the flesh" (12:12). Yet here is one more—one about the spiritual Christology of Joseph Ratzinger. What kind of Christology might this be? How does it seek to answer our simple question?

Some attempts to answer our question pose it in this form—can we know anything about Jesus, and, if so, how can we know it? Ratzinger's spiritual Christology does attempt to answer the question in this form. It is, in part, an investigation of what the Sacred Scriptures, the Sacred Liturgy, the Symbols of Faith, the Ecumenical Councils, the Fathers and Doctors, and various other theologians can give in answer to the question in this form. It has been carried out by Ratzinger in the study and the library, and presented in homilies, lectures, papers, journal articles, and books.

Yet, Ratzinger's spiritual Christology is much more than this. It also seeks to answer our question in *this* form—can we know Jesus, and, if so, how can we know him? In this form it has been carried out by Ratzinger in church, chapel and inner room, in private and liturgical prayer, in *lectio divina*, and in the celebration of the sacraments, above all in the celebration of the Eucharist. He has also carried it out in his living of *communio* with his brothers and sisters in Christ. Reports of it have found their way into his writings, most comprehensively in his *Jesus of Nazareth*. This spiritual Christology does not fall within the normal contemporary categories. It is neither objective nor subjective, high nor low, incarnational nor cruciform. Rather, it is personal. It is relational. It is a Christology of participation, of *communio*. It is an exercise in *theoria*, in contemplation. It is a beholding of the Pierced One.

In sharing his spiritual Christology with us, Ratzinger's purpose has been to invite us to join him in this beholding, so that eventually we can say: "It is no longer I who live, but Christ who lives in me" (Gal 2:20). It is an invitation to *theosis*. I hope that this attempt to explain and evaluate his spiritual Christology will go some way towards realizing his intention. I also hope that it will not cause the reader any weariness in the flesh, but rather, give life in the Spirit.

Acknowledgments

I wish to thank the principal supervisor of the doctoral embryo of this book, Dr. Damien Casey of Australian Catholic University, for his availability, advice, and friendly encouragement. I also wish to thank my second supervisor, Professor Tracey Rowland of the John Paul II Institute for Marriage and the Family, for the same reasons, as well as for sharing with me her expertise in the theology of Joseph Ratzinger, and especially for her companionship over the whole course of this odyssey, from the day I first knocked on her door seeking a topic.

My thanks go also to Dr. Adam Cooper (John Paul II Institute for Marriage and the Family), Professor Matthew Levering (Mundelein Seminary), Dr. Aaron Riches (Instituto de Filosofía Edith Stein), and Dr. Robert Tilley (Catholic Institute of Sydney), for their thoughtful comments upon this work in its various incarnations.

I also wish to thank Dr. Christopher Ben Simpson, the editor of *Radical Orthodoxy: Theology, Philosophy, Politics*, for publishing earlier versions of parts of this book in that journal.

Material in "Insight on the way," and chapters one, three, five, six, seven, and fourteen also appear in Peter John McGregor, "Is there a Pneumatological Lacuna in the 'Spiritual Christology' of Joseph Ratzinger, *Pro Ecclesia*, 25 (2) 2016: 200–219. This article was accepted for publication shortly before the publication of this book.

Finally, I wish to dedicate this book to my wife, Mary, for her long-suffering patience, unflagging encouragement, meticulous proof-reading, and for going out to "win the bread" so that I could study full-time. Without her this book would not have been written.

An Insight on the Way

In *Behold the Pierced One*, a collection of christological addresses and homilies published in 1984, Joseph Ratzinger recounts how the composition of one of these addresses, a 1981 paper on the Sacred Heart of Jesus, had led him to "consider Christology more from the aspect of its spiritual appropriation" than he had done previously. Upon realizing that this same year was the 1300th anniversary of the Third Council of Constantinople, he decided to study the pronouncements of this council, and came to believe, "much to [his] astonishment, that the achievement of a spiritual Christology had also been the Council's ultimate goal, and that it was only from this point of view that the classical formulas of Chalcedon appear in the proper perspective."[1] Ratzinger's conclusion in attempting to define a spiritual Christology was that "the whole of Christology—our speaking of Christ—is nothing other than the interpretation of his prayer: the entire person of Jesus is contained in his prayer."[2]

What Is Ratzinger's Spiritual Christology?

Ratzinger's spiritual Christology is composed of three elements: seven christological theses, a theology of the heart, and a eucharistic spirituality. All three elements are to be found in *Behold the Pierced One*. The theses delineate his spiritual Christology. In order to arrive at an authentic Christology, they outline "certain fundamental characteristics of the indivisible unity of Jesus and Christ, Church and history."[3] Ratzinger simply numbers his theses one to seven. Herein, they have been named for the sake of easier identification. The first "filial" thesis is that the center of Jesus' life and

---

1. *Behold*, 9. The paper referred to commemorates the twenty-fifth anniversary of Pope Pius XII's encyclical on the Sacred Heart, *Haurietis aquas*.
2. Ibid., 20.
3. Ibid., 15.

person is his intimate communion with the Father, his prayer. The second "soteriological" thesis is that Jesus died praying. Who he is (Christology) and what he does (soteriology) come together in his sacrificial offering of himself on the Cross. The third "personal" thesis is that since prayer is the center of the person of Jesus "it is essential to participate in his prayer if we are to know and understand him." The fourth "ecclesial" thesis is that "sharing in Jesus' praying requires communion with all his brethren." The fifth "dogmatic" thesis is that the teaching of Chalcedon faithfully interprets the data of biblical Christology. The sixth "volitional" thesis is that it is only the teaching of Constantinople III regarding the will of Jesus which enables the dogma of Chalcedon to yield its full meaning. The seventh "hermeneutical" thesis is that only a hermeneutic of faith is able to "hold fast [to] the entire testimony of the sources" and overcome the temporal, cultural and national differences between people. Ratzinger's conclusion to his theses is that: "Christology is born of prayer or not at all."[4]

An analysis of these seven theses reveals that four of them—the filial, soteriological, dogmatic, and volitional—constitute the content of Ratzinger's spiritual Christology. The remaining personal, ecclesial, and hermeneutical theses are methodological.

The second element, a theology of the heart, also has its content and method. The content is—an anthropology of the human heart, a theology of the Father's heart, and a Christology and ecclesiology of the heart of Jesus.[5] Ratzinger's anthropology of the heart, rather than treating the heart as identical with the human person or as a particular faculty of the person, treats it as the integrating principle of the person. This anthropology is drawn from the presentation of the heart in Sacred Scripture as well as Stoic philosophy, and the teachings of Origen, St. Augustine, Blaise Pascal, Bl. John Henry Newman, and Romano Guardini. Ratzinger's theology of the Father's heart privileges the symbolic theology of images over the rational theology of concepts. This theology proposes that the bodily image of the heart gives us a greater insight into the nature of God's heart than do concepts. Ratzinger's Christology and ecclesiology of the heart of Jesus develop a synthetic biblical/Stoic understanding of this heart rather than following an analytic Thomistic/Platonic one.

The method of this element is *theoria* (contemplation). This *theoria* is not just an activity of the mind, but of the heart. It is a heart to heart beholding—the believer's heart beholding the pierced heart of Jesus, who, since he is the one nearest to the Father's heart, reveals that heart in his own. Nor is it

---

4. The seven theses are explained on pages 15–46 of *Behold*.
5. Ibid., 47–69.

an isolated beholding. It is a personal beholding in a corporate personality, the Body of Christ. The prerequisite for this beholding is a pure heart.

The third element is a eucharistic one.[6] This too has its content and method. The content is that the core of eucharistic spirituality and ecclesial spirituality is to be found in the communion between the divine and the human found in the Incarnate Word. In the Word, human nature has been assumed into the being of God. When one receives Jesus in the Eucharist, one enters into a community of being with him, a communion which is a precondition of communion between human beings. Grasping the spirituality of the Eucharist means grasping "the spiritual tension which marks the God-man: only in the context of a spiritual Christology will the spirituality of the sacrament reveal itself."[7] The method of this element is *communio*. It is participation in the celebration of the Eucharist, and the continuation of the *koinonia* of the Eucharist through devotions such as adoration of the Blessed Sacrament, and through continuing to love the brethren, especially the poor. In *Behold the Pierced One* these three elements are not integrated but treated separately.

We shall see that Ratzinger's spiritual Christology is neither high nor low, but one of *communio*. It is one of participation. Indeed, it is one of *theosis*. Through a personal and ecclesial participation in the prayer of Jesus, exercised in purity of heart, and consummated in the eucharistic celebration, one comes into communion with Jesus Christ and all the members of his Body, so that eventually one can say truly: "It is no longer I who live, but Christ who lives in me" (Gal 2:20).

How Did Ratzinger's Spiritual Christology Develop?

Ratzinger's statement that his 1981 paper on the Sacred Heart had led him to consider Christology *more* from the aspect of its spiritual appropriation than previously would seem to indicate that he had already given *some* consideration to this aspect of Christology. This is exactly what an investigation of his earlier Christology reveals.

For Ratzinger, authentic theology "understands itself as interpreting the common faith of the Church."[8] In the case of his earlier Christology, the content of an authentic Christology is the faith of the church as encapsulated in the christological articles of the Creed. Its method is the rational investigation of the Christian faith. Ratzinger's Christology is not to be

6. Ibid., 71–100.
7. Ibid., 90.
8. Ibid., 15.

found in a systematic treatise, but primarily in the christological sections of *Introduction to Christianity* (1968), and *The God of Jesus Christ* (1976). Yet, this earlier Christology also contains aspects of Ratzinger's later spiritual Christology, although expressed in an inchoate way. In the case of its first element, in *Introduction to Christianity*, one finds him emphasizing the importance of the prayer of the Son in the Christology of the Gospel according to John. In *The God of Jesus Christ*, he characterizes the Incarnation of the Son as an act of prayer.[9] In the same work he maintains that the prayer of Jesus in the Gospel according to Luke is the central christological category of that gospel. Regarding its second element, one can discern an anthropological prolegomenon to Ratzinger's theology of the heart in his commentary on the first part of *Gaudium et spes* (1969). Finally, in *Eucharistie: Mitte der Kirche* (1978), in a sermon entitled "The Eucharist as the Wellspring of Life," elements of a Christology and ecclesiology of the heart of Jesus, in connection with a eucharistic spirituality, make their appearance.

On the development of his spiritual Christology, Ratzinger remarked: "I had no time [in 1981] to make a study of this particular theme, but the thought of a spiritual Christology remained with me and found its way into other works."[10] The essential theory of this spiritual Christology is to be found in three papers given by Ratzinger between 1981 and 1983, collected into the first part of *Behold the Pierced One*, each paper outlining one of the elements of this spiritual Christology. One is the 1981 paper on the Sacred Heart referred to already. Another is an address given in 1982 to a congress on Christology, wherein one finds the seven christological theses. The third is a paper on the connection between the Eucharist, parish community and the mission of the church, wherein one finds the eucharistic spirituality.

Besides the papers referred to above, some of the "other works" are three homilies which Ratzinger includes in the second part of *Behold the Pierced One*. Subsequent to 1983, one can perceive instances of Ratzinger's spiritual Christology in many other works, including his *Principles of Catholic Theology*, *The Nature and Mission of Theology*, *Verbum Domini*, *Spe salvi*, *A New Song for the Lord*, *The Spirit of the Liturgy* and *God is Near Us*. However, the most comprehensive presentation of it is to be found in his three-volume *Jesus of Nazareth*, and in *Deus caritas est* and *Sacramentum caritatis*.

There has been much disagreement about the nature of *Jesus of Nazareth*. Is it exegesis or biblical theology? Is it scholarship or devotion? Herein it will be argued that it is, in fact, an exercise in *theoria*, in contemplating the Pierced One. Within it one can discern the seven christological theses being

---

9. Ratzinger makes the same point in his *Principles of Catholic Theology*, 20.
10. *Behold*, 9.

applied in the various meditations upon the mysteries of Jesus' life. This *theoria* is not just an activity of the mind, but of the heart. Whereas in *Behold the Pierced One* the three elements of Ratzinger's spiritual Christology are presented separately, in *Jesus of Nazareth* the application of Ratzinger's christological theses and his theology of the heart are woven together. What then of the eucharistic element of Ratzinger's spiritual Christology? Although intimations of it can be found in *Jesus of Nazareth*, the main places to find it being given expression are the encyclical *Deus caritas est* and the apostolic exhortation *Sacramentum caritatis*.

Why Is Ratzinger's Spiritual Christology Important?

In 1979, the International Theological Commission asserted that the quest for the historical Jesus carried out by some biblical scholars, combined with a tendency to make our humanity the prime analogate of Christ's humanity, was leading towards a certain dualism in Christology. The Commission encouraged Catholic theologians to overcome this dualistic separation between the "Jesus of history" and the "glorified Christ" by turning towards the dyothelitism of Constantinople III in order to reassert the intrinsic unity of divinity and humanity in Christ.[11]

Overcoming this dualism has been a fundamental goal in Ratzinger's christological reflections. He himself has characterized this debate, sometimes framed in terms of a high Christology which emphasizes the divinity of Christ versus a low Christology which emphasizes his humanity, as being focused on questions about the relation between christological dogma and the testimony of Sacred Scripture, between biblical Christology and the real historical Jesus, and between Jesus and the church.[12] Ratzinger thinks that the penchant of some for speaking of "Jesus" rather than "Christ" "reveals a spiritual process with wide implications, namely, the attempt to get behind the Church's confession of faith and reach the purely historical figure of Jesus."[13] A faithfulness to Jesus which has no place for the church is the result of this division between the Jesus of (the theologian's) history and the Christ of (the church's) faith. According to Ratzinger: "This in turn goes be-

---

11. See "Selected Questions on Christology," 185–206. Ratzinger was a member of the Commission which drafted the document. Constantinople III taught that Christ had two wills, one human and the other divine (dyotheletism), not just one, the divine. See Denzinger, nos. 553–59. Aaron Riches draws attention to the significance of "Selected Questions on Christology" for suggesting a way out of the impasse between the Jesus of history and the Christ of faith. See Riches, "After Chalcedon," 201–3.

12. *Behold*, 13–14.

13. Ibid., 14.

yond Christology and affects soteriology, which must necessarily undergo a similar transformation. Instead of 'salvation' we find 'liberation' taking pride of place . . . [which] automatically adopts a critical stance over against the classical doctrine of how man becomes a partaker of grace."[14] By contrast, for Ratzinger, authentic theology "understands itself as interpreting the common faith of the Church, not as reconstructing a vanished Jesus, at long last piecing together his real history."[15] He sees his task as presenting "in some way the inner totality and unity . . . of Christology . . . [since] the loss of a total view is the real central problem of the contemporary christological debate."[16]

Ratzinger's response to this debate has been to seek to overcome *every* dualism in Christology. Here dualism means elements of Christology which have been set in opposition to or isolated from each other. Not, for example, the valid duality of the two natures of Christ. These sundered elements Ratzinger seeks to reintegrate. The dualisms which he seeks to overcome include the contemporary ones mentioned above, as well as a more longstanding one, namely, that of a theology of the Incarnation and a theology of the Cross, which also could be identified as a separation between Christology and soteriology. Besides this, he has worked to expose the basis of these dualisms, which he sees as the division between ontology and history, or as he also puts it, the separation of being from act.[17]

Ratzinger's desire to overcome every dualism reaches beyond Christology to theology as a whole. Indeed, the dualisms in Christology cannot be overcome in isolation. These dualisms are part of a larger division between theology and anthropology, which various theological anthropologies have sought to overcome.

Yet, Ratzinger seeks to overcome an even deeper dualism. According to him, since Vatican II, the axis of theological debate has shifted from particular *quaestiones disputatae* to the very nature of theology itself.[18] As he sees it, there has arisen a fundamental opposition in the practice of theology, that between spirituality and theology. He sees much contemporary theology as having become de-spiritualized. One of his aims in developing a spiritual Christology has been to overcome *this* dualism, a division between contemplative and systematic theology, between what he calls a "theology of the heart" and a "theology of reason." Related to this dualism is that which

14. Ibid.
15. Ibid., 15.
16. Ibid., 13.
17. Ratzinger, *Principles of Catholic Theology*, 153–90.
18. *Behold*, 13.

divides Christians, supposedly, into theologians and non-theologians. As Ratzinger sees it, this is a false dichotomy. Theology is not the preserve of a Christian *intelligentsia*. All Christians are called to be theologians.

As a part of his spiritual Christology, Ratzinger seeks to overcome not a dualism, but a disintegration of the Christian who theologizes. This disintegration is both individual and corporate. Rather than being an activity that is purely intellectual, theologizing is one which engages the whole human person—intellect, will, body, and emotions. For Ratzinger, the place of integration is the "heart." This human heart, in turn, must be integrated with the "heart" of God, an integration which takes place in the "heart" of Jesus. Finally, the heart of the individual believer must be integrated with those of all other believers. This integration too takes place in the heart of Jesus, made present for us in the Eucharist.

A Roadmap for this Investigation

The essential aims of this investigation are to reveal the content and method of Ratzinger's spiritual Christology, demonstrate how he applies method to content, assess the integrity and validity of the resulting Christology, and attempt, in a modest way, to develop it.

This work is divided into four sections—theory, *theoria*, evaluation, and development. In the theory section, chapter 1 briefly presents Ratzinger's earlier Christology in order to give a context for his spiritual Christology, and to enable us to see what continuities or discontinuities might be found in this Christology vis-à-vis his earlier Christology. It includes an assessment of various critiques which have been made of his earlier Christology. Chapter 2 gives an account of the embryonic presence of Ratzinger's spiritual Christology in his earlier Christology. Chapter 3 analyzes the theory of Ratzinger's spiritual Christology as set out in *Behold the Pierced One*. After a brief account of extant explanations of his spiritual Christology, it expounds and analyzes its three elements.

In the *theoria* section, chapter 4 examines various critiques of *Jesus of Nazareth*, concluding with a presentation of its purpose. Chapter 5 presents the method of Ratzinger's spiritual Christology as practiced in *Jesus of Nazareth*—how Ratzinger applies his three methodological theses to the mysteries of Jesus' life. Chapter 6 shows how he applies the four content theses and his theology of the heart to the various meditations upon the mysteries of Jesus' life contained in that work. Chapter 7 addresses a number of questions raised by critiques of *Jesus of Nazareth*, looks at two *lacunae* in Ratzinger's spiritual Christology, and also investigates the aspect of Ratzinger's spiritual Christology which is largely absent from *Jesus of Nazareth*, but is to be found in *Deus caritas est* and *Sacramentum caritatis*, his eucharistic spirituality.

In the evaluation section, chapter 8 gives an assessment of Ratzinger's christological theses, beginning with the three methodological theses, followed by the four content theses. Chapter 9 critiques Ratzinger's use of the dyothelitism of St. Maximus the Confessor. Chapter 10 seeks to establish that freedom is the ultimate goal of Ratzinger's spiritual Christology. Chapter 11 assesses his anthropology of the human heart, chapter 12 his theology of the Father's heart, and chapter 13 his Christology and ecclesiology of the heart of Jesus.

The development section, chapter 14, finishes with an assessment of the degree to which Ratzinger's spiritual Christology is complete and integrated. Finding that Ratzinger's spiritual Christology is incomplete, an unfinished symphony as it were, an attempt is made to develop further its "cardiacal," "pneumatological," and "eucharistic" potentialities. The final chapter should be regarded as a reconnaissance in force rather than a grand offensive.

It has been a daunting task to analyze and critique the work of such a consummate theologian as Joseph Ratzinger. Given the lucidity and clarity of his prose, I have tried herein to let him speak for himself as much as possible. I offer what follows as a contribution to the conversation about the value of Ratzinger's theological endeavors in the service of Christ, the church, and the world to which the church is sent. I hope that it will stimulate further discussion about the possibilities opened up by a spiritual Christology for the life and mission of the church.

Abbreviations

Church Documents

CCC	*Catechism of the Catholic Church*
DCE	*Deus caritas est*
Denzinger	*Enchiridion symbolorum definitionum et declarationum de rebus fidei et morum*
DV	*Dei Verbum*
GS	*Gaudium et spes*
HA	Encyclical Letter *Haurietis aquas* (Catholic Truth Society edition)
SC	*Sacramentum caritatis*
SS	*Spe salvi*
VD	*Verbum Domini*
Vatican II	*The Documents of Vatican II with Notes and Index: Vatican Translation*

Other Documents

Behold	*Behold the Pierced One*
Bockmuehl	"Saints' Lives as Exegesis"
"Church and Man's"	"The Church and Man's Calling—The Dignity of the Human Person—Pastoral Constitution on the Church in the Modern World"
DP	*Disputation with Pyrrhus*

Abbreviations

Jesus I	*Jesus of Nazareth: From the Baptism in the Jordan to the Transfiguration*
Jesus II	*Jesus of Nazareth: Holy Week*
Introduction	*Introduction to Christianity*
Jesus Christ	*The God of Jesus Christ*
McFarland	*"'Willing is not Choosing': Some Anthropological Implications of Dyothelite Christology"*
PG	*Patrologia Graeca*
PL	*Patrologia Latina*
OTP	*Opuscula et Polemica*
ST	*Summa Theologica*

Theory

1

Doctor of Reconciliation

In order to gain a more thorough understanding of Ratzinger's spiritual Christology, it is necessary to investigate the seedbed within which it germinates—his earlier Christology. Later this will enable us to find substantial continuities between the two, and a couple of discontinuities. We shall also find that his earlier Christology contains one *lacuna*—the substantial absence of the Holy Spirit.

The Problems Faced by Pre-1968 Christology according to Ratzinger

The mention of "1968" may lead one to jump to certain conclusions. However, the date is coincidental. It is simply that of the publication of *Einführung in das Christentum* (*Introduction to Christianity*). In Ratzinger's earlier Christology, as set out in this work, the investigation of who Jesus is does not begin with an analysis of what Sacred Scripture says about him, but with the Apostles' Creed: "I believe in Jesus Christ, his only Son, our Lord." Ratzinger's starting point is the church's profession of faith, that the man Jesus is the Christ of God, his own Son. For Ratzinger, the second article of this Creed "proclaims the absolutely staggering alliance of *logos* and *sarx*, of meaning and a single historical figure."[1] This alliance is not only of word and flesh, but of faith and history, since: "The historical man Jesus is the Son of God, and the Son of God is the man Jesus."[2]

---

1. *Introduction*, 193. Cf. Collins, *The Word Made Love*, 71–72.
2. *Introduction*, 194.

Theory

Faith in Jesus Christ and the Difficulties Raised by "Positivism"

However, confronting this faith in a single historical figure, Ratzinger sees a mental obstacle which he calls "positivism." According to him, this obstacle is endemic to human reasoning, but it has been intensified by the modern rejection of metaphysics in favor of physics, a renunciation of the investigation of being itself for that of what can be demonstrated by the scientific method. This leads to the rejection of the possibility of knowing ontological truth, leading in turn to a philosophical retreat into phenomenology, the investigation of appearances.[3]

According to Ratzinger, the historical-critical method is an adaptation of this methodology, bearing in mind that historical studies cannot reach the same degree of certainty as can be reached by empirical experimentation. Strictly speaking, one should say historical-critical *methods*. However, these methods are often referred to in the singular. Like the natural sciences, this methodology can reveal only the phenomenal aspect of what has happened in past history. Also, while this scientific approach can lead to greater historical accuracy, it suffers from a serious limitation. Its data are limited to what written documents happen to have survived, and are therefore incomplete. The temptation is to treat this incomplete picture as complete. Any past event which cannot be tested and passed by this method is rejected as invalid. The method can investigate documentary evidence about a man called Jesus, but it cannot tell us from this evidence if he is the Christ.[4]

The Dilemma Created by the Historical-Critical Method

Ratzinger holds that the historical-critical method tends to divide faith from history. This has led to two different attempts to find a secure basis for Christology. The first is that typified by Wolfhart Pannenberg, whereby historical investigation is seen as being capable of getting behind the demonstrable (phenomenal) in order to establish an accurate picture of Jesus, one which perceives not just the facts about him, but his significance. A variation of this, exemplified by Adolf von Harnack, limits itself to the demonstrable. Ratzinger dismisses these attempts as imperfect. Historical investigation can only arrive at the demonstrable, but since we do not have all the data, the gaps in our knowledge are closed by the personal opinion of the scholar. The failure of this approach leads to a second course, pioneered

---

3. Ibid., 194–95.
4. Ibid., 195–96.

by Rudolf Bultmann, which abandons the historical altogether and confines itself to the idea or the kerygma.[5] As Ratzinger states:

> The dilemma of the two courses—on the one hand, that of transposing or reducing Christology to history and, on the other, that of escaping history completely and abandoning it as irrelevant to faith—could be quite accurately summarized in the two alternatives by which modern theology is vexed: Jesus or Christ? Modern theology begins by turning away from Christ and taking refuge in Jesus as a figure who is historically comprehensible, only to make an about-turn at the climax of this movement . . . and flee in the opposite direction back to Christ, a flight, however, that at the present moment is already starting to change back into the new flight from Christ to Jesus.[6]

For Ratzinger, this shuttling back and forth between Jesus and Christ is a very useful pointer to the fact that "Jesus" cannot exist without "Christ," and that "one is bound to be continually pushed from one to the other because in reality Jesus only subsists as Christ and the Christ only subsists in the shape of Jesus."[7] Ratzinger's solution to this supposed dilemma is to recognize these two courses as theories, or reconstructions, which are supplementary artificial creations. The firm foundation for Christology is the Christian faith, which is neither a theory nor a reconstruction, but "a present, living reality," a phenomenon which has always aimed at "understanding who and what Jesus really was."[8] It is in order to enable the rediscovery of the authentic Jesus that Ratzinger eventually proposes the development of a spiritual Christology. We should note that the above critique is only of what is called the "first Quest" for the historical Jesus, the reaction to it, and the "second Quest."

Jesus Is the Christ: The Foundation of Ratzinger's Christology

The Identification of Office/Work/Teaching and Person in Jesus Christ

How does the Christian faith understand who and what Jesus really was? Ratzinger initially looks for the answer to this question in the Creed. He

5. Ibid., 196–98.
6. Ibid., 198.
7. Ibid., 201.
8. Ibid., 201–2.

notes that in the Apostles' Creed the word "Christ" is still the title of an office. It is becoming but has not yet entirely become a proper name.

> [This becoming] spotlights the very heart of that process of understanding that the faith went through with regard to the figure of Nazareth. For what faith really states is precisely that, with Jesus, it is not possible to distinguish office and person . . . The person is the office and the office is the person.[9]

Jesus does not possess a private, off-duty aspect of himself. Nor did he leave behind a body of teaching that could be separated from himself. Ratzinger makes the point that the Creed contains no teachings of Jesus. Faith understands that Jesus has put himself into his work and word. Thus:

> Here there is no "I" . . . that utters words; he has identified himself so closely with his word that "I" and word are indistinguishable: he *is* word. In the same way, to faith, his work is nothing else than the unreserved way in which he merges himself into this very work; he performs *himself* and gives himself; his work is the giving of himself . . . In other words, faith's decisive statement about Jesus lies in the indivisible unity of the two words "Jesus Christ," a unity that conceals the experience of the identity of existence and mission.[10]

Thus faith in Jesus Christ is a personal faith. Rather than faith in a system or a body of teaching, it is faith in a person who *is* his word.

The Cross as the Taproot for Faith in Jesus Christ

Although Ratzinger asserts that the church answers the question of who and what Jesus was in the Apostles' Creed, he also asserts the need to go back beyond this Creed in order to reach the origin of the Christian faith. For him it is an established fact that "the birthplace of the faith in Jesus as the Christ, that is, the birthplace of 'Christ'-ian faith as a whole, is the Cross."[11] For Ratzinger, it was not Jesus who declared himself to be the Messiah, but Pilate, in the execution notice which he had fastened to the Cross. For the first Christians, Pilate's ironic declaration became their fundamental profession of faith—that this man executed as a criminal was indeed the King, the Messiah. According to Ratzinger, Christ's crucifixion is his coronation, and

---

9. Ibid., 203.
10. Ibid., 203–4.
11. Ibid., 205.

his kingship is his surrender of himself to us. In him, word, mission and existence are identified in the yielding up of this existence.

> His existence is thus his word. He *is* word because he is love. From the Cross faith understands in increasing measure that this Jesus did not just do and say *something*; that in him message and person are identical, that he is all along what he says. John needs only to draw the final straightforward inference: if that is so—and this is the Christological basis of his Gospel—then this Jesus Christ is "word"; but a person who not only *has* words but *is* his word and his work, who is the *logos* ("the Word," meaning, mind) itself; that person has always existed and will always exist; he is the ground on which the world stands—if we ever meet such a person, then he is the meaning that comprises us all and by which we are all sustained.[12]

Ratzinger holds that the reality of the Cross caused the first Christians to identify the person, word and work of Jesus as being one reality. Thus to say that Jesus was the Christ became a simple, but valid, profession of faith. This was followed by a second step. In the light of this understanding Christians looked back on the words of Jesus. As Ratzinger asserts, there they found that if one studies the words of Jesus one will find that they always lead to and flow from his "I" into the identity of word and person. Ratzinger further asserts that it was John the Evangelist who was able to make the link between "word" and "person." His Gospel is "the thorough reading of the words of Jesus from the angle of the person and of the person from the words." John "treats 'Christology,' the assertion of faith in Christ, as the message of the story of Jesus and, vice-versa, the story of Jesus as Christology indicates the complete unity of Christ and Jesus, a unity that is and remains formative for the whole further history of faith."[13]

In the light of these assertions, Ratzinger reassesses the aforementioned attempts to find a secure basis for Christology. He declares that, to a point, one can follow Bultmann. One can focus on the fact of Jesus' existence, "a fusion of the fact of Jesus with faith in the Christ."[14] Furthermore, the challenge delivered by von Harnack: "Not the Son but only the Father belongs in the Gospel as Jesus preached it," can also be revisited.[15] Christology need not exclude the message about God the Father. It need not find a

---

12. Ibid., 206.
13. Ibid., 207.
14. Ibid.
15. Harnack, *Das Wesen des Christentums*, 86. Cf. Razinger, *Introduction*, 198–99 and 207–8.

contradiction between faith in Christ and "the love of all men that oversteps and surmounts the boundaries of faith."[16] To grasp the total oneness of person and work in Jesus is to abandon the dialectic between faith and love. The sacrifice of Jesus shows that his "I" "is Being completely derived from the 'Thou' of the Father and lived for the 'You' of men. It is the identity of *logos* (truth) and love and thus makes love into the *logos*, the truth of human existence."[17] As Ratzinger states:

> [the Matthean interpretation in Matt 25] of the christological profession of faith into the unconditionality of human service and mutual help is not to be regarded, after what we have said, as an escape from otherwise prevailing dogma; it is in truth the logical consequence of the hyphen between Jesus and Christ and, therefore, comes right from the heart of Christology itself.[18]

Jesus Christ: True God and True Man

The Formulation of the Dogma

In turning to the dogma that Jesus is true God and true man, Ratzinger maintains that this dogma is not simply about ideas or an independent body of teaching, but concerns "the 'I' of Jesus, [and] leads toward an 'I' that is complete openness, all 'Word,' all 'Son.'"[19] These concepts are meant to convey the dynamic character of Jesus' existence. Words always come "from" someone and are uttered "for" someone. The same can be said of sons. In Ratzinger's formulation of the Christian faith the central focus is not an idea but a person, an "I" who is defined as "word" and "son," and hence as "total openness." This brings to light the drama of faith in Jesus as the Christ, and its necessary historical development into faith in Jesus as the divine Son of God.[20]

However, this formulation also brings to light three questions for Ratzinger. First, if this "I," who is pure openness, totally deriving his being from the Father, one whose whole existence is as "Son," must this person not only *have* love but *be* love, and therefore be identical with God, who alone is love? Second, if Jesus is all that he does, the one who has sacrificed himself completely for others, is he not the most human of us, the fulfillment of what

---

16. *Introduction*, 208.
17. Ibid.
18. Ibid., 209.
19. Ibid., 210.
20. Ibid., 210–11. Cf. 149–50 and 184–90.

it means to be human? In other words, these first two questions seem to present a choice between resolving Christology into either theology or anthropology. Third, "should the real man, precisely because he *is* wholly and properly such, be God, and God be the real man? Ought it to be possible for the most radical humanism and faith in the God who reveals himself to meet and even merge here?"[21]

Ratzinger asserts that the ecumenical councils of Christianity's first five centuries answered each of these questions in the affirmative. In the developed christological dogma "the radical Christship of Jesus presupposes the Sonship and . . . the Sonship includes the Godship."[22] Thus the dogma remains "*logos*-like," logically consistent, a rational statement, while at the same time acknowledging "that in the radicality of his service Jesus is the most human of men, the true man, and [the dogma] thus subscribes to the coincidence of theology and anthropology."[23]

Ratzinger recognizes that this position can be, and often is, categorized as being idealistic and pre-critical. He acknowledges that "we must ask whether the findings of the Bible and its critical illumination of the facts empower us to conceive the Sonship of Jesus in the way we have just done and in the way christological dogma does." However, he asserts that an acceptance of the approach he has outlined, which he describes as the biblical faith in the Son as expounded in the early Church, is necessary to avoid "rationalistic trivialities or mythological son-ideas."[24]

The False Historical Jesus

Before delving deeper into the fundamental christological dogma, Ratzinger sketches a vignette of a "historical Jesus" which he claims to be widespread. This Jesus was an eschatological prophet who preached the proximity of the Kingdom of God. However, his first interpreters emphasized the "now" of this kingdom, the need to make a decision about establishing this kingdom in the present. Although dying a failure, his teaching somehow became concretized in a belief that he himself was in some way "risen," and would return in the future as the Son of Man, the Messiah. This hope in a coming kingdom was then projected back onto the historical Jesus. When this belief travelled from a Semitic to a Greek world, the categories of Son of Man and Messiah, incomprehensible to the Greek mind, were replaced by those of

21. Ibid., 211.
22. Ibid.
23. Ibid., 211–12.
24. Ibid., 212.

"divine person" and "God-man." Since the Hellenic God-man, demi-god, and demi-man was a miracle worker of divine origin, miracles were now ascribed to the historical Jesus. Since he must be of divine origin, the "myth" of the Virgin Birth was added to the picture. Finally, this myth became the Chalcedonian concept of the ontological divine sonship of Jesus.[25] According to Ratzinger, this whole picture is false. The concept of the divine man or God-man is not to be found in the New Testament. Nor is the Hellenistic divine man ever described as the "Son of God." The Bible knows nothing of a divine man, and the Greeks had no concept of a Son of God. There was no connection between the two in either language or conceptual content.[26] For Ratzinger, this false historical Jesus is neither the Christ nor the true Son of God.

Son of God

Having looked at how Jesus is the Christ, Ratzinger takes up the dogmatic identification of Jesus as Son of God and seeks to ground it in biblical terminology. He immediately makes the point that there are actually two designations which must be analyzed, designations which bear a resemblance to each other but which, in fact, "belong to quite different contexts, have different origins, and express different things."[27] They are Son of God, and simply, Son.

Ratzinger claims that: "The expression 'Son of God' stems from the 'king' theology of the Old Testament, which itself rests upon the demythologization of oriental 'king' theology and expresses its transformation into the 'Chosen People' theology of Israel."[28] The Davidic court set the mythological sense aside and replaced it with the idea that the king became "son of God" through election by God rather than procreation by him. This idea was a concentrated form of the whole theology of the Chosen People. In the successor of David the whole of Israel's vocation was summed up.[29]

According to Ratzinger, the classic example of this development and identification is Psalm 2:7: "You are my son, today I have begotten you. Ask of me, and I will make the nations your heritage, and the ends of the earth your possession." Given the incongruity of the later proclamation in the

25. Ibid., 213–15.
26. Ibid., 215–16. Ratzinger claims that the concept of a divine man "can hardly be attested in the pre-Christian period but only turns up later" (216).
27. Ibid., 216.
28. Ibid.
29. Ibid., 216–17.

light of the actual situation of the king of Judah, it was inevitable that this verse be interpreted as a promise for the future. Thus the theology moves from being one of begetting to one of election, until it finally becomes a theology of hope in a king to come.[30] Ratzinger holds that the original Christian community probably applied these words of the Psalm to Jesus' Resurrection. Israel's hope is fulfilled in the one who died on the Cross. This leads to a radical reinterpretation of the nature of kingship. In the crucified Christ the meaning of being chosen is revealed to be that of being chosen for the service of others. Furthermore, the true meaning of kingship is not ruling but "representation," standing in the place of others. This New Testament development of the Son of God idea is the second stage in the demythologization of the oriental concept of kingship which had begun in the Old Testament.[31]

Finally, the development of this theology led to the intertwining of the idea of the royal Son of God as servant, exemplified in Philippians 2:5-11.[32] The one who became the servant of all, who emptied himself for others, in doing so, has become the Lord of all.

Ratzinger concludes his account of the development of the Son of God theology by pointing out that the true parallel for Son of God in the Graeco-Roman world was not the "divine man" but the "divine Augustus." It is in the cult of the Roman emperor that we find a return of the oriental concept of monarchy. Thus both the Christian and the imperial understanding of Son of God spring from the same root—the former being demythologized myth and the latter remaining myth.[33]

Son

Unlike Son of God, for Ratzinger, "Son" is Jesus' self-description. It is founded upon what Ratzinger calls the language of the "coded parable," and is to be found in Jesus' private conversations with the inner circle of disciples rather than his public preaching.[34] For Ratzinger, the probable source or this term is the prayer of Jesus. "Son" forms the natural corollary to "*Abba.*" Ratzinger agrees with Joachim Jeremias' proposition that the words of Jesus handed down to us in Aramaic are a good indication of Jesus' original

---

30. Ibid., 218.
31. Ibid., 218–20.
32. Ibid., 220.
33. Ibid., 221–23.
34. Ibid., 223.

mode of speech.[35] Such intimate familiarity with God would not have been possible for a Jew. It expressed an intimacy with God which was unique to Jesus. For Ratzinger, *Abba* and Son "express the distinctive way in which Jesus prayed, his awareness of God, into which . . . he let his closest circle of friends have an insight."[36] Unlike Son of God, this self-description of Jesus is completely new—something much more simple, personal and profound. As an insight into Jesus' experience of prayer, it reveals a nearness to God which is unique to him, but one in which he wishes to incorporate others so that they too can experience the intimacy of knowing God as *Abba*.[37]

According to Ratzinger, it is John who gives center stage to this self-description of Jesus. That which in the Synoptics was reserved for catechetical moments with the disciples becomes the heart of John's portrait of Jesus. Son is the "guiding thread" of John's depiction of Jesus. It reveals the total relativity of his existence—"being from" and "being for." It is identical with the designations "Word" and "the one sent." In describing Jesus as "I am," he is shown to be in total unity with God because of his self-surrender. Ratzinger concludes:

> The heart of this Son-Christology of John's, the basis of which in the synoptic Gospels and through them in the historical Jesus (*Abba*!) was made plain earlier, lies accordingly in what became clear to us at the outset as being the starting point of all Christology: in the identity of work and being, of deed and person, of the total merging of the person in his work and in the total coincidence of the doing with the person himself, who keeps back nothing for himself but gives himself completely in his work.[38]

Ratzinger holds that John "ontologizes" the "phenomenal" character of what Jesus says and does. These phenomena reveal the truth about his being—that he is Son, Word and mission. This ontological dimension of Jesus does not replace "the Christology of service with any kind of triumphalist Christology of glorification."[39] Rather, Jesus is "servant" not just in his actions but in his being itself—and because Jesus is nothing but service, he is Son. The anthropological conclusion to be drawn from this is that "he who surrenders himself completely to the service of others, to complete selflessness and self-emptying, literally *becomes* these things—that this very person is the true man, the man of the future, the coinciding of man and God."[40]

---

35. Ibid.
36. Ibid., 224.
37. Ibid., 224–25.
38. Ibid., 225–26. Cf. Collins, *The Word Made Love*, 80–85.
39. Ibid., 226.
40. Ibid.

Thus Ratzinger holds that the dogmas of Nicaea and Chalcedon "intend to express nothing else than this identity of service and being, in which the whole content of the prayer relationship '*Abba*-Son' comes to light."[41] The christological dogmas do not arise from mythological notions of origin, but from John's testimony, which presents Jesus' self-sacrifice for human beings as a prolongation of his converse with the Father. Thus the ontology of John and the ancient Creeds express a radical "actualism." Unlike Bultmann's actualism, in this there is no static "being" behind the "event" of "being God" and "being Lord." For if that were the case, an encounter with God would remain on the level of event and never penetrate to the level of being. It would deny that being can become act.[42] Rather, the Christology of John and the church's Creed, in saying that Jesus is his work, acknowledges in him the identity of being and act. Thus Ratzinger states:

> [that] precisely because this "being" is no longer separable from its *actualitas*, it coincides with God and is at the same time exemplary man, the man of the future, through whom it becomes evident how very much man is still the coming creature, a being still, so to speak, waiting to be realized; and what a short distance man has even now progressed toward being himself. When this is understood, it also becomes clear why phenomenology and existential analysis, helpful as they are, cannot suffice for Christology. They do not reach deep enough, because they leave the realm of real "being" untouched.[43]

The Different Paths Taken by Christology

Theology of the Incarnation and Theology of the Cross

Having proposed an intrinsic relationship between being and act in Jesus, Ratzinger then seeks to apply it to a fundamental christological dispute—that between the theology of the Incarnation and the theology of the Cross. According to Ratzinger, the former came from Greek thought and became dominant in the church of both the east and west. It concerns itself with "being," and sees God becoming man as the decisive, redemptive factor to which all else is secondary. This theology "tends toward a static, optimistic

---

41. Ibid., 227.
42. Ibid.
43. Ibid., 228.

view."⁴⁴ The importance of sin is downplayed. The decisive factor is not the need of atonement for the past, but future divinization.⁴⁵

On the other hand, the theology of the Cross is based on St. Paul and the earliest faith of Christians, and was taken up especially by the Protestant Reformers. It focuses on "event" rather than "being," specifically God's activity in the Cross and Resurrection. It leads to "a dynamic, topical, anti-world interpretation of Christianity, which understands Christianity only as a discontinuously but constantly appearing breach in the self-confidence and self-assurance of man and of his institutions, including the Church."⁴⁶

Ratzinger's comment on this conundrum is that there is no simple solution. No simple synthesis can avoid the loss of crucial insights. The polarities mutually correct and complement each other. What ultimately unites these polarities is the fact that the "being" of Christ is *actualitas*—not "a being that rests in itself, but the act of being sent, of being son, of serving. Conversely, this 'doing' is not just 'doing' but 'being'; it reaches down into the depths of being and coincides with it." Thus a "Christology of being and of the Incarnation must pass over into the theology of the Cross and become one with it; conversely, a theology of the Cross that gives its full measure must pass over into the Christology of the Son and of being."⁴⁷

Christology and Soteriology

Ratzinger believes that the antithesis between a theology of the Incarnation and a theology of the Cross is related to another division that developed in Christology—that between Christology perceived as the doctrine of Jesus' being, and soteriology perceived as a doctrine of redemption in isolation from the ontology of the Incarnation. This antithesis of being and act having led to a separation of Christology and soteriology, questions of how Jesus could be God and man, and how he could save us, became incomprehensible and insoluble.⁴⁸ The form in which the latter came to be answered was most often St. Anselm's satisfaction theory. Ratzinger asserts that this theory had a partial validity, inasmuch as it took into account key biblical and human insights.

> [Its] guiding thread remains that truth which the Bible expresses in the little word "for" . . . And who could fail to see that thus

44. Ibid., 229.
45. Ibid., 228–29.
46. Ibid., 229–30.
47. Ibid., 230.
48. Ibid., 230–33. Walter Kasper makes a similar point in *Jesus the Christ*, 22–23.

in the schematization of the "satisfaction" theory the breath of the biblical idea of election remains clear, the idea that makes election, not a privilege of the elected, but the call to live for others?[49]

The drawback of the theory is the way in which it "distorts the perspectives and with its rigid logic can make the image of God appear in a sinister light."[50] However, when this division of Jesus into person and work, with the person as being under an obligation to perform the work of satisfaction, is replaced with that of the oneness of person and work, then the true image of God is revealed.[51]

Christ the Exemplary Man

Ratzinger sums up his Christology in two parts. First, Christian faith believes in Christ as the "last Adam," the "exemplary man." He is the exemplary man because he has gone beyond the limits of humanity. He is the exemplar of humanity because it is only "through 'the other' and 'being' with 'the other' [that he comes] to himself."[52] Furthermore: "Man is finally intended for *the* other, the truly other, for God; he is all the more himself the more he is with the *entirely* Other . . . [It is] Jesus Christ . . . who has moved right out beyond himself and, *thus*, [has become] the man who has truly come to himself."[53] For Ratzinger, the first step in "hominization" was that from animal to *logos*. But this step is only completed when *logos* is merged with *Logos*. Full hominization only occurs when God becomes man. Ratzinger states that:

> [Only] by this event is the Rubicon dividing "animal" from the "logical" finally crossed forever and the highest possible development accorded to the process that began when a creature of dust and earth looked out beyond itself and was able to address God as "You" . . . [Man] is most fully man, indeed *the* true man, who is most unlimited, who not only has contact with the infinite—the Infinite Being!—but is one with him: Jesus Christ.[54]

The goal of hominization is divinization, and in Jesus the Christ it has been reached.

49. Ibid., 233.
50. Ibid.
51. Ibid., 233–34.
52. Ibid., 234.
53. Ibid., 234–35.
54. Ibid., 235.

The second part concerns the abolition of another frontier. If Jesus the Christ is the exemplary man he cannot be an exception. In calling him "Adam," the New Testament "expresses the unity of the whole creature 'man,' so that one can speak of the biblical idea of a 'corporate personality.'"[55] The whole of "Adam" is to be gathered into Christ. What St. Paul calls the Body of Christ is "an intrinsic postulate of this existence, which cannot remain an exception but must 'draw to itself' the whole of mankind."[56]

Ratzinger finds Pierre Teilhard de Chardin's approach to the questions of hominization and "corporate personality" helpful. While maintaining some reservation about what he perceives to be Teilhard de Chardin's tendency towards a biological approach, Ratzinger focuses upon his emphasis on the movement towards greater complexity being directed from above rather than below, a movement which is also one of each human ego towards the climax of a super ego, although without a monism which obliterates individuality.[57] Ratzinger sees this as a modern reworking of Pauline Christology, where in Jesus the breakthrough out of a "monadic enclosure . . . has occurred."[58] For Ratzinger:

> [Jesus is the one] in whom personalization and socialization no longer exclude each other but support each other; the man in whom perfect unity . . . and perfect individuality are one; the man in whom humanity comes into contact with its future and in the highest extent itself becomes its future, because through him it makes contact with God himself, shares in him, and thus realizes its most intrinsic potential.[59]

Ratzinger believes that Johannine theology points in the same direction. For John, the meaning of Jesus' death is contained in the words: "And I, when I am lifted up from the earth, will draw all men to myself" (John 12:32). The outstretched arms of Jesus on the Cross are a sign that he is the one who draws all people into his embrace, and that union with him is the goal of all people. Also, it is this complete openness that makes Jesus the "man of the future" as opposed to the one "who wants to stand only in himself, [who] is then the man of the past." Christ is the one "in whom the dividing walls of existence are torn down, who is entirely 'transition' (Passover, 'Pasch')."[60]

For Ratzinger, this transitional nature of Christ brings us back to the Cross and Easter. The image *par excellence* for an existence which completely

55. Ibid., 236.
56. Ibid.
57. Ibid., 236–39.
58. Ibid., 239.
59. Ibid.
60. Ibid., 240.

destroys human separation is that which forms the climax of John's crucifixion scene, and indeed, the whole of Jesus' life: "One of the soldiers pierced his side with a spear, and at once there came out blood and water" (John 19:34). The spear which confirms that the earthly life of Jesus has ended also indicates that "his existence is completely open; now he is entirely 'for'; now he is truly no longer a single individual but 'Adam,' from whose side Eve, a new mankind, is formed."[61] In the blood and water, John points to the two sacraments from which the church is formed as a sign of a new mankind.

Ratzinger holds that the crucified Jesus reveals the crucial difference between mere optimism and Christian hope. The future does not belong to human progress but to those who can become a sacrifice, thereby being "for others." One can enter this new existence only "by letting the walls of [one's] existence be broken down, by looking on him who was pierced (John 19:37), and by following him who as the pierced and opened one has opened the path into the future."[62] This means that Christianity is concerned with both the Alpha and the Omega—that it recognizes the primacy of the *logos* both as the creative meaning of the origin of all things, and the future end summed up in the coming one. Christian faith does not merely look back. It is not just a Platonic and metaphysical view of what is eternal. It also, and pre-eminently, looks forward, not to a utopian hope based on humanly produced progress, but in a hope grounded in the past, present and future—Jesus Christ, who was, who is and who is to come.

Finally, Ratzinger draws an insightful conclusion about the relationship between history and being: "From the standpoint of Christian faith one may say that for *history* God stands at the end, while for *being* he stands at the beginning." It is this that distinguishes it from "mere metaphysics and from the future-oriented ideology of Marxism."[63]

Various Assessments of Ratzinger's Earlier Christology

Kasper's Charge that Ratzinger's Theology Is Idealistic

Walter Kasper gave a critique of *Introduction to Christianity* immediately after its publication. He claimed that the book was permeated with Platonic Idealism. According to him, Ratzinger's starting point was the Platonic dialectic between the sensual and super-sensual worlds, the visible and invisible. Claiming that a better starting point would have been the human

---

61. Ibid., 241.
62. Ibid., 242.
63. Ibid.

being's concrete location in nature, society, culture and history, Kasper asserted that this visible/invisible dialectic led Ratzinger to an idealism which identified the historically contingent with the necessary, and freedom with necessity.[64] Although Kasper's critique was not of an explicitly christological nature, it is relevant to a study of Ratzinger's Christology because it touched upon the question of *Cur Deus Homo*.[65] As Ratzinger stated in *Introduction to Christianity*: "God's disguise as man in history 'must' be—with the necessity of freedom."[66]

In his account of the dispute between Ratzinger and Kasper over the supposed idealistic character of Ratzinger's theology, James Corkery claims that, *pace* Kasper, Ratzinger does have a concrete-historical focus—not Kasper's placing of the human being within the context of nature, society, culture and history, but rather human nature marred by sin. Corkery thinks that Ratzinger's position is reminiscent of Plato's cave, where people live in blindness and must turn around to see the truth. Just as the prisoners in the cave must turn from shadow to reality, so Christians must turn from the visible to the invisible. According to Corkery:

> Ratzinger starts from human beings in need of change; Kasper suggests starting from human beings' concrete historical situatedness—and seeking the mediation of the divine, the invisible, in and through it. For Ratzinger, to encounter God we must *turn* around; for Kasper, to encounter God we must *look* around. The consequences of the Platonic-Ratzingerian position are severe in relation to praxis; for we begin by turning *from* the world, not *to* it. The consequences of Kasper's position are that praxis is truly central: Christianity, Kasper points out, is concerned with *doing* the truth (John 3:21).[67]

---

64. Kasper, "Das Wesen des Christlichen. B,'" 184–86. See also Kasper, "Theorie und Praxis innerhalb einer *theologia crucis*," 155. Krieg also accuses Ratzinger of idealism, but one in the likeness of Max Scheler rather than Plato. Krieg's critique is more christologically pointed than Kasper's, since he faults Ratzinger with proposing a Christology from above which assumes anthropology into Christology. See Krieg, "Cardinal Ratzinger," 205–19. By way of contrast, de Gaál holds that, for Ratzinger, "the Christ of faith and the historical Jesus are not unrelated realities but circumscribe one person. Christology is not a Platonic discipline detached from the earthly Jesus." See de Gaál, *The Theology of Pope Benedict XVI*, 80.

65. Ratzinger, "Schlusswort zu der Diskussion mit W. Kasper," 158.

66. Ratzinger, *Introduction*, 269. For an account of the debate between Kasper and Ratzinger on this issue, see Corkery, *Joseph Ratzinger's Theological Ideas*, 69–74.

67. Corkery, *Joseph Ratzinger's Theological Ideas*, 71. Cf. Kasper, "Das Wesen des Christlichen. B,'" 187; and "Theorie und Praxis," 155.

At first sight, there seems to be some justification for this accusation. For Ratzinger states that:

> Christian belief . . . means opting for the view that what cannot be seen is more real than what can be seen. It is an avowal of the primacy of the invisible as the truly real, which holds us and hence enables us to face the visible with calm composure—knowing that we are responsible before the invisible as the true ground of all things.[68]

However, when one looks at the context for this statement, one finds that this context is the difficulty confronting coming to faith in God, given the nature of human knowing. As Ratzinger explains:

> [This difficulty exists because] there is an infinite gulf between God and man; because man is fashioned in such a way that his eyes are only capable of seeing what is not God, and thus for man God is always outside his field of vision. God is essentially invisible, something lying outside his field of vision . . . In this area of things that can be seen and grasped, the area that determines the living space as man, God does not occur and never will occur, however much the area may be extended. I believe that it is important that in principle the Old Testament contains this assertion: God is not just he who at present lies in fact outside the field of vision but could be seen if it were possible to go farther; no, he is the being who stands *essentially* outside it, however far our field of vision may extend.[69]

In speaking of the invisible as "more real," and saying that "God does not occur and never will occur" in the visible world, should one take Ratzinger literally, or in a hyperbolic sense? Is Ratzinger saying anything that is not implied by the statement that "faith is the assurance of things hoped for, the conviction of things not seen . . . By faith we understand that the world was created by the word of God, so that what is seen was made out of things that do not appear" (Heb 11:1–3)?

An answer to these questions can be found in an excursus which Ratzinger takes before he works through the christological statements of the Creed. This excursus is on "Christian structures." Ratzinger attempts to summarize the basic content of Christianity in a few simple statements, in order to give an overall context for looking at the individual articles.[70]

---

68. *Introduction*, 74.
69. Ibid., 49–50.
70. Ibid., 243–44.

One of these statements he calls the "law of disguise." This seeks to explain what is truly "entirely other" about God. In Ratzinger's version of what he thinks of as an inadequate negative theology, we think that we know the nature of God's being entirely other, that it lies in a total dissimilarity and complete unknowability. This philosophical negative theology is overthrown by "the peculiarity of the Christian form of negative theology, the form determined by the Cross."[71] When the Word becomes flesh he makes visible the entirely other, invisible, unrecognizable God in a way that we did not expect, the Alpha who becomes the Omega, in the sense of the lowliest. God "shows himself to be the *really* entirely Other, the one who casts overboard our notions of otherness and thereby shows himself to be the only one who genuinely is entirely other."[72]

Ratzinger asserts that, in the Bible, "one can find again and again the notion of God's double mode of appearing in the world."[73] On the one hand, he appears as the creative Logos of the world who surpasses all our thoughts. One the other, he appears under the sign of the lowly. This sign, "by concealing him more, shows more truly his intrinsic nature" as the unexpected truly other. Ratzinger states that: "One could cite in this connection the series Earth-Israel-Nazareth-Cross-Church, in which God seems to keep disappearing more and more and, precisely in this way, becomes more and more manifest as himself." It is in the Cross, on which hung "a man whose life had been a failure," that we find "the point at which one can actually touch God."[74]

Just as he does with the theologies of the Incarnation and the Cross, in this law of disguise, Ratzinger is attempting a balancing act between the knowability and unknowability of God by human beings.

> [He is wrestling with] polarities that cannot be surmounted and combined in a neat synthesis without the loss of the crucial points in each . . . [but must] remain present as polarities that mutually correct each other and only by complementing each other point toward the whole.[75]

The infinite can never be *comprehended* by the finite. We can only eternally strive to grasp him. The chief element of our knowledge of God is wonder.

The fact that Ratzinger and Kasper do not entirely agree on this point does not necessarily invalidate either of their positions. What both must do

71. Ibid., 255.
72. Ibid.
73. Ibid.
74. Ibid., 256.
75. Ibid., 230.

is have positions that are rationally and biblical defensible. They must be able to account for the following: "He who has seen me has seen the Father (John 14:9)," and "For flesh and blood has not revealed this to you, but my Father who is in heaven (Matt 16:17)." In Jesus, God is both visible and invisible.

Kasper also asserts that this supposed visible/invisible dialectic leads Ratzinger to an idealism which identified the historically contingent with the necessary, and freedom with necessity.[76] As Ratzinger states: "God's disguise as man in history 'must' be—with the necessity of freedom." However, once again, Ratzinger is attempting to balance two truths, the complete synthesis of which is beyond us. On the one hand, we are truly free. On the other, "man does not create his specific quality out of his own resources; it has to come to him as something not made by himself; not as his own product, but instead as a free exchange that gives itself to him."[77] We are both completely free and completely created. Ratzinger believes that an acceptance of these two truths enable us to "square the theological circle." Thus:

> the intrinsic necessity of the apparently historical contingency of Christianity can be shown, the "must" of its—to us—objectionable positivity as an event that comes from the outside. The antithesis . . . between . . . contingent factual truth . . . and . . . necessary intellectual truth . . . there becomes surmountable. The contingent, the external is what is necessary to man; only in the arrival of something from outside does he open up inwardly.[78]

Although it is a great blow to our pride, we cannot simply create ourselves. What seems to be contingent, what seems to be open to the possibility of having been otherwise, is necessary. We cannot become truly human apart from the *necessary* exemplary Man.

The Charge that Ratzinger's Earlier Christology Is "High"

Before proceeding with an assessment of the validity of the claim that Ratzinger's Christology is "high," it will be helpful to point out that, in contemporary theology, there seems to be more than one understanding of what is meant by Christology-from-above and Christology-from-below. One is that

---

76. Kasper, "Das Wesen des Christlichen. B,'" 184–86. See also Kasper, "Theorie und Praxis," 155.
77. *Introduction*, 268.
78. Ibid., 268–69.

which Ratzinger himself exemplifies. For him, theology of the Incarnation is high Christology, and theology of the Cross is low Christology.[79] Those who criticize Ratzinger's Christology as high see such a Christology as beginning with the church's Creeds, and low Christology with the historical Jesus.

Reflecting upon the definition of high and low Christologies, Roger Haight makes the astute observation that Karl Rahner's approach to Christology did not exactly follow this high-low dichotomy. As Haight explains, Rahner did distinguish between two types of Christology, one from below and one from above. However:

> This distinction of Rahner does not correspond with another similar sounding contrast between a so-called "high" christology and a "low" christology. A high christology generally refers to an understanding of Jesus Christ that highlights his divinity, whereas a low christology would so stress Jesus' humanity that his divinity appears to be compromised. Rahner's point is really quite different from the high-low contrast referring to the content of an understanding of Jesus Christ. He sought to clarify something prior to content, namely, a major difference in the possible method or approach that one followed in order to form such an understanding. In a method *from* below, one begins one's reflection with the testimony of Scripture to Jesus of Nazareth and experience of him today, and one as it were "ascends" to an understanding of Jesus' saving work and divinity. A method from below could also be called an ascending christology. In a method *from* above, one begins with the authoritative teaching about Christ's divine status, and from this dogmatic and metaphysical platform one interprets the issues connected with christologically understanding Jesus of Nazareth. Both methods of christology can yield a "high" christology.[80]

In focusing upon method, Haight helps us to clarify an essential point, although it is a point which he does not mention. Beginning one's reflection upon who Jesus is from Sacred Scripture is not necessarily the same as beginning from a historical Jesus. Nor, for that matter, is beginning one's reflection upon who Jesus is from faith in him necessarily the same as beginning from dogmatic propositions in the Creed.

Proceeding to the charge, Thomas Rausch claims that, in *Introduction to Christianity*, Ratzinger begins his Christology from the Apostles' Creed rather than the Jesus of history, rejecting attempts to establish it on a secure

---

79. Ratzinger, *Behold*, 32.

80. Haight, *The Future of Christology*, 165. Haight refers the reader to Rahner, "Two Basic Types of Christology," 213–23.

historical basis, because Ratzinger thinks that "such efforts were restricted to the phenomenal or demonstrable and were thus unable to produce faith, or . . . were based more on personal opinion than historical research."[81] Robert Krieg claims that, in the same work, Ratzinger pursues a high Christology which emphasizes the divinity of Christ.[82] Krieg contrasts Ratzinger's Christology with that of Kasper, holding that while the former emphasizes the "retrieval of Scripture and tradition and all but ignores dialogue," the latter is able to bring "Scripture and tradition into conversation with today's church and contemporary life."[83] That is to say, Kasper is able to combine high and low Christologies, whilst Ratzinger is not. Krieg maintains that: "Ratzinger is troubled not only by specific christological texts but also by Christology from below in general, especially when it relies heavily on the historical-critical method."[84]

Here, there are three distinct, albeit related, charges. The first charge is a failure to properly embrace the historical-critical method, and hence, the historical Jesus. According to Rausch, despite his best intentions, Ratzinger's Christology is not sufficiently critical to be properly grounded in the historical Jesus.[85] Neither Rausch nor Krieg claim that Ratzinger has a problem with the historical-critical method itself.[86]

What Ratzinger does object to is the exclusive use of the method, the failure of some to recognize its limitations, and the premises which some bring to it. Ratzinger sees the historical-critical method as an attempt to apply the scientific method to the study of history. He rejects the exclusive use of this method for the study of Sacred Scripture since it is capable of revealing the phenomenal aspect of what has happened in past history, but not the ontological aspect. In other words, it can tell us about what Jesus

---

81. Rausch, *Pope Benedict XVI*, 86. Cf. Ratzinger, *Introduction*, 197.

82. Krieg, "Who do you say I am?," 12–13. Krieg defines Christology from above as beginning with "the Second Person of the Trinity, with the pre-existing divine Word in relation to the Father and the Holy Spirit. This methodology then proceeds 'downward' to the Incarnation, to the event in which the Word or Logos became man in Jesus Christ. Finally, this approach to Christology draws our attention to how the Word made flesh suffered and died for our sins, and then rose from the dead and returned to God's 'right hand.'"

83. Ibid., 15.

84. Ibid., 16.

85. Rausch, *Pope Benedict XVI*, 100. Ratzinger's use of the historical-critical method in particular instances is not beyond criticism. For example, in spite of his awareness of how biblical scholars are prone to theorize beyond the biblical data, he himself occasionally uses the language of probability rather than that of possibility.

86. Krieg comes closest to doing so in "Who do you say I am?," 16.

said and did, but not who he really was, that is to say, whether or not he was a mere man or God incarnate.[87]

This is one of the two limitations of the method which Ratzinger sees, limitations which scholars need to recognize. The second is that the method cannot reach the same degree of certainty as can the scientific method of experimental verification, even with regard to the phenomenal, since its data are limited to what written documents happen to have survived, and are therefore incomplete. At a distance of 2,000 years and more, whatever one can say historically must be very incomplete. As has been said, the temptation is to treat this incomplete picture as complete. Furthermore, any past event which cannot be tested and passed by this method is rejected as invalid.

Besides the premise that the historical-critical method is self-sufficient, Ratzinger recognizes two other premises which can lie unexamined by the scholar. One is the rationalistic premise, associated with the self-sufficient premise, and epitomized by von Harnack, that Jesus was a prophetic Jewish teacher who was eventually transformed by the church into a Hellenistic God-man. The second is the idealistic premise, epitomized by Bultmann, which rejects the search for historical certainty and assumes that the reality of Jesus is contained not in who he was, but by what he means, and that this meaning is revealed in his preaching of the Gospel.

All of the above objections to the ways in which the historical-critical method can be used enable us to understand why Ratzinger rejects the premise that one can begin Christology from the historical Jesus. Full access to this Jesus is impossible. The historical-critical method can help us to a better understanding of a Jesus who we already know through faith. It is this faith which led to the writing of the New Testament and the reinterpretation of the Old, and is made explicit in the Creed.

The second charge is that Ratzinger's Christology takes as its starting point the Creed rather than the historical Jesus. Ratzinger's starting point *is* the Creed, because his starting point is neither the Jesus of history nor the Christ of faith, but Christ Jesus, Jesus the Christ. The accusation is true, but the premise is not. For Ratzinger, the christological articles of the Creed declare the church's faith in the one who is true God and true man; and this faith includes the historical Jesus Christ, who was born of the Virgin Mary; suffered under Pontius Pilate; was crucified, died and was buried; who descended into Hell; and who on the third day rose again from the dead and ascended into Heaven where he is seated at the right hand of the Father, from whence he shall come to judge the living and the dead. It is the same

---

87. *Introduction*, 194–95.

faith of the church which also holds that Sacred Scripture is the inspired written word of God, thus giving us a motive for reflecting upon the Jesus about whom we read therein.

The third charge is that Ratzinger is unable to bring Scripture and tradition into conversation with today's church and contemporary life, that he is unable to combine high and low Christologies. The charge is that Ratzinger's Christology is that of a past age, that it is not existential. This is a more subjective charge. What does Krieg mean by "today's church" and "contemporary life?" One could answer that Ratzinger's starting point is explicitly existential. The first chapter of *Introduction to Christianity* is not on "God, the Father, the Almighty," or "Jesus Christ, his only Son, our Lord," but on "Belief in the World of Today." In *Introduction*, his Christology begins with "The Problem of Faith in Jesus Today."[88] The success of Ratzinger's attempt to communicate with the people of today is open to question. That he is aware of the importance of the need to make the attempt, and makes it, is not. What also is open to question is Krieg's identification of conversation with today's church and contemporary life with a low Christology. Ratzinger does not want to bring the historical Jesus into that conversation. He wishes it to be between Jesus Christ and contemporary man.

As Ratzinger has pointed out, prior to the Second Vatican Council, theologians such as Karl Adam, Josef Jungmann, Karl Rahner and F. X. Arnold spoke of "a factual monophysitism among pious people, about monophysitism as a danger in the Church of their times."[89] That may have been true at the time, but Ratzinger sees the danger, since Vatican II, of "a new Arianism, or, to put it more mildly, at least a quite pronounced new Nestorianism."[90] This neo-Nestorianism is a form of dualistic Christology which splits Christ into "a human model and a Son of God who does not concern us existentially." We can "only imitate the human being Jesus, not the Son of God."[91]

---

88. Ibid., 193–96.

89. Ratzinger, *A New Song for the Lord*, 7–8 and 26–27. Ratzinger gives a reference for this point but the endnote is missing from the English translation.

90. Ibid., 27. The view of Riches on this question is that "a quasi-Nestorianism that expressed itself in neoscholasticism before Vatican II (paralleling 'grace' and 'nature') is reincarnated after the Council among those theologians who would dispense with the impassible Logos and attempt to find comfort in the dissociated 'humanity' of Jesus who merely 'suffers with us.'" See Riches, "After Chalcedon," 208.

91. Ibid., 7.

Contradictory Accusations

Looking at the dispute between Kasper and Ratzinger, alongside the claim that Ratzinger's Christology is high, leads to an interesting realization, namely, that there seem to be contradictory accusations leveled at Ratzinger. On the one hand, we have seen that Ratzinger is accused of having a high Christology which focuses on the divinity of Christ, a too great an emphasis on a theology of Incarnation. On the other hand, Corkery, basing his conclusion on Kasper, claims that Ratzinger's theology is too pessimistic and anti-world. One would expect such a position to come from an over-emphasis on a theology of the Cross.

However, there are two points on which Corkery's conclusion can be questioned. First, he can make this claim because he accepts Kasper's appraisal that the starting point for Ratzinger's theological synthesis is the Platonic dialectic between the visible and invisible.[92] However, this has just been shown to be false. Second, although Corkery accepts that Ratzinger's position does have a concrete historical focus, which Corkery interprets as the need for human beings to turn from the world, he claims that Ratzinger's position, as opposed to Kasper's, is not praxis.[93] However, Ratzinger does posit a praxis. It is called *metanoia*. He proposes a "turning from" sin. This is a turning from "the world," not in an undifferentiated sense, but in the Johannine sense of the primordial human rebellion against God. Furthermore, Corkery does not mention who Ratzinger might consider to be the one "to whom we turn." Ratzinger's position is not Platonic. Rather, one could say that Plato, in his allegory of the cave, perceived a facet of the truth, a truth that is more completely revealed in the command to "repent and believe in the Gospel" (Mark 1:15).

The Charge that Ratzinger's Christology Is too Johannine

Related to the charge of a high Christology is that of a Johannine Christology. Emory de Gaál thinks that Ratzinger has a preferential option for John's theology, but defends this supposed preference on the basis that it is John who achieves a synthesis, a christological symphony, of Greek philosophy and Judeo-Christian faith.[94] De Gaál also points to Ratzinger's identification of the concept of *logos* as decisive for the Christian image of God and as forming the core of Christology, a vein of thought which de Gaál identi-

---

92. Corkery, *Joseph Ratzinger's Theological Ideas*, 70.
93. Ibid., 71.
94. De Gaál, *The Theology of Pope Benedict XVI*, 120.

fies as Johannine.⁹⁵ Rausch agrees that Ratzinger's Christology is essentially Johannine, thinking that Ratzinger reads the synoptic Gospels through a Johannine lens, and consequently, is able to find a high Christology in the Synoptics as well.⁹⁶ However, that of which de Gaál approves, Rausch questions. For Rausch, Ratzinger's Jesus is too Johannine, too focused on Jesus the Logos to do full justice to Jesus the servant of the kingdom. Where de Gaál sees a christological symphony, Rausch perceives a hellenized Christology, a Jesus transmuted from a teacher and healer to a god.⁹⁷

It cannot be denied that Ratzinger's earlier Christology is extensively influenced by the Gospel of John. Indeed, he sees the Christology of Nicaea and Chalcedon as being, in essence, that of John's Gospel.⁹⁸ Yet, in the Preface to the new edition of *Introduction to Christianity* (2000), Ratzinger states that he is "firmly convinced that a renewal of Christology must have the courage to see Christ in all of his greatness, as he is presented by the four Gospels together in the many tensions of their unity."⁹⁹

Does Ratzinger broaden the evangelical base of his earlier Christology? In *The God of Jesus Christ* there is some indication that he has begun to do so. There he draws upon the prayer of Jesus as portrayed in the Letter to the Hebrews in order to expand an understanding of the *kenosis* of the Son, and as presented in Luke so as to show the uniqueness of Jesus' relationship with the Father.¹⁰⁰ Ratzinger goes so far as to claim that Luke raises "the prayer of Jesus to the central christological category from which he describes the mystery of the Son."¹⁰¹ We shall see in due course whether or not this broadening continues.

The Alpha of Ratzinger's Earlier Christology—Faith in Christ

The most substantial account of Ratzinger's earlier Christology is to be found in *Introduction to Christianity*. This Christology is more than an intellectual exercise. It has been developed for a purpose—to strengthen the faith of those who believe in Christ. The very structure of the *Introduction* reveals this. Ratzinger does not begin his introduction to *Christianity* with

95. Ibid., 84. Cf. Bonagura, "*Logos* to Son," 475–88.
96. Rausch, *Pope Benedict XVI*, 87–88.
97. Ibid., 99.
98. *Introduction*, 227–28.
99. Ibid., 29.
100. *Jesus Christ*, 66–68.
101. Ibid., 82.

Christ. Rather, he begins with the nature of faith. Faith in Christ is the starting point for Ratzinger's Christology. He does not see Christology in terms of the Bible versus the Creed. For him, this is a false dichotomy. The starting point for Christology is the faith of the church. It is an ecclesial faith, to which the believer gives assent in the *credo*. It is this faith which gives rise to both the New Testament and the Creed. It is in the light of this faith that the Old Testament is reinterpreted.

The Practical Goal of a Balanced Christology

If one had to find a title for Ratzinger as a theologian, Doctor of Reconciliation might not be a poor choice. Because Christian doctrine is an attempt to explain the divine mystery, it must consist in trying to bring together truths which, if examined perfunctorily, can appear contradictory. The perennial temptation is to accept one and reject the other. Finding the "narrow way" which is able to combine them rationally is the theologian's greatest challenge. Ratzinger is one theologian whose ability to unite apparently disparate concepts is profound, and well worthy of imitation. The account given below of his reconciling aptitude, as demonstrated in his earlier Christology, is not exhaustive.

Reconciling the Understanding of Faith and History in the Creed

According to Ratzinger, the historical-critical method tends to divide faith and history. The immediate temptation, in face of this division, is to abandon faith and trust history. Thus the "school" of Harnack idealizes history. It is taken up out of the world of existential faith. At the other extreme, the "school" of Bultmann idealizes faith. It is taken up out of the world of existential history. We are left with the apparent dilemma of being forced to choose between the Jesus of History and the Christ of Faith. Ratzinger claims to resolve this dilemma in the Creed. Here, the Christ of Faith, the Christ in whom we believe, is the Jesus of History, who the conceived and born, suffered and died, rose and ascended.[102]

Reconciling the Understanding of Being and Act in Jesus Christ

Underlying the reconciliation of the understanding of faith and history in the Creed is the reconciliation of the understanding of being and act in Jesus

102. Cf. Collins, *The Word Made Love*, 66–68.

Christ. This could also be called the reconciliation of ontology and history. According to Ratzinger, in Jesus Christ, it is not possible to distinguish between person and office. Jesus is his word, and this word is Jesus. This is why, in the first instance, one does not believe in the teachings of Jesus, but in Jesus himself. Faith in Jesus Christ is a personal faith. Rather than faith in a body of teaching, it is faith in a person who *is* his teaching.

Reconciling Theology and Anthropology in Christology

Ratzinger recognizes the perennial tension between doing full justice to both the humanity and divinity of Jesus. This tension has existed since the early church. Sometimes it has been possible to maintain this tension within the household of faith, as demonstrated by the so-called schools of Antioch and Alexandria. Sometimes this tension has led to a sundering of the bonds of faith—Docetism or Ebionism, Apollinarianism or Arianism, Monophysitism or Nestorianism. Ratzinger's basic framing of the dilemma is this—the choice seems to be between resolving Christology into theology or into anthropology.

In recent times, attempts have been made to resolve this tension through what is called theological anthropology, that is, through theological reflection upon the human person. It is based on the conviction that the human person can be fully understood only from a theological perspective. According to this view, human persons are defined and determined by their relationship to God. Their relation to God is essential to and constitutive of their nature. True knowledge of human persons begins with the relationship between them and God.[103] According to Karl Rahner and Herbert Vorgrimler, "theological anthropology resolves all other anthropologies into theology (the doctrine of God) and Christology (the doctrine of the God-Man)."[104]

There are a number of contemporary approaches to theological anthropology, but ultimately they can be resolved into two basic models. One begins with the human person in relation to God, and then moves to investigate how this relationship is expressed in the person of Jesus Christ. Rahner takes this approach.[105] The other focuses first on the divine-human relationship as it is expressed in the person of Jesus Christ, the one who is both human and divine, and then moves to examine how the nature of all human persons is revealed in Jesus Christ. This is the approach taken by

---

103. Cortez, *Theological Anthropology*, 5–7.
104. Rahner and Vorgrimler, "Man," 270.
105. See Rahner, *Hearer of the Word*.

Hans Urs von Balthasar.[106] Rahner's theological anthropology moves from anthropology to Christology, whilst von Balthasar's moves from Christology to anthropology.

The problem with Rahner's beginning with theological anthropology and then proceeding to Christology is that anthropology is the noun and theology the adjective. Nor would its opposite, an anthropological theology which begins with God and then moves to man, resolve this dilemma. The danger of the first is an over-emphasis on the humanity of Christ, and of the second, an over-emphasis on his divinity. Ratzinger chooses neither. Rather, he sees the reconciliation of the two in Christology, more specifically, in the christological dogmas of the Creed. The being of God and human action, as well as the action of God and being human, are reconciled in Christ. The one who says "I" in Jesus is both fully divine and fully human.[107] Rather than Christology resolving itself into either anthropology or theology, anthropology and theology are harmonized in Christology. Only in Christology can both anthropology and theology be most fully understood. Jesus shows us what it is to be human, and what it is to be divine. He does divine things humanly, and human things divinely.

Reconciling the Theologies of the Incarnation and the Cross in the Crucified One

The reconciliation of faith and history, being and act, theology and anthropology, all lead to the ultimate reconciliation of the theology of the Incarnation with the theology of the Cross. In Ratzinger's thinking, such reconciliation is needed, since the former tends towards a static, optimistic view in which the importance of sin and the need for atonement is downplayed and future divinization emphasized, whilst the latter tends towards a dynamic, topical, pessimistic view in which the goodness of the world is downplayed and human sinfulness emphasized.[108]

Ratzinger believes that, until recently, it is the theology of the Incarnation which has held a dominant position in the Catholic Church. He believes this to be shown by the separation of soteriology from Christology, with the latter becoming substantially a theology of the Incarnation.[109]

---

106. See Balthasar, *A Theological Anthropology*. Furthermore, like John Paul II, who wrote three separate encyclicals which address the human person's relationship with each particular Person of the Trinity, von Balthasar also offers a Trinitarian Christocentrism—Christ is only understood in his relations with the other divine Persons.

107. *Introduction*, 211. Cf. Collins, *The Word Made Love*, 65–66.

108. *Introduction*, 228–30.

109. Ibid., 232–33.

Consequently, in spite of accusations that he is the purveyor of an essentially high Christology, he wishes to reconcile a theology of the Incarnation with a theology of the Cross. How else can one explain the apparently contradictory accusation of a high Christology and an excessive focus on human sinfulness?

The ultimate *locus* wherein Ratzinger seeks to reconcile the theology of the Incarnation with the theology of the Cross is in the Crucified One himself. This is why he calls the Cross the birthplace of Christian faith. For him, the crucifixion is the *locus* for recognizing that Jesus is the Christ.[110] He believes that *this* is the basis of John's Christology, not simply that Jesus is the *Logos*, but that, in John's Gospel, there is an identity between *Logos* and *Agape*.[111]

The Omega of Ratzinger's Christology—Divinization as Authentic Hominization

The classic patristic understanding of the reason for the Incarnation is this—God became man so that man might become divine. Ratzinger agrees with this position, and draws from it the following conclusion—divinization is true hominization. Jesus is the last Adam, the exemplary man. In this exemplary man, being and act, *logos* and *agape*, God and man, become one. This exemplary man is also the Crucified One. In his total self-giving on the Cross, Jesus has gone beyond the limits of humanity. On the Cross, Jesus has fulfilled human nature, for: "Man is finally intended for *the* other, the truly other, for God; he is all the more himself the more he is with the *entirely* Other . . . [It is] Jesus Christ . . . who has moved right out beyond himself and, *thus*, [has become] the man who has truly come to himself."[112] For Ratzinger, man alone can never be fully human. It is only when the human *logos* becomes one with the divine *Logos* that man becomes fully human.[113]

Man alone can never be fully human. For Ratzinger, this is true both individually and corporately, humanly and divinely. In Jesus, two frontiers are abolished, that between God and man, and that between individual human persons. According to Ratzinger, Jesus cannot be the exemplary man

---

110. Ibid., 205–6.

111. Ibid., 208. Cf. Collins, *The Word Made Love*, 82–85. In a later work, Ratzinger draws our attention to the patristic interpretation of the Passion and Cross of Jesus as marriage, "as that suffering in which God takes upon himself the pain of the faithless wife in order to draw her to himself irrevocably in eternal love." See Ratzinger, *Daughter Zion*, 29.

112. *Introduction*, 234–35.

113. Ibid., 235.

if he is an "exception," and that in two senses. The first is that, in the individual sense, he cannot be the only individual man who has become fully human. The second is that, if he remains an individual, he cannot be fully human. Ratzinger appeals to St. Paul's identification of Christ with Adam, and redeemed humanity as the Body of Christ, in order to emphasize the corporate personality of Christ. The whole human race, in being "drawn into" Christ, does not remain a set of isolated individuals in him, but is caught up into the unity of trinitarian *agape*, and, in so being caught up, each individual human person becomes fully human.[114]

Ratzinger's focus on divinization could lead one to believe that, despite his attempt to achieve a balance between the theology of the Incarnation and a theology of the Cross, he has ultimately swung back to the former—God became man so that man might become divine. However, such is not the case. This is because the exemplary man and his mission are ultimately revealed in the Crucified One, the one who was pierced. Ratzinger's understanding of John's Christology leads him to the conclusion that the climax of John's portrayal of Jesus is the account of the piercing of his side with a lance. For Ratzinger, this image is the ultimate expression not only of the complete self-giving of Jesus, but also of the drawing of all human persons into union with God through union with Jesus himself, a union which is also one of all human persons with one another.[115] For Ratzinger, John's Gospel has achieved the balance between the Word who became flesh and was lifted up, and the One who was pierced—between a theology of the Incarnation and a theology of the Cross.

In *Introduction to Christianity*, Ratzinger draws upon the "complexification" thesis of Teilhard de Chardin in order to help explain the nature of hominization and corporate personality. Whilst avoiding Teilhard de Chardin's biological approach, Ratzinger finds his emphasis upon a movement towards a greater complexity, which is directed from above, rather than by a blind "evolutionary impulse," to be a reworking of St. Paul's "Body of Christ." On this point, Ratzinger's ideas are not dependent upon Teilhard de Chardin's, but find there a contemporary expression of Pauline Christology.[116] Where Ratzinger does seem to depend upon Teilhard de Chardin is in the notion of the taking up of *bios* into *zoe*.[117] Ratzinger thinks that Teilhard de Chardin has overcome an anthropological/cosmic dualism, has enabled the reconciliation of anthropology and cosmology within Christology, by

114. Ibid., 236.
115. Ibid.
116. Ibid., 236–39.
117. Ibid., 305.

demonstrating that full hominization includes not only the union of God and man, and the creation of the corporate man, but the unification of the cosmos with the personal, of the ultimate union of all matter with spirit in the person of Jesus Christ.[118]

The Absence of the Holy Spirit

When looking at the beginnings of a spiritual Christology in Ratzinger's earlier Christology, it becomes apparent that there is a substantial *lacuna* in this Christology—the almost complete absence of the Holy Spirit. This is not to say that there are no other deficiencies in his earlier Christology. For example, while drawing attention to Jesus' self-description as Son, found mainly in John's Gospel, it needs to be said that Ratzinger does not give the same attention to another self-descriptive term used by Jesus, found mainly in the synoptic Gospels—"Son of Man." This is not to say that his understanding of the significance of Son is incorrect, only that there is more to the story of Jesus' self-understanding. The lack of attention to Son of Man can be explained by Ratzinger's focus on the two key creedal expressions of Christian belief, neither of which use this term. When Ratzinger takes a more scripturally based approach to the self-identification of Jesus, he does not make the same omission.[119]

Be that as it may, in the case of the Holy Spirit, except for the briefest of references to the role of the Spirit in the Incarnation and Resurrection, the Spirit plays no part in Ratzinger's understanding of the *Christ*.[120] That is to say, Ratzinger speaks of the Anointed One, and of the Father who anoints him, but of the One with whom he is anointed there is hardly a sign. In both *Introduction to Christianity* and *The God of Jesus Christ*, the respective sections on the Holy Spirit are little more than appendices and, even then, in these sections Ratzinger focuses exclusively on the relationship between the Holy Spirit and the church.[121] In his exposition of Jesus as the Christ, he finds the fundamental significance of the title in that it identifies Jesus as the Logos, the person who is his word. He emphasizes the sonship but not the anointed aspect of the title Christ.[122]

---

118. Ibid., 319–22.
119. *Jesus I*, 321–35.
120. *Introduction*, 272; and *Jesus Christ*, 99.
121. *Introduction*, 331–59; and *Jesus Christ*, 103–13.
122. By contrast, Kasper is much more aware of the pneumatological dimension of Christology, that a "pneumatologically defined Christology can in fact best convey the uniqueness of Jesus Christ and his universal significance" (252). See Kasper, *Jesus the Christ*, 230–68, especially 249–57.

Moving on to the practical outworking of the Christ-ship of Jesus, even where we would reasonably expect to find some reference to the relationship between Jesus and the Holy Spirit, none is to be found. When Ratzinger turns to Luke and looks at his accounts of Jesus praying, one would expect that some attention would be paid to the Holy Spirit, given the prominence of the role of the Spirit in the person and mission of Jesus as portrayed in that Gospel. Yet such is not the case. For example, in Ratzinger's analysis of the Transfiguration, as found in Luke, there is no mention of the prominent place of the Holy Spirit, manifested in the form of the cloud, which overshadows Jesus and the three disciples, and from which the Father's voice is heard, testifying to the Son (cf. Luke: 9:34–35). Even though Ratzinger speaks of the dialogue between the Son and his Father as being a "total dialogue of love, [transformed by] the fire of love," the person who is the love of the Father for the Son and the love of the Son for the Father is not mentioned.[123] Again, when Ratzinger analyzes Matthew 11:27 in terms of the light it sheds upon how the Son is able to reveal the Father to us, although he places a great emphasis upon the self-giving of the Father and Son to each other in an "exchange of eternal love, both the eternal gift and the eternal return of this gift," there is no allusion to the One who is "gift" personified.[124] Finally, in looking at the Son's dialogue with the Father as the reason for the Resurrection of Jesus, Ratzinger stated that the Resurrection brings the human existence of Jesus "into the trinitarian dialogue of eternal love itself."[125] Once again, even though a specific reference is made to the Trinity, the personal nature of this eternal love, and his role in bringing the humanity of Jesus into the divine *perichoresis*, is not addressed. The question of whether or not Ratzinger, in developing a spiritual Christology, fills in this *lacuna*, is of crucial importance for assessing the validity of that Christology. For how can one have a spiritual Christology without the Holy Spirit?

---

123. *Jesus Christ*, 82.
124. Ibid., 91.
125. Ibid., 84.

2

Prolegomena to a Spiritual Christology

In this chapter no attempt will be made to give a comprehensive analysis of Ratzinger's understanding of the development of the christological articles of the Creed. Rather, it will concentrate on those aspects of his analysis which in some way are relevant to the development of his spiritual Christology.

The Development of the Christian Faith in the Christological Articles of the Creed

Conceived by the Power of the Holy Spirit and Born of the Virgin Mary

Having investigated the belief that Jesus is the Christ and the Son of God, Ratzinger attempts to show how this belief is explained in the christological articles of the Apostles' and Nicene Creeds. According to him, the conception of Jesus in the womb of Mary was neither the New Testament's nor the church's foundation for belief in the real divinity, the divine sonship, of Jesus. Rather:

> [The] Divine Sonship of which faith speaks is not a biological but an ontological fact, an event not in time but in God's eternity; God is always Father, Son, and Holy Spirit; the conception of Jesus means, not that a new God-the-Son comes into being, but that God as Son in the man Jesus draws the creature man to himself, so that he himself "is" man.[1]

1. *Introduction*, 275.

For Ratzinger, the church's teaching about the divine sonship of Jesus is based ultimately "on the *Abba*-Son dialogue and on the relationship of Word and love that we found revealed in it."[2]

He Came Down from Heaven

According to Ratzinger, the second article of the Creed does not abolish the first. The lordship and majesty of God above exists, and even in coming down from Heaven in humility and hiddenness, God remains "above," remains God. Indeed, this is the greatness of the descent of God.[3] In order to understand the "descent," one must understand the "height." The descent is not cosmological but metaphysical and existential. It is "the movement of God's being into the being of man and ... the movement out of glory into the Cross."[4] The Incarnation is the culmination of the descent of God which has been occurring throughout human history.

In order to illustrate the nature of this descent, one of the texts which Ratzinger uses is the tenth chapter of the Letter to the Hebrews, which he thinks especially apt in that it addresses only the personal and spiritual side of this descent, not the spatial. In the text's theology of the Incarnation, the "descending" and "entering" of Jesus are presented as an act of prayer (cf. Heb 10: 5–7; Ps 40: 5–7), a real "act." "Christ's entry into the cosmos is understood here as a voluntary and verbal event, as the concrete realization of the kind of thinking and believing that emerges in the piety of so many psalms."[5] Ratzinger asserts that the Psalm quoted in this passage of Hebrews is the prayer of thanksgiving of one raised from the dead. His sacrifice is not that of animals, but of hearing and obedience. True thanksgiving means entering into the will of God.[6]

Ratzinger sees this passage in Hebrews as presenting the Incarnation as a dialogue between the Father and the Son, as an event within the Trinity, a spiritual event. The one change in the text between the psalm and this passage is the replacement of "ear" with "body," which Ratzinger interprets as human existence itself. In Jesus, obedience has become incarnate.

> The theology of the Word becomes the theology of the Incarnation. The Son's gift of himself to the Father emerges from the

---

2. Ibid., 276. Collins, in *The Word Made Love*, characterises the whole of Ratzinger's theology, not just his Christology, as dialogic in form.
3. *Jesus Christ*, 61.
4. Ibid., 62.
5. Ibid., 66.
6. Ibid., 66–67.

dialogue within the Godhead; it becomes the acceptance, and thus the gift, of that creation that finds its synthesis in man. This body, or more correctly the humanity of Jesus, is the product of obedience, the fruit of the loving response of the Son; it is, so to speak, prayer that has taken on a concrete form. In this sense, Jesus' humanity is something wholly spiritual, something that is "divine" because of its origin.[7]

For Ratzinger, this reveals a profound link between the Incarnation and the Cross. The divine sonship of Jesus is the release and handing back of himself to the Father. Within creation, it becomes "obedience unto death" (Phil 2:8). For us, this indicates that our divinization comes through sharing in this obedience, when our "body" has entered into this prayer of Jesus, and this prayer has taken flesh in our daily lives. We become the Body of Christ by descending and ascending with him in his obedience to his Father.[8]

And Became Man

Rather than address the nature of the Incarnation through what he calls the basic components of human existence—"spirit and body, Creator and creation, the individual and the community, or history as the sphere in which we live," in the Nicene Creed Ratzinger approaches the question via what have traditionally been called the "mysteries" of Jesus' life, working on the premise that it is the totality of a person's life, rather than a single moment, which reveals who that person is.[9] He reminds us that this approach to the mysteries must be, first and foremost, a contemplative prayer.[10] He will recapitulate and greatly expand this approach in *Jesus of Nazareth*.

In looking at Jesus' public ministry, Ratzinger begins by focusing on two consequences of it. First, that it exposes Jesus to opposition in the forms of contradiction, misunderstanding and abuse. Second, that it entails the paradox of isolation, even in the midst of friends and disciples. Jesus experiences their misunderstanding, and even betrayal. Furthermore, Jesus is alone in another and unique sense. His life is lived "on the basis of a point that others could not reach, namely, on the basis of his being alone with God."[11] It is this last point to which Ratzinger devotes special attention. He believes that, of the four evangelists, Luke treats this subject most pen-

7. Ibid., 67.
8. Ibid., 67–68.
9. Ibid., 69.
10. Ibid., 70.
11. Ibid., 79.

etratingly. However, his analysis begins with an instance in Mark of Jesus praying, in order to show that, on this point, Luke is not unique.

For Ratzinger, the Marcan account of Jesus praying alone on the mountain, while the disciples are struggling against a headwind on the lake (cf. Mark 6:45–52; and Matt 14:22–33), reveals an important insight into the prayer of Jesus. Unlike in the Matthean account, when Jesus is alone and praying to the Father, here he also "sees" the disciples' lack of progress against the wind. The ecclesiological symbolism reveals that when Jesus is with the Father, he is not absent from the disciples: "Where Jesus is with the Father, the Church too is present."[12] This sheds light on the perception of Jesus' absence until his Second Coming. On a trinitarian level: "Jesus sees the Church in the Father, and on the basis of the Father's might, in the power drawn from his speaking with the Father, he is present to the Church." Ratzinger concludes this point by saying that: "It is precisely his speaking with the Father, his being on the mountain, that makes him present, and so we can say that the Church is, as it were, the object of the conversation between the Father and the Son and is thereby anchored in theology."[13]

In Luke, Ratzinger first looks at the calling of the Twelve (cf. Luke 6:12–16). Comparing this with the similar account in Matthew (cf. Matt 10:1–4), he states that rather than being an anticipatory response to the disciples' prayer to send laborers into God's harvest, Luke locates the act of calling the Twelve in the nocturnal prayer of Jesus, alone on the mountain. The apostolate is "the fruit of the dialogue between the Son's will and the Father's will."[14]

The second Lukan text is the account of the Transfiguration (cf. Luke: 9:28–36). Ratzinger thinks that this text shows that the "innermost essence of the mystery of Jesus becomes visible" in his prayer on the mountain.[15] Rejecting the position that the Transfiguration must be a transposition of a Resurrection narrative back into the earthly life of Jesus, Ratzinger characterizes it as a "Resurrection appearance."

> [Such an appearance is possible because] the inner foundation of the Resurrection is already present in the earthly Jesus, that is, the immersion of the core of his existence in his dialogue with the Father, an immersion that is also the glory of the Son and is indeed the very form his sonship takes. His Passion and death would then mean that his entire earthly existence, too, is

12. Ibid., 80.
13. Ibid.
14. Ibid., 81.
15. Ibid.

poured out into the total dialogue of love, where the fire of love transforms it.[16]

According to Ratzinger:

> Luke has raised the prayer of Jesus to the central christological category from which he describes the mystery of the Son. What Chalcedon expressed by means of a formula drawn from the sphere of Greek ontology is affirmed by Luke in an utterly personal category based on the historical experience of the earthly Jesus; in substantial terms, this corresponds completely to the formula of Chalcedon.[17]

Ratzinger holds that this is confirmed by Luke's account of Peter's profession of faith (cf. Luke 9:18–20), where this profession "proceeds from Jesus' praying and is a response to it."[18] Luke says that Jesus was *alone*, yet his disciples were with him. According to Ratzinger, this is a theological, and not just historical, statement. It shows that only those who share in the solitude of Jesus in this dialogue with the Father can profess who Jesus really is.[19]

Suffered Under Pontius Pilate, Was Crucified, Died, and Was Buried

In expounding this article in the Apostles' Creed, Ratzinger first wishes to refute what he calls "a much coarsened version of St. Anselm's theology of atonement."[20] He maintains that this theology distorts our understanding of the true meaning of the Cross by creating a conflict between God's righteousness and his love. On the contrary, the Cross is not "part of a mechanism of injured right . . . [but] the expression of the radical nature of love that gives itself completely, of the process in which one is what one does and does what one is."[21] Ratzinger claims that the scriptural theology of the Cross revolutionizes the notion of expiation and redemption held by other world religions, a notion which "usually means the restoration of the damaged relationship with God by means of expiatory actions on the part of men."[22] This, Ratzinger claims, is the opposite of the situation described in

16. Ibid., 81–82.
17. Ibid., 82.
18. Ibid.
19. Ibid.
20. *Introduction*, 281.
21. Ibid., 282.
22. Ibid.

the New Testament. There it is God who takes the initiative, restoring human righteousness through grace, through Christ, in whom God reconciled the world to himself (cf. 2 Cor 5:19).[23]

For Ratzinger, the Cross is presented in the New Testament as primarily a movement from above to below. Because it changes the whole axis of religion, the whole of human existence, including worship, is given a new direction in Christianity. Rather than a plea for atonement it becomes *"first of all* [a] thankful acceptance of the divine deed of salvation," hence, *Eucharistia*.[24] Rather than glorifying God by offering him our gifts, we do so by receiving *his* gifts, thus recognizing him as the only Lord. Christian sacrifice is total receptivity and self-surrender to God, allowing him to act upon us.

However, Ratzinger maintains that the Cross is also presented as a movement from below to above, in that it is an obedient offering of a sacrifice to the Father by Jesus. Ratzinger seeks a reconciliation of these two movements in what he calls the point of departure for the New Testament's interpretation of the Cross. According to him, the disciples' understanding of the Cross had to undergo a radical transformation—from a disaster to a victory. Besides the Resurrection, which gave them the certainty that Jesus was truly the King of the Jews, the means for the achievement of this transformation were images and concepts contained in the Old Testament. The disciples saw the Torah and the prophets being fulfilled in Jesus. The Old Testament, in turn, could now be reinterpreted in the light of Christ.[25]

In particular, Ratzinger focuses on the reinterpretation of Old Testament cult theology, especially as found in the Letter to the Hebrews.[26] This presents the Day of Atonement as the hermeneutical lens for viewing the Cross. All human cultic attempts to conciliate God are futile, because God does not desire what we are able to offer—the flesh of bulls and the blood of goats—but a sacrifice of thanksgiving (cf. Ps 50: 9–14). However, we are incapable of giving this true worship, which is our unqualified Yes to God. This is the only worship or sacrifice that has meaning. Yet it is an impossible task. We cannot give anything in return for our lives (cf. Mark 8:37). All pre-Christian cults, based on the idea of substitution, of representation, are attempts to replace the irreplaceable. However, "in Christ the idea of substitute . . . has acquired a new meaning."[27] Jesus is the one true priest. For Ratzinger:

23. Ibid., 282–83.
24. Ibid., 283.
25. Ibid., 284–85.
26. Ibid., 285.
27. Ibid., 286.

> [Jesus' death on the cross was] in reality the one and only liturgy of the world, a cosmic liturgy, in which Jesus stepped, not in the limited arena of the liturgical performance, the Temple, but publically, before the eyes of the world, through the curtain of death into the real temple, that is, before the face of God himself, in order to offer, not things, the blood of animals, or anything like that, but himself (Heb 9:11ff.).[28]

Jesus did not offer "things," he offered himself. His blood is not a material gift, "it is simply the concrete expression of a love of which it is said that it extends 'to the end'" (John 13:1).[29]

The implications of this for Christian worship are as follows. Such worship does not consist in the surrender or destruction of things, but in the absoluteness of love. In Jesus, God's own love has become human love. In Jesus, a new form of representation has come into existence. Rather than rely on attempts at self-justification, we can "accept the gift of love of Jesus Christ, who 'stands in' for us, allow ourselves to be united in it, and thus become worshippers with him and in him."[30] Furthermore, this demonstrates the error of resolving Christianity into a religion of *philia* alone, without *agape* directed to God. Indeed such brotherly love would not be the truly human love of a true humanity. Such a love must be open to redemption through Jesus, who alone loves sufficiently. One cannot become fully human unless one cooperates in the disinterested love by which Jesus glorifies God himself.[31]

Ratzinger next raises the question of the relationship between sacrifice/worship and suffering. For him, Christ's sacrifice establishes the fundamental principle of Christian worship as being "for" both God and one's fellow man, and that Christ, in his sacrifice, "has smelted the body of humanity into the Yes of worship."[32] This worship is completely anthropocentric *because* it is radically theocentric; that is, in completely delivering his "I" to God, Jesus has completely delivered "the creature man to God." Ratzinger sees this love as "the ec-stacy of man outside himself, in which he is stretched out infinitely beyond himself, torn apart, as it were, far beyond his apparent capacity for being stretched." Therefore, worship/sacrifice "is always at the same time the Cross, the pain at being torn apart, the dying of the grain of wheat that can come to fruition only in death."[33] However,

28. Ibid.
29. Ibid., 287.
30. Ibid., 288.
31. Ibid.
32. Ibid., 289.
33. Ibid.

in this sacrifice, pain is only a secondary element. According to Ratzinger: "The fundamental principle of sacrifice is not destruction but love. And even this principle only belongs to the sacrifice to the extent that love breaks down, opens up, crucifies, tears."[34]

In order to elucidate this further, Ratzinger quotes Jean Daniélou:

> This feeling of being torn asunder, which is a cross to us, this inability of our hearts to carry within itself simultaneously love of the most holy Trinity and love of a world alienated from the Trinity, is precisely the death agony of the only begotten Son, an agony he calls on us to share.[35]

Ratzinger explains the hellish experience of Jesus expressed in the cry, "My God, why have you forsaken me?" (Mark 15:34) as follows: "Anyone who has stretched his existence so wide that he is simultaneously immersed in the God and in the depths of the God-forsaken creature is bound to be torn asunder, as it were; such a one is truly 'crucified.'"[36] For Ratzinger, the Cross reveals the nature God, who, for our sake, becomes the smallest worm (cf. Ps 22:6). It also reveals the fallen nature of man in what happens to the truly just one. Such a one must be crucified by universal human injustice.[37]

Ratzinger asserts the contradictory nature of human death—on the one hand, it is biologically necessary, but on the other, spiritually unnatural and illogical, since the human spirit is ordered towards eternal loving communion.[38] This contradiction reaches its most acute manifestation in Jesus, the one "whose whole existence is in the shared dimension of his dialogue with the Father."[39] Yet this same communion is the unavoidable cause of his death, being the ultimate outcome of human failure to understand this communion.

According to Ratzinger's earlier Christology, the death of Jesus interrupts his dialogue with the Father, since the body is the human instrument of communication, and when the body dies, the intellectual act of communication ceases. Thus, compared with the death of any other human being, for Jesus, a far greater isolation occurs. Yet this dialogue with the Father is also the reason for the Resurrection of Jesus, since "it is through the Resurrection that his human existence is brought into the trinitarian dialogue

---

34. Ibid.
35. Ibid., 290. The quotation is from Daniélou, *Essai sur le mystère de l'histoire*. No pagination given.
36. Ibid.
37. Ibid., 291–93.
38. *Jesus Christ*, 83.
39. Ibid.

of eternal love itself."[40] Ratzinger claims that the Resurrection discloses the ultimate meaning of the Incarnation. In the Resurrection of Jesus the contradictory nature of man is overcome. In him, we can be one with the utterly other—God. With him we are *in* God. "When we say 'Father' with Jesus, we say it in God himself."[41] We shall see that this idea of the death of Jesus as an interruption of his dialogue with the Father is not to be found in *Jesus of Nazareth*. This is one discontinuity between Ratzinger's earlier Christology and his spiritual Christology. Rather, the death of Jesus will be portrayed as the culmination of the *Abba*-Son dialogue. Furthermore, in *Jesus of Nazareth*, Ratzinger will give a new emphasis to the corporate dimension of Jesus' prayers from the Cross and prayer of the Cross. The soteriological significance of Psalm 22 will be more developed, in that the prayer of Jesus will be shown as also expressing his identification with the suffering of Israel, and all who suffer.

Descended into Hell

In looking at this article in the Apostles' Creed, Ratzinger takes up the meaning of the term "hell." Although he holds it as correct to say that this statement denotes that Jesus entered into the state of death, it also raises the question of what death really is. We do not know from experience. In order to address this ignorance, Ratzinger turns to the psychological passion of Jesus on the Mount of Olives. Here, the heart of his Passion is revealed as radical loneliness, a complete abandonment which is again revealed in Jesus' cry to his Father on the Cross. The Passion of Jesus reveals "the abyss of loneliness of man in general, of man who is alone in his innermost being."[42] This loneliness is a fundamental contradiction of human nature, for it is not good for us to be alone. This results in a fear which is not of any particular threat, but an experience of human vulnerability which cannot be overcome by any rational means. This "fear peculiar to man cannot be overcome by reason but only by the presence of someone who loves him."[43] Ultimately, this leads to an understanding of the true nature of Hell. It is the state of loneliness which no "you" can reach, no love penetrate. That such is the truth about human nature is reflected in those modern philosophies which hold that all human encounters are superficial, and this all human existence is, at bottom, hellish.[44]

40. Ibid., 84.
41. Ibid.
42. *Introduction*, 298.
43. Ibid., 299–300.
44. Ibid., 300.

For Ratzinger, the ultimate human fear is fear of the loneliness of death, which is why the Old Testament has only one word for both Hell and death—*sheol*. "Death is absolute loneliness . . . [and] the loneliness into which love can no longer advance is—hell."[45] In going down into Hell, Jesus has penetrated our final loneliness and abandonment. He has entered the place where there is no "you." Death is no longer Hell. Rather, now life and love dwell in death. Now the only Hell is the "second death" (cf. Rev 20:14). Such a perspective enables us to understand both the Matthean opening of the tombs (cf. Matt 27:52), and the patristic imagery of Christ opening the gates of Hell and fetching forth the dead.[46]

Rose Again from the Dead

In looking at the article in the Apostles' Creed on the Resurrection of Jesus, Ratzinger does not start with the accounts of the empty tomb or the appearances of Jesus to his disciples. Rather, he begins with a quotation from the Song of Songs: "Love is strong as death" (8:6). For him, this sentence expresses the "boundless demands of *eros*."[47] It expresses the paradox of love which constitutes the fundamental problem of human existence—love demands infinity and indestructibility, but it seems that this demand cannot be satisfied. The human person is not immortal. Yet it is only by being immortal that love can be *stronger* than death.

According to Ratzinger, this paradox points to a disruption in human nature. At this point, we need to realize that, for Ratzinger, true humanity means to exist in the other. It was the striving for autonomy, to be like God, which led to death. Sin is the refusal to recognize the need for the other, and this attempt to be self-sufficient leads to death. Yet this, in part, is recognized by us. Knowing that absolute autonomy is a chimera, we attempt to exist in the other, but on our own terms. First, we attempt it in our progeny. When this is found to be unreal, we seek immortality in fame. But this is no better than the immortality of Hades, "more non-being than being."[48] Both one's children and one's fame will also perish. Finally, we must recognize that the only one in whom we can continue to exist is the one whose essence is to exist—he who is.

Ratzinger holds that, from another point of view, love is stronger than death only when someone values love more highly than life. However, the

45. Ibid., 301.
46. Ibid.
47. Ibid., 302.
48. Ibid., 303.

only way that this can be so is if love can be superior to and encompass mere *bios*. In a way that acknowledges an insight of Teilhard de Chardin, Ratzinger states that such a "mutation" or "evolution" would take *bios* up into *zoe*—a definitive life which is not subject to death. This last development would not be achieved "within the realm of biology but by the spirit, by freedom, by love."[49]

Ratzinger asserts that the two aspects of living in the other and the love of the other are mirrored in the two ways in which the Resurrection is described in the New Testament: that Jesus has risen and that he has been raised by the Father. Jesus lives in the Father, and the love of the Father has drawn him out of death.[50] Furthermore, if love establishes immortality, if immortality is the specific character of love, then immortality proceeds from love. This principle applies most properly to God, who is eternal *because* he is relational. As Ratzinger states:

> God, too, is absolute permanence, as opposed to everything transitory, for the reason that he is the relation of three Persons to one another, their incorporation in the "for one another" of love, act-substance of the love that is absolute and therefore completely "relative," living only "in relation to."[51]

For Christianity, "absolute" means "absolute relatedness."

Since Ratzinger holds that "love is the foundation of all immortality, and immortality proceeds from love alone," he concludes that, since Jesus is the one who truly has love, he has established immortality for all.[52] That is to say, *his* Resurrection is *our* life (cf. 1 Cor 15:16–19). The love of Jesus is the foundation of our immortality. He is the one who possesses *zoe*, a life beyond the realm of *bios* and history, a reality borne out by the Resurrection narratives. However, his new life has been begotten in history. These two insights enable us to work out the correct hermeneutic for interpreting the biblical Resurrection narratives.[53]

According to Ratzinger, this hermeneutic enables us to see that the Resurrection of Jesus is no mere resuscitation. His new life is no longer governed by the laws that govern *bios*. Hence, encounters with Jesus are

49. Ibid., 305.

50. Ibid.

51. Ibid., 305–6.

52. Ibid., 306. Kasper calls this Ratzinger's "phenomenology of love, which is stronger than death." Kasper contrasts it with a phenomenology of human freedom advocated by Rahner, Pannenberg's phenomenology of hope, and Moltmann's phenomenology of hope for justice. See Kasper, *Jesus the Christ*, 136.

53. Ibid., 307.

termed "appearances." In these, the recognition of Jesus is his initiative. He must open hearts and minds to recognize his *zoe* in the midst of *bios*. Herein lies the difficulty of the witnesses in recounting their experience of Jesus. The result is a dialectic character to statements about the appearances, "in the simultaneity of touching and not touching, or recognizing and not recognizing, of complete identity between the crucified and risen Christ and complete transformation."[54]

By way of example, Ratzinger examines the Emmaus story. Ultimately, the risen Lord can only be recognized by faith—"he sets the hearts of the two travellers aflame by his interpretation of the Scriptures and by breaking bread he opens their eyes." By attempting to describe this encounter in liturgical terms, Luke "provides both a theology of the Resurrection and a theology of the liturgy: one encounters the risen Christ in the word and in the sacrament; worship is the way in which he becomes touchable to us and recognizable as the living Christ."[55] However, the Resurrection narratives are not simply disguised liturgical scenes. Rather, they make visible the founding event of all Christian liturgy.

In his exposition of the Nicene Creed, Ratzinger recognizes that there is a contemporary tendency to view the traditional understanding of the Resurrection of Jesus as historically conditioned and in need of reinterpretation, a view supported by the seeming discrepancies in the Resurrection narratives. In response to this, he begins by dividing the biblical testimony into two types of tradition—the "confessional" and the "narrative." The first is exemplified by passages such as 1 Corinthians 15:3–8, the second is to be found in the Gospel accounts. The fundamental difference between the two types lies in the different questions which they were written to address.[56] The confessional tradition grew out of the simple liturgical acclamation that the Lord had risen (cf. Luke 24:34). It is a profession of faith, and in that sense, not informational, but creedal. The narrative tradition grew out of the desire for information, to know what had happened. In part, it served an apologetic purpose, enabling Christians to give an answer for the hope that was in them (cf. 1 Pet 3:15). However, although both traditions are necessary, it is the confessional which is superior. It is "the faith" "that provides the criteria for every interpretation."[57]

---

54. Ibid., 308.

55. Ibid.. 309.

56. *Jesus Christ*, 92–93. Cf. Kasper, *Jesus the Christ*, 125–29, where Kasper calls these confessional and narrative traditions the Easter kerygma and the Easter stories.

57. *Jesus Christ*, 94.

Turning to the Pauline text (cf. 1 Cor 15:3–8), which begins with the death of Jesus, Ratzinger thinks that it contains six key points which reveal the significance of this death. First, that this event was "in accordance with the Scriptures." It is a *logical* event, in the sense that it proceeded from and was the fulfillment of God's Word in history, specifically, the fulfillment of the Old Testament covenants.[58] Second, it is not a death which originates in the human desire to "be like God," but is a death "for our sins." It is a death that brings about our reconciliation with God. In the death of Jesus, death dies.[59] Third, "he was buried"—he experienced death to the full.[60] However, this experience of human death does not mean that the Resurrection was simply an overcoming of physical death through a return to his previous physical life. This is borne out by the fourth point—that "he appeared." Ratzinger asserts that a better translation of the Greek text would be "he allowed himself to be seen." According to Ratzinger, this phrase reveals that, after his Resurrection: "Jesus belongs to a sphere of reality that is normally inaccessible to our senses," hence, the persistent failure of his disciples to recognize him.[61] He can only be seen if he allows it, and if there is an inner openness of heart in the seer. Even on the natural level, one person may perceive the beauty of things whilst another only perceives their usefulness. Seeing makes demands upon both the senses and the mind. This leads Ratzinger to the fifth point, that the risen Jesus was not simply resuscitated, but now lives "out of the very heart of the divine power, above the zone of that which is physically and chemically measureable."[62] This is the underlying meeting of two more affirmations. The first is that: "He was raised on the third day in accordance with the Scriptures." Ratzinger sees the phrase "on the third day" as an allusion to Psalm 16:10: "You did not give me up to Sheol, or let your godly one see the Pit" of corruption, the very words quoted by Peter in order to demonstrate that Jesus is the one who fulfils the Old Testament prophecies. Since the Jews believed that corruption set in after the third day (cf. John 11:39), the fact that Jesus does die but does not "see corruption" shows that his death has conquered death.[63] The second phrase is: "He appeared to Cephas, then to the Twelve." Ratzinger states that:

> The Resurrection and the appearing are clearly separate, independent elements in the profession of faith. The Resurrection is

58. Ibid., 94–95.
59. Ibid., 95–96.
60. Ibid., 96.
61. Ibid., 98.
62. Ibid.
63. Ibid., 99.

more than appearances; and the appearances are not the Resurrection but are only its radiant splendor. First, the Resurrection is an *event* that happens to Jesus himself, between the Father and him in the power of the Holy Spirit; then this event that happens to Jesus himself becomes *accessible* to men, because he makes it accessible.[64]

According to Ratzinger, the Resurrection of Jesus shows that, contrary to appearances, death "does not belong fundamentally and irrevocably to the structure of creation, to matter." But only "the creative power of the Word and of love . . . [is] strong enough to change the structure of matter so fundamentally that it becomes possible to overcome the barrier of death."[65] In the Resurrection, God unconditionally affirms creation and matter. His Word penetrates matter, and he calls us to responsibility not only to the spiritual, but to the whole of creation.

Ascended into Heaven and Is Seated at the Right Hand of the Father

Ratzinger begins his analysis of this article in the Apostles' Creed by addressing what he sees as a modern misconception of the Ascension, a misconception from which the Descent into Hell also suffers, derived from a strictly empirical view of the cosmos. Such a view regards the "three-storied" view of Heaven, Earth and Hell, of "above" and "below," as mythical. Ratzinger asserts that these dimensions are metaphysical rather than physical. In holding them to be metaphysical dimensions, he maintains that they are also existential. For example, Ratzinger points out that in "the prayer of the crucified Christ to the God who has abandoned him, there is no trace of any cosmic reference."[66] The Hell into which Christ descends "is not a cosmographical destination but a dimension of human nature."[67] It is the dimension of loneliness and rejected love. This existential depth is the common patrimony of the human race, a burden which the new Adam undertakes to bear with us.

Conversely, in his Ascension, Jesus enters the divine love itself, and thus is opened to the possibility of reaching out in love to all other human beings. This is what Heaven is. It is communion with others through communion

64. Ibid.
65. Ibid., 100–101.
66. *Introduction*, 311.
67. Ibid., 312.

with God. As Hell is wanting only to be oneself, and is something that one can only give to oneself, so Heaven is that which one cannot make or give to oneself, but can only be received from another. In other words, it is grace.[68]

Thus for Ratzinger, Heaven is not physically above the world. Nor is it an eternal metaphysical region independent of the world. Rather, Heaven and the Ascension of Jesus are indivisible. The Ascension brings Heaven into existence. Ratzinger puts it thus:

> Heaven is to be defined as the contact of the being "man" with the being "God"; this confluence of God and man took place once and for all in Christ when he went beyond *bios* through death to new life. Heaven is accordingly that future of man and of mankind which the latter cannot give to itself, which is therefore closed to it so long as it waits for itself, and which was first and fundamentally opened up in the man whose field of existence was God and through whom God entered into the creature "man."[69]

From this it follows that Heaven is not a private destination, but the destiny of all those who are incorporated in the last Adam.[70]

From this position, Ratzinger claims to derive what he calls important hermeneutical insights. First, it enables one to properly understand the "eschatology of Imminence." Rather than driving a wedge between the preaching of Jesus about the end of the world, and his death and Resurrection, it enables us to understand his Resurrection and Ascension as "the beginning of 'eschatology,' or the end of [this] world."[71] Christ is the "end," the "center" of history, in that the immortality of both the human individual and race are to be found in him.

Second, it enables us to understand the true relationship between the finite and the infinite, the temporal and the eternal. It enables us to break out of the dualism of antiquity which saw eternity as "before" time, and God as a kind of prisoner of his eternal nature, unable to enter into a relationship with us. Rather, it is "the power of the present in all time."[72] The Incarnation manifests God's dominion over time. In Jesus, our time and God's eternity become one. It is this that renders our prayers effective.[73]

---

68. Ibid., 312–13.
69. Ibid., 313–14. Kasper expresses the same idea in *Jesus the Christ*, 152.
70. *Introduction*, 314.
71. Ibid.
72. Ibid., 317.
73. Ibid., 315 and 318.

He Will Come Again to Judge the Living and the Dead

In addressing this article, Ratzinger begins with the modern rejection of the end of the world and the Lord's return in judgment. Yet, unlike the accounts of the Descent and Ascension of Jesus, those of his Second Coming do contain cosmological elements, those concerning the world. However, Ratzinger maintains that "world" means primarily the human world, human history. It is this that God will bring to an end. Be that as it may, this essentially anthropological event is presented in cosmological and political imagery.[74]

According to Ratzinger, in the Bible, the cosmos is not merely a setting for human existence. Rather, "world and human existence necessarily belong to one another, so that neither a worldless man nor even a world without man seems thinkable."[75] Although the first proposition seems obvious, Ratzinger holds that the work of Teilhard de Chardin has rendered the second also comprehensible. Thus, rather than an anthropology in cosmic dress, or an anthropological/cosmic dualism, Ratzinger holds the following:

> [The] total biblical view [depicts] the coincidence of anthropology and cosmology in definitive Christology and, precisely *therein*, portrays the end of the "world," which in its two-in-one construction out of cosmos and man has always pointed to this unity as its final goal.[76]

This means that the cosmos itself is a kind of "history," both before human history and embracing human history. In this cosmic history, matter forms the precursor of spirit or mind.[77] Continuing to follow Teilhard de Chardin, Ratzinger sees the world as advancing to an "omega" point, in which it will be revealed that the true ground of reality is not matter but mind. This "process of 'complexification' of material being through spirit . . . [brings about] a new kind of unity."[78] The human ability to change the world through technology hints at the true relationship between spirit and matter, in which the former draws the latter into itself. This leads to a conception of Christ's return as the ultimate unification of reality by spirit.

---

74. Ibid., 318–19.

75. Ibid., 319.

76. Ibid. Kasper makes the same point when he characterizes Teilhard de Chardin as trying to show how cosmogenesis and anthropogenesis find fulfilment in Christogenesis. See Kasper, *Jesus the Christ*, 18.

77. *Introduction*, 320.

78. Ibid., 321.

This complexification of the world through mind/spirit can only be in the reality of the personal. This means "that the cosmos is moving toward a unification in the personal," and also demonstrating the precedence of the individual over the universal.[79] All is drawing towards unity in the person. It is the personal which gives meaning to the whole cosmos. Christianity sees "one individual [as] the center of history and of the whole."[80] This ultimate "triumph" of spirit is the triumph of truth, freedom and love. That which finally embraces the whole cosmos is not a collectivity or idea, but one with a human face.[81]

Since the ultimate consummation of the cosmos is based on spirit and freedom, it includes responsibility. It is not materially determined, but is based on decisions. Hence, the Lord's second coming brings not only salvation, but also judgment. The "works" are wrought in freedom, and this freedom is not cancelled out by grace. This also points to the universality of the offer of salvation and refutes the idea that it is the church alone which offers salvation.[82] Ratzinger muses that this paradox of judgment according to human freedom and the doctrine of grace may only be solved by one who actually lives his or her life based on faith. "Anyone who entrusts himself to faith becomes aware that both exist: the radical character of grace that frees helpless man and, no less, the abiding seriousness of the responsibility that summons man day after day."[83] What enables us to live with this paradox is our conviction of the infinitely greater power of Christ to save us. This leads to a profound freedom and tranquility. Yet it does not do away with our responsibility for our own actions, for how we have responded to God's grace.[84]

Because Christ will judge the living and the dead we know that grace will not simply wipe out our injustice, but will preserve true justice. This is so that justice can be reconciled with perfect love, a love which does not create injustice. However, one must also avoid the opposite error, which sees only the wrath of God punishing injustice, without any fulfillment of the promise of mercy. Ratzinger calls this the "contrast between *Maran atha* and *Dies irae*."[85] Furthermore, he asserts that if we take this article of the Creed from its original context in the Christian tradition, there can be a tendency

79. Ibid., 322.
80. Ibid.
81. Ibid.
82. Ibid., 322–24.
83. Ibid., 324.
84. Ibid., 324–25.
85. Ibid., 326.

for us to emphasize judgment rather than mercy. However, this imbalance can be redressed if we remember that it is *Jesus* who judges. It is not simply the infinite, eternal God who judges us, but Jesus our brother. Remembering this will enable us to recapture the attitude to judgment expressed in the words *Maran atha*.[86]

Consubstantial with the Father

Ratzinger thinks that this christological aspect of the Nicene Creed currently is perceived as no longer relevant to Christology, that it makes Jesus inaccessible to people today and reduces faith to philosophy. According to Ratzinger, this modern view wishes to abandon the Greek search for "essence," and find Jesus in history.[87] Contrary to this view, he maintains that the bishops at Nicaea and Chalcedon saw themselves as addressing a very basic question of believers—who is Jesus? Was he simply a man, or something more? If the answer is the former, then ultimately the faith of the church will not endure, since he can offer no supreme guidance for our lives. If in Jesus God has not become man, then the man Jesus is of no consequence. Paradoxically, Ratzinger holds that it is only if Jesus is the Son of God, is God made man, that history has been made. The ontological and historical are linked: "Precisely this *Being* is the tremendous *event* on which everything depends."[88]

Ratzinger believes that modern public opinion has the same reason for rejecting the full divinity of Jesus as had that of the educated world of Arius' time—an idealistic or deistic concept of God, one which sees God as necessarily excluded from history. He claims that the Fathers of the church regarded this position as atheism, "since a God to whom man has no access whatsoever, a God who in reality cannot play a role in the world, is no God."[89] Ratzinger holds that the true reason many have retreated to a great but only human Jesus is that their understanding of God is "impersonal," and that the *kenosis* of God is impossible.

Be that as it may, Ratzinger asks that, although the question "Who is Jesus" may be simple, is not the answer *homoousios* unnecessarily complex? His answer is that this term is simply a translation of the metaphor "Son" into a concept—that Son is meant to be taken literally. To say that Jesus is

---

86. Ibid., 326–27.
87. *Jesus Christ*, 85–86.
88. Ibid., 88.
89. Ibid.

consubstantial with the Father, that he has the same substance as the Father, is to say that he is truly, and not just figuratively, the Son of God.[90]

How can the church make this profession of faith? To answer this question, Ratzinger turns to the rather Johannine statement of Jesus in Matthew's Gospel, "no one knows the Son except the Father, and no one knows the Father except the Son and anyone to whom the Son chooses to reveal him (Matt 11:27)." No one knows God except God. The Son is the act of God knowing himself. It is "God's giving of himself as Father and God's receiving of himself and giving back of himself as Son, the exchange of eternal love, both the eternal gift and the eternal return of this gift."[91] Therefore, the Son can choose to reveal the Father. However, he can only do so to one who has voluntarily accepted to be in his, the Son's, will by living in it. Such a one lives as God's child, and is therefore able to call God "Father." Sonship, knowledge, and freedom mean being able to say Father to God.

Identifying the Prolegomena

In the Preface to *Behold the Pierced One*, Ratzinger states that it was a talk given by him in 1981 on the Sacred Heart of Jesus which was the occasion for his considering Christology *more* from the aspect of spiritual appropriation than he had previously done. This means that he had previously given *some* thought to this aspect of Christology. In his analysis of the christological articles of the Creed as examined in *Introduction to Christianity*, and more so in *The God of Jesus Christ*, one can already find a marked emphasis upon the prayer of Jesus and our participation in it. To begin with, Ratzinger identifies "Son" as Jesus' self-description, and sees this title as the completely new element in our understanding of the Messiah. This self-identification flows out of Jesus' prayer relationship with his *Abba*, a relationship into which he wishes to incorporate others. According to Ratzinger, the christological dogmas arise from the identity of service and being in Jesus which is revealed in this converse with his Father, a "conversation" which reaches its culmination on the Cross. Furthermore, Ratzinger sees the Johannine image of the pierced side of Jesus as the climax of not only the crucifixion, but of the whole of Jesus' life, and the image *par excellence* of the effect of Jesus' sacrifice—the destruction of our estrangement from God, and the openness of Jesus' existence which draws a new human race into himself. This new human race in turn is drawing the whole of the cosmos into a unity which

---

90. Ibid., 89–90.
91. Ibid., 91.

is personal—the ultimate triumph of the spirit, of truth, freedom and love, revealed in the face of Jesus the Christ.

What follows is a presentation of the obvious *prolegomena* of Ratzinger's spiritual Christology. However, we shall see that all of the fundamental *leitmotifs* of Ratzinger's earlier Christology are recapitulated in his spiritual Christology.

The Prayer of Jesus and Our Participation in It

Ratzinger maintains that the church's teaching about the divine sonship of Jesus is based ultimately on the *Abba*-Son dialogue. He presents the Incarnation as an act of prayer. Our divinization comes through sharing in the obedience found in this prayer of Jesus. Ratzinger approaches the question of the Incarnation's nature via the mysteries of Jesus' life, and advocates that this approach to the mysteries should begin with contemplative prayer. Contemplating these mysteries reveals that the whole orientation of Jesus' life is towards his *Abba*. Yet there is an ecclesial dimension to this relationship. Although the *Abba*-Son relationship is utterly unique, when Jesus is "alone" with the Father he is also with the disciples. Indeed, Ratzinger maintains that the church is the object of the *Abba*-Son dialogue. Hence, the calling of the Twelve, as presented by Luke, follows from this dialogue. Furthermore, Peter's profession of faith in Jesus proceeds from the prayer of Jesus made manifest on the mount of the Transfiguration. Ratzinger presents the death of Jesus on the Cross as a "cosmic liturgy," a sacrificial act of worship. Christian worship is to worship in and with Christ. Jesus' death is also presented as an interruption of his dialogue with the Father. This dialogue is the reason for his Resurrection. Because of Jesus' Resurrection those who are in Christ are in God, and can address God as Father. Because Jesus has ascended to the Father and, in his humanity, is completely one with him, our time and God's eternity have become one, thus rendering our prayers effective. In looking for this emphasis on the prayer of Jesus in Ratzinger's earlier Christology, one can identify three main biblical sources—in *Introduction to Christianity* the Gospel of John, and in *The God of Jesus Christ* the Letter to the Hebrews and the Gospel of Luke.

The Prayer of the Son in the Gospel according to John

As has been seen, for Ratzinger, "Son" is the guiding thread in John's Christology. He believes that it reveals the total relativity of Jesus' existence as the one sent "from" the Father "for" us. It reveals "the starting point of all

Christology: in the identity of work and being, of deed and person, of the total merging of the person in his work and in the total coincidence of the doing with the person himself."[92] For Ratzinger, the description of Jesus as Son comes from the prayer of Jesus, in that it is the natural corollary to *Abba*. If Jesus addressed God thus, then he is the Son in a unique way. Ratzinger holds that John ontologizes the phenomenal character of what Jesus says and does. These phenomena reveal the truth about his being—that he is Son, Word and mission. Foundational amongst these phenomena is how Jesus prays. Thus Ratzinger traces the foundation of John's Christology back to the prayer of Jesus. Furthermore, he sees the dogmas of Nicaea and Chalcedon as developing out of John's Christology, which presents Jesus' self-sacrifice for human beings as a prolongation of his converse with the Father. He thinks that these dogmas put into ontological terms that which is revealed by the prayer relationship *Abba*-Son, and the actions of Jesus which arise from this relationship. These acts reveal the being of Jesus, and an identity of these acts with that being.

The Prayer of the Son and the Theology of the Incarnation

One would expect that a concentration upon the prayer of Jesus would contribute to a theology of the Cross, especially as most examples in the Gospels of Jesus praying are in the context of his Passion (cf. Matt 26:39–44, 27:46; Mark 14:35–40, 15:34; Luke 22:31–32, 40–44, 23:34, 46; John 17:1–26). Yet, in looking at the Incarnation, Ratzinger characterizes it as an act of prayer. He bases this on his reading of Hebrews 10:5–7. He sees this passage as presenting the Incarnation as a dialogue between the Father and the Son, as an event within the Trinity. He interprets the "body" which is given to Jesus as human existence itself. In Jesus, obedience has become incarnate. The dialogue between the Father and the Son in the Godhead becomes the Son's obedient acceptance of a body. The humanity of Jesus is "prayer that has taken on a concrete form. In this sense, Jesus' humanity is something wholly spiritual, something that is 'divine' because of its origin."[93] While one may ask how the Father-Son dialogue within the Trinity can also be prayer, and how human existence itself can be prayer, there can be no denying that this passage from Hebrews seems to present the *kenosis* of the Son as prayer. For Ratzinger, this reveals a profound link between the Incarnation and the Cross. Divine sonship is "the release and handing back of himself" to the Father. Within creation, it becomes "obedience unto death" (Phil 2:8). This

---

92. *Introduction*, 225–26.
93. *Jesus Christ*, 67.

aspect of Ratzinger's earlier Christology is a second discontinuity with his later spiritual Christology. It does not make a re-appearance in *Behold the Pierced One* or *Jesus of Nazareth*.

The Prayer of Jesus in the Gospel according to Luke

The most explicit precursor of a spiritual Christology is to be found in Ratzinger's exposition of the public ministry of Jesus as portrayed by Luke. Indeed, he goes so far to say that: "Luke has raised the prayer of Jesus to the central christological category from which he describes the mystery of the Son." Ratzinger holds that: "What Chalcedon expressed by means of a formula drawn from the sphere of Greek ontology is affirmed by Luke in an utterly personal category based on the historical experience of the earthly Jesus; in substantial terms, this corresponds completely to the formula of Chalcedon."[94] Ratzinger sees the prayer of Jesus as a dialogue between the Son's will and the Father's will. It reveals the innermost essence of the mystery of Jesus. It reveals that "the inner foundation of the Resurrection is already present in the earthly Jesus," that the core of his existence is revealed in his dialogue with the Father. Only those "who share in the solitude of Jesus in this dialogue with the Father can profess who Jesus really is."[95]

The Eucharist as the Wellspring of Life

The two other aspects of Ratzinger's spiritual Christology, a theology of the heart and a eucharistic spirituality, can also be found earlier than *Behold the Pierced One*. In 1978 Ratzinger published four sermons under the title *Eucharistie: Mitte der Kirche*. Of particular relevance is a homily entitled "The Wellspring of Life from the Side of the Lord, opened in Loving Sacrifice." Here Ratzinger focuses upon the pierced side of Jesus as the source of both the church and the sacraments which up-build it. He notes that the word which John uses for the side of Jesus is the same as that used for Adam's rib, making it clear that Jesus is the new Adam, from whose side, in the sleep of death, issues a new human race. From the self-sacrifice of Jesus issues the blood and water which symbolize the Eucharist and Baptism, the source of the church.[96] Ratzinger links this outpouring with both Jesus' offering of his Body and Blood at the Last Supper and with his Resurrection. For

94. Ibid., 82.
95. Ibid.
96. Ratzinger, *God is Near Us*, 42–43.

Ratzinger, the Last Supper alone was not sufficient for the institution of the Eucharist. The words spoken then by Jesus were an anticipation of his death. They transformed his death into an event of love. Furthermore:

> [They] did not remain mere words but were given content by his actual death . . . [and] the death would remain empty of meaning, and would also render the words meaningless, if the Resurrection had not come about . . . [Thus] only the three together [Last Supper, Crucifixion and Resurrection] make up a whole, only these three together constitute a veritable reality, and this single mystery of Easter is the source and origin of the Eucharist.[97]

For Ratzinger, the Eucharist is a sacrifice, the presentation of Jesus' sacrifice on the Cross. It is a sacrifice in which God himself provides the offering which we are incapable of providing. Ratzinger sees the essence of this offering as prayer. He recounts how Israel came to understand the true nature of sacrifice as prayer, grasping that "the sacrifice pleasing to God is a man pleasing to God and that prayer, the grateful praise of God, is thus the true sacrifice in which we give ourselves back to him, thereby renewing ourselves and our world."[98]

Ratzinger sees the heart of Israel's worship as being expressed in the word "memorial" (remembrance). This was the essence of the Passover celebration, to remember the great works of God for Israel. At the time of Jesus, he believes that the idea of true sacrifice as "word was increasingly impressing itself upon the consciousness of Israel"; that "the man who in thanksgiving gave a spiritual dimension both to things and to himself, purified them, and thereby rendered them fit for God."[99]

For Ratzinger, Jesus transforms this sacrificial prayer of Israel. He transforms the thanksgiving prayer of the Passover, which remained merely verbal, into a concrete sacrifice. "Jesus Christ now gave this prayer a heart that opens the locked door; this heart is his love, in which God is victorious and conquers death." Our Eucharistic Prayer is the "continuation of this prayer of Jesus at the Last Supper and is thereby the heart of the Eucharist."[100] This transformation of Jesus' death into a verbal prayer in the Last Supper, and its continuation in the Eucharist, enables this death to remain present for us, since it continues to be present in the Eucharist. We can share in this death because we can participate in this prayer. "Because he turned death

---

97. Ibid., 43–44.
98. Ibid., 48.
99. Ibid., 48–49.
100. Ibid., 49.

into a proclamation of thanksgiving and love, he is now able to be present down through the ages as the wellspring of life, and we can enter into him by praying with him."[101] In the Eucharist, Jesus has given us a "new heart" whereby we can unite our entire selves with his sacrifice. His sacrifice becomes ours, and "our own life and suffering, our own hoping and loving, can also become fruitful, in the new heart he has given us . . . when the Eucharist is celebrated, the whole mystery of the Church, her living heart, the Lord, is present."[102] Ratzinger concludes his homily by turning to John 19:37/Zechariah 12:10: "They shall look on him whom they have pierced." This is not just a statement about the Day of Judgment (cf. Rev 1:7), but a description of the inner direction of the Christian life. By looking upon him, by keeping the eyes of our heart turned to him, we become more like him.[103]

Looking back upon this understanding of the Eucharist we can see references to the pierced side of Jesus, and to the Eucharist as a "heart." Jesus transforms the thanksgiving prayer of the Passover into a concrete sacrifice, thereby giving this prayer a heart which opens the locked door of death. This heart is his love. As a continuation of this prayer of Jesus, the Eucharistic Prayer becomes the heart of the Eucharist. In the Eucharist, Jesus has given us a "new heart." In this new heart his sacrifice becomes ours. When the Eucharist is celebrated, the whole mystery of the church, her living heart, the Lord, is present. However, there is a general absence of reference to the heart in any other context besides this homily. Two exceptions to this can be found. First, there is Ratzinger's reference to a passage from Daniélou, which likens the death agony of Jesus to a feeling of being torn asunder, of the heart being unable to carry within itself simultaneously love of the Trinity and love of a world alienated from the Trinity. Second, we are invited to look upon the Pierced One with the "eyes of our heart."

An Anthropological Prolegomenon to a Theology of the Heart

In order to find the beginnings of Ratzinger's anthropology of the heart, one must turn from *Introduction to Christianity* and *The God of Jesus Christ* to his commentary on the first chapter of *Gaudium et spes* on the dignity of the human person. There, Ratzinger offers a critique of the document's understanding of that person. In doing so he introduces some thoughts on the nature of the human heart. These specifically address the relationship between the heart and "interiority," the heart and man's relationship to God,

---

101. Ibid., 49–50.
102. Ibid., 50 and 52.
103. Ibid., 55.

the heart and human embodiment, the heart and conscience, and the heart and reason. Ratzinger's initial reference to the human heart is in his commentary on article 14, within the context of overcoming a body-soul dualism through a concept of "*interioritas*."[104] This concept reminds Ratzinger of Teilhard de Chardin's *intériorité*, that is, the inner dimension of things which is a fundamental principle of all reality. Ratzinger thinks that the Pastoral Constitution partly draws upon this idea "in order to suggest a sort of intuitive representation of what 'interiority' in man, his mind and spirit, means and is."[105] Nevertheless, Ratzinger thinks that Pascal's Fragment 793 is a stronger influence on the concept.[106] Finally, Ratzinger sees Augustine's theology of the interior life behind the mention of *conversio ad cor*, and how God awaits man in the depths of man's being. Here are echoes of Augustine's spiritual experience of God being closer to man than man is to himself, "that man finds himself and God by accomplishing a pilgrimage to himself, into his own inner depths, away from self-estrangement among things."[107] Thus Ratzinger sees this text:

> [as being] influenced by two fundamental concepts of Augustinian thought, by which [he] aimed at a synthesis of biblical anthropology, more historical in tendency, with the metaphysical conception of antiquity. The first is the distinction between the "homo interior" and "exterior." As compared with the corpus-anima schema, this introduces a greater element of personal responsibility and decision regarding the direction of life. It

---

104. Ratzinger, "Church and Man's," 127–28. The relevant passage in GS, no. 14 reads: "*Interioritate enim sua universitatem rerum excedit: ad haec profundam interioritatem redit, quando convertitur ad cor, ubi Deus eum exspectat, qui corda scrutatur.*" Austin Flannery's popular English translation of the Vatican II documents renders this as: "For by his power to know himself in the depths of his being he rises above the whole universe of mere objects. When he is drawn to think about his real self he turns to those deep recesses of his being where God who probes the heart awaits him." A less "dynamic" translation could be: "For in his interiority he exceeds the whole universe of things: he returns to this deep interiority when he is turned within to the heart, where the God who probes the heart awaits him." One can see that in attempting to render the Latin text into idiomatic English, Flannery has largely lost the Augustinian flavor of the original. See Flannery, *Vatican Council II*, 915. The Vatican translation of this passage is much closer to the original Latin. See *The Documents of Vatican II: Vatican Translation*, 134.

105. "Church and Man's," 128.

106. Ibid. Ratzinger refers the reader to Pascal, *Pensées*, in the edition of Léon Brunschvicg, 697, where Pascal writes: "All bodies, the firmament, the stars, the earth and its kingdoms do not equal the least of spirits; for the latter know all things, whereas bodies know nothing."

107. "Church and Man's," 128.

therefore analyzes man more on historical and dynamic than on metaphysical lines. The second is the concept of the "philosophia cordis," the biblical concept of the heart which for Augustine expresses the unity of the interior life and corporeality. This again becomes a key concept with Pascal and here enters the conciliar text, bringing with it by implication a good deal of what Karl Rahner and Gabriel Marcel have had to say on other grounds and from other angles.[108]

Ratzinger regards these concepts of heart and interiority as "the real theology of the body presented by this section," in contrast to a theology of the body which consists "of a purely regional theology concerning the body in contradistinction to the soul."[109] Rather, a genuine theology of the body must regard it in its full humanity, as the corporeal embodiment of mind and spirit, the way in which the human spirit has concrete existence. So Ratzinger concludes:

> It must therefore be a theology of the unity of man as spirit in body and body in spirit, so that a genuine theology of the body will be achieved in proportion as the "cor" is spoken of as spirit "to the extent that it has come close to the blood" and therefore no longer merely spirit but embodied and therefore human.[110]

Ratzinger's comments upon the relationship between the heart and conscience are brief. He sees the Constitution's teaching on the nature of human conscience in article 16 as taking "its place in a line of thought deriving from Newman" in that it avoids "any purely sociological or psychological interpretation of conscience," instead affirming "its transcendent character."[111] This character is described as a law written in the human heart by God. This makes the conscience a holy place, where one is alone with God and hears the voice of God. It is the innermost core of the human person.

Finally, Ratzinger looks at the relationship between the human reason and heart within the context of his comments on the attitude of the church towards atheism in article 21. In discussing the difficulties presented by the article with regard to its presentation of the roles of experience and reason in coming to a natural knowledge of God, Ratzinger points out that there were two requests to modify the text, one which wanted a reaffirmation of

---

108. Ibid., 128–29.

109. Ibid., 129.

110. Ibid. The interior quotation given by Ratzinger is taken from a book on Pascal by Guardini, *Christliches Bewußtsein*, 187. This has been translated into English as *Pascal for our Time*.

111. "Church and Man's," 134.

Prolegomena to a Spiritual Christology 61

the definition of Vatican I regarding natural knowledge of God, and the other that despite the revelation of Christ, God remains inaccessible, that in our present state we cannot intellectually see God in his essence.[112] In response to the second request, the commission responsible for adjudicating such requests gave the remarkable answer that the *theologia negativa* was a *disputata quaestio!*[113] Ratzinger remarks that in passing over the essentials of the *theologia negativa*, the Council "took no account of Augustine's epistemology, which is much deeper than that of Aquinas."[114] He goes on to state that:

> [Augustine] is well aware that the organ by which God can be seen cannot be a non-historical "*ratio naturalis*" [natural reason] which just does not exist, but only *ratio pura*, i.e. *purificata* [purified reason] or, as Augustine expresses it echoing the Gospel, the *cor purum* ("Blessed are the pure in heart, for they shall see God"). Augustine also knows that the necessary purification of sight takes place through faith (Acts 15:9) and through love, at all events not as a result of reflection alone and not at all by man's own power.[115]

It is important to note that Ratzinger does not question the existence of "natural reason," but only that of "non-historical" natural reason. He wishes "to limit the neo-scholastic rationalism contained in the formula of 1870 [by placing] its over-static idea of 'ratio naturalis' in a more historical perspective."[116]

---

112. Cf. Denzinger, nos. 3004–5.
113. "Church and Man's," 154.
114. Ibid., 155.
115. Ibid. Cf. Rowland, *Ratzinger's Faith*, 4.
116. "Church and Man's," 153.

3

The Spiritual Christology of *Behold the Pierced One*—Theory

Commentary on Ratzinger's Spiritual Christology

Ratzinger's spiritual Christology has not hitherto been investigated in any great depth. Although there have been some perceptive commentaries, they have, with one exception, only touched upon it *en passant*. De Gaál attends to it briefly, but gives some important insights. He asserts that, for Ratzinger, the prayer of Jesus is the basic affirmation of his person, that it is Jesus' filial relationship with his Father which is at the root of the question of human freedom and liberation, that we must participate in the prayer of Jesus if we are to know and understand him, that both the church and the Eucharist have their origin in the prayer of Jesus, that only in a spiritual Christology will a spirituality of the Eucharist reveal itself, and that theology is ultimately grounded in prayer. He points out that Ratzinger regards prayer as the indispensable starting point for any Christology.[1] Apart from these points, de Gaál comments upon the dyotheletic roots of Ratzinger's spiritual Christology and its implication for human volition, claiming that, for Ratzinger, the teaching of the Constantinople III "implies that there exists a proper dignity of Christ's human nature, which is being absorbed into the divine will; both blend into one will. The human and divine identities

---

1. De Gaál, *The Theology of Pope Benedict XVI*, 4–5 and 86–88. Cf. Ratzinger, *Behold*, 46 and 90.

move into one subject as a pure affirmation of the Father's will. In Jesus, human volition acquires a divine form, and an 'alchemy of being' occurs."[2]

De Gaál thinks that it is Ratzinger's view of the nature of revelation which enables him to "accept both the divinity of the historical Jesus and the historical method without limiting faith to the historical method's range."[3] Going further, Cong Quy Joseph Lam has proposed that Ratzinger's spiritual Christology is a direct result of his theology of revelation, a "theological-practical consequence of his earlier study of the Bonaventurian concept of revelation."[4] For Lam, Ratzinger's Christology is situated within the divine dialogue. It is neither a Monophysitic "theology from above," nor a Nestorian "theology from below," but a "theology from within," a *vade mecum*.[5] Lam sees the influence of the pastor-theologians Augustine and Bonaventure leading Ratzinger to view theology as embedded in proclamation and complemented by prayer, and thus being a performative rather than merely informative undertaking, one which calls its audience (and presumably its practitioner) to conversion. According to Lam, for Ratzinger, it is the prayer of Jesus that reveals his inner reality, a reality of constant dialogue with his Father wherein Jesus is revealed as the Word of the Father. Through his sending of the Holy Spirit, the one who is both Word and Son draws believers into his prayer and thus into communion with God.[6]

Lam goes on to propose that Ratzinger's spiritual Christology is fully disclosed in the three volumes of *Jesus of Nazareth*.[7] Therein, he claims, the clearest disclosure of Jesus' inner reality is to be found in the Lord's Prayer and the prayer of Jesus in the garden of Gethsemane. The former reveals the heart of the relationship between Jesus and God, his *Abba*, a relationship which is unique to them. This latter reveals the synergy of the divine and human wills in Christ which makes salvation possible. For Christians, participating in the prayer of Jesus is a soteriological event. Worship is the bridge between Christology and soteriology.[8]

2. De Gaál, *The Theology of Pope Benedict XVI*, 219. Joseph Murphy, in a brief exposition of Ratzinger's Christology, is also aware of the importance of the prayer of Jesus in that Christology, and indeed, makes the assertion that the Church's christological dogmas owe much to "her reflection on [Jesus'] relationship with God, particularly as expressed in his prayer." Murphy looks at the dyothelitic teaching of St. Maximus the Confessor and Constantinople III, and how, in *Behold*, "Ratzinger develops the theme [of the Council as to] how our freedom is realized through its insertion into Christ's prayer" (Murphy, *Christ our Joy*, 120–21, and 124).

3. De Gaál, *The Theology of Pope Benedict XVI*, 80.
4. Lam, *Joseph Ratzinger's Theological Retractations*, 89.
5. Ibid., 21 and 90–91.
6. Ibid., 113–16.
7. Ibid., 135–43.
8. Ibid., 117–23.

In an essay on the human and divine wills of Christ, Aaron Riches draws upon Ratzinger's work on the dyothelite Christology of Maximus and Constantinople III. Riches refers to Ratzinger's endorsement in *Behold the Pierced One* of the Maximian Christology of Constantinople III—stating that this Christology overcomes "a residual binary logic in Chaldedonian Christology" by clarifying the mode of unity of the humanity and divinity of Christ. According to Riches:

> [Ratzinger holds that] a theology of the filial prayer of Jesus specifies the mode of mutual indwelling of divinity and humanity in the Son's singular synthetic Person. Therefore, speculative reflection on the prayer of the Son concretely abolishes whatever latent binary logic is unwittingly preserved at Chalcedon ... [for Ratzinger] the Maximian achievement lies pre-eminently in the abolition of every dualism of the two natures in Christ.[9]

Riches maintains that Ratzinger is attracted to the Maximian Christology because he thinks it will help overcome a certain dualism in the contemporary liturgy which springs from a dualism in Christology. On this point Riches states:

> [In this dualism there is] a discretely dissociated anthropology that presumes it is possible to imitate the "human" Jesus apart from the "divinity" of the Son of God. Under this condition, the Liturgy becomes increasingly focused on "our" humanity (the self-evident "given" of our nature). The Liturgy is thus inclined to become a "self-enclosed" parody of *latreia*, a parody that fails to doxologically open in *metanoia* to the divine horizon of the filial-union Jesus gifts to the world in gifting himself (i.e. his own personhood). In this way, the contemporary form of the Liturgy is posited as betraying a Nestorian dissociation of humanity and divinity in Christ. Attempting to discretely follow the "pure" humanity of Jesus, the Liturgy loses the Person of the Son and in so doing loses the personal pattern of humanity's divine *sequela*.[10]

Riches claims that "the quasi-Nestorianism that expressed itself in neoscholasticism before Vatican II (paralleling 'grace' and 'nature') is reincarnated after the Council among those theologians who would dispense with the

---

9. Riches, "After Chalcedon," 207.

10. Ibid., 208. Helmut Hoping also sees a relationship between Ratzinger's Christology and his understanding of the Liturgy, in that the former is the basis for the latter. See Hoping, "Gemeinschaft mit Christus," 558.

impassible Logos and attempt to find comfort in the dissociated 'humanity' of a Jesus who merely 'suffers with us.'"[11]

A fourth and more extensive commentary on Ratzinger's spiritual Christology is that of Sara Butler, who looks at the place of the Sacred Heart of Jesus in this Christology. This is the only commentary which is concerned solely with Ratzinger's spiritual Christology. Butler notes that Ratzinger's favorite devotional image is the pierced heart of Jesus, that gazing upon this heart is a central theme in his Christology, and that he sees this heart as revealing the Father's love, and being the fountain of salvation from which the Holy Spirit streams forth. She notes the affinity between Ratzinger's understanding of the Sacred Heart and that of Pope Pius XII in his encyclical *Haurietis aquas*.[12] Like Riches, Butler draws attention to the influence of Constantinople III on the development of Ratzinger's spiritual Christology. She also takes up a point similar to that of Riches, the connection between this spiritual Christology and Ratzinger's understanding of the liturgy, whereby devotion to the pierced heart of Jesus becomes a "necessary counterpart to the objective spirituality of the liturgical movement."[13] Butler also takes note of Ratzinger's conviction that the way to faith in Christ, to our knowing and loving him, is not through the historical-critical method, but through "participating in his prayer, that is, by acts of self-surrender and love."[14] Furthermore, she draws attention to Ratzinger's linking of the biblical texts which speak of the Savior's pierced heart (cf. John 19:34, 37; Zech 12:10; and Rev 1:7) with the sacrificial nature of the Eucharist.[15]

Butler maintains that Ratzinger sees an abandonment of devotion to the Sacred Heart being caused by a loss of appreciation for more emotional and subjective forms of piety in the wake of the liturgical movement's emphasis on more sober and objective liturgical forms. His response is to claim that objections to the devotion had been already answered in *Haurietis aquas*. This encyclical grounded the devotion in the Bible, establishing a pedigree which goes back to the Fathers. In particular, Ratzinger draws on the work of Hugo Rahner, who uncovered two patristic traditions which connected the piercing of Jesus' side on the Cross (cf. John 19:34) with the promise of "fountains of living water" given in John 7:37–39. The "Ephesian" interpretation of this latter passage saw the promise as referring to the pierced side of Jesus, whilst the "Alexandrian" interpretation saw it as

---

11. Riches, "After Chalcedon," 208.
12. Butler, "Benedict XVI," 145. Cf. Pius XII, *Haurietis aquas*, 309–53.
13. Butler, "Benedict XVI," 148.
14. Ibid.
15. Ibid., 148–49.

referring to the believer's heart as the source of living water. Rahner argued that it was the Ephesian reading which correctly interpreted the evangelist's intention.[16]

However, as Butler points out, Ratzinger observes that the word "heart" does not occur in the Johannine texts. Since worshippers can participate in the Paschal Mystery through the Eucharist, is not devotion to the Sacred Heart superfluous? His rejoinder is that the only worthy response to the passion of the heart of God revealed on the Cross is one which engages the passions of the human heart. Believers need an affective "beholding" and "touching." Their hearts need to be engaged. Ratzinger sees the "heart" as the "hub" of the senses and emotions. A spirituality of the senses is a spirituality of the heart. Since the incarnate Word experienced the human passions in his heart, incarnational spirituality must be a spirituality of the passions, a spirituality of "heart to heart." What is more, the heart of Jesus reveals the heart of God, a heart which, in the estimation of Origen, can even suffer. This heart-centered spirituality reveals a God who loves us passionately, a heart which is "overturned" by this passionate love (cf. Songs 4:9 and 8:16; and Hos 11:1–9), an overturning ultimately made manifest in the heart of Jesus on the Cross, a heart which is concerned with self-surrender rather than self-preservation.[17]

Butler sees Ratzinger's focus on a spirituality of the heart, along with his reading of the christological doctrine of the Constantinople III, as leading him to attempt the development a spiritual Christology. In response to a historical Jesus who cannot be the object of personal faith and devotion, Butler holds that Ratzinger's spiritual Christology presents a biblical Jesus, proclaimed in the church and appropriated by faith, one who can be known and experienced as the risen Lord through participation in his mysteries. According to her, Ratzinger's aim is to develop a new christological synthesis, a Christ-centered spirituality. She sees Ratzinger grounding a devotional knowledge of Christ through faith in a participation in the prayer of Jesus. Ultimately, this is a participation in Jesus' relationship with his Father. Butler sees the seven theses of Ratzinger's spiritual Christology as developing this basic insight.[18]

---

16. Ibid., 151–53. Cf. Rahner, "On the Biblical Basis of the Devotion," 15–35; and "The Beginnings of the Devotion in Patristic Times," 37–57.

17. Butler, "Benedict XVI," 153–57. Cf. *Behold*, 50–69.

18. Butler, "Benedict XVI," 157–59. Cf. *Behold*, 13–46. Also cf. Hahn, *Covenant and Communion*, 143–46. In this study, Hahn focuses briefly on Ratzinger's spiritual Christology. His conviction is that Ratzinger's emphasis on the relationship between the person and the prayer of Jesus is one of his "most unique and important contributions to Christology." Hahn specifically identifies the first two published volumes of *Jesus of Nazareth* as a work of spiritual Christology (14–15).

The Spiritual Christology of *Behold the Pierced One*—Theory

Butler goes on to ask how we can participate in the prayer of Jesus. She sees Ratzinger's answers essentially saying that this participation can take place through the living Lord present and living in the church, which is the living subject of our knowledge of Jesus, and in which the memory of the past is present. For Butler, the significance of Ratzinger's emphasis upon the union of the human and divine wills of Jesus, a union affirmed by the Constantinople III, is that it demonstrates how this union does not destroy the human freedom of Christ. On the contrary, it fulfils it. Therefore, our participation in the prayer relationship between Jesus and his Father means that our wills too must come into union with the divine will, and this union becomes the source of a new human freedom which is ultimately that of divinization.[19]

Butler sees Ratzinger's spiritual Christology influencing the Christology of the *Catechism of the Catholic Church*, Pope Benedict XVI's encyclical *Deus caritas est*, and *Jesus of Nazareth*. In the *Catechism*, the sub-section on the christological councils concludes with a paragraph on the Sacred Heart. Ratzinger's commentary on the *Catechism* explains that this is a fitting climax to an account of the teaching of the seven christological councils, since the heart of Jesus is the chief sign and symbol of the Redeemer's love for the Father and for each one of us.[20] In *Deus caritas est*, Butler sees Ratzinger proposing the pierced heart of Jesus as a recurring *leitmotif*, the icon *par excellence* of God's love for us, and she sees Ratzinger's spiritual Christology as a hermeneutical key to *Jesus of Nazareth*.[21]

We can see that those who have investigated Ratzinger's spiritual Christology have drawn attention to some very significant aspects of it. De Gaál and Butler have commented upon the connection between this spiritual Christology and the question of human freedom, and, in Butler's case, human divinization. Riches, Lam and Butler have realized its importance for liturgical questions. All four have stressed the importance of its dyotheletic aspect. De Gaál has mentioned its ecclesial and eucharistic relevance. Lam, in particular, has pointed out the connection between Ratzinger's theology of revelation and his spiritual Christology.[22] Both Butler and Lam have grasped that Ratzinger's spiritual Christology provides a hermeneutical key to *Jesus of Nazareth*. However, it is Butler who has had the most

---

19. Butler, "Benedict XVI," 160–62. Cf. Denzinger, nos. 553–59.

20. Butler, "Benedict XVI," 163. Cf. *CCC*, no. 478; and Ratzinger, *Gospel, Catechesis, Catechism*, 70–71.

21. Butler, "Benedict XVI," 165–67. Cf. *DCE*, nos. 7, 9–10, 12, 19, and 39.

22. Collins makes a similar point, it being that Ratzinger's Christology follows the same dialogical framework as does his theology of revelation. See Collins, *The Word Made Love*, xiii and 56–59.

comprehensive insights. She has been able to look beyond the importance of the christological theses of Ratzinger's spiritual Christology and see the fundamental place which the heart of Jesus occupies in it. In what follows, an attempt will be made to analyze and evaluate in a systematic way, and hopefully go beyond, that which these commentators have commented upon.

The Principles of Ratzinger's Spiritual Christology

We have seen that, in order to arrive at an authentic Christology, Ratzinger proposes seven christological theses.[23] They might also be called the principles of a renovated Christology as well as the principles of a spiritual Christology. This is so because Ratzinger's spiritual Christology is not an addition to his normal Christology. Rather, he sees it as a way to more effectively arrive at an authentic Christology which overcomes the many divisions currently present in that theology. It is leaven in the dough, not icing on the cake. Although Ratzinger only numbers his theses, they can be denominated as follows—filial, soteriological, personal, ecclesial, dogmatic, volitional and hermeneutical.

The Filial Thesis: "According to the testimony of Holy Scripture, the center of the life and person of Jesus is his constant communication with the Father."

In this first thesis Ratzinger reiterates, in a condensed form, his thinking on the development of the title "Son" as the church's ultimate confession of who Jesus truly is.[24] Contrary to the view that can be found in modern exegesis and history of doctrine that "this kind of concentration of the historical inheritance may be a falsification of the original phenomenon simply because the historical distance is too great," Ratzinger puts forward the view that,

---

23. These Christological theses were not the first proposed by Ratzinger. In "Thesen zur Christologie," 133–36, he gives ten Christological theses. However, the only bibliographical detail given for this article is "Unveröffentlicht" (Unpublished). No date is given. Reading these theses, I get the impression that they were composed prior to *Introduction to Christianity*. In them the starting point for Christology in the New Testament is the Resurrection. The Crucifixion, the Lordship of Jesus and his claim to divinity are grounded in the Resurrection. The formula of the Father's identification of Jesus as his Son is presented as an interpretation of the Resurrection and what it reveals about Jesus. John's Gospel is presented as giving the clearest view of the identity of Jesus as the Word and Son of God. The Church's professions of faith and Christological creeds reach a certain completion in the Council of Chalcedon.

24. *Behold*, 15–17. Cf. *Introduction*, 213–28.

The Spiritual Christology of *Behold the Pierced One*—Theory

in the use of this term, "the Church was responding precisely to the basic historical experience of those who had been eyewitnesses of Jesus' life." He is convinced of this because he maintains that "the entire Gospel testimony is unanimous that Jesus' words and deeds flowed from this most intimate communion with the Father."[25]

Once again, Ratzinger goes back to Luke's stressing of this point. He recalls the three examples which he gave in *The God of Jesus Christ*—the calling of the Twelve (cf. Luke 6:12–17), Peter's profession of faith (cf. Luke 9:18–20), and the Transfiguration (cf. Luke 9:28–36).[26] In the first of these, Ratzinger sees not just the calling of the Twelve as proceeding from the Son's converse with the Father, but the church as being "born in that prayer in which Jesus gives himself back into the Father's hands and the Father commits everything to the Son." The communication of the Son and Father constitutes the "true and ever-new" origin and foundation of the church.[27]

In Peter's confession of faith, Ratzinger sees the second stage of the church's development. It is when the disciples begin "to share in the hiddenness of [Jesus'] prayer . . . [that they grasp and express] the fundamental reality of the person of Jesus as a result of having seen him praying, in fellowship with the Father."[28] Ratzinger holds that, according to Luke:

> The Christian confession of faith comes from participating in the prayer of Jesus, from being drawn into his prayer and being privileged to behold it; it interprets the experience of Jesus' prayer, and its interpretation of Jesus is correct because it springs from a sharing in what is most personal and intimate to him.[29]

In essence, Ratzinger identifies the Christian profession of faith in Jesus, not as a proposition, but as prayer. It is from participation in the prayer of Jesus that the church arises.[30] In the third example, the Transfiguration makes visible what actually takes place in Jesus' prayer—revelation. As Ratzinger says: "Jesus' proclamation proceeds from this participation in God's radiance, God's glory, which also involves a seeing with the eyes of God—and therefore the unfolding of what was hidden."[31] Revelation and prayer are united in the person of Jesus in the mystery of his sonship. Furthermore,

---

25. Ibid., 17.
26. See *Jesus Christ*, 66–68.
27. *Behold*, 18.
28. Ibid., 19.
29. Ibid.
30. Ibid.
31. Ibid., 20.

Jesus' communication with the Father is the true reason for his Resurrection. The Son, who shares in the glory of the Father, cannot remain in death. Taking these three examples together, Ratzinger concludes that, for Luke, "the whole of Christology—our speaking of Christ—is nothing other than the interpretation of his prayer: the entire person of Jesus is contained in this prayer."[32]

Ratzinger gives three more examples from the other Evangelists to illustrate that this view is not unique to Luke. He calls attention to Mark's preservation of Jesus addressing the Father as *Abba*, a familiarity which demonstrates the absolute uniqueness of Jesus' relationship with the Father, and makes the term "Son" the only possible one for fully expressing the relationship from Jesus' side (cf. Mark 14:36).[33] Further illustrating the uniqueness of this relationship is the account of Jesus teaching his disciples to pray (cf. Matt 6:9–13). The fact that the disciples are told to address God as "Our Father" shows that although the disciples pray as a community and through their common prayer participate in Jesus' relationship with God, nevertheless, the mode of their relationship with God is not absolutely identical with that of Jesus, who is able to pray "my Father" in a unique way.[34] Finally, having seen that this relationship is not only expressed in the word "Son," but also in a series of formulas found throughout Jesus' preaching in the synoptic Gospels which express his awareness that he speaks and acts, not from himself, but from another, we can see that the emphasis in John's Gospel on "Word," "Son," and "send" is not alien to the synoptic tradition. For Ratzinger, the fourth Gospel shows who Jesus is from the experience of intimate friendship with him.[35]

The Soteriological Thesis: "Jesus died praying. At the Last Supper he had anticipated his death by giving himself, thus transforming his death, from within, into an act of love, into a glorification of God."

Ratzinger believes that in the prayer of Jesus we have the clue which links together Christology and soteriology, "the person of Jesus and his deeds and sufferings," and that Jesus fashioned his death into an act of prayer, of worship.[36] The fact that the "death cry" of Jesus was misunderstood by the

32. Ibid.
33. Ibid., 20–21.
34. Ibid., 21.
35. Ibid., 21–22.
36. Ibid., 22.

bystanders serves to demonstrate that only faith can recognize the messianic fulfillment of Psalm 22. Ratzinger holds that all the Evangelists agree on this Psalm being uniquely and completely fulfilled in the Passion of Jesus, and that it was the key christological text of the early Christians.[37] The last words of Jesus were an expression of his innermost essence, which was to be in dialogue with the Father. His death was his handing himself over to the Father completely. He fulfils Scripture in that Scripture becomes flesh in him.[38]

According to Ratzinger, once we see this, we can understand the indissoluble bond between the Last Supper and the death of Jesus. When Jesus anticipates his death by sharing his body and blood, he transforms his death into an act of love. This is why John sees the death of Jesus as a glorification of God and of the Son (cf. John 12:28; 17:22). What by nature is the destruction of communication is transformed into the supreme act of communication, having the power to redeem because it "signifies the triumph of love over death."[39]

The personal thesis: "Since the center of the person of Jesus is prayer, it is essential to participate in his prayer if we are to know and understand him."

Following the axiom of the co-naturality of the knower and the known, and what follows from it regarding the knowing of a person—that there needs to be an entering into to, a becoming one with, the one who is known in order to reach an understanding of that one—Ratzinger applies this axiom to religion.[40] According to Ratzinger, the fundamental act of religion is prayer, and in Christianity, prayer is "the act of self-surrender by which we enter the Body of Christ," and thus an act of love.[41]

Since the prayer of Jesus, his communication with the Father, is the central act of his person, "it is only possible really to understand this person by entering into this act of prayer, by participating in it." Ratzinger sees Jesus' comment that no one can come to him unless drawn by the Father (cf. John 6:44) as confirmation of this. Unless one has a relationship with God "there can be no understanding of him who, in his innermost self, is nothing but relationship with God, the Father."[42] One may know things *about* him,

37. Ibid., 22–24.
38. Ibid., 24.
39. Ibid., 25.
40. Cf. *ST* I, q. 12, a. 1.
41. *Behold*, 26.
42. Ibid.

but intimate knowledge of the person himself will elude us. Thus Ratzinger states that:

> [A] participation in the mind of Jesus, i.e., in his prayer, which ... is an act of love, of self-giving and self-expropriation to men, is not some kind of pious supplement to reading the Gospels, adding nothing to knowledge of him or even being an obstacle to the rigorous purity of critical knowing. On the contrary, it is the basic precondition if real understanding, in the sense of modern hermeneutics—i.e., the entering-in to the same time and meaning—is to take place.[43]

Ratzinger calls what he is proposing a "theological epistemology." As he claims to find in the conversion of St. Paul (cf. Acts 9:11): "The person who prays begins to see ... as Richard of St. Victor says—'Love is the faculty of seeing.'"[44] While critical exegesis, the history of doctrine and the anthropology of the human sciences are necessary, they are not sufficient. They "must be complemented by the theology of the saints, which is theology from experience. All real progress in theological understanding has its origin in the eye of love and in its faculty of beholding."[45]

The Ecclesial Thesis: "Sharing in Jesus' praying involves communion with all his brethren. Fellowship with the person of Jesus, which proceeds from participation in his prayer, thus constitutes the all-embracing fellowship that Paul calls the 'Body of Christ.' So the Church—the 'Body of Christ'—is the true subject of our knowledge of Jesus. In the Church's memory the past is present because Christ is present and lives in her."

In his exposition of his filial thesis, Ratzinger already touches upon the need for Christians to participate in the prayer of Jesus. However, Ratzinger holds that, for us, God is not "my Father" as he is for Jesus, but "our Father." We have the right to call God "Father" because we have been created by him and for each other. "To recognize and accept God's Fatherhood always means accepting that we are set in relation to one another: man is entitled to call

---

43. Ibid.

44. Ibid., 27. For the quotations from Richard of St. Victor, Ratzinger cites *De Gradibus Charitatis* (PL 196:1203).

45. *Behold*, 27.

God 'Father' to the extent that he participates in the 'we'—which is the form under which God's love seeks him."[46]

Besides a biblical foundation for this experience, Ratzinger posits two supporting existential ones—human reason and historical experience. For him, the "history of religion and of the mind . . . [reveals] a peculiar dichotomy in the question of God."[47] On the one hand, there has been an acceptance of rational evidence for the existence of God (cf. Wis 13:4; Rom 1:19-20), and on the other, "a tremendous obscuring and twisting of the image of God," a point which St. Paul also takes up in the passage from Romans. When people try to name and describe the God who we know to exist, "the image of God falls apart in contradictory aspects. They do not simply eliminate the primary evidence, but they so obscure it as to make it unrecognizable; indeed, in the extreme cases, they can actually destroy it entirely."[48] In addition, Ratzinger posits a recurring theme of revelation in the history of religions, showing that although man himself cannot create a relationship with God, ancient communities realized that the means which they had of relating to God ultimately came from God. "To that extent, even the awareness that religion must rest on a higher authority than one's own reason, and that it needs a community as a 'carrier,' is part of mankind's basic knowledge, though found in manifold forms and even distortions."[49] Ratzinger then applies these biblical and existential insights to Jesus, maintaining that although Jesus' personal relationship to God was unique, it did not depart from the pattern just described. For Ratzinger, Jesus' dialogue with the Father was also a dialogue with Moses and Elijah, the Law and the Prophets (cf. Mark 9:4). Jesus revealed the "spirit" of the Old Testament and, in doing so, revealed the Father "in the Spirit." Thus he fulfilled rather than destroyed the "letter" of the Old Testament. He did not destroy the People of God, but renewed it, and gave "the nations" access to the "Spirit of revelation," and hence to God the Father. Jesus did not found a new "People of God." Rather: "Jesus made the old People of God into a new People by adopting those who believe in him into the community of his own self (of his 'Body')." According to Ratzinger, this adoption was made possible by the death of Jesus, which he transformed "into an act of prayer, an act of love, and thus by making himself communicable."[50] Putting it another way, Ratzinger states that:

46. Ibid., 27-28.
47. Ibid., 28.
48. Ibid.
49. Ibid., 29.
50. Ibid., 30.

> Jesus has entered into the already existing subject of tradition, God's people of Israel, with his proclamation and his whole person, and by doing so he has made it possible for people to participate in his most intimate and personal act of being, i.e., his dialogue with the Father.[51]

For Christians, this means "that we are in communication with the living subject of tradition," the church.[52] According to Ratzinger, the New Testament bears witness to this reality in presupposing that the church is its subject, in the sense of the one who "speaks" it. The Johannine corpus expresses this in what Ratzinger calls the "ecclesial we" (cf. 1 John 5:1–20; John 3:11), a "we" that "points to the Church as the subject of knowledge in faith."[53]

Ratzinger also points to the concept of "remembrance" in John's Gospel, as demonstrating how "the Church's tradition is the transcendental subject in whose memory the past is present." Over time, the Holy Spirit leads the church to a deeper and clearer understanding of what she remembers, not an absolutely new knowledge, but "the process whereby the memory becomes aware of itself (cf. John 14:26; 16:13)."[54]

For Ratzinger, this "memory" of the church provides the hermeneutical context for the individual's exercise of reason in understanding the faith of the church. In understanding, as well as in love, there needs to be a "fusing" of the I with the other. The memory of the church is enriched and deepened in two ways, "by the experience of love which worships . . . [and by being] continually refined by critical reason." In other words, theology has an ecclesial quality which is "not an epistemological collectivism, not an ideology which violates reason, but a hermeneutical context which is essential to reason if it is to operate at all."[55]

---

51. Ibid.
52. Ibid.
53. Ibid., 31.
54. Ibid.
55. Ibid., 32.

The Spiritual Christology of *Behold the Pierced One*—Theory

The Dogmatic Thesis: "The core of the dogma defined in the councils of the early Church consists in the statement that Jesus is the true Son of God, of the same essence as the Father and, through the Incarnation, equally of the same essence as us. Ultimately this definition is nothing other than an interpretation of the life and death of Jesus, which was preordained from the Son's primal conversation with the Father. That is why dogmatic and biblical Christology cannot be divorced from one another or opposed to one another, no more than Christology and soteriology can be separated. In the same way, Christology 'from above' and 'from below,' the theology of the Incarnation and the theology of the Cross, form an indivisible unity."

For Ratzinger, this thesis follows from the filial and soteriological theses—the testimony of Sacred Scripture regarding the prayer of Jesus, especially his prayer on the Cross. Ratzinger holds that the dogma that Jesus is the true Son of God, of the same essence of the Father and of us, simply puts the meaning of Jesus' prayer into the language of philosophical theology.[56]

Ratzinger is aware of the charge that dogma has distorted the original "Hebraic" faith in Jesus by replacing trust in saving grace with a "Greek" doctrine about ontology. His response is to address the nature of salvation. His argument runs thus: If Christ saves man, "liberates" him, what is the nature of this liberation? What is human freedom? Freedom without truth is not true freedom. Moreover, human freedom means being "like God," "becoming like God," even "being God." All human programs of liberation have this as their goal, since "the yearning for freedom is rooted in man's being."[57] Therefore, when we ask questions about truth and freedom we are asking ontological questions. Ratzinger maintains that, because the question of being arises from the desire for freedom and the need for truth, it does not belong to any particular stage of man's intellectual development, but is perennial.[58]

According to Ratzinger, the contemporary rejection of ontological questions does not spring from a desire for a return to a simple Hebraic faith, but from a positivist position which only looks at the phenomenal level and rejects the possibility of knowing the truth of being. However: "The question of truth and the question of freedom are involved in the

---

56. Ibid., 32–33.
57. Ibid., 33.
58. Ibid., 34.

question of being and therefore also in the question of God."[59] Ultimately, these questions *are* the question of God. Particular times may develop particular methods of addressing these questions, but they can never be put aside, and any interpretation of the New Testament which does so is theologically irrelevant.

Concretely, when we address the question of Jesus' prayer we are asking about the nature of his person, that which is central to his humanity. For Ratzinger:

> [The] New Testament designates [the prayer of Jesus] as the place where man may actually become God, where his liberation may take place; it is the place where he touches his own truth and becomes true himself. The question of Jesus' filial relationship to the Father gets to the very root of the question of man's freedom and liberation, and unless this is done, everything else is futile. Any liberation of man which does not enable him to become divine betrays man, betrays his boundless yearning.[60]

To the charge that "of one substance with the Father" departs from the biblical understanding of who Jesus is, Ratzinger replies that it simply translates the word "Son" into philosophical language. According to him, such a translation became necessary when faith began to reflect upon and ask questions about what exactly the word "Son" meant when applied to Jesus. Was it being used metaphorically, or did it have a more concrete meaning? According to Ratzinger, "of one substance" means that the term "Son" is to be understood literally, not metaphorically. Thus, the phrase does not add to the testimony of the New Testament, rather, it defends it from being allegorized. "Jesus is not only *described* as the Son of God, he *is* the Son of God."[61]

The Volitional Thesis: "The so-called Neo-Chalcedonian theology which is summed up in the Third Council of Constantinople (680–681) makes an important contribution to a proper grasp of the inner unity of biblical and dogmatic theology, of theology and religious life. Only from this standpoint does the dogma of Chalcedon (451) yield its full meaning."

According to Ratzinger, the Council of Chalcedon left a residual parallelism of the two natures in Christ. It was this parallelism which brought about

59. Ibid., 35.
60. Ibid.
61. Ibid., 36.

the genesis of certain post-conciliar divisions. What needed to be clarified was the mode of unity of the true humanity and divinity of Jesus. This meant a clarification of the nature of the one Person in Christ so that there could be seen a unity of mutual indwelling and not just a juxtaposition. For Ratzinger: "Only in this way can there be that genuine 'becoming like God,' without which there is no liberation and no freedom."[62]

In Ratzinger's view, the achievement of Constantinople III was twofold. First, it preserved the human nature of Christ from any amputation or reduction. Second, it abolished any dualism or parallelism of the two natures which had been adopted in order to protect the human freedom of Jesus. Ratzinger maintains that this attempt to safeguard Jesus' human freedom forgot that "when the human will is taken up into the will of God, freedom is not destroyed; indeed, only then does genuine freedom come into its own."[63] Ratzinger's reading of Constantinople III is that when the human will of Jesus follows the divine will it is not absorbed into the divine will, but becomes one, not in a "natural" manner, but in freedom. The metaphysical twoness of the wills remain, but unity is achieved in the realm of the person. The two wills become one, not naturally, but personally. This free unity, a form of unity created by love, is "higher and more interior than a mere natural unity," corresponding to the highest form of unity, the trinitarian.[64]

The text which the Council cites in order to illustrate this unity is John 6:38: "I have come down from Heaven, not to do my own will, but the will of him who sent me." Ratzinger understands this passage thus:

> Here it is the divine Logos who is speaking, and he speaks of the human will of the man Jesus as his will, the will of the Logos. With this exegesis of John 6:38 the Council indicates the unity of the subject in Christ. There are not two "I"s in him, but only one. The Logos speaks in the I-form of the human will and mind of Jesus; it has become his I, has become adopted into his I, because the human will is completely one with the will of the Logos. United with the latter, it has become a pure Yes to the Father's will.[65]

At this point, attention should be drawn to a certain ambiguity in Ratzinger's account of the relationship between the human and divine wills in Christ. In speaking of the human will of the Logos, and the divine will of the Logos, can he be saying that the Logos and the Father have *separate wills*,

62. Ibid., 38.
63. Ibid.
64. Ibid.
65. Ibid., 39.

or does he hold to the position that there is only one will in God, that the divine will of the Logos and the will of the Father are the selfsame will? We shall have cause to return to this ambiguity.

Ratzinger maintains that this distinction between the human will which is that of human nature, but exercised by a divine Person, and the divine will which is exercised by a divine Person, a distinction which he thinks has received little attention until now, was worked out by St. Maximus the Confessor. Maximus made a distinction between:

> [the] θέλημα φυσικόν [natural will] which belongs to the nature and thus exists separately in Christ's godhead and manhood, from the "gnomic" θέλημα [will] "which is identical with the *liberum arbitrium* [free decision] and pertains to the person; in Christ it can only be a single θέλημα since he subsists in the divine person."[66]

According to Ratzinger, Maximus illuminates the context of the Council's teaching by reference to the prayer of Jesus on the Mount of Olives, a prayer in which the inner life of the Word-made-man is revealed. In the prayer, "Not what I will, but what thou wilt (Mark 14:36)," we see the human will of Jesus assimilating itself to the will of the Son. Ratzinger states that:

> In doing this, [Jesus] receives the Son's identity, i.e., the complete subordination of the I to the Thou, the self-giving and self-expropriation of the I to the Thou. This is the very essence of him who is pure relation and pure act. Wherever the I gives itself to the Thou, there is freedom because this involves the reception of the "form of God."[67]

Ratzinger thinks that this is even clearer if we approach it from the side of the Logos. He is the one who humbles himself in adopting a human will as his own. Thus:

> [He] addresses the Father with the I of this human being; he transfers his own I to this man and thus transforms human speech into the eternal Word, into his blessed "Yes, Father." By imparting his own I, his own identity, to this human being, he liberates him, redeems him, makes him God. Now we can take the real meaning of "God has become man" in both hands, as it were: the Son transforms the anguish of a man into his own

---

66. Ibid., 39–40, n. 18.
67. Ibid., 40.

filial obedience, the speech of the servant into the Word which is the Son.[68]

Ratzinger is convinced that it is only our participation in this freedom of Jesus, the Son, this unity of our will with that of God, which meets our desire to become divine. The prayer "which enters into the praying of Jesus and becomes the prayer of Jesus in the Body of Christ [is] freedom's laboratory."[69] The only way to the right-ordering of the world is through a conscience that has been radically re-created through this participation.

The Hermeneutical Thesis: "The historical-critical method and other modern scientific methods are important for an understanding of Holy Scripture and tradition. Their value, however, depends on the hermeneutical (philosophical) context in which they are applied."

Ratzinger thinks that an incorrect use of the historical-critical method can lead to a divorce between scholarship and tradition, reason and faith. Critical exegesis does not *ipso facto* poison faith, but nor is it the real magisterium. Faith and reason are not contradictory if exercised properly. Rather, an irrational faith is inhuman, and a faithless reason is blind.[70]

Ratzinger holds that, like any tool, the effectiveness of the historical-critical method depends on how it is used, that is, on the hermeneutical and philosophical presuppositions one brings to its application. Such a context always exists, whether the historical critic is aware of it or not. There is no difficulty with a critical investigation of history, only with unexamined presuppositions.[71] The initial presupposition was that of the Enlightenment, which thought that history could correct dogma, could uncover a genuine historical Jesus who would correct the Christ of faith. Despite continual attempts

---

68. Ibid., 41.

69. Ibid., 42. Given the context, there can be little doubt that Ratzinger's use of the term "laboratory" is a reference to Maximus' identification of the human person as "the laboratory in which everything is concentrated and in itself naturally mediates between the extremities of each division [of being]." See Maximus, *Ambiguum* 41 (*PG* 1305: A–B). As Andrew Louth explains, "human beings are found on both sides of each division: they belong in paradise but inhabit the inhabited world; they are earthly and yet destined for heaven; they have both mind and senses; and though created, they are destined to share in the uncreated nature by deification." See Louth, *Maximus the Confessor*, 74 and, for the translation of this passage from Maximus, 156–57.

70. *Behold*, 42–43.

71. Ibid., 43.

to purge the method of rationalistic presuppositions, attempts which have yielded many important insights into the biblical testimony, the rationalistic approach which sidelines faith has led to multiple divorces, not just of Jesus and Christ, but of the inner unity of the New Testament books, of the New and the Old Testaments, and of the historical Jesus himself. Rather than establishing who the "real" Jesus is, this approach has produced multiple and conflicting portraits of Jesus, "the Jesus of the logia, the Jesus of this or that community, Jesus the philanthropist, Jesus the Jewish rabbi, the apocalyptic Jesus, Jesus the Zealot, Jesus the revolutionary, the political Jesus, etc."[72] According to Ratzinger, these divisions reflect the divisions in human thinking and action, divisions which the real Jesus came to overcome.

Ratzinger then raises the question of how one can discern if a hermeneutic is valid or not. He takes a "scientific" view, that "the legitimacy of an interpretation depends upon its power to explain things."[73] Hence, the less an interpretation "needs to interfere with the sources, the more it respects the corpus as given and is able to show it to be intelligible from within, by its own logic, the more apposite such an interpretation is."[74] The more an interpretation can truly unify, truly achieve a synthesis, the more it is to be trusted.

Ratzinger holds that only the hermeneutics of faith can do this, and that this hermeneutic has a two-fold unifying power. First, it alone has the unity of vision that can accept the whole testimony of the sources, with all their nuances, pluriformity, and apparent contradictions. For example: "Only the doctrine of the two natures joined together in one Person is able to open up a vista in which the apparent contradictions found in the tradition each have enough scope and can be molded together into a totality."[75] All rationalistic pictures of Jesus are partial, surviving only by absolutizing a portion of the sources, or by postulating theoretical sources behind the sources. Paradoxically, this involves "throwing doubt on some part of the historical corpus."[76]

The second unifying power of faith is that only it can transcend the differences between cultures, times and peoples. Their particular values find a higher unity in the incarnate Word. Only the hermeneutics of faith can "initiate a spiritual fellowship in which everything belongs to everyone and

---

72. Ibid., 44.
73. Ibid.
74. Ibid., 45.
75. Ibid.
76. Ibid.

there is a mutual relationship of giving and receiving, because of him who has given us himself and, in and with himself, the whole fullness of God."[77]

Ratzinger concludes his elucidation of this thesis by stating that the unity of the person of Jesus, who embraces the human and divine, "prefigures that synthesis of man and world to which theology is meant to minister." The theologian's task is to "bring to light the foundations for a possible unity in a world marked by divisions . . . [and] to answer the question of how this unity can be brought about today."[78] Ratzinger thinks that this can only be done in the following way.

> [The theologian must enter] that "laboratory" of unity and freedom of which we have spoken, i.e., where his own will is refashioned, where he allows himself to be expropriated and inserted into the divine will, where he advances toward that God-likeness through which the kingdom of God can come. Thus we have arrived back at our starting point: Christology is born of prayer or not at all.[79]

An Analysis of the Theses

In our examination of Ratzinger's earlier Christology we have seen how he sought to reconcile some fundamental divisions in Christology—between faith and history, being and act, theology and anthropology, Christology and soteriology, theology of the Incarnation and theology of the Cross. An investigation of the above seven theses present us with three immediate questions. First, how are these theses intended to help overcome the divisions just mentioned? Second, to what extent are these theses applied in Ratzinger's earlier Christology? Third, can one of the seven theses be regarded as a first principle?

The Reconciling Intention of the Theses

The project of theological reconciliation in Ratzinger's earlier Christology is continued and expanding in his spiritual Christology. All of the theses are intended to help overcome fundamental divisions in Christology, and indeed, can be applied to theology as a whole. The filial thesis seeks to overcome the division between faith and history; the soteriological thesis, that

77. Ibid., 46.
78. Ibid.
79. Ibid.

between Christology and soteriology. The personal thesis introduces the reconciliation of a division which Ratzinger sees as the ultimate division, that between theology and spirituality. This division has led to a rationalistic theology. It also has the potential, although this is not mentioned, of leading to an irrational piety. Another way of putting this is that this thesis intends to reconcile faith and reason.

This reconciliation between theology and spirituality could be likened to the replanting of a rootless theology—rootless, and hence lifeless and unable to give life. In this, Ratzinger is putting in contemporary terms a common patristic insight into the nature of theology; the theologian is one who prays. This insight was succinctly expressed by Evagrius Ponticus: "If you are a theologian, you will pray. And if you pray truly, you are a theologian."[80] Before one can have an insightful conversation *about* God, one must have a conversation *with* God. This is the most fundamental reconciliation which needs to take place in contemporary practice of theology. This estrangement is the ultimate reason behind the other estrangements—the Jesus of history and the Christ of faith, theology and anthropology, and even the theology of Incarnation and the theology of the Cross. Ultimately, one should be able to see how all of the seven theses are related to the reconciliation of theology and spirituality—we can only come to the real Jesus through faithful prayer, through praying truly.

The ecclesial thesis aims at the reconciliation of faith and history, and also of the faith of the individual and that of the *ecclesia*. The dogmatic thesis continues the work of the soteriological thesis in seeking to reconcile Christology and soteriology, the theology of the Incarnation with the theology of the Cross. It also aims to address a divorce between dogmatic and biblical Christology. The volitional thesis contributes to reconciling biblical and dogmatic Christology, theology and spirituality, faith and reason. The hermeneutical thesis also seeks to reconcile reason and faith, in the forms of scholarship (reason) and tradition (ecclesial faith).

The Earlier Applications of the Theses

We can see that the filial thesis is not new. In *Introduction to Christianity*, Ratzinger had identified the prayer of Jesus as the probable source of his self-description as Son, since it is the corollary to *Abba*, revealing the uniqueness of this communion with God. In *The God of Jesus Christ*, Ratzinger had already come to the conclusion that Luke in particular revealed that the center of Jesus' life and person was his prayer. When we come to

---

80. Evagrius Ponticus, *De oratione*, 61.

The Spiritual Christology of *Behold the Pierced One*—Theory

the soteriological thesis, we find that Ratzinger has simply applied the filial thesis to the defining act of Jesus' life—his death. When we come to the personal thesis we find that it is an application of Ratzinger's position, that the foundation of Christology is faith, to his position that the defining act of faith is participation in the prayer of Jesus. The ecclesial thesis originates from Ratzinger's understanding that as Christians we are incorporated into the exemplary man being united to the personal thesis. The dogmatic thesis, as Ratzinger tells us, flows from the filial and ecclesial theses, united with his prior position that the christological dogma in the Creed reveals to us that the real Jesus of history is the Christ of faith. The volitional thesis is the one which appears to be genuinely new. It is a realization that Ratzinger claims he did not come to until he began to study the teaching of the Constantinople III and St. Maximus the Confessor. The hermeneutical thesis regarding the historical-critical method pre-existed Ratzinger's spiritual Christology, but Ratzinger's understanding of personal and ecclesial faith, and consequently of hermeneutics, has been given a new depth owing to his perception of the fact that, as a believer, the theologian's task is rooted in participation in the prayer of Jesus.

The First Principle of Ratzinger's Spiritual Christology

A first principle is a principle that is not or cannot be deduced from another principle, but is the basis for the deduction of all other principles. However, a first principle is not simply plucked out of thin air. Before deduction comes induction. Induction is demonstration by experience, while deduction is demonstration by argument. For example, the first principle of epistemology is that we know that things exist. We know the reality of being. We know that things, including ourselves, exist because we experience their existence. To give a more mundane example, a man does not arrive at the knowledge of his wife's love for him through a syllogism, but through the experience of being loved by her. From that, he can deduce certain things about the nature of spousal love.

One would expect that the first principle of Ratzinger's spiritual Christology would be the first that he gives. But this is not so. In his filial thesis Ratzinger proposes that, despite the claims of "modern exegesis and the history of doctrine" to the contrary, we know that in the testimony of Sacred Scripture "the church was responding precisely to the basic historical eyewitnesses of Jesus' life." But how can we claim this knowledge? It has not been arrived at by inductive reasoning, since we have no direct experience of how the church responded to the eyewitnesses of Jesus' life. Nor is this conclusion deduced from prior propositions. Must it be placed in the category of knowledge accepted on trust from eyewitnesses, not on the basis of personal verification, a category into which much of human knowledge falls? The soteriological thesis is a development of the filial. It too is based on the "testimony of Holy Scripture."

It would seem that the actual first principle of Ratzinger's spiritual Christology is, in fact, a combination of the personal and ecclesial theses—that we can only know and understand who Jesus truly is if we participate in his prayer, and that we do not participate in this prayer as isolated individuals, but as members of his Body, the church. This is where Ratzinger claims to ground knowledge of Christ—in a personal experience which is also a corporate experience. This is knowledge which is "personally verified" and not simply accepted on the word of another. The difficulty that another person has in accepting this kind of knowledge is that the other person can only be certain that it is true through their own personal verification. They too must discover the real Jesus in prayer.

Human beings have a tremendous capacity for misunderstanding and self-deception. If this is true of things to which we are ontologically equal or superior, how much more so when it comes to our knowledge of the mystery of God. However, we do not come to know God as isolated individuals. One's experience of Christ is not just the experience of the encounter with Christ in personal prayer, but the experience of encountering him when praying as a member of the Body of Christ. It is the experience of being drawn by Christ to himself in communion with other believers. Ultimately, the believer only comes to know Christ without misconception or self-deception through his Body. Faith comes through hearing the witness of other believers, and having that witness verified in one's own personal experience. Faith comes through the witness of the Holy Spirit *and* the teaching of the Apostles (cf. Acts 2:37; 15:28); or rather, through the witness of the Holy Spirit through the teaching of the Apostles being personally verified by the Holy Spirit in one's own heart and mind. As St. Paul says: "For we know brethren, beloved of God, that he has chosen you; for our gospel came to you not only in word, but also in power and in the Holy Spirit and with full conviction (1 Thess 1:4–5)."

The dogmatic thesis, that the "dogma defined in the councils of the early church consists in the statement that Jesus is the true Son of God, of the same essence as the Father," is a consequence of the filial and soteriological theses. The volitional thesis, on the neo-Chalcedonian theology of the Constantinople III, builds on the dogmatic thesis. Finally, the hermeneutical thesis on the correct use of the historical-critical method follows from accepting the personal and ecclesial theses. So, as to the correct order of the theses, if one begins with the "testimony of Holy Scripture," then the logical order is the one that Ratzinger gives—filial, soteriological, personal, ecclesial, dogmatic, volitional, and hermeneutical. But if one begins with the "testimony of the Holy Spirit," then the logical order is personal, ecclesial, hermeneutical, filial, soteriological, dogmatic, and volitional. The first three make up the "method" of Ratzinger's spiritual Christology, and the following four the "content."

A Theology of the Heart in Ratzinger's Spiritual Christology

The Crisis in Devotion to the Sacred Heart—A Crisis in Method

In *Behold the Pierced One*, Ratzinger begins his investigation of the relationship between the heart of Jesus and a spiritual Christology with the rejection of "the emotionalistic piety of the nineteenth century and its symbolism" by the sobriety and objectivity of the liturgical movement, which wanted to be led entirely by Scripture and the Fathers.[81] Subsequently, there arose a desire to "preserve the inheritance of more recent ages of the Church and involve it in the return to Christian origins."[82] In the case of devotion to the Sacred Heart it was Hugo Rahner who sought to provide a new basis for the devotion by connecting it with the patristic interpretation of John 7:37–39 and 19:34. Ratzinger comments on the significance of these passages as follows.

> Both passages are concerned with the opened side of Jesus, with the blood and water which flow from it. Both passages are an expression of the Paschal Mystery: from the Lord's pierced Heart proceeds the life-giving stream of the sacraments ... Both texts also express the connection between Christology and pneumatology: the water of life which springs from the Lord's side is the Holy Spirit, the spring of life which makes the desert blossom. This also brings out the connection between Christology, pneumatology and ecclesiology: Christ communicates himself to us in the Holy Spirit; and it is the Holy Spirit who makes the clay into a living Body, i.e., fuses isolated men into the one organism of the love of Jesus Christ. It is also the Holy Spirit who imparts new meaning to Adam's becoming "one flesh" with Eve, applying it to the Second Adam: "He who is united to the Lord becomes one spirit with him" (1 Cor 6:17). The liturgical

---

81. *Behold*, 47.
82. Ibid., 48.

movement had discovered the center of Christian spirituality in the Paschal Mystery. In his researches, Hugo Rahner had tried to show that devotion to the Sacred Heart, too, is nothing but devotion to the mystery of Easter and thus concentrates on the core of the Christian faith.[83]

Next, Ratzinger turns to Pope Pius XII's 1956 encyclical on the Sacred Heart, *Haurietis aquas*. According to Ratzinger, the aim of the encyclical is the same as that of H. Rahner—to "overcome the dangerous dualism between liturgical spirituality and nineteenth-century devotion, to let each of them stimulate the other to bring forth fruit, to bring them into a fruitful relationship without simply dissolving one in the other."[84] However, Ratzinger maintains, although Rahner had made it clear that devotion to the Sacred Heart is an Easter spirituality, that the blood and water flowing from the side of Jesus is the biblical icon of this devotion, contemplation of which can fulfill the prophecy of Zechariah: "They shall look on him whom they have pierced" (Zech 12:10), Rahner's work left two objections unanswered. First, neither of the Johannine passages actually mention the word "heart." Although they interpret the mystery of the heart: "Of themselves, however, they cannot explain why it is the Lord's *Heart* that is the center of the Easter image." The second and more radical question is this: "If devotion to the Sacred Heart is a mode of Paschal spirituality, what is there that is specific to it?" That is to say, if one can participate in the Easter mystery where it is really present, in the sacraments, why the need to participate in it in an emotional way, "a secondary form of mysticism, compared with the primary mysticism of the 'mystery'?"[85]

The Relationship between Method and Content—The Devotion's Foundation in a Theology of the Incarnation

According to Ratzinger, the questions which *Haurietis aquas* actually replied to were those presupposed by the liturgical reform of Vatican II. The whole thrust of the encyclical was to develop an anthropology and theology of bodily existence as the philosophical and psychological basis for devotion to the Sacred Heart. Ratzinger summarizes the teaching of the encyclical as follows: The body is the self-expression of the spirit, its "image," the place where the spirit can be discerned, the visible form of the person. The person

---

83. Ibid., 48–49.
84. Ibid., 49.
85. Ibid., 50.

exercises personhood in the body. Since the person is the image of God, the body, "in its whole context of relationships, is the place where the divine is portrayed, uttered and rendered accessible to our gaze." When "the Bible represents the mystery of God in the metaphors of the body and its world," it is following this principle that God is visible and expresses himself in the bodily world.[86] It is this context in which the Bible presents the Incarnation. The representation of God in the parables and imagery of the bodily world of the human person is an anticipation of the Incarnation. The Incarnation is actually the fulfillment of the Word's continually drawing all flesh towards himself and making it his own flesh. "On the one hand the Incarnation can only take place because the flesh has always been the Spirit's outward expression and hence a possible dwelling for the Word; on the other it is only the Son's Incarnation that imparts to man and the visible world their ultimate and innermost meaning."[87]

According to Ratzinger, the encyclical balances the work of H. Rahner, in which the Easter aspect tended to dominate, to the detriment of the incarnational aspect. However, the Incarnation does not exist for its own sake, but is ordered to the transcendence and dynamism of the Easter mystery. In the Incarnation: "God transcends himself and enters the realm of flesh, the realm of the passion of the human being." What this self-transcendence also brings to light is the inner transcendence of the whole of creation, that "body is the self-transcending movement toward spirit, and through the spirit, to God." Under the shadow of Kasper's critique of his supposed Platonism, Ratzinger states that: "Beholding the invisible in the visible is an Easter phenomenon."[88] The encyclical sees this principle summed up in John 20:26–29: Thomas beholds the invisible in the visible. According to Ratzinger's reading of the encyclical, its illustration of this principle, as applied to devotion to the Sacred Heart, is to be found in its quotation of St. Bonaventure's *Mystical Vine*: "The wound of the body also reveals the spiritual wound . . . Let us look through the visible wound to the invisible wound of love!"[89]

The conclusion that Ratzinger draws is that the ontological and psychological basis of the Easter mystery is "the connection of body and spirit, of Logos, Spirit and body, making the incarnate Logos into a 'ladder' which we can climb as we behold, touch and experience."[90] When we "look on the

---

86. Ibid., 52.
87. Ibid.
88. Ibid., 53.
89. Ibid.
90. Ibid., 54.

one whom we have pierced," when we "touch" the exposed Heart of Jesus, we behold and touch the Logos, God himself.

Enfleshing the Method—The Importance of the Senses and the Emotions in Spirituality

Building on this conclusion, Ratzinger holds that what he identifies as a so-called spirituality, based on the celebration of the liturgy, is insufficient. If the liturgy is to be properly celebrated it must be "prepared for, and accompanied by, that meditative 'abiding' in which the heart begins to see and to understand, drawing the senses into its beholding."[91] According to Ratzinger, the encyclical gives an apologia for a spirituality of the heart, senses and emotions. Reason has its limits. This is borne out by Ephesians 3:18–19 on comprehending the love of Christ, and the pseudo-Dionysian tradition which develops into the *ignote cognoscere*, knowing in unknowing. The basis of this mysticism is that it is love alone that sees.[92]

Ratzinger points out that, according to the encyclical, the love of God, as presented in the New Testament, is not just "spiritual"—that in Jesus, divine love has become tangible in the form of human love. Thus a spirituality of the senses corresponds to the bodily nature of the divine-human love of Jesus. Ratzinger holds that, according to the encyclical, this spirituality of the senses is actually a spirituality of the heart, "since the heart is the hub of all the senses, the place where sense and spirit meet, interpenetrate and unite."[93] It is the spirituality exemplified by Newman's motto—*Cor ad cor loquitur*.

Besides the heart being the hub of the senses, Ratzinger's reading of the encyclical is that the heart is also the epitome of the human passions. By this he means not just the individual passions, but also the "passion" of being human. He contrasts this understanding with the *apatheia* of the Stoa and the Aristotelian God who is Thought thinking itself. Without the heart there could be no Passion.[94]

Although, as Ratzinger points out, the encyclical quotes many patristic expressions of this insight, he also maintains that the Fathers experienced a particular difficulty in synthesizing this biblical insight with Greek thought. Owing to the Stoic ideal of the impassivity of the wise man, they had difficulty reconciling the "passionate" God of the Old Testament with impassive

91. Ibid.
92. Ibid., 55.
93. Ibid., 56.
94. Ibid.

The Spiritual Christology of *Behold the Pierced One*—Theory

God of Greek philosophy. This helps explain the temptation to a Gnosticism which separated the God of the Old Testament from that of the New. When faced with the figure of a "passionate" Jesus who incarnates the passions of the Old Testament God, the temptation was to a Docetism more congenial to Stoic thought. However, such a solution completely undermined the mystery of Easter. As Ratzinger states: "It was impossible to excise Christ's sufferings, but there can be no Passion without passions: suffering presupposes the ability to suffer, it presupposes the faculty of the emotions."[95]

According to Ratzinger, it was Origen who had the most profound grasp of the idea of a suffering God. Origen held that this idea could not be restricted to a suffering Jesus. Thus Ratzinger says: "The Father suffers in allowing the Son to suffer, and the Spirit shares in this suffering . . . (Rom 8:26f.)"[96] For Ratzinger, Origen gave the normative way for understanding the theme of the suffering God—he is a sufferer because he is a lover.

Ratzinger holds that the resurgence of this theme in contemporary theology is, in fact, a reaction against the current separation of faith and reason, spirituality and theology. It is a reaction against a rationalistic picture of God. However, this theme must be firmly anchored in prayerful love *for* God. (Although Ratzinger does not state it, it can be presumed that this is also necessary if one is to avoid the opposite extreme, that of a sentimental, irrational piety). Ratzinger thinks that the encyclical sees the passions of Jesus, summed up and set forth in his heart, as the reason why the human heart, that is, "the capacity for feeling, the emotional side of love, must be drawn into man's relationship with God. Incarnational spirituality must be a spirituality of the passions, a spirituality of 'heart to heart.'"[97]

Ratzinger maintains that the importance of this theme has been confirmed since Vatican II, since the rejection of emotion now comes in the form of a technological rationalism which marginalizes the emotions and instrumentalizes the body. Eventually, the emotions have their revenge in the form of a chaotic spiritual emotionalism, pathos rendered pathological. Rather than neglect a meditative, contemplative spirituality in favor of a community-based activism, we need to integrate our emotions into the totality of our human existence, including the totality of our relationship with God. We have come to this pass because we looked upon the spirituality of the second Christian millennium as inherently inferior to that of the first.[98]

95. Ibid., 57.

96. Ibid., 58. On the subject of the "passion" of the Holy Spirit, Ratzinger refers the reader to what he calls "the profound interpretation of Romans 8:26" in Schlier, *Der Römerbrief*, 268.

97. *Behold*, 59–60.

98. Ibid., 60.

Content—Ratzinger's Anthropology and Theology of the Heart in the Bible and the Fathers

Ratzinger concludes that, in genuine Christian spirituality, the senses "are structured by and united in the heart," while the emotions "are focused on the heart."[99] He holds that there is a correspondence between a heart-centered spirituality and our understanding of the Christian God who has a heart, and that this is what expresses and elucidates the Paschal Mystery. However, the further task is to see if this emphasis on the heart accords with the biblical and patristic tradition.

Ratzinger makes the following observations about the biblical tradition. The Song of Songs played a preeminent role in the development of the medieval mysticism of the heart. The Fathers also saw the language of this book as expressing God's love for the church and the soul, as well as the human response to this love. These words "were thus fitted to integrate all the passion of human love into man's relationship with God." Unfortunately, a "straitened historical mode of thought" led to a loss of the ability to enter into this movement.[100] The recovery of the ability to enter this mystery via the biblical route depends upon the recovery of an understanding of the Bible as a whole, including a lifting of the embargo on an allegorical understanding.[101]

As a preeminent example of the biblical basis for understanding the "heart of God" Ratzinger proposes Hosea 11. After portraying the immense proportions of God's love for Israel, his son, there follows God's lament for the lack of response from this son. After declaring that the result of this refusal to respond to God's love will be banishment, enslavement and destruction, there comes a complete change of key, a blatant contradiction—"How can I give you up, O Ephraim! How can I hand you over, O Israel! . . My heart recoils within me, my compassion grows warm and tender. I will not execute my fierce anger . . . for I am God and not man, the Holy One in your midst, and I will not come to destroy" (Hos 11:8–9).

In Ratzinger's view, this passage exemplifies the Old Testament's teaching about the heart of God. It is the organ of his will and the measuring rod of human behavior. The Flood demonstrates that the pain in God's heart at human sinfulness causes him to send destruction. But the insight into human weakness on the part of the same heart causes God to refrain from repeating that judgment. Hosea 11 takes these insights to a new level.

---

99. Ibid., 61.
100. Ibid.
101. Ibid., 61–62.

"God's Heart turns around—here the Bible uses the same word as in the depiction of God's judgment on the sinful cities of Sodom and Gomorrha (Gen 19:25); the word expresses a total collapse . . . The same word is applied to the havoc wrought by love in God's Heart in favor of his people."[102] Regarding this point, Ratzinger cites Heinich Gross thus: "The upheaval occasioned in God's Heart by the divine love has the effect of quashing his judicial sentence against Israel; God's merciful love conquers his untouchable righteousness (which, in spite of everything, remains untouchable)."[103]

According to Ratzinger, the resolution of this riddle is to be found in the New Testament in the Passion of Christ. In this Passion: "God himself, in the person of his Son, [suffers] Israel's rejection."[104] There, God takes the place of the sinner, and gives us sinners the place of the Son. The words of Hosea 11: "My heart recoils within me, my compassion grows warm and tender," reveal the drama of God's heart in the Passion of Jesus. "The pierced Heart of the crucified Son is the literal fulfillment of the prophecy of the Heart of God, which overthrows righteousness by mercy and by that very action remains righteous."[105] Someone like St. Bernard can begin the establishment of devotion to the Sacred Heart because, in his time, the two Testaments were still read as a unity. Hence, we can only grasp the true nature of this devotion if we return to that comprehension.

In the patristic tradition there is no direct reference to the "heart of Jesus." However, the Fathers do have a "theology and philosophy of the heart." For example, Augustine's anthropology has been called a *philosophia cordis*.[106] According to Ratzinger, a reading of the *Confessions* reveals that, for Augustine, "the stream of biblical theology and anthropology, has entered into his thought and combined with an entirely different, Platonic conception of man, a conception unacquainted with the notion of 'heart' [in the sense of] "a dialogic anthropology."[107]

Ratzinger maintains that much patristic writing reveals a failure to fully synthesize the biblical image of the heart with the Platonic world of ideas. However, the Fathers were often aware of these two contradictory anthropologies, the Platonic anthropology having its center in the intellect, and the Christian in the heart. Furthermore, Ratzinger sees not just this opposition, but also an opposition between Platonic and Stoic anthropologies,

---

102. Ibid., 62.
103. Gross, "Das Hohelied der Liebe Gottes," 89. Cf. *DCE*, no. 10.
104. *Behold*, 64.
105. Ibid.
106. Ibid., 65.
107. Ibid.

an opposition which actually presented the Fathers with "the opportunity of drawing on the Bible to create a new anthropological synthesis."[108]

Ratzinger then goes on to develop an understanding of the "heart" which draws upon Stoic anthropology in particular. Whilst Platonic anthropology distinguishes the individual potencies of the soul—intellect, will, and sensibility—and relates them in a hierarchical order, Stoic thought is closer to the anthropology of the Bible, focusing, as it does, on the heart rather than the intellect. Stoic thought conceives of man as a microcosm corresponding to the macrocosm. As this cosmos is fashioned by a formless primal fire which adopts the form of that which it creates, so the human body is fashioned and enlivened by this divine, primal fire, becoming hearing, sight, thought and imagination. This primal fire in the cosmos is called logos. In us it is called "the logos in us." For the Stoics, as the sun is the "heart of the cosmos," the human heart is the body's sun, the seat of the logos in us.[109]

Notwithstanding the banal naturalism of some of this thinking, Ratzinger maintains that it also displays a profound philosophical intuition, which offered the Fathers the opportunity of reaching a new synthesis of Platonic thought and biblical faith. For Ratzinger, it was Origen who made the most of this opportunity. Basing his thinking on John 1:26: "Among you stands one whom you do not know," Origen went on to assert that,

---

108. Ibid., 66. Dietrich von Hildebrand comments upon the neglect of the heart in philosophical enquiry. See von Hildebrand, *The Sacred Heart*, 19–20 and 25–33. However, as Rowland points out: "A theological anthropology which pays due regard to the intellectual and affective dimensions of human action is now in the course of development. Here the mid-twentieth century work of Dietrich von Hildebrand is a valuable source of insights on what the document [*In Search of a Universal Ethic: A New Look at the Natural Law*, 57] calls 'emotional intelligence'. The contemporary work of Robert Sokolowski has also drawn attention to this neglected element in presentations of the natural law. With reference to the notion of the law being written on the hearts of the gentiles, Sokolowski has argued that the word *kardia* in the passage from St. Paul's *Letter to the Romans* (usually translated in the Vulgate as *cor*), does not connote the separation of heart and head that we take for granted in a world shaped by Descartes [Sokolowski, *Christian Faith and Human Understanding*, 230]. He concurs with Robert Spaemann's claim that in the New Testament the heart is taken to be a deeper recipient of truth than even the mind or intellect in Greek philosophy since it deals with the person's willingness to accept the truth [Sokolowski, "What Is Natural Law?" 525]. These insights of von Hildebrand, Spaemann and Sokolowski are consistent with what Aidan Nichols has discerned as Benedict XVI's desire to unite 'philosophy and theology in a single, internally differentiated but also internally cohesive, intellectual act' [Nichols, *From Hermes to Benedict XVI*, 228]. What one finds in Pope Benedict's many publications is 'a convergence of the mainly philosophical disclosure of *logos* with the chiefly theological revelation of love' [ibid., 222–31]" (Rowland, "The Rôle of Natural Law," 164–65).

109. *Behold*, 66–67.

The Spiritual Christology of *Behold the Pierced One*—Theory

unbeknownst to us, the Logos is at the center of all human beings, since the Logos is present in the center of every man, the heart. As Ratzinger states:

> It is [this] Logos which enables us to be logic-al, to correspond to the Logos; he is the image of God after which we were created. Here the word "heart" has expanded beyond reason and denotes "a deeper level of spiritual/intellectual existence, where direct contact takes place with the divine." It is here, in the heart, that the birth of the divine Logos in man takes place, that man is united with the personal incarnate Word of God.[110]

Following Endre von Ivánka, Ratzinger maintains that it is this stream of thought and spirituality which ultimately leads to the medieval beginnings of devotion to the Sacred Heart and to that mysticism wherein "the heart takes precedence over reason, love over knowledge."[111] It leads to Pascal's principle—"God sensible in the heart, not in the reason," and "the heart has reasons that the reason does not know."[112] It leads to Newman's motto—"Heart speaks to heart." Ratzinger's conclusion is that, in patristic thought, there developed a synthesis which enabled the Fathers to see the heart as the place of the saving encounter with the Logos.

Ratzinger draws one further conclusion from his investigations of Stoic thought regarding the heart. In this thinking it was the function of the heart, as the life force and preserving energy of the human organism, to hold that organism together. That is, the task of the heart was the self-preservation of the human being. However:

> The pierced Heart of Jesus has also truly "overturned" (cf. Hos 11:8) this definition. This Heart is not concerned with self-preservation but with self-surrender. It saves the world by opening itself. The collapse of the opened Heart is the content of the Easter mystery. The Heart saves, but it saves by giving itself away. Thus, in the Heart of Jesus, the center of Christianity is set before us. It expresses everything, all that is genuinely new and revolutionary in the new Covenant. This Heart calls to our heart. It invites us to step forth out of the futile attempt of self-preservation and, by joining in the task of love, by handing ourselves over to him and with him, to discover the fullness of love which alone is eternity and which alone sustains the world.[113]

---

110. Ibid., 67–68. Here Ratzinger cites von Ivánka, *Plato christianus*, 326.

111. Ibid., 68.

112. We should note that the reason of which Pascal speaks is the shrivelled reason of the Enlightenment, reason reduced to reasoning.

113. Ibid., 69.

The Eucharist in Ratzinger's Spiritual Christology

Included in *Behold the Pierced One* is a paper given by Ratzinger at a continuing education course for priests.[114] This paper looks at the relationship between the Eucharist, the parish community and mission in the church. Ratzinger begins by looking at the ecclesiology of Luke. According to him, Luke sees the church as having three fundamental characteristics. It is pneumatological, being created by the Holy Spirit. It is catholic, having a dynamic mission to bring the Good News of salvation to the ends of the earth. It is liturgical, since the gathered community receives the gift of the Spirit in the act of prayer.[115] Having said this, Ratzinger then focuses on what he takes to be another thread in Luke's ecclesiology, his fundamental ecclesial definition given in Acts 2:42. This definition consists of four concepts which identify the essence of the church—the Apostles' teaching and fellowship, the breaking of bread and the prayers. Here Ratzinger sees two pairs of concepts—the linking of the teaching of the Apostles with fellowship with the Apostles, and the linking of the Eucharist and praying. The teaching of and fellowship with the Apostles is continued in the successors of the Apostles. Apostolicity is deepened and given concrete expression in the abiding structure of the church. Furthermore, the "praying" of the church finds its center of gravity in the "breaking of the bread." Ratzinger sees the Eucharist being revealed as the heart of church life. Yet he sees one concept as uniting all of these aspects—*koinonia (communio)*. This concept unites the two realities of "Eucharist" and "community," "communion as sacrament and communion as a social and institutional reality."[116] *Koinonia* is the method of the eucharistic aspect of Ratzinger's spiritual Christology.

Ratzinger sees *koinonia* as being linked with apostolic teaching on the one hand, and the breaking of the bread on the other. Thus "it is portrayed as something going beyond the practice of worship, something essentially rooted in the fundamental fact of constantly maintained tradition and its ecclesial form."[117] According to Ratzinger, this *koinonia* with the Apostles, this continuing in the teaching of the Apostles, is essential for the continuing unity of the church. This unity includes the ability of both Jews and Gentiles to participate in "table fellowship." However, this "institutional fellowship" has what Ratzinger calls a spiritual dimension. When Paul and Barnabas

---

114 Ratzinger, "L'eucaristia al centro della communità e della sua missione." A reworked version is to be found in *Behold*, 71–100, under the title "Communion, Community and Mission."

115. *Behold*, 71–74.

116. Ibid., 75.

117. Ibid., 76–77.

The Spiritual Christology of *Behold the Pierced One*—Theory

were given "the right hand of fellowship" by the "pillars of the church," one particular injunction was laid upon them, to be solicitous for the poor of Jerusalem. Communion in the Body of Christ means communion with other believers. This means giving both spiritual and physical life to each other. Social relations are at the core of the concept of *koinonia*. It embraces "the sacramental and spiritual as well as the institutional and personal."[118]

Ratzinger sees the vertical dimension of *koinonia* as being the ultimate foundation of its horizontal dimension. For the Jewish people there could be no *communio* relationship between God and man. Rather, that relationship was designated by the word "covenant." But for Christians the church is a communion between human beings only "as a result of the death and Resurrection of Jesus, communion with Christ, the incarnate Son, and hence communion with the eternal, triune Love of God."[119] In his Son, the transcendent God reveals his innermost life as a dialogue of eternal love.

> Since he himself is relationship—Word and Love—he can speak, feel, answer, love. Since he is relationship, he can open himself and provide his creatures with a relationship to him. In the Incarnation of the eternal Word there comes about that communion between God and the being of man, his creature, which up to now had seemed irreconcilable with the transcendence of God.[120]

In the person of Jesus Christ, divine and human nature interpenetrate. God enters into communion with human beings by taking flesh in human nature. Thus, for Ratzinger, the source of *communio* is in Christ.

> [The] incarnate Son is the "communion" between God and men. Being Christian is in reality nothing other than sharing in the mystery of the Incarnation, or as St. Paul puts it: the Church, insofar as she is the Church, is the "Body of Christ" (i.e., a participation on the part of men in that communion between man and God which is the Incarnation of the Word). Once this has been grasped, it is clear that there can be no separation of Church and Eucharist, sacramental communion and community fellowship.[121]

---

118. Ibid., 78. On this and the previous page, Ratzinger refers to Gal 1:13–2:14 and Acts 15:1–35.
119. Ibid., 86.
120. Ibid., 86–87.
121. Ibid., 88.

In the Eucharist we have *koinonia* in the body and blood of Christ. We are one body because we all partake of the one bread (cf. 1 Cor 10:16–17). Ratzinger sees these words as the core of St. Augustine's theological thought. By eating the one bread we become what we eat. The eucharistic food is stronger than we. It reverses the whole normal process of eating. Rather than it becoming assimilated to us, we become assimilated by it. We become the bread that we eat. Consequently, we become members of each other.[122] As Ratzinger concludes:

> The goal of eucharistic communion is a total recasting of a person's life, breaking up a man's whole "I" and creating a new "We." Communion with Christ is of necessity a communication with all those who are his: it means that I myself become part of this new "bread" which he creates by transubstantiating all earthly reality.[123]

The church is no merely human sociological reality. It only exists because the Lord is its origin and goal. The essence of the church is "relationship," one created by the love of Christ, which in turn creates a new relationship between human beings.

Ratzinger thinks that the core of eucharistic spirituality and ecclesial spirituality is to be found in the communion between God and man to be found in the Incarnate Word. In him, human nature has been infused into the being of God. When one receives the Lord in the Eucharist, one enters into a community of being with him, a communion which is a precondition of communion between human beings. Grasping the spirituality of the Eucharist means grasping "the spiritual tension which marks the God-man: only in the context of a spiritual Christology will the spirituality of the sacrament reveal itself."[124]

Ratzinger believes that western theology has neglected this spiritual Christology, which is "the link between the various disciplines of theology and between theological reflection and the concrete, spiritual working out of Christianity."[125] Once again, Ratzinger proposes the teaching of the Constantinople III as opening up our way to a spiritual Christology, as well as enabling us to properly interpret the teaching of the Council of Chalcedon.[126] Whereas that council described the ontological content of the Incarnation as being two Persons in one nature, Constantinople III grappled with

---

122. Ibid., 88–89.
123. Ibid., 89.
124. Ibid., 90.
125. Ibid.
126. See Denzinger, nos. 553–59.

the question of what the spiritual substance of such an ontology might be. So Ratzinger asks:

> What does it mean, in practical and existential terms, to speak of "One Person in Two Natures"? How can a person live with two wills and a twofold intellect? These were by no means questions posed out of theoretical curiosity; the question affects us too, for the issue is this: How can *we* live as baptized people, to whom Paul's words must apply: "I live, yet not I, but Christ liveth in me" (Gal 2:20)?[127]

Ratzinger describes the teaching of the council thus: It proposed that in the ontological union of the human and divine wills in Jesus, each remains independent within the unity of Person. At the existential level, there is a communion (*koinonia*) of the two wills. This is union as communion, an ontology of freedom. "The two 'wills' are united in the way in which two wills can be united, namely, in a common affirmation of a shared value. In other words, what unites the two wills is the Yes of Christ's human will to the divine will of the Logos."[128]

Existentially, the two wills become one, whilst ontologically they remain two independent wills. The council added that as the flesh of Jesus may be called the flesh of the Logos, so his human will may be called the will of the Logos. Ratzinger states that:

> In practice the Council is here applying the trinitarian model (with the mandatory ever-greater difference in the analogy) to Christology: the highest unity there is—the unity of God—is not the unity of unstructured, amorphous substance but unity by communion, a unity which both creates and is love.[129]

The Logos speaks of the will of Jesus as his own will (cf. John 6:38). In the Son's obedience, both the human will and Logos' will (which is the will of the Father, there being only one will in God), become a single Yes. Thus comes into being the ultimate communion between Creator and creature. In this painful obedience a fundamental change takes place in human nature, a change which redeems the world. Therefore Ratzinger states: "Here community is born, here the Church comes into being."[130]

Ratzinger ends by saying that: "This communion between God and man, which is realized in the Person of Jesus Christ, itself becomes

---

127. *Behold*, 91.
128. Ibid., 92.
129. Ibid.
130. Ibid., 93.

communicable in the Easter mystery, i.e., in the Lord's death and Resurrection. The Eucharist is our participation in the Easter mystery, and hence it is constitutive of the Church, the Body of Christ."[131] Hence, the Eucharist is necessary for salvation. Its necessity is identical with the necessity of the church, and vice versa (cf. John 6:53). As Ratzinger states: "The most intimate mystery of communion between God and man is accessible in the sacrament of the *Body* of the Risen Lord; conversely, then, the mystery lays claim to our *bodies* and is realized in a *Body*."[132]

Conclusion

As has been seen, even prior to 1981 (the paper on the Sacred Heart) and 1984 (*Behold the Pierced One*), Ratzinger had begun to develop a spiritual Christology, without explicitly identifying it as such. It can be seen that this spiritual Christology is more developed in 1976 (*The God of Jesus Christ*) and 1978 (*Eucharistie: Mitte der Kirche*) than in 1968 (*Introduction to Christianity*). Almost all the elements of Ratzinger's spiritual Christology, bar his insight into the significance of the neo-Chalcedonian theology of Constantinople III, are present before 1981, although it must be said that his theology of the heart is present mainly in his anthropology of the human heart, his image of the Eucharist as the "heart" of the church, and an awareness of the significance of the pierced side of Jesus for the Eucharist. The heart of God, the Father's heart, has yet to make an appearance.

Turning to the explicit expression of Ratzinger's spiritual Christology, analyzing its theory reveals that it is composed of three elements which have not been explicitly integrated. Also, the theological method of Ratzinger's spiritual Christology has been identified, as it pertains to his seven christological theses, his theology of the heart, and his eucharistic spirituality.

It has also been shown that there is a pneumatological deficiency in Ratzinger's earlier Christology, including his implicit spiritual Christology, noting that his focus on the activity of the Holy Spirit is almost entirely limited to the ecclesial activity of the Spirit, while neglecting the Spirit's christological activity. Looking back on his explicit spiritual Christology, it can be seen that this pattern is repeated in Ratzinger's christological theses, his theology of the heart, and his eucharistic spirituality—the Holy Spirit is mentioned almost exclusively in relation to the church. The Spirit flows to us from the pierced heart of Jesus, but there is still a marked absence of reference to the activity of the Holy Spirit in Jesus himself. The concern is with the pneumatological nature of the church, but not of the Christ.

131. Ibid.
132. Ibid., 93–94.

Theoria

4

Understanding *Jesus of Nazareth*

Commentary on *Jesus of Nazareth*

The Christology of *Jesus of Nazareth*

Most analyses of Ratzinger's Christology have focused upon the first published volume of *Jesus of Nazareth*. In assessing Ratzinger's portrayal of Jesus, these commentaries range from giving it unmitigated praise to claiming that Ratzinger has tried to "steal ... Jesus of Nazareth" from the commentator.[1] Rausch sees the Christology of *Jesus of Nazareth*, like that of Ratzinger's earlier Christology, as essentially Johannine. For him, John is the lens through which Ratzinger reads the synoptic tradition, represented largely by Matthew, enabling Ratzinger to find a high Christology in the Synoptics as well.[2] Rausch criticizes Ratzinger's Christology in a number of ways, in particular, asking if Ratzinger's portrait of Jesus fails to take sufficiently into account the best historical-critical scholarship. For Rausch, Ratzinger's Jesus is too Johannine, focusing "far more on the full christological meaning of Jesus as the logos, the Torah in person, and the new Temple than he does on the Jesus of the ministry and his call to discipleship in the service of the kingdom."[3] Rausch claims that ultimately, while Ratzinger "presupposes the importance of historical-critical scholarship and makes some use of it, his Christology is not critically grounded in the historical Jesus. He often subscribes more to him than many scholars would be able

---

1. Wostyn, "Pope Benedict XVI" 96.
2. Rausch, *Pope Benedict XVI*, 87–88.
3. Ibid., 99.

to acknowledge."[4] Rausch further charges that because Ratzinger does not ground his Christology in the Jesus of history, this "leaves [Ratzinger's Christology] open to the often-heard charge that the church's christological doctrine underwent a 'Hellenization,' divinizing Jesus the teacher and healer by turning him into a god."[5]

Richard Hays paints a similar picture. He claims that Ratzinger's Jesus is strongly Johannine, and that this character is grounded in high christological claims, namely, that Jesus was one with God, proclaiming a universalism which broke the boundaries of Judaism, as well as a realized eschatology. Yet the teaching of this Jesus contains little in the way of social ethics. However, Hays thinks that Ratzinger makes a serious case that these "high" emphases are not confined to John's Gospel but can be found in the Synoptics as well. In the end he concludes that "it is the Gospel of John that imparts the fundamental shape to Ratzinger's portrayal of Jesus."[6]

George Denis O'Brien maintains that one will tend to see Christology through an ecclesiological lens. He thinks that what he calls Ratzinger's "canonic" reading of the Scriptures in *Jesus of Nazareth* leads to a high Christology, which nonetheless is given its framework by John's Gospel.[7] O'Brien has three criticisms of Ratzinger's canonic reading. First, he thinks that it seeks to impose a unity which is not actually present in the Bible.[8] Second, he believes that it presents a rigid either/or choice between a subjectivity which measures the Bible against the "dogma" that God cannot act in history, and an objectivity which has Jesus teaching propositional truths. O'Brien thinks that Ratzinger's supposed high Christology (Jesus *the* Truth), by neglecting a low Christology (Jesus experiencing history), runs the risk

---

4. Ibid., 100.

5. Ibid.

6. Hays, "Ratzinger's Johannine Jesus," 113–14. Cf. Miles, "Between Theology and Exegesis," 20. Like Hays, Miles claims that Ratzinger reads the Gospels through a high Christological lens. Wostyn goes much further than either Rausch or Hays, attributing to Ratzinger not just a Christology from above, but "a high 'Christology-from-above.'" In Wostyn's view, Ratzinger borders on being a Docetist. In his review of *Jesus of Nazareth*, he claims that: "Ratzinger's Christology goes beyond the Councils of Nicaea-Chalcedon by simply erasing all the disagreements and ambiguities that appeared during these Councils. He presents the *homoousios* of Nicaea as somehow the norm." Wostyn thinks that Ratzinger, in his attempt to avoid a new Arianism, has actually veered too far in the direction of a new Docetism, seeing in Jesus "the appearance" of a human being. He sees him as a new Cyril of Alexandria, "exiling" Christology-from-below theologians such as Edward Schillebeeckx, Roger Haight, and Jon Sobrino for their supposed Arianism. See Wostyn, "Pope Benedict XVI," 95–96.

7. O'Brien, "Who's Listening?," 266–68.

8. Ibid., 268–69.

of tending towards a form of Gnosticism, a Christian Platonism.⁹ Third, he believes that *Jesus of Nazareth* fails to do justice to the paradox of Jesus of Nazareth as very man and very God. He believes that Ratzinger constantly states this dogma, but never defends it.¹⁰ To sum up, O'Brien concludes that *Jesus of Nazareth* "is light on historicity and light on theology."¹¹

The Hermeneutics of *Jesus of Nazareth*

Some commentators have attempted to uncover the hermeneutical key of Ratzinger's Jesus. For example, Peter Casarella thinks that Ratzinger's literary, hermeneutical and theological key is the "search for a discrete face of an otherwise invisible God," as revealed in the Suffering Servant of that God.¹² A number of commentators raise important questions about Ratzinger's principles of biblical interpretation, his use of the historical-critical method, and his attempt to integrate it with a theological exegesis, which Daniel Harrington describes as Ratzinger's "project to integrate the historical hermeneutic practiced in much biblical scholarship today and a properly developed faith or theological hermeneutic and thus to restore biblical study to its identity as a theological discipline."¹³ Indeed, the focus of commentators

---

9. Ibid., 268–71.

10. Ibid., 271–72.

11. Ibid., 275.

12. Casarella, "Searching for the Face," 84. Casarella thinks that Ratzinger's methodology bears some similarity to that used by Frank Matera in his *New Testament Christology* in that they both claim to recognise a canonical unity in the distinct New Testament portraits of Jesus. See Casarella, "Searching for the Face," 91–92. Simon Oliver argues that Ratzinger's hermeneutical key for reading the Gospel narratives is the kenotic descent of Christ, wherein Ratzinger extends von Balthasar's emphasis on Christ's descent to the dead on Holy Saturday. See Oliver, "Christ, Descent and Participation," 68. For R. W. L. Moberly, the key is Ratzinger's "striking and unusual engagement with the Old Testament" as demonstrated in his messianic interpretation of Deuteronomy 18:15 and 34:10, where the people of Israel are promised a "new Moses"; and of Exodus 33, where Moses is portrayed as speaking with God "as with a friend"; and his linking of these passages to John 1:18, where Jesus is presented as the one who "lives before the face of God." See Moberly, "The Use of the Old Testament in *Jesus of Nazareth*," 98–101. Hays claims to see four major themes in *Jesus of Nazareth*—Jesus' intimate unity with the Father, the universal scope of his mission, a reduction of the apocalyptic content of Jesus' message, and the removal of the concrete political and social order from the explicitly sacred realm. See Hays, "Ratzinger's Johannine Jesus," 112–13. Cf. *Jesus I*, 6, 22, 58, 114, 118, and 126.

13. Harrington, "Benedict's Passion," 28. While generally positive, Harrington's analysis sounds a cautionary note. He writes: "In carrying out his theological exegesis of the Gospels, the pope joins historical exegesis, patristic theological insights, more recent theological concerns, liturgical practice and contemporary experience. The

upon Ratzinger's hermeneutics seems to be the most common one. How successful the integration to which Harrington refers is an important question for this study since the historical accuracy of Ratzinger's portrayal of Jesus includes the question of how Jesus prays and what conclusions validly can be drawn from his prayer.

A wide spectrum of analysis of Ratzinger's hermeneutics is revealed. Rausch thinks that, in the first published volume of *Jesus of Nazareth*, Ratzinger "makes clear that he takes for granted everything that the Second Vatican Council and modern exegesis teaches about literary forms and authorial intent."[14] According to Rausch, for Ratzinger's biblical hermeneutics, the historical-critical method remains indispensable so long as one recognizes its limits. He begins not with a historical but with a theological datum of the unity of the Bible, which datum presupposes an act of faith. He applauds canonical exegesis, which seeks to read individual texts within the totality of Scripture, and which, in turn, sheds new light on individual texts. This allows room for what biblical scholars have called the "fuller sense," a properly theological interpretation which may go beyond the precise sense the words were intended to convey at their time and place of origin. Since Scripture is not simply historical literature it must always be read within the living tradition of the church. According to Rausch, Ratzinger attempts to portray the Jesus of the Gospels as the real, historical Jesus in the strict sense of the words. He takes faith as his starting point, though he reads the texts with the help of historical methodology.[15]

Hays is critical of Ratzinger's attempt to integrate the historical-critical method with a theological hermeneutic. He thinks that Ratzinger's approach results in an "ambivalence about 'history' that runs like a fault line through the whole book."[16] He criticizes Ratzinger for wanting to make the

---

dangers involved in theological exegesis include trying to do too many things at once, blurring the distance between the ancient text and life today and moving too quickly from textual study to homiletics" (29). For a comprehensive overview of other reviews, both scholarly and popular, of the first *Jesus of Nazareth*, see Joseph S. O'Leary's homepage: www.josephsoleary.typepad.com. As well as his own review, O'Leary discusses reviews from English, French, German, Italian and Portuguese sources. By O'Leary's account, much of the debate in these reviews has focused on Ratzinger's alleged use or misuse of the historical-critical method, and his alleged success or failure in uniting the Jesus of history with the Christ of faith.

14. Rausch, *Pope Benedict XVI*, 86.

15. Ibid.

16. Hays, "Ratzinger's Johannine Jesus," 114. Cf. Miles, "Between Theology and Exegesis," 22. Miles also is critical of Ratzinger's use of the historical-critical method, which he regards as breaking too absolutely with science and modernity. However, Markus Bockmuehl, although he regards Ratzinger's historical portrait of Jesus as weak and sometimes indefensible, finds the great strength of the book to be its theological

conviction of faith the starting point for reading the texts, since this would, in the eyes of many historical critics, compromise a historical methodology. Hays states that, if Ratzinger's aim is to retain a serious engagement with history, "he owes us a more careful explanation of how he proposes to reconceive the practice of historical criticism to allow for the historical claims he wants to make."[17] Rather than doing so, Hays sees Ratzinger as giving insufficient attention to the theological and literary differences between the different Gospels, a fault he attributes partly to an insufficient grasp of more recent biblical scholarship.[18] However, Hays sees many positive points in Ratzinger's book—it is a synthetic theological reading of the canonical New Testament which is often subtle and illuminating, it grounds the interpretation of Jesus in the Old Testament as well as the New, and it achieves a sympathetic appropriation of patristic exegesis, drawing it into conversation with modern exegesis.[19]

Luke Timothy Johnson gives a thoughtful, though on the whole critical, review of the first published volume of *Jesus of Nazareth*. Johnson recognizes that Ratzinger, in principle, embraces the historical-critical method, avoiding the use of Sacred Scripture as a quarry containing proof texts for building a dogmatic edifice, and he praises Ratzinger for his deployment of patristic and liturgical resources in the interpretation of specific biblical passages.[20] However, Johnson thinks that Ratzinger pays no more than lip service to the historical-critical method, claiming that he does not engage in genuine historical enquiry. He criticizes Ratzinger for what he does not do—determine the relationship of the Gospels to each other, come to grips with the distinctive portrayal of Jesus in each, or address the development of the Resurrection faith in the light of the Resurrection experience. In short,

---

hermeneutic, "in equal measure history-affirming and insistent on the great christological questions that the Church Fathers posed." See Bockmuehl, 122. Moberly makes two particular criticisms of Ratzinger's exegesis, namely that his reading of Deuteronomy 18:15 and 34:10 does not take into account the different meanings of "like" in the two passages, and that Exodus 33 does not imply the desirability of a prophet greater than Moses. Moberly thinks that Ratzinger "is starting from his Johannine perspective of Jesus' surpassing Moses, and is looking for a textual warrant for this with the Old Testament." See Moberly, "The Use of the Old Testament in *Jesus of Nazareth*," 106. Cf. *Jesus I*, 5–6. For Moberly, this is indicative of a failure to respect the historical dimensions of the biblical text. He proposes a renewed hermeneutic of typology or figuration which does not give up a historical-critical awareness. See ibid., 107–8.

17. Ibid., 114–15.

18. Ibid., 115–16. Cf. Bockmuehl, "Saints' Lives as Exegesis," 122, where Bockmuehl makes a similar assessment of Ratzinger's engagement with more recent biblical scholarship.

19. Ibid., 117–18.

20. Johnson, "Jesus of Nazareth," 318 and 319.

he sees Ratzinger as opting for continuity and harmony in his portrait of Jesus, rather than discontinuity and dissonance.[21] Furthermore, Johnson too sees Ratzinger's Christology as being high—a thoroughly incarnational Christology which sees the distinguishing character of Jesus as the one who brings God to the world.[22] Hence, Ratzinger pays much more attention to the words of Jesus than he does to his deeds or his human character. Yet he is unable to see "the incongruity of inquiring into the original linguistic sense of 'rule of God' from one who has chosen to read the Gospels from the perspective of a fully incarnational Christology."[23] Ultimately, Johnson sees *Jesus of Nazareth* as a noble failure because it "falls between the worlds of scholarship and devotion."[24]

At the opposite end of the spectrum, Angus Paddison thinks that *Jesus of Nazareth* is sometimes "too beholden to historical-critical readings of Scripture and so ends up confusing the historical *reality* of Jesus with the historical *authenticity* of the Gospels as precise transcripts of what Jesus did and said."[25] He thinks that, in some ways, the practical outworking of the hermeneutical methodology given in the Foreword of the book does not measure up to the expectations raised. He also thinks that Ratzinger could have done more to link the correspondences between Scripture and doctrine.[26]

More positively, Thomas Weinandy thinks that Ratzinger's chief contribution to biblical exegesis is in providing it with a "christological hermeneutic" whereby Jesus Christ becomes the key to understanding the Bible as a unity, both historically and theologically, when that understanding is preceded by an act of faith. In particular, Weinandy focuses on the fact that Ratzinger presents Jesus himself as the model exegete, teaching us how to understand the unity of biblical revelation through his interpretation of

---

21. Johnson, "Jesus of Nazareth," 319. Johnson is not alone in voicing this lament. Cf. Deines, "Can the 'Real' Jesus?," 219, nos. 50 and 51, and 220, nos. 52, 53, and 54, where Deines gives an overview of the reaction of some German feminist, liberation, ecumenical, inter-religious and Judeophile theologians to Ratzinger's neglect of their perspectives. Cf. also Hays, "Ratzinger's Johannine Jesus," 116, where Hays makes a similar observation about the questions which Ratzinger has not raised. Cf. also Bockmuehl, 122.

22. Johnson, "Jesus of Nazareth," 318.

23. Ibid., 319–20. Cf. Huovinen, "The Pope and Jesus," 149.

24. Johnson, "Jesus of Nazareth," 320. Cf. Huovinen, "The Pope and Jesus," 151. Huovinen sees *Jesus I*, as a book with two aims—to give "a historically, theologically, and philosophically consistent view of Jesus," as well as "a pious book calling the reader to fellowship with Christ."

25. Paddison, "Following Jesus," 193. Cf. Deines, "Can the 'Real' Jesus,?" 213–14.

26. Paddison, "Following Jesus," 194.

the Old Testament.[27] Michael Root thinks that Ratzinger shows a skill in theological exegesis that few can match. Like Weinandy, he sees Ratzinger's christological hermeneutic as the basis of his appeals to typology, lifting it out of a mere appeal to typology as such. The historical-critical method must not be abandoned, but taken up into a theological method.[28] Root further maintains that Ratzinger's hermeneutic is not just theological, but also ecclesial. The inspiration of the individual biblical authors has an ecclesial dimension. That dimension is the "subject" of the People of God, which is the deeper "author," a subject itself subject to the guidance of the Holy Spirit.[29]

David Lincicum goes about the task of attempting to show how Ratzinger engages in canonical criticism. For Lincicum, one of the keys to understanding *Jesus of Nazareth* is "the canonical judgment that enables a figural reading of the two-testament canon of Christian Scripture to function as a witness to Jesus."[30] For Ratzinger, the ultimate subject of all Scripture is Jesus Christ. Lincicum sees this as a circular process. The chief presupposition which undergirds this way of reading Scripture is "that very 'wholeness' that emerges as the *result* of figural reading."[31] This circularity is justified as an act of faith seeking understanding. The unity of Scripture, obscure to historical criticism, is a theological datum which follows from a prior act of faith.[32] This theological datum opens the way to canonical exegesis.

Denis Farkasfalvy believes that the ultimate issue at stake in *Jesus of Nazareth* is "the legitimacy, the limitations, and the usefulness of the historical critical method."[33] According to Farkasfalvy, Ratzinger makes four

---

27. Weinandy, "Pope Benedict XVI," 21–22. Weinandy further develops his analysis of Ratzinger's Christological hermeneutic in "The Son's Filial Relationship,"253–64.

28. Root, "Jesus and the Pope," 154–55. Hans Boersma makes the same point, while drawing attention to the similarity of Ratzinger's approach to that of *ressourcement* theologians such as De Lubac and Daniélou, who "argued for a sacramental relationship between the realities of history and faith, and therefore between historical exegesis and spiritual interpretation." See Boersma, "History and Faith," 987.

29. Root, "Jesus and the Pope," 155–56.

30. Lincicum, "Benedict's Jesus," 286.

31. Ibid., 287.

32. Ibid. Cf. *Jesus I*, xviii–xix.

33. Farkasfalvy, "*Jesus of Nazareth*," 440. Cf. Wright, "A 'New Synthesis,'" 35–66. Wright asserts that *Jesus of Nazareth* is Ratzinger's substantive effort to carry out a new synthesis in biblical exegesis. According to Wright, this synthesis includes "a philosophically renovated historical criticism [which] would be more open to the text's claim and not exclude certain possibilities (such as divine intervention in the world) on philosophical grounds. Other features of this program include the consideration that events are meaningful in themselves, and awareness of the exegete's location within the Church community, and the acceptance of the Church's faith as an interpretive key,

pertinent points about this method. First, it is essential, since the "facticity" of the Incarnation is indispensable. Second, the most important limitation of the method is that it must approach its subject as belonging to the past. It cannot make it a part of the present. Third, it "*a priori* assumes that history is homogeneous," it is a closed system "which excludes by definition the possibility of divine intervention."[34] Finally, Ratzinger's way out of these confines is through a theology of inspiration. This theology has two aspects. First: "Experience teaches us that human utterances express and signify more than what their speakers or writers intend."[35] Therefore, in view of the transcendence of the human word, the historical-critical method must recognize that the Bible is, *ipso facto*, open to transcendental intervention. Second, the method itself reveals that the Bible contains "a dynamic of 'remembering and retelling' as well as anticipation and prophetic interpretation, a framework in which texts point beyond themselves both back into the past and forward into the future."[36] Farkasfalvy asserts that Ratzinger's exegetical system can be traced back to the pre-Vatican II insights of theologians such as Rahner, de Lubac, Congar and Daniélou.[37] However, he maintains that one must look to other publications by Ratzinger for further presuppositions of his exegetical system. He identifies these presuppositions as a theological anthropology which "connects man's historical existence with his capability for transcendence," along with a concept of revelation as itself being history. It is only though the pilgrim people of God in its journey through history that the words of the Bible can become "present."[38]

not an impediment, for understanding Scripture" (36). Wright characterises *Jesus of Nazareth* as a work of Christian theological exegesis, one which harmonizes reason and faith, that is to say, historical criticism and the faith of the Church (50–51).

34. Farkasfalvy, "*Jesus of Nazareth*," 440.

35. Ibid., 441.

36. Ibid.

37. Ibid. Farkasfalvy maintains that Ratzinger's placing of Scripture as emerging from the heart of a living subject, the Church, "summarizes Rahner's theology of inspiration in a more accessible language than Rahner himself was able to do." See ibid., no. 8.

38. Ibid., 442. Cf. Casarella, "Searching for the Face," 88, where Casarella says: "From a hermeneutical standpoint, what merits particular attention is the notion that an ecclesial reading of certain words may uncover 'a deeper value' to those words as they are read and re-read over time (pp. xix–xx). If the genetic fallacy is the unmasking of the view that only what is exposed in its pristine originality is what counts as true, then Ratzinger has hereby proposed a fairly original approach to understanding the relationship of Scripture and tradition. In a sense, Ratzinger draws out the christological and interpersonal implication of what Maximus the Confessor called 'the thickening of the Word.' The speech of the Word as it unfolds in history carries within it a performative dimension that allows for more mature understandings to take root and blossom

Eero Huovinen covers some of the same ground as Farkasfalvy, maintaining that Ratzinger wishes to retain the historical and scientific aspects of biblical research, while at the same time recognizing its limits. First, that it is bound by its very nature to the analysis of past events. Second, that it can make no provision for events which deviate from immanent events, although it may sense a transcendent reality behind human words and events. Third, it is limited to the individual contexts of each book in the Bible, but it cannot be used to investigate that Bible as a single entity.[39] In looking at Ratzinger's understanding of theological exegesis, Huovinen draws attention to the fact that Ratzinger is aware of the difficulties concerning the unity of Scripture—that the integration of individual texts into one entity calls for the rereading of these texts. Thus Huovinen says: "Goethe spoke about 'sleeping texts' (*Schläfertexte*), texts that are to be better understood later on. The 'deeper values' hidden behind words open up within the history in which the speaker lives."[40] Huovinen makes an especially perceptive observation when he says that Ratzinger approaches biblical inspiration not "by appealing to the divine nature of the Word but begins 'from below.'" Hence: "Inspiration is an understandable concept even from the viewpoint of profane historical research. The biblical authors do not speak as private individuals . . . but rather as a part of a living community and historical movement with its own dynamics."[41] Huovinen thinks that Ratzinger sees, within the Bible, three "subjects" which mutually indwell each other—the individual author or group of authors, the people of God, and God himself.[42] Finally, Huovinen asserts that although criticizing a rationalistic interpretation of Jesus, Ratzinger uses the concept "reason of faith" (*Vernunft des Glaubens*) in a positive way. According to Huovinen:

> In Ratzinger's thinking, *Vernunft* does not primarily mean reason in the modern sense but rather *intellectus* in the classical philosophical sense, namely, understanding and wisdom. *Vernunft des Glaubens* means the *intellectus fidei*. As an old student of St. Augustine, Ratzinger's intention is to emphasize the striving to understand the object of faith (*fides quaerens intellectum*) and to see this object with the eyes of faith (*fides abet oculos suos*).[43]

within the community of faith."

39. Huovinen, "The Pope and Jesus," 143–44.
40. Ibid., 144.
41. Ibid., 145.
42. Ibid.
43. Ibid., 149.

Henri-Jérôme Gagey claims to uncover the epistemological principles behind Ratzinger's balance between exegesis and theology, principles based on the demand to pursue the dialogue between faith and reason. He believes that Ratzinger engages in reasoning which is circular, although Gagey thinks that such reasoning is justifiable. As Gagey claims:

> Without basic confidence in the truthfulness of the Gospels, it is very difficult to grasp their coherence. But such basic confidence can only come from accepting the truth of the gospel. This fits with the theological hermeneutical principle that only tradition gives access to the Scriptures.[44]

The objection is raised that this approach immerses one in dogmatic assumptions. According to Gagey, Ratzinger's response is to point out that historical-critical thinking is itself circular in form. The "scientific" portrayal of Jesus put forward by some biblical scholars was itself dependent on exegetical and historical options which were expressions of "dogmatic" philosophical and theological assumptions.[45] However, Gagey thinks that, in presenting only two alternatives, Ratzinger oversimplifies the situation. He holds that in the third quarter of the twentieth century, particularly amongst German Protestant biblical scholars, the gap between Jesus the preacher of the kingdom and Jesus as the risen Lord preached by his disciples was bridged by stressing the most peculiar feature of Jesus' earthly ministry—his claim to authority. The christological faith of the disciples "proved to be no longer an arbitrary addition to his simple preaching of a moralistic gospel."[46] Rather, by preaching Jesus as the Christ they were accepting his self-identification as the one with authority to announce the Kingdom and interpret the will of God.

Roland Deines addresses the issue of whether or not Ratzinger's *Konstruktionspunkt* (point of construction) of his approach to the historical Jesus is, as many reviewers have claimed, a Johannine approach. He concludes that such is not the case. Rather, it is the close relationship between Jesus and God, a relationship for which he finds support in John's Gospel. Deines thinks that Ratzinger begins with an inherited tradition about Jesus' relation to God, because he is convinced that the traditional faith correctly formulates an "ontological truth-claim." According to Deines:

---

44. Gagey, "Once there was no Historical Jesus," 16. Cf. Martínez, "Christ of History," 23–24.
45. Ibid., 16–17. Cf. Ratzinger, "Schriftauslegung im Widerstreit," 15–44.
46. Ibid., 19.

Following an ostensibly circular argument, he then attempts to go one step further: if the understanding of Jesus inherited from the tradition can be corroborated with historical evidence, then it is legitimate to integrate the transempirical elements of the ontological claims about Jesus into the historical question as well (pp. xiii–xiv).[47]

Although generally positive about Ratzinger's attempt to integrate the "transempirical" with the historical, Deines has some reservations about Ratzinger's definition of the limits of the historical method. He thinks that Ratzinger "defines historical research within the secular paradigm"—that it can only treat the biblical words as human words, and leave the past in the past. Deines asks: "Why is 'faith,' understood as a specific, precisely defined approach to reality, incongruent with a sound historical approach?"[48]

According to Anthony Sciglitano, one of Ratzinger's goals in *Jesus of Nazareth* is "to reunite devotion and intellect by way of a neopatristic theology grounded in Scripture but open to the sorts of public reason advocated by the neo-Thomist tradition in Catholic theology that can recognize a legitimate if relative autonomy for reason and the secular sphere."[49] In particular, Sciglitano draws attention to Ratzinger's use of "symbol" (*Vorstellung*) in *Jesus of Nazareth*. He sees Ratzinger's discussion of maternal images of God in Scripture as an instance of this approach. He quotes Ratzinger thus: "The image language of the body furnishes us . . . with a deeper understanding of God's disposition toward man than any conceptual language could."[50] Sciglitano also takes note of Ratzinger's retrieval of the patristic and medieval hermeneutic which recognized four senses of Sacred Scripture as manifestations of one, christological sense.[51] For Sciglitano, this is a manifestation of neo-patristic *ressourcement* theology as practiced by de Lubac, Congar, von Balthasar, and Chenu, which systematically elevated symbol (*Vorstellung*) over concept (*Begriff*). As Sciglitano explains:

> This does not mean that they turn to an irrationalist form of theology, but rather that human reason needs to be regulated by the symbolic world of Scripture and Christian worship, within which a deeper reason is disclosed that can heal and perfect distortions of inadequate human reason. This divine

---

47. Deines, "Can the 'Real' Jesus?," 206.

48. Ibid., 207 n. 22.

49. Sciglitano, "Pope Benedict," 160. Wright too characterises Ratzinger's theology in *Jesus is Nazareth* as "neo-Patristic." See Wright, "A 'New Synthesis,'" 66.

50. *Jesus I*, 139. Quoted by Sciglitano, "Pope Benedict," 177.

51. Sciglitano, "Pope Benedict," 177. Cf. *Jesus I*, xx.

reason, however, cannot be reduced to human propositions and univocal statements; rather, it presents itself in the paradoxical joinings of spirit and matter, meaning and expression that can disclose a reality that transcends human rationality, yet does not destroy it.[52]

Intimations of Ratzinger's Spiritual Christology in *Jesus of Nazareth*

A number of commentators have highlighted the importance of the prayer of Jesus for understanding Ratzinger's portrayal of him. For example, Casarella sees the first two chapters of *Jesus of Nazareth*, in treating of the face-to-face dialogue between the Father and the Son, and the iconic dimension of the Baptism of Jesus in the Jordan, as being a kind of blue-print for the whole book, the aim of which is to reveal in the "face of the Lord" his revelation of the Father.[53]

Markus Bockmuehl takes up the question of how the saints interpret Sacred Scripture. In looking at Ratzinger's christological interpretation of the Beatitudes, Bockmuehl draws particular attention to what appears to be

---

52. Ibid., 175.

53. Casarella, "Searching for the Face," 88. Fergus Kerr compares Ratzinger's treatment of the self-knowledge of Christ with that of Aquinas, Rahner, von Balthasar, and Weinandy. Kerr concludes that Ratzinger thinks that Jesus knew he was God, that his approach to this question is closest to that of Weinandy, and that it was "above all through his intimate communion with his Father in prayer [that] Jesus came to understand who he was." See Kerr, "If Jesus Knew?," 66. Cf. Weinandy, *Jesus the Christ*, 30–39. Huovinen claims that Jesus' relationship with the Father is the underlying theme of *Jesus of Nazareth*, and that this theme colours all that Ratzinger says about Jesus therein. See Huovinen, "The Pope and Jesus," 146–47. Cf. *Jesus I*, 44, 66, 95, 265–66, 291, 304, 310, and 316. Root recognises participation in God through Jesus as a constant theme of the book. See Root, "Jesus and the Pope," 157. Hays asserts that the "single most dominant theme throughout *Jesus of Nazareth* is Jesus' 'intimate unity with the Father.' The key to interpreting Jesus' identity lies in his relation to God, which is ontologically grounded in his pre-existent unity with the Father and expressed in his communion with the Father in prayer." See Hays, "Ratzinger's Johannine Jesus," 112. Weinandy believes the major theme of *Jesus of Nazareth* to be that "Jesus is the incarnate Son of God who bestows upon all believers what he himself shares—a filial intimacy and knowledge of the Father," and that this revelation "results from his human prayer, which is 'a participation in this filial communion with the Father.'" In particular, when we pray the Our Father, or the *Psalms*, or participate in the liturgy, "our words of prayer precede our thoughts . . . [our words] conform our minds to the truths expressed in such prayers and so we actually pray in conformity with the inspiration of the Holy Spirit (cf. 130–31)." Weinandy, "Pope Benedict XVI," 24, 23, and 28. The internal quote is from *Jesus I*, 7.

a detour into the presentation of the life of St. Francis of Assisi as the most intense illustration of a Christian being truly poor in spirit. For Bockmuehl, this excursus is not to be dismissed as pious hagiography. Rather, it sets the stage for a hermeneutical principle of Ratzinger's: "The saints are the true interpreters of Scripture. The meaning of a given passage of the Bible becomes most intelligible in those human beings who have been totally transfixed by it and have lived it out."[54] Bockmuehl sees in this proposition more than Gadamer's emphasis on the "hermeneutical force of the text's aftermath," or "popular insistences on diachronic communities of interpretation and on the necessarily self-involving nature of exegesis."[55] Rather, he sees an emphasis on biblical interpretation as performance.[56] He likens Ratzinger's proposition to one hinted at in *The Art of Reading Scripture*, that the saints can guide us in the interpretation and performance of Sacred Scripture. Their communion can form our own reading. We can learn from them the centrality of interpretive virtues, such as receptivity, humility, truthfulness, courage, charity, humor and imagination. This guidance is to be found in both their writings and the holiness of their lives. "[Faithful] interpretation of Scripture requires its faithful performance."[57] However, Bockmuehl believes that Ratzinger goes beyond this position. He thinks that what Ratzinger is advocating is the idea that the praxis of a saint "can be a lived exposition or commentary on their specific encounter with the Jesus of the Sermon on the Mount."[58] Some specific "performances" can expound particular biblical texts. An example in the Bible itself would be the way in which the death of St. Stephen is an exposition of Christ's death—as St. Paul says, "it is no longer I who live, but Christ who lives in me" (Gal 2: 20). In their own lives, the saints interpret the Scriptures, just as Christ did in his.[59] Bockmuehl regards this hermeneutical approach as having an ancient pedigree, being found in St. Augustine's notion of biography-as-exposition in *On Christian Doctrine*, and in the concluding paragraph of St. Athanasius' treatise on the Incarnation. So Bockmuehl says: "The object of the text is the proper object of interpretation, and the life transparently

---

54. *Jesus I*, 78. Quoted in Bockmuehl, "Saints' Lives as Exegesis," 125.

55. Bockmuehl, 125.

56. Ibid. Cf. Barton, "New Testament Interpretation," 179–208; Fowl and Jones, *Reading in Communion*; and Lash, "Performing the Scriptures," 37–46.

57. Davis and Hays, "Nine Theses," 4. Quoted in Bockmuehl, "Saints' Lives as Exegesis," 126.

58. Bockmuehl, "Saints' Lives as Exegesis," 126.

59. Ibid., 126–27.

formed by the object is the most apposite commentary on it."[60] However, he does see a potential danger in this kind of hermeneutical approach. Rather than providing a true interpretation of Sacred Scripture, such an approach may yield, to those who attempt this kind of praxis, no more than a mirror for the interpreter's own thoughts and feelings.[61]

Paddison offers a variation upon Bockmuehl's theme. Instead of limiting the interpretive task to the saints, he proposes that, in *Jesus of Nazareth*, Ratzinger employs a "hermeneutic of discipleship." Paddison thinks that "disciples enjoy an interpretative privilege because they participate in the world which Scripture makes known."[62] Following Jesus and reading Sacred Scripture are mutually informing practices. Paddison sees Ratzinger following this hermeneutic when he writes that the Sermon on the Mount "can be understood and lived out only by following Jesus and accompanying him on his journey."[63] He sees Ratzinger proposing a "hermeneutic of faith," since faith is a way of knowing which is more truly "scientific" than historical-criticism, as it renders a more intelligible understanding of the biblical text.[64] However, this hermeneutic of faith is not in competition with a historical hermeneutic, because the Son of God has become incarnate. Rather, it prioritizes the church "as the subject through which Scripture emanates and liturgy as Scripture's native habitat."[65]

Paddison gives an excellent summary of Ratzinger's understanding of the foundation of discipleship, as sketched out in *Jesus of Nazareth*.

> The Jesus whose face the Pope seeks "lives in the most intimate unity with the Father" and communicated this closeness to those who listened to him (p. 6). Again and again Benedict locates the centre of Jesus in his ceaseless, prayer-rich communion with his Father, a communion into which disciples are invited to enter. Jesus' "unity of will with the Father's will is the core of his very being" (p. 149). This unity is the ground and basis of the authority of Jesus' teaching, a teaching whose hidden reality "can truly be discovered through discipleship" (p. 324). Jesus communicates God. Jesus' life is marked by his ascent into the Father's presence through prayer and his suffering descent into the form and shape of our human life (p. 68). And just as Jesus' communion is sustained by prayer, so too the disciple who prays

60. Ibid., 132.
61. Ibid., 132–33.
62. Paddison, "Following Jesus," 176.
63. *Jesus I*, 69; quoted in Paddison, "Following Jesus," 186.
64. Paddison, "Following Jesus," 189. Cf. *Behold*, 45.
65. Ibid.

is caught up in Jesus' filial relationship with his Father. The disciple is taken up into communion between the Father and the Son; indeed our communion with the Father is possible only on the basis of the mutual knowing between the Father and the Son. Those who follow Jesus see God (John 14.9), startlingly so in the Transfiguration which, in the Lukan account, is the climatic unfolding to Jesus' disciples of his prayerful communion with the Father (p. 310).[66]

In attempting to explain what kind of book *Jesus of Nazareth* is, Roch Kereszty says that it resists classification into exegetical study, systematic Christology, homily, or mystical theology, although it also includes all of these *genres*.

> Though not a work of scholarly exegesis, it discloses the profound unity between the Old and New Testaments, as well as among the Synoptic, Johannine, and Pauline Christologies. It presents no systematic christological treatise, yet it lays the foundations for a future christological synthesis. It is not a collection of homilies, but by drawing on its insights, homilists can revitalize their preaching. It is not a treatise of mystical theology either, yet it springs from an intimate friendship with Christ and intends to lead its readers to such a friendship.[67]

According to Kereszty, Ratzinger's blend of theology, exegesis and contemplation is reminiscent of the style of the Church Fathers and St. Augustine in particular. It expresses the deepest theology in a language comprehensible to educated lay believers, yet still challenging for scholars. It is a style which held sway before the high Middle Ages, when theologians were also pastors and preachers, "competent and willing to lead the faithful toward and intimate and personal union with God."[68] However, a subsequent trend towards specialization and differentiation has marginalized the influence of theologians on the thinking, life and spirituality of the church, limiting their audience largely to other theologians and their students. While there have been exceptions to this rule, *Jesus of Nazareth* challenges contemporary theologians "to embrace a more integral ecclesial vocation."[69] Kereszty

---

66. Ibid., 189–90.

67. Kereszty, "The Challenge of *Jesus of Nazareth*," 456.

68. Ibid., 457. Cf. Martínez, "Christ of History," 21–22.

69. Ibid., 458. Cf. Casarella, "Searching for the Face," 91. Bockmuehl puts a different, through witty slant on this question when he says: "There is an open, if sometimes awkward and one-sided conversation [in biblical scholarship] between two partners still too often alternately boycotted by different groups of scholars: twentieth-century scholarship on the one hand and 20 centuries of scholarship on the other" (Bockmuehl,

sees Ratzinger as advocating a contemporary expression of the patristic model, one which utilizes the genuine fruits of the specialization which has occurred since the late Middle Ages, including the positive results of historical-critical exegesis.[70] He characterizes the theology of *Jesus of Nazareth* as "contemplative." He believes that, on the one hand, it avoids the tendency of the "Jesus of history" literature to reduce Jesus to a single idealistic category, while on the other it avoids the neo-scholastic attempt to build a complex Christology of abstract concepts. Although aware of the importance of metaphysics, Kereszty believes that Ratzinger's more personalist, concrete language leads to encountering Christ rather than just speculating about him.[71] He holds that Ratzinger's book is a book which is *unterwegs*, on the way; that it presents both the author and the church as still on the way to a fuller relationship with Jesus.[72] For Kereszty, the goal of Ratzinger's book is a renewed theology which "goes beyond the articulation of concepts for expressing the metaphysical dimension of the Christian mystery . . . [Rather it] aims at helping the 'I' of the reader die to its limits and enter into the 'I' of Jesus so that the reader may also 'see' the Father."[73]

The Puzzle of *Jesus of Nazareth*

As can be seen, there has been much disagreement as to the nature of *Jesus of Nazareth*. Is it exegesis or biblical theology? Is it scholarship or devotion? Kereszty defines it as "contemplative." Johnson regards it as a failed attempt to be two things at once, scholarship and devotion. Huovinen sees it as a successful attempt to be both scholarly and pious. Weinandy sees it as being a "robust theological work that addresses authentic contemporary biblical, historical, philosophical and doctrinal issues," rather than a book of meditations.[74] Hays asks if it is a scholarly study of the historical figure of Jesus, an interpretive theological account of the biblical foundations of the church's trinitarian doctrine, a devotional mediation on the person of Jesus for prayerful appropriation by the faithful, or a Christian *apologia* in the face of secularism's barren and destructive view of humanity?[75] Hopefully, this study of Ratzinger's spiritual Christology will help to solve this puzzle.

123).
70. Kereszty, "The Challenge of *Jesus of Nazareth*," 458.
71. Ibid., 471.
72. Ibid., 471–72.
73. Ibid., 472.
74. Weinandy, "Pope Benedict XVI," 19.
75. Hays, "Ratzinger's Johannine Jesus," 111.

The Purpose of *Jesus of Nazareth*

What is Ratzinger's Hermeneutic in *Jesus of Nazareth*?

The hermeneutical key to *Jesus of Nazareth* has been variously defined as the kenotic descent of Christ, the search for the face of God in the Suffering Servant, and Jesus as the new Moses.[76] Ratzinger's hermeneutic has been variously defined as being a "hermeneutic of faith," a "christological hermeneutic," a "theological hermeneutic," and an "ecclesial hermeneutic."[77] There are elements of truth in all of these definitions. The very fact that so many different definitions have been proposed would seem to suggest that each proposer has perceived a facet of the truth. However, here it will be proposed that Ratzinger's hermeneutic ultimately should be defined as one of "communion" in that it begins with a prayerful communion with the Pierced One, a communion which is then lived out by the Christian. We "behold the Pierced One," and move towards the point where it is Christ, and no longer we, who live.

Some have commented upon the importance of participation in the prayer of Jesus, whether individually or ecclesially, in Ratzinger's spiritual Christology in *Jesus of Nazareth*.[78] However, most of the commentators on Ratzinger's hermeneutical method have not raised the question of the place that prayer might have in it. For the exceptions, like Kereszty, the goal of *Jesus of Nazareth* is to encounter Jesus Christ, not just speculate about him.[79] Weinandy skirts around the borders of the question when he draws

---

76. See Oliver, "Christ, Descent and Participation," 68; Casarella, "Searching for the Face," 84; and Moberly, "The Use of the Old Testament in *Jesus of Nazareth*," 98–101.

77. For example, for "Christological hermeneutic," see Weinandy, "Pope Benedict XVI," 21–22; and Root, "Jesus and the Pope," 154–55. For "theological hermeneutic," see Harrington, "Benedict's Passion," 28; and Hays, "A Challenge to Enlightenment Historiography," 114. For "ecclesial hermeneutic," see Root, "Jesus and the Pope," 155–56. For both "faith" and "ecclesial hermeneutic," see Wright, "A 'New Synthesis,'" 41–45.

78. For individual participation, see de Gaál, *The Theology of Pope Benedict XVI*, 5; Weinandy, "Pope Benedict XVI," 23 and 24; Root, "Jesus and the Pope," 157; and Paddison, "Following Jesus," 189. For ecclesial participation, see de Gaál, *The Theology of Pope Benedict XVI*, 86–87; and Hoping, "Gemeinschaft mit Christus," 558.

79. Kereszty, "The Challenge of *Jesus of Nazareth*," 471–72. Kereszty is the commentator who seems to be most aware of what Ratzinger is attempting to do in *Jesus of Nazareth*. In characterizing its theology as "contemplative," and seeing its goal as a renewed theology, he has perceived the purpose of Ratzinger's spiritual Christology without mentioning the term—its goal is to enable the "I" of believer to enter into the "I" of Jesus, and so "see" the Father. This is the solution to the puzzle of *Jesus of Nazareth*. Cf. Wright, "A 'New Synthesis,'" 56–61. As Sciglitano has asserted, the ultimate goal of spiritual Christology is a reconciliation of theology and spirituality, a "respiritualization" of theology. See Sciglitano, "Pope Benedict," 160.

attention to Ratzinger's insight that, when we pray the prayers of the church, "our words of prayer precede our thoughts . . . [our words] conform our minds to the truths expressed in such prayers and so we actually pray in conformity with the inspiration of the Holy Spirit (cf. 130–131)."[80] A few have an awareness of the role that a "lived" Christology might play in such a hermeneutic. So, Bockmuehl has drawn our attention to the hermeneutics of the saints, and Paddison to the hermeneutics of discipleship.[81]

In the Foreword to the second volume of *Jesus of Nazareth*, Ratzinger states that he has not attempted to write a Christology. Rather, he says that his intention has been closer to that of writing a theological treatise on the mysteries of the life of Jesus. He compares it with the treatise of St. Thomas Aquinas (*ST* III, qq. 27–59), with the caveat that his *Jesus of Nazareth* is situated in a different historical and spiritual context from that of Aquinas, and that it also has "a different inner objective that determines the structure of the text in essential ways."[82] If one compares *Introduction to Christianity* with *Jesus of Nazareth*, one cannot dispute the assertion that the latter work is more in the *genre* of a meditation on the mysteries of Christ's life, or more in the form of a biblical Christology, than the earlier work. However, whilst it is not a fully worked out Christology, it cannot help *revealing* a Christology. How is Ratzinger's spiritual Christology revealed in *Jesus of Nazareth*? How can one discern this spiritual Christology in each of the mysteries addressed by Ratzinger in his personal search "for the face of the Lord"?

---

80. Weinandy, "Pope Benedict XVI," 28.

81. Bockmuehl, "Saints' Lives as Exegesis," 125–33; and Paddision, "Following Jesus," 176–90.

82. *Jesus II*, xvi. Jared Staudt maintains that we should take Ratzinger at his word when he compares his *Jesus of Nazareth* with Aquinas' treatise on the mysteries of the life of Jesus. On this point, Staudt comments: "Although this may be surprising, upon further reflection it is clear that the two theologians hold much in common, including the importance of the Greek philosophical tradition and realist metaphysics for theology, a strong reliance on the Fathers of the Church, and a great devotion and attention to the Word of God. These connections produce in them similar attention to Scripture, centered on Christ who is the *Logos*, the fullness of truth manifest to reason and contained within the Word of God. One key reason for the similarity of approach is their common reliance on the exegetical principles of St. Augustine. In particular, Augustine's *De doctrina christiana* lays out a crucial hermeneutical principle concerning signs (*signa*) and the thing or reality (*res*) they signify" (Staudt, "Reality and Sign," 332).

5

The Spiritual Christology of *Jesus of Nazareth*— Method

An Initial Reflection on the Mystery of Jesus in *Jesus of Nazareth*

It is no accident or poetic flight of fancy which causes Ratzinger to call *Jesus of Nazareth* his personal search for the face of Jesus. Right from the beginning he introduces two foundation stones of his spiritual Christology, the prayer of Jesus and the heart of God. His reflection on the mystery of Jesus focuses on him as the one who sees God "face to face" in prayer, and thus is the one who can truly reveal him: "No one has ever seen God; it is the only Son, who is nearest to the Father's heart, who has made him known" (John 1:18).[1] Ratzinger sees Jesus as the one who is the ultimate prophet, the one who goes beyond Moses, the greatest of the Old Testament prophets. Moses *spoke* to God "face to face" as to a friend (cf. Exod 33:11 and Deut 34:10). He spoke with God "mouth to mouth" and beheld "the form of the Lord" (cf. Num 12:8). Yet he did not *see* God "face to face." He entered into the cloud of God's presence, but he could not see God's face. He had to be hidden in the cleft of a rock and only see God's back (cf. Exod 33:20–23).[2] Because Jesus *sees* the Father "face to face," because he is the one "closest to the Father's heart," he can make the Father known in a definitive way. Jesus' teaching originates in this "face to face" dialogue with the Father, "from the vision of the one who rests close to the Father's heart."[3] According to

---

1. *Jesus I*, 6.
2. Ibid., 3–6.
3. Ibid., 6–7.

Ratzinger: "We have to start here if we are truly to understand the figure of Jesus as it is presented to us in the New Testament; all that we are told about his word, deeds, sufferings, and glory is anchored here."[4]

Ratzinger goes on to state that the prayer of Jesus is fundamental for our understanding of who he is. The descriptions in the Gospels of Jesus praying alone with his Father are fundamental passages for our understanding of him. According to Ratzinger:

> [They] lift the veil of mystery just a little; they give us a glimpse into Jesus' filial existence, into the source from which his action and teaching and suffering sprang. This "praying" of Jesus is the Son conversing with the Father; Jesus' human consciousness and will, his human soul, is taken up into that exchange, and in this way human "praying" is able to become a participation in this filial communion with the Father.[5]

Pace von Harnack, Jesus' message is not just about the Father.

> [Rather,] Jesus is only able to speak about the Father in the way he does because he is the Son, because of his filial communion with the Father. The Christological dimension—in other words, the mystery of the Son as revealer of the Father—is present in everything Jesus says and does. Another important point appears here: We have said that in Jesus' filial communion with the Father, his human soul is also taken up into the act of praying. He who sees Jesus sees the Father (cf. John: 14:9). The disciple who walks with Jesus is thus caught up with him into communion with God. And that is what redemption means: this stepping beyond the limits of human nature, which had been there as a possibility and an expectation in man, God's image and likeness, since the moment of creation.[6]

Here, at the very beginning of his meditations, Ratzinger delves into the divinization of Jesus' humanity as effected by and revealed in his dialogue with the Father, and the divinization of our humanity through participation in his prayer. One can also see three of Ratzinger's theses being given flesh—the personal, volitional and filial. Jesus' communication with the Father is the center of his life and person, his human consciousness and will are taken up into that communication, and one who is in communication with Jesus is caught up into communion with God.

---

4. Ibid., 6.
5. Ibid., 7.
6. Ibid., 7–8. Cf. *Introduction*, 234–35.

The Approach to *Jesus of Nazareth*

What method should one use to discern Ratzinger's spiritual Christology in *Jesus of Nazareth*? In *Behold the Pierced One*, the three aspects of this Christology are addressed separately—first his seven theses, then his theology of the heart, and finally, his eucharistic spirituality. Yet in *Jesus of Nazareth* only the first two are substantially involved, and these two aspects are not separated. How then should they be analyzed? Since they are not treated separately in *Jesus of Nazareth* they will not be treated separately here. Rather, an attempt will be made to integrate them. At the conclusion of the chapter we shall examine *Deus caritas est* and *Sacramentum caritatis*, wherein one gets some insight into the place of the Eucharist in Ratzinger's spiritual Christology.

Jesus of Nazareth is composed of "meditations" on the "mysteries" of Jesus' life. One approach could be to examine each of these meditations in turn and seek to discover how the seven theses are applied therein. Throughout these meditations Ratzinger also introduces a number of "prayer events" in Jesus' life—his Baptism, the Sermon on the Mount, the calling of the Disciples, the giving of the Lord's Prayer, Peter's Confession of Faith, the Transfiguration, the High Priestly Prayer of Jesus, the Last Supper, Gethsemane and even the Crucifixion itself. One could examine these and try to see how the theses are applied to them. However, the method employed here will be to use the theses themselves as the point of departure for our investigation. Also, the investigation of how the theses are applied in *Jesus of Nazareth* will follow the "spiritual" sequence given in chapter 3— the personal, ecclesial, and hermeneutical in this chapter; the filial, soteriological, dogmatic, and volitional in the following chapter.

The Personal Thesis

This thesis states that: "Since the center of the person of Jesus is prayer, it is essential to participate in his prayer if we are to know and understand him."[7] With this thesis, Ratzinger proposes the necessity of a *lived* Christology for any intellectual Christology, a living which begins with praying. The danger of failing to do this is brought out in his analysis of the second temptation faced by Jesus in the desert. It is a temptation that every believer also faces. Like the others, the temptation to "put God to the test" is also about one's relationship with God. Ratzinger sees this temptation as ultimately being about our understanding of who God is. In refusing to

---

7. Ibid., 25.

put God to the test, Jesus refuses to treat God as an "object" which can be submitted to experiment. As Ratzinger says:

> We are dealing here with the vast question of how we can and cannot know God, how we are related to God and how we can lose him. The arrogance that would make God an object and impose our laboratory conditions upon him is incapable of finding him. For it already implies that we deny God as God by placing ourselves above him, by discarding the whole dimension of love, of interior listening.[8]

For Ratzinger, this treating God as an object ultimately leads to an entirely "subjective" view of God, to a God who is created in the image of our own "truth." This is a danger which entering into the prayer of Jesus can overcome. Our hearts must set out on an "exodus" from "Egypt" and recognize that rather than living on bread alone we live by obedience to God's word.[9]

The Lord's Prayer and the Believer's Heart

In *Jesus of Nazareth* Ratzinger devotes considerable attention to an analysis of the Lord's Prayer. He notes that Luke, in particular, places the context of the communication of this prayer to the disciples within the context of Jesus' own praying. The entire ministry of Jesus is sustained by his prayer, and defining events in his life are revealed as prayer events. Thus: "Peter's confession that Jesus is the Holy One of God is connected with encountering Jesus at prayer (cf. Luke 9:18ff.); [and] the Transfiguration of Jesus is a prayer event (cf. Luke 9:28ff.)."[10] By placing the Our Father within the context of Jesus' own praying, Luke shows us that Jesus draws us into his own prayer. The words of the Our Father "train us in the inner attitude of Jesus (cf. Phil 2:5)."[11] Since the Our Father originates in Jesus' own dialogue with the Father, it reaches depths which can "never be fully fathomed by a purely historical exegesis, however important this may be."[12]

In his analysis of the Lord's Prayer, Ratzinger continually uses the term "heart." We are to be "prompted by a joyful heart."[13] Our prayer should

---

8. Ibid., 37.
9. Ibid., 34.
10. Ibid., 132.
11. Ibid.
12. Ibid., 133.
13. Ibid., 129.

arise "above all from our heart."[14] When one opens one's spirit to the Word of God in prayer, "[one's] own heart will be opened, and each individual will learn the particular way in which the Lord wants to pray with him."[15] In praying the Our Father, "we pray totally with our own heart."[16] Solomon prays for a "listening heart" so that he "may discern between good and evil,"—such a heart is the ultimate way for the Kingdom of God to come, and a request for union with Jesus.[17] Man "has knowledge of God's will in his inmost heart, that anchored deeply within us there is a participation in God's knowing, which we call conscience."[18] One could continue to present examples like these, from both the chapter on the Lord's Prayer and *Jesus of Nazareth* as a whole.

Ratzinger also speaks of praying "in the Spirit." The words of the Psalms and the Our Father are words "given by God." For Ratzinger, when we pray the Our Father, we enter into communion with the Father, the Son and the Holy Spirit.

> Jesus' promise regarding true worshippers, those who adore the Father "in spirit and truth" (John 4:23), is fulfilled in us. Christ, who is the truth, has given us these words, and in them he gives us the Holy Spirit ([St Cyprian] *De dominica oratione* 2; *CSEL* III, I, pp. 267f.). This also reveals something of the specificity of Christian mysticism. It is not in the first instance immersion in the depths of oneself, but encounter with the Spirit of God in the word that goes ahead of us. It is encounter with the Son and the Holy Spirit and thus a becoming-one with the living God who is always both in us and above us.[19]

Ratzinger recognizes that *because* the Our Father is a prayer of Jesus, it is a trinitarian prayer—with Christ through the Holy Spirit to the Father.[20] Furthermore, the good thing that we should ask for and which the Father will give us is the gift of the Holy Spirit (cf. Matt 7:9; Luke 11:13). The gift of God is God himself. Ultimately, prayer is opening ourselves to God and asking for the "one thing necessary," the gift of God himself which is the indwelling of the Holy Spirit.[21]

14. Ibid., 130.
15. Ibid., 133.
16. Ibid., 141.
17. Ibid., 146–47. Cf. 1 Kgs 3:9.
18. Ibid., 148.
19. Ibid., 131–32.
20. Ibid., 135.
21. Ibid., 136–37.

The Kingdom of God

Ratzinger's antidote to a "subjective" view of God is brought out especially in his investigation of the preaching of the Gospel. There, he begins by examining the actual meaning of *evangelium*. Noting that the Evangelists adopted a term which expressed the salvific power of the Roman emperors, he asserts that in contemporary linguistic theory it would be called performative speech, "not just the imparting of information, but action, efficacious power that enters into the world to save and transform."[22] It is, as Mark calls it, the "Gospel of God." It is God's word, which is simultaneously word and deed. This is reminiscent of the passage in Isaiah, where, speaking in God's name, the prophet tells us how the word that comes forth from God's mouth does not return to him empty, but accomplishes his purpose (cf. 55:10–11).

Next, Ratzinger examines the nature of the kingdom which is proclaimed. First, he goes through the various interpretations of what the phrase "kingdom of God" means. Beginning with Origen's christological one, which identifies the kingdom with Jesus himself, and his idealistic or mystical one which identifies its location in human interiority, Ratzinger moves to the ecclesiological interpretation of the nineteenth and early twentieth centuries, which tended to identify it with the church, then the ethical interpretation of early twentieth century liberal theology. He follows these with the post First World War radically eschatological interpretation, until he reaches the contemporary secular interpretation and its rejection of Christocentrism to embrace theocentrism, and ultimately regnocentrism, in its efforts to include all religions in the kingdom. Ratzinger concludes that this last secular interpretation has ended in a bizarre contradiction—the proclamation of the kingdom of God without God.[23] He sees this interpretation as having an entirely subjective view of religion. It does not matter if the various religious traditions actually contradict each other. What counts is the objective which religion can serve, an attitude which he finds alarmingly close to Jesus' third temptation.

Ratzinger observes that, in both Hebrew and Greek, the meaning of the word we normally translate as "kingdom" is active—it means the regal function, the active lordship of the king.[24] Thus the proclamation of this kingdom is the proclamation of the God who is acting *now*. This lordship was recognized by Israel pre-eminently in the act of adoration, a recognition demonstrated daily in the praying of the *Shema Israel*. Through this

---

22. Ibid., 47.
23. Ibid., 49–55.
24. Ibid., 55.

The Spiritual Christology of *Jesus of Nazareth*—Method

prayer "one accepts God's lordship, which consequently, through the act of praying, enters into the world. The one who is praying helps to bear it on his shoulders, and through his prayer, God's lordship shapes his way of life, his day-to-day existence, making it a locus of God's presence in the world."[25] This divine lordship transcends the moment and thus history. Yet it also belongs absolutely to the present. It is present in the liturgy as an anticipation of the next world, and "it is present as a life-shaping power through the believer's prayer and being: by bearing God's yoke, the believer already receives a share in the world to come."[26]

Ratzinger concludes that this "divine lordship" is a very complex reality, something which is borne out by the variety of interpretations which "kingdom of God" has received. There are elements in the words of Jesus that seem to express an "imminent expectation" (cf. Mark 1:15; Matt 12:28; and Luke 17:21). The kingdom is also spoken of as something apparently insignificant and yet of great value, something which is present and yet mysterious. Ultimately, Ratzinger supports Origen's interpretation, which identifies the divine lordship with Christ who is in our midst (cf. Luke 17:20–21), yet with this nuance. The kingdom is not simply located in Jesus' physical presence, but rather through his action, accomplished in the Holy Spirit, it "is drawing near" (cf. Luke 11:20).[27] The "now" of the divine lordship, this fullness of time (cf. Mark 1:15), is not a worldly lordship.

> [Rather, Jesus] rules through the love that reaches "to the end" (John 13:1), to the Cross. It is from this center that the different, seemingly contradictory aspects can be joined together. In this context we understand Jesus' statements about the lowliness and hiddenness of the Kingdom . . . his invitation to follow him courageously, leaving everything else behind. He himself is the treasure; communion with him is the pearl of great price.[28]

It is in this "communion" with Jesus that we come to understand the kingdom. This communion is the lived prayer of discipleship, a discipleship which is particularly portrayed in the Beatitudes.

---

25. Ibid., 57.
26. Ibid.
27. Ibid., 60.
28. Ibid., 61.

The Sermon on the Mount

A prayed Christology leads to a lived Christology. This lived Christology Ratzinger finds in the Sermon on the Mount. Moreover, he holds that in this Sermon one finds a hidden Christology, that the one most eminently portrayed in the Beatitudes is Jesus himself.[29] According to Ratzinger:

> [The] Beatitudes present a sort of veiled interior biography of Jesus, a kind of a portrait of his figure. He who has no place to lay his head (cf. Matt 8:20) is truly poor; he who can say, "Come to me . . . for I am meek and lowly in heart" (cf. Matt 11:28–29) is truly meek; he is the one who is pure of heart and so unceasingly beholds God. He is the peacemaker, he is the one who suffers for God's sake.[30]

In Ratzinger's reading of Matthew's account of the Sermon, the "mountain" on which Jesus, the one greater than Moses, teaches, is also the "mountain" on which he prays, the place where he is with the Father face to face. Likewise, Ratzinger sees Luke's account of the Sermon as ultimately grounded in the prayer of Jesus, as it follows immediately upon the calling of the Twelve after a night spent by Jesus on the mountain, watching in prayer with the Father. Unlike Mount Sinai, the Mount of the Beatitudes is a place which completes the transformation of meeting God, from the fire and earthquake encountered by Moses to the still small breeze experienced by Elijah. God is now revealed in mildness, simplicity and closeness.

Ratzinger sees the Beatitudes as "the transposition of the Cross and Resurrection into discipleship. But they apply to the disciple because they were first paradigmatically lived by Christ himself."[31] What St. Paul describes as the "Cross" of his sufferings and the joy of his "Resurrection" (cf. 2 Cor 4:8–11 and 6:8–10), is paralleled by St. John, who calls the Cross an "exaltation," an elevation to God's throne. John brings the Cross and Resurrection together in a single word, the "hour" of Jesus, since for John they are inseparable. For Ratzinger: "The Cross is the act of the 'exodus,' the act of love that is accomplished to the uttermost and reaches 'to the end' (John 13:1). And so it is the place of glory—the place of true contact and union with God, who is love (cf. 1 John 4:7, 16)."[32] Just as they reveal the meaning of discipleship, the Beatitudes also have a christological character. "The disciple is bound to the mystery of Christ. His life is immersed in communion

---

29. Ibid., 99.
30. Ibid., 74.
31. Ibid.
32. Ibid., 73.

with Christ: 'It is no longer I who live, but Christ who lives in me'" (Gal 2:20).[33]

Following this general assessment of the meaning of the Beatitudes, Ratzinger proceeds to examine each in turn. Regarding the first, he holds the "poor in spirit" to be those who recognize their spiritual poverty. This is most easily done when one is also materially poor, but material poverty, in and of itself, does not guarantee salvation. Such poverty can lead to avarice and covetousness, a hardness of heart. Rather, the poor in spirit are those who, in their humility, have a generosity of heart which is also an openness of heart to Christ. They have an interior poverty. Their hands are empty for two reasons—they are generous and give, and they come to God as beggars—"they are lovers who simply want to let God bestow his gifts upon them and thereby to live in inner harmony with God's nature and word."[34] Those who are materially well off can live this poverty by putting their possessions at the service of others. Ratzinger calls this having a culture of inner freedom.[35]

In examining this Beatitude, Ratzinger makes a brief excursus into the life of St. Francis of Assisi as an illustration of it. This excursus, far from having little direct relevance to Ratzinger's spiritual Christology, goes to the very heart of it. As has been said, for Ratzinger, spiritual Christology is not just an intellectual exercise—it is first a *lived* Christology.

> For Francis, [his] extreme humility was above all freedom for service, freedom for mission, ultimate trust in God . . . It was the deepest possible openness to Christ, to whom Francis was perfectly configured by the wounds of the stigmata, so perfectly that from then on he truly no longer lived as himself, but as one reborn, totally from and in Christ.[36]

One could say that, for Ratzinger, *the* key text for the *practice* of a spiritual Christology is: "It is no longer I who live, but Christ who lives in me" (Gal 2:20).

Ratzinger now passes over the second Beatitude to the third because he sees it as closely connected with the first. He begins with an analysis of the Greek word *praus* which translates the Hebrew *anawim*, meaning God's poor, rather than merely "non-violent." He points to the designation of both Moses and Jesus as "meek" (cf. Num 12:3 and Matt 11:29), and coupled with the prophecy of Zechariah, which announces the coming of a humble king

33. Ibid., 74.
34. Ibid., 76.
35. Ibid., 77.
36. Ibid., 79.

who will establish peace (cf. Zech 9:9–10; Matt 21:4–5; and John 12:15), identifies Jesus as the king who comes with divine rather than earthly power to establish peace, the one whose "inmost being is humility and meekness before God and men." He establishes peace through his "filial obedience: by renouncing violence and accepting suffering until he was released from it by the Father."[37]

Ratzinger next looks at the second part of this Beatitude and its promise of inheriting the land. Recalling an interpretation of the Exodus which he gave in *The Spirit of the Liturgy*, he sees "the land" as the place where the people of God are free to worship.[38] This worship is carried out in obedience to God. Ratzinger states that: "The concept of obedience to God, and so of the right ordering of the earth, is an essential component of freedom and the concept of the land." Even the *diaspora* fulfils this obedience to God in that it turns the whole world into "a zone of response to his love, a zone of obedience and freedom."[39]

These reflections on the relationship between meekness and peace lead Ratzinger onto the seventh Beatitude. The peacemakers will be called sons of God. Ratzinger compares Jesus with Solomon, whose name is derived from *shalom*, and to whose father David, God had promised a reign of peace (cf. 1 Chron 22:9–10). Ratzinger sees a connection between being the Son of God and being the Prince of Peace—establishing peace is part of the very essence of sonship. In the life of each person, peace comes from being reconciled with God (cf. 2 Cor 5:20). Only by such a reconciliation can one be reconciled and in harmony with oneself, and consequently, with others. This lasting peace comes from "abiding in God's *eudokia*, his 'good pleasure.'"[40]

Turning to the second Beatitude, Ratzinger identifies three kinds of authentic "mourning." The first is that of conversion in the face of one's own sinfulness, exemplified by the bitter tears of Peter. The second is that of those who mourn over the wicked deeds of others, like those who have the *tau* traced on their foreheads (cf. Ezek 9:4). The last kind is that of those who stand at the foot of the cross, who have "com-passion," who "suffer with" the one condemned.

> [These] place themselves on his side, and by their "loving with" they are on the side of God, who is love. This "com-passion" reminds us of the magnificent saying of Saint Bernard of

---

37. Ibid., 81.
38. Ibid., 82. Cf. Ratzinger, *The Spirit of the Liturgy*, 15–23.
39. Ibid., 83.
40. Ibid., 85.

> Clairvaux's commentary on the Song of Songs (sermon 26, no. 5): "Impassibilis est Deus, sed non incompassibilis"—God cannot suffer, but he can "suffer *with*" . . . Those who do not harden their hearts to the pain and need of others, who do not give evil entry to their souls, but suffer under its power and so acknowledge the truth of God—they are the ones who open the windows to the world to let the light in.[41]

Ratzinger links the second Beatitude with the last, "those who are persecuted for righteousness' sake." He identifies "righteousness" as the Old Covenant term for fidelity to the Torah. The equivalent term in the New Testament is "faith." The man of faith is the "righteous man" who walks in God's ways (cf. Ps 1; Jer 17:5–8).[42] The christological basis for this Beatitude is the crucified Christ. Ratzinger sees this Beatitude as promising something new—those persecuted for the sake of righteousness are promised a great reward. In promising this reward, Jesus goes beyond the prophets of old. The criterion of righteousness and salvation is the "I" of Jesus himself, and fidelity to his person. According to Ratzinger:

> In the other Beatitudes, Christology is present, so to speak, in veiled form; here, however, the message that he himself is the center of history emerges openly. Jesus ascribes to his "I" a normative status that no teacher in Israel—indeed, no teacher in the Church—has a right to claim for himself. Someone who speaks like this is no longer a prophet in the traditional sense; he himself is the reference point of the righteous life, its goal and center.[43]

Ratzinger continues with the theme of righteousness by turning to those who thirst for it. He sees this desire exemplified in the presentation of Daniel as a *vir desideriorum*, a man of longings (cf. Dan 9:23 in the *Vulgate*). They have a restless heart that points them towards something greater. They have an interior sensitivity which enables them "to see and hear the subtle signs that God sends into the world to break the dictatorship of convention."[44] This hunger and thirst, this passion for righteousness, comes from an openness of heart—a heart which has an inner watchfulness, humble piety and patient longing.[45]

---

41. Ibid., 87.
42. Ibid., 89.
43. Ibid., 90.
44. Ibid., 91.
45. Ibid.

The Beatitude which Ratzinger addresses last is that which tells us that the pure in heart will see God. This is the point to which his mediations on the Beatitudes have been leading. We have seen how, in his analysis of the other Beatitudes and the Lord's Prayer, Ratzinger constantly speaks of the human heart. It is a theme which permeates both volumes of *Jesus of Nazareth*. In the parable of the Prodigal Son, the conversion of the prodigal is a "change of heart."[46] In telling the parable, Jesus seeks to woo the hearts of the murmuring Pharisees and scribes through the words of the father to his prodigal.[47] Jesus also wishes to speak to the hearts of the poor and downtrodden, like Lazarus (cf. Luke 16:19–31). Rather than leave them with embittered hearts (cf. Ps 73:13–22), he wishes them to behold the form of God (cf. Ps 77:14–15), that their hearts may be "sated by the encounter with infinite love."[48] We are called to become like the "little ones" in the temple, who are able to praise Jesus with Hosannas because they see with pure and undivided hearts.[49] The alternative to faith in Jesus is a hardening of the heart. Whether it is in response to the parables, or to a miracle of Jesus (cf. John 11:45–53), putting God "to the test" leads to a "non-seeing" and "non-understanding," a "hardening of heart."[50] We are all in a position of "not knowing" what we do (cf. Luke 23:34, Acts 3:14–17; and 1 Tim 1:13).[51] It is the failure to recognize this ignorance which is fatal, because it blinds one to the need for repentance. It is a danger which especially threatens the learned. As Ratzinger writes:

> Are we not blind precisely as people of knowledge? Is it not on account of our knowledge that we are incapable of recognizing Truth itself, which tries to reach us through what we know? Do we not recoil from the pain of that heartrending Truth of which Peter spoke in his Pentecost sermon? Ignorance diminishes guilt, and it leaves open the path to conversion. But it does not simply excuse, because at the same time it reveals a deadening of the heart that resists the call of Truth.[52]

The essential question which must be answered is this: What exactly does Ratzinger mean by the "heart?" Is he simply speaking in a poetic,

---

46. Ibid., 205.
47. Ibid., 209.
48. Ibid., 214.
49. *Jesus II*, 23.
50. *Jesus I*, 193 and 216.
51. *Jesus II*, 206–8.
52. Ibid., 208.

metaphorical, or unreflective way; or does he endow this term with a more substantial meaning? His understanding of the heart he explains thus:

> "Blessed are the pure in heart, for they shall see God" (Matt 5:8). The organ for seeing God is the heart. The intellect alone is not enough. In order for man to become capable of perceiving God, the energies of his existence have to work in harmony. His will must be pure and so too must the underlying affective dimension of his soul, which gives intelligence and will their direction. Speaking of the *heart* in this way means precisely that man's perceptive powers play in concert, which also requires the proper interplay of body and soul, since this is essential for the totality of the creature we call "man." Man's fundamental affective disposition actually depends on just this unity of body and soul and on man's acceptance of being both body and spirit. This means he places the body under the discipline of the spirit, yet does not isolate intellect or will. Rather, he accepts himself as coming from God, and thereby also acknowledges and lives out the bodiliness of his existence as an enrichment for the spirit. The heart—the wholeness of man—must be pure, interiorly open and free, in order for man to be able to see God.[53]

We can see that this definition of the human heart is in keeping with the description of it given in *Behold the Pierced One*.[54] The heart is not to be identified simply with the intellect, or the will, or the passions, or the senses, or the body, or the soul. Nor is it to be identified with the *ego*. The heart is not identical with the person. One can speak of *my* heart, the heart as something which *I* possess. Rather, for Ratzinger, it is the "place" of the integration of the intellect, will, passions, and senses, of the body and the soul. One could say that, for Ratzinger, the human heart *is* the personal integration, the integration by the person, of these aspects of their human nature.

Ratzinger then asks how the purification of the heart can take place. He finds the answer especially in Psalms 24 and 15. A pure heart is one which inquires after God, which seeks his face (cf. Ps 24:6). But a pure heart also means "clean hands," one whose love of neighbor is not just outward, but penetrates to its depths. It is one which searches first for God (the first tablet of the Decalogue), and then hungers to do justice to its neighbor (the second tablet).[55]

---

53. *Jesus I*, 92–93.
54. *Behold*, 55–56.
55. *Jesus I*, 94. Cf. Gadenz, "Jesus the New Temple," 211–12. Gadenz points out that, in his discussion of the face of Christ in *On the Way to Jesus Christ*, Ratzinger states that, in the Old Testament, the face of God was encountered in the Temple. Germane

Since Ratzinger regards the Beatitudes as above all christological, these insights apply first and foremost to Jesus.

> On Jesus' lips ... these words acquire new depth. For it belongs to his nature that he sees God, that he stands face-to-face with him, in permanent interior discourse—in a relation of Sonship ... We will see God when we enter into the "mind of Christ" (Phil 2:5). Purification of heart occurs as a consequence of following Christ, of becoming one with him. "It is no longer I who live, but Christ who lives in me" (Gal 2:20). And at this point something new comes to light: The ascent to God occurs precisely in the descent of humble service, in the descent of love, for love is God's essence, and is thus the power that truly purifies man and enables him to perceive God and to see him. In Jesus Christ, God has revealed himself in his descending: "Though he was in the form of God," he "did not count equality with God a thing to be grasped, but emptied himself, taking the form of a servant, being born in the likeness of men ... He humbled himself and became obedient unto death, even death on a cross. Therefore God has highly exalted him" (Phil 2:6–9).[56]

According to Ratzinger, it is in the Cross that God descends, and reveals himself in his true divinity. Our ascension to God can only happen when we follow him on his descending path, in purity of heart.

> The pure heart is the loving heart that enters into communion of service and obedience with Jesus Christ. Love is the fire that purifies and unifies intellect, will, and emotion, thereby making man one with himself, inasmuch as it makes him one in God's eyes. Thus, man is able to serve the uniting of those who are divided.[57]

The greatest obstacle to a pure heart which sees God is human hubris, "the arrogant presumption of autonomy that leads man to put on the airs of divinity, to claim to be his own god, in order to possess life totally and to draw from it every last drop of what it has to offer."[58]

---

to this is Geoffrey Wainwright's observation that, according to the second volume of *Jesus of Nazareth*, "the most striking feature introduced by Christ into the world and human history was—in an oft repeated phrase —a "new worship," "ein neuer Kult."" See Wainwright, "The 'New Worship,'" 993.

56. *Jesus I*, 95.
57. Ibid., 95–96.
58. Ibid., 98.

The Spiritual Christology of *Jesus of Nazareth*—Method

After the Beatitudes, Matthew presents what Ratzinger calls the "Torah of the Messiah," suggesting that this may be what St. Paul is alluding to when he speaks of the "law of Christ" (Gal 6:2). This law calls us to freedom, which is freedom from the slavery of sin, freedom in the service of good, allowing oneself to be led by the Spirit of God. The "law" of Christ is the "freedom" of the Spirit. Christ "spiritualizes" the law. This spiritualized law calls us to a greater righteousness than the Torah of Moses.[59]

Having established that Christ brings a new, spiritualized law which fulfils the law given to Moses, Ratzinger goes further, through means of a reflection upon Rabbi Jacob Neusner's analysis of the teaching of Jesus.[60] According to Ratzinger, Neusner concludes that Jesus is actually claiming to be the new Sabbath, the new Temple, indeed the new Torah, the word of God in person.[61] Moreover, Neusner sees that Jesus proposes the formation of a new "family," not one based on descent from Abraham or adherence to the Torah, but on Jesus himself. The brothers and sisters and mothers of Jesus are those who do the will of the Father in Heaven (cf. Matt 12:46–50).[62]

For Ratzinger, communion with Jesus is communion in God's will.

> For Jesus' "I" is by no means a self-willed ego revolving around itself alone . . . Jesus' "I" incarnates the Son's communion of will with the Father. It is an "I" that hears and obeys. Communion with him is filial communion with the Father . . . It is entry into the family of those who call God Father and who can do so because they belong to a "we"—formed of those who are united with Jesus and, by listening to him, united with the will of the Father, thereby attaining to the heart of the obedience intended by the Torah.[63]

Furthermore, by being established in God's will, man is taught to see the right and good, and attains freedom. However:

> [we are called] not to a blind and arbitrary freedom "understood according to the flesh," as Paul would say, but to a "seeing" freedom, anchored in communion of will with Jesus and so with God himself . . . [a] new way of seeing . . . [This] search for God's will in communion with Jesus is above all a signpost for [man's]

---

59. Ibid., 99–101.
60. See Neusner, *A Rabbi Talks with Jesus*.
61. *Jesus I*, 103–11.
62. Ibid., 111–17.
63. Ibid., 117.

reason, without which it is always in danger of being dazzled and blinded.[64]

Ultimately, we are called to the seeming paradox of a "free obedience."[65]

The Ecclesial Thesis

We have just seen Ratzinger point to Neusner's insight that Jesus proposes the formation of a new family. The ecclesial thesis is that sharing in the prayer of Jesus brings us into communion with all his brethren. The fellowship which comes from participating in the prayer of Jesus, and that which St. Paul calls the Body of Christ, is one and the same fellowship. Hence, this Body of Christ is the true subject of our knowledge of Jesus. In the "memory" of this subject the past is present because Christ is present and lives in it.[66]

The Church as a Corporate Personality

This union with Jesus and the brethren in prayer begins with Israel and continues with the church. Ratzinger sees this exemplified in Jesus' praying of the Psalms. He holds that, even under the Old Covenant, the Psalms were not just the prayers of individual subjects, but were "uttered in union with all who suffer unjustly, with the whole of Israel, indeed with the whole of suffering humanity."[67] Jesus is the real David, the one whose prayer is not merely intercession on Israel's behalf, but the one who, in praying *for* them *is* also them. Ratzinger appeals to the teaching of the Fathers, which today is called corporate personality, in support of this assertion. Referring to the teaching of St. Augustine, Ratzinger writes:

> Christ prays as both head and body (cf., for example, *En. in Ps.* 60:1–2; 61:4; 85:1, 5). He prays as "head," as the one who unites us all into a single common subject and incorporates us all into himself. And he prays as "body," that is to say, all of our struggles, our voices, our anguish, and our hope are present in his praying. We ourselves are the ones praying this psalm [22],

---

64. Ibid., 119.
65. Ibid., 120.
66. *Behold*, 27.
67. *Jesus II*, 215.

but now in a new way, in fellowship with Christ. And in him, past, present, and future are always united.[68]

As well as praying in the church, Jesus continues to suffer in the church, and the church to suffer in Jesus.

> Jesus' agony, his struggle against death, continues until the end of the world . . . We could also put it the other way around: at this hour, Jesus took upon himself the betrayal of all ages, the pain caused by betrayal in every era, and he endured the anguish of history to the bitter end.[69]

This union is consummated upon the Cross, and revealed to our understanding through the narrative's allusion to Psalm 22. However, one particular aspect of this revelation seems to point to another expression of corporate personality—the Eucharist. Referring to verse 26, that the afflicted shall eat and be satisfied, Ratzinger maintains that the early church recognized in this "a sign of the mysterious new meal that the Lord had given them in the Eucharist."[70] It is from the blood and water flowing from the pierced heart of Jesus that the church is created. "In this double outpouring of blood and water, the Fathers saw an image of the two fundamental sacraments—Eucharist and Baptism—which spring from the Lord's pierced side, from his heart."[71]

Another way of describing this corporate personality, as grounded in the communion of prayer, is in the reality of Jesus as the New Temple, the definite place of worship. The rejection and crucifixion of Jesus brings about the end of the former Temple. A new worship is introduced in the Temple of Christ's body, he who as the Risen One gathers the peoples and unites them in the sacrament of his body and blood.[72]

Again, another way in which Ratzinger speaks of this corporate personality is through his analysis of the obedience of Jesus, especially as it is portrayed in the Letter to the Hebrews. Coming from God as man, he establishes the true form of man's being. Through the obedience of Jesus the reconciliation of God and man takes place. Jesus is the ultimate, definitive man, the "heavenly" man, the "life-giving spirit" (cf. 1 Cor 15:45–49). "He is

---

68. Ibid., 215. See also 146–47.
69. Ibid., 68.
70. Ibid., 205.
71. Ibid., 226.
72. Ibid., 21–22. See also 35–40. Cf. Gadenz, "Jesus the New Temple," 211–30.

not just one individual, but rather he makes all of us 'one single person' (Gal 3:28) with himself, a new humanity."[73]

Finally, this corporate personality is expressed in the image of the Woman, the New Eve: "This at last is bone of my bones and flesh of my flesh" (Gen 2:23). Just as Paul sees Jesus as the New Adam, so John sees, in the figure of Mary, the New Eve. As Ratzinger explains:

> When the Book of Revelation speaks of the great sign of a Woman appearing in heaven, she is understood to represent all Israel, indeed, the whole Church. The Church must continually give birth to Christ in pain (cf. Rev 12:1–6). Another stage in the evolution of this idea is found in the Letter to the Ephesians, where the saying about the man who leaves his father and mother to become one flesh with his wife is applied to Christ and the Church (cf. 5:31–32). On the basis of the "corporate personality" model—in keeping with biblical thought—the early Church had no difficulty recognizing in the Woman, on the one hand, Mary herself and, on the other hand, transcending time, the Church, bride and mother, in which the mystery of Mary spreads out into history.[74]

Furthermore, this New Eve, the church, was seen by the Fathers as being born from the open side, the pierced heart, of the New Adam.[75]

The Memory of the Church

This corporate personality "remembers." It possesses a "collective memory." Ratzinger refers to the disciples "remembering," after the Resurrection, events from the life of Jesus, and in this remembering, understanding the teaching or event in its full depth. He refers to this memory as "the collective memory of the community of disciples enlightened by the Holy Spirit, that is, the Church."[76]

The most extensive exposition of the nature of this collective memory is given in Ratzinger's investigation of the specific character of John's Gospel, wherein he sees Jesus' divinity as being unveiled.[77] Beginning with Martin Hengel's analysis of the composition of this Gospel, Ratzinger takes up four of the five elements which Hengel identifies as being decisive for the

73. *Jesus I*, 334.
74. *Jesus II*, 222.
75. Ibid., 226.
76. Ibid., 21. See also 137; and *Jesus I*, 324.
77. See *Jesus I*, 218–38.

The Spiritual Christology of *Jesus of Nazareth*—Method

Gospel's composition. They are the personal recollection of the Evangelist, the historical reality of the events recounted, the tradition of the church, and the guidance of the Holy Spirit.[78] Ratzinger groups these four into two pairs—first historical reality and personal recollection, then church tradition and the guidance of the Holy Spirit. According to Ratzinger:

> Together [the first pair] constitute what the Fathers of the Church call the *factum historicum* that determines the literal sense of the text: the exterior side of the event, which the Evangelist knows partly from personal recollection and partly from Church tradition . . . His intention is to act as a "witness" reporting the things that happened. No one has emphasized this particular dimension of what actually happened—the "flesh" of history—to such an extent as John.[79]

Ratzinger sees these two factors leading, by their inner dynamic, to the second pair. On the one hand, he holds that the remembrance of the Evangelist is very personal, as testified to by his testimony to the water and the blood flowing from the side of Christ (cf. John 19:35). On the other hand, Ratzinger sees the Evangelist's remembering as never merely private. It is a remembering in and with the "we" of the church. The church is the subject who remembers. Furthermore: "Because the personal recollection that provides the foundation of the Gospel is purified and deepened by being inserted into the memory of the church, it does indeed transcend the banal recollection of facts."[80] In a way, this is similar to the "personal" and "corporate" found in the personal and ecclesial theses.

Next, Ratzinger seeks to establish exactly what John means by "memory" through an analysis of three occasions where he uses the word "remember." The first is in his account of the cleansing of the Temple. There, the disciples remember a passage from the Old Testament (cf. Ps 69:9). Ratzinger holds that:

> The event that is taking place calls to mind a passage of Scripture and so the event becomes intelligible at a level beyond the merely factual. Memory sheds light on the sense of the act, which then acquires a deeper meaning. It appears as an act in which the Logos is present, an act that comes from the Logos and leads to it. The link connecting Jesus' acting and suffering

---

78. Ibid., 229–31. Hengel's fifth element is the theological concern of the author. See Hengel, *The Johannine Question*, 132.

79. *Jesus I*, 230.

80. Ibid., 231.

with God's word comes into view, and so the mystery of Jesus himself becomes intelligible.[81]

The second and third occurrences bring out the connection between remembering and the Resurrection. The disciples hear Jesus prophesy that he will raise the destroyed temple in three days. They remember it after Jesus is raised from the dead (cf. John 2:22). Again, after Jesus has been glorified, the disciples remember the events of Palm Sunday, and come to realize the true meaning of the words: "Fear not, daughter of Zion; behold, your king is coming, sitting on an ass's colt!" (John 12:15; cf. Zech 9:9). For Ratzinger: "The Resurrection evokes remembrance, and remembrance in light of the Resurrection brings out the sense of this hitherto puzzling saying and reconnects it to the overall context of Scripture. The unity of Logos and act is the goal at which the Gospel is aiming."[82]

According to Ratzinger, this remembering is a pneumatic remembering. It fulfills the prophecy of Jesus that: "When the Spirit of truth comes, he will guide you into all the truth; for he will not speak on his own authority, but whatever he hears he will speak, and he will declare to you the things to come" (John 16:13). It is no mere psychological or intellectual process. This pneumatic remembering of the church is no merely private affair, but transcends the sphere of human understanding and knowing. "It is a being-led by the Holy Spirit, who shows us the connectedness of Scripture, the connection between word and reality, and, in doing so, leads us 'into all the truth.'"[83]

As well as a memory, does this corporate personality also have a heart? In his meditation on the "Our Father," Ratzinger writes that it is "at once a fully personal and a thoroughly ecclesial prayer. In praying the Our Father, we pray totally with our own heart, but at the same time we pray in communion with the whole family of God."[84] He also writes of Jesus speaking "to the heart of his people" in his ministry.[85] Finally, in the most pointed instance, he characterizes the authors of the Scriptural books as not being autonomous writers in the modern sense. Rather, "they form part of a collective subject, the 'People of God,' from within whose heart and to whom they speak."[86] Yet, beyond these brief allusions to an ecclesial heart Ratzinger does not go.

81. Ibid.
82. Ibid., 232.
83. Ibid., 234.
84. Ibid., 141.
85. Ibid., 256.
86. Ibid., xx–xxi.

However, he sees the progression from remembering to understanding, to being led "into all truth" (John 16:13), taking place in the heart of Mary. In the account of the Annunciation, he sees Mary entering into an interior dialogue as she ponders what the angel's greeting could mean. Mary keeps all the events of Jesus' nativity in her memory, and ponders them in her heart (cf. Luke 2:19), as she does with the events surrounding her finding Jesus in the Temple (cf. Luke 2:51).[87] Since Ratzinger sees the corporate personality of the church as being embodied in Mary, this raises the possibility that he would see an analogous process taking place in the church.

Given Ratzinger's emphasis upon the importance of remembering in the church, it is surprising that in *Jesus of Nazareth* he makes no mention of this remembering in his reflections on the Eucharist. Despite the fact that he recognizes the Eucharist as the memorial of Jesus' death and Resurrection, that the promise of the Holy Spirit leading the disciples into all truth is given in the context of the Last Supper, and that the apostles were commanded to "do this as a memorial of me," Ratzinger does not draw any explicit connection between the church's coming to understand who Jesus really is through its remembering in a general sense, and its remembering in the celebration of the Eucharist.

The Church Participates in the Prayer of Jesus

In his treatment of the High Priestly Prayer of Jesus, Ratzinger identifies four major themes in this prayer which outline how the church participates in this prayer of Jesus. First, Jesus prays that his disciples may have *zoe*—"life." This life is eternal. It is not life after death, but it is a real "life" which can be lived in this life. This life is obtained through "recognition," one which creates communion. The "key to this life is not *any kind of* recognition, but to 'know *you* the only true God, and Jesus Christ whom you have sent' ([John] 17:3)."[88] In the encounter with Jesus "we experience the recognition of God that leads to communion and thus to 'life.'"[89]

The second thing for which Jesus prays is that his disciples may be "sanctified" in the truth. In his analysis of this prayer, Ratzinger identifies a triple sanctification. Jesus himself is sanctified by the Father. He sanctifies himself. And he prays that his disciples may be sanctified in the truth. Ratzinger identifies sanctity as "holiness," which in its fullest sense can be attributed only to God. Apart from God, to sanctify means to hand someone

---

87. Ibid., 233–34.
88. *Jesus II*, 83.
89. Ibid., 84.

or something over to God, especially for worship. It can be the consecration of something for sacrifice, or the consecration of someone as a priest. This sanctification has two apparently opposite aspects—being set apart from the world, but paradoxically, being set apart for the world.[90] Hence, the Father sends the Son into the world and consecrates him for the world. This consecration is identical with the Incarnation, expressing "both total unity with the Father and total existence for the world."[91] When Peter acknowledges Jesus as the Holy One of God, it is a comprehensive christological confession (cf. John 6:69). When Jesus says that he consecrates himself (cf. John 17:19), Ratzinger, following Bultmann and Feuillet, interprets this as being consecrated as a sacrifice.[92] Thus, the second consecration is connected with the first. As a sacrifice, Jesus exists "for the world." He is both priest and sacrifice for the world. The second consecration is for the sake of the third—that the disciples be sanctified (cf. John 17:17 and 19). Ratzinger sees a double aspect to this sanctification. First, to be consecrated *in truth* means to participate in the consecration of Jesus Christ, into his union with the Father and his mission in the world (cf. John 17:19). Yet the disciples are also to be consecrated *in the truth*. As the sons of Aaron were bathed, robed and anointed in their investiture as priests, so the disciples must be purified, robed and anointed *in Christ*. They must "put on" Christ. According to Ratzinger, this consecration "takes place through union of will and union of being with [Christ]."[93]

The third theme of the high priestly prayer is that Jesus has revealed the "name" of God to the disciples. According to Ratzinger, this name means the immanence of God, his presence among men. God's name is God entering into a relationship with us. Jesus has made God known in a radically new way. In him, God's immanence has become ontological—"in Jesus, God has truly become man."[94]

Finally, Jesus prays that his disciples, and all who believe in him through their word, may be one, as he and the Father are one. Ratzinger holds that this unity comes from the Father, through the Son, and springs from the "glory" which the Son gives to the Father. It comes from the presence of Jesus, "granted through the Holy Spirit, which is the fruit of the Cross, the fruit of Jesus' transformation through death and Resurrection."[95]

90. Ibid., 86.
91. Ibid., 87.
92. Ibid.
93. Ibid., 90.
94. Ibid., 92.
95. Ibid., 95–96.

The Hermeneutical Thesis

Building on a Personal/Ecclesial Theological Epistemology

This thesis states that: "The historical-critical method and other modern scientific methods are important for an understanding of Holy Scripture and tradition. Their value, however, depends on the hermeneutical (philosophical) context in which they are applied."[96] For Ratzinger, this thesis follows from the previous two theses, the personal and the ecclesial. The theological interpretation of the Bible springs from a personal/ecclesial theological epistemology. The composition of the Scriptures involves three "subjects"—the individual author or authors, the church, and God himself. Thus, Ratzinger states that:

> The Scripture emerged from the heart of a living subject—the pilgrim People of God—and lives within this same subject. One could say that the books of Sacred Scripture involve three interacting subjects. First of all, there is the individual author or group of authors to whom we owe a particular scriptural text. But these authors are not autonomous writers in the modern sense; they form part of a collective subject, the "People of God," from within whose heart and to whom they speak. Hence this subject is actually the deeper "author" of the Scriptures. And yet likewise, this people does not exist alone; rather, it knows that it is led, and spoken to, by God himself, who—through men and their humanity—is at the deepest level the one speaking.[97]

As the word of God, Scripture is the power which directs his people. As a word which lives within his people, Scripture enables it, this people, to transcend itself. They become the people of God in whom the words of Scripture are always present.[98]

Using the composition of John's Gospel as an example, Ratzinger says that it rests upon the remembering of the disciple which is also a co-remembering with the "we" of the church. This remembering of the church is the context for the promise that the Holy Spirit will guide the disciples into all the truth (cf. John 16:13). As we have seen, this remembering is therefore a pneumatic event, not one which is merely psychological or intellectual. Nor is it merely a private remembering. Rather, it is led by the Holy Spirit, who shows us the connection between word and event, and thus leads us "into all

---

96. *Behold*, 42.
97. *Jesus I*, xx–xxi.
98. Ibid., xxi.

the truth." The Holy Spirit can lead us through the Sacred Scriptures, from generation to generation, "ever anew into the depth of all the truth."[99]

However, being within the body of Christ is not sufficient in itself to guarantee an authentic personal understanding of Sacred Scripture. In his exposition of the Our Father, Ratzinger makes the point that we need to become involved in Jesus' own prayer. He says that while it is important to listen as carefully as we can to the words of Jesus as presented to us in Scripture and try to recognize his thoughts, we must also remember that this prayer originates in Jesus' own dialogue with the Father. "This means that it reaches down into depths far beyond the words. It embraces the whole compass of man's being in all ages and can therefore never be fully fathomed by a purely historical exegesis, however important this may be."[100]

These words are meant for all believers, academic theologians included. In *Behold the Pierced One*, Ratzinger ends his exposition of the hermeneutical thesis with an exhortation to theologians. They are to enter into the laboratory of unity and freedom. They must allow their own wills to be refashioned. They must allow themselves to be expropriated and inserted into the divine will. They must move towards the God-likeness that will allow the kingdom of God to come. "Thus we have arrived back at our starting point: Christology is born of prayer or not at all." This very last sentence of the hermeneutical thesis is testimony to the fact that the first principle for Ratzinger's spiritual Christology is the personal/ecclesial one. Its starting point is a lived Christology. The most authentic theologians, the most accomplished interpreters of Sacred Scripture, are the saints. Thus Ratzinger states: "Interpretation of Scripture can never be a purely academic affair, and it cannot be regulated to the purely historical. Scripture is full of potential for the future, a potential that can only be opened up when someone 'lives through' and 'suffers through' the sacred text."[101]

Ratzinger's Hermeneutical Method

Ratzinger sees a pressing need to restore the theological nature of hermeneutics. He goes so far as to characterize a certain kind of hermeneutic as "Antichrist." He is using this term in a literal rather than pejorative sense. A positivistic hermeneutic makes access to Jesus as the *Christ* impossible. Of this hermeneutic, he writes:

99. Ibid., 234.
100. Ibid., 133.
101. Ibid, 78.

The Spiritual Christology of *Jesus of Nazareth*—Method

> The common practice today is to measure the Bible against the so-called modern worldview, whose fundamental dogma is that God cannot act in history—that everything to do with God is to be regulated to the domain of subjectivity. And so the Bible no longer speaks of God, the living God; no, now *we* alone speak and decide what God can do and what we will and should do. And the Antichrist, with an air of scholarly excellence, tells us that an exegesis that reads the Bible from the perspective of faith in the living God, in order to listen to what God has to say, is fundamentalism; he wants to convince us that only *his* kind of exegesis, the supposedly purely scientific kind, in which God says nothing and has nothing to say, is able to keep abreast of the times.[102]

The Foreword of the first published volume of *Jesus of Nazareth* is devoted largely to explaining Ratzinger's hermeneutical method. The goal of this method is the reunification of the Jesus of History with the Christ of Faith. According to Ratzinger, the achievement of this goal is of the utmost importance, because the end result of an exclusive use of the historical-critical method has been that this separation is so conclusive that intimate friendship with the real Jesus is impossible. One can have so little certain knowledge of him that he has become little more than a mirage.[103] Ratzinger wishes to avoid a Marcionian reading of the Bible, which he sees as one of the great temptations of modernity. The fact that an exclusive use of the historical-critical method makes a christological interpretation of the Old Testament impossible leads either to an exclusively spiritual interpretation of the New Testament which has no political or social relevance, or conversely, an interpretation of the New Testament which sees Jesus exclusively in terms of a political theology.[104]

It is Ratzinger's conviction that the necessary starting point for a recovery of the real historical Jesus is focus on what Rudolf Schnackenburg identified as a genuine historical insight: Jesus' relatedness to God and his closeness to God.[105] Ratzinger says that this is his starting point in *Jesus of Nazareth*: the filial thesis that Jesus' communion with the Father is the

---

102. Ibid., 35–36.

103. Ibid., xii–xiii.

104. Ibid., 121–22 and xvi. Cf. Ratzinger, *Many Religions—One Covenant*, 18: "The historico-critical method makes Christian interpretation of the Old Testament seem largely dubious; New Testament exegesis has increasingly relativized Christology . . . now (it might appear) the Jewish interpretation of the Old Testament is the only one that can be regarded as historically valid."

105. *Jesus I*, xiii–xiv.

true center of his personality, that unless we realize this we will be unable to understand him, and that "it is from this center that he makes himself present to us still today."[106]

Ratzinger claims that he draws his hermeneutical methodology from *Dei Verbum* and two subsequent documents of the Pontifical Biblical Commission, *The Interpretation of the Bible in the Church* and *The Jewish People and their Sacred Scriptures in the Christian Bible*.[107] His first point is that, given the nature of theology and faith, the historical-critical method is indispensable. The Christian faith is about real historical events. It is faith in the Incarnation of God.

Faith demands the historical method. However, the limits of this method must be recognized. First, being a *historical* method, it can tell us about "what the author could have said and intended to say in the context of the mentality and events of the time."[108] It can attempt to apply this "word from the past" to the present, but it cannot make it into something which is present *today*. Second, it must treat the biblical words as no more than human words. It can open itself up to self-transcendence, but "its specific object is the human word as human."[109] Third, it must treat the individual books of Scripture as individual. It cannot recognize the unity of these writings as one Bible. Although it can look at the process by which the individual texts were brought together, "it always has to begin by going back to the origin of the individual texts, which means placing them in their past context."[110] Our efforts to know the past are limited. Humanly speaking, we cannot bring the past into the present.

Ratzinger holds that the inner nature of the historical-critical method points beyond itself, being open to complementary methods. Although it investigates words from the past, these words raise the question of their meaning today. This method does not exhaust the interpretive task, since the biblical writings form a single corpus which is inspired by God. This realization has led to the development of canonical exegesis, which aims to read the individual texts within the totality of the Bible. This unity of the Bible is a theological datum. The words in the Bible *become* Scripture. Through constant rereading deeper meanings are revealed.[111]

106. Ibid., xiv.

107. Ibid., xv. As well as co-drafting these two works, Ratzinger was the Chairman of the Pontifical Biblical Commission which promulgated them, and as a *peritus* at Vatican II he worked on *Dei Verbum*.

108. Ibid., xvi.

109. Ibid., xvii.

110. Ibid.

111. Ibid., xviii–xix.

The Spiritual Christology of *Jesus of Nazareth*—Method

This process is complex. It is a christological hermeneutic. Scripture unfolds in the light of Jesus Christ. He is the key which allows one to see the Bible, both Old and New Testaments, as a unity. This process presupposes a prior act of faith in Jesus Christ. It cannot be based on a purely historical method. Rather, it bears historical reason within itself, enabling us to see the unity of Scripture.[112] It also gives us a new understanding of its original elements, without destroying their historical originality. Canonical exegesis carries the historical-critical method towards becoming authentic theology.

Essentially, Ratzinger is opposing an exclusively positivistic hermeneutic, a dual hermeneutic which grasps history through faith. Thus:

> [Scholarly exegesis] must take a methodological step forward and see itself once again as a theological discipline, without abandoning its historical character. It must learn that the positivistic hermeneutic on which it is based does not constitute the only valid and definitely evolved rational approach; rather, it constitutes a specific and historically conditioned form of rationality that is both open to correction and completion and in need of it. It must recognize that a properly developed faith-hermeneutic is appropriate to the text and can be combined with a historical hermeneutic, aware of its limitations, so as to form a methodological whole.[113]

Ratzinger's personal and ecclesial theses, his theological epistemology, provide us with the necessary hermeneutic of faith.

The Application of the Method

It is not possible within the confines of this study to give a comprehensive account of how Ratzinger applies his hermeneutical method in *Jesus of Nazareth*. Rather, only a few points will be touched upon. First, as Weinandy has pointed out, Ratzinger's model exegete is Jesus himself.[114] As Ratzinger states:

---

112. Ibid., xix. In the English translation of *Jesus I*, a sentence has been mistranslated in such a way that it seems that Ratzinger is engaging in a circular argument. The translation reads, "this act of faith is based upon reason—historical reason" (xix). However, the German original reads, "dieser Glaubensentscheid trägt Vernunft—historische Vernunft—in sich," (18); that is to say, "this act of faith bears reason—historical reason—in itself." The German verb *tragen* cannot bear the sense of "to be based upon." On this point, see Root, "Jesus and the Pope," 155.

113. *Jesus II*, xiv–xv.

114. Weinandy, "Pope Benedict XVI," 22.

> The announcement of God's lordship is, like Jesus' entire message, founded on the Old Testament. Jesus reads the Old Testament, in its progressive movement from the beginnings with Abraham right down to his own time, as a single whole; precisely when we grasp this movement as a whole, we see that it leads directly to Jesus himself.[115]

Ratzinger gives a number of examples of Jesus' re-lecturing of the Torah, and indeed, the whole of the Old Testament, including his explanation of the "law and the prophets" to the disciples on the road to Emmaus, his claim to be the subject of Moses' discourse, his identification of himself with the Suffering Servant and the Son of Man, his Palm Sunday entry into Jerusalem, and his rereading of the apocalyptic discourses of Daniel, Ezekiel and Isaiah.[116] Following the example of Jesus himself, Ratzinger treats the Old and New Testaments as a unity. Jesus Christ is the key to interpreting the Bible as a whole, and one "learns from him how to understand the Bible as a unity."[117]

Ratzinger sees Jesus as continuing and bringing to completion an already established practice of reinterpretation. According to him:

> Modern exegesis has brought to light the process of constant rereading that forged the words transmitted in the Bible into Scripture: Older texts are reappropriated, reinterpreted, and read with new eyes in new contexts. They become Scripture by being read anew, evolving in continuity with their original sense, tacitly corrected and given added depth and breadth of meaning. This is a process in which the word gradually unfolds its inner potentialities, already somehow present like seeds, but needing the challenge of new situations, new experiences and new sufferings, in order to open up.[118]

Ratzinger gives the example of how prophets such as Isaiah, Hosea, Amos and Micah, in the light of changed historical circumstances, came to condemn caustic law (developed for specific judicial issues), which, although it was contained in the Torah, had become a form of injustice.[119] He also draws attention to how the apocalyptic passages from the books of Daniel, Ezekiel and Isaiah are interconnected, with old images being reinterpreted

---

115. *Jesus I*, 56.
116. Ibid., 102, 121, 235, and 331–33; and *Jesus II*, 5, 17, and 49–52.
117. *Jesus I*, xix.
118. Ibid., xviii–xix.
119. Ibid., 123–24.

The Spiritual Christology of *Jesus of Nazareth*—Method

in situations of hardship and further developed—a process which Jesus continues in his own apocalyptic discourse.[120]

Ratzinger sees the early church continuing the Jewish practice of reinterpretation. In looking at the Gospels, he sees a constant witness to the fact that the Old Testament refers to Jesus. Accordingly:

> From the start of his Gospel, Matthew claims the Old Testament for Jesus, even when it comes to apparent minutiae. What Luke states as a fundamental principle, without going into detail, in his account of the journey to Emmaus (cf. Luke 24:25ff.)—namely, that all the Scriptures refer to Jesus—Matthew, for his part, tries to demonstrate with respect to all the details of Jesus' path.[121]

Ratzinger sees this witness being continued in the Acts of the Apostles, for example, in St. Paul's address to the Jews of Antioch in Pisidia (cf. Acts 13:32–34) where he appeals to the verse in Psalm 2, "You are my Son, today I have begotten you," as testimony to God's fulfillment of his promises to them in the Resurrection of Jesus. This Ratzinger sees as "a typical example of early missionary preaching to the Jews, in which we encounter the nascent Church's christological reading of the Old Testament."[122]

One detailed example which Ratzinger gives of the unity of the Old and New Testaments are the allusions in the Passion narrative to Psalm 22 and Isaiah 53. According to him, they "are of fundamental significance, because they span, as it were, the whole of the Passion event and shed light upon it theologically."[123] Taking Psalm 22 in particular, Ratzinger sees Israel's anguished cry in the midst of its sufferings echoed in the great cry of Jesus in Mark's Gospel (cf. 15:34). The mockery directed at the Psalmist as one in whom the Lord takes no delight, and the casting of lots for his garments, is prophetically fulfilled on the Cross. So, Ratzinger continues, attesting to the church's recognition of the Resurrection in the granting of the suppliant's prayer (cf. Ps 22:25), Christ brings a salvation which comes to all (cf. Ps 22:26–27). In the afflicted eating and being satisfied, the early church recognized an allusion to the Eucharist, and in all the nations worshiping the God of Israel, it perceived all peoples converted to the God of Jesus Christ (cf. Ps 22: 6–8, 18, 25–27). As Ratzinger states: "Eucharist (praise and

---

120. *Jesus II*, 49–50.

121. *Jesus I*, 64. Cf. *Jesus II*, 203 and 252, where Ratzinger reiterates Luke's position that, in the light of the Resurrection, Christ's followers need to learn to read the Old Testament afresh.

122. *Jesus I*, 337.

123. *Jesus II*, 204.

thanksgiving: v. 25; eating and being satisfied: v. 26), and universal salvation (v. 27) appear as God's great answer to prayer in response to Jesus' cry."[124]

Ratzinger also wishes to retrieve the patristic and medieval hermeneutic of a fourfold sense of Sacred Scripture, each thought of as an individual manifestation of the one, christological sense. Thus: "There are dimensions of the word that the old doctrine of the fourfold sense of Scripture pinpointed with remarkable accuracy. The four senses of Scripture are not individual meanings arrayed side by side, but dimensions of the one word that reaches beyond the moment."[125] For example, in the petition in the Lord's prayer that we should be given our daily bread, over and above the literal sense of the bread with which God wishes to maintain our natural lives, there is the allegorical sense that Jesus himself is our true bread, foreshadowed in the daily manna which fed the people of Israel in the desert, tropologically lived out in our celebration of the Eucharist, which anagogically prefigures the Supper of the Lamb.[126]

Finally, there is the question of how Ratzinger applies the historical-critical method in particular instances. One prominent example is his addressing of the Johannine Question. Ratzinger notes that because John's Gospel presents the mystery of Jesus' person through extended discourses built around images rather than the parables of the Synoptics, and shifts the main focus of Jesus' activity from Galilee to Jerusalem, that modern critical scholarship has denied the historicity of much of the text. Rather than constituting a reliable source for knowledge of the historical Jesus, the Christology of John's Gospel is regarded as being too highly developed to be anything other than a later theological construction.[127] In response to Bultmann's characterization of John's Gospel as rooted in Gnosticism, Ratzinger draws upon the scholarship of Hengel to argue that the theological framework for the Gospel is to be found rather in the Torah and Jewish piety. Hengel locates the cultural milieu of the Gospel in a Hellenized Jewish upper class, a priestly aristocracy. According to Hengel, the author of the fourth Gospel was someone with an excellent firsthand knowledge of the Palestine of Jesus' time, and someone connected with the household of the high priest.[128]

Ratzinger's response to this debate is to pose two questions which he sees as decisive for the "Johannine Question": Who is the author of this

124. Ibid., 204–5.
125. *Jesus I*, xx.
126. Ibid., 150–57. Cf. Sciglitano, "Benedict XVI," 177.
127. *Jesus I*, 219.
128. Ibid., 219–22.

The Spiritual Christology of *Jesus of Nazareth*—Method

Gospel and how historically reliable is it? In answer to the first question, Ratzinger draws upon the internal testimony of the Gospel that the author is a disciple who stood at the foot of the Cross and saw the blood and water which issued from the pierced side of Jesus (cf. John 19:26, 34–35 and 21:24). This disciple is the one who reclined beside Jesus at the Last Supper and "leaned back on Jesus' breast" (John 13:25). According to Ratzinger:

> These words are intended to parallel the end of the prologue of John's Gospel, where it is said apropos of Jesus: "No one has ever seen God; it is the only Son, who is nearest to the Father's heart, who has made him known" (John 1:18). Just as Jesus, the Son, knows about the mystery of the Father from resting in his heart, so too the Evangelist has gained his intimate knowledge from his inward repose in Jesus' heart.[129]

Once more we see the defining principle of Ratzinger's spiritual Christology. The Evangelist knows the truth about Jesus not just because he is an eyewitness to the blood and water, but because of his prayerful communion with the heart of Jesus. As to whether the "beloved disciple" is actually John, son of Zebedee, Ratzinger rejects the thesis of Ulrich Wilckens that the beloved disciple is not a historical figure but a symbol for the basic structure of the faith.[130] Ratzinger believes that unless the beloved disciple is a real witness to the events described, faith in Jesus would be without historical grounding. As he says:

> If the favorite disciple in the Gospel expressly assumes the function of a witness to the truth of the events he recounts, he is presenting himself as a living person. He intends to vouch for historical events as a witness and he thus claims for himself the status of a historical figure. Otherwise the statements we have examined, which are decisive for the intention and quality of the entire Gospel, would be emptied of meaning.[131]

Appealing to the unanimous tradition of the church in identifying the partner of Peter as both the beloved disciple and the author of John, Ratzinger also acknowledges the questioning of that identification on the basis of doubts over whether a Galilean fisherman could have had both the theological capability and the necessary connections with the priestly aristocracy of

---

129. Ibid., 222–23. This passage is strongly reminiscent of a passage from Guardini's *The Word of God*, 28: "We can love Him [Jesus] and He is able to give us a communion which reflects the intimacy in which He lies upon the bosom of the Father, and which St John experienced when His Master permitted him to lay his head upon His heart."

130. *Jesus I*, 223.

131. Ibid.

Jerusalem needed by the Gospel's author. On the basis of specific exegetical research, Ratzinger argues that such an identification would be possible.[132] Ultimately, Ratzinger deduces that the Fourth Gospel is historically credible, since it goes back to the original testimony of an eyewitness which was redacted by one of his followers. In the Gospel of John we have access to the historical reality of the substance of Jesus' discourses, and the authentic content of his life.[133]

---

132. Ibid., 224–25.
133. Ibid., 225–29.

6

The Spiritual Christology of *Jesus of Nazareth*—Content

The Filial Thesis

The Father's Heart

The filial thesis of Ratzinger's spiritual Christology is that the center of the life and person of Jesus is his constant communication with the Father. Jesus' words and deeds flow out of this intimate communion. For Ratzinger, the key text which expresses this communion is John 1:18: "No one has ever seen God; it is the only Son, who is nearest the Father's heart, who has made him known." In the first volume of *Jesus of Nazareth*, this text is quoted or alluded to no fewer than eight times.[1]

As we have seen, the term heart is constantly employed by Ratzinger in his personal search for the face of Jesus. It is used to refer to four different hearts—the heart of God the Father, the heart of Jesus, the hearts of human persons, and even the heart of the church. This raises two immediate questions. First, what kind of meaning is Ratzinger seeking to communicate through the use of this term? Is he simply mimicking in an unreflective or equivocal way the use of the term in Sacred Scripture? Second, if the term has a definite meaning, is it univocal, whether it is applied to the Father, the Son, or to human persons; or does it have a different meaning when applied to human hearts, including the human heart of Jesus, than when it is applied to the heart of the Father; and are these meanings related in a metaphorical or analogical manner?

---

1. *Jesus I*, 6, 7, 75, 132, 222–23, 236, 265–66, and 340.

We have already found a partial answer to the first question. With regard to the human heart, it is the place of the integration of the intellect, will, passions and senses, of the body and the soul. It is the personal integration, the integration by the person, of these aspects of their human nature.

However, what does Ratzinger mean by the term heart as applied to God? When addressing the significance of the word Father as applied to God, he raises the question of whether God is also Mother. It is within the context of his answer that he makes a point which is of relevance to his understanding of the term heart as applied to God. He recounts how the Hebrew word for "womb" came to be used to mean the mercy of God. Ratzinger states that:

> The Old Testament constantly uses the names of organs of the human body to describe basic human attitudes or inner dispositions of God, just as today we use *heart* or *brain* when referring to some aspect of our own existence. In this way the Old Testament portrays the basic attitudes of our existence, not with abstract concepts, but in the image language of the body. The womb is the most concrete expression of the intimate interrelatedness of two lives and of loving concern for the dependent, helpless creature whose whole being, body and soul, nestles in the mother's womb. The image language of the body furnishes us, then, with a deeper understanding of God's dispositions toward man than any conceptual language could.[2]

Ratzinger draws attention to the use of womb as a synonym for heart when speaking of the compassion of the Good Samaritan. There he says that: "His heart is wrenched open. The gospel uses the word that in Hebrew had originally referred to the mother's womb and maternal care. Seeing this man in such a state is a blow that strikes him 'viscerally,' touching his soul."[3] "Womb" indicates the Good Samaritan's inner disposition of mercy.

Ratzinger expresses himself more plainly on the subject of God's heart when he recounts the compassion of God for his people as expressed by the prophet Hosea: "How can I give you up, O Ephraim! How can I hand you over, O Israel! . . My heart turns itself against me, my compassion grows warm and tender" (Hos 11:8).

> Because God is God, the Holy One, he acts as no man could act. God has a heart, and this heart turns, so to speak, against God himself: Here in Hosea, as in the Gospel, we encounter once

---

2. Ibid., 139.
3. Ibid., 197.

The Spiritual Christology of *Jesus of Nazareth*—Content

again the word *compassion*, which is expressed by means of the image of the maternal womb.[4]

As Ratzinger had said earlier: "This 'com-passion' reminds us of the magnificent saying of Saint Bernard of Clairvaux's commentary on the Song of Songs (sermon 26, no. 5): 'Impassibilis est Deus, sed non incompassibilis'—God cannot suffer, but he can 'suffer *with*.'"[5]

The Prayer of Jesus

In describing Jesus at prayer, the Gospels momentarily lift the veil from his constant, intimate communion with the Father. So, we find in *Jesus of Nazareth* that certain prayer events of Jesus' life are given great prominence. According to Ratzinger, Luke tells us that Jesus was praying while he received baptism (cf. Luke 3:21).[6] The calling of the Twelve is also a prayer event, emerging from the Son's dialogue with the Father (cf. Luke 6:12–16).[7] In Ratzinger's analysis of the Lord's Prayer he notes that Luke, in particular, places the context of the communication of this prayer to the disciples within the context of Jesus' own praying. He thinks that Luke draws particular attention to the fact that Jesus' prayer is the source of his preaching and action. They issue from "his inner oneness with the Father, from the dialogue between Father and Son."[8]

As we have seen, Ratzinger holds that in the Sermon on the Mount one finds a hidden Christology, that the one pre-eminently portrayed in the Beatitudes is Jesus himself. In his reading of Matthew's account of the Sermon, the mountain on which Jesus, the one greater than Moses, teaches, is also the mountain on which he prays, the place where he is with the Father face to face.[9] Likewise, Ratzinger sees Luke's account of the Sermon as ultimately grounded in the prayer of Jesus, as it follows immediately upon the calling of the Twelve after a night spent by Jesus on the mountain, watching in prayer with the Father.[10] As has been seen, Ratzinger holds that the entire

---

4. Ibid., 207.
5. Ibid., 87.
6. Ibid., 18. In fact, although Jesus may have been praying when he was baptized, Luke tells is that it was *after* Jesus was baptized that he was praying.
7. Ibid. 170.
8. Ibid., 182.
9. Ibid., 66.
10. Ibid., 68.

ministry of Jesus is sustained by his prayer, and defining events in his life are revealed as prayer events.[11]

For Ratzinger, Jesus is the one who has seen God and, therefore, can make him known (cf. John 1:18). He is the one greater than Moses, who completes what Moses began—the revelation of God. His identity as the new and definitive Moses is especially revealed on the mountain of the Beatitudes.[12] Yet, this mountain is only one of numerous mountains in the life of Jesus. Besides the "mountain of his great preaching" there is also "the mountain of temptation . . . the mountain of his prayer; the mountain of the Transfiguration; the mountain of his agony; the mountain of the Cross; and finally, the mountain of the Risen Lord."[13] Granted, one does not witness Jesus explicitly praying during his temptations in the desert, or on the mountain of his Ascension, and there are instances of Jesus praying, addressed by Ratzinger, which are not set on mountains—his baptism in the Jordan, his *Jubelruf* (joyful cry) upon the return of the seventy, before Peter's confession of faith, and his high priestly prayer at the Last Supper. However, for Ratzinger, the symbolism of the mountain is important. "The mountain is the place of ascent—not only outward, but also inward ascent." It is the place where one experiences "the God who speaks."[14] So it seems that, for Ratzinger, all of these mountains are places where Jesus encounters the Father.

In Ratzinger's mind, Jesus' prayer encounters with his Father reveal Jesus' divinity. At the Jordan, the heavenly voice reveals that Jesus is the Son of God.[15] For the disciples, witnessing these encounters become occasions for realizing that this is who Jesus is. Ratzinger sees Peter's confession as a key example of this. He sees Luke's account of this event as beginning with a deliberate paradox: that Jesus was praying alone *and* the disciples were with him (cf. Luke 9:18). As Ratzinger says:

> The disciples are drawn into his solitude, his communion with the Father that is reserved to him alone. They are privileged to see him as the one who . . . speaks face-to-face with the Father, person to person. They are privileged to see him in his utterly filial being—at the point from which all his words, his deeds, and

---

11. Ibid., 132.
12. Ibid., 66.
13. Ibid., 308.
14. Ibid., 309.
15. Ibid., 19.

The Spiritual Christology of *Jesus of Nazareth*—Content

his powers issue . . . This seeing is the wellspring of their faith,
their confession; it provides the foundation of the Church.[16]

Here, one can see the personal, ecclesial and filial theses being applied to the account of Peter's confession of faith.

Ratzinger sees this confession of Peter in the synoptic Gospels as linked with the Transfiguration. In both, the issue for Ratzinger is that the divinity of Jesus as the Son is made manifest.[17] Ratzinger notes that Luke is the only one of the synoptic Gospels to say that the purpose of Jesus' ascent of the mountain of the Transfiguration was to pray (cf. Luke 9:28).[18] The radiance of Jesus' glory as he prays to the Father makes manifest "the profound interpenetration of his being with God, which then becomes pure light."[19] According to Ratzinger:

> In his oneness with the Father, Jesus is himself "light from light." The reality that he is in the deepest core of his being, which Peter tried to express in his confession—that reality becomes perceptible to the senses at this moment: Jesus' being in the light of God, his own being-light as Son.[20]

Ratzinger sees a connection between the Transfiguration and the Feast of Tabernacles. Following an argument of Daniélou, he concludes that in each of the synoptic Gospels the Transfiguration is presented as occurring on the last day of this feast. According to Daniélou, the tents of this feast had an eschatological symbolism. Jesus' manifestation of his glory to Peter is the sign that the times of the Messiah have arrived. In messianic times the just will dwell in tents, signified by the huts of the Feast of Tabernacles.[21] Ratzinger sees here a link with the prologue to John's Gospel, "where the Evangelist sums up the mystery of Jesus: 'And the Word became flesh and pitched his tent among us'" (John 1:14).[22]

One final example of the connection between the prayer of Jesus and the manifestation of his divinity is Mark's account of Jesus' walking on the water. Ratzinger notes that Jesus withdraws to pray "on the mountain." While he is praying, he sees that the disciples, in their boat on the lake, can make no headway against the wind. It is then that he comes to them across

---

16. Ibid., 291.
17. Ibid., 305. Cf. Gadenz, "Jesus the New Temple," 222.
18. Ibid., 309.
19. Ibid., 310.
20. Ibid.
21. Ibid., 306.
22. Ibid., 315.

the water. In response to the disciples' cry of "total confusion," Jesus says to them: "Take heart, it is I; have no fear" (Mark 6:50). Ratzinger thinks that "it is I" is an echo of the Johannine "I am he."[23] However, when Jesus gets into the boat and the wind ceases, the disciples' fear and astonishment increase! (cf. Mark 6:51). Ratzinger sees their increased fear as a response to a theophany, a recognition of the presence of God himself in Jesus—"an encounter with the mystery of Jesus' divinity. Hence, Matthew quite logically concludes his version of the story with an act of adoration (*proskynesis*) and the exclamation of the disciples: 'Truly, you are the Son of God.'"[24]

The Soteriological Thesis

This thesis is a refinement of the filial thesis, focusing upon the final and definitive self-offering of Jesus to the Father in the Passion. Ratzinger maintains that: "Jesus died praying. At the Last Supper he had anticipated his death by giving himself, thus transforming his death, from within, into an act of love, into a glorification of God."[25] However, this does not mean that it is only the events of the Passion which are relevant to this thesis. Ratzinger's meditations on the life of Jesus are permeated with a theology of the Cross. For him, from the time of Jesus' Baptism, the Cross is never absent from the Lord's life. Ultimately, he is revealed in "the form of the Cross, of the suffering God, who calls us to step into [a] mysterious fire, the fire of crucified love."[26] Ratzinger speaks of a "descent" and an "ascent." "God now speaks intimately, as one man to another. Now he descends into the depths of human sufferings."[27] The entering of Jesus into communion with his Father, "the inward ascents of his life . . . are then prolonged in his descents into communion of life and suffering with men."[28] It should be noted here that the volitional thesis, the union of Jesus' will with that of the Father, most fully revealed in the garden of Gethsemane, is also seen by Ratzinger as taking place throughout Jesus' post-baptismal life.

23. Ibid., 352.
24. Ibid.
25. *Behold*, 22.
26. *Jesus I*, 67.
27. Ibid.
28. Ibid., 68.

The Baptism of Jesus

Beginning with the Baptism of Jesus, there are three aspects of Ratzinger's account of it which are pertinent to his soteriological thesis. First, he focuses on two words of Jesus' reply to John the Baptist—"now" and "righteousness." According to him, here the Greek word for "now" implies an action in the face of specific and temporary circumstances. Concerning "righteousness," Ratzinger sees it as the key to interpreting Jesus' answer. Righteousness must be fulfilled. It is the answer to the Torah, the acceptance of the whole of God's will, the bearing of the yoke of God's kingdom. By this reply, Jesus is acknowledging it as "an expression of an unrestricted Yes to God's will, as an obedient acceptance of his yoke . . . In a world marked by sin, this Yes to the entire will of God also expresses solidarity with men, who have incurred guilt and yearn for righteousness."[29]

Ratzinger holds that Christians came to look at Jesus' baptism in the light of the Cross and Resurrection, and thus interpreted it as Jesus taking man's guilt on his shoulders, taking the place of sinners. It is an anticipation of the Cross. Thus:

> The Baptism is an acceptance of death for the sins of humanity, and the voice that calls out "This is my beloved Son" over the baptismal waters is an anticipatory reference to the Resurrection. This also explains why, in his own discourses, Jesus uses the word *baptism* to refer to his death (cf. Mark 10:38; Luke 12:50).[30]

Second, Ratzinger focuses on the understanding of Jesus' baptism in the Eastern Church as revealed in its liturgy and icons. There, he sees a deep connection between the Epiphany and Easter, the heavenly voice proclaiming Jesus to be the Son of God and the Resurrection demonstrating the same. According to Ratzinger, the Eastern Church "sees Jesus' remark to John that 'it is fitting for us to fulfill all righteousness' (Matt 3:15) as the anticipation of his prayer to the Father in Gethsemane: 'My Father . . . not as I will, but as thou wilt' (Matt 26:39)."[31]

Third, Ratzinger looks at the Baptist's identification of Jesus as the "Lamb of God, who takes away the sin of the world" (John 1:29). This reference identifies Jesus as the Passover Lamb and interprets his baptism, his descent into the Jordan, as prefiguring his descent into the abyss of death, an interpretation taken up by the Fathers and by eastern iconography. Ratzinger

---

29. Ibid., 17.
30. Ibid., 18.
31. Ibid., 19.

sees this as an expression of John's theology of the Cross.³² He focuses on the fact that all the Evangelists give a prominent place to this theophany. Thus:

> All four Gospels recount in their different ways that, as Jesus came up from the water, heaven was "torn open" (Mark 1:10) or "was opened" (Matt 3:16; Luke 3:21); that the Spirit came down upon him "like a dove"; and that in the midst of all this a voice from heaven resounded. According to Mark and Luke, the voice addresses Jesus with the words "Thou art . . . "; according to Matthew, the voice speaks about him in the third person, saying, "This is my beloved Son, with whom I am well pleased" (Matt 3:17). The image of the dove may be a reminiscence of what the creation account says about the Spirit brooding over the waters (Gen 1:2); the word *like* ("like a dove") suggests that it is "a simile for something that ultimately cannot be described" (Gnilka, *Matthäusevangelium*, I, p. 78). The same heavenly voice sounds out again at the Transfiguration of Jesus, though with the addition of the imperative to "listen to him."³³

Ratzinger examines, in particular, three aspects of this scene. The first is the image of the heavens being torn apart. He sees this as an affirmation that Jesus' "communion of will with the Father, his fulfillment of 'all righteousness' opens heaven, which is essentially the place where God's will is perfectly fulfilled."³⁴ The second is that the Father proclaims *what* Jesus' mission is by proclaiming *who* Jesus is, the beloved Son on whom God's pleasure rests. Finally, Ratzinger sees in this scene the beginnings of the revelation of the three Persons of the Trinity, a revelation which will only be fully revealed at the Resurrection.³⁵ He maintains that these texts enable us to ascertain the connection between Jesus and "Moses and the Prophets," and to recognize the unity of his life's trajectory from its first moment to the Cross and Resurrection.

The Temptations of Jesus

Looking at the temptations of Jesus in the desert provides one with ample opportunity for examining the humanity of Jesus in his intellect, will and passions. Ratzinger takes up his examination with the descent of the Holy Spirit upon Jesus after his baptism. He holds that this event "is to be

32. Ibid., 19–22.
33. Ibid., 22–23.
34. Ibid., 23.
35. Ibid.

The Spiritual Christology of *Jesus of Nazareth*—Content 159

understood as a kind of formal investiture with the messianic office," and refers to the patristic understanding of it as "analogous to the anointing by which kings and priests in Israel were installed in office," a visible sign of investiture with the gifts of these offices and with the Spirit of God.[36] Jesus fulfils the hope of Isaiah 11:1–9 for the coming of the true Anointed One, the one on whom the Spirit of God comes down to rest, a hope presented by Luke as fulfilled by Jesus' presentation of himself and his mission in the synagogue at Nazareth (cf. Luke 4:18; Isa 61:1).

Ratzinger speaks of the anointing with the Spirit within the context of Jesus' temptations because the first act of the Spirit, which Ratzinger calls a command, is to lead Jesus into the desert "to be tempted by the devil" (Matt 4:1; cf. Mark 1:12–13 and Luke 4:1–2). This temptation by the devil "is prefaced by interior recollection, and this recollection is also, inevitably, an inner struggle for fidelity to the task, a struggle against all the distortions of the task that claim to be its true fulfillment."[37]

Ratzinger sees the temptations of Jesus as a "descent" into the "perils" faced by mankind. Jesus must penetrate this "drama" to its "uttermost depths." It is a descent "into Hell," a descent that accompanied Jesus throughout his whole life. In it, he recapitulates the whole of human history—he suffers through the whole of it so as to transform it. This solidarity with human suffering as Jesus' mission is especially emphasized in the Letter to the Hebrews: "Therefore he had to be made like his brethren in every respect, so that he might become a merciful and faithful high priest in the service of God, to make expiation for the sins of the people. For because he himself has suffered and been tempted, he is able to help those who are tempted" (Heb 2:17–18; cf. Heb 4:15). Ratzinger sees the story of Jesus' baptism as being intimately connected with that of his temptations, for in both he enters into solidarity with sinners. The temptations of Jesus do not just occur at the beginning of his ministry. They simply give us an insight into the temptations which he suffered throughout his ministry, culminating in his agony in Gethsemane.[38] The temptations of Jesus "reflect the inner struggle over his own particular mission."[39]

Ratzinger then goes on to address the three temptations depicted in Matthew and Luke. He sees the first words addressed by the devil to Jesus as significant—"If you are the Son of God." He sees this demand for some proof as a constantly recurring theme in the life of Jesus. Ratzinger thinks

36. Ibid., 25.
37. Ibid., 26.
38. Ibid., 27.
39. Ibid., 28.

that Matthew presents this first temptation in broader terms than Luke who, according to Ratzinger, sees this temptation simply in terms of Jesus' hunger. He regards the more extended reply of Jesus in Matthew's account—"Man shall not live by bread alone, *but by every word that proceeds from the mouth of God*"—as pointing to a broader meaning. If Jesus is the Redeemer of mankind, should he not fulfill the promise implied by God's feeding of his people with manna in the desert?[40]

For Ratzinger, the second temptation also is about one's relationship with God. He sees this temptation as ultimately being about our understanding of who God is. In refusing to put God to the test, Jesus refuses to treat God as an "object" which can be submitted to experiment. The "leap" of Jesus was not from the pinnacle of the Temple, but a leap into "the abyss of death, into the night of abandonment, and into the desolation of the defenseless."[41] The Cross is Jesus' act of God's love for human persons and an act of complete human trust in his Father. It is following the will of God in the face of the abyss.

Ratzinger sees the third temptation as the climax of the whole story. It presents a choice between two different kinds of Messiah, one who has worldly power, and one who empties himself of power. Like the other temptations, it accompanies Jesus throughout his life. It is manifested again after Peter's confession of faith in Jesus as the Messiah-Christ, the Son of the living God, when Peter takes on the role of tempter. Jesus recognizes this for what it is—a temptation, a hindrance, an exhortation to choose the path of worldly power rather than that of humble submission to the Father's will.

If Jesus does not bring world peace, universal prosperity and a better world, what then does he bring? Ratzinger's answer to this rhetorical question is simple—God. Jesus brings the final revelation, the final unveiling of the face of God.

> He has brought God, and now that we know his face, now we can call upon him. Now we know the path that we human beings have to take in the world. Jesus has brought God and with God the truth about our origin and destiny: faith, hope, and love. It is only because of our hardness of heart that we think this is too little."[42]

Ratzinger sees this temptation as the false divinization of power and prosperity, the invitation to worship power. Hence, the Lord's *riposte* that: "You

---

40. Ibid., 31.
41. Ibid., 38. Cf. Gadenz, "Jesus the New Temple," 218–19.
42. Ibid., 44.

The Sermon on the Mount

As we have seen, Ratzinger holds that in the Sermon on the Mount one finds a hidden Christology, that the one pre-eminently portrayed in the Beatitudes is Jesus himself. Ratzinger sees the Beatitudes as "the transposition of the Cross and Resurrection into discipleship. But they apply to the disciple because they were first paradigmatically lived by Christ himself."[43] What St. Paul describes as the Cross of his sufferings and the joy of his Resurrection (2 Cor 4:8–11 and 6:8–10), is paralleled by St. John, who calls the Lord's Cross an "exaltation" to God's throne. According to Ratzinger:

> John brings Cross and Resurrection, Cross and exaltation together in a single word, because for him the one is in fact inseparable from the other. The Cross is the act of the "exodus," the act of love that is accomplished to the uttermost and reaches "to the end" (John 13:1). And so it is the place of glory—the place of true contact and union with God, who is love (cf. 1 John 4:7, 16).[44]

Since Ratzinger regards the Beatitudes as above all christological, his insights into them apply first and foremost to Jesus, and only then to his disciples. We have seen this in his meditation on the third Beatitude where he expounds upon the meekness of Jesus, the one whose "inmost being is humility and meekness before God and men." He is the one who establishes peace through his "filial obedience."[45] In his meditation on the seventh Beatitude, Ratzinger presents Jesus as the ultimate peacemaker. He sees a connection between being the Son of God and being the Prince of Peace—establishing peace is part of the very essence of Jesus' sonship.[46]

Looking at the final Beatitude, Ratzinger identifies "righteousness" as the Old Covenant term for fidelity to the Torah. The equivalent term in the New Testament is "faith." The christological basis for this Beatitude is the crucified Christ. According to Ratzinger: "In the other Beatitudes, Christology is present, so to speak, in veiled form; here, however, the message

---

43. Ibid., 74.
44. Ibid., 73.
45. Ibid., 81.
46. Ibid., 85.

that he himself is the center of history emerges openly."[47] On Jesus' lips the words of the Beatitudes acquire new depth. "For it belongs to his nature that he sees God, that he stands face-to-face with him, in permanent interior discourse—in a relation of Sonship . . . In Jesus Christ, God has revealed himself in his descending."[48]

The Transfiguration of Jesus

We have seen how Ratzinger regards both Peter's Confession and the Transfiguration of Jesus as prayer events. He also sees these events as being deliberately linked in the synoptic Gospels. In both cases the issue is the divinity of Jesus as the Son. Also, in both cases, the appearance of his glory is connected with a Passion motif. Only when we combine Jesus' divinity with the Cross can we recognize who he really is.[49]

In the three disciples who Jesus takes with him up the mountain of the Transfiguration, Ratzinger sees a counter-image to the Mount of Olives.[50] He also sees it as a repetition of Jesus' baptism.[51] In Luke's account, Jesus' "exodus" through the Cross is the topic his conversation with Moses and Elijah.[52] As the disciples come down from the mountain with Jesus, they learn that the messianic age revealed by the Transfiguration is "first and foremost the age of the Cross."[53]

The Passion of Jesus

As has been said, Ratzinger sees the Cross being present in the life of Jesus from his baptism onwards. The Cross is both descent and ascent (cf. Phil 2:6–9).[54] It is in the Cross that God descends, and reveals himself in his true divinity. The entering of Jesus into communion with his Father, "the inward ascents of his life . . . are . . . prolonged in his descents into communion of life and suffering with men."[55] This "descending ascent" is revealed through-

---

47. Ibid., 90.
48. Ibid., 95.
49. Ibid., 305–6.
50. Ibid., 308.
51. Ibid., 316.
52. Ibid., 311.
53. Ibid., 315.
54. Ibid., 95.
55. Ibid., 68.

out Jesus' life—beginning with his descent into the Jordan, and revealed in the temptations which accompanied him throughout his life, and in the "mountains" which he ascended.[56] In Luke's Gospel, Ratzinger sees the ascent of Jesus to Jerusalem as ultimately his ascent into the presence of God. For Ratzinger:

> The ultimate goal of Jesus' "ascent" is his self-offering on the Cross, which supplants the old sacrifices; it is the ascent that the Letter to the Hebrews describes as going up, not to a sanctuary made by human hands, but to heaven itself, into the presence of God (9:24). This ascent into God's presence leads via the Cross—it is the ascent toward "loving to the end" (cf. John 13:1), which is the real mountain of God.[57]

We come now to this self offering on the Cross, this "loving to the end." According to Ratzinger, the Passion of Jesus is "prayer," an act of worship. Jesus "transforms his violent death into the free offering of his life (cf. [John] 10:18)."[58] His body is the new Temple, the *locus* of a new worship.[59] He is the new Ark of the Covenant, the place of atonement. He is the *hilastērion*, the seal of the Ark of the Covenant, "the locus of the presence of the living God."[60] As Ratzinger sees it:

> [In him,] the entire Old Testament theology of worship (and with it all the theologies of worship in the history of religions) is "preserved and surpassed" [*aufgehoben*] and raised to a completely new level. Jesus himself is the presence of the living God. God and man, God and the world, touch one another in him. In his self-offering on the Cross, Jesus, as it were, brings all the sin of the world deep within the love of God and wipes it away.[61]

In the "hour" of Jesus, Ratzinger finds once more the descending ascent of Jesus. He finds its essence captured in John 13:1: "Now before the feast of the Passover, when Jesus knew that his hour had come to depart out of this world to the Father, having loved his own who were in the world, he loved them to the end." For Ratzinger: "The essence of this hour is described by John with two key words: it is the hour of his 'departing' (*metabaínein/*

---

56. Ibid., 19–22, 26–27, and 309.
57. *Jesus II*, 2.
58. Ibid., 71.
59. Ibid., 21–22.
60. Ibid., 39.
61. Ibid., 39–40.

metábasis); it is the hour of the love that reaches to the end (*agápē*)."[62] According to Ratzinger, these two concepts shed light upon each other and cannot be separated. As he says:

> Love is the very process of passing over, of transformation, of stepping outside the limitations of fallen humanity—in which we are all separated from one another and ultimately impenetrable to one another—into infinite otherness. "Love to the end" is what brings about the seemingly impossible *metábasis*: stepping outside the limits of one's closed individuality, which is what *agape* is—breaking through into the divine. The "hour" of Jesus is the hour of the great stepping beyond, the hour of transformation, and this metamorphosis is being brought about through *agape*. It is *agape* "to the end"—and here John anticipates the final word of the dying Jesus: *telélestai*—"it is finished" (19:30). This end (*télos*), this totality of self-giving, of remolding the whole of being—this is what it means to give oneself even unto death.[63]

The High Priestly Prayer of Jesus

Ratzinger continues his meditation upon the Passion of Jesus by looking at what has been called Jesus' high priestly prayer. He sees Jesus revealed in this prayer as "the one making atonement as well as the expiatory offering, both priest and sacrifice."[64] According to Ratzinger, Jesus' prayer realizes that which the rite of the feast of Atonement signified. The object of the Feast was to restore Israel as God's holy people in the midst of the world. This leads us to an essential point in Ratzinger's theology of worship. He holds that "the inner purpose of the whole of creation [is] to open up a space to God's love, to his holy will."[65] He draws on the rabbinic thought that "the idea of establishing a holy people to be an interlocutor for God in union with him—is prior to the idea of the creation of the world and supplies its inner motive."[66] The cosmos was created so that there might be a space for the covenant, for the loving Yes between God and man.

Ratzinger sees the high priestly prayer of Jesus as exactly reproducing the structure of the ritual for the feast of Atonement. Therein:

---

62. Ibid., 54.
63. Ibid., 54–55.
64. Ibid., 76.
65. Ibid., 78.
66. Ibid.

> Jesus prays for himself, for the Apostles, and finally for all who will come to believe in him through their word—for the Church of all times (cf. John 17:20). He sanctifies "himself," and he obtains the sanctification of those who are his. The fact [is] that, despite a certain demarcation from the "world" (cf. John 17:9), this means the salvation of all, the "life of the world" as a whole (cf. 6:51).[67]

For Ratzinger, the high priestly prayer of Jesus reveals him as the high priest of the Day of Atonement for the world, achieved in his Cross and exaltation. In the words of Jesus, the ritual of this day is transformed into prayer. Sacrificial animals have been made redundant. Rather:

> In their place are what the Greek Fathers called *thysia logike*—spiritual sacrifices [literally: sacrifices after the manner of the word]—and what Paul described in similar terms as *logike latreia*, that is, worship shaped by the word, structured on reason (Rom 12:1).[68]

This "word" is the word of him who is "*the* Word." It draws all human words into God's inner dialogue of reason and love. This Word has become flesh, has offered up his body and poured out his blood. The high priestly prayer of Jesus also reveals a renewed understanding of priesthood. This priesthood, prefigured in the Suffering Servant Songs of Isaiah, is one wherein the priest is also victim. He achieves reconciliation by laying down his life for his sheep.[69]

The Last Supper

Looking at the Last Supper itself, Ratzinger holds that, as it is presented in the Gospels, this meal was not the old Passover, but the new one. It

---

67. Ibid., 78–79.

68. Ibid., 80. The *logike latreia* of St. Paul is a key concept in Ratzinger's liturgical theology. As he states in *A New Song for the Lord*: "Paul coined the expression *logike latreia* (Rom 12:1), which is quite difficult to translate into our modern languages because we do not have a real equivalent for the concept of logos. One could translate it 'spiritual worship' and so refer at the same time to the saying of Jesus about worshiping in spirit and truth (John 4:23). One could, however, translate it 'divine worship shaped by the word,' but would then of course have to add that 'word' in the biblical sense (and also in the Greek sense) is more than language and speech, namely, creative reality. It is also certainly more than mere thought and mere spirit. It is self-interpreting, self-communicating spirit" (152). See also Ratzinger, *The Spirit of the Liturgy*, 58; *Pilgrim Fellowship of Faith*, 114–18; and "Bilan et perspectives."

69. *Jesus II*, 81.

was Jesus' Passover, possessing an inner connection with Jesus' death and Resurrection. It was a real anticipation of the Cross and Resurrection. The old Passover has been brought to its full meaning. Jesus is now the Paschal Lamb (cf. 1 Cor: 5:7).[70]

To those who propose that the words and actions attributed to Jesus at the Last Supper cannot be authentic, on the basis of a contradiction between Jesus' Galilean proclamation of the kingdom of God and his teaching in Jerusalem about vicarious expiatory death, Ratzinger makes the following response, a response which has already been touched upon—the Gospels are permeated with a theology of the Cross. From Jesus' prophecy about the days when the Bridegroom will be taken from them (cf. Mark 2:20), through his prophecies of his coming rejection (cf. Mark 4:10–12), to the interpretation of the parables of the Kingdom (cf. Matt 13:10–17; Luke 8:9–10), a theology of the Cross is constant. Not only is the Sermon on the Mount colored with the language of the Cross, especially in the final beatitude (cf. Matt 5:10–12), but Luke begins his account of Jesus' ministry with his rejection in Nazareth (cf. Luke 4:16–29).[71]

When we come to the nature of Jesus' prayer at the Last Supper, in Jesus' action Ratzinger identifies two strands—thanksgiving and blessing. It is *eucharistía* (as in Paul and Luke), and *eulogia* (as in Mark and Matthew). Jesus' prayer is thanks and praise for God's gift. Praise returns as blessing over the gift (cf. 1 Tim 4:4–5). At the Last Supper: "Jesus takes up this tradition. The words of institution belong within this context of prayer; the thanksgiving leads to blessing and to transformation."[72] He then breaks the bread and gives it to the disciples. For Ratzinger, when Jesus speaks of his "body," he is referring to his whole person. It is himself in his entirety which he is giving. He is laying down his life of his own accord (cf. John 10:18). Although his life will be taken from him on the Cross, already, at the Last Supper, he is laying it down. His violent death he transforms into a free act of self-giving for others and to others.[73] He gives thanks because his prayer has been heard (cf. Heb 5:7), because he knows that his Father will not abandon him to death (cf. Ps 16:10). He gives thanks for the gift of the Resurrection. Hence he can already give his body and blood in the form of bread and wine as a pledge of resurrection and eternal life (cf. John 6:53–58).[74] The reason that Jesus can already give himself in his body is that, according to

---

70. Ibid., 114–15.
71. Ibid., 118–24.
72. Ibid., 128.
73. Ibid., 130.
74. Ibid., 140.

Ratzinger, in the very act of laying it down he is also taking it up again (cf. John 10:18).[75] Once again we have the descending ascent of Jesus.

With the words spoken by Jesus over the chalice, Ratzinger sees an interweaving of three Old Testament texts—the sealing of the Covenant (cf. Exod 24:8), the promise of a New Covenant (cf. Je 31:31), and the promise of a Suffering Servant (cf. Isa 53:12). Jesus is the one who can truly seal the Covenant with his blood because he is the only one who can fulfill the promise of obedience. He is able to establish a New Covenant because his obedience is irrevocable and inviolable. He is the Suffering Servant, whose obedience, "now located at the very root of human nature, is the obedience of the Son, who made himself a servant and took all human disobedience upon himself in his obedience even unto death, suffered it right to the end, and conquered it."[76]

Rather than ignore man's disobedience and the terrible evil which springs from it, in Jesus, God has done what we cannot do, confronted evil and taken it upon himself. In the obedience of the Son, God has himself suffered our evil. The blood of Jesus atones for our sin. His blood is "the total gift of himself, in which he suffers to the end all human sinfulness and repairs every breach of fidelity by his unconditional fidelity." His blood shed "for you" and "for many" reveals that: "His entire being is expressed by the word 'pro-existence'—he is there, not for himself, but for others. This is not merely a dimension of his existence, but its innermost essence and its entirety. His very being is 'being-for.'"[77]

Gethsemane

When we come to Jesus' prayer in the Garden of Gethsemane, we come to the experiential aspect of Ratzinger's volitional thesis, the union of the human and divine wills in Jesus. However, Ratzinger does not wait until this point to introduce the subject of the union of these two wills. We have already seen him introduce it in his account of Jesus' baptism in the Jordan.[78] When speaking of the "Torah of the Messiah" in the Sermon on the Mount, Ratzinger says that Jesus' "I" "is by no means a self-willed ego revolving around itself alone . . . Jesus' 'I' incarnates the Son's communion of will with the Father. It is an 'I' that hears and obeys."[79] In his account of

75. Ibid., 130–31.
76. Ibid., 132.
77. Ibid., 134.
78. *Jesus I*, 23.
79. Ibid., 117.

the petition in the Lord's Prayer that the Father's will be done, he asserts that when Jesus says that his food "is to do the will of the one who sent me, and to accomplish his work" (John 4:34), he means that his oneness with the Father's will is the absolute foundation of his life.

> The unity of his will with the Father's will is the core of his very being. Above all, though, we hear in this petition an echo of Jesus' own passionate struggle in dialogue with his Father on the Mount of Olives . . . [This prayer will allow us] a glimpse into his human soul and its "becoming-one" with the will of God.[80]

Ratzinger sees a continual submission of Jesus to the will of the Father. Even before he reaches the Mount of Olives, Jesus continues his self-offering, praying the Psalms of Israel for Israel.[81] Jesus' praying of the Psalms is no minor matter for Ratzinger. In this act he sees a process of appropriation and reinterpretation. Jesus is the new David. He "appears as the one who leads and inspires the prayer of Israel, who sums up all Israel's sufferings and hopes, carries them within himself, and expresses them in prayer."[82] When Jesus prays, "he is completely in union with Israel, and yet he is Israel in a new way."[83] He is the one who "truly prays these psalms; he is their real subject. Jesus' utterly personal prayer and his praying in the words of faithful, suffering Israel are . . . seamlessly united."[84]

For Ratzinger, Gethsemane confronts us with a supremely dramatic moment in the life of Jesus.

> [It] was here that Jesus experienced that final loneliness, the whole anguish of the human condition. Here the abyss of sin and evil penetrated deep within his soul. Here he was to quake with foreboding of his imminent death. Here he was kissed by the betrayer. Here he was abandoned by all his disciples. Here he wrestled with his destiny for my sake.[85]

Ratzinger identifies five versions of the prayer of Jesus on the Mount of Olives—in the three synoptic Gospels (cf. Matt 26:36–46; Mark 14:32–42; Luke 22:39–46), in the Letter to the Hebrews (cf. 5:7–10), and a version which John places in the Temple at the beginning of Holy Week (cf. 12:27–28). He begins his meditation by quoting the Marcan version, that Jesus

---

80. Ibid., 149.
81. *Jesus II*, 145–46 and 150.
82. Ibid., 146.
83. Ibid., 147.
84. Ibid., 153.
85. Ibid., 149.

"began to be greatly distressed and troubled," and that he told his disciples, "My soul is very sorrowful, even to death" (14:33–34), a quotation from Psalm 43:5. Ratzinger sees this and other quotations from the Psalms by Jesus during his Passion as "fully personal; they have become the intimate words of Jesus himself in his agony. It is he who truly prays these psalms; he is their real subject."[86]

In Matthew's and Mark's versions, Jesus falls on his face. Ratzinger regards this as expressing extreme submission to the will of God, a radical self-offering.[87] In Luke's version, Jesus kneels, and this Ratzinger regards as an expression of martyrdom, which can only be overcome with prayer.[88] When it comes to the actual prayer itself, he begins with Mark's version. Jesus asks the Father that, if it is possible, this hour might pass him by (cf. 14:35). The essential content of the prayer is: "Abba, Father, all things are possible to you; remove this chalice from me; yet not what I will, but what you will" (14:36).

Ratzinger then identifies three elements in this prayer. The first is the fear of death which Jesus shares with our created nature.[89] It is the primordial experience of fear in the face of the power of death. It is "terror before the abyss of nothingness that makes him tremble to the point that, in Luke's account, his sweat falls to the ground like drops of blood (cf. 22:44)."[90]

In John's version (cf. 12:27), the verb *tetárakai* is used. Ratzinger understands this to mean that John is indicating the deepest of human fears, the fear of created nature face to face with death. However, over and above this is "the particular horror felt by him who is Life itself before the abyss of the full power of destruction, evil, and enmity with God that is now unleashed upon him."[91] This is the second element of Jesus' prayer. For Ratzinger, Jesus' experience in Gethsemane is not simply the same as any other human being facing an imminent death. It is a more radical fear, one which flows from his sonship. It is the more radical fear of Life itself before the abyss of evil and enmity with God which is unleashed upon him, one which he takes into himself in such a way that he is "made to be sin" (cf. 2 Cor 5:21).

> Because he is Son, he sees with total clarity the whole foul flood of evil, all the power of lies and pride, all the wiles and cruelty of

86. Ibid., 153.
87. Ibid.
88. Ibid., 154.
89. Ibid., 154–55.
90. Ibid., 154.
91. Ibid., 155.

the evil that masks itself as life yet constantly serves to destroy, debase, and crush life. Because he is Son, he experiences deeply all the horror, filth, and baseness that he must drink from the "chalice" prepared for him: the vast power of sin and death. All this he must take into himself, so that it can be disarmed and defeated in him.[92]

At this point, Ratzinger begins his analysis of the relationship between the will of Jesus and the will of the Father. He sees Jesus' prayer as presenting a confrontation between two wills, which he calls the "natural will" of Jesus and his "filial will." The natural will of Jesus resists what is about to happen to him and pleads that he might avoid it. The filial will of Jesus abandons itself completely to the Father's will. In John's version, Jesus first asks to be saved from this "hour," then that the Father's name be glorified (cf. John 12:27–28). Jesus' anguish of soul causes him to pray for deliverance, but his knowledge that this is the Father's will enables him to pray that God be glorified. It is through his acceptance of the horror of the Cross that God's name *is* gloried: "For in this way, God is manifested as he really is: the God who, in the unfathomable depth of his self-giving love, sets the true power of good against all the powers of evil."[93]

It must be said that Ratzinger's speaking here of two wills could lead to a misunderstanding, as if Jesus had two human wills. It would have been better had he said that the one human will of Jesus undergoes two successive movements; the first in keeping with the "natural" human desire to avoid such an evil, followed by the "filial" desire to do the will of the Father. He expresses himself more felicitously when he says that: "Jesus uttered both prayers, but the first one, asking for deliverance, merges into the second one, asking for God to be glorified by the fulfillment of his will—and so the conflicting elements blend into unity deep within the heart of Jesus' human existence."[94]

Finally, Ratzinger views the prayer of Jesus in the Letter to the Hebrews as referring not exclusively to the night in Gethsemane, but to the whole of Jesus' *Via Dolorosa*, up to and including the crucifixion. The "prayers and supplications, with loud cries and tears" (Heb 5:7) refer also to Jesus' crying out the opening words of Psalm 22, and the loud cry with which he expired. According to Ratzinger: "The Letter to the Hebrews views the whole of Jesus' Passion—from the Mount of Olives to the last cry from the Cross—as

---

92. Ibid.
93. Ibid., 157.
94. Ibid.

thoroughly permeated by prayer, one long impassioned plea to God for life in the face of the power of death."[95]

This being the case, Ratzinger sees Hebrews as treating the entire Passion of Jesus as a prayer, one "in which Jesus wrestles with God the Father and at the same time with human nature."[96] That being so, it sheds further light upon the prayer in Gethsemane. In this prayer, Jesus is exercising his high priesthood, holding up to God the anguish of human existence. The language of Hebrews underlines this. The verb *prosphérein* (to bring before God, bear aloft—cf. Heb 5:1) is used in the sacrificial cult. In offering himself to do the will of the Father, Jesus offers himself as a sacrifice.[97] A second verb, *teleioūn* (to make perfect) is used exclusively to mean "to consecrate as priest." Jesus is consecrated as high priest by learning obedience through his sufferings (cf. Heb 5:8–9).

The Letter to the Hebrews says that the prayer of Jesus was granted. On account of Jesus' "godly fear" he was saved from death. Ratzinger identifies this with the Resurrection of Jesus, which was his definitive and permanent salvation from death. Yet he also sees something more in this text: "[The] Resurrection is not just Jesus' personal rescue from death. He did not die for himself alone. His was a dying 'for others'; it was the conquest of death itself."[98] Ratzinger sees this text as a parallel to that of John 12:27–28. When Jesus says to the Father, "glorify your name," the response of the Father is "I have glorified it, and I will glorify it again." The Cross becomes the glory of God. In the love of the Son the glory of God is revealed. The Cross becomes the conquest of death and the source of life for all. Jesus becomes the source of salvation for all who obey him (cf. Heb 5:9–10; Ps 110:4).[99] We can see in this another expression of a corporate personality. In exercising his high priesthood, "bearing-aloft human existence to God," he "becomes the source of salvation for all who obey him."

The Crucifixion of Jesus

We have seen how Ratzinger sees the Passion of Jesus as prayer, an act of worship—how Jesus transforms his violent death into the free offering of his life (cf. John 10:18).[100] Hence, he sees not just the words of Jesus, but

---

95. Ibid., 163.
96. Ibid.
97. Ibid., 164.
98. Ibid., 165.
99. Ibid., 165–66.
100. Ibid., 71.

his very act of dying on the Cross, as prayer. The crucifixion of Jesus is the summit of the prayer which his whole life has been. Here too Jesus is not spared from the temptation to turn aside from the Father's will. His mockers imitate the devil by trying to lead him into temptation, that of saving himself and coming down from the Cross, thereby revealing his power as the Son of God.[101] Likewise, in his prayer for his crucifiers, "Father, forgive them, for they know not what they do" (Luke 23:34), he puts his preaching in the Sermon on the Mount into practice, revealing that he is ultimately the one who keeps the new Torah perfectly. The hidden Christology of the Sermon is made manifest.[102]

A fundamental aspect of Ratzinger's understanding of Jesus' prayer on the Cross is that it cannot be fully understood if it is regarded as no more than a personal prayer. Rather, his prayer must be seen as also expressing his identification with the suffering of Israel, and indeed, all who suffer. Thus:

> Psalm 22 is Israel's great cry of anguish, in the midst of its sufferings, addressed to the apparently silent God. The word "cry," which is of central importance, especially in Mark's account, for the story of the crucifixion, sets, as it were, the tonality of this psalm . . . we can hear the great anguish of the one suffering on account of God's seeming absence.[103]

However, Ratzinger does not agree with those, like Bultmann, who suggest the possibility that Jesus himself may have experienced an apparent abandonment by God.[104] Rather, it is an act of vicarious intercession. In praying the Psalm of suffering Israel he takes upon himself not just the tribulation of Israel, but of all those who suffer from God's concealment.

> He brings the world's anguished cry at God's absence before the heart of God himself. He identifies himself with suffering Israel, with all who suffer under "God's darkness"; he takes their cry, their anguish, all their helplessness upon himself—and in so doing he transforms it.[105]

Ratzinger sees the whole of Jesus' Passion anticipated by this Psalm, including the certainty of being answered in the Resurrection, where the poor will have their fill in the gathering of the "great assembly" (cf. Ps 22:24–26). "The cry of extreme anguish is at the same time the certainty of an answer

---

101. Ibid., 208–10.
102. Ibid., 206. Cf. *Jesus I*, 99.
103. *Jesus II*, 203.
104. Ibid., 213.
105. Ibid., 214.

from God, the certainty of salvation—not only for Jesus himself, but for 'many.'"[106] It is in the same light that Jesus' cry "I thirst" must be understood, echoing Psalm 69, the "Passion Psalm." "Jesus is the just man exposed to suffering. The Passion of the just, as presented in Scripture through the great experiences of praying amid suffering, is fulfilled in him."[107]

The final prayer of Jesus is uttered at the moment of his death. In Luke it is, "Father, into your hands I commit my spirit" (23:46; cf. Ps 31:5), and in John, "It is finished" (19:30). Ratzinger points out that the word *telélestai*, which was found in the account of the washing of the feet, where we are told that Jesus loved his own "to the end," is used once more at this moment. Jesus has gone as far as can be gone in loving. "He has truly gone right to the end, to the very limit and even beyond that limit. He has accomplished the utter fullness of love—he has given himself."[108] Ratzinger also links this word with the word *teleioūn*, which he connects with Hebrews 5:9. In the Torah it means consecration, the bestowal of priestly dignity, total dedication to God. In offering himself to God through his death, an offering which he expressed in this high priestly prayer, Jesus has enacted the ultimate worship of God.

> Jesus has accomplished the act of consecration—the priestly handing-over of himself and the world to God—right to the end (cf. John 17:19). So in this final word, the great mystery of the Cross shines forth. The new cosmic liturgy is accomplished. The Cross of Jesus replaces the other acts of worship as the one true glorification of God, in which God glorifies himself through him in whom he grants us his love, thereby drawing us to himself.[109]

The Heart of Jesus

We have already seen Ratzinger refer to the pierced heart of Jesus in his application of the ecclesial thesis—to the outpouring of blood and water from the heart of Jesus as an image of the Eucharist and Baptism, to the church being born from the pierced heart of the New Adam, and to the "remembrance" of the Evangelist in his testimony to the water and the blood flowing from the side of Christ (cf. John 19:35).[110] Yet, considering the prominence

---

106. Ibid.
107. Ibid., 218.
108. Ibid., 223.
109. Ibid.
110. Ibid., 226; and *Jesus I*, 231 and 243.

which Ratzinger gives to the pierced heart of Jesus in the title of his book on spiritual Christology, one might have expected a more substantial meditation at this point. What Ratzinger does say is that "the Church in every century has looked upon this pierced heart and recognized therein the source of the blessings which are symbolized in blood and water."[111] Another surprise is that although Ratzinger quotes the First Letter of John to the effect that there are *three* witnesses who agree that Jesus is the Christ; the Spirit, the water and the blood; in relation to the pierced heart of Jesus, Ratzinger makes little mention of the witness of the Holy Spirit, beyond asserting the necessity of the Holy Spirit to complete this triple testimony in and through the church (cf. 1 John 5:6–8; and John 15:26, 16:10).[112] However, when looking at the words of Jesus at the Feast of Tabernacles, "out of his heart shall flow streams of living water" (John 7:38), Ratzinger identifies this "water" with the Holy Spirit, the "pneumatic drink" of which St. Paul speaks (cf. 1 Cor 10:4).[113]

Ratzinger does have more to say about the heart of Jesus. He is the one who is meek and lowly of heart (cf. Matt 11:28–29).[114] In the hidden Christology of the Beatitudes, he is the one who "is truly meek; he is the one who is pure of heart and so unceasingly beholds God."[115] Since Jesus is the one who beholds God, he is the one who can reveal him, but only to the "little ones." Jesus himself proclaims this in his prayer—only he knows the Father and only he can reveal him (cf. Matt 11:25–27; and Luke 10:21–22). His knowledge of the Father comes from his oneness with the Father. Thus Ratzinger states:

> Every process of coming to know something includes in one form or another a process of assimilation, a sort of inner unification of the knower with the known. This process differs according to the respective level of being on which the knowing subject and the known object exist. Truly to know God presupposes union with him, it presupposes oneness of being with him. In this sense, what the Lord himself now proclaims in prayer is identical with what we hear in the concluding words of the prologue of John's Gospel ... "No one has ever seen God; it is

---

111. *Jesus I*, 25.
112. Ibid., 243.
113. Ibid., 244.
114. Ibid., 74, 80, and 109.
115. Ibid., 74.

the only Son, who is nearest to the Father's heart, who has made him known" (John 1:18).[116]

This perfect communion in knowledge is simultaneously perfect communion in being. Indeed, the former is only made possible by the latter. Therefore, all real knowledge of the Father must come from participation in the Son's knowledge of him. Revealing this knowledge is the will of the Son, a will in union with the will of the Father (cf. Matt 11: 25 and 27).[117] However, this knowledge can only be revealed to the little ones, the simple, for the "clever of heart" (cf. 1 Cor 1:18–20, 26, 29; Isa 29:14) are "too caught up in the intricacies of their detailed knowledge."[118] Here, Ratzinger takes us back to the Beatitudes in order to show how participation in the knowledge of the Son is based on participation in his will. The key to participation in the Son's knowledge of the Father is purity of heart (cf. Matt 5:8). "Purity of heart enables us to see. Therein consists the ultimate simplicity that opens up our life to Jesus' will to reveal. We might also say that our will has to become a filial will. When it does then we can see."[119] This is how the three hearts—the Father's heart, the heart of Jesus and the believer's heart—come into union. According to Ratzinger:

> The fact that Luke places the Our Father in the context of Jesus' own praying is . . . significant. Jesus thereby involves us in his own prayer; he leads us into the interior dialogue of triune love; he draws our human hardships deep into God's heart . . . each one of us with his own *mens*, his own spirit, must go out to meet, open himself to, and submit to the guidance of the *vox*, the word that comes to us from the Son. In this way his own heart will be opened, and each individual will learn the particular way in which the Lord wants to pray with him.[120]

As we have seen, Ratzinger sees a parallel between the description of the beloved disciple leaning back on Jesus' breast at the Last Supper, and the remark that it is only the Son who knows God, since he is nearest to the Father's heart (cf. John 13:25 and 1:18). He states that: "Just as Jesus, the Son, knows about the mystery of the Father from resting in his heart, so too

---

116. Ibid., 340.
117. Ibid., 340–41.
118. Ibid., 342.
119. Ibid., 343.
120. Ibid., 132–33.

the Evangelist has gained his intimate knowledge from his inward repose in Jesus' heart."[121]

The Resurrection of Jesus

Given Ratzinger's focus throughout *Jesus of Nazareth* on the prayer of Jesus, it is surprising that, when he comes to the chapter devoted to the Resurrection of Jesus, he makes no explicit reference to these events as the Father's *response* to this prayer. We have seen how, in his account of Gethsemane, Ratzinger identifies the Resurrection as the granting of Jesus' prayer, not just the prayer on the Mount of Olives, but the prayer that he offered "with loud cries and tears" throughout his whole life (cf. Heb 5:7–10).[122] It is through the Resurrection that Jesus is accredited by God as "Son."[123] Furthermore, he sees the granting of this prayer in the Resurrection as the conquest of death itself, which is now made available to all. Ratzinger sees a parallel text in John 12:27–28, where Jesus says to the Father, "glorify your name," and Father responds, "I have glorified it, and I will glorify it again." Here Ratzinger focuses on the Cross becoming the glory of God, on the love of the Son revealing the glory of God, of the Cross becoming the conquest of death and the source of life for all.[124] Yet, although there is no explicit mention of the Resurrection being these things, we should recall that throughout *Jesus of Nazareth* Ratzinger consistently links the Cross and Resurrection together as one event.[125]

---

121. Compare this with the three reported revelations of the Sacred Heart of Jesus to St. Margaret Mary Alacoque. In the popular devotion to the Sacred Heart most attention is given to the second and third revelations, which Margaret Mary claimed to be apparitions of Jesus showing his Sacred Heart, and wherein he speaks of human ingratitude for his love and asks to be consoled. However, of the first reputed revelation, on December 27, 1673, Margaret Mary reports: "Once, being before the Blessed Sacrament ... I felt wholly filled with [the] Divine Presence, and so powerfully moved by it that I forgot myself and the place in which I was. I abandoned myself to this Divine Spirit, and yielded my heart to the power of His love. He made me rest for a long time on His Divine Breast, where He discovered to me the wonders of His love and the inexplicable secrets of His Sacred Heart, which He had hitherto kept hidden from me. Now He opened it to me for the first time, but in a way so real, so sensible, that it left me no room to doubt ... " See Margaret Mary's "Mémoire," in *Life and Works of Blessed Margaret Mary Alacoque*, 325. For the above English translation, see *Revelations of the Sacred Heart to Blessed Margaret Mary and the History of Her Life*, 163–64.

122. *Jesus II*, 164–65 and 205.

123. Ibid., 210.

124. Ibid., 165–66.

125. In the first two volumes of *Jesus of Nazareth* the Cross and Resurrection are referred to as one event at least two dozen times.

The answer to this prayer of Jesus is divinization—first of the humanity of Jesus, then of our humanity. Ratzinger portrays the Resurrection of Jesus as a universal event, one which opens up our own resurrection (cf. 1 Cor 15:15–20). It is an "evolutionary leap."[126] It opens up a new possibility of human existence, a new kind of future for the human race. According to Ratzinger, creation is actually waiting for this evolutionary leap, for this "union of the finite with the infinite, for the union of man and God, for the conquest of death."[127] When the Risen Lord appears, he comes not from the realm of the dead but from that of pure life, from God. He is the one who is truly alive, who is himself the source of life.[128] This evolutionary leap is an "ontological leap."[129] The humanity of Jesus, including his body, now belongs completely to the sphere of the divine and the eternal. Although man was created for immortality, "it is only now that the place exists in which his immortal soul can find its 'space,' its 'bodiliness,' in which immortality takes on its meaning as communion with God and with the whole of reconciled mankind."[130] This "place" is the cosmic body of Christ (cf. Eph 1:3–23 and Col 1:12–23). The transformed body of Christ is the place wherein we enter into communion with God and each other, and are able to live an indestructible life.

The Ascension of Jesus to the Right Hand of the Father

Ratzinger calls the final chapter of *Jesus of Nazareth* an Epilogue, yet it would be a mistake for us to see it as no more than a brief tidying up of his meditations. Rather, with a few deft strokes, he brings us back full circle to the first principle in his spiritual Christology, our participation in the prayer of Jesus. He had already begun to do this in the previous chapter on the Resurrection, where he dwelt on the new presence of Jesus as manifested in his post-Resurrection table fellowship with his disciples. Ratzinger sees these accounts as pre-eminently eucharistic. He sees Luke's choice of the term *synalizómenos*, "eating salt with them," as a deliberate sign of the new and everlasting life which Jesus brings. It is a covenant event, having an inner association with the Last Supper, with the establishment of a New Covenant.[131] For Ratzinger, this table fellowship is a new covenant fellow-

---

126. *Jesus II*, 244.
127. Ibid., 247.
128. Ibid., 269.
129. Ibid., 274. Cf. *Introduction*, 305.
130. Ibid.
131. Ibid., 271.

ship with Jesus and God—"he is giving them a share in real life, making them truly alive and salting their lives through participation in his Passion, in the purifying power of his suffering."[132] This table fellowship continues in the celebration of the Eucharist.

In looking at the Ascension of Jesus to the Father, Ratzinger does not see it as causing a separation of Jesus from his disciples, but the inauguration of a new mode of his presence with them. He emphasizes that the early disciples, while they spoke of the return of Jesus, concentrated upon bearing witness to him as being alive, as Life itself, and our sharing in this life (cf. John 14:19).[133] In an astute reading of the account of the Ascension in Luke's Gospel, he notes that after this event the disciples return to Jerusalem "full of joy" (Luke 24:52). He understands this to mean that, rather than being despondent over the departure of Jesus, they are convinced that he is present with them in a new way. Ratzinger puts it thus: "They know that 'the right hand of God' to which he 'has been exalted' includes a new manner of his presence."[134] Jesus promises that his disciples will receive the gift of the Holy Spirit, which is also the gift of God's inner closeness.

Ratzinger then focuses on the cloud which took Jesus from the sight of the disciples. He compares it with the cloud at the Transfiguration, the overshadowing of Mary at the Annunciation, and the cloud of God's presence over the Tent of Meeting. For him, the cloud of the Ascension is unambiguously theological: "It presents Jesus' departure, not as a journey to the stars, but as his entry into the mystery of God. It evokes an entirely different order of magnitude, a different dimension of being."[135] For Ratzinger, "sitting at the right hand of God" (cf. Ps 110:1), being placed beside the throne of God, means participating in God's divine dominion over all "space." Therefore, Jesus has not "gone away" but is now with us in a new kind of presence. His "going away" is also a "coming" (cf. John 14:28). The mystery of his Cross, Resurrection and Ascension is the mystery of "a new form of closeness, of continuing presence."[136]

This new presence of Jesus with us is also a new presence of the Father. Ratzinger uses the account of Jesus' walking on the water to illustrate this point (cf. Mark 6:45–52 and parallel passages). When Jesus ascends the mountain to pray he seems to be far away from the disciples and their difficulties. But because he is with the Father he is able to see them, and hence

132. Ibid., 272.
133. Ibid., 278.
134. Ibid., 281.
135. Ibid., 282.
136. Ibid., 283.

come to them. *Because* the Lord is now with the Father he can see us, hear our prayers, and come to us. Likewise, in his reading of the account of Jesus' appearance to Mary Magdalene (cf. John 20:17), he draws the same conclusion. It is only when Jesus has ascended to the Father that we can truly "touch" him in a new way.[137]

This new presence of Jesus and the Father in us is also a new presence of us in them. With Jesus, we have been raised up to the right hand of God. Through baptism, our life is already hidden with Christ in God (cf. Col 3:1–3). Our "ascension," our "exaltation," like that of Christ, also takes place through the Cross. In communion with him, we move from a dimension of self-enclosed isolation to one of world-embracing divine love, what Ratzinger calls a "space travel of the heart."[138]

Ratzinger concludes *Jesus of Nazareth* with a focus upon prayer—our prayer for the return of Jesus in glory. Jesus has "eternally opened up within God a space for humanity," and calls everyone into that space, that God may be all in all (cf. 1 Cor 15:20–28).[139] Ratzinger notes that we are not to neglect this prayer—that such a prayer, *maran atha*, has been uttered by Christians since apostolic times (cf. Rev 22:20 and 1 Cor 16:22). Moreover, it has been a eucharistic prayer, as the testimony of the *Didachē* reveals.[140] According to Ratzinger, this prayer for the Lord's return always includes an experience of his presence (cf. Matt 28:20), a presence which is especially made manifest in the Eucharist. This coming, which is also a coming of the Father, is that of which Jesus spoke at the Last Supper: "If a man loves me, he will keep my word, and my Father will love him, and we will come to him" (John 14:23). Jesus comes to us in word and sacrament, especially in the Eucharist. He comes to us in the words and events of our lives. He comes to us in his saints. In praying for this coming as well as his final coming in glory we fulfill the words of the prayer which he taught us—"Your kingdom come"! In the final analysis, the Ascension of Jesus has not only torn Heaven open that we may enter it, but has torn the world open so that Heaven may enter and become present within that world.[141]

---

137. Ibid., 284–86.
138. Ibid., 286.
139. Ibid., 287.
140. Ibid., 289.
141. Ibid., 290–93.

The Dogmatic Thesis

This thesis is applied far less than the others. In fact, it is Ratzinger's stated conviction that *Jesus of Nazareth* was not the place for a debate about christological dogmas, since this work is concerned with understanding Jesus' earthly path and preaching, "not their theological elaboration in the faith and reflection of the Church."[142] However, Ratzinger does not avoid reflecting upon the "exalted christological titles." He does so in the final chapter of the first volume, which is devoted to the identity of Jesus. There he partially recapitulates his analysis in *Introduction to Christianity* of the formulation of the dogma that Jesus is true God and true man. He does this by looking briefly at three titles by which Jesus continued to be identified after Easter—Christ, Lord and Son of God. He then proceeds to look at two titles which, according to the Gospels, Jesus used for himself—Son of Man and Son—followed by an analysis of the significance of the "I am" sayings of Jesus for a comprehension of his identity.

The Volitional Thesis

In his analysis of the petition in the Our Father wherein we pray that the Father's will be done, Ratzinger raises a point with which he will deal in much greater depth in the second volume of *Jesus of Nazareth*, the union of Jesus' will with that of the Father. When Jesus says that his food "is to do the will of the one who sent me, and to accomplish his work" (John 4:34), it means that "his oneness with the Father's will is the foundation of his life. The unity of his will with the Father's will is the core of his very being."[143] Jesus' prayer in Gethsemane will allow us "a glimpse into his human soul and its 'becoming-one' with the will of God."[144] This becoming-one has already been addressed in the analysis of the Agony in Gethsemane given above. Now we shall look at its dogmatic development in the Constantinople III, and the significance Ratzinger attributes to that development.[145]

For Ratzinger, the prayer of Jesus in Gethsemane is relevant to contemporary Christology. According to him, some theologians suggest that in this prayer, the man Jesus is addressing the Trinitarian God.[146] However, Ratzinger holds that it actually reveals the Son addressing the Father. The

---

142. *Jesus I*, 320–21.
143. *Jesus II*, 149.
144. Ibid.
145. Denzinger, nos. 553–59.
146. *Jesus II*, 162.

interplay between the will of Jesus and the will of the Father gives the deepest insight into the mystery of who Jesus is, and the early church's attempts to understand him "took their final shape as a result of faith-filled reflection on his prayer on the Mount of Olives."[147]

When the Council of Chalcedon stated that in Jesus Christ the one person of the Son of God possessed two natures "without confusion or change, without division or separation," it left unanswered questions.[148] What is meant by "nature" and "person"? Some had preferred to emphasize the unity of the person, which opened the door to the one divine nature of Monophysitism. Others had feared that the true humanity of Jesus would be compromised, and thus insisted on two natures somewhat at the expense of the one person, leaving an opportunity for the heresy of Nestorius.[149] The key questions proved to be: What is the status of Jesus' human nature? Must this nature inevitably be absorbed by a divine person, at least at its highest point, the will (Monotheletism)? But how could a man with no human will be truly a man?

For Ratzinger, it is St. Maximus the Confessor who solved this conundrum through his reflections upon Jesus' prayer on the Mount of Olives. Jesus' humanity remains complete. He has a truly human will. But he does not thereby have a dual personality. The "natural will" of human nature is drawn into union with the one "personal will." This does not result in an annihilation of the natural will, "because the human will, as created by God, is ordered to the divine will. In becoming attuned to the divine will, it experiences its fulfillment, not its annihilation. Maximus says in this regard that the human will, by virtue of creation, tends towards synergy (working together) with the divine will."[150]

In sinful human beings one finds opposition rather than synergy, since sinners see this synergy as a threat to, rather than the fulfillment of, their freedom. According to Ratzinger:

---

147. Ibid., 157.

148. Denzinger, no. 302.

149. In the past, these positions have been attributed to the so-called "schools" of Alexandria and Antioch. However, recent research suggests that this two schools *schema* is a distortion of historical reality. The Antiochene Christology of Diodore of Tarsus, Theodore of Mopsuestia, and Nestorius was an eccentric and minority view, whereas the Alexandrian Christology of St. Athanasius and St. Cyril of Alexandria expressed the authentic Catholic tradition. For more on this issue see Riches, *Ecce Homo*, 31, no. 45; 68, no. 190; 72–73; 87–93; 163, no. 492; and 167, no. 504. In support of his position, Riches refers to Louth, "Why Did the Syrians?," 107–16; Fairbairn, *Grace and Christology*, 3–11; Gavrilyuk, *The Suffering of the Impassible God*, 137–139; Behr, *The Case Against Diodore and Theodore*, 3–129; and Wallace-Hadrill, *Christian Antioch*.

150. *Jesus II*, 160.

> The drama of the Mount of Olives lies in the fact that Jesus draws man's natural will away from opposition and back toward synergy, and in doing so he restores man's true greatness. In Jesus' natural human will, the sum total of human nature's resistance to God is, as it were, present within Jesus himself. The obstinacy of us all, the whole opposition to God is present, and in his struggle, Jesus elevates our recalcitrant nature to become its real self.[151]

Here, Ratzinger brings us back to the theme of corporate personality. The movement of will from opposition to union is accomplished through the sacrifice of obedience. The prayer "not my will, but yours" is truly the Son's prayer to the Father. Through it, the natural human will is completely subsumed into the "I" of the Son.

> Indeed, the Son's whole being is expressed in the "not I, but you"—in the total self-abandonment of the "I" to the "you" of God the Father. This same "I" has subsumed and transformed humanity's resistance, so that we are all now present within the Son's obedience; we are all drawn into sonship.[152]

In answer to the proposition that, in Gethsemane, the man Jesus is praying to the trinitarian God, Ratzinger sees the address of Jesus to the Father as key. His addressing God as *Abba* reveals the heart of his relationship with God. It is "the Son speaking here, having subsumed the fullness of man's will into himself and transformed it into the will of the Son."[153]

---

151. Ibid., 161.
152. Ibid.
153. Ibid., 162.

7

Questions about Ratzinger's *Theoria*

Critiquing the Critiques

A High Johannine Christology?

In chapter 1 we noted that although the Christology of *Introduction to Christianity* was extensively influenced by the Gospel of John, in *The God of Jesus Christ* there is evidence that Ratzinger had begun to broaden the evangelical base of his Christology. There is no doubt that, in *Jesus of Nazareth*, Ratzinger has broadened this base even further. The Gospels of Matthew and Luke figure much more prominently than in *Introduction to Christianity* and *The God of Jesus Christ*. The Christologies of St. Paul and of the Letter to the Hebrews are also drawn upon. Yet the question remains, are these all read through a Johannine lens? Has there been any significant movement on Ratzinger's part from seeing the Christology of Nicaea and Chalcedon as being, in essence, that of John's Gospel?

This is a difficult question to answer, and, as we have seen, there are arguments for and against a Johannine hermeneutic. Kereszty sees a profound unity in *Jesus of Nazareth* between synoptic, Johannine and Pauline Christologies. De Gaál observes what he thinks to be a justifiable preferential option for John's theology. Rausch thinks that Ratzinger reads the synoptic tradition, represented mostly by Matthew, through a Johannine lens. Hays believes that although Ratzinger's overall portrait of Jesus is strongly Johannine in character, he also makes a good case that particular Johannine emphases such as Jesus' oneness with God, a universalism that breaks the boundaries of Judaism, a realized eschatology, and a kingdom which is not of this world, can be found in the synoptic Gospels as well. Yet, Hays still maintains that Ratzinger's Christology is essentially Johannine in character. Deines concludes that the *Konstruktionspunkt* of Ratzinger's approach to the historical Jesus is not Johannine, but rather the close relationship between Jesus and God, a relationship for which Ratzinger finds support in John's Gospel. He thinks that Ratzinger's starting point is an inherited tradition about Jesus' relation to God which correctly formulates an "ontological truth-claim."

In *The God of Jesus Christ*, Ratzinger drew upon the prayer of Jesus as portrayed in Hebrews in order to expand an understanding of the *kenosis* of the Son, and as presented in Luke so as to show the uniqueness of Jesus' relationship with the Father, claiming that Luke raises "the prayer of Jesus to the central christological category from which he describes the mystery of the Son." In the first volume of *Jesus of Nazareth* he has continued this broadening process. There he draws especially upon Matthew for his reflections on the Temptations of Jesus, the Sermon on the Mount, and the Lord's Prayer. The chapter on the Message of the Parables is almost entirely Lucan. All the synoptic Gospels are represented in the chapters on the Baptism of Jesus, the Gospel of the Kingdom of God, the Disciples, and Peter's Confession and Transfiguration. In the final chapter on the Identity of Jesus, Ratzinger draws upon all four Gospels. John's Gospel only comes to the fore in a single chapter which deals specifically with its principle images. Indeed, taken as a whole, it could be argued that the greatest overt influence is Matthean. There is rather more of John in the second volume of *Jesus of Nazareth*, specifically in the Washing of the Feet, the High Priestly Prayer of Jesus, and the account of Jesus before Pilate, but all four Gospels are well represented in that work as a whole.

Be this as it may, there remains the question of whether or not *Jesus of Nazareth* is pervaded by a *covert* Johannine influence. Deines has identified the close relationship between Jesus and the Father as the starting point of Ratzinger's Christology. As we have seen, Ratzinger sees this relationship as being made manifest in the prayer of Jesus, although the ultimate starting point of his spiritual Christology is our participation in this prayer. Certainly, two of the key texts in Ratzinger's spiritual Christology are John 1:18, and 19:37. Has Ratzinger simply found more support in them for his original *Introduction to Christianity* emphasis on John's Gospel, more grist for the Johannine mill? Or should one refrain from such speculations and weigh Ratzinger's arguments for a synoptic basis for the divinity of Jesus on their merits? For my part, I find convincing his argument that the synoptic Gospels portray Jesus as saying the kinds of things and making the kinds of changes that only God could make, identifying himself as the new Torah and the Lord of the Sabbath.

Questions about Ratzinger's *Theoria*

Those who think that Ratzinger has a high Christology ultimately reach this conclusion on the basis of their understanding of the historical Jesus supposedly revealed by the historical-critical method.[1] This is normally joined to the position that Ratzinger's Christology is too Johannine, that is to say, that it concentrates too much on the divine nature of Jesus, as revealed in John, and not enough on his human nature, as revealed in the Synoptics. The fact is, although Ratzinger uses the historical-critical method, he does not *begin* his Christology with the "historical Jesus." In his earlier Christology his starting point was the church's faith as expressed in the christological articles of the Creed. This starting point was characterized as existential, as beginning not with dogma as such, but with faith in Jesus Christ. In his spiritual Christology the starting point remains existential, but has moved back a step to be more explicitly grounded in the *praxis* of faith, of praying and living in Christ.

At its starting point, Ratzinger's spiritual Christology should be characterized neither as high nor low, but as existential and participatory, a Christology of communion. If we recall Haight's observation about method, we could say that Ratzinger's christological method is to be found in his personal, ecclesial and hermeneutical theses. One could call it a "Christology from inside," from within a personal/corporate relationship with Jesus, rather than a Christology from outside such a relationship. However, there remains the possibility for such a Christology to veer too much in an "incarnational" or "crucial" direction. Ratzinger emphasizes the crucial, since he sees a longstanding over-emphasis on the incarnational direction in Catholic theology. His ultimate focus is not on Christ as the *Pantocrator*, but as the Pierced One. He does not emphasize the divine nature of Christ over his human nature. In fact, as we shall see, the purpose of the volitional thesis is to bring about an ultimate reconciliation between our notions of the two.

Circular Reasoning?

Either implicitly or explicitly a number of theologians have intimated that, in his hermeneutics, Ratzinger engages in circular reasoning. Curiously, all of them have an essentially positive attitude towards his biblical hermeneutics. Lincicum sees Ratzinger's figural reading of Sacred Scripture as a circular process. The "wholeness" which emerges from this figural reading, a wholeness which sees Jesus Christ as the ultimate subject of Scripture,

---

1. For example, see Krieg, "Who do you say I am?," 16; Rausch, *Pope Benedict XVI*, 100; Wostyn, "Pope Benedict XVI," 95–96; O'Brien, "Who's Listening?," 268–71; and Johnson, "Jesus of Nazareth," 318.

becomes the presupposition for reading the self-same Scriptures. Lincicum sees this circularity as being justified, since it is a "theological datum" which follows from a prior act of faith. This theological datum enables one to see the unity of Scripture and opens the way to canonical exegesis.

Gagey claims to see a justifiable circular reasoning based on Ratzinger's attempt to balance exegesis and theology in a way that allows a dialogue between faith and reason. According to Gagey, Ratzinger holds that the basis of an exegesis which can recognize the coherence of the Gospels must be confidence in the truth of the Gospels themselves. This confidence goes with a theological hermeneutical principle that only tradition gives access to the Scriptures. In the face of the objection that this reliance on tradition immerses one in dogmatic assumptions, and is hence a circular argument, Gagey identifies Ratzinger's response as being that the historical-critical method is also circular. The "scientific" portrayal of Jesus is itself dependent on exegetical and historical options which were expressions of "dogmatic" philosophical and theological assumptions.

Both Deines and Paddison also read Ratzinger in this way. Paddison sees Ratzinger trusting Sacred Scripture because it is mediated through the church. Deines sees the basis of Ratzinger's approach to the historical Jesus as his relationship with God. However, Deines claims that Ratzinger's knowledge of this relationship comes from an inherited tradition correctly formulating an "ontological truth claim" about the nature Jesus revealed by this relationship, which in turn he accepts on the basis of convincing arguments advanced by many scholars. Deines claims that Ratzinger "then attempts to go one step further: if the understanding of Jesus inherited from the tradition can be corroborated with historical evidence, then it is legitimate to integrate the transempirical elements of the ontological claims about Jesus into the historical question as well."[2] The difficulty here is not so much circular reasoning, but an inconsistency in Ratzinger's understanding of historical certainty. On the one hand, he identifies the decisive point, made by Schnackenburg, as being "Jesus' relatedness to God and his closeness to God," a point which Schnackenburg regards as a genuinely historical insight.[3] While constructing his book around seeing "Jesus in light of his communion with the Father, which is the true center of his personality," Ratzinger also holds that:

> We have to keep in mind the limit of all efforts to know the past: We can never go beyond the domain of hypothesis, because we cannot bring the past into the present. To be sure, some

---

2. Deines, "Can the 'Real' Jesus?," 206. Cf. *Jesus I*, xiii–xiv.
3. *Jesus I*, xiii–xiv.

hypotheses enjoy a high degree of certainty, but overall we need to remain conscious of the limit of our certainties.[4]

On the one hand, Ratzinger seems to agree with Schnackenburg that an insight can be "genuinely historical," while on the other he holds that "one can never go beyond the domain of hypothesis." He then speaks of some hypotheses as enjoying a "high degree of certainty," whilst we must remain conscious of the "limit of our certainties."

Given that Ratzinger states that the real hermeneutic of Sacred Scripture is the rule of faith, and that this hermeneutic is derived from Scripture itself, there is some justification for the above mentioned theologians reaching the conclusion that Ratzinger's hermeneutical method engages in circular reasoning. If one takes Ratzinger's starting point as the "rule of faith" or the "tradition" or the dogmatic teaching of the church, then such a conclusion is justified. This is the case in Ratzinger's earlier Christology. In *Introduction to Christianity*, he states that "the birthplace of the faith in Jesus as the Christ, that is, the birthplace of 'Christ'-ian faith as a whole, is the Cross."[5] It is Pilate who declares Jesus to be the Messiah through the execution notice which he had fastened to the Cross. This ironic declaration became the fundamental profession of faith of the first Christians—this man executed as a criminal is the Messiah. Yet this "testimony" of Pilate is to be found in Sacred Scripture. One must have faith in what the Scriptures have Pilate saying, yet historically, one cannot establish with certainty whether or not Pilate ever said it. However, this is not the *Konstruktionspunkt* of Ratzinger's spiritual Christology. If we are to truly know "Jesus in light of his communion with the Father, which is the true center of his personality," then we need another method than the historical-critical one. This starting point is the personal and ecclesial participation in this communion. As we shall see, such a starting point begins to break the "hermeneutical circle."

Why Some Historical-Critical Issues and not Others?

We have seen Johnson criticize Ratzinger for what he does not do in the first volume of *Jesus of Nazareth*—determine the relationship of the Gospels to each other, come to grips with the distinctive portrayal of Jesus in each, or address the development of the Resurrection faith in the light of the Resurrection experience. One could reply that all of these questions have been addressed almost to a point of exhaustion, and that Ratzinger wishes to take a different approach. Johnson has divined this partially when he sees

4. Ibid., xiv and xvii.
5. *Introduction*, 205.

Ratzinger's Jesus as the one who brings God to the world. As we have seen, Ratzinger regards him as much more than that. Yet the question remains— why does Ratzinger address certain historical-critical issues and not others? For example, why does he devote so much attention to the identity of the author of John's Gospel, but not of the other Gospels? The answer is that he sees John's Gospel suffering from a denial of its historicity in a way that the Synoptics do not.[6] And the essential historicity of the Gospels is a key conviction of Ratzinger. What about the dating of the Last Supper? Here again, the issue is one of historicity. Ratzinger sees a contradiction on this point between the Synoptics and John.[7] Thus he states:

> From a theological standpoint, it must be said that if the historicity of the key words and events [of the Last Supper] could be scientifically disproved, then the faith would have lost its foundation. Conversely, we may not expect . . . to find absolutely certain proof of every detail, given the nature of historical knowledge. The important thing for us, then, is to ascertain whether the basic convictions of the faith are historically plausible and credible when today's exegetical knowledge is taken in all seriousness.[8]

A Thaumaturgic Lacuna in *Jesus of Nazareth*

Rausch claims that, in *Jesus of Nazareth*, Ratzinger has neglected the Jesus of ministry and the call to discipleship in the service of the kingdom.[9] As regards the second point, Ratzinger does look at the call to discipleship in the service of the kingdom in some detail—how a disciple should pray (the Our Father), what a disciple should proclaim (the Gospel of the Kingdom of God), what a disciple should learn (the Parables), how a disciple should live (the Beatitudes). However, Ratzinger does neglect an aspect of Jesus' ministry. Notably absent from *Jesus of Nazareth* is any meditation upon the exorcisms, healings and miracles of Jesus. If, as Ratzinger claims, "the whole of Christology—our speaking of Christ—is nothing other than the interpretation of his prayer: the entire person of Jesus is contained in this prayer," how does this claim account for the christologically significant activities just mentioned?

---

6. *Jesus I*, 219.
7. *Jesus II*, 106.
8. Ibid., 104–5.
9. Rausch, *Pope Benedict XVI*, 99.

In fact, some account can be given of the relationship between the prayer of Jesus and his works of spiritual power. Although most accounts of these works make no mention of Jesus praying, there are a few that do. We could begin with the most obvious one, the raising of Lazarus from the dead. "And Jesus lifted up his eyes and said, 'Father, I thank you that you have heard me. I knew that you always hear me, but I have said this on account of the people standing by, that they may believe that you did send me'" (John 11:41–42). Here, we are given an indication that these works of Jesus are not performed independently of Jesus' ongoing communion with the Father. Furthermore, we could go to the accounts of the feeding of the five thousand. In the synoptic Gospels, Jesus "looked up to heaven, and blessed" (Mark 6:41; Matt 14:19; Luke 9:16), whereas John tells us that Jesus gave thanks (cf. 6:11). If one thinks that the eucharistic implications of this miracle are the main reason for the references to Jesus praying, there is still the curious account in Mark's Gospel of the healing of a deaf man with a speech impediment, where Jesus looks up to heaven and sighs before he says *ephphatha* (cf. 7:34). In most accounts of Jesus' exorcisms, healings and miracles, the emphasis is placed upon the power that has been given to him by God. He utters a command and the work is done. Perhaps in this particular Marcan healing, since it was performed in private, away from the crowds, we are allowed to see the interior reality of Jesus' prayer, which was present in all his words and actions.

Beholding the Pierced One in *Deus Caritas Est* and *Sacramentum Caritatis*

At about the same time as Ratzinger was writing *Jesus of Nazareth*, as Pope Benedict XVI he was composing his first encyclical and first apostolic exhortation. A pope's first encyclical can be expected to set forth the essence of what he wishes to promote during his pontificate. As it happens, the central point of the encyclical is the importance of beholding and entering into communion with the Pierced One. We come to know that *Deus caritas est*. We come to know the love of God, the love of the Father, through the pierced heart of Jesus. As Benedict XVI states: "By contemplating the pierced side of Christ (cf. John 19:37), we can understand the starting-point of this Encyclical Letter: 'God is love' (1 John 4:8). It is from there that this truth can be contemplated. It is from there that our definition of love must begin."[10]

10. *DCE*, nos. 12 and 39.

In order to set the scene for this revelation of love, Benedict XVI returns to Hosea's account of God's love for his people in the face of their infidelity (cf. Hos 11:8–9).[11] For Benedict XVI, Hosea reveals that God's love for his people is a "passionate" and forgiving love. "It is so great that it turns God against himself, his love against his justice." This turning against himself dimly prefigures the Cross. "[By] becoming man he follows him even unto death, and so reconciles justice and love."[12]

The first part of the encyclical is concerned with defining the true nature of Eros and Agape, which Benedict characterizes as "ascending and descending love." Both are necessary for us. If we wish to give love we must receive it as a gift. Certainly, one can become a source from which rivers of living water flow (cf. John 7:37–38). "Yet to become such a source, one must constantly drink anew from the original source, which is Jesus Christ, from whose pierced heart flows the love of God (cf. John 19:34)."[13]

Through contemplating the pierced side of Jesus a Christian comes to discover the path of love for his life. However, we can do more than contemplate. As Benedict XVI says:

> Jesus gave this act of oblation an enduring presence through his institution of the Eucharist at the Last Supper. He anticipated his death and resurrection by giving his disciples, in the bread and wine, his very self, his body and blood as the new manna (cf. John 6:31–33). The ancient world had dimly perceived that man's real food—what truly nourishes him as man—is ultimately the *Logos*, eternal wisdom: this same *Logos* now truly becomes food for us—as love. The Eucharist draws us into Jesus' act of self-oblation. More than just statically receiving the incarnate *Logos*, we enter into the very dynamic of his self-giving.[14]

Contemplating the pierced heart of Jesus is our way into participation in the eucharistic mystery of Jesus' self-oblation. Otherwise we can receive without recognition. We should recall the practice of so many saints of looking upon the Crucified One when they pray, as well as the popular practice of adoration of the Blessed Sacrament.

For Benedict XVI, the Eucharist brings together the whole of salvation history. It is the ultimate "making visible" of God. God's loving pursuit of our hearts throughout the history of Israel culminates in the Last Supper, the piercing of the heart of Jesus on the Cross, his appearances after

---

11. Ibid., no. 10.
12. Ibid., nos. 10 and 12. Cf. *SC*, no. 9.
13. Ibid., no. 7.
14. Ibid., no. 13. Cf. *SC*, no. 11.

the Resurrection, and the great ministry of the Apostles through which he guided the nascent church.[15]

Our communion with Christ in his Body and Blood is also our communion with each other. In the one Bread and one Body, love of God is united with love of neighbor. Communion (*koinonia*) with the Lord becomes communion with each other (cf. Acts 2:42–45). This communion of love is not meant to be mere sentiment, but a communion born of a union of our wills with the will of God. We can enter into this communion because the Lord is present with us, in those who reflect his presence in his word, the sacraments and especially in the Eucharist.[16]

> [Our contact with these] visible manifestations of God's love can awaken within us a feeling of deep joy born of the experience of being loved. But this encounter also engages our will and our intellect. Acknowledgement of the living God is one path towards love, and the "yes" of our will to his will unites our intellect, will and sentiments in the all-embracing act of love. [This] communion of will increases in a communion of thought and sentiment, and thus our will and God's will increasingly coincide.[17]

According to Benedict XVI, this communion of will even affects one's feelings. I can love even the person who I do not like or even know. One begins to see with the eyes of Christ. His friend is my friend.[18] This transformation of one's entire person is ultimately brought about by the Holy Spirit. As Benedict XVI explains:

> In the foregoing reflections, we have been able to focus our attention on the Pierced one (cf. John 19:37, Zech 12:10), recognizing the plan of the Father who, moved by love (cf. John 3:16), sent his only-begotten Son into the world to redeem man. By dying on the Cross—as Saint John tells us—Jesus "gave up his Spirit" (John 19:30), anticipating the gift of the Holy Spirit that he would make after his Resurrection (cf. John 20:22). This was to fulfill the promise of "rivers of living water" that would flow out of the hearts of believers, through the outpouring of the Spirit (cf. John 7:38–39). The Spirit, in fact, is the interior power which harmonizes their hearts with Christ's heart and moves

---

15. Ibid., no. 17. Cf. *SC*, no. 10, where Benedict XVI writes: "In instituting the sacrament of the Eucharist, Jesus anticipates and makes present the sacrifice of the Cross and the victory of the Resurrection."

16. Ibid.

17. Ibid. Cf. *SC*, no. 9, where Benedict XVI states: "In [Jesus'] crucified flesh, God's freedom and our human freedom met definitively in an inviolable, eternally valid pact."

18. Ibid., no. 18.

them to love their brethren as Christ loved them. The Spirit is also the energy which transforms the heart of the ecclesial community, so that it becomes a witness before the world to the love of the Father, who wishes to make humanity a single family in his Son.[19]

In *Sacramentum caritatis*, Benedict XVI draws out one final implication of gazing upon the Pierced One. Looking at the patristic meditations on the blood and water which flowed from the pierced side of Christ as symbolizing the sacraments, Benedict XVI reminds us of the allegory which the Fathers drew from the relationship between "Eve's coming forth from the side of Adam as he slept (cf. Gen 2:21–23) and the coming forth of the new Eve, the Church, from the open side of Christ sleeping in death." This contemplative gaze "leads us to reflect on the causal connection between Christ's sacrifice, the Eucharist and the Church."[20] We come to realize that since the Eucharist makes present Christ's redeeming sacrifice, and in the Eucharist Christ gives himself to us and builds up his Body, the Eucharist is the "cause" of the church. As Benedict XVI expresses it:

> [In] the striking interplay between the Eucharist which builds up the Church, and the Church herself which "makes" the Eucharist, the primary causality is expressed in the first formula: the Church is able to celebrate and adore the mystery of Christ present in the Eucharist precisely because Christ first gave himself to her in the sacrifice of the Cross. The Church's ability to "make" the Eucharist is completely rooted in Christ's self-gift to her.[21]

A Pneumatological Lacuna in Ratzinger's Spiritual Christology?

When looking at the beginnings of Ratzinger's spiritual Christology we found an almost complete absence of the Holy Spirit in his understanding of the *Christ*. His focus on the Holy Spirit was almost exclusively on the relationship between the Spirit and the church. As we have seen, Benedict

19. Ibid., no. 19. Cf. *SC*, no. 8, where Benedict XVI writes: "Jesus Christ, who 'through the eternal Spirit offered himself without blemish to God' (Heb 9:14), makes us, in the gift of the Eucharist, sharers in God's own life."
20. *SC*, no. 14.
21. Ibid. Cf. John Paul II, *Redemptor hominis*, no. 20; and *Dominicae cenae*, no. 4. Cf. also de Lubac, *Corpus Mysticum*, 88. In contemporary terms, de Lubac is the source of this idea.

XVI is aware of the role of the Holy Spirit in transforming the heart of the believer and the heart of the church in the Eucharist. However, does the absence of the role of the Holy Spirit in divinizing the humanity of Christ himself continue in Ratzinger's more developed spiritual Christology? In *Sacramentum caritatis* we find a greater concentration upon the presence and activity of the Holy Spirit in Jesus the Christ. There Benedict XVI states:

> The Paraclete, Christ's first gift to those who believe, already at work in Creation (cf. Gen 1:2), is fully present in the life of the incarnate Word: Jesus Christ is conceived by the power of the Holy Spirit (cf. Matt 1:18; Luke 1:35); at the beginning of his public mission, on the banks of the Jordan, he sees the Spirit descend upon him in the form of a dove (cf. Matt 3:16 and parallels); he acts, speaks and rejoices in the Spirit (cf. Luke 10:21), and he can offer himself in the Spirit (cf. Heb 9:14). In the so-called "farewell discourse" reported by John, Jesus clearly relates the gift of his life in the paschal mystery to the gift of the Spirit to his own (cf. John 16:7). Once risen, bearing in his flesh the signs of the passion, he can pour out the Spirit upon them (cf. John 20:22), making them sharers in his own mission (cf. John 20:21).[22]

Benedict XVI goes on to recount what the outpoured Spirit will accomplish in the disciples (cf. John 14:26; 15:26; 16:13 and Acts 2:1–4). He emphasizes that it is through the working of the Spirit that Christ himself continues to be present and active in the church, and that this presence and activity begins from the Eucharist.[23]

When we go to *Jesus of Nazareth* we find a greater emphasis on the Holy Spirit than was to be found in *Introduction to Christianity* and *The God of Jesus Christ*. In the application of the personal thesis, how Jesus draws us into his own prayer, Ratzinger addresses the role of the Holy Spirit in so drawing us. We pray "in the Spirit." We enter into communion with the Father, with the Son and Holy Spirit. True worshippers adore the Father "in spirit and truth" (John 4:23). In prayer we become one with God through an encounter with the Son and the Holy Spirit.[24] We pray with Christ through the Holy Spirit to the Father.[25] The gift we ask of the Father is the gift of the

---

22. *SC*, no. 12.
23. Ibid.
24. *Jesus I*, 132.
25. Ibid., 135.

Holy Spirit (cf. Matt 7:9; Luke 11:13). In receiving this gift we receive God himself, dwelling in us.[26]

However, when we come to the application of the ecclesial thesis there is still a gap. In looking at the Spirit's role in the genesis of the church, Ratzinger refers to the gift of the Spirit from the resurrected Lord (cf. John 20:22) and the outpouring of the Spirit at Pentecost (cf. Acts 2:1–4), but not to the water that flows from the pierced heart of Jesus. Although he recognizes that it is from the blood and water flowing from that pierced heart that the church is created, he sees in this double outpouring an image of the Eucharist and Baptism, but he does not mention the gift of the Holy Spirit per se.[27] Although in *Behold the Pierced One* Ratzinger follows the Ephesian reading of John 7:37–39, whereby the source of the Spirit is the heart of Jesus, in *Deus caritas est* he follows the Alexandrian reading whereby it is

26. Ibid., 136–37.

27. *Jesus II*, 226; and *SC*, no. 14. This is not to say that Ratzinger makes no connection between the Cross and the gift of the Holy Spirit. In a meditation on Pentecost he states that the Holy Spirit creates in man an understanding of God, the world, one's fellowman and one's self "because he is the Love that flows from the Cross, from the self-renunciation of Jesus Christ" (Ratzinger, "Mind, Spirit, and Love," 319). Furthermore, commenting on John 14:15–16 in his Pentecost Homily of 2010, Benedict XVI says: "Here the praying heart of Jesus is revealed to us, his filial and fraternal heart. This prayer reaches its apex and its fulfilment on the Cross, where Christ's invocation is one with the total gift that he makes of himself, and thus his prayer becomes, so to speak, the very seal of his self-gift out of love of the Father and humanity. Invocation and donation of the Holy Spirit meet, they permeate each other, they become one reality. 'And I will pray the Father, and he will give you another Counsellor, to be with you for ever.' In reality, Jesus' prayers, that of the Last Supper and that on the Cross, form a single prayer that continues even in Heaven, where Christ sits at the right hand of the Father. Jesus, in fact, always lives his intercessional priesthood on behalf of the people of God and humanity and so prays for all of us, asking the Father for the gift of the Holy Spirit" (Benedict XVI, "Homily of His Holiness Benedict XVI"). Cf. how the piercing of the side of Jesus is treated in Congar, *The Mystery of the Church*, 112–19 and 152–56. In John 19:34 "water" does not just symbolize baptism, through which we receive the gift of the Holy Spirit (cf. St. John Chrysostom, *Catechesis* 3, 13–19: *Sources Chrétiennes* 50, 174–77), but the gift of the Holy Spirit himself. Cf. also St. Ambrose, *Expositio Evangelii secundum Lucam* 2, 85–89: (*PL* 15, 1666–668). As George Montague writes: "Whatever symbolism lies behind the blood, there can be little doubt that John sees in the water coming from Jesus' side a fulfillment of the prophecy of [John] 7:37–39. As Moses stuck the rock in the desert and water flowed (Num 20:11), so Jesus' side is pierced and from it flows water, symbol of the Spirit. It is very interesting to note that according to Jewish midrash on Exod 4:9 (*Midrash Rab.* 3:13) Moses struck the rock twice, first bringing out blood and then water." See Montague, *The Holy Spirit*, 349. In *HA*, 213, Pius XII also refers to the water flowing from the rock struck by Moses as a prophetic sign of the living water that shall flow from within Jesus. For a very thoughtful account of how the water and blood flowing from the side of Jesus symbolize both the expiatory and life-giving effect of the death of Jesus, with the gift of life being the gift of the "life-giving" Spirit, see Heer, "The Soteriological Significance," 38–39.

from the hearts of believers that the Spirit flows.[28] When looking at the role played by the Holy Spirit in the eucharistic celebration, Ratzinger focuses upon the role of the Spirit through the epiclesis in transubstantiation, and in gathering the faithful into one Body, but not on the outpouring of the Holy Spirit into the hearts of believers from the heart of Jesus.[29]

Furthermore, in his meditations upon Jesus as the source of the Holy Spirit for believers, Ratzinger neglects to mention the other two Johannine references to this, the conversation of Jesus with the Samaritan women at the well (cf. John 4:10–24), where he gives the promise of a gift of "living water," and within the context of the blood and water flowing from the side of Jesus (cf. John 19:28–37), the remark that, upon dying, Jesus "gave over the spirit" (John 19:30).[30] Taken together, to which reading of John 7:37–39 does this triptych point, the Ephesian or the Alexandrian? To the women at the well, Jesus indicates that *he* will give the living water, which will *then* become a spring of living water within the recipient (cf. John 4:13–14). John 19:28–37 indicates that Jesus is the source of the Holy Spirit, the living water. In John 7:37–39 Jesus invites the thirsty one to come to him and drink, indicating that Scripture promises a flow of living water from within either himself or the believer. As it happens, there is no passage in the Old Testament which promises this in so many words. This would mean that Jesus is referring to the substance of the Scriptural teaching on the gift of living water. There are many particular passages to which one could refer in order to find the substance of this teaching. They are—the two instances when Moses brings forth water from a rock by striking it (cf. Exod 17:6 and Num 20:11–12), the promise of drawing water joyfully from the wells of salvation (cf. Isa 12:3), that of water gushing forth in the wilderness (cf. Isa 35:6), the promise of water poured out on the thirsty land and the Spirit of God on the peoples' offspring (cf. Isa 44:3), the invitation to come and drink at the waters (cf. Isa 55:1), the statement that the people will be like a well-watered garden, like a spring that never fails (cf. Isa 58:11), the prophecy of the water flowing east from under the threshold of the temple (cf. Ezek 47:1), and of water flowing out from Jerusalem (cf. Zech 14:8). Whilst all of these texts could have contributed to the teaching of Jesus about the "living water," the

---

28. *Behold*, 48–49; and *DCE*, no. 19. Ratzinger also follows the Alexandrian reading of John 7:37–39 in Ratzinger, "Geist und Freiheit—Freiheit und Bindung," 63. In *Haurietis aquas*, Pius XII follows the Ephesian reading. The fountain of living water rises from within Jesus. See *HA*, 213.

29. *SC*, no. 13.

30. On the question of the identification of the living water with the Holy Spirit, see Montague, *The Holy Spirit*, 344–46. On the question of what is meant by Jesus handing over his spirit, see Heer, "The Soteriological Significance," 37–38.

most explicit antecedent would seem to be Isaiah 58:11b: "And you shall be like a watered garden, like a spring of water, whose waters fail not." Taken with the fact that the metaphor of living water welling up within a person is to be found in Jewish writings, the evidence seems to point towards the Alexandrian reading.[31] Taking the Johannine triptych together, the full picture seems to be that the ultimate source of the "spring of water that wells up to eternal life" (John 4:14) is the glorified humanity of Jesus. The fountain of the Spirit which flows from the heart of Jesus to the believer in turn becomes a fountain of the Spirit within the believer.[32]

When we come to the portrait of Jesus himself in *Jesus of Nazareth* through the application of the filial and soteriological theses, we find that his nature as the Christ, as the Messiah anointed by the Father with the Holy Spirit, is still somewhat under-emphasized. Beginning with the Epiphany of Jesus as the Christ following his baptism, Ratzinger sees in the descent of the Holy Spirit an affirmation of the communion between Jesus' will and the will of the Father, a proclamation of Jesus' identify and mission, and a revelation of the Trinity. Yet, he makes no reference to that descent of the Holy Spirit from the Father as an *experience* by Jesus of his sonship—"You are my beloved Son; with you I am well pleased" (Mark 1:11 and Luke 3:22). This is a surprising omission, given the importance of sonship in Ratzinger's Christology.[33]

When looking at the temptations of Jesus, although Ratzinger notes that the Spirit led Jesus into the desert to be tempted by the devil, and thus "descend" into the uttermost depths of the human struggle against sin, the struggle to remain faithful to his mission, he does not embark upon any conjecture as to what the role of the Holy Spirit might be in that struggle to fulfill his mission as the Christ, that is to say, the relationship between the Holy Spirit and the human will of Jesus.[34] Finally, in speaking of the "Torah of the Messiah," the "law of Christ" (cf. Gal 6:2), the law which Christ "spiritualizes," the law which "calls us to freedom, which is freedom from the slavery of sin, freedom in the service of good, allowing oneself to be led by the Spirit of God," Ratzinger makes no mention of the role of the Holy Spirit in "spiritualizing" Jesus himself, allowing his humanity to be free to serve the good.[35]

---

31. Cf. Bloomfield, "Η ΚΑΙΝΗ ΔΙΑΘΗΚΗ," in *Greek New Testament*, 373.
32. For John, Jesus' glorification begins with the Cross (cf. John 12:23-24).
33. *Jesus I*, 25.
34. Ibid., 25-28.
35. Ibid., 99-101.

Following his reflections on the Temptations in the desert, Ratzinger makes no mention of Jesus returning "full of the Holy Spirit" (Luke 4:1). Nor in his account in *Jesus of Nazareth* of Jesus' great *Jubelruf* at the return of the seventy is there any allusion to the claim that Jesus "rejoiced in the Holy Spirit" (Luke 10:21). Although Ratzinger does note the Lucan reference to the "finger of God" as a reference to the Holy Spirit, recognizing the action of the Holy Spirit in the thaumaturgic acts of Jesus, he largely passes over the Lucan emphasis on the action of the Spirit in the life of Jesus (cf. Luke 11:20).[36]

We have seen how Ratzinger views the Transfiguration as the central panel in a triptych, flanked by the Baptism of Jesus and his agony on the Mount of Olives. Unlike in the Baptism account, the Holy Spirit receives no mention in his account of the Transfiguration. This is despite the fact that in Luke's account the word which indicates the overshadowing of the cloud is the same as that used for the overshadowing of Mary by the Holy Spirit (cf. Luke 1:35 and 9:34), as well as the longstanding theological identification of the cloud as a manifestation of the Holy Spirit.[37] Even though Ratzinger sees a connection between the Transfiguration and the Feast of Tabernacles, with the manifestation of Jesus' glory as a sign that the messianic times have arrived, he does not acknowledge the action of the Holy Spirit in making those times present.[38]

The pneumatological lacuna in Ratzinger's spiritual Christology does not invalidate that Christology. From what we have seen, this lacuna could more accurately be called a weakness in the pneumatological dimension of his spiritual Christology rather than a complete absence of the Holy Spirit from it. As a part of the concluding chapter an attempt will be made to give a brief sketch of how this weakness might be remedied.

Conclusion to Ratzinger's *Theoria*

In examining how Ratzinger's seven christological theses, theology of the heart, and eucharistic spirituality are put into practice, there is a danger that, in subjecting the various parts to scrutiny, we lose sight of the goal of his spiritual Christology as a whole. That goal is eucharistic. Although the

---

36. Ibid., 60.

37. For example, see *ST* III, q. 45, 4, ad 2; and *CCC*, no. 555. The *Catechism*, in identifying cloud and light as symbols of the Holy Spirit, raises the possibility that the cloud which took Jesus out of the sight of the disciples at the Ascension is not only a symbol of divine glory, but also of the Holy Spirit (cf. nos. 659 and 697).

38. *Jesus I*, 306 and 315.

Eucharist does not play an especially obvious role in most of *Jesus of Nazareth*, it has a place in the ecclesial, hermeneutical and soteriological theses, and it does become prominent in the Epilogue to the Holy Week volume, which we should see as the conclusion to all three volumes. However, we must look to *Deus caritas est* and *Sacramentum caritatis* for a fuller flowering of Ratzinger's eucharistic spirituality.

The goal of Ratzinger's spiritual Christology is a practical one, to participate in Christ, to enter into communion with God through Christ. The place of communion *par excellence* is the celebration of the Eucharist. It is the Eucharist which brings together Christ and the church. The pierced heart of Jesus is the "cause" of the Eucharist, it is the celebration of the Eucharist which "causes" the church, and that communion of love which is the church, the Body of Christ, is meant to include the "yes" of our will to the will of Jesus, uniting our intellect, will and sentiments, in an all-embracing act of love.

Evaluation

8

Assessing Ratzinger's Christological Theses

Prayer as an Integrating Principle of Ratzinger's Spiritual Christology

The burden of the previous section has been that *Jesus of Nazareth* is an exercise in *theoria*, in beholding. However, Ratzinger's *theoria* is more than Aristotle's.[1] It is not just an activity of the mind, but of the heart. It is a "heart to heart" beholding—the believer's heart beholding the pierced heart of Jesus, who, since he is the one nearest to the Father's heart, reveals that heart in his own. Nor is it an isolated beholding. It is a personal beholding in a corporate personality, the Body of Christ. "It is no longer I who live, but Christ who lives in me" (Gal 2:20). Christ lives in the believer, and the believer lives in Christ. Christ prays in the believer, and the believer prays in Christ. Nor is it a contemplative beholding alone. It is a "lived Christology," not just a "prayed Christology." Christ lives in the believer, and in his Body, and continues to love through them.[2]

This personal and corporate beholding, leading to a lived Christology, leads in turn to knowledge and love of the one beheld. An integrating

---

1. See Aristotle, *Nicomachean Ethics*, 431–34, where Aristotle presents *theoria* as an entirely self-contained activity of the mind.

2. Cf. Augustine, *Expositions on the Book of Psalms*, 86, 1, 409–10. Cf. also with Ratzinger, *Feast of Faith*, 29, where in expounding upon how believers find their true identity in Christ, he states: "In finding my own identity by being identified with Christ, I am made one with him; my true self is restored to me, I know that I am accepted, and this enables me to give myself back to him. On this basis the theology of the Middle Ages proposed that the aim of prayer (and the movement of being in which it consists) was that, through it, man should become an *anima ecclesiastica*—a personal embodiment of the Church."

principle of this beholding is communion with God the Father through prayer. This is a communion with the prayer of Jesus. The seven theses are meant to contribute to this integration. They cover the prayer of Jesus' entire life, including the prayer of his Passion, death and Resurrection, the prayer of the believer, the prayer of the church, dogma as the conceptualization of what the prayer of Jesus reveals, the role of the will of Jesus in his prayer, and the role of prayer for the theologian. Prayer is an integrating principle of the seven theses. It remains to be seen how effectively Ratzinger applies this integrating principle, and how sufficient it is for a spiritual Christology.

The Personal and Ecclesial Theses

The seven theses propose an exercise in *theoria*. In assessing the validity of the theses, and Ratzinger's skill and consistency in applying them, it is logical to assess the personal, ecclesial and hermeneutical theses first, since they pertain to the *interpretation* of the other four theses. Furthermore, since a Christian participates in Christ simultaneously as an individual and as a member of his Body, and the personal and ecclesial theses together constitute the first principle of Ratzinger's spiritual Christology, although one could examine them separately, here they will be examined together.

Descending and Ascending with Jesus

The infancy of the personal and ecclesial theses can be seen in Ratzinger's earlier Christology. In that Christology, the Alpha is faith. The birthplace of faith in Jesus is identified as the Cross. Ratzinger moves back from the Creed to the Cross, and his knowledge of the Cross comes from the "tradition," the oral and written testimony of the Apostles. Yet we also find the beginnings of the personal thesis—we come to know God as our *Abba* through participation in the prayer of Jesus. In Ratzinger's spiritual Christology it is brought out even more forcefully and explicitly that we come to know the Father, we come into communion with the Father, not just through a personal faith in Jesus but by participation in his prayer. We also find in this spiritual Christology a re-casting of the Omega of Ratzinger's earlier Christology. Our *theosis* takes place through participation in the prayer of Jesus. The humanity of Jesus himself is divinized through his dialogue with the Father, and the divinization of our humanity takes place through participation in this dialogue.

We have seen in *The God of Jesus Christ* how Ratzinger approached the nature of the Incarnation via the mysteries of Jesus' life, working on the premise that it is the totality of a person's life which reveals who that person is. There he asserted that this approach to the mysteries, first and foremost, must be one of contemplative prayer. Furthermore, he also indicated that our divinization comes through sharing in the obedience of Jesus the Son in handing himself back to the Father, his "obedience unto death" (Phil 2:8). When our "body," our humanity, has entered into this prayer of Jesus, and this prayer has taken flesh in our daily lives, we become the "body of Christ." We "descend" and "ascend" with him in his obedience to his Father. The ascent to God takes place precisely in the descent of loving obedience. Communion with Jesus in his ascent and descent means communion in God's will. Thus: "Communion with him is filial communion with the Father . . . It is entry into the family of those who call God Father and who can do so because they belong to a 'we'—formed of those who are united with Jesus and, by listening to him, united with the will of the Father."[3] Ultimately, it is in the Cross that God descends and reveals his true divinity. Our ascension to God can only happen when we follow him on his descending path. When Jesus prays, and this includes the "prayer" of the Cross, his whole humanity is taken up into communion with the Father. This is why he who sees Jesus sees the Father (cf. John 14:9). As Ratzinger says:

> We have said that in Jesus' filial communion with the Father, his human soul is also taken up into the act of praying. He who sees Jesus sees the Father (cf. John: 14:9). The disciple who walks with Jesus is thus caught up with him into communion with God. And that is what redemption means: this stepping beyond the limits of human nature, which had been there as a possibility and an expectation in man, God's image and likeness, since the moment of creation.[4]

An essential element of this descent and ascent with Jesus, this stepping beyond the limits of human nature, is our integration into a new corporate personality. We have seen Ratzinger emphasize the prayerful element of this incorporation, how Christ prays as both head and body, uniting us with him when he prays as head, and uniting himself with us, with "all of our struggles, our voices, our anguish, and our hope."[5] This union is made manifest in Jesus' prayer on the Cross, and encompasses past, present, and future. Because he continues to pray in the church, Jesus continues to suffer in the church, and the church to suffer in Jesus. As Ratzinger asserts:

3. *Jesus I*, 117.
4. Ibid., 7–8.
5. *Jesus II*, 215.

> Jesus' agony, his struggle against death, continues until the end of the world . . . We could also put it the other way around: at this hour, Jesus took upon himself the betrayal of all ages, the pain caused by betrayal in every era, and he endured the anguish of history to the bitter end.[6]

However, there is an aspect of Ratzinger's understanding of the descent and ascent of Jesus which is addressed in his earlier Christology but not in his spiritual Christology—the Incarnation as prayer. We have seen how, in his earlier Christology, Ratzinger sought to reconcile the theology of the Incarnation with the theology of the Cross. One of the ways in which he attempted to do this was by looking at the Incarnation of Jesus as an act of prayer. This prayer is the "body," the humanity, of Jesus. Ratzinger characterized the text in Hebrews, "Sacrifices and offerings you have not desired, but a body you prepared for me; in burnt offering and sin offerings you have taken no pleasure. Then I said, 'Lo, I have come to do your will, O God'" (10:5–7), as presenting Jesus' descent as an act of prayer, as "a voluntary and verbal event," as a real "act."[7] In the Incarnation, not just in the Cross and Resurrection, Jesus exceeds the limits of humanity. When we participate in his descent and ascent we become fully human by exceeding the limits of *our* humanity. We become truly human by becoming more than human, by being divinized.

The Nature of Theology as Personal and Ecclesial Participation in the Prayer of Jesus

In 1979, Ratzinger published a talk entitled "*Was ist Theologie?*"[8] There he drew attention to the ancient Greek use of the word θεολογία (*theologia*) to designate, not a human science, but the divine discourse itself. For this reason the Greeks designated as "theologians" only those who could be regarded as instruments of the divine discourse. So, Aristotle drew a distinction between θεολογία and θεολογιχή (*theologiche*)—between theology and the study of theology, between the divine discourse and human effort to understand it. Pseudo-Dionysius used the word "theology" to designate Sacred Scripture—the discourse of God rendered into human words.[9] According to him, Scripture alone is theology in the fullest sense of the word. The writers of Sacred Scripture are *theologoi*, "through whom God as subject, as the word

---

6. Ibid., 68.
7. *Jesus Christ*, 66.
8. Ratzinger, "Was ist Theologie?," 121–28.
9. Ratzinger, *Principles of Catholic Theology*, 320–21.

that speaks itself, enters into history."[10] Thus the Bible becomes the model of all theology, and the biblical writers the norm for the theologian. Because theology is ultimately the word which God speaks to us, it can never be a merely "positive" science, but rather a "spiritual" one. Even when studied in the academe, theology must be studied "in the context of a corresponding spiritual praxis and of a readiness to understand it, [and] at the same time, as a requirement that must be lived . . . just as we cannot learn to swim without water, so we cannot learn theology without the spiritual praxis in which it lives."[11] It must include "the necessary self-transcendence of contemplation into the practice of the faith."[12] If theology is a spiritual science, if it requires a spiritual praxis, then what is the significance of a spiritual Christology for it? The answer is this—Ratzinger's spiritual Christology *is* a spiritual praxis. Or, in other words, it is a lived Christology. One could say that the starting point for theology is being a "Christologian." The theologian, that is to say, the one who prays, must begin by living the personal thesis—contemplating the Pierced One, and then bearing the fruits of this contemplation. What Ratzinger has said of Christology would be applied by him to theology as a whole—it is born of prayer or not at all. This is reminiscent of Evagrius' definition of a theologian: "If you are a theologian, you will pray. And if you pray truly, you are a theologian."[13] For Ratzinger, the starting point for Christology, indeed, for all theology, is a lived Christology. Anyone who prays truly, who allows Christ to live in them, is a theologian. Every Christian is called to be a theologian in this fundamental sense. So, for Ratzinger, the phrase "academic theologian" would not be a tautology.

For Ratzinger, theology presupposes faith. This faith regards the truth of our being itself and "what we must do to attain the rectitude of our being," the truth of what we are and how we must live. This truth "becomes accessible only in the act of faith and that faith is the gift of a new beginning for thought which it is not in our power either to set in existence or to replace . . . once accepted, this truth illuminates our whole being and, therefore, also appeals to our intellect and even solicits our understanding."[14]

---

10. Ibid., 321.

11. Ibid., 322.

12. Ibid., 321.

13. Evagrius Ponticus, *De oratione*, 61. Ratzinger expresses the same thought in his commentary on *GS*, no. 22, when, in the article's final focus on adoration ("Christ has risen again, destroying death by his death, and has given life abundantly to us so that, becoming sons in the Son, we may cry out in the Spirit: Abba, Father!"), he says that the "culmination in adoration [is] theo-logy in the strictest sense of the term" ("Church and Man's," 163).

14. Ratzinger, *The Nature and Mission of Theology*, 56.

According to Ratzinger, both faith and rational reflection are integral to theology. However, theology is a new beginning of thought which is not self-generated but has its origin in the encounter with the Word. The act of accepting this new beginning is called "conversion," a conscious affirmation of this new beginning which turns the "I" to the "no-longer-I." As Ratzinger states:

> It is immediately obvious that the opportunity for creative theology increases the more that faith becomes real, personal experience; the more that conversion acquires interior certainty thanks to a painful process of transformation; the more that it is recognized as the indispensable means of penetrating into the truth of one's own being.[15]

For Ratzinger, this connection between faith and theology is not "some sort of sentimental or pietistic twaddle but is a direct consequence of the logic of the thing."[16]

This conversion has an ongoing character, and reverses the direction of normal knowing. Ratzinger states that it is:

> an act of obedience toward a reality which precedes me and which does not originate from me. Moreover, this obedience continues, inasmuch as knowledge never transforms this reality into a constituent element of my own thought, but rather the converse is true: it is I who make myself over to it, while it always remains above me. For Christians, this prior reality is not an "it" but ... a "thou." It is Christ, the Word made flesh. He is the new beginning of our thought. He is the new "I" which bursts open the limits of subjectivity and the boundaries dividing subject from object, thus enabling me to say: "It is no longer I who live."[17]

What is the relationship between this kind of theology and "academic" theology? In two successive general audiences in 2009, Benedict XVI spoke about two types of theology, which he called "monastic" and "scholastic."[18] He also called them, respectively, the "theology of the heart" and the "theology of reason."[19] According to him, during the twelfth century Latin theology flourished in two milieus—monasteries and *scholae*—which followed two different theological models. The monks practiced what he calls

---

15. Ibid., 57.
16. Ibid.
17. Ibid., 58–59.
18. Benedict XVI, "Monastic Theology and Scholastic Theology."
19. Benedict XVI, "Two Theological Models."

a biblical theology, which entailed the devout listening to, and reading of Sacred Scripture, that is to say, *lectio divina*, a prayed reading of the Bible. It was a biblical theology practiced in docility to the Holy Spirit. The aim was to read Sacred Scripture in the same spirit in which it was written. This praxis demanded a purification of the heart if it was to reach its ultimate goal, an encounter with the Lord, knowing and loving God. By it: "Theology thus becomes meditation, prayer, a song of praise and impels us to sincere conversion."[20]

On the other hand, according to Benedict XVI, the aim of scholastic theology was "to train professionals of culture in a period in which the appreciation of knowledge was constantly growing." Central to the scholastic method was the *quaestio*, the questions that arise from Scripture and Tradition and give rise to debate. Scholastic theology sought to achieve a synthesis between arguments based on authority and those based on reason "in order to reach a deeper understanding of the Word of God." The aim of this kind of theology was to add "the dimension of reason to the word of God and thus [create] a faith that is deeper, more personal, hence also more concrete in the person's life."[21] The creation of syntheses led to the birth of "systematic" theology. The scholastic method sought to present the unity and harmony of Christian revelation through the use of human reason.

In looking at these two methods, Benedict XVI does not play one off against the other. Scholastic theology enables us to give an account of the hope that is in us (cf. 1 Pet 3:15). He agrees with St. John Paul II, that: "Faith and reason are like two wings on which the human reason rises to the contemplation of the truth." However, the essential insight of monastic theology concerns the ultimate goal of all theology. Both faith and reason must be "inspired by the search for intimate union with God."[22] Taking St. Bernard and Abelard as representatives of the two methods of theology, Benedict XVI states that, in pursuing the goal of *fides quaerens intellectum*, St. Bernard put the emphasis on faith, while Abelard put it on reason. Thus:

> For Bernard faith itself is endowed with deep certitude based on the testimony of Scripture and on the teaching of the Church Fathers. Faith, furthermore, is reinforced by the witness of the Saints and by the inspiration of the Holy Spirit in the individual believer's soul. In cases of doubt and ambiguity, faith is

---

20. Benedict XVI, "Monastic Theology and Scholastic Theology." Cf. *VD*, no. 86.
21. Ibid.
22. Ibid. The quotation is from the beginning of *Fides et ratio*.

> protected and illumined by the exercise of the Magisterium of the Church.[23]

The dangers which Bernard saw in Abelard's approach were an arrogant intellectualism, a relativization of truth, and even a questioning of the truths of the faith. He saw the danger of a lack of intellectual humility wherein the theologian could come to believe in the ability of reason to "grasp" the mystery of God. Monastic, that is to say, contemplative theology, must form the basis of scholastic theology. As Benedict XVI says:

> [In] the theological field there must be a balance between what we may call the architectural principles given to us by Revelation, which therefore always retain their priority importance, and the principles for interpretation suggested by philosophy, that is, by reason, which have an important but exclusively practical role.[24]

For Benedict XVI, in theology, humble love must direct the intellect. Thus:

> When love enlivens the prayerful dimension of theology, knowledge, acquired by reason, is broadened. Truth is sought with humility, received with wonder and gratitude: in a word, knowledge only grows if one loves truth. Love becomes intelligence and authentic theology wisdom of heart, which directs and sustains the faith and life of believers.[25]

However, theology is not just born from the individual believer—it is also born from the church. Here, the ecclesial thesis must be lived. In *The Nature and Mission of Theology*, Ratzinger has a section entitled: "The New Subject as the Precondition and Foundation of All Theology." Therein, he goes to the example of St. Paul in the *apologia pro vita sua* to be found in his Letter to the Galatians. There he sees St. Paul describing "the distinctive element of Christianity as a personal experience which revolutionizes everything and at the same time is as an objective reality: 'It is no longer I who live, but Christ who lives in me'" (Gal 2:20)."[26] This conversion is a "death-event." That which in *Jesus of Nazareth* was viewed as an individual renewal of the mind and purification of the heart is here seen as an ecclesial event.[27] It is

---

23. Benedict XVI, "Two Theological Models." In this talk Benedict makes the point that it was Abelard "who introduced the term 'theology' in the sense in which we understand it today."

24. Ibid.

25. Benedict XVI, "Monastic and Scholastic Theology."

26. Ratzinger, *The Nature and Mission of Theology*, 50.

27. Cf. *Jesus I*, 95.

the exchange of the old subject for a new subject. The autonomous "I" now stands within a greater "I," and in doing so, receives itself anew. Those who have been baptized into this new subject, Christ, have put on Christ (cf. Gal 3:27–29). The Christian has become "a new, singular subject together with Christ."[28] This exchange of subjects is not something that one can bring about by oneself. Rather:

> The exchange of subjects includes a passive element, which Paul rightly characterizes as death, in the sense of receiving a share in the event of the Cross. It can come to someone only from the outside, from another person. Because Christian conversion throws open the frontier between the "I" and the "not-I," it can be bestowed upon one only by the "not-I" and can never be achieved solely in the interiority of one's personal decision. It has a sacramental structure. The "I no longer live" does not describe a private mystical experience but rather defines the essence of baptism. What takes place is a sacramental event, an event involving the Church. The passive side of becoming a Christian calls for the acting Church, in which the unity of believers manifests itself in its bodily and historical dimensions.[29]

However, the new subject is not simply the church by itself. It is "in no wise a separate subject, endowed with its own subsistence. The new subject is much rather 'Christ' himself, and the church is nothing more but the space of this new unitary subject."[30]

According to Ratzinger, in the Gospel of John, this new subject is the place of right understanding. Rather than coming to know Jesus through retracing his history, the Christian comes to know him through being in him. John "affirms that only the Paraclete, the Spirit, who is the Spirit both of the Father and the Son himself, can make Jesus known. Someone can be understood only through himself."[31] The Holy Spirit works to bring the church to understanding. How does the Spirit work?

> First of all, by bestowing remembrance, a remembrance in which the particular is joined to the whole, which in turn endows the particular, which hitherto had not been understood, with its genuine meaning. A further characteristic of the Spirit is listening: he does not speak in his own name, he listens and teaches how to listen. In other words, he does not add anything

28. Ratzinger, *The Nature and Mission of Theology*, 52.
29. Ibid.
30. Ibid., 54.
31. Ibid., 54–55.

> but rather acts as a guide into the heart of the Word, which becomes light in the act of listening. The Spirit does not employ violence; his method is simply to allow what stands before me as an other to express itself and enter into me. This already entails an additional element: the Spirit effects a space of listening and remembering, a "we," which in the Johannine writings defines the Church as the locus of knowledge. Understanding can only take place within this "we" constituted by participation in the origin. Indeed, all comprehension depends on participation.[32]

This reality does not lead into a private relationship with Jesus. It has a "we character." Only when we enter this "we" can our obedience to the truth become concrete. God must become "concrete" if we are to avoid making him a projection of our own selves. God has become concrete, has become flesh, in Jesus Christ. And Christ remains concrete, in the flesh, in the church. Therefore, rather than following an autonomous "search for God" wherein the individual need only obey his or her own thoughts and judgments about God: "Obedience to the Church is the concreteness of our obedience. The Church is the new and greater subject in which past and present, subject and object come into contact. The Church is our contemporaneity with Christ: there is no other."[33] Consequently:

> [The] Church is not an authority which remains foreign to the scientific character of theology but rather is the ground of theology's existence and the condition which makes it possible . . . This subject [the church] is by nature greater than any individual person, indeed, than any single generation. Faith is always a participation in a totality and, precisely in this way, conducts the believer to a new breadth of freedom.[34]

Because the church is the inner foundation and wellspring of theology, it must be competent to pass judgment on the work of individual theologians. This is a part of her pastoral office, wherein she preaches to the faithful, amongst whose number academic theologians are included. For all are believers. There is no special caste of theologians. Rather, *all* can be theologians. As Ratzinger says: "Through not all men can be professional theologians, access to the great fundamental cognitions is open to everyone."[35] The proclamation of the faith teaches bindingly for all, including theologians working in the academe. It is the normative criterion for theology.

32. Ibid., 55.
33. Ibid., 60.
34. Ibid., 61.
35. Ibid., 63.

Indeed, it is the object of theological reflection. Proclamation is the measure of theology, not vice versa. Another way of putting this is that there is, in fact, only one Theologian, one Doctor, one *Magister*. "You have one Teacher, the Christ" (Matt 23:10). One is a theologian only to the extent that one theologizes in Christ, and Christ theologizes in one. It is no longer I who theologize, but Christ who theologizes in me.

What Ratzinger says about the nature of theology could be taken further. If the Word of God is theology in the original, most fundamental sense, then Jesus the Christ is theology incarnate. And if the church is the Body of Christ, the new subject who makes Christ contemporary, then the church is the body of theology. It is the place where theology is made present in the present. To participate in the prayer, life and mission of the church is to participate in theology.

The Hermeneutical Thesis

A Theological Hermeneutic

The discussion above of Ratzinger's understanding of theology is necessary if one is to understand his hermeneutical thesis. To address what is meant by a theological hermeneutic it was necessary to determine first what Ratzinger means by "theological." We have seen Ratzinger's hermeneutic variously defined as being a "hermeneutic of faith," a "christological hermeneutic," a "theological hermeneutic," and an "ecclesial hermeneutic." As Root has stated, Ratzinger holds that the historical-critical method must not be abandoned, but taken up into a theological method.[36] However, we have seen that, for Ratzinger, theology has a more radical meaning than faith seeking understanding through concepts. Rather, theology beings with faith seeking understanding through personal and ecclesial participation in the prayer of Jesus.[37] Theology begins with prayer, and must be lived as well as conceptualized. All that was said above regarding the personal and ecclesial theses form the epistemological basis for the hermeneutical thesis.

---

36. As Hahn so concisely explains in *Covenant and Communion*, 14: "Benedict has articulated a biblical theology that synthesizes modern scientific methods with the theological hermeneutic of spiritual exegesis that began in the New Testament writers and patristic commentators and has continued throughout the Church's tradition."

37. Although commentators such as Rausch, Weinandy and Lincicum identify the starting point of Ratzinger's hermeneutical method as faith, in Ratzinger's spiritual Christology this faith exists within the context of a personal and ecclesial participation in the prayer of Jesus.

True to his "ministry of reconciliation," Ratzinger wishes to see biblical exegesis become a truly theological activity. His method for achieving this goal begins with prayer—not prayer as a laudable adjunct to biblical scholarship, but as its very genesis. In an address commemorating the fortieth anniversary of *Dei Verbum*, Benedict XVI drew attention to the fact that the opening sentence of that dogmatic constitution begins thus: "Hearing the Word of God with reverence and proclaiming it with faith." He noted that the church is a community that listens to and proclaims the Word of God. This practice must be applied by every Christian, since "only those who first listen to the Word can become preachers of it." As a way of facilitating this, he recommends the ancient practice of *lectio divina*, "the diligent reading of Sacred Scripture accompanied by prayer [which] brings about that intimate dialogue in which the person reading hears God who is speaking, and in praying, responds to him with trusting openness of heart (cf. *Dei Verbum*, n. 25)."[38] This is hermeneutics practiced after the manner of the personal thesis.

This practice he especially recommends to those engaged in biblical ministry. A number of commentators, even those who are more critical of Ratzinger's biblical exegesis, have remarked upon the inspiring insights and interpretations that he often brings to this exegesis. For example, Hays characterizes Ratzinger's synthetic theological reading of the canonical New Testament as often subtle and illuminating. It would not be unreasonable to draw the inference that Ratzinger has diligently practiced that which he preaches.

The Hermeneutics of the Saints and Discipleship

Bockmuehl sees Ratzinger presenting St. Francis as an interpreter of Sacred Scripture—as Ratzinger states: "The saints are the true interpreters of Scripture. The meaning of a given passage of the Bible becomes most intelligible in those human beings who have been totally transfixed by it and have lived it out."[39] Bockmuehl understands this to mean that the saints can guide us in the interpretation and living out of the teaching of Sacred Scripture. The praxis of a saint "can be a lived exposition or commentary on their specific encounter with the Jesus of the Sermon on the Mount," a performance which can expound particular biblical texts.[40] However, we need to recall that, for Ratzinger, this "interpretation" is not merely an intellectual exercise, but a

---

38. Benedict XVI, "Address of his Holiness Benedict XVI."
39. *Jesus I*, 78. Quoted in Bockmuehl, 125. Cf. *VD*, nos. 48–49.
40. Bockmuehl, 126.

contemplative and relational one. We have seen in his brief excursus into the life of St. Francis that, before anything else, his spiritual Christology is a *lived* Christology. Francis' interpretation of Sacred Scripture followed upon his contemplation of the Pierced One in the Church of San Damiano, was lived out in his radical embrace of poverty, and was completed in his reception of the stigmata on Mt. Alverna.

Paddison's "hermeneutic of discipleship" expands upon this notion, for saints are first disciples. This hermeneutic is not one of "detached objectivity." One does not bring one's own standard of judgment to the text. Rather than we interpreting the text, the text "interprets" us. We come to know Jesus in the activity of following him and participating in the life of the community which is his Body.

An Ecclesial Hermeneutic

However, this theological hermeneutic is not a private practice. One cannot be a disciple on one's own. The hermeneutic of discipleship must also be an ecclesial hermeneutic. It is carried on by "theologians" who are members of Christ's body. As both Root and Huovinen have pointed out, for Ratzinger, there is an ecclesial dimension to this hermeneutic. This dimension begins with the original Chosen People. Within the Bible there are three subjects which mutually indwell each other—the individual author or group of authors, the people of God, and God himself.[41] The inspiration of the individual biblical authors has an ecclesial dimension. Furthermore, there is a hierarchy amongst these three authors. The biblical author or authors are subject to a deeper author, the people of God, which in turn is subject to the guidance of the Holy Spirit.

How are these three authors to be interpreted? Ratzinger follows the premise of *Dei Verbum*—that Sacred Scripture "must be read and interpreted in the sacred spirit in which it was written."[42] As Sacred Scripture is inspired, its interpretation must also be inspired. As both Huovinen and Farkasfalvy have pointed out, Ratzinger begins his theology of inspiration from "below," with the potential of the human utterance to transcend itself. The *Schläfertexte* are open to expressing and signifying more than what their speakers

---

41. Huovinen, "The Pope and Jesus," 145. Cf. *VD*, nos. 29–30 and 50–55.

42. *DV*, no. 12. Cf. *Jesus I*, xviii. In this instance, the translation of this passage from *DV* in Flannery, "since Sacred Scripture must be read and interpreted with its divine authorship in mind," is not just inadequate, but downright misleading. Again, the Vatican translation is far better. See *The Documents of Vatican II: Vatican Translation*, 83. Cf. also with *VD*, nos. 15–16.

or writers intended. Even on the merely human level, a deeper meaning and significance can be discovered in the words of the individual authors by that living and ongoing community. Therefore, the human words of Sacred Scripture are open to transcendent intervention. We see this process taking place within the Bible—a remembering and retelling of past events, as well as a prophetic reinterpretation of events which looks both back into the past and forward into the future.[43] Both Paddison and Lincicum have drawn attention to Ratzinger's figural reading of Sacred Scripture. Furthermore, according to Ratzinger, the church continues this remembering and retelling. This is hermeneutics practiced after the manner of the ecclesial thesis.

A Hermeneutic of Faith

Ratzinger speaks of a combination of a faith hermeneutic with a historical hermeneutic. In the second volume of *Jesus of Nazareth* he states:

> Naturally, this combination of two quite different types of hermeneutic is an art that needs to be constantly remastered. But it can be achieved, and as a result the great insights of patristic exegesis will be able to yield their fruit once more in a new context . . . I would not presume to claim that this combination of the two hermeneutics is already fully accomplished in my book. But I hope to have taken a significant step in that direction. Fundamentally this is a matter of finally putting into practice the methodological principles formulated for exegesis by the Second Vatican Council (in *Dei Verbum* 12), a task that unfortunately has scarcely been attempted thus far.[44]

What does Ratzinger mean by a faith hermeneutic? *Dei Verbum* speaks of taking into account the analogy of faith when interpreting Sacred Scripture.[45] In *Behold the Pierced One* Ratzinger states that "the inner unity of the books of the New Testament, and that of the two Testaments, can only be seen in the light of faith's interpretation."[46] In the second volume of *Jesus of Nazareth*, Ratzinger explains what he considers to be the *real* hermeneutic of Sacred Scripture. Faith in Jesus "is something more than a word, an idea: it

---

43. Huovinen, "The Pope and Jesus," 144–45; and Farkasfalvy, "*Jesus of Nazareth*," 441. This supposed potential of human utterance to transcend itself is simply accepted by Ratzinger. Whether or not it is so is a question which requires further investigation. Cf. *VD*, nos. 40–41.

44. *Jesus II*, xv. Cf. Wright, "A 'New Synthesis,'" 41–43.

45. *DV*, no. 12.

46. *Behold*, 44. Pages 45–46 expand upon this understanding.

involves entering into communion with Jesus Christ and through him with the Father."[47] This faith is the real foundation of the disciples' communion and the basis of church's unity. It is the "flesh" which knits individual believers into one "body" and perpetuates the Incarnation of the *Logos* until Christ's "full stature" is attained (cf. Eph 4:13).[48]

This faith in Jesus Christ as the one sent by the Father includes mission. The whole identity of Jesus is "being sent." This characteristic identity is extended to include the Holy Spirit (cf. John 14:26, and 15:26). After the Resurrection, Jesus draws the disciples into this mission (cf. John 20:21) in which they are guided by the Holy Spirit (cf. John 16:13). Apostolic succession is the sacramental continuation of this mission, an incorporation into the mission of the Word that existed from the beginning (cf. 1 John 1:1).[49] Ratzinger makes the point that the Greek word for succession (*diadochē*) refers both to structure and to content: "It points to the continuation of the mission in the witnesses; but it also points to the content of their testimony, to the word that is handed down, to which the witness is bound by the sacrament."[50]

With this apostolic succession in the service of mission, the early church discovered two other elements fundamental for her unity—the canon of Sacred Scripture and the rule of faith. This rule encapsulated the essential content of the faith, "which in the early Church's baptismal confessions took on a liturgical form." It is this rule of faith, this creed, which, in Ratzinger's eyes, constitutes "the real 'hermeneutic' of Scripture, the key derived from Scripture itself by which the sacred text can be interpreted according to the Spirit."[51]

We can see that Ratzinger is using the term "faith" in two different, albeit related, senses. There is the personal faith of the believer in which he or she enters into communion with Jesus Christ and, through him, with the Father. This faith is a lived faith, a faith which works: "The term that in the New Testament corresponds to the Old Testament concept of righteousness is *faith*: The man of faith is the 'righteous man' who walks in God's ways (cf. Ps 1; Jer 17:5–8). For faith is walking with Christ, in whom the whole Law is fulfilled; it unites us with the righteousness of Christ himself."[52] This

---

47. *Jesus II*, 97. Cf. *VD*, no. 36.
48. Ibid.
49. Ibid., 98.
50. Ibid., 99.
51. Ibid.
52. *Jesus I*, 89. Cf. Root, "Jesus and the Pope," 157 n. 9. Root maintains that: "Benedict uses faith most often as a comprehensive term for the Christian's total attitude toward God, in line with *Dei Verbum* no. 5 and the Reformation, rather than as the

faith is shared in communion with other believers, and it succeeds through the apostolic successors, who recognize it in the canon of Scripture and encapsulate it in the rule of faith, faith in the second sense. Thus the hermeneutic of faith is also an expression of the personal and ecclesial theses.

Some Over-Confidence in the Historical-Critical Method

We have seen Ratzinger warn practitioners of the historical-critical method that they need to be attentive to their hermeneutical and philosophical presuppositions. What he does not warn about is a need to be attentive to the apparent presuppositions of some about the nature of historical methodology. What can the historical-critical method actually tell us about the historical Jesus? If one applies to it the same rigor that one would apply to the investigation of secular history, the answer is—not very much. In order to establish the reality of a past event with certainty, we need to meet certain criteria. We need to have sufficient independent witnesses, we need to establish their reliability, these witnesses need to agree, and when they do not, we need to make a judgment as to whom we should believe. The further one goes back into the past, the more difficult it becomes to establish historical certainty. History is not a "science" like the natural sciences. One cannot conduct historical experiments in order to test one's hypotheses. When we come to Jesus, our primary sources are the Gospels and the rest of the New Testament, with almost no independent sources which can be used to verify or disprove the data which they provide. Our main independent sources are polemical ones, such as those of Trypho, Celsus, Porphyry and Julian the Apostate, and some of these are provided for us by Christian sources. Even those which are purportedly independent witnesses (Josephus, Tacitus and Suetonius) have been provided for us by Christian scribes.[53] Furthermore, many of them are considerably later than the events which they dispute.

---

epistemic element in the triad faith, hope and love, as is most often the case in Scholastic usage."

53. For example, see Justin Martyr's *Dialogue with Trypho*; and Celsus' *True Account*, parts of which are preserved in Origen's *Contra Celsum*; Josephus, *Antiquities of the Jews*, 18. 3. 3. and 5. 2., and 20. 9. 1., in *The Works of Josephus*, 25–426; Tacitus, *Annals*, 15. 44., in *Great Books of the Western World* 14, 168; Suetonius, "Claudius," 25. 4., in *The Twelve Caesars*, 197. The remains of three books of Julian the Apostate's *Against the Galileans* are to be found in St. Cyril of Alexandria, *Contra Julianum* (PG 76: 503–1058). Only fragments of Porphyry's *Against the Christians* are to be found in the works of early Christian writers such as Eusebius of Caesarea, St. Jerome, Macarius, and others.

In reality, the results of the application of the historical-critical method to the New Testament Gospels in search of the "historical Jesus" are most meager. They leave us in what is close to an agnostic position as regards that figure. One could argue that the "Jesus Seminar" is not rigorous enough in its dismissal of those words and deeds of Jesus which cannot be established with historical certainty. This is not to say that the historical-critical method can be dispensed with. As Benedict XVI himself has said, the methods of historical study are important and indispensable for our understanding of how the biblical texts came to be written and what they meant to their original audiences.[54] Their value lies in giving us a "context" for Jesus, a more general cultural, political or linguistic understanding, not in telling us with certainty who Jesus was, what he did, what he said, and what happened to him.

There are two other points to which practitioners of the historical-method need to pay attention. One is the lamentable habit which many have of first stating a conjecture, then later treating this conjecture as a fact, and proceeding to use this supposed fact as a premise for a theological argument. The other is the inadvertent practice of using the language of probability when discussing these conjectures—terms such as "probably" and "likely" are commonly used. However, history is not a statistical science. One cannot validly use such terms literally in this science. Rather than "probabilities" we have "possibilities." The evidence may "seem" or "appear" to point to a particular conclusion, but such may not be the case. The only two valid categories in history are "certain" and "uncertain." Often these two errors are found together. A historical conjecture is deemed to be "probable," and is later treated as having definitely happened.

Occasionally, Ratzinger falls into both these traps. Regarding the second, in *Jesus of Nazareth* he defines events in the Gospels as "probable" more than a dozen times, although some of the events so defined are of minor importance. Of more consequence is his apparent understanding of historical methodology, whereby he seems to think that historical research can establish that some events are more "probable" than others. For example, in his meditation on the Last Supper, with regard to whether or not Jesus gave his disciples bread and wine as his body and blood, Ratzinger says: "This naturally raises once more the question of the possible and appropriate forms of historical verification. We must be clear about the fact that historical research can at most establish high probability but never final and absolute certainty over every detail." And again: "Today . . . it is becoming

---

54. Benedict XVI, "Homily, Mass of Possession," 3.

increasingly clear that John's chronology is more probable than the Synoptic chronology."[55]

We can see Ratzinger falling into the first trap of treating conjecture as fact in his dealing with the Johannine Question. In response to the denial of the historicity of much of the Johannine text and therefore its reliability as a source for knowledge of the historical Jesus, Ratzinger argues for its historicity. In response to Bultmann's characterization of John's Gospel as rooted in Gnosticism, Ratzinger argues that its theological framework is to be found rather in the Torah and Jewish piety. Such an approach is valid, since one can directly compare John's Gospel with the Torah and Jewish piety presented in the Old Testament. Yet then Ratzinger argues, on the basis of an account by Eusebius of Caesarea about bishop Papias, that a certain Presbyter John *may have been* the leader of a Johannine School at Ephesus, which traced its origins to John the Apostle. Ratzinger *suggests* that Presbyter John was closely connected with the John the Apostle and became the bearer of his heritage. From these *conjectures* Ratzinger *deduces* that the Fourth Gospel is historically credible, since it ultimately goes back to the testimony of an eyewitness which was redacted by one of his followers.[56] In criticizing this reasoning, I am not saying that the Fourth Gospel is not historically credible, or that this is the only way in which Ratzinger seeks to establish its credibility, only that its credibility cannot be established in this way.

Beginning to Break the Hermeneutical Circle

The personal, ecclesial and hermeneutical theses constitute Ratzinger's theological epistemology. With regard to the hermeneutical thesis, in his earlier Christology, Ratzinger proposed that the historical-critical method as sometimes practiced had led to a separation of faith from history. He sought to reconcile the two in the faith of the church, as expressed in the symbol of faith, the Creed. He saw the faith of the Creed as ultimately being grounded in the realization of Jesus as the Christ which was made manifest on the Cross. The difficulty with this proposal is that it involves us in a kind

---

55. *Jesus II*, 104 and 109.

56. Ratzinger is by no means the worst offender when it comes to the problems of attributing probability to events described in the Gospels, or turning conjecture into certainty. For more egregious examples, see Kasper's discussion of the historicity of Jesus' miracles and death in *Jesus the Christ*, 89–91 and 113–21. Hays makes a valid point when he says that Ratzinger owes us "a more careful explanation of how he proposes to reconceive the practice of historical criticism to allow for the historical claims he wants to make" (Hays, "Ratzinger's Johannine Jesus," 114–15).

of circular argument, for our knowledge of Jesus as the Messiah which Ratzinger proposed as the ground of our faith, and hence our starting point for interpreting Sacred Scripture, is itself derived from the testimony of Sacred Scripture, the historicity of which is a question addressed by the historical-critical method.

Does Ratzinger overcome this difficulty in the hermeneutical method which he has developed as a part of his spiritual Christology? In his later hermeneutical method he identifies three elements—apostolic succession, the canon of Sacred Scripture and the liturgical rule of faith. The rule of faith is the real hermeneutic of Sacred Scripture, even though it is derived from Scripture itself. However, this faith is a faith which is professed liturgically, and in the living of a righteous life in communion with Jesus Christ and, through him, with the Father. It is also a faith which is shared in communion with other believers, and it succeeds through the apostolic successors, who recognize it in the canon of Scripture and encapsulate it in the rule of faith.

This hermeneutic of faith is an expression of the personal and ecclesial theses. With regard to these two theses, what begins to remove the *probability*, as Ratzinger puts it, from the ultimate foundation of the dogmas of Nicaea and Chalcedon, are the personal and ecclesial theses. Because we are not limited to only reading about Jesus' prayer relationship with the Father in texts, the historicity of which we cannot establish with certainty, or be taught about it by a church which bases its dogma on those texts, but can participate in the prayer relationship of Jesus and the Father both personally and ecclesially, we can *know* the truth about the relationship between Jesus and the Father. This epistemology begins to break the hermeneutical circle of sacred text and ecclesial dogma. It establishes the priority of a contemplated and lived Christology for an intellectual Christology, and the superiority of an ecclesial one over an individualistic one. It is my conclusion that this later hermeneutical method goes some way towards breaking the hermeneutical circle, but that it still requires further development. It needs to become a "eucharistic" hermeneutic "in the Holy Spirit."

The Four Content Theses

As the three interpretive theses reveal the method of Ratzinger's spiritual Christology, so the remaining four theses reveal its content. However, within the four content theses it is the last, the volitional thesis, which enables us to understand fully the filial, soteriological and dogmatic theses. Indeed, it and the other content theses will also help us to understand the personal, ecclesial and hermeneutical theses. For method and content mutually condition each other. As we grow in a deeper understanding of our faith in Jesus, our method for approaching that faith is refined. Ratzinger notes the importance of the volitional thesis for practice of the other theses when he says that: "The so-called Neo-Chalcedonian theology which is summed up in the Third Council of Constantinople makes an important contribution to a proper grasp of the inner unity of biblical and dogmatic theology, of theology and religious life."[57] Therefore, in what follows, brief critiques will be offered of the filial, soteriological and dogmatic theses, followed by a critique of the volitional thesis and its implications for the other theses.

The Filial Thesis

In the filial thesis Ratzinger moves back beyond Pilate's unknowing proclamation that Jesus is the Christ, back from the word of Jesus to us and work of Jesus for us, to the revelation of his identity in his relationship with the Father, a revelation made in his prayer. He moves the basis of his Christology back from Jesus' preaching (Bultmann) and his message about God the Father (von Harnack) to the revelation of his identity in his relationship with the Father.

In *Introduction to Christianity* Ratzinger saw the Creed as encapsulating the Christian understanding of who and what Jesus really is. The faith professed by the Creed recognizes that in Jesus the Christ, the person is the office and the office is the person. Faith understands that Jesus has put himself into his word and work, that he is his word and work. There is an identity between his message and his person. Faith in Jesus is a "personal faith," faith in a person who is his word. However, Ratzinger saw the need to look back beyond the Creed to what Sacred Scripture says about the Cross. Herein he finds the birthplace of faith in Jesus as the Christ, which is then expressed in the Creed. In the canon of Sacred Scripture the church recognizes its own faith. Therein, Jesus is presented as the Christ.

Ratzinger understood christological dogma to be about a person rather than an idea, a person who is defined as total openness to God and to others by the terms "Word" and "Son." In the latter term, Ratzinger saw Jesus' self-description. He saw the source of this term as the prayer of Jesus himself, since Son is the natural corollary to *Abba*. This self-description reveals a unique nearness to and intimacy with God. Also revealed in the Gospels is a desire on the part of Jesus to incorporate others into this experience. "Son" reveals the total relativity of Jesus' existence, of "being from" and "being for,"

---

57. *Behold*, 37.

and is identical with the designations "word" and "being sent." Ratzinger saw this Son Christology:

> [as] the starting point of all Christology: in the identity of work and being, of deed and person, of the total merging of the person in his work and in the total coincidence of the doing with the person himself, who keeps nothing back for himself but gives himself completely in his work.[58]

Ratzinger stated that the dogmas of Nicaea and Chalcedon "intend to express nothing else than this identity of service and being, in which the whole content of the prayer relationship *Abba*-Son comes to light."[59] For Ratzinger, the terms "*Abba*" and "Son" expressed the distinctive way in which Jesus prayed, his awareness of God, into which he drew his disciples. As an insight into Jesus' experience of prayer it reveals both a nearness to God which is unique to him, but one in which he wishes to incorporate others so that they too can experience the intimacy of knowing God as *Abba*.

In his filial thesis Ratzinger builds upon work already done in his earlier Christology. In the application of this thesis in *Jesus of Nazareth* he expands on his earlier conviction that the church's teaching about the divine sonship of Jesus is based ultimately on the *Abba*-Son dialogue. We have seen how Ratzinger identifies the prayer of Jesus as Luke's central christological category, how Luke grounds the calling of the disciples in the prayer of Jesus, and how the innermost essence of Jesus becomes visible in his prayer on the mount of the Transfiguration. The prayer of Jesus in Mark reveals that when Jesus is present with the Father he is not absent from the disciples, a point which is also emphasized in Luke in his account of Peter's profession of faith. All of these points are taken up in Ratzinger's application of his filial thesis in *Jesus of Nazareth*, to which are added the prayer of Jesus in his Baptism, and the Lukan grounding of the Sermon on the Mount in the prayer of Jesus.

The Soteriological Thesis

Are the roots of Ratzinger's soteriological thesis also to be found in his earlier Christology? Certainly, in *Introduction to Christianity*, Jesus' death on the Cross is presented as an act of worship. It is an act of sacrifice whereby God in Christ reconciles the world to himself (cf. 2 Cor 5:19). The true nature of the sacrifice of Jesus, his "I" completely derived from the "Thou" of the

---

58. *Introduction*, 225–26.
59. Ibid., 227.

Father and lived for the "You" of human beings, is revealed in his sacrificial action which is also prayer. His revelation of the identity of *logos* (truth) and *agape* (love), the truth of human existence, is revealed in his sacrificial prayer. Jesus is presented as the one true priest. His death on the cross was a cosmic liturgy carried out, not in the Temple, but before the face of God, offering not the blood of animals, but himself (cf. Heb 9:11–14).

However, Ratzinger's soteriological thesis takes this insight and develops it in four ways. The first is by fleshing it out much more thoroughly. Not only the prayers of Jesus on the Cross, but his very act of dying on the Cross, is prayer. Earlier, Ratzinger had seen the death of Jesus as an interruption in his dialogue with the Father. Now he sees it as the culmination of that dialogue. Furthermore, Ratzinger gives a new emphasis to the corporate dimension of Jesus' prayers from the Cross and prayer of the Cross, upon which Jesus vicariously intercedes for suffering Israel and for all who suffer.

Second, the soteriological significance of Psalm 22 is more developed. Jesus' prayer on the Cross is more than a personal prayer. Rather, his prayer must be seen as also expressing his identification with the suffering of Israel, and all who suffer.

Third, a fundamental theme in Ratzinger's earlier Christology is that of "descending" and "ascending," to which he refers in *The Spirit of the Liturgy* and elsewhere as *exitus* and *reditus*, going out and returning.[60] In his earlier Christology, besides the obvious Descent into Hell and Ascension into Heaven, this descending and ascending of Jesus the Christ focused upon the Incarnation and the Cross. Jesus descends from Heaven. The Cross is a movement primarily from above to below, God reaching down to us in mercy. Only then is it a movement from below to above, in Jesus' obedient sacrifice of himself to the Father. However, in his soteriological thesis, this understanding of *exitus* and *reditus* is seen in all the actions of Jesus' life. The entering of Jesus into communion with his Father are the inward ascents of his life, while his entry into a communion of life and suffering with us are the descents of his life. This "descending ascent" is revealed throughout his life. It is revealed in his descent into the Jordan. In his Baptism he prefigures his descent into the abyss of death. It is revealed also in his temptations, temptations which accompany him throughout his life, wherein he descends into the perils faced by mankind. Furthermore, it is revealed in all the mountains of prayer which he ascended, and subsequently, descended.

Fourth, the emphasis on the role of the will of Jesus is not just limited to the volitional thesis, which Ratzinger examines most explicitly in Jesus' Agony in the Garden, but is traced out in all the actions of Jesus' life. His

---

60. Ratzinger, *Spirit of the Liturgy*, 29–34.

food is to do the will of God (cf. John 4:34). In his Baptism he fulfils all righteousness by taking on the yoke of God's will for him. In his Temptations he submits to God's will, refusing to put him to the test. These temptations do not stop after the forty days in the desert. The devil returns at "opportune times" (cf. Luke 4:13), most notably, in the Garden of Gethsemane.

The Dogmatic Thesis

Turning to the dogmatic thesis, in *Jesus of Nazareth* Ratzinger reiterates and develops his earlier explanation of how the christological dogmas of Nicaea and Chalcedon were ultimately grounded in the church's awareness of the sonship of Jesus. For example, he partially recapitulates his analysis of the formulation of the dogma that Jesus is true God and true man when he looks at the title which, according to the Gospels, Jesus used for himself, the "Son" sayings of Jesus, and how these enable us to comprehend his identity.[61] Again, in his account of the doctrine of the Resurrection, Ratzinger recapitulates and expands his earlier grounding of it in the narrative and confessional traditions.[62] These examples could be multiplied. Essentially, in *Jesus of Nazareth*, Ratzinger greatly expands his earlier account of the biblical grounds for holding the dogma that Jesus is truly human and truly divine, as in the case of Jesus' self-identification with God through his self-identification with the Torah, as found by Rabbi Neusner in the Sermon on the Mount.[63]

The Volitional Thesis

What is new in *Jesus of Nazareth*, as compared with his earlier Christology, is that, in spite of the fact of his stated conviction that it is not the place for a debate about christological dogmas, Ratzinger wishes to clarify the christological dogma of Chalcedon, that "one and the same Lord Jesus Christ, the only begotten Son, must be acknowledged in two natures, without confusion or change, without division or separation."[64] He seeks to do this by means of his volitional thesis which, in fact, is also a dogmatic thesis. He holds that the teaching of Constantinople III on the wills of Jesus can help to eliminate a certain parallelism of the two natures of Christ whereby it remains unclear

---

61. *Jesus I*, 335–45. Cf. *Introduction*, 223–28.
62. Cf. *Jesus Christ*, 92–94, with *Jesus II*, 248–72.
63. *Jesus I*, 99–127. Cf. Neusner, *A Rabbi Talks with Jesus*, 59–108.
64. Denzinger, no. 302.

how the one divine person acted by virtue of these two natures.[65] He also holds that there remained a certain tension in the dogma of Chalcedon over the definition of "person" and "nature." This tension came to be centered specifically on the status of Jesus' human nature. It led to divisions in the wake of Chalcedon—monenergism and monothelitism.

Rather than remaining in the past, this tension has once more become palpable in recent theological debate. The dualism between the Jesus of history and the Christ of faith has tended towards a privileging of the "human" Jesus, "a tendency to read Christ's humanity as pre-eminently an identification with our humanity—an error that necessarily inverts the prime analogate of Christology, as if 'our' humanity could be the criterion by which to judge the Incarnation of God."[66] Thomas Watts has outlined seven contemporary objections to the dyothelite teaching of Constantinople III.[67] 1) The New Testament never speaks of Jesus as having two wills. 2) There is no such thing as will—rather, persons engage in acts of willing. 3) Two wills in Jesus would make him two persons. 4) Two wills in Jesus would either oppose one another, which is unacceptable, or conform to one another, which makes one of them superfluous. 5) Two wills in Jesus would compromise either his full humanity or full divinity or both. 6) Arguments for two wills do not rule out speaking about Jesus as having one will in another sense. 7) The debate over whether Jesus had two wills is an example of the worst sort of theological debate, affecting little of substance in the Christian faith.[68] In presenting these objections I do not intend to offer a point by point rebuttal of them here. My aim is merely to show that this teaching is once more being disputed. How well Ratzinger provides an antidote to this dualism *redivivus* is the subject of the next chapter.

---

65. See Denzinger, nos. 302 and 553–59

66. Riches, "After Chalcedon," 201.

67. For this teaching, see Denzinger, nos. 553–59.

68. Watts, "Two Wills in Christ?," 446–48. References for these objections are as follows: 1) Moreland and Craig, *Philosophical Foundations for a Christian Worldview*, 611; 2) and 3) Macquarrie, *Jesus Christ in Modern Thought*, 166–67; 4) Pannenberg, *Jesus: God and Man*, 294; 5) Macquarrie, *Jesus Christ*, 166; and Pannenberg, *Jesus*, 294; 6) No reference given; 7) Macquarrie, *Jesus Christ*, 166.

9

Ratzinger and the Dyothelitism of St. Maximus the Confessor

Ratzinger's Reading of the Dyothelitism of Maximus and Constantinople III

In the Preface to *Behold the Pierced One*, Ratzinger stated that he came to realize that the achievement of a spiritual Christology had been the ultimate goal of Constantinople III. However, as Marie-Joseph le Guillou points out, if the *Terminus* of the Council is to be fully understood, it must be read through a Maximian lens.[1] In focusing upon the prayer of Jesus in the Garden of Gethsemane, St. Maximus the Confessor provided a historical context for the dogma of Chalcedon. What Ratzinger ultimately wishes to achieve through his spiritual Christology is that "we come to grasp the manner of our liberation, our participation in the Son's freedom ... We can ... describe the prayer which enters into the praying of Jesus and becomes the prayer of Jesus in the Body of Christ as freedom's laboratory."[2] This means that through entering into the praying of Jesus, both personally and ecclesially, we come to participate in his freedom. The question to be asked at this point is: How well does Ratzinger understand and expound the dyothelitism of Maximus and Constantinople III in order to achieve his goal?

---

1. Guillou, "Quelques Réflexions sur Constantinople III et la Sotéreriologie de Maxime," 235–37. For this reference, see Riches, "After Chalcedon," 204. As Riches says: "[A] Maximian reading of Constantinople III yields a full 'narrativisation' of Chalcedon ontology, a blending of historical event and metaphysical speculation, of story and ontology" (204). This is precisely how Ratzinger reads the pronouncements of the Council.

2. *Behold*, 42.

In order to answer this question it will be helpful to recapitulate Ratzinger's understanding of the two wills in Christ. In *Behold the Pierced One* Ratzinger's exposition of the teaching of Maximus and Constantinople III is fairly brief. For Ratzinger, it is essential to clarify the mode of unity of the humanity and divinity of Christ since it is through this unity that salvation comes to us. It must be a mutual indwelling rather than a mere juxtaposition if we are to become like God, if we are to be truly free. The teaching of Constantinople III on the unity of God and man in Christ abolishes the Chalcedonian dualism or parallelism of the two natures, which had seemed necessary in order to safeguard Jesus' human freedom.³ This unity does not reduce Christ's human nature but brings his humanity for the first time to the fullness of freedom. When the human will is taken up into the will of God its freedom is not destroyed, but fulfilled. The human will of Jesus is not absorbed by the divine will. Rather, "this human will follows the divine will and thus becomes one with it, not in a natural manner but along the path of freedom."⁴ In the realm of the person, of freedom, the two wills become one will, not naturally, but personally. This free unity, which is created by love, is higher and more interior that a merely natural unity, and corresponds to trinitarian unity. When Jesus says that: "I have come down from heaven, not to do my own will but the will of him who sent me" (John 6:38), his "own will" is the human will of the Logos. The human will and mind of Jesus are adopted into his "I" and are completely one with the divine will of the Logos. Ratzinger says of this human will that: "United with the latter [the will of the Logos], it has become a pure Yes to the Father's will."⁵ In a footnote to this last point, Ratzinger says that:

> [Maximus distinguishes] the θέλημα φυσικόν [natural will] which belongs to the nature and thus exists separately in Christ's godhead and manhood, from the "gnomic" θέλημα "which is identical with the *liberum arbitrium* and pertains to the person; in Christ it can only be a single θέλημα, since he subsists in the divine Person."⁶

---

3. Ibid., 38.
4. Ibid., 39.
5. Ibid.
6. Ibid., 39–40, no. 18. The interior quotation is taken from Beck, in *Handbuch der Kirchengeschichte II* 2, 41. Peter Lombard defines the *liberum arbitrium* as follows: "Liberum vero arbitrium est facultas rationis et voluntatis, qua bonum eligitur, gratia assistente, vel malum, eadem desistente. Et dicitur liberum quantum ad voluntatem, quae ad utrumlibet flecti potest; arbitrium vero quantum ad rationem, cuius est facultas vel potentia illa, cuius etiam est discernere inter bonum et malum" ("*Liberum arbitrium* is the faculty of reason and will, by which good is chosen with the assistance of grace,

In looking at Maximus' interpretation of the prayer of Jesus at Gethsemane, Ratzinger states the following.

> [In praying: "Not what I will, but what thou wilt (Mark 14:36)"] Jesus' human will assimilates itself to the will of the Son. In doing this, he receives the Son's identity, i.e., the complete subordination of the I to the Thou, the self-giving and self-expropriation of the I to the Thou. This is the very essence of him who is pure relation and pure act. Wherever the I gives itself to the Thou, there is freedom because this involves the reception of the "form of God."[7]

Ratzinger goes on to describe this process from what he calls "the other side."

> [The] Logos so humbles himself that he adopts a man's will as his own and addresses the Father with the I of this human being; he transfers his own I to this man and this transforms human speech into the eternal Word, into his blessed "Yes, Father." By imparting his own I, his own identity, to this human being, he liberates him, redeems him, makes him God. Now we can take the real meaning of "God has become man" in both hands, as it were: the Son transforms the anguish of a man into his own filial obedience, the speech of the servant into the Word which is the Son.[8]

Finally, the union of the human and divine wills in the Son reveals the manner of our participation in the Son's freedom. Here Ratzinger takes us back to the personal and ecclesial theses. In order for us to become divine we must enter into the praying of Jesus, a prayer that becomes the prayer of Jesus in the Body of Christ. This is "freedom's laboratory"—it is "only along this path that conscience attains its fundamental soundness and its unshakable power."[9]

At this point, four comments are called for. First, we should notice Ratzinger's focus on human freedom. As we shall see, this is a fundamental concern for him in his understanding of the significance of the union of

---

or evil, when grace is not there to assist. And it is called 'liberum' with respect to the will, which can be turned toward either [good or evil], while [it is called] 'arbitrium' with respect to reason, as it has to do with that power or faculty to which the discerning between good and evil belongs.") See Peter Lombard, *Sententiarum Quatuor Libri*, 549–53.

7. *Behold*, 41.
8. Ibid.
9. Ibid., 42.

wills in Jesus. In fact, in the next chapter, we shall see that human freedom is the terminus of Ratzinger's spiritual Christology. Second, there is some imprecision in Ratzinger's terminology. It would be incredible for a theologian of Ratzinger's quality to inadvertently fall into tri-theism through attributing separate wills to the divine persons, but his speaking of the human and divine wills becoming one "personally," followed by reference to the divine will of the Logos, and then the Father's will, leaves some ambiguity.[10] He would be aware that the will of the Logos and of the Father are one and the same will, the divine will, and that "will" in God pertains to his relation with his creatures. In a similar way, some of his language concerning the assumption of human nature by the Logos has a distinctly Nestorian flavor. However, I take it to mean that when he says that the Logos adopts *a man's will* he means *a human will*, and when he says that the Logos liberates, redeems, and makes *this man* God, he means liberates, redeems, and deifies *this human nature*. Third, the reference to Maximus' teaching about the gnomic will of Christ requires clarification. It will be essential for us to understand this teaching. Fourth, there is an awareness on Ratzinger's part that the unity of the human and divine wills in Jesus has a relationship to the trinitarian unity of the divine persons. In the mutual indwelling of the human and divine wills it is a trinitarian God in whose image we are made. The assimilation of the human will to the divine will is a reflection of the Son's relation to the Father, in which the Son is pure relation and pure act.

Ratzinger's application of this teaching to the prayer of Jesus in Gethsemane is also fairly brief. This prayer has great significance for Ratzinger. He believes that in it "the whole drama of our redemption is made present."[11] He identifies three elements in this prayer. One is that Jesus undergoes the primordial fear of created nature when confronted with imminent death, an experience which, in his case, is far more radical than the fear that everyone else experiences in the face of death. This is because, unlike us, the one who is Life, the Son, *knows completely* what he is facing. As Ratzinger so passionately writes:

> [Jesus] sees with total clarity the whole flood of evil, all the power of lies and pride, all the wiles and cruelty of the evil that masks itself as life yet constantly serves to destroy, debase, and crush

---

10. Ratzinger's use of the terms "person" and "personally" are different from Maximus,' and this difference, a conceptual and terminological one, needs to be clarified. Judgement about its validity depends on whether Ratzinger is intending to interpret Maximus simply, or whether he is trying to articulate a better Christology that is not inconsistent with Maximus' position. I am obliged to Dr. Adam Cooper for this clarification.

11. *Jesus II*, 154.

life. Because he is Son, he experiences deeply all the horror, filth, and baseness that he must drink from the "chalice" prepared for him: the vast power of sin and death. All this he must take into himself, so that it can be disarmed and defeated in him.[12]

A second element in the Gethsemane prayer of Jesus is that which Ratzinger regards as its interpretive key, the form of address: "*Abba*, Father" (Mark 14:36). This way of addressing God reveals the heart of Jesus' relationship with God. It is not the address of "the man Jesus . . . addressing the Trinitarian God . . . No, it is the Son speaking here, having subsumed the fullness of man's will into himself and transformed it into the will of the Son."[13] Once more, Ratzinger's terminology is ambiguous and potentially misleading. It can give the impression that the divine Logos has a will distinct from that of the Father. What the Son, the Logos, actually does is transform his human willing so that it is one with God the Father's willing, which is the divine will total possessed by each of the divine persons.

A third element concerns that which Ratzinger sees as presented in the two petitions of Jesus' prayer, a confrontation between two wills. These are "the 'natural will' of the man Jesus, which resists the appalling destructiveness of what is happening and wants to plead that the chalice will pass from him; and there is the 'filial will' that abandons itself totally to the Father's will."[14] Ratzinger explains what takes place in Jesus by reference to a Gethsemane-like moment in John's Gospel—"Father, save me from this hour . . . Father, glorify your name" (John 12:27–28). The anguish of Jesus' soul impels him to pray for deliverance. Yet his awareness of his mission enables him to pray that God will glorify his name through his, Jesus,' embrace of the Cross. The first prayer merges into the second, asking that God be glorified through the fulfillment of his will. The result is a deep unity within the heart of Jesus' human existence.

Previously, the problem of the terminology which Ratzinger uses here was commented upon. He could be read as saying either that Jesus has two human wills, or that the Logos has a separate will from the divine will (a glance at the German original shows that this is not a mistranslation). It beggars belief that he means either. Rather, he could have expressed himself more precisely by saying that in the prayer of Jesus we encounter a confrontation of two *desires*, or two *volitional motions*.[15] The one human will

12. Ibid., 155.
13. Ibid., 162.
14. Ibid., 156.

15. In fact, Maximus himself distinguishes between a number of different volitional movements in the human being, some of which belong to the "natural will" by

of Jesus is moved by two emotions—desire to escape the particular death which faces him, and desire to glorify the Father in and through that death, and it is the second desire which Jesus humanly *wills*. The use of the term "will" as a noun can mislead us into thinking of it as a thing rather than an act. In fact, the only real "noun" is the one who wills. In Jesus there is only one person, one agent who wills. When we speak of the divine will of Jesus, we mean that God the Logos wills divinely, that is, according to his divine nature. This will is the one divine will which is totally willed by each of the divine persons. When we speak of the human will of Jesus, we mean that the divine Logos wills humanly, that is, according to his assumed human nature.

What is needed here is an elucidation of the relationship between the human passions and human willing in Jesus. In the Garden we do not see a confrontation between the two wills of Jesus. Rather, we see a confrontation between two human desires impinging upon the human willing of Jesus. At this point a brief exposition of the human passions could be helpful. The *Catechism of the Catholic Church* defines passions as "emotions or movements of the sensitive appetite that incline us to act or not to act in regard to something felt or imagined to be good or evil."[16] Passions move us towards what is good or believed to be good and away from what is evil or believed to be evil. According to the *Catechism*:

> The most fundamental passion is love, aroused by the attraction of the good. Love causes a desire for the absent good and the hope of obtaining it; this movement finds completion in the pleasure and joy of the good possessed. The apprehension of evil causes hatred, aversion, and fear of the impending evil; this movement ends in sadness at some present evil, or in the anger that resists it.[17]

One human desire experienced by Jesus in the Garden is the negative desire of fear—the desire to flee from evil, in this case, death. The other is to do the will of the Father, to glorify the Father, to bring about our salvation. We see this desire expressed in John 12:28—"Father, glorify your name." We see it also expressed in Luke 12:49–50—"I came to cast fire upon the earth; and would that it were already kindled! I have a baptism to be baptized with; and

---

which we instinctively shun suffering and death. In Jesus' prayer in Gethsemane, one movement is manifest in the "let this cup pass from me." Another movement is more rational and self-determinative. This volitional power is manifest in the second part of the prayer, "not my will but yours." Again, I am grateful to Cooper for this insight. See also Bathrellos, *The Byzantine Christ*, 17–147.

16. CCC, no. 1763.
17. Ibid., no. 1765.

how I am constrained until it is accomplished!" This desire of Jesus, a desire stronger than the fear of death, is that we be filled with the fire of the Holy Spirit. This is the Father's glorification and our salvation. Jesus set his face towards Jerusalem (cf. Luke 9:51) because of his eagerness to undergo his baptism into death, his eagerness to break the constraint of the Father's will unfulfilled, his eagerness to accomplish the Father's will (cf. John 19:30). It is this latter desire which moves his will to accept his arrest rather than calling upon the Father to defend him. "Do you think that I cannot appeal to my Father, and he will at once send me more than twelve legions of angels?" (Matt 26:53). This is the first temptation of the Passion. This is the moment of decision, of willing. It is at this point that Jesus conforms his human willing to the will of his Father. And Jesus continues to humanly will the will of the Father, in spite of the further temptation to prove himself by coming down from the Cross, until the Father's will is accomplished (cf. Matt 27:41 and John 19:30).

Ratzinger continues his analysis of the prayer of Gethsemane by raising the question of exactly *who* is praying, and to whom. Is it the Son addressing the Father, or the man Jesus addressing the triune God? In order to answer this question, Ratzinger makes the assertion that the dogma of Chalcedon was "ahead of its time."[18] It stated that there is "one and same Christ, Son, Lord, Only-Begotten, known in two natures, without confusion, without change, without division, without separation." Yet it did not define exactly what was meant by "person" and "nature." This led to Monophysitism one the one hand, which sought to protect the full divinity of Jesus, and Nestorianism on the other, which sought to protect his full humanity. The key issue came to center on the status of Jesus' human nature. As Ratzinger writes: "If it subsists within the one divine person, can it be said to have any real, specific existence in itself? Must it not inevitably be absorbed by the divine, at least at its highest point, the will?"[19] The Monothelites held that, since it is ultimately in the will that one manifests oneself, a person can only have one will. However, the response to this was that if Jesus has no human will he cannot be fully human. Ratzinger presents Maximus' solution to this dilemma in the following terms.

> Jesus' human nature is not amputated through union with the Logos; it remains complete. And the will is part of human

---

18. *Jesus II*, 158. Essentially, the unresolved legacy of Chalcedon is that it leaves the *communicatio idiomatum* unspecified. That is to say, it does not specify how the properties of the divinity of the Logos can be ascribed to Jesus, nor how the properties of the humanity of Jesus can be predicated of the Logos.

19. Ibid., 159.

> nature. This irreducible duality of human and divine willing in Jesus must not, however, be understood to imply a dual personality. Nature and person must be seen in the mode of existence proper to each. In other words: in Jesus the "natural will" of the human nature is present, but there is only *one* "personal will," which draws the "natural will" into itself. And this is possible without annihilating the specifically human element, because the human will, as created by God, is ordered to the divine will. In becoming attuned to the divine will, it experiences its fulfillment, not its annihilation.[20]

Thus far, Ratzinger's summary of Maximus' position, though brief, is accurate, at least if we understand the "personal will" to be the one divine will. However, in what follows, Ratzinger does not capture all the nuances of Maximus' teaching.

> Maximus says in this regard that the human will, by virtue of creation, tends towards synergy (working together) with the divine will, but that through sin, opposition takes the place of synergy: man, whose will attains fulfillment through becoming attuned to God's will, now has the sense that his freedom is compromised by God's will. He regards consenting to God's will, not as his opportunity to become fully himself, but as a threat to his freedom against which he rebels... The drama of the Mount of Olives lies in the fact that Jesus draws man's natural will away from opposition and back towards synergy, and in doing so he restores man's true greatness. In Jesus' natural will, the sum total of human nature's resistance to God is, as it were, present within Jesus himself. The obstinacy of us all, the whole of our opposition to God is present, and in this struggle, Jesus elevates our recalcitrant nature to become its real self.[21]

In the last two sentences of this quotation Ratzinger has not represented Maximus' actual position. We shall need to grasp what Maximus truly holds regarding which aspects of our human nature Jesus assumes, and which he does not.

---

20. Ibid., 160.

21. Ibid., 160–61. See Maximus, *Ambiguum* 42 (*PG* 91: 1316A–1349B); and Blowers and Wilken, *On the Cosmic Mystery*, 119–22.

The Need for a More Thorough Understanding of the Dyothelitism of Maximus

We need to undertake a more thorough exposition of the dyothelitism of Maximus and Constantinople III in order to address the aforementioned ambiguities in Ratzinger's dyothelitism—in particular, his claim that: "In Jesus' natural will, the sum total of human nature's resistance to God is, as it were, present within Jesus himself. The obstinacy of us all, the whole of our opposition to God is present, and in this struggle, Jesus elevates our recalcitrant nature to become its real self." The Council of Chalcedon established that Jesus Christ was to be confessed as one person (*hypostasis*) in two natures, human and divine.[22] Since will belongs to the nature rather than the *hypostasis*, a dyothelite extension of Chalcedon is that Jesus Christ must be confessed as having two wills. A human person wills according to his or her human nature. In Christ, one agent, the divine Logos, wills according to his human nature and his divine nature. If will was in the *hypostasis*, then Christ could only have one will, the divine, and there would be three wills in God, corresponding to the three trinitarian *hypostases*. Furthermore, following the principle that Christ cannot redeem what he has not assumed, he must have assumed a human will, the ability to will humanly, in order to bring about its redemption.

Within human willing itself, Maximus makes a distinction between the natural will and the gnomic will. Although prior to the monothelite controversy Maximus treated *thelema* and *gnome* as synonyms, and had no difficultly in ascribing *gnome* to Christ, his arguments with monothelites required him to make a distinction between them.[23] As Ian McFarland explains:

> Maximus' dyothelite arguments includes a further distinction within human willing between the "natural will" (*thelema phusikon* or *thelema*) and the "gnomic will" (*thelema gnomikon* or *gnome*). According to Maximus, all human beings possess both a natural and a gnomic will; yet while he insists that Christ's full humanity dictates that he, too, has a natural will, he repeatedly denies that Christ has a gnomic will.[24]

---

22. See Denzinger, nos. 300–303.

23. McFarland, "Willing Is Not Choosing," 8–9. For my understanding of Maximus' dyothelitism I am greatly indebted to McFarland's analysis. For Maximus' treatment of *thelema* and *gnome* as synonyms, see his *Commentary on the Our Father* (*PG* 90: 900A), in Berthold, *Maximus the Confessor: Selected Writings*, 114. See also Bathrellos, *The Byzantine Christ*, commonly regarded as the standard text on these questions.

24. McFarland, "Willing Is Not Choosing," 8. McFarland bases this understanding upon his reading of Maximus' *OTP* 7 (*PG* 91: 81C–D) and *DP* (*PG* 91: 308D–309A,

For Maximus, Christ can only redeem the human will if it is part of the nature which he assumed at the Incarnation. This natural will Maximus identifies with human agency.[25] The primary manifestation of the natural will is in our natural appetites. As Maximus states:

> For by this power [of the will] alone we desire being, life, movement, understanding, speech, perception, nourishment, sleep, refreshment, as well as not to suffer pain or to die—quite simply to possess fully everything that sustains nature and to lack whatever harms it.[26]

For Maximus, the gnomic will is associated with the powers of deliberation and decision, the ability to choose between options.[27] However, the natural will does not "choose" the above-mentioned desires. Although we share these desires with the animals, what is distinctive for human beings is that we desire these things not through a compulsive instinct, but freely, through the will. As well as this instinctive dimension of the natural will, Maximus holds that it has a rational aspect. Thus he writes:

> For that which is rational by nature has a natural power that is a rational appetite, which is also called the will of the intellective soul. And by this power we reason willingly; and when we have reasoned, we desire willingly.[28]

This is the kind of human will possessed by Jesus. By contrast, the gnomic will is the capacity to choose between options, including good and evil options, that is, with the possibility of sin. Sin is a product of a *gnome* which has turned from what is natural, or rather, *gnome* is a manifestation of a sinful propensity. Yet the gnomic will should not simply be identified as fallenness, since it can conform to God's will.[29] According to McFarland:

329D).

25. *DP* (*PG* 91: 304C). McFarland states that: "'Agency' is preferable to 'self-determination' or 'freedom of choice' as translations for *autoexousiotes* precisely because Maximus contrasts *autoexousiotes* as the defining feature of the natural will with the gnomic qualities of *prohairesis* (*OTP* 1 [*PG* 91: 13A]) and *autoairesis* (*OTP* 16 [*PG* 91: 192B–C]), both of which much more clearly have the sense of autonomous freedom of choice" (McFarland, "Willing Is Not Choosing," 9, no. 22).

26. *OTP* 16 (*PG* 91: 196A). See McFarland, "Willing Is Not Choosing," 9. Bathrellos (*inter alia*) takes this description of the θέλημα φυσικόν to refer to "it's vital . . . non-rational, instinctive and desirous aspect. Reason does not play any significant role here (123)."

27. *OTP* 1 (*PG* 91: 16D–17B). See McFarland, "Willing Is Not Choosing," 10.

28. *DP* (*PG* 91: 293B). See McFarland, "Willing Is Not Choosing," 10.

29. *OTP* 7 (*PG* 91: 80A), and 16 (*PG* 91: 193B). McFarland maintains that: "This

> Maximus associates this capacity [of the gnomic will] with a will that does not enjoy the eschatological state of complete conformity to God's will, arguing that short of this state willing is a complex process that moves from desire (*boulesis*) through deliberation (*boule* or *bouleusis*) to the actualization of the results of deliberation in choice (*prohairesis*).[30]

For Maximus, deliberation is associated with ignorance and doubt. Thus one can deviate from one's natural end. Through the fall this possibility has been actualized, rendering us disposed to sin. Even if we do not sin our actions are characterized by deliberation and choice.

Having a gnomic will and a natural will does not mean that human beings have two wills. Rather, for Maximus, the gnomic will is the *tropos*, the mode, in which one wills, not an inherent *logos*, or property, of the will. *Gnome* is a kind of modality in the deployment of our natural faculties. It is not another will, but how willing takes place. As McFarland explains: "In the same way that hypostasis is defined as the *tropos* (that is, mode of being) of a particular *logos* (that is, type of entity), so the gnomic will refers to the mode in which the natural will is instantiated by human hypostases prior to its eschatological transformation into a condition of immediate conformity to God's will."[31]

According to Maximus, Christ does not have a gnomic will since he does not suffer from the kind of ignorance and doubt which we do. Therefore, he wills without deliberation and decision. Christ's willing lacks these characteristics because his humanity is already deified. His *tropos* is different from ours.[32] Jesus' human will is oriented to God in such a way that it does not need to deliberate. However, although this makes his will different from ours, according to McFarland:

> [It] does not compromise Christ's consubstantiality with us, because the latter is a function of the will's *logos* rather that its *tropos*. In short, in the same way that Christ's having a genuinely human body is not compromised by the fact that the agent who is the subject of his bodily movements is God, neither is the claim that his incarnate acts are humanly willed compromised

---

distinction between the exercise of the gnomic will and sin also shows that Maximus does not subscribe to an Augustinian version of fallen humanity as *non posse non peccare*" (McFarland, "Willing Is Not Choosing," 10, no. 25).

30. McFarland, "Willing Is Not Choosing," 10. In support, McFarland refers to *OTP* 1 (*PG* 91: 13A–16C).

31. Ibid., 11. McFarland refers to *DP* (*PG* 91: 308D) for this position.

32. *OTP* 20 (*PG* 91: 236D). See McFarland, "Willing Is Not Choosing," 11.

by the fact that God is the subject of the willing. As a property of human nature, the humanity of the will—like that of the mind or body—is logically distinct from (and thus ontologically unaffected by) the divinity of the hypostasis.[33]

Maximus bases his argument for a distinct human will in Jesus on the testimony of Sacred Scripture. Therein, Jesus is depicted as willingly submitting to things which could not be ascribed to the divine nature—hunger and thirst, labor and weariness, and so on.[34] Furthermore, Jesus is depicted as being obedient to the Father, obedient to the point of death. In his *Disputation with Pyrrhus* Maximus writes: "Was [Jesus] obedient willingly or unwillingly? If unwillingly, then it should be described as compulsion and not obedience. But if willingly, obedience is not a property of God but of human beings."[35] Both petitions in Jesus' prayer in the Garden are acts performed by virtue of his human will. In the first petition, Jesus expresses the instinctive aversion to and fear of death natural to human nature. In the second, he conquers that fear of death and submits himself to the divine will. He is able to do this because his human will is wholly deified—it is the human will of a divine person.[36]

Maximus has been criticized for denying a gnomic will to Jesus, on the grounds of *quod non est assumptum, non sanatum*. This criticism takes three forms. First, how can Jesus be truly consubstantial with human beings if his human willing lacks the ability to deliberate upon and make choices between different options, an ability which our contemporaries are inclined to view as the essence of human freedom?[37] Second, if Jesus has no deliberative *gnome*, how can he redeem our sinful *gnome*?[38] Third, since the two petitions of Jesus differ in content, how can they be ascribed to the same human will if Jesus' "lack of a gnomic will precludes the possibility that doubt and deliberation be used to account for the shift from resistance to acceptance"?[39] McFarland's rebuttal of the third objection, in fact, answers all three. In making a distinction between what is natural to the human

---

33. McFarland, "Willing Is Not Choosing," 12.

34. *OTP* 7 (*PG* 91: 77A); and *DP* (*PG* 91: 320D–324A). See McFarland, "Willing Is Not Choosing," 12–13.

35. *DP* (*PG* 91: 324A–B). See McFarland, "Willing Is Not Choosing," 13.

36. *OTP* 7 (*PG* 91: 80C–D). See McFarland, "Willing Is Not Choosing," 14.

37. McFarland, "Willing Is Not Choosing," 8. McFarland attributes this criticism to Schwager in *Der wunderbare Tausch*, 157–58.

38. Schwager, *Der wunderbare Tausch*, 141–47 and 157–58. Cf. Blowers, "The Passion of Jesus Christ," 372–74.

39. McFarland, "Willing Is Not Choosing," 14.

will, and this same will being, as it is, deified and immovably fixed on God, McFarland holds the following.

> [Maximus] insists that though Christ's two petitions are clearly different from one another, the fact that God, as the common author of created nature and deifying grace, is the source of both movements of the will means that this difference cannot be interpreted in terms of the process of choosing between sin and righteousness characteristic of gnomic deliberation.[40]

Nor can Jesus' second petition be seen as interfering with his humanity, since divinization does not change human nature into something non-human. Rather, "the movement from rejection of the cup to its acceptance illustrates a progression from human nature as it operates according to its own powers and human nature enabled to transcend those powers through grace."[41]

McFarland points out that "the distinction between the natural power (*logos*) of Christ's human will and the particular way (*tropos*) it moves in Gethsemane parallels the distinction between the natural and gnomic wills."[42] However, there are three interrelated differences. First, the deified will is fixed upon the divine will, whereas the gnomic will is not. Second, the gnomic process of deliberation and decision is not found in the deified will. I should point out that gnomic deliberation between objects of choice is of a *moral* kind. Jesus has no moral indecisiveness. Third, and this is the crucial point:

> [While] the distance from God that is definitive of gnomic willing means that in itself freedom of choice consists in the possibility of willing that which is *against* nature (and which is therefore opposed to God), the freedom of the deified will consists in the God-given capacity to will that which is *beyond* but—crucial for Maximus—*not against* nature. In other words, the gnomic will has the capacity either to follow nature or to sin. By contrast, the deified will's deviation from its "natural" object is not sin, because it is not a rejection of nature; on the contrary, it wills whatever it wills (in this case, the cup of suffering) precisely out of obedience to God who is recognized as the author of human nature and thus as the one whose calling must

---

40. Ibid. Cf. *OTP* 3 (*PG* 91: 48D).
41. Ibid. McFarland refers to *OTP* 3 (*PG* 91: 48C), 4 (*PG* 91: 60C), and 7 (*PG* 91: 31D and 84 A–B) for these insights.
42. Ibid., 14–15.

be understood as a fulfillment of that nature even as it exceeds that nature's inclinations and capacities.[43]

The divine will of God moves the human will of Jesus that, in turn, accepts this moving "in an act of obedience which both reflects and constitutes its deification."[44] The deified will of Jesus remains free and human because God does not cancel or override it but, through his grace, enables Jesus to will an object which is beyond the natural capacity of a human will. The transcendence is in *mode*, not in *object*. To put it more simply, the conditional petition, "If it be possible . . . " is not an act of deliberation on the part of Jesus. He intends to do the Father's will, whatever it may be.

In fact, the saints in glory will engage in the same kind of willing.[45] They will not engage in gnomic choosing since their willing will be fixed on God. However, they will retain their individual integrity since although their willing now transcends nature each will be drawn to God according to his or her own particular calling. Because the being of God is infinitely good, true and beautiful, and each human person is a unique creature of God, obedience to God's will shall differ for each person.[46]

It is this which constitutes true human freedom. Our problem is that we are not used to thinking of freedom in these terms. We associate freedom with gnomic willing, the ability to choose between this or that moral option according to our own particular desires. However, for Maximus, human freedom is associated with the natural will. It is this will which constitutes us as free and responsible agents. Whereas one with an un-deified, gnomic will makes choices through deliberation and decision, one with a deified will has no need for this process, but is moved by the grace of God. However, God's grace takes nothing away from the integrity of the will. The person is *moved* by God, not *compelled*. The source of our problem is that we tend to think of ourselves as autonomous, self-creating beings, ones who are the

---

43. Ibid., 15. Cf. *OTP* 6 (*PG* 91: 65A), and *DP* (*PG* 91: 297A). It is in this sense that Jesus exhibits Augustine's *non posse peccare* of the beatified state. This raises another question regarding the relative character of temptation for such a person. Once again, I am indebted to Cooper for this insight.

44. Ibid. McFarland clarifies this point in a footnote where he says that: "This is not to say that Christ in any way increases—let alone achieves—his deification in Gethsemane; but it is to stress that for Maximus deification combines steadfastness with movement and is therefore not a static condition. See, e.g., *The Church's Mystagogy* 19 [*PG* 91: 696B–C], where Maximus characterizes human experience of the glorified state as 'the identity of an inflexible eternal movement around God' (in *Maximus Confessor*, p.202)."

45. *OTP* 1 (*PG* 91: 24C). See McFarland, "Willing Is Not Choosing," 17.

46. Ibid., (*PG* 91: 25A); and Maximus, *Ambiguum* 31 (*PG* 91: 1280D–1281A). See McFarland, "Willing Is Not Choosing," 17.

source of their own identities. However, the actual source of our identities is God. Our wills are the means by which we live out our identities as God's creatures. One with a deified will has been loved into existence by God, is called to love God in return, and does so *willingly*.[47]

It is important to realize that the gnomic will is devoid of *content*. It does not "create" or "determine" the person. As McFarland explains:

> Its objects come to it from without, either (positively) from divine promptings and the intrinsic drives of human nature on the one hand, or (negatively) from the soul's disordered passions on the other. From this perspective, the idea that human beings make themselves is true only to the extent that they drift away from their natural end toward self-destruction. By contrast, in so far as human beings follow their nature, they are emphatically not self-made, but God-made—and never more so than in their deification. At the same time, because what God first makes and then deifies are human beings—rational, responsible, self-conscious agents—the saint's relationship with God is a manifestation of personal freedom as one who, by grace, not only knows and loves God, but does so willingly.[48]

We can now see that, for Maximus, in Jesus' natural will, the sum total of human nature's resistance to God is *not* present within Jesus himself. The obstinacy of us all, the whole of our opposition to God is *not* present. Gnomic will, which includes the possibility, though not the inevitability, to sin, is *not* present in Jesus. What is present in Jesus' natural will are the natural desires of that will, natural desires which every human being has. In the struggle of Gethsemane, Jesus does elevate human nature to become its real self, but he does this by taking upon himself our authentic human nature. He takes upon himself the *consequences* of sin, but neither concupiscence nor sinfulness. Jesus is the Second Adam, who has become like us in all things but sin. Our divinization consists in being raised by grace to willingly love God as he does.

Ratzinger holds that the struggle of Jesus in Gethsemane to conform his human will to that of the Father occurs throughout his entire ministry—from the time he is driven into the wilderness by the Holy Spirit until the moment of his death upon the Cross.[49] However, what are we to make of the Gospel accounts of this continuing struggle, especially as portrayed in

---

47. McFarland, "Willing Is Not Choosing," 17–20.
48. Ibid., 20.
49. See Ratzinger's reference to Heb 5:7 in *Jesus II*, 162–63, and his account of the Temptations of Jesus in *Jesus I*, 26–45.

the temptations of Jesus? For if, for Jesus, it is *non posse peccare*, what is the point of his being tempted? That he was tempted is so deeply imbedded in the synoptic Gospels and the Letter to the Hebrews that we must give some explanation for it. The temptations are to sin, which, according to Maximus, in fallen creatures requires deliberation based on ignorance and doubt. As the reason for Jesus being tempted, Ratzinger gives the necessity of his entry into the drama of human existence, penetrating it to its uttermost depths. For Ratzinger, the descent of Jesus into Hell, of which the Apostles' Creed speaks, does not take place only in and after his death, but accompanies him throughout his entire life. "He must recapitulate the whole of history from its beginnings—from Adam on; he must go through, suffer through, the whole of it, in order to transform it."[50] He must become like his brethren in every respect—"For because he himself has suffered and been tempted, he is able to help those who are tempted" (Heb 2:18), and: "For we have not a high priest who is unable to sympathize with our weaknesses, but one who in every respect has been tempted as we are, yet without sin" (Heb 4:15).[51] Yet, if it was impossible for Jesus to sin, how can he be tempted as we are in every respect? How can he help us and sympathize with us in our temptations? Ratzinger portrays Jesus as entering into solidarity with us sinners through his baptism and wrestling with his mission through its whole duration.[52] But what is the nature of this solidarity, this wrestling? According to Ratzinger:

> Matthew and Luke recount three temptations of Jesus that reflect the inner struggle over his own particular mission and, at the same time, address the question as to what truly matters in human life. At the heart of all temptations, as we see here, is the act of pushing God aside because we perceive him as secondary, if not actually superfluous and annoying, in comparison with all the apparently far more urgent matters that fill our lives. Constructing a world by our own lights without reference to God, building our own foundation; refusing to acknowledge the reality of anything beyond the political and material, while setting God aside as an illusion—that is the temptation that threatens us in many varied forms.[53]

For Ratzinger, the question which Jesus must respond to in his temptations is the question of God—is he, Jesus, truly God or not? Yet in his account

50. *Jesus I*, 26.
51. Quoted by Ratzinger in ibid., 26–27.
52. Ibid., 27.
53. Ibid., 28.

of the three temptations themselves, Ratzinger does not go into what we might call their "inner workings." Jesus is tempted, and he does not give in to them. What, then, is their significance? Is he setting us an example, teaching us? How does his resistance help us? Or does some kind of change take place in Jesus through these temptations? The Letter to the Hebrews tells us that: "Although he was a Son, he learned obedience though what he suffered; and being made perfect he became the source of salvation to all who obey him" (5:8–9). Do the temptations of Jesus have a soteriological and deifying significance?

Once more, Maximus can come to our aid. He states that in the Incarnation the Logos assumed the passible element of human nature, yet without sin.[54] This raises the questions—if Jesus has become like us in *all things* but *sin*, what is meant by "sin," and what is left as "all things?" When we say "sin," do we only mean that he did not engage in sinning, or that he was incapable of sinning? Jesus did not experience concupiscence, that effect of original sin which inclines us towards sin. Nor, as we have seen, did he experience our gnomic will, our ignorance about what is truly good, and hence our need to deliberate over it. In a state of original justice, our first parents knew what was truly good, their passions moved them towards the truly good, and, knowing, loving and desiring the truly good, they willingly chose it. This original justice Jesus possessed. However, in becoming passible, the Son laid himself open to experiencing one of the effects of original sin, which was suffering and death. Besides the good to be loved, desired and enjoyed, there was now the evil to be hated, feared, angered by, and grieved by.

Jesus possessed the passible element of human nature. Therefore, he could suffer. But in what sense could he be tempted? The standard patristic answer to this question is to present the temptations of Jesus as "proofs" of his humanity, concessions to our incredulity concerning the reality of his humanity. To this question, neither Ratzinger nor Maximus give an answer.

Ratzinger's grasp of the dyothelitism of Maximus and Constantinople III is fundamentally sound, but it seems that he is not aware of all of its nuances. In particular, in saying that Jesus took upon himself all of human nature's resistance and opposition to God, he has not fully distinguished those aspects of human nature which Jesus did, and did not, take to himself. This is a point which needs to be clarified, since it may affect one's understanding of how human freedom can participate in the freedom of Jesus Christ. To that understanding we know turn.

---

54. Maximus, *61st Question to Thalassius* (PG 90: 629A–636B).

10

Human Freedom as the Terminus of Ratzinger's Spiritual Christology

"We can ... describe the prayer which enters into the praying of Jesus and becomes the prayer of Jesus in the Body of Christ as freedom's laboratory."[1] Maximus identifies the human person as "the laboratory in which everything is concentrated and in itself naturally mediates between the extremities of each division [of being]."[2] The ultimate division overcome in this laboratory is that between the created and uncreated in the divinization of Jesus' humanity. Our freedom/divinization is brought about through our personal/corporate participation in the prayer of Jesus. Ratzinger holds that to be a child of God, to possess the "sonship" of knowledge and freedom, means being able to say "Father." The ultimate consummation of the cosmos, the ultimate triumph of spirit, is the triumph of truth, freedom, and love in Jesus Christ. Human freedom in Christ is the terminus of Ratzinger's spiritual Christology, a freedom which is our divinization.

A number of those who have commented upon Ratzinger's spiritual Christology have drawn our attention to its significance for our understanding of human freedom. For example, de Gaál asserts that, for Ratzinger, it is Jesus' filial relationship with his Father which is at the root of the question of human freedom and liberation. A more explicit connection with Ratzinger's volitional thesis is made by Joseph Murphy, who sees Ratzinger developing the dyothelic teaching of Constantinople III as to how our freedom is realized through its insertion into Christ's prayer.[3] Butler, too, focuses on how

---

1. *Behold*, 42.
2. Maximus, *Ambiguum* 41 (*PG* 91: 1305 A–B).
3. Murphy, *Christ Our Joy*, 124.

Ratzinger emphasizes that the dyothelitism of Constantinople III affirms the human freedom of Christ, and that our participation in the prayer relationship between Jesus and his Father becomes the source of a new human freedom which is ultimately that of divinization.

We have seen the question of freedom being raised in Ratzinger's earlier Christology. Likewise, in the exposition of his christological theses, the question of divine freedom and human freedom, including the human freedom of Jesus, comes to the fore in the dogmatic and volitional theses. In *Jesus of Nazareth*, although the term "freedom" is used mainly in relation to human participation in the freedom of God, the human freedom of Jesus, as expressed in the union of his will with that of God, is meditated upon in the mysteries of his life, especially in his Passion. In what follows, an attempt will be made to show that, through both his earlier and spiritual Christology, Ratzinger has developed a theology of God's freedom, and an anthropology of human freedom, which are then brought together in a Christology of the freedom of Jesus, a freedom in which we are called to participate ecclesially.

Some False Ideas of Freedom according to Ratzinger

In his commentary on the section of *Gaudium et spes* which addresses the nature of human freedom, Ratzinger maintains that the intention of the text is to affirm the value of freedom on the basis of faith. The particular aspect of freedom which he addresses is psychological rather than social or political. He seeks to find a firm basis for human freedom which is subject neither to external coercion nor to the compulsion of instinct. He also seeks to oppose the idea that freedom is simply the absence of commitment. Ratzinger sees the negation of freedom through coercion and instinct, or the identification of freedom with license, as potential means for the social manipulation of the human person through control of the intellectual and economic markets. Finally, he thinks that the text wished to uphold the reality of human moral responsibility in opposition to any kind of determinism. Regarding this last point, Ratzinger sees a contemporary paradox—on the one hand, the demand for freedom without responsibility, and on the other, a materialistic belief that human behavior is biologically determined. In opposition to this, Ratzinger sees the text as professing human moral freedom, not only against biological, but also theological determinism. As he states:

> However much the New Testament . . . may speak of the decadence and impotence of man, it nevertheless always expressly affirms the moral responsibility of *all* men; despite the important aspects calling for consideration which it expresses, Luther's

> "servum arbitrium" [unfree will] cannot be maintained on New Testament grounds.[4]

In Ratzinger's analysis one can discern the false freedom of license, which can so often become chimeric through propaganda, and which leads to the enslavement of the will in sin, as well as both the materialist and theological denials of freedom. In *Feast of Faith* he identifies another denial of freedom which springs not from a materialistic but a rationalistic worldview shaped by science and technology. There he states that:

> [A] rationally constructed world is determined by rationally perceived causality. The notion of personal intervention [by God] is both mythical and repugnant. But if this approach is adopted, it must be followed consistently, for what applies to God applies equally to man. If there is only *one* kind of causality, man too as a person is excluded and reduced to an element in mechanical causality, in the realm of necessity; freedom too, in this case, is a mythical idea. In this sense it can be said that the personalities of God and of man cannot be separated. If personality is not a possibility, i.e., not present, with the "ground" of reality, it is not possible at all. Either freedom is a possibility inherent in the ground of reality, or it does not exist.[5]

In *A New Song for the Lord*, Ratzinger identifies a false notion of freedom in liberation theology. While recognizing the contemporary appeal of Christ the liberator for our times, he thinks that liberation theology tends to read salvation history the wrong way round. Instead of moving from Moses to Christ, and from Christ to the kingdom of God, it goes in the opposite direction through the application of political criteria to Christ. This leads to a political interpretation of the Exodus rather than a christological one. What Ratzinger wishes to do is "make comprehensible the new dimension of the concepts of exodus, freedom, and liberation that came into the world through Christ."[6]

The Contemporary Dilemma of Human Freedom

Ratzinger's must comprehensive analysis of false notions of freedom are to be found in an essay entitled "*Freiheit und Wahrheit*" (Freedom and Truth),

---

4. "Church and Man's," 139–40.
5. Ratzinger, *Feast of Faith*, 20.
6. Ratzinger, *A New Song for the Lord*, 6.

and, as Benedict XVI, in his encyclical *Spe salvi*.[7] In the first he maintains that the fundamental difficulty with the contemporary concept of freedom is that it has been separated from that of truth. The general notion of freedom is that expressed by Karl Marx, when he says that in the future Communist society one will be able "to do one thing today and another tomorrow; to hunt in the morning, fish in the afternoon, breed cattle in the evening and criticize after dinner, just as I please . . ."[8] This concept of freedom as the ability to do or to have anything which we desire, to have one's own will as the sole norm of our action, presupposes that one's will is truly free. Yet, Ratzinger asks, if the will is irrational, can it be truly free? Can it be truly good? He proposes the need for a definition of freedom which says that it is "the capacity to will and to do what we will in the context of reason."[9] Such an interplay between reason and will shall enable us to find that common reason shared by all people, and thus ground the compatibilities of personal liberties.

Ratzinger points out that both Marxism and Liberalism have failed to deliver the freedom which they have promised. Although Marxism claimed to have discovered a scientifically guaranteed way to freedom, it instituted a gigantic system of slavery. Despite the promises of the liberal system of politics and economics, many people in democratic societies are excluded from freedom by unemployment and material poverty, as well as being "haunted by the specter of meaninglessness."[10] Ratzinger cites the Polish philosopher Andrej Sziztpiorski's reaction to the fall of communism in Eastern Europe and the apparent triumph of western liberal democracy, which is that this triumph has raised the possibility that there is no way to human liberation. If neither East nor West can give an answer to the human desire for freedom, perhaps there is no answer.[11] So, for Ratzinger, there are actually two questions which need to be answered, not just "what is truth?" but also "what is freedom?"

Ratzinger sees the idea of freedom as the defining theme of post-mediaeval European society. The issue which Luther raised was that of the most intimate of all human freedoms, the freedom of conscience vis-à-vis the authority of the church. The concept of freedom came to be individualized. Rather than something found in the church, it meant "liberation from the

   7. Published in English as Ratzinger, "Truth and Freedom," 16–35. See also *SS*, nos. 16–23.
   8. Marx and Engels, *Werke*, 3:33. Cited in Ratzinger, "Truth and Freedom," 17. Ironically, Marx's concept of freedom is thoroughly bourgeois.
   9. Ratzinger, "Truth and Freedom."
   10. Ibid., 18.
   11. Ibid., 19.

yoke of a supra-individual order."[12] Yet this liberation was confined to the "religious" sphere. In the political sphere the contrary happened—liberation was curtailed by a growing secular authority which, more and more, attempted to subjugate the church.

In *Spe salvi*, Benedict XVI gives a complementary account of this individualization of freedom through showing its connection with the individualization of salvation. According to him, this reduction of redemption to the "salvation of the soul" arose from the development of the scientific method. The new correlation of experiment and method introduced the possibility of what Francis Bacon called "the triumph of art over nature."[13] The potential to dominate creation occasioned by the new correlation between science and praxis lead to an attempt to rebuild the Tower of Babel, an attempt to return to Eden via science rather than faith. This displaced faith onto another level—that of the private and other-worldly which proves to be irrelevant to the world. Publically, faith in Christ is replaced by "faith in progress." The kingdom of God now becomes the kingdom of man. According to Benedict XVI, the two categories which become increasingly central to this idea of progress are reason and freedom. It is reason which drives progress towards the perfect realization of freedom. Since this realization of perfect freedom comes about through the establishment of a kingdom of man, which could also be called a kingdom of reason, both these concepts of reason and freedom are politicized. These concepts were interpreted as being in conflict with both the faith and the church, and the reigning political structures.[14]

Initially, this faith in reason was *naïf*. The French Revolution seemed to promise the establishment of the rule of reason and freedom as a political reality. Only later did some begin to doubt this new-found faith. Benedict XVI illustrates this point through appealing to two essays in which Kant reflects upon the Revolution. In his 1792 *Der Sieg des guten Prinzips über das Böse und die Gründung eines Reiches Gottes auf Erden* (The Victory of the Good over the Evil Principle and the Founding of a Kingdom of God on Earth), Kant claims that: "The gradual transition of ecclesiastical faith to the exclusive sovereignty of pure religious faith is the coming of the Kingdom of God."[15] Yet three years later, in *Das Ende aller Dinge* (The End of All Things), he is wondering if the transition from an "ecclesiastical" faith could also lead to an "irrational" faith. As Benedict XVI puts it: "Now Kant considers the

---

12. Ibid., 20.
13. Bacon, *Novum Organum* 1:117. Cited in SS, no. 16.
14. SS, no. 18.
15. Kant, *Werke* 4:777. Cited in SS, no. 19.

possibility that as well as the natural end of all things there may be another that is unnatural, a perverse end."[16]

The Enlightenment challenged not just religious but also political authority by proposing the emancipation of the human will through reason, a reason to which even political authority must bow. Only that which is reasonable is valid. Paradoxically, this led to two, antithetical social philosophies with their attendant political programs. The first, anglo-saxon current, emphasized natural rights and constitutional democracy as the only realistic way to freedom. For this way of thinking: "Freedom is not bestowed on man from without. He is a bearer of rights because he is created free."[17] Thus we can see that this idea has a Christian origin. It is a principle which can be found in Romans 2:14: "When Gentiles who have not the law do by nature what the law requires, they are a law to themselves . . ." It is based on a theology of creation. And yet, in the Enlightenment recasting of this idea, the individual is set in opposition to the community. Human rights must be protected from the community—"the institution seems to be the polar opposite of freedom, whereas the individual appears as the bearer of freedom, whose goal is seen as his full emancipation."[18]

The second current, exemplified by Rousseau, also begins with the idea of nature. Yet this nature is anti-rational. According to Ratzinger, for Rousseau, "everything which owes its origin to reason and will is contrary to nature, and corrupts and contradicts us."[19] Rousseau's concept of nature is anti-metaphysical. Nature is a state of total, unregimented freedom. This anarchic concept of freedom eventually comes to dominate the French Revolution, and resurfaces in Nietzsche and National Socialism. Although it is inimical to the Enlightenment appeal to reason, it is, nonetheless, the Enlightenment cry for freedom in its most radical form.

Ratzinger sees Marxism as a continuation of this radical line, in that it gives precedence to the community rather than the individual. For Marxism, freedom is indivisible. Unless there is equality, freedom for all, there is freedom for none. Therefore, individual liberties must give way to solidarity with those struggling for freedom. Yet the endpoint of this struggle is the unbounded freedom of the individual. The precedence of the community only stands until the freedom of equality is achieved.[20]

16. *SS*, no. 19. See Kant, *Werke*, 4:190.
17. Ratzinger, "Truth and Freedom," 21.
18. Ibid., 22.
19. Ibid. Although Ratzinger does not explicitly make a link, perhaps we could see Rousseau's position as a fulfilment of Kant's fear of an anti-rational faith.
20. Ibid., 23. Cf. *SS*, no. 20.

As Ratzinger sees it, the problem for Marxism is simply that, at its heart, it contains a contradiction. It claims to be the rational means of bringing about a change in the very structure of society, yet those who are to bring about the change are unable to attain the altruism necessary for such a change. Consequently, Marxists took refuge in a "mythology"—the new structure would bring forth a new, altruistic man. Yet this "new man" is the necessary prerequisite for the achievement of the new structure. This "lie" at the heart of Marxism reveals that there can be no freedom without truth. The lie neutralizes even those elements of truth which do exist in Marxism.[21]

Turning to that element of truth, Ratzinger confronts the democratic concept of freedom. The Marxist critique of democracy has some validity. How free are elections when they can be manipulated by propaganda in the guise of advertising, underwritten by capital? How much does a supposedly enlightened oligarchy rule through control of the media? How representative is representative democracy, with its rule by what is often a narrow majority? How much power do interest groups exercise compared to the unorganized individual? How often does the will of individuals prevail over the freedom of the whole? The freedom of total autonomy, of doing what one pleases, is impossible for all. Ultimately, it means an imposition of the will of the strong upon the weak. The inability of democratically ordered freedom to give freedom to all increases the anarchic calls for freedom.

As Benedict XVI, Ratzinger also reflects upon the twentieth century's critique of the nineteenth century's faith in progress. Referring specifically to Theodor Adorno's observation that "progress" means progress from the sling to the atom bomb, he states what should be obvious to any thoughtful person, that because of the human potential for either good or evil, we can only speak of true progress in the sense of technical progress. Without a corresponding moral progress this technical progress is, in fact, a regression, and potentially, annihilation.[22]

Ratzinger maintains that the grand promises of modernity to establish freedom for all flow from a failure to penetrate to the foundations of what man is, and how he can live rightly, both individually and collectively. Modernity separated the philosophical and hence political concept of freedom from the religious concept. This has led ultimately to the most radical philosophy of freedom, what might be called the nadir of freedom, that of Sartre.

21. Ibid., 23–24. Cf. SS, no. 21, where he points out that Marx's deepest error was to forget the reality of human nature. Since Marx was a materialist, he assumed that human evil was a product of economic conditions.

22. SS, no. 22.

Sartre regards man as condemned to freedom. In contrast to the animal, man has no "nature." The animal lives out its existence according to laws it is simply born with; it does not need to deliberate what to do with its life. But man's essence is undetermined. It is an open question. I must decide myself what I understand by "humanity," what I want to do with it, and how I want to fashion it. Man has no nature, but is sheer freedom. His life must take some direction or other, but in the end comes to nothing. This absurd freedom is man's hell. What is unsettling about this approach is that it is a way through the separation of freedom and truth to its most radical conclusion: there is no truth at all. Freedom has no direction and no measure. But this complete absence of truth, this complete absence of any moral and metaphysical bond, this absolutely anarchic freedom—which is understood as an essential quality of man—reveals itself to one who tries to live it not as the supreme enhancement of existence, but as the frustration of life, the absolute void, the definition of damnation. The isolation of a radical concept of freedom, which for Sartre was a lived experience, shows with all desirable clarity that liberation from the truth does not produce pure freedom, but abolishes it. Anarchic freedom, taken radically, does not redeem, but makes man a miscarried creature, a pointless being.[23]

The Inadequate Answer of *Gaudium et Spes*

In his commentary on *Gaudium et spes*, Ratzinger criticized the section which dealt with freedom.[24] An analysis of his criticisms can help us to grasp his understanding of human freedom. His first criticism is that its exposition of the nature of human spirituality in terms of intellect (the human capacity for truth), conscience (the human capacity for good), and freedom, excluded the inter-subjectivity of the human person, our essential ordination to love. The concept of person does not ground its presentation of freedom.[25] His second criticism is that the document excluded the New

23. Ratzinger, "Truth and Freedom," 25–26.
24. "Church and Man's," 136–40. The biblical texts referred to are Eccl 15:14 and 2 Cor 5:10. However, we should note that, at the 1985 Synod, Ratzinger affirmed the importance of GS, no. 22 as the hermeneutical lens for the rest of the document. This being the case, the point of the document is to affirm the contemporary longing for human freedom and self-fulfilment which can only be realised through union with Christ. See Rowland, *Ratzinger's Faith*, 32–33 and 38.
25. Ibid., 130–31. On this point, Rowland comments: "Regrettably for Ratzinger

Testament doctrine of freedom. It linked the idea of freedom with the doctrine of man as being in the image and likeness of God, but without any reference to Christ. In Ratzinger's estimation, the document should have set out the New Testament teaching on the gift of freedom which is conferred in Christ. Instead, even in its use of biblical texts, it grounded the meaning of freedom in natural theology rather than faith. It developed something which Ratzinger calls "a *theologia naturalis*, or, even more, an *ethica naturalis*."[26] Rather than simply follow the ethical optimism of late Jewish wisdom theology, it should have read the biblical texts in the light of the critical wisdom theology of Ecclesiastes and especially Job. It should have attended to the Jewish ethical doctrine of the two ways, which is grounded on the theology of the Covenant. When one looks at the actual history of the Covenant, one encounters the inability of Israel to fulfill it. Ultimately, the way of life came not from a freedom which could fulfill the Law but Christ's fulfillment of the Law through his death on the Cross.[27]

Essentially, Ratzinger's dissatisfaction with the account of freedom given in *Gaudium et spes* is that it is inadequate on both theological and philosophical levels. Its theological understanding of freedom is neither historically faithful to the biblical witness, nor to actual human history. It neglects to address the slavery to sin so dramatically described in Romans 7:13–25. Ratzinger goes so far as to say the following.

> It even falls into downright Pelagian terminology when it speaks of man "sese ab omni passionum captivitate liberans finem suum persequitur et apta subsidia ... procurat." That is not balanced by the following sentence, which logically is scarcely linked with it and which speaks of a wound inflicted by sin but regards grace only as a help to make the will once more "plene actuosam." The extent of the human dilemma, which is not constituted by the modest difference between "plene actuosus" and "actuosus" but calls man in question to his very depths and makes him unfree, is not taken even roughly into account here. Fundamentally,

---

... the young Karol Wojtyla's personalism did not carry through to articles 15–17 of *Gaudium et spes* ... Neither the concept of person nor the idea of love was mentioned here. The philosophy of interpersonal love, the whole set of I-Thou questions, are practically absent for the treatment of spirituality within this section of the document, and Ratzinger was quite appalled that anyone could attempt to speak of spirituality without thinking that Christian love might have something to do with it" (Rowland, *Ratzinger's Faith*, 41).

26. "Church and Man's," 137.

27. Ibid., 137–38.

the formula "plene actuosus" means that an at all events semi-Pelagian representational pattern has been retained.[28]

On the philosophical level Ratzinger asserts that the document presents what he calls "a colorless philosophical doctrine of freedom" which takes no account of the contemporary awareness that human freedom is constrained by numerous psychological and sociological factors. According to Ratzinger, it could even have been improved by taking into account the Marxist perception of "the extent of human alienation and decadence."[29]

As Ratzinger sees it, *Gaudium et spes* did not really deal with the problems of human freedom. It only dealt with "freedom of choice." As he states:

> The actual ontological content of the idea of freedom, the capacity to accept one's own nature and to become identified with it, is just as little realized as the dialogue character of human freedom, which is only brought to the full possibilities of its realization by that appeal of love which can never be forced upon it. But only on this basis would it have been possible to show that God's summons, under which man stands, is not in opposition to his freedom but makes it truly possible; that human freedom does not consist in abstract selection between different possibilities of behavior, but by its very nature lives in the presence of God and can only be really understood in relation to this vis-à-vis. Only on this basis would it also be possible to explain the perfect fulfillment of Christian freedom in the "freedom of the children of God."[30]

The Theology of Freedom

The purpose of Ratzinger's focus upon the prayer of Jesus in the Garden is to establish the outcome of that prayer for Jesus and for us. He maintains that, "Wherever the I gives itself to the Thou, there is freedom because this involves the reception of the 'form of God,'" and that "the Son transforms

---

28. Ibid., 138. The Vatican translation of the relevant passage from GS, no. 17 is :"Man achieves such dignity when, emancipating himself from all captivity to passion, he pursues his goal in a spontaneous choice of what is good, and procures for himself through effective and skilful action, apt helps to that end. Since man's freedom has been damaged by sin, only by the aid of God's grace can he bring such a relationship with God into full flower." See *Vatican II*, 135.

29. Ibid.

30. Ibid., 138–39.

the anguish of a man into filial obedience, the speech of the servant into the Word which is the Son."³¹ Consequently:

> [We] come to grasp the manner of our liberation, our participation in the Son's freedom. As a result of the unity of wills . . . the greatest possible change has taken place in man, the only change which meets his desire: he has become divine. We can therefore describe the prayer which enters into the praying of Jesus and becomes the prayer of Jesus in the Body of Christ as freedom's laboratory.³²

If we are to understand what Ratzinger means by our participation in the Son's freedom, we must discover two things—what he means by freedom, and how he understands it to be exercised by the Son.

In Ratzinger's earlier Christology, we came across a paradoxical reference to freedom: "God's disguise as man in history 'must' be—with the necessity of freedom."³³ However, if we are to understand this paradox we must go back to its foundation in Ratzinger's understanding of God. We begin with what he calls the primacy of the *logos*. This *logos* he identifies as "the idea," "freedom," and "love." It is "the originating and encompassing power of all being."³⁴ All being is derived from thought and, indeed, the innermost structure of being is thought. All being is "being-thought." What we find present in all things is "objective mind," which is the product of "subjective mind." All of our thinking about being is actually a rethinking of what has already been thought. This being-thought-ness of things is discoverable by philosophers, that is to say, they can discover the God of the philosophers. Ratzinger sums up thus: "The world is objective mind; it meets us in an intellectual structure, that is, it offers itself to our mind as something that can be reflected upon and understood."³⁵ From this follows the conviction of the existence of God, since being-thought is not possible without thinking, and hence a thinker.

In arriving at this conclusion, Ratzinger rejects the materialist solution to the question of being and accepts the idealist solution: "All being is ultimately being-thought and can be traced back to mind as the original reality."³⁶ Ratzinger defines matter as "being that does not itself comprehend being," and mind as "being that understands itself, as being that is

31. *Behold*, 41.
32. Ibid., 42.
33. *Introduction*, 269.
34. Ibid., 152.
35. Ibid., 155.
36. Ibid., 156.

present to itself," and consequently: "The idealist solution to the problem of being accordingly signifies the idea that all being is the being-thought by one single consciousness. The unity of being consists in the identity of the one consciousness, whose impulses constitute the many things that are."[37]

From the God of the philosophers, Ratzinger moves to the God of Jesus Christ. This God is not completely identical with the idealist's God as outlined above. The Christian God is being which is being-thought, but does not remain thought alone, only giving rise to the appearance of an independent existence in things. Rather:

> Christian belief in God means that things are the being-thought of a creative consciousness, of a creative freedom, and that the creative consciousness that bears up all things has released what has been thought into the freedom of its own, independent existence. In this it goes beyond any mere idealism. While the latter ... explains everything real as the content of a single consciousness, in the Christian view what supports it all is a creative freedom that sets what had been thought in the freedom of its own being, so that, on the one hand, it is the being-thought of a consciousness and yet, on the other hand, is true being itself.[38]

Thus, for Ratzinger, God is being, not just as consciousness, but as creative freedom that creates further freedoms. Hence:

> To this extent one could very well describe Christianity as a philosophy of freedom. For Christianity, the explanation of reality as a whole is not an all-embracing consciousness or one single materiality; on the contrary, at the summit stands a freedom that thinks and, by thinking, creates freedoms, thus making freedom the structural form of all being.[39]

We should note that, thus far, Ratzinger has been speaking in terms of being as such, not personal being. All being, both uncreated and created, participates in freedom. "To be" is "to be free."

According to Ratzinger, the Christian belief in the primacy of the *logos* leads to a belief in the personal nature of original being. Such being, as original thought, expressed as being-thought in the world, means that this original being "is not an anonymous, neutral consciousness but rather freedom, creative love, a person."[40] For Ratzinger, the acceptance of the *logos* as

---

37. Ibid., 157.
38. Ibid.
39. Ibid., 158.
40. Ibid.

personal and creative means the acceptance of the primacy of the particular over the universal. The difference between the "personal" and the "individual" is that the latter is understood as arising out of and secondary to the universal, whereas the personal means it is the particular being which is the primary reality.[41] To accept the primacy of the person means to accept the primacy of freedom rather than that of cosmic necessity. It is this primacy of freedom which marks the division between idealism and Christian belief.[42]

At this point, Ratzinger moves from an economic view of freedom as expressed in creation back to an immanent view of freedom in God, and how that freedom issues forth in establishing economic freedom. Since the creative thinking which is the precondition and ground of all being is conscious thinking, it must know not only itself but also its whole thought. Furthermore:

> It means further that this thinking not only knows but loves; that is it is creative because it is love; and that, because it can love as well as think, it has given its thought the freedom of its own existence, objectivized it, released it into distinct being, loves it and, loving, upholds it.[43]

Ratzinger identifies the *logos* of all being as "consciousness," "freedom," and "love." The world is not grounded on cosmic necessity, but on freedom. Freedom is the "necessary structure" of the world. Yet this very fact renders the world "incomprehensible." If the world is upheld by a freedom which wills, knows and loves the world *as freedom*, then incalculability becomes an essential part of the world. This freedom creates the possibility of the rejection of freedom. The world is willed and created on the "risk" of freedom and love. "As the arena of love it is also the playground of freedom and also incurs the risk of evil. It accepts the mystery of darkness for the sake of the greater light constituted by freedom and love."[44]

---

41. Ibid., 160.
42. Ibid., 158–59.
43. Ibid., 159.
44. Ibid., 160. In *Principles of Catholic Theology*, Ratzinger is critical of Rahner's concept of freedom because, he argues, it leaves no room for the "incomprehensible" and "incalculable." According to Ratzinger, in his attempt to reconcile history and ontology, Rahner has attempted to do too much. The particular is reduced to the universal. Initially, this looks like liberation. The Christian "is freed from the burden of Christian particularity, led into the freedom of universal philosophy and its rationalism" (167). However, Christianity itself becomes a "burden." All that is needed is "self-acceptance," just being human. For Ratzinger, this is "damnation" rather than "salvation." We do not merely want to accept our own humanity, but transcend it. What is needed is a spirituality of "conversion," of "self-transcendence," which is one of Rahner's

Ratzinger makes his paradoxical statement about the necessity of freedom in the context of a section of *Introduction to Christianity* called: "The

---

basic concepts, one which, according to Ratzinger, he loses sight of in his synthesis. Ratzinger thinks that Rahner went astray in attempting to provide "a philosophical and theological world formula on the basis of which the whole of reality can be deduced cohesively from necessary causes" (169). However, such a solution is contrary to the "mystery" of freedom. Hegel's conviction that there is a "spiritual world formula" is wrong. According to Ratzinger, Rahner adopted the concept of freedom that is proper to idealistic philosophy—a concept which can only be applied to God. Rahner defines freedom as "the ultimate self-responsibility of the person . . . as self-action [*Grundkurs des Glaubens*, 47]. Freedom is the ability to be oneself [*Grundkurs*, 49]. According to Ratzinger, for Rahner, human freedom seems to have been absorbed into divine freedom, having an efficacy which belongs to God alone. Furthermore, in calling human freedom an "always already accomplished freedom" [*Grundkurs*, 138], freedom seems to be assimilated by predestination. Ultimately, Ratzinger sees Rahner as the advocate of a different kind of identification of freedom with necessity. Thus, "the attempt to depict cohesively with a logical necessity the unity and totality of the real leads unquestionably to an identification of freedom and necessity . . . Ultimately, then, a synthesis that combines being and history in a single compelling logic of the understanding becomes, by the universality of its claim, a philosophy of necessity, even though this necessity is then explained as a process of freedom" (170). For Ratzinger's complete analysis of Rahner's position on the nature of freedom in the context of the relationship between ontology and history, see *Principles of Catholic Theology*, 153–90, especially 161–71. Let it be said that, although we can participate in the freedom of God, and to some extent understand it, we cannot comprehend it. It remains a divine mystery. A passage from *The Great Divorce* captures this mystery admirably. Therein, the Teacher, George MacDonald, in answer to the question of the Ghost whether or not all will be saved, says: "[All] answers deceive. If ye put the question from within Time and are asking about possibilities, the answer is certain. The choice of ways is before you. Neither is closed. Any man may choose eternal death. Those who choose it will have it. But if ye are trying to leap on into eternity, if ye are trying to see the final state of all things as it *will* be (for so ye must speak) when there are no more possibilities left but only the Real, then ye ask what cannot be answered to mortal ears. Time is the very lens through which ye see—small and clear, as men see through the wrong end of the telescope—something that would otherwise be too big for ye to see at all. That thing is Freedom: the gift whereby ye most resemble your Maker and are yourselves parts of eternal reality. But ye can see it only through the lens of Time, in a little clear picture, through the inverted telescope. It is a picture of moments following one another and yourself in each moment making some choice that might have been otherwise. Neither the temporal succession nor the phantom of what ye might have chosen but didn't is itself Freedom. They are a lens. The picture is a symbol: but it's truer than any philosophical theorem (or, perhaps, than any mystic's vision) that claims to go behind it. For every attempt to see the shape of eternity except through the lens of Time destroys your knowledge of Freedom. Witness the doctrine of Predestination which shows (truly enough) that eternal reality is not waiting for a future in which to be real; but at the price of removing Freedom which is the deeper truth of the two. And wouldn't Universalism do the same? Ye *cannot* know eternal reality by a definition. Time itself, and all acts and events that fill Time, are the definition, and it must be lived. The Lord said we were gods. How long could ye bear to look (without Time's lens) on the greatness of your own soul and the eternal reality of her choice?" (Lewis, *The Great Divorce*, 114–15).

primacy of acceptance and Christian positivity."[45] There he writes of "the primacy of acceptance over action, over one's own achievement, when it is a question of man's final end."[46] Essentially, the human person only becomes wholly human through the free reception of the gift of love. This love "represents simultaneously both man's highest possibility and his deepest need," and "this most necessary thing is at the same time the freest and most unenforceable means . . . for his 'salvation.'"[47] Attempting self-salvation, self-liberation, destroys one's humanity. This is the attempt to be like God which misunderstands the true nature of God, which thinks of him as an independent, autonomous, self-sufficient being. This is "loneliness," but God is "fellowship." Freedom is not independence, but a freely willed exchange, the freedom of self-giving communion.[48]

The Anthropology of Freedom

In *"Freiheit und Wahrheit,"* Ratzinger develops the anthropological understanding of freedom at further length. Taking the example of a woman who aborts her child in response to a false notion of freedom which sees it as the right to autonomy, to self-determination, which in turn annuls the right of another to freedom, Ratzinger points to the interdependent nature of being human. The mother-child relationship is a particularly vivid example of the true nature of human freedom. As Ratzinger explains:

> The being of another person is so closely interwoven with the being of this person, the mother, that for the present it can survive only by physically being with the other, in a physical unity with her. Such unity, however, does not eliminate the otherness of this being or authorize us to dispute its distinct selfhood. However, to be oneself in this way is to be radically from and through another. Conversely, this being-with compels the being of the other—that is, the mother—to become a being-for, which contradicts her own desire to be an independent self and is thus experienced as the antithesis of her own freedom.[49]

---

45. *Introduction*, 266–69.
46. Ibid., 266.
47. Ibid., 267. Cf. Ratzinger, "Loi de l'Eglise et liberté du chrétien," where he states: "In the Church, the debate (about freedom) concerns liberty in its deepest sense, as openness to the divine Being in order to become a sharer in its life." This is from an unpublished paper, and is cited by Nichols in "Walter Kasper," 22.
48. *Introduction*, 267–68.
49. Ratzinger, "Truth and Freedom," 27.

For Ratzinger, this "being-from," "being-with," and "being-for" is the essence of "being-human." We must all accept the limitation of our freedom, meaning that we must live out our freedom in communion rather than competition. The temptation which faces us is to accept the being-for of others in the sense of others being-for us, but reject the reality of being-from and the responsibility of being-for others. According to Ratzinger, the radical demand for freedom which springs from the Enlightenment regards what is actually the fundamental reality of human existence as an attack on freedom. Thus, "[the] radical cry for freedom demands man's liberation from his very essence as man, so that he may become the 'new man.'"[50]

Ratzinger sees this attempt to achieve a freedom of radical autonomy as a kind of false attempt at *theosis*—"the implicit goal of all of modernity's struggles for freedom is to be at last like a god who depends on nothing and no one, and whose own freedom is not restricted by that of another." This is a false attempt at divinization because behind it lies a false image of God, an idol, a conception of divinity as pure egoism. It is a demonic antithesis of the real God, who is "by his very nature entirely being-for (Father), being-from (Son), and being-with (Holy Spirit). Man, for his part, is God's image precisely insofar as the 'from,' 'with,' and 'for' constitute the fundamental anthropological pattern."[51] Any attempt to free ourselves from this pattern leads not to divinization but dehumanization. We destroy our being through a destruction of the truth about our being. The Enlightenment ideal of freedom leads in the end to Sartre's "hell is other people" from which there is "no exit."

What is Ratzinger's antidote for this freedom which poisons itself? For him:

> [Human freedom] can consist only in the ordered coexistence of liberties, this means that order—right—is not the conceptual antithesis of freedom, but rather its condition, indeed, a constitutive element of freedom itself. Right is not an obstacle to freedom, but constitutes it. The absence of right is the absence of freedom.[52]

---

50. Ibid., 28.
51. Ibid.
52. Ibid., 29. The translator of this essay points out that here the term "right" renders the German *Recht*. This term can mean "right" in the sense of "human rights," but may also mean "law," with the more or less explicit connotation of "just order," "order embodying what is right." It is in this latter sense that Ratzinger uses *Recht* here and in what follows.

This raises the question of how one identifies that "right" which accords with freedom. Right must be in accord with truth and thus with freedom. The truth of our being includes its moral truth. Ratzinger seeks to answer this question inductively rather than deductively by beginning with how a small community discovers "which order best serves the shared life of all the members, so that a common form of freedom emerges from their joint existence."[53] He then observes that no small community is self-contained. The same is true of nation states. Yet, the common good of a particular community, even if it be a nation state, cannot be true, genuinely human freedom. The whole of humanity, both today's and tomorrow's, must be kept in mind. Citing Augustine, Ratzinger says that "a state which measures itself only by its common interests and not by justice itself, by true justice, is not structurally different from a well-organized robber band."[54]

The true right which accords with freedom Ratzinger calls the good of the whole, the good itself. For him, the central concept in ethics is "responsibility." Ratzinger defines responsibility as "the anchoring of freedom in the truth of the good, of man and of the world."[55] Rather than consisting of an ever growing expansion of individual rights in isolation from the whole, freedom can only increase if there is an increase in a responsibility which includes the claims of a shared human existence and of true human nature. Such a responsibility must include a religious understanding, for philosophy, by itself, is unable to obtain a comprehensive view of the common good, including the good of the future.[56] The two alternatives to this are a consequentialism which overreaches itself, since we are unable to foresee all the consequences of our actions, or an elitist "consensus" of those who deem themselves capable of rational argument, who will engage in "advocacy" on behalf of lesser mortals.

For Ratzinger, one cannot understand freedom as long as one only sees the human person in his or her individuality without reference to the other person and to the whole of mankind. There is a single humanity, present in every human person, which we call human nature. From faith in creation comes the conviction that "there is one divine idea, 'man,' to which it is our task to answer. In this idea, freedom and community, order and concern for the future, are a single whole." Therefore, "[responsibility] would thus mean

---

53. Ibid.
54. Ibid., 30.
55. Ibid., 31. Cf. *Introduction*, 322–24.
56. Ibid. Cf. *SS*, no. 28: "Love of God leads to participation in the justice and generosity of God towards others. Love of God requires an interior freedom from all possessions and all material goods: the love of God is revealed in responsibility for others."

to live our being as an answer—as a response to what we are in truth."[57] We can find this truth in the Decalogue, which is the self-presentation and self-exhibition of both God and man. It is the mirror of God's essence. In living the Decalogue we bring our being into correspondence with the truth and thus do the good. The definition of freedom is to live our divinity, which comes through the union of our being with that of God.

Ratzinger's concern for history breaks through in his analysis of freedom because, for him, there is a history of freedom. There is a history of liberation, an "ongoing purification for the sake of the truth. The true history of freedom consists in the purification of individuals and of institutions through this truth [of responsibility]."[58] Returning to his notion that there is always an excess in the meaning of human words of which the speaker is unconscious, but which comes to the surface over time, Ratzinger states that this must, *a fortiori*, be true of the Word which comes out of the depths of God. Hence, the Decalogue, although it has received its definitive and authoritative exegesis in the words, life, Passion and Resurrection of Christ, continues to reveal unexpected depths. Consequently, "man's listening to the message of faith is not the passive registering of otherwise unknown information, but the resuscitation of our choked memory and the opening of the powers of understanding which await the light of the truth in us."[59] Therefore, our reason is on a quest for responsibility. There is a real history of freedom.

The Biblical Meaning of Freedom

Ratzinger has also sought to establish the meaning of freedom on a secure biblical basis. In a 1981 essay entitled "Freedom and Constraint in the Church," he identified two biblical terms which express the concept of freedom—*eleutheria* (freedom) and *parresia* (frankness, candor).[60] The first term does not refer to freedom of choice, but the fullness of membership and possession of rights in a family or society. The free person is the one who "belongs," who fully participates. In the allegory of Sarah and Hagar on the nature of Christian freedom, to be free one must truly belong to the household (cf. Gal 4:21–31). It does not consist in having different privileges from the slave but in having a different status, that of an heir and an owner (cf. Gal 4:1). In short, to be free means to be a son (cf. Gal 4:5). For

---

57. Ibid., 31.
58. Ibid., 30. Cf. *SS*, nos. 24–25.
59. Ibid., 33.
60. Ratzinger, "Freedom and Constraint in the Church," 186.

the Christian, an ontological difference leads to a difference in behavior. Because one has put on Christ (cf. Gal 3:27), one participates in his way of acting. Hence, one does not use one's freedom as an opportunity for the flesh but, like Christ, through love becomes a servant of the other (cf. Gal 5:13). One fulfils the law of Christ (cf. Gal 6:2). As Ratzinger explains:

> This is a consequence of their ontological status, that is, of the fact that through the Spirit of Christ they participate in the ontological status of Jesus Christ himself. They are "spiritual" (6:1). To live the law of Christ means, therefore, to live according to the ontological status of the spiritual man, in the way of the Spirit. This includes crucifying the flesh "with its passions and desires" (5:24).[61]

From a biblical perspective, freedom is not indeterminacy, nor participation in a given social structure, but participation in being itself. From this perspective, God is freedom in person, since he is in possession of being in its totality. To be free means to participate in the gift of love and the reception of love which takes place in God. To be free is to be divinized, to participate in the life of the trinitarian God. To be free means to be like Christ crucified.[62]

The "frankness" or "candor" of this freedom is based on a term which in its original context of Greek political vocabulary meant the right to say everything publically. It springs from the responsibility of the free individual as an heir and owner. The right of freedom flows from the responsibility of freedom. According to Ratzinger, in the First Letter to the Thessalonians, St. Paul develops a Christian rhetoric for freedom which "interprets a characteristic basic right of freedom in a Christian and ecclesial way."[63] Ratzinger's reading of St. Paul attributes to him an understanding of the rhetoric of antiquity as characterized by flattery, covetousness and glory-seeking. It sought self-promotion, material gain and the good opinion of others. The last mentioned, in particular, is contrary to truth. "Seeming suppresses being. The appearance becomes the universal standard. Man lives for appearance, and so his life becomes a semblance of life. In this the Bible rightly sees the essence of slavery, of the lack of freedom." Thus, there can be no freedom where there is no truth. Because St. Paul speaks the truth to a world ruled by appearances, he faces "great opposition" (1 Thess 2:2). This expression of freedom presupposes a freedom from oneself, a detachment from oneself.

---

61. Ibid., 188.
62. Ibid.
63. Ibid., 189.

Here again, Ratzinger locates freedom in being, which then takes concrete forms "in active freedoms, in rights to do things."[64]

If to be free means to be like Christ crucified then, by implication, Christ exercises his true freedom in saying yes to the Father's will that he drink of the cup of death. Ratzinger has drawn our attention to our participation in the freedom of Christ, in the life of the Trinity, through participation in the Cross, *through the Spirit of Christ*. Yet he has not given much attention to *Christ's* participation in the Cross *through the Spirit*.

The Freedom of Jesus in His Passion and Death

How does Jesus' exercise of human freedom in his Passion save us and lead to our divinization? When we compare Ratzinger's treatment of the Passion and death of Jesus in *Introduction to Christianity* and *The God of Jesus Christ* with that found in *Jesus of Nazareth*, we can see that although there are some elements in common there are also some differences in emphasis. Some things which are given great prominence in the earlier works receive less in the latter, wherein one finds new emphases as well as some development of earlier points.

In his earlier works Ratzinger finds the key to the Passion in what he calls the "brokenness" of Jesus, a brokenness which is worship. In this worship there is a two-fold movement, from God to man and from man to God. Christian sacrifice is receiving, "becoming totally receptive and letting ourselves be completely taken over by him."[65] It is also the gift of the Son to the Father. The Cross is the sacrifice which Jesus offers the Father in obedience. It is "man's unqualified Yes to God" which alone is "true worship."[66] We have been "lent the freedom to say Yes or No, the freedom to love or to reject; love's free Yes is the only thing for which God must wait—the only worship of 'sacrifice' that can have any meaning."[67] Though Ratzinger does not state it here, on the basis of his understanding of freedom, what this implies is that sin has destroyed true human freedom. Only the man who is truly free can offer this sacrifice. Jesus is the one true priest, and the worship he offers is "the one and only liturgy of the world, a cosmic liturgy."[68] What Jesus sacrifices is his own "'I,' his own self. It is love "to the end" (John 13:1).

---

64. Ibid., 190.
65. *Introduction*, 283.
66. Ibid., 285.
67. Ibid., 285–86.
68. Ibid., 286.

What is the nature of this love? It is God's own love become human love. Again, this implies that the freedom of God, the one who is freedom itself, becomes the freedom of the human love of Jesus. According to Ratzinger, it is a new form of representation. Jesus stands in our place, not in a legal sense but in an ontological one. In order to participate in this sacrifice we must let ourselves be taken over by him, allow ourselves to be united with this gift of love from Jesus to the Father, "and thus become worshippers with him and in him."[69] For Ratzinger, Jesus' worship of the Father through the Cross "has smelted the body of humanity into the Yes of worship. It is completely 'anthropocentric,' entirely related to man, because it was radical theocentricity, delivery of the 'I' and therefore the creature man to God."[70]

At this point, Ratzinger comes to the heart of his understanding of sacrifice. It is "the form that love takes in a world characterized by death and self-seeking." The love of Jesus for the Father becomes "the ec-stacy of man outside himself, in which he is stretched out infinitely beyond himself, torn apart, as it were, far beyond his apparent capacity for being stretched."[71] In a sinful world worship must be sacrificial, it must be the Cross, it must be the pain of being torn apart. This pain of the Cross is necessary, not because the Father wills it, but because love can take no other form in the face of sin and death. Although the fundamental principle of sacrifice is love, in the face of evil, love is crucified. However, this love is active, not passive. Jesus freely drinks from the cup. So, Ratzinger can say that this love "breaks down, opens up, crucifies, tears."[72]

We need to return to Ratzinger's statement that in Jesus' natural will, the sum total of human nature's resistance to God, our obstinacy, our opposition to God, our recalcitrant nature, is present within Jesus himself. This idea does not fit with Ratzinger's portrayal of the human freedom of Jesus which has just been presented. Whatever is in the natural will of Jesus is in Jesus himself. If human resistance, obstinacy, opposition and recalcitrance towards God are present in Jesus, how can he be truly free to offer the sacrifice of himself? It seems that this particular idea of Ratzinger contradicts the rest of his understanding of the human freedom of Jesus. It is the one significant point of contradiction in his spiritual Christology.

It is in looking at the article of the Creed which says that Jesus descended into Hell that Ratzinger attempts to lay bare the meaning of Jesus being torn asunder. Quoting Jean Daniélou, he portrays the death agony of

69. Ibid., 288.
70. Ibid., 289.
71. Ibid.
72. Ibid.

Christ, as a sharing in "[our] feeling of being torn asunder, which is a cross to us, this inability of our heart to carry within itself simultaneously the love of the most holy Trinity and love of the world alienated from the Trinity." Ratzinger presents us with the paradox of the crucified Christ, in the words "My God, why have you forsaken me?" being "simultaneously immersed in God and in the depths of the God-forsaken creature."[73] This is the "crucifixion" of Jesus, the realization of love.

In *The God of Jesus Christ*, Ratzinger reflects further on this paradox. He states that, for Jesus, "the destruction of the bodily instrument of communication interrupts his dialogue with the Father. When the bodily instrument is crushed, the intellectual act that is based on this instrument disappears for a time." Since the whole existence of Jesus "is in the shared dimension of his dialogue with the Father, the absolute solitude wrought by death is incomprehensible."[74] In true Marcelian fashion, Ratzinger does not attempt to solve this apparent problem, only to clarify the mystery. The "silence" of God, as well as the "speech," is a part of Christian revelation—"God is not only the comprehensible word that comes to us; he is also the silent, inaccessible, uncomprehended, and incomprehensible ground that eludes us."[75]

For Ratzinger, Jesus' descent into Hell begins on the Mount of Olives. Here, the innermost heart of his Passion is revealed not as "physical pain but radical loneliness, complete abandonment." Ratzinger believes that this loneliness is nothing other than the human condition. We dwell in an "abyss of loneliness"—we are "alone in [our] innermost being."[76] Created by God for communion, we are unable to exist alone. Yet paradoxically we are alone. We experience the fear of loneliness, which is not a rational fear of some identifiable threat, but a fear of a state which is a contradiction of our very nature. For Ratzinger, this is a "hellish" state.

> If there were such a thing as a loneliness which could no longer be penetrated by the word of another; if a state of abandonment were to arise that was so deep that no "You" could reach into it

---

73. Ibid., 290; quoting Daniélou, *Essai sur le mystère de l'histoire*, no pagination given.

74. *Jesus Christ*, 83.

75. *Introduction*, 296. Cf. Marcel, *The Mystery of Being*, 211–12.

76. *Introduction*, 298. We could even say that the Descent into Hell begins with Jesus' baptism in the Jordan. Ratzinger speaks of the descent into the waters of baptism as an anticipation of the descent of Holy Saturday, saying that in the ultimate descent Jesus does not descend in the role of a spectator, as is presented in Dante's Inferno. Thus he agrees with von Balthasar that the descent is a not a triumphal one, but rather a suffering-with-others one. See *Jesus I*, 19–20.

any more, then we should have real, total loneliness and dreadfulness, what theology calls "hell."[77]

By Ratzinger's account, the fact that the Old Testament has one word for Hell and death, *Sheol*, reveals a profound insight. Death is Hell. It is absolute loneliness, the place that no love can reach. Or rather, it was such a place. For now Jesus has descended into this Hell. It is no longer the place that no love can reach. Life has gone down into Hell. Love now dwells there.[78]

When we come to the crucifixion and death of Jesus in *Jesus of Nazareth*, we find, as has been said, some elements in common with Ratzinger's earlier Christology, as well as some different emphases. Overall, the later work does not reach the intellectual depths of the earlier ones, although it covers a broader expanse. It is more biblically based. So, although Ratzinger covers much the same ground in looking at the Cross as an act of worship, he does so with a much more explicitly biblical flavor.[79] His approach might be termed more pastoral in intent. It is concerned not just with the actions of Jesus but also the reactions to him from the onlookers.

One aspect which is more developed is the ecclesial significance of Psalm 22. Attention is focused not just on one verse in the Psalm, but upon the whole Psalm.[80] When Ratzinger does look at Jesus' cry of abandonment from the Cross, he moves beyond the attention which he gave earlier to exclusively concentrating upon "the mystery of his person in his final agony."[81] While not denying the validity of this approach, he characterizes it as too narrowly individualistic. Now he emphasizes the intercessory aspect of this cry, and the reality of "corporate personality."[82] There is also a greater emphasis upon the priesthood and kingship of Jesus.[83]

There are also new elements. In the cry "I thirst" (John 19:28), the lament of God over the failure of his people to requite his love is made present

---

77. *Introduction*, 300.

78. One can see both similarities and differences between Ratzinger's and von Balthasar's portrayals of the descent into Hell. Although Ratzinger shares von Balthasar's focus on the loneliness of Jesus and his solidarity with us, he does not go so far as to lay himself open to a charge of universalism. Furthermore, he identifies the descent into Hell with the whole of the Passion, rather than Holy Saturday alone. Cf. Balthasar, *Mysterium Paschale*, 148–88. Von Balthasar's thesis is contemporaneous with that of Ratzinger, since it was first mooted in his *Theologie der Drei Tage*.

79. *Jesus II*, 229–39.

80. Ibid., 204–5.

81. Ibid., 214–15.

82. Ibid., 213–16.

83. Ibid., 209–12, 216–17, and 223.

in Jesus.[84] Also, Ratzinger points out that an aspect of corporate personality is that we can be purified by participating in the suffering of Jesus, by gazing upon the pierced one (John 19:37; Zech 12:10), while another is that the church and its sacraments are born from this same pierced side.[85]

The Consummation of Jesus' Freedom in His Resurrection

Like goodness, truth, and beauty, for Ratzinger, love and freedom are convertible. They are coterminous—love is freedom, freedom is love. In our fallen world, in the face of sin, this love/freedom must take the form of obedient sacrificial worship. This worship transforms the un-freedom/loneliness of sin, and its consummation, death, into true freedom, the freedom/love of God.

This new consummation takes place first in Jesus, in his Resurrection from the dead and his Ascension to the Father's right hand. In order to grasp Ratzinger's understanding of this consummation, we must again address his understanding of that love which is freedom. The love which Ratzinger focuses upon is that spoken of in the Song of Songs. It is the love that is as strong as death (cf. Song 8:6). This love is not *agape*, but *eros*. This love Ratzinger typifies as making boundless demands which give expression to the basic problem of human existence, the demand of human love for infinity and indestructibility, a demand which must remain unsatisfied in a world of sin and death, a world of loneliness and destruction.

Why does Ratzinger focus upon *eros* rather than *agape*? He himself admits that the term *eros* is used only twice in the Septuagint and not at all in the New Testament.[86] To begin with, he sees *eros* as having been subjected to a false divinization in the ancient world. Rather than being a true ascent in ecstasy to the divine, it was warped and degraded. It needs to be disciplined and purified so that it can give "a certain foretaste of the pinnacle of our existence, of that beatitude for which our whole being yearns."[87] Ratzinger focuses upon *eros* rather than *agape* because the human person is not pure spirit, but body and soul. It is this "unified creature composed of body and soul, who loves."[88] *Eros* is meant to ascend to the divine. We are meant

---

84. Ibid., 217–19.
85. Ibid., 219–22 and 225–26.
86. *DCE*, no. 3.
87. Ibid., no. 4.
88. Ibid., no. 5.

to rise in ecstasy above ourselves in a love which is meant to realize both a human and divine promise.[89]

In the Song of Songs, love moves from an insecure, indeterminate and searching love to a love which really discovers the other and seeks the good of the beloved. *Eros* is transformed in a twofold sense—it becomes exclusive and eternal. It becomes ecstasy, not in terms of intoxication, "but rather as a journey, an ongoing exodus out of the closed inward-looking self towards liberation through self-giving, and thus towards authentic self-discovery and indeed the discovery of God." This path is travelled first by Jesus through the Cross and Resurrection. Thus Ratzinger states: "Starting from the depths of his own sacrifice and of the love that reaches fulfillment therein, he ... portrays ... the essence of love and indeed of human life itself."[90]

In looking at *agape* and *eros*, which he often contrasts as "descending" love and "ascending" love, Ratzinger rejects a distinction which would classify the first as Christian and the second as non-Christian. Rather, the two can never be completely separated. When the two are united, the true nature of love is revealed. *Agape* enters into *eros*, which consequently seeks the good of the other more and more. Human love cannot be pure *agape*, since, as a creature, the human person must receive love as well as give it. One must receive the descending *agape* of God in order to pass on an *agaped eros* to both God and other human beings.[91] For Ratzinger, the love of God for man is simultaneously both *eros* and *agape*. He not only "gives," "creates"—he also "desires," "elects," "chooses." God's *eros* is *agape* because it is gratuitous and it forgives.[92]

We have said that, for Ratzinger, the path by which *eros* is transformed into *agape* is firstly the Cross and Resurrection. In the Resurrection this love is shown to be greater than the power of death. Indeed, the Resurrection "*is* the greater strength of love in the face of death."[93] The human paradox is that man is not by nature immortal. Heaven is a grace added over and above our human nature.[94] The striving for autonomy which has fallen to our lot

---

89. Ibid., no. 6.
90. Ibid.
91. Ibid., nos. 7–8. C. S. Lewis also holds that *eros* needs to be "agaped." See his *The Four Loves*, 7–14 and 85–106.
92. *DCE*, nos. 9–10.
93. *Introduction*, 302.
94. Ibid., 313.

owing to original sin must end in death, since autonomy is impossible for us.[95]

How can love be stronger than death? According to Ratzinger, it is only when someone is ready to put life second to love. In the Resurrection of Jesus, the power of love has risen to be superior to the power of mere biological life. In him, *bios* has been encompassed by and incorporated in the power of love. This love of Jesus for us has become the love that actually keeps us alive. In this "evolutionary leap," *bios* has become *zoe*, definitive life. This leap is achieved "by the spirit, by freedom, by love. It would no longer be evolution but decision and gift in one."[96]

From the human perspective, immortality is only possible through living in another, and it is only the other who, through taking us up into his own being, can make immortality possible for us. Ratzinger sees these two perspectives mirrored in the two New Testament descriptions of the Resurrection of Jesus—that he has risen, and that the Father has raised him up. Thus he writes that:

> The two formulas meet in the fact that Jesus' total love for men, which leads him to the Cross, is perfected in totally passing beyond to the Father and therein becomes stronger than death, because it is at the same time total "being held" by him.[97]

From this, Ratzinger draws the point that love and immortality are intrinsically linked. Indeed, the specific character of love is to establish immortality. The reverse of this principle is that immortality always proceeds from love. It cannot proceed from an autarchy which is sufficient unto itself. This principle even applies to God. Because God is the relation of three Persons to each other in the "one for another" of love, because he lives only "in relation to," he is absolute permanence. The absolute is "absolute relatedness."[98]

Returning to the Resurrection, Ratzinger argues that it is on the basis of love as the foundation of immortality that the Resurrection of Jesus *is* our life.[99] For him, this is the reasoning which lies behind St. Paul's argument

---

95. Ibid., 302. The positions that we are by nature mortal and have lost immortality through original sin are not contradictory. The rebellion of our first parents precluded our reception of eternal life. We should remember that there were two special trees in Eden, the tree of the knowledge of good and evil and the tree of life. Had we not eaten from the first we would have been free to eat of the fruit of the second (cf. Gen 3:22).

96. Ibid., 305.

97. Ibid.

98. Ibid., 305–6.

99. Ratzinger refers to "the biblical statement that *his* Resurrection is *our* life"; in *Introduction*, 306. He seems to be referring to the statement of Jesus in John 11:25—"I am the Resurrection and the Life."

that if the dead are not raised nor is Christ (cf. 1 Cor 15:12–19). Only if Christ has risen can love be stronger than death. In Jesus, it is love *for us* that is stronger than death.[100]

What conclusion can we draw from all of this concerning the freedom of Jesus? We have seen how Ratzinger regards love and freedom in God as identical. We can now add to this that he sees the life of God as identical with his love and freedom. In the Cross and Resurrection of Jesus, *bios* has been transformed into *zoe* through the transformation of human *eros* into divine *agape*, human freedom into the freedom of God. This new state of affairs Ratzinger attributes also to "the spirit."

Freedom and the Eschaton

In *Introduction to Christianity* a deliberate contrast is made between the descent of Jesus into Hell and his ascension into Heaven. According to Ratzinger, these two states form the two poles of the total range of possible human existence. These two poles are existential rather than cosmic. It is possible for any human person to move to the hellish pole through the definite rejection of being-for the other.[101] At the opposite pole, the Ascension opens up the possibility for human persons of communion with others through communion with divine love. As Hell can only be self-inflicted,

---

100. Ibid.

101. Ibid., 311–12. At this point, Ratzinger makes the following remark: "We know today better than ever before that everyone's existence touches these depths; and since in the last analysis mankind is '*one* man,' these depths affect not only the individual but also the one body of the whole human race, which must therefore bear the burden of them as a corporate whole. From this angle it can be understood once again how Christ, the 'new Adam,' undertook to bear the burden of these depths with us and did not wish to remain sublimely unaffected by them; conversely, of course, total rejection in all its unfathomability has only now become possible" (312). Unfortunately, Ratzinger does not expound upon this analysis of the corporate personality of the human race, although, in his commentary on GS, no. 22, he does write, "[in this section the] idea of the 'assumptio hominis' is touched upon in its full ontological depth. The human nature of all men is one; Christ's taking to himself the one human nature of man is an event which affects every human being; consequently human nature in every human being is henceforth Christologically characterised. This idea is then extended to the real plane of actual concrete human existence. Human action, thought, willing and loving have become the instrument of the Logos; what is first present on the plane of being also gives new significance to the plane of action, to the actual accomplishment of human personal life" ("Church and Man's," 160). We should note how Ratzinger grounds the "creation" of Hell for human persons on Christ's taking upon himself the burden of the "corporate man." Hell becomes possible for us only after Christ has "descended into Hell." Recall the account of Christ going to preach "to the spirits in prison, who formerly did not obey" (1 Pet 3:19–20).

Heaven by nature can only be received as a gift. Thus Heaven only comes into existence through the ascension of Christ. To say that he "ascended into Heaven" is simply to say that he brought about the communion "of the being 'man' with the being 'God.'"[102] Since Jesus is the "last Adam" his "creation" of Heaven is for the corporate human race, not simply private individuals.

Since the communion of God and man in the Resurrection and Ascension of Christ has broken down the frontier of *bios* and transformed it into *zoe*, the *eschaton* has already begun. Ratzinger identifies the Resurrection as *the* eschatological event.[103] In Christ the temporal has been taken up into the eternal. The barrier between "being" and "becoming" has been breached. Time has been drawn into God. For Ratzinger, our prayers are effective because:

> In Jesus we temporal beings can speak to the temporal one, our contemporary; but in him, who with us is time, we simultaneously make contact with the Eternal One, because with us Jesus is time, and with God he is eternity.[104]

Jesus is "in actual fact 'the throne of grace' to which at any time we can 'with confidence draw near'" (Heb 4:16).[105]

In *Jesus of Nazareth*, Ratzinger develops his understanding of the new presence of Jesus which has been brought about by his Resurrection and Ascension. The "heaven" into which Jesus has ascended is not some inaccessible place, but a sharing in God's dominion over space as well as time. Jesus' "going away" is also his "coming" (cf. John 14:28). Because Jesus is with the Father he can "see" us. We can only "touch" Jesus because he is now present with the Father. Through baptism our life is now hidden with God in Christ (cf. Col 3:1–3).[106] However, one fact which must be mentioned at this point is that Ratzinger makes no mention of the new presence of Jesus being the result of the gift of the Holy Spirit.

Previously it was said that, for Ratzinger, the two poles of possible human existence are existential and not cosmic. This position needs to be clarified further. For Ratzinger, anthropology and cosmology coincide in Christology. That is to say, in Christ, man and the cosmos have been reconciled. In the assumption of *eros* into *agape*, *bios* has been taken up into

---

102. *Introduction*, 313.
103. Ibid., 320.
104. Ibid., 317.
105. Ibid., 318.
106. *Jesus II*, 279–86.

zoe.[107] The cosmos was not created as a mere container for human history. Rather, "the cosmos is movement . . . it is not just a case of history *existing in* it . . . cosmos itself *is* history."[108] This history is moving towards its omega point, the second coming of Jesus Christ.

In his earlier Christology, Ratzinger made much use of Teilhard de Chardin's complexification thesis to explain this movement. This movement is driven from above by mind, not from below by unconscious matter. There is a process taking place by which the material is taken up into a new kind of unity through spirit. The return of Christ will be "the final unification of reality by spirit or mind."[109] This increasing coalescence of spirit and matter, of anthropology and cosmology, implies unification in a person, since there can be no mind which does not subsist as person. For the omega of the world to be "the triumph of spirit, that is, the triumph of truth, freedom, and love," this omega must be a person, since only a person can be truthful, free and loving. If reaching this omega "is based on spirit and freedom," it must include responsibility.[110] For this reason the second coming of the Lord brings judgment as well as salvation. The "final stage of the world is not the result of a natural current but the result of responsibility that is grounded in freedom."[111] At this point Ratzinger introduces what he sees as the paradox of freedom.

> There is a freedom that is not cancelled out even by grace and, indeed, is brought by it face to face with itself: man's final fate is not forced upon him regardless of the decisions he had made in his life . . . It is not part of our task to consider in detail how [the assertion that we will be judged according to our works] can coexist with the full weight of the doctrine of grace. Perhaps in the last analysis it is impossible to escape a paradox whose logic is completely disclosed only to the experience of a life based on faith. Anyone who entrusts himself to faith becomes aware that both exist: the radical character of grace that frees helpless man and, not less, the abiding seriousness of the responsibility that summons man day after day. Both mean together that the Christian enjoys, on the one hand, the liberating, detached tranquility of him who lives on that excess of divine justice known as Jesus Christ. There is a tranquility that knows: in the last analysis, I

---

107. *Introduction*, 318–20.

108. Ibid., 320.

109. Ibid., 321.

110. Ibid., 322. Note once more the equation of spirit, freedom, love, and now truth.

111. Ibid., 323.

cannot destroy what *he* has built up. For in himself man lives with the dreadful knowledge that his power to destroy is infinitely greater than his power to build up. But this same man knows that in Christ the power to build up has proved infinitely stronger. This is the source of a profound freedom, a knowledge of God's unrepentant love; he sees through all our errors and remains well disposed to us. It becomes possible to do one's own work fearlessly; it has shed its sinister aspect because it has lost its power to destroy: the issue of the world does not depend on us but is in God's hands. At the same time the Christian knows, however, that he is not free to do whatever he pleases, that his activity is not a game that God allows him and does not take seriously.[112]

The question which arises from this position is the following—can this apparent paradox be dissolved or must it remain insoluble? How can freedom be love and at the same time the choice to reject love? Perhaps the term freedom is being used in different senses. If freedom is love, then not loving is unfreedom. Rejecting God's grace is not an exercise in freedom, but a rejection of freedom. This is so even though we may say that we are free to reject God's grace, his offer of himself. When Ratzinger says that "there is a freedom which is not cancelled out even by grace," we can say that such a freedom is actually unfreedom. In Maximian terms it is an exercise of a gnomic rather than a natural will. This freedom is actually a perversion of true freedom, a perversion which ultimately leads to its negation.

Our Liturgical Participation in the Freedom of Jesus

Ratzinger holds that there is indeed a genuine theology of liberation. In *A New Song for the Lord* he explains this theology in the context of the statement of Jesus that he is "the way, the truth and the life" (John 14:6). Regarding the first aspect of this liberation, when Jesus calls himself "the way," this entails a "theology of liberation." As the true Moses, Jesus does more than lead us along the way, he *is* the way. This liberation theology is shaped by the connection between the Old and New Testaments, which Ratzinger sees as the "two stages of the divine-human history of freedom."[113] Although a new theology of "exodus" was first developed in countries wherein suffering

---

112. Ibid., 324–25. Here again we can see the practical, existential nature of Ratzinger's spiritual Christology. The apparent contradiction between God's grace and human freedom is "a paradox whose logic is completely disclosed only to the experience of a life based on faith."

113. Ratzinger, *A New Song for the Lord*, 5.

from political and economic oppression is especially prevalent, Ratzinger claims that the desire for the promised land of freedom is just as strong in those nations which enjoy the greatest political, economic and social freedom.

Ratzinger sees a particular manifestation of the meeting of the two stages of the divine-human history of freedom in the accounts of the Transfiguration. He notes that the one place in the Gospels wherein the word "exodus" appears is in the Lucan account of the Transfiguration. The two men who appear talking with Jesus about his coming exodus through his Passover in Jerusalem are Moses and Elijah. That Moses foreshadows this exodus hardly needs to be pointed out. Yet Ratzinger presents Elijah too as a type of exodus. Although in his time the people of Israel lived in the Promised Land, in their way of life they had returned to Egypt, and ironically, were living under a tyrannical king and experiencing a tyrannical existence even in the Promised Land. Throwing off the Covenant, their self-made freedom had proved to be a new tyranny. It is for this reason that Elijah must go to Sinai in order to symbolize a new exodus. A true exodus means living according to the Covenant.[114]

Ratzinger sees the mount of the Transfiguration as a new Sinai. In Matthew and Mark it occurs six days after Peter's profession of faith. Just as, six days after coming to Sinai, Moses, accompanied by the two priests Nadab and Abihu, ascends into the divine presence where his face is transfigured (cf. Exod 24:1 and 16), so Jesus, accompanied by Peter, James and John, ascends the new Sinai, where his whole body is transfigured. Rather than receiving a new Decalogue, the disciples are presented with a new living Torah, the Son, the beloved of the Father, to whom they must listen. Ratzinger goes on to further identify the Feast of Booths, the feast of thanksgiving for the gift of the land, with the three tents of the Transfiguration. For Ratzinger, the Transfiguration of Jesus signifies that: "The exodus of Israel and the exodus of Jesus touch each other: all the feasts and all the ways of Israel lead to the Passover of Jesus Christ."[115]

According to Ratzinger, Luke depicts the entire public life of Jesus as an exodus. It is a going up to Jerusalem in order to passover to the Father. It is "the real and definitive exodus in which Christ walks the path into the open and himself becomes the way for humanity into the open, into freedom."[116] However, this road does not end in Jerusalem but continues into the Resurrection. Jesus opens "the new and living way for us . . . through the curtain

114. Ibid., 16–17.
115. Ibid., 18.
116. Ibid.

Human Freedom as the Terminus 273

(that is, through his flesh)" (Heb 10:20). He leads us into the "tent not made by hands" into the presence of the living God (cf. Heb 9:11). For Ratzinger, this is the freedom that we desire, the freedom that cannot be satisfied by any earthly thing or experience. Rather: "The thirst for freedom is the voice of our being made in the image and likeness of God; it is the thirst 'to sit at the right hand of God,' to be 'like God.'"[117]

How can we participate in the freedom of God? What is the alternative to the serpent's temptation to "be like God" through a self-made freedom? One way Ratzinger explains it is that this freedom is based on a new "substance." Referring to the Letter to the Hebrews, as Benedict XVI, he points out that the definition of faith given there in Hebrews 11:1 is: "Faith is the *hypostasis* (in the Vulgate, *substantia*) of things hoped for; the proof of things not seen." Following St. Thomas, Benedict XVI points out that faith is a *habitus*, a stable disposition of the spirit, "through which eternal life takes root in us and reason is led to consent to what it does not see."[118] This is to say that the substance of eternal life for which we hope is already present in us through faith. This presence of eternal life creates a certainty that, although it does not yet appear in the external world, can be perceived interiorly. *Pace* Luther, this substance is objectively present, not just subjectively present as an expression of an interior attitude. It is not just subjective conviction, but objective *elenchos*, proof. The fact that we have this new "possession" (hyparxin—Vg. *substantiam*) enables Christians, in the face of persecution, to give up their normal source of security, their "property" (hyparchonton—Vg. *bonorum*).[119] In linking these two kinds of substance, Benedict XVI maintains that the *habitus* of faith, based as it is on the possession of eternal life, creates a new freedom which transcends the possessions which are the habitual foundation of life. This new freedom is not only revealed in martyrdom, but in all those who renounce their own wills in order to bring the Gospel to others. Touched by the hope of Christ, "hope has arisen for others who [are] living in darkness and without hope."[120]

Furthermore, in explaining the meaning of this freedom, Ratzinger identifies two sayings of Jesus which refer to being placed on the right hand of God. The first is the promise to those who gave Jesus food when he was hungry, drink when he was thirsty, welcomed him when he was a stranger, and visited him when he was sick or in prison (cf. Matt 25:31–40). The second is in response to the request of the sons of Zebedee, who are told that

---

117. Ibid., 19.
118. *SS*, no. 7. Citing *ST* II–II, q. 4, a. 1.
119. Ibid., no. 8. Cf. Heb 11:34.
120. Ibid.

whosoever may sit to the right and left of the Christ, their call is to drink the cup that Jesus drinks and receive the baptism that he receives (cf. Mark 10:35-40). These two passages are paradigmatic of Ratzinger's understanding of how we become truly free. They point to more than a mere moral imitation of Christ. The imitation of Jesus is a christological category. We are not just called to imitate the human Jesus. We are called to imitate him in his divinity—as Ratzinger quotes: "Therefore be imitators of God" (Eph 5:1).[121] The way which Jesus opens for us "through the curtain" is ontological. By denying oneself and taking up one's cross, through entering into the Paschal dimension of Jesus' exodus, we are reborn into a new life. This is a life of conversion wherein the old self is put to death, and the new creature enters into the freedom of God.[122]

Ratzinger briefly touches upon the other aspects of this liberation—Jesus as the truth and the life. As we have seen, for Ratzinger, truth and freedom are inseparable. We are now friends of Jesus rather than mere servants because we can *know* everything that Jesus has heard from his Father (cf. John 15:15). As Ratzinger explains:

> Ignorance is dependency, slavery: whoever does not know remains a servant. Only when understanding opens up, when we begin to comprehend what is essential, do we begin to be free. Freedom from which truth has been removed is a lie. Christ the truth, this means: God who makes friends out of unknowing servants by letting us become, to some degree, sharers in the knowledge of himself.[123]

The alternative to this kind of freedom is not a self-made freedom but the negation of freedom. If God is not the author of the world, then the world does not originate in freedom, and any appearance of freedom in it is an illusion. If we cannot know the truth about God, the true God, "then we are not free people in a creation that is open to freedom, but elements in a system of necessities in which, inexplicably, the cry for freedom will not die out."[124]

To Ratzinger, this is another manifestation of the refusal to accept the call to divinization. It is the heresy of Arius, who refused to abandon the idea of God's absolute transcendence, and hence, our inability to know him. This transcendent God cannot be the creator of the world, but must act

---

121. Ratzinger, *A New Song for the Lord*, 20-21.
122. Ibid., 22.
123. Ibid., 23.
124. Ibid., 24.

through a less then divine intermediary. We cannot become the friend of such a God.[125]

Using the example of iconography, Ratzinger argues that the transcendence of God does not prevent him from being visible in Christ. He takes the words of Jesus, "He who has seen me has seen the Father" (John 14:9), to be true. "Whoever sees Christ really sees the Father; in that which is visible one sees that which is invisible, the invisible in person."[126] The human life of Jesus is the love of the Father made visible. The Crucified One is the image of the invisible God (cf. Col 1:15). Those who look upon Christ are taken up into his exodus. In Ratzinger's estimation, the whole Christology of St. Maximus the Confessor is one great interpretation of John 14:9: "He who has seen me has seen the Father." If one sees the Father in Christ Crucified, then one sees through the torn curtain of the Temple. The God who is thus revealed is a Trinity. In becoming a friend of this God, one is initiated into the very heart of truth. Yet this truth is also a way, "it is the fatal, yet precisely through losing oneself life-giving adventure of love which alone is freedom."[127]

Even more briefly, Ratzinger looks at the third aspect of this liberation, Christ as the life. Of particular interest is his focus upon John 7:37–38, Jesus' invitation to come and drink from the fountain of living waters. He points out that this reception is not merely passive. If we come and drink, out of our own hearts living waters will flow. Thus: "To drink from the living water of the rock means to consent to the salvific mystery of water and blood . . . It is consenting to love; it is entering the truth. And exactly this is life."[128]

It is no coincidence that the freedom of this way, truth and life is addressed in a book on the Liturgy because, for Ratzinger, the Sacred Liturgy is the ultimate *locus* of our participation in freedom. In *The Spirit of the Liturgy*, Ratzinger reiterates much of what he has said about freedom in earlier works, although here it is within the context of the connection of the liturgy to both the cosmos and history.[129] His first point is that Christian worship is related to both the cosmos and history, to God the Creator as well as to God the Savior. Thus: "Creation moves toward the Sabbath, on the day on which man and the whole created order participates in God's rest, in his freedom."[130] For Ratzinger, the Sabbath is a "vision of freedom." This

---

125. Ibid., 24–25.
126. Ibid., 25.
127. Ibid., 26.
128. Ibid., 32.
129. Ratzinger, *The Spirit of the Liturgy*, 24–34.
130. Ibid., 25.

freedom is not only anthropological, that is to say, freedom from subordination to another and to work. For Ratzinger, the Sabbath is the sign of the Covenant, and is intrinsically linked with Creation. Accordingly:

> [Creation] exists to be a place for the covenant that God wants to make with man. The goal of creation is the covenant, the love story of God and man. The freedom and equality of men, which the Sabbath is meant to bring about, is not a merely anthropological or sociological vision; it can only be understood *theo*-logically. Only when man is in covenant with God does he become free. Only then are the equality and dignity of all men made manifest. If, then, everything is directed to the covenant, it is important to see that the covenant is a relationship: God's gift of himself to man, but also man's response to God. Man's response to the God who is good to him is love, and loving God means worshipping him.[131]

In Ratzinger's understanding, the completion of the Tabernacle by Moses after seven days mirrors the completion of creation—in fact, the completion of the Tabernacle anticipates the completion of creation. The glory of the Lord which fills the Tabernacle anticipates the fullness of God dwelling in his creation. As Ratzinger sees it:

> Creation and history, creation, history and worship are in a relationship of reciprocity. Creation looks toward the covenant, but the covenant completes creation and does not simply exist along with it. Now if worship, rightly understood, is the soul of the covenant, then it not only saves mankind but is also meant to draw the whole of reality into communion with God.[132]

In Ratzinger's estimation, the heart of worship is sacrifice. But true worship does not mean destruction. Rather, it means union through true surrender to God, the union of man and creation with God. Belonging to God does not entail destruction, that is, non-being, but is a way of being. It means moving from a state of separation, or autonomy, to one of finding oneself through losing oneself (cf. Mark 8:35; Matt 10:39). Ratzinger calls upon St. Augustine in maintaining the following.

> [The] true "sacrifice" is the *civitas Dei*, that is, love-transformed mankind, the divinization of creation and the surrender of all

---

131. Ibid., 26.
132. Ibid., 27.

things to God: God all in all (cf. 1 Cor 15:28). That is the purpose of the world. That is the essence of sacrifice and worship.[133]

Thus divinization is the goal of both worship and creation. For Ratzinger, a divinized world is a world of freedom and love.

In support of this position, Ratzinger calls upon both modern and ancient witnesses. The complexification thesis of Teilhard de Chardin is the former. As it pertains to Christian worship, this thesis ends in giving a new meaning to that worship, "the transubstantiated Host is the anticipation of the transformation and divinization of matter in the christological 'fullness.'... the Eucharist provides the movement of the cosmos with its direction; it anticipates its goal and at the same time urges it on."[134]

The ancient witness is the pattern of *exitus* and *reditus*, found in its most impressive form in Plotinus. In Christian thought, this pattern of an *exitus* as a fall from the infinite into finitude, to be redeemed by a *reditus* which liberates from finitude, is recast. The Christian *exitus* is one in which the Creator engages in a free act of creation. Rather than being something negative, non-divine being is the positive fruit of the divine will. Thus Ratzinger states:

> The act of God's being, which causes created being, is an act of freedom. In this respect, the principle of freedom is present in being itself, from the ground upward. The *exitus*, or rather God's free act of creation, is indeed ordered toward the *reditus*, but that does not now mean the rescinding of created being ... [Instead, the] creature, existing in its own right, comes home to itself, and this act is an answer in freedom to God's love.[135]

The creature accepts its creation from God as an offer of love, and thus enters into a dialogue of love, with the new kind of unity which is the unique creation of love. Rather than being absorbed by the other, in giving itself, the creature becomes fully itself. This *reditus*, instead of abolishing creation, results in its full and final perfection.[136]

In spite of this freedom, the creature has the freedom to rupture the *reditus* through the rejection of love which is seen as dependence. This is the autonomy of the attempt at self-divinization. Since we have all in fact

133. Ibid., 28.
134. Ibid., 29.
135. Ibid., 32–33.
136. Ibid., 33. Cf. Ratzinger, "The End of Time," 20–21. Rowland contrasts Ratzinger's understanding of human participation in the freedom of God with both the extrinsicist separation of nature and grace, and Rahner's alternative of naturalising the supernatural. See Rowland, *Ratzinger's Faith*, 37.

suffered this rupture in the Fall, sacrifice, which "in its essence is simply returning to love and therefore divinization," now takes on a new form. As Ratzinger explains:

> [Worship] now has a new aspect: the healing of wounded freedom, atonement, purification, deliverance from estrangement. The essence of worship, of sacrifice—the process of assimilation, of growth in love, and this the way into freedom—remains unchanged. But now it assumes the aspect of healing, the loving transformation of broken freedom, of painful expiation. Worship is directed to the Other in himself, to his all-sufficiency, but now it refers itself to the Other who alone can extricate me from the knot that I myself cannot untie.[137]

The sacrifice of the Cross of Christ, "the love that in dying makes a gift of itself," is an act of new creation, "the restoration of creation to its true identity." All worship is now a participation in this passover "from divine to human, from death to life, to the unity of God and man."[138] In the sacrifice of Jesus, and our participation in it through the Sacred Liturgy, the gift of freedom has become the center not only of divine being, but of created being as well. So now we have come full circle, from the freedom of Jesus as expressed in the volitional thesis back to our participation, personally and corporately, in that freedom though our participation in the prayer of Jesus, and this participation is in the freedom of God.

---

137. Ratzinger, *The Spirit of the Liturgy*, 33. Cf. Ratzinger, *Feast of Faith*, 30. Cf. also *Introduction*, 289, where we saw that, for him, Christ's sacrifice "has smelted the body of humanity into the Yes of worship."

138. Ibid., 34.

11

Ratzinger's Anthropology of the Heart

In *Behold the Pierced One* Ratzinger notes that the Fathers had a theology and philosophy of the heart, and speaking of St. Augustine's understanding of *cor*, he noted that it is "the center of a dialogical anthropology. It is quite clear that . . . the stream of biblical terminology, and, with it, the stream of biblical theology and anthropology, has entered into his thought."[1] We have just seen that Ratzinger has a theology, anthropology and Christology of freedom. In the next three chapters we shall investigate his *anthropology* of the human heart, followed by his *theology* of the Father's heart, and then see how he brings them together in a *Christology* and *ecclesiology* of the heart of Jesus.[2]

The Symbol of the Human Heart

For Ratzinger, the metaphor of the human "heart" is not to be identified simply with the intellect, or the will, or the passions, or the senses, or the body, or the soul. Nor is it to be identified with the "I," the *ego*. It is not identical

---

1. *Behold*, 65.

2. In his commentary on *GS*, no. 22, Ratzinger alluded to a Christocentric theology which united anthropology and theology in Christ: "We are probably justified in saying that here for the first time in an official document of the magisterium, a new type of completely Christocentric theology appears. On the basis of Christ this dares to present theology as anthropology and only becomes radically theological by including man in discourse about God by way of Christ, thus manifesting the deepest unity of theology. The generally theologically reserved text of the Pastoral Constitution here attains very lofty heights and points the way to theological reflection in our present situation" ("Church and Man's," 159). This approach he now applies to the "heart."

with the person. Rather, Ratzinger defines the human heart as the "place" of the integration of the intellect, will, passions and senses, of the body and the soul, as being the personal integration of these aspects of human nature.[3] It must be said that this is not what people ordinarily mean when speaking of the human heart. Yet, by using this metaphor, people are trying to express something which eludes their conceptualization. They are speaking of something which involves their emotions, but also something which is more than, or deeper than, emotion. Both the poets and the prophets, both we and Sacred Scripture, also speak of the heart as thinking, discoursing, and choosing. We even speak of our hearts being "broken" or "crushed." So, when people use the term "heart," even though they may not have in mind a definition such as Ratzinger's, it does not follow necessarily that Ratzinger's definition is invalid. He may have uncovered, in a more explicit way, what the "average" person is trying to express. Not only is God a mystery, but the human person, the image of God, is also mysterious. We cannot fully comprehend ourselves. Our self-understanding approaches, but does not completely encompass, our own nature.

For his understanding of the heart, Ratzinger's main sources seem to be the way the term is used in Sacred Scripture, the Fathers, especially Origen and St. Augustine, as well as in the writings of Blaise Pascal, Bl. John Henry Newman, Romano Guardini, and Pope Pius XII in his encyclical *Haurietis aquas*. Therefore, we shall examine these sources in order to see what commonalities and differences they share with Ratzinger's understanding. Since Ratzinger also refers to the medieval devotion to the heart of Jesus we shall also briefly examine that understanding. We shall also look at the understanding of Karl Rahner, whose theology is often a great contrast to that of Ratzinger, but which, in this instance, shows some congruence with it. By way of contrast, we shall look also at a definition of "heart" which, at first glance, appears to be quite different from Ratzinger's—that of Dietrich von Hildebrand.

The Biblical Understanding

When we come to Sacred Scripture we find that "heart" is used in many different senses. It is the place of knowing (cf. Gen 31:20 and 26; Deut 29:3; Judg 16:17; 2 Sam 15:6; Song 4:9; Isa 6:10; Job 12:3; Hos 4:11 and 7:11; Sir 8:19 and 21:6; Matt 13:15, John 12:40, Luke 2:19, 34–35, 51, and 24:38), of faith (cf. Rom 10:10; 1 Cor 2:9 and 3:15; Eph 1:18 and 3:17), of the will (cf. 1 Sam 14:6; 2 Sam 7:3; Matt 5:28), and of conscience (cf. 1 Sam 24:6 and

---

3. See *Behold*, 55–56; and *Jesus I*, 92–93.

25:31; 2 Sam 24:10; 1 Kgs 8:38; Jer 17:1). It is sometimes qualified in terms of the inner disposition of the will (cf. 1 Kgs 11:2–4; Ps 112:7). It is drawn to what seems good and beautiful (cf. Num 15:39; Job 31:7 and 9; Sir 5:2 and 9:9; Matt 6:21; Luke 12:34). It is the place of *koinonia* (cf. Acts 4:32; 2 Cor 3:2, 6:11, and 7:3; Phil 1:7). It is the seat of the emotions, especially of joy and sorrow (cf. Gen 42:28; 2 Sam 17:10; Josh 7:5; Pss 22:14, 29:4, 38:10, and 40:12; Isa 7:2; Jer 4:9 and 19). It can be broken (cf. Pss 34:19, 51:17, and 69:20; Isa 57:15 and 61:1; Jer 23:9; Ezek 6:9). It is the place of pity and mercy (cf. 1 Kgs 3:26; Phil 1:7).[4] It is "the locus of everything that is innermost, genuine, precious and essential in man."[5]

Following the *Theological Dictionary of the New Testament*, Hugo Rahner claims that, in the Old Testament:

> Heart is the principle and organ of the personal life of man, the center in which the being and the activity of man as a spiritual personality are concentrated, and consequently the source and center of his religious and ethical life.[6]

According to the *Theological Dictionary*, in the New Testament:

> [The] heart is the centre of the inner life of man and the source or seat of all the forces and functions of the soul and spirit . . . [In it] dwell feelings, desires and passions . . . [It is] the seat of understanding, the source of thought and reflection . . . the seat of the will, the source of resolves . . . supremely the one center in man to which God turns, in which the religious life is rooted, which determines moral conduct.[7]

Drawing upon the biblical use of the term "heart," Rahner draws the following conclusion.

> "Heart" is . . . the key word for expressing the newness and redemptive message of the New Testament. It is in the heart, in the depths of the righteous man who is penetrated by the love

---

4. Becker, "The Heart," 24–30. With regard to the heart as the place of pity and mercy, Becker makes the following point: "Biblical language prefers to assign to these feelings other terms, meaning approximately 'bowels'" (30). Hugo Rahner regards this term as equivalent to "heart." See Rahner, "On the Biblical Basis," 17–26. Rahner states that: "In the language of Revelation, the hallowed word 'heart' and its almost synonymous equivalents (Hebrew: *leb, lebab, beten, me(j)'im, kereb*; Greek: *kardia, koilia, splanchna*; Latin: *cor, venter, viscera*) have the same primal meaning as in all human language" (17).

5. Becker, "The Heart," 27.

6. Rahner, "On the Biblical Basis," 17. Cf. Baumgärtel and Behm, "καρδια," 605–11.

7. Baumgärtel and Behm, "καρδια," 611–12.

of God, that the encounter of Revelation and faith, of grace and response to grace, takes place. The grace of Christ is a circumcision of the heart (Acts 7:51; Rom 2:29). Justification is in faith "from the heart" (Rom 10:10; Heb 10:22). The Spirit is poured out in our hearts (Gal 5:6). Love from the heart constitutes perfection (Matt 22:37; 1 Tim 1:5). The Christian is called simply "the hidden self of the heart" (1 Pet 3:4).[8]

Rahner, following Viktor Warnach, sees the heart as ultimately a spiritual reality. As Warnach says:

> The *pneuma* is that profound element in man, at once godlike and intensely personal, which is repeatedly called "heart" (*kardia*) in Holy Scripture because it constitutes the real directive center of the person, from which spring all thoughts and feelings, all cares and decisions (Mark 7:21f.; Rom 8:27; 10:10; 1 Cor 14:25; 1 Thess 2:4; 2 Thess 3:5). The same meaning attaches to the equivalent term *leb* (or later *lebab*), which is frequently used in the Old Testament; and in the Liturgy and spirituality of the Church down the centuries, "heart" has generally retained this spiritual sense.[9]

The Patristic Understanding

Origen's understanding of the "heart" is in keeping with that of Sacred Scripture. The heart is more than reason. It is deeper than reason. It is the center of man. It is the place where the Logos is born in man, where contact with the divine takes place, where one is united with the personal, incarnate Word of God.[10]

As both von Hildebrand and Ratzinger have pointed out, "heart" is a key term in St. Augustine's *Confessions*.[11] For Augustine, the love of the heart

---

8. Rahner, "On the Biblical Basis," 17.

9. Warnach, *Agape*, 231, quoted by Rahner, "On the Biblical Basis," 18. Rahner sees Pascal's "*Coeur qui trouve Dieu* (the heart which finds God) as having the same meaning" (18).

10. See *Behold*, 67–68, where Ratzinger refers the reader to Origen, *In Joa*, 94, 18; 494, 22; and 497; and Ivánka, *Plato christianus*, 325–326. Similarly, as Ratzinger points out, in opposition to the Platonic identification of the intellect as the center of man, St. Jerome places the heart. See St. Jerome, *Epist.* 64, 587. Cf. Rahner, *Symbole der Kirche*, 148, were he points out related passages in St. Gregory of Nyssa, *De hominis opificio*, 156 CD, and Lactantius, *De opificio Dei*, 51.

11. Cf. von Hildebrand, *The Sacred Heart*, 28–29: "It is true that there is one great tradition in the stream of Christian philosophy in which full justice is done in a concrete

is deeper than language, and can convey that which words cannot. "[The] word which sounds without is a sign of the word which shines within, which (in the heart) is much more worthy of the name 'word.'"[12] We do not know our own hearts. They are an "abyss," a "great deep."[13] According to John Rist:

> At the philosophical level Augustine is probably adopting the Platonic idea that words (or propositions) can only inadequately represent their subject-matter, and that propositional knowledge about the Good only gives us a poor image of the Good itself. On the theological level he believes that the inadequacies of speech are made up for by love (*On Catechizing the Simple* 12.17).[14]

Augustine sometimes seems to speak of the heart as equivalent to the "self." His famous *fecisti nos ad te et inquietum est cor nostrum donec requiescat in te* (you have made *us* for yourself, and our *hearts* are restless until they rest in you) indicates as much.[15] At other times he seems to equate the heart with the soul. In his account of the death of a friend, Augustine speaks of the heart as the place of the passions—it was black with grief. Then: "I became a great enigma to myself and I was forever asking my soul why it was sad and why it disquieted me so sorely."[16] He also sees the heart as the place of encounter with God: "*Redeamus ad cor, ut inveniamus Eum* (let us return to the heart, that we may find Him)."[17] As we have seen, Ratzinger himself pointed out the following in his 1969 commentary on *Gaudium et spes*.

> Augustine's epistemology . . . is well aware that the organ by which God can be seen cannot be a non-historical "ratio naturalis" which just does not exist, but only the *ratio pura*, i.e. *purificata* [purified reason] or, as Augustine expresses it echoing the gospel, the *cor purum* ("Blessed are the pure in heart, for they shall see God"). Augustine also knows that the necessary purification of sight takes place through faith (Acts 15:9) and

---

way to the affective sphere and to the heart. St. Augustine's work from the *Confessions* onward is pervaded by deep and admirable insights concerning the heart and the affective attitudes of man." Von Hildebrand goes so far as to wonder why, when Augustine speaks of the reflection of the Trinity in the human soul, he "fails to give to the affective sphere and to the heart a standing analogous to that granted to the reason and will" (28). Cf. also *Behold*, 65.

12. Rist, *Augustine*, 33.
13. Ibid., 37.
14. Ibid., 38.
15. Augustine, *Confessions*, 1. 1. 1.
16. Ibid., 4. 4. 9.
17. Ibid., 4. 12. 19. Quoted by Ratzinger in *Behold*, 68.

through love, at all events not as a result of reflection alone and not at all by man's own power.[18]

Beyond this, Augustine never precisely defines what he means by heart. He simply describes it in action. For him, ultimately, it is an enigma, a mystery.

The Medieval Understanding

Ratzinger maintains that medieval devotion to the Sacred Heart leads "to that mysticism which is aware that the heart takes precedence over reason, love over knowledge."[19] Certainly, one can find a concentration on the wounded heart of Jesus as the source of love and mercy for the disciple in the writings of such luminaries as John of Fécamp, St. Bernard and St. Bonaventure, and many other medieval writers.[20] The love of Jesus is poured into the hearts of believers from his wounded heart.

By way of contrast, St. Thomas Aquinas sometimes uses the term *cor* to mean the principle of animal life and movement,[21] but not of cognition.[22] Yet when speaking of it in its biblical sense he equates *cor* with *spiritus*.[23] He also thinks of it as the organ of the passions. As Leo Elders has pointed out, St. Thomas "thinks of the heart as the organ of the passions, in the sense that the motions and affections of the sensitive part of the soul are joined with a powerful motion (*commotio*) of the body, and in particular of the heart. In this way love produces a *dilatatio cordis*. Grief has the greatest effect."[24] Experience tells us that this is true.

---

18. "Church and Man's," 155.

19. *Behold*, 68.

20. For an overview of medieval devotion to the heart of Jesus, see Baier, "Key Issues," 81–99.

21. Elders, "The Inner Life," 79.

22. Ibid.

23. Ibid. In prayers attributed to St. Thomas one can sometimes find a more "spiritual" understanding of the term "heart." For example, in a Prayer for a Priestly Heart we read: "Give me, O Lord, an ever watchful heart which no subtle speculation may ever lure from you. Give me a noble heart that no unworthy affection shall ever draw downwards to earth. Give me a heart of honesty that no insincerity shall warp. Give me a heart of courage that no distress shall ever crush or quench. Give me a heart so free that no perverted or impetuous affection shall ever claim it for its own."

24. Ibid.

Pascal's Understanding

In the *Pensées* we find the famous, frequently quoted, and frequently misunderstood statement: "The heart has its reasons of which the reason knows nothing."[25] In saying this, Pascal is being neither sentimental nor irrational. By "reason" he means Cartesian "reasoning" by scientific analysis and calculation, what Scholastic-Aristotelian logic called the third act of the mind, the discursive reasoning by which one proves one truth, the conclusion, from another, the premise.[26] Pascal says that the heart has its *reasons*. These are first principles, self-evident truths.

> We know the truth not only through our reason but also through our heart. It is through the latter that we know first principles, and reason, which has nothing to do with it, tries in vain to refute them . . . For knowledge of first principles, like space, time, motion, number, is as solid as any derived through reason, and it is on such knowledge, coming from the heart and instinct, that reason has to depend and base all its argument . . . Principles are felt, propositions proved, and both with certainty by different means.[27]

For Pascal, the first act of the mind, understanding the meaning of an essence, is carried out by the "heart." Furthermore, it is the heart which "feels" God. This is Pascal's definition of faith. "It is the heart which perceives [feels] God and not the reason. That is what faith is: God perceived by the heart, not by the reason."[28] The heart "sees" God, it knows God. God gives

---

25. Pascal, *Pensées*, 423 (277). There are two common ways of numbering Pascal's "thoughts." The Krailsheimer number is given first, followed by the Brunschvicg number in parentheses.

26. Cf. Descartes, *Discourse on the Method*, 265–72. For Pascal's understanding of "reason" and "heart," see Kreeft, *Christianity for Modern Pagans*, 228–34. For a clear, lucid and comprehensive explanation of the three acts of the mind, 1) understanding the meaning of an essence, 2) affirming the truth of a proposition, and 3) or proving one truth from another, see Kreeft, *Socratic Logic*, 28–199. Kreeft thinks that Pascal's understanding of reason as "reasoning" is consistent with the rest of his thought, unlike Edward Oakes, who thinks that Pascal, in his use of the term "reason," sometimes rejects "the scholastic fusion between faith and reason, as here: 'It is the heart that perceives God and not the reason'" (424). See Oakes, *Infinity Dwindled to Infancy*, 293. On this point I concur with Kreeft.

27. Pascal, *Pensées*, 110 (282).

28. Ibid., 424 (278). It should be noted that what Pascal actually says is: "*C'est le Coeur qui sent Dieu, et non la raison.*" (It is the heart which feels God, and not the reason). The French verb *sentir* normally means to smell or taste, but can be used figuratively to mean "to feel" in the sense of being aware of something. Hence Krailsheimer's translation of *sent* as "perceives" is true to Pascal's meaning.

faith to people by moving their hearts.[29] It is also the heart which chooses, which wills, to love God or self. "I say that it is natural for the heart to love the universal being or itself, according to its allegiance, and it hardens itself against either as it chooses."[30] Finally, for Pascal, the heart is "the unified center of inner life."[31]

Ultimately, Pascal's understanding of the heart is derived from his experience of the love of God for him, what St. Paul calls "the love of God poured into our hearts through the Holy Spirit who has been given to us" (Rom 5:5).

> Fire—"God of Abraham, God of Isaac, God of Jacob," not of the philosophers and scholars. Certainty, certainty, heartfelt, joy, peace. God of Jesus Christ. God of Jesus Christ . . . Joy, joy, joy, tears of joy . . . "And this is life eternal, that they might know thee, the only true God, and Jesus Christ whom thou has sent." Jesus Christ. Jesus Christ.[32]

This is the extraordinary "memorial" which Pascal had sown into his coat over his physical heart, to remind him of the one who dwelt in his "heart."

Newman's Understanding

Although, like Augustine, John Henry Newman frequently uses the term "heart," he does not give an explicit definition of what he means by it. We must infer the definition from the manner in which he uses the term. Newman's approach to theology is not scholastic. As Graham Shute observes:

> His language is that of the ordinary educated person of his day. He often employs terms having a quasi-technical use in philosophy, but these—terms like "heart" . . . "nature," "the passions"—have their place in the tradition of British empiricism and had become so much a part of educated parlance, that it is a nice question as to whether they may be counted as technical terms at all.[33]

For Newman, "reason," in the sense of that faculty which is used in logic, mathematics, the scientific method and historical investigations, cannot

---

29. Ibid., 110 (282).
30. Ibid., 423 (277).
31. Ibid., 110 (282).
32. Ibid., 913. There is no Brunschvicg number for the "memorial."
33. Shute, "Newman's Logic of the Heart," 232.

establish faith in God. Even though Newman holds that conscience can establish the "reasonableness" though not the rationality of faith, it too is not capable of establishing faith.[34] Reacting against an eighteenth century reduction of faith to nothing more than an acceptance of evidence, Newman argues from "existential" evidence that: "The Word of Life is offered to a man; and, on its being offered, he has Faith in it . . . Faith is the reasoning of a religious mind, or of what Scripture calls a right or renewed heart."[35]

In a sermon entitled "Love the Safeguard of Faith against Superstition," Newman states:

> Right faith is the faith of a right mind. Faith is an intellectual act; right faith is an intellectual act, done in a certain moral disposition. Faith is an act of Reason, viz. a reasoning upon presumptions; right Faith is a reasoning upon holy, devout, and enlightened presumptions.[36]

Again, in the same sermon, he says:

> [This faith does not need] what is popularly called Reason for its protection,—I mean processes of investigation, discrimination, discussion, argument, and inference. It itself is an intellectual act, and takes its character from the moral state of the agent. It is perfected, not by intellectual cultivation, but by obedience.[37]

Like Pascal, Newman held that there were two modes of reasoning, that already discussed, and a "logic of the heart." The latter is an insight or intuition.[38] Conversion comes, not by overcoming the reason, but by touching the heart.[39] Furthermore: "The heart is commonly reached, not through the reason, but through the imagination, by means of direct impressions, by the testimony of facts and events, by history, by description. Persons influence us, voices melt us, looks subdue us, deeds inflame us."[40] Rather than "reasoning," Newman sees that:

> The safeguard of Faith is a right state of heart. This it is that gives it birth; it also disciplines it. This is what protects it from bigotry, credulity, and fanaticism. It is holiness, or dutifulness,

---

34. Ibid., 233–35.
35. Newman, *Newman's University Sermons*, 202–3.
36. Ibid., 239. Cf. Sands, *The Justification of Religious Faith*, 121.
37. Ibid., 249–50.
38. Hughes, "*Une Source Cachée*," 29–44.
39. Newman, *An Essay in Aid*, 425.
40. Ibid., 92. Cf. Ferreira, "The Grammar of the Heart," 129.

> or the new creation, or the spiritual mind, however we word it, which is the quickening and illuminating principle of true faith, giving it eyes, hands, and feet. It is Love which forms it out of the rude chaos into an image of Christ.[41]

Like Augustine, Newman is convinced that it is only the "heart" which can "see" God. It is only the love-purified reason that can perceive him. Thus in a sermon entitled "Faith and Reason contrasted as Habits of Mind" he states:

> For is not this the error, the common and fatal error, of the world, to think itself a judge of Religious Truth without preparation of heart? "I am the good Shepherd, and know My sheep, and am known of Mine." "He goeth before them, and the sheep follow Him, for they know His voice." "The pure in heart shall see God:" "to the meek mysteries are revealed;" "he that is spiritual judgeth all things." "The darkness comprehendeth it not." Gross eyes see not; heavy ears hear not. But in the schools of the world the ways towards Truth are considered high roads open to all men, however disposed, at all times. Truth is to be approached without homage.[42]

Rahner's Understanding

Like Ratzinger, Karl Rahner understands the heart as signifying an anthropological totality. For him, "[the heart] falls into the category of words for the whole man; that is, it signifies a human reality predicable of the whole man as a person of body and spirit, a reality which is therefore prior to any possible distinction between body and soul."[43] As he puts it:

> [The formal source of "heart"] is the original, concrete, ontological unity of body and soul. Since man in his entirety is a bodily being, the concept "heart" includes the idea of bodiliness, and therefore includes also a bodily heart. Not for its own sake is the bodily heart thus included; still less is it taken as a merely external symbol for something else, for what we really mean . . . "Heart," taken in this primal sense, denotes that center which is the origin and kernel of everything else in the human person . . . Here is the focal point of a man's primal and integral relations with others and above all with God; for God is concerned with

---

41. Newman, *Newman's University Sermons*, 234. Cf. Shute, "Newman's Logic," 235.
42. Ibid., 198.
43. Rahner, "Some Theses," 132.

the whole man, and in his divine actions it is to man's center, his heart, that he addresses his graces or his judgments.[44]

According to Rahner, the representation of the physical heart is a symbol of this personal center. It is a natural symbol, since "[the] nature of man as a creature of body and soul gives the body a symbolic character."[45] The obvious symbol for the center of this composite creature, confirmed by psychological experience, is the heart.

Rahner goes on to explain that every human person not only has innate, unalterable "qualities," but also "attitudes" towards themselves and others, attitudes which can be empirically "experienced" but not metaphysically deduced. According to him:

> [These attitudes] show a multiplicity, under which there exists, or ought to exist, a formal unity, joining together the attitudes of a person into an articulate, meaningful whole. This process of free, formative unification takes place in the concrete living person. His innate qualities, if we can imagine them prior to this process, are taken over by this free and formative act of self-understanding, they are "understood" (in one way or another), and actuated.[46]

The original, form-giving unity of a person's attitudes is the "heart." The "heart" is not simply a "piece" of a person, but the primal, unifying center of the whole. Ultimately, a person is indivisible. Thus: "In the person, the 'part,' because it is taken over and 'understood' by the personal center, can be seen correctly only in the whole, and the whole person can be judged adequately only from his 'heart-center.'"[47]

Guardini's Understanding

In looking at what has been called Ratzinger's anthropological prolegomenon to a theology of the heart, we noted that one of the sources he drew upon was a book on Pascal by Guardini. In looking at the concepts of the heart and interiority as grounding a true theology of the body, he appealed to Guardini for support of the notion that the heart must be understood as

---

44. Ibid., 133.
45. Ibid. For Rahner's understanding of "symbol," see Rahner, "The Theology of Symbol," 221–52.
46. Ibid., 135–36.
47. Ibid., 138.

embodied spirit.[48] We shall now investigate Guardini's anthropology of the heart in order to assess the extent to which Ratzinger's is based upon it.

Guardini identifies a focus upon the heart which he calls the noblest tradition of the Christian Occident—a *philosophia* and *theologia cordis*. According to him, the pedigree of this tradition begins with Plato, and runs through Paul, Ignatius of Antioch, Augustine, Bernard of Clairvaux, Francis of Assisi, Gertrude the Great, Elizabeth of Thuringia and Catherine of Siena. Its "system" is created by Bonaventure and its "poetry" by Dante. After a hiatus in the Renaissance it continues through Teresa of Avila, Francis de Sales, Pascal, the Oratorians Condren, Bérulle, Gratry and Rosmini, and culminates in Newman. In the East it has been cultivated by Soloviev, Khomyakov and Florensky. Guardini also sees it, "in a strange Nordic modification," in Kierkegaard, and, in an anti-Christian manifestation, in Nietzsche.[49]

Our two main sources for Guardini's anthropology of the heart are his book on Pascal and another on the conversion of St. Augustine, both published in 1935. Although it is the work on Pascal to which Ratzinger refers, the more thorough-going exposition of Guardini's understanding of the human heart is to be found in that on Augustine. This is because, in the case of Pascal, Guardini focuses mostly upon Pascal's reflections about the heart, whereas in the case of Augustine his canvas is much broader. With Pascal, he analyzes an explicit anthropology of the heart and seeks to develop it, whereas with Augustine he seeks to draw out such an anthropology from analyzing what Augustine confesses about his conversion. He seeks to give a basis for understanding the whole of Augustine's development as described in *The Confessions*. As Guardini puts it:

> The long slow process of experience, of growth, unfolding, seizure and struggle, action and suffering by which the young man with his unfree sensuality on the one hand, his abstract, idealistic-aesthetic intellectuality on the other, pries open the realm of the heart; the manner in which that realm, strengthened, purified, and instructed, gains power and knowledge and

---

48. "Church and Man's," 129. Cf. Guardini, *Christliches Bewußtsein*, 187.

49. Guardini, *Pascal for Our Time*, 128–29. This is a fascinating provenance, especially when compared with the theological influences which have helped to shape Ratzinger's theology. However, there are some surprising omissions from Guardini's list. What of Sts. Margaret Mary Alacoque, Claude de la Colombière and John Eudes? Also, besides the focus on the heart of later Orthodox theologians such as Soloviev, Khomyakov and Florensky, it could be fruitful to study the understanding of the heart found in some of their patristic and medieval confreres—for instance, Evagrius Ponticus, Macarius the Egyptian, Diadochus of Photiki, and St. Gregory Palamas. For an introduction to their understanding of the "heart," see Monk Vartholomaeos, "The Heart in the Hesychastic Treatises of St. Gregory of Palamas," 1–18.

certainty—all this forms the central skein of Augustine's rich and complicated development.⁵⁰

In Guardini's analysis of St. Augustine's "inner world," we have presented to us an anthropology of the heart in embryonic form, one which Guardini himself calls not even a sketch.⁵¹ In what follows an attempt shall be made to reproduce the main lines of this sketch. However, Guardini's prose is so pithy, his thought so profound, and his terminology so idiosyncratic, that one almost despairs of giving a just account of it. Part of the challenge in understanding it is that, in order to do so, one must theologize in the same way that Guardini does. It is a challenge to the whole heart, not just that manifestation of the heart which we call the mind.

In the quotation given above, Guardini identifies two "halves" to Augustine, one sensual and the other intellectual. His analysis will concern itself with how these two halves come to be reconciled in the "realm of the heart." According to Guardini, in Augustine's anthropology the "lower" can only be understood from the "higher"—the body can only be understood from the intellectual soul, the soul only in relation to its ultimate end in the true and the good, and these only understandable in God. The soul is only truly spiritual when it is drawn Godward. The human person is only comprehensible and attains the fullness of his or her own human being in God.⁵²

Besides the lower and the higher in the above sense, Guardini also identifies in Augustine another "lower" and "higher." The lower "depth" he calls the inner world, or interiority.⁵³ Of this inwardness he identifies two manifestations—the psychic-ethical and the religious-spiritual. The former is the place of moral struggle. Yet, compared with true "inwardness," it is, in fact, still "outside." It can become a place of retreat from true inwardness, the religious-spiritual where God dwells. The grace of God shines into the psychic-ethical, revealing the moral abyss therein, at the bottom of the heart, bringing one face to face with oneself, with one's self-deceptions.⁵⁴ In this inwardness one also finds "the conflict between the commanding and obeying functions of the will, between the will's ideal and its reality."⁵⁵

---

50. Guardini, *The Conversion of Augustine*, 45.

51. Ibid., 66.

52. Guardini, *The Conversion of Augustine*, 5. Guardini refers the reader to St. Augustine, *Civitas Dei*, 19, 26: "Wherefore, as the soul is the flesh's life, so is God the beatitude of man."

53. Guardini, *The Conversion of Augustine*, 18–20. Cf. GS, no. 14.

54. Ibid., 19–20.

55. Ibid., 21.

One also finds there the interiority of the emotions. Referring to Augustine's account of the death of a close friend in Book Four of the *Confessions*, Guardini draws our attention to Augustine's inability to endure his misery, a misery which could only be lifted by God, though only by the true God, and not Augustine's false notions of him.

> For my God was not yet You but the error and vain fantasy I held. When I tried to rest my burden upon that, it fell as through emptiness and was once more heavy upon me; and I remained to myself a place of unhappiness, in which I could not abide, yet from which I could not depart. For where was my heart to flee from my heart? Whither was I to fly from myself?[56]

Augustine seeks to escape himself by going "elsewhere," to another town. Yet, as Guardini explains, the only true escape from oneself is God: "God's heights would have been the only truly liberating power, the real 'elsewhere' to the self's sinful and sorrowful 'here,' genuine 'above' and 'within' to the worldly 'below' and 'without.'"[57] True inwardness, which is also "aboveness," is the presence of God both within and above oneself. This interiority is not present in us until we come to know, through the religious act of faith, the God who is present in us. As Guardini writes: "Christian inwardness is that living 'area' which comes into being when God's deeper-than-any-human depths assert themselves in an actual person, when he experiences them, participates in them, appropriates them—how, is the unanswerable question."[58] Here, a new heart, a new interiority, comes into existence. Instead of a "natural" interiority, a "spiritual" interiority comes into existence. This new interiority transforms its natural predecessor. As Guardini puts it:

> The point is that such interiority is not psychologically deeper, or spiritually nobler, but essentially different from any natural interiority; it is a gift of grace from the Spirit. Within it, again, there are infinite degrees of profundity, but issuing, all of them, from that primary disposition. Such inwardness realizes itself in the person; thus inevitably the whole content of his existence enters into it; conversely, it leavens that whole existence, deepening and developing it into what might be termed a second Christian psychological inwardness.[59]

---

56. Augustine, *Confessions*, 4.7. Quoted by Guardini in *The Conversion of Augustine*, 21–22.

57. Guardini, *The Conversion of Augustine*, 21.

58. Ibid., 23. Cf. Augustine, the famous passage in book 10.27 of the *Confessions*: "Late have I loved Thee . . ."

59. Guardini, *The Conversion of Augustine*, 24.

As has been said, for Guardini, this inwardness is also an aboveness. It is God who is both within and above. For Guardini, this is the axis of human existence:

> that [one] becomes truly human precisely to the degree that its order asserts itself upon him. As he grows "inward," he lives, no longer he, "but Christ in him"—and again, as he is elevated, seeking "what is above," where Christ thrones [sic] at His Father's right.[60]

According to Guardini, the *Confessions* is a narrative of Augustine's interior drama, an inner dialogue. Thus, in him:

> In memory and consciousness the dialectic of the self takes place, not merely existing, but actively confronting itself with itself. Spirituality or inwardness includes all life's levels with their divisions into the plains and realms where consciousness, remembrance, self-possession, and self-confrontation take place.[61]

Beneath the moral conflict, as epitomized in Augustine's attempt to turn away from his lust, lies a deeper religious conflict, which Guardini calls "the substance of the inner drama at its deepest level."[62] This is the struggle between human self-assertion and the grace of God, a grace which demands self-surrender and obedience to faith and love. Rather than threatening one's natural, autonomous personality, this surrender enables one to find one's truest self. It is the replacement of the natural personality by the spiritual personality.[63]

At this point in his analysis Guardini makes a key assertion. According to him, Augustine's struggle to surrender to God involved simultaneous movements of every faculty, every aspect of his personality. Thus:

> [Augustine] is unable to attain to a clear relation of his will and heart to God because he is incapable of reaching the concept of pure spirit. The reason is that an inmost will prevents any such concept, urging him therefore to ignore as "unfeasible" the demand to surrender himself. In the course of the struggle, one process sustains the other. The ultimate escape of the will from its bonds; the final clarification of Augustine's concept of God; the readiness which results from that clarification; the road it

---

60. Ibid., 25.
61. Ibid., 27.
62. Ibid., 30.
63. Ibid., 31.

> opens and the growing ease with which he can now properly conceive of God—all these processes take place simultaneously, with and through one another.[64]

Having said this, Guardini embarks upon an analysis of the relationship between the body and the mind. He begins with the claim that, prior to Augustine's conversion, he experienced a conflict between the life of the senses and the life of the mind, between sensual desire and the desire for wisdom. Eventually, this conflict becomes one between the life of the senses and that of Christian faith.[65] According to Guardini:

> Augustine is straining with all the strength of his will and feeling toward the "*vita beata*," that existence replete with value, hence with supreme fulfillment. This beatific or blissful life can issue only from truth, for truth and value are profoundly one, as are knowing and loving. Basically, knowing and real life—indeed even knowing and real being—are one.[66]

Here, Guardini makes some fundamental assertions about the unity of knowing and loving, even knowing and being. Furthermore, he uses two terms which we must define if we are to understand what he means by the "heart." They are "value" and "instinct."

According to Guardini, "instinct" culminates in the religious act. Instincts are "the same fundamental human forces which nourish our organic life [and] nourish our spiritual as well."[67] Guardini identifies the "organic" and the "spiritual" as two "realms." The instinctive, which he also calls the "vital powers," is contrasted with the "intellectual." However, the effect of the instincts is not limited to the organic, but empowers the life of the mind. Conversely:

> [If] the flow of these powers is to be salutary, the senses must be enlightened by the mind [as in the creation of a great artistic masterpiece]: stimulated, controlled by a mind transformed. This is possible only when an intermediate realm exists in which the mind may become "flesh and blood," an intellectual realm in which it is appropriated by the organic, which in turn reaches out to the mind, eager to be transformed by it. This intermedial realm is the heart.[68]

64. Ibid.
65. Ibid., 35–38.
66. Ibid., 38–39.
67. Ibid., 41–42.
68. Ibid., 42.

Whilst it is true that mere instinct is not sufficient for the "religious act," that religious experience requires the mind to make it intelligible, for Guardini this is possible only when the mind is enlivened with that which springs from our bodily being. According to Guardini, the mind must maintain "close contact with the roots of existence, nature, and the life processes," it must abandon "its isolation to participate in the living event."[69] When it does, a dimension will appear within it "in which the world of instinct opens itself to the spirit, offering itself as grist for its mill, as protective norm and motive power. This intermedial dimension is the heart." Guardini goes on to say that: "From the standpoint of instinct, the heart is height; from that of the mind, it is inwardness, fervor. To the first it brings freedom; to the second, contact with reality."[70]

Standing in opposition to the union of the instinctive and intellectual in the form of the "heart" is sin. Both the instinctive and the intellectual harbor sin. The sin which springs from the instinctive is "reckless self-assertion with its blindness, stubbornness, unreasonableness, and treachery."[71] Mere intellect cannot simply take over the sensual since it will tend to constrain, distort and rationalize it. This is so because the mind also harbors sin, for example, pride. In order for the two to be reconciled, they must pass through the intermediate realm of the heart. The sensual must enliven the mind through love, selflessness and sacrifice. The mind must "permeate the world of the senses creatively, forming it in truth and freedom . . . through love, inwardness, and humility."[72]

The heart is the center of Guardini's anthropology. It is the heart which makes us truly human. It is the key to a genuine anthropology rather than a pseudo-anthropology, a kind of disguised angelism. It is the loving heart which establishes the human person as an embodied spirit, not just a spirit in a body, a ghost in a machine. The humanizing of both the intellect and the senses takes place in the heart. Thus Guardini writes:

> The heart is the vital center of a man. Herein is rooted his humanity; from here he is continually renewed. Here instinct rises to be spiritualized, and the mind or spirit becomes flesh and blood . . . through love. The heart is love's vital organ. From love issues the human being. Everything in him which falls out of the range of love's radiance falls into inhumanity, bestiality. It loses

69. Ibid.
70. Ibid., 43.
71. Ibid.
72. Ibid.

> its loftiness and inwardness, the two poles of the axis on which humanity is spanned.[73]

However, for the heart to be the center of our humanity it must purify and transform itself. Significantly, Guardini sees the chief danger which threatens the heart to be emotional rather than intellectual, "that self-glorification of emotion which sets itself up as infallible." The heart can err "more profoundly, fatefully, and incorrigibly than the mind, because it so easily mistakes the immediacy of its experience for truth." Purity of heart, that purity which "sees God," is "the purity of freedom from selfishness, from the subtler selfishness of the emotions."[74]

According to Guardini, it is the heart which enables the intellectual and sensual life to merge with the religious life. In order to live this life the heart must elevate the instinct and humble the intellect. When love has become the center of one's life: "Then, warmed by its proximity to the blood, the mind can become soul. Leavened by the mind, corporeity becomes body: body enlightened and transformed. Now both, humanized, are ready for the religious life."[75]

It was said earlier that we need to define two terms which Guardini uses. One has been defined— instinct. Now the other must be defined— value. Initially, Guardini speaks of "value" within the context of the Kantian separation of metaphysics and morality. In Guardini's reading of Kant's moral doctrine the only good is the good will, the good intention. Moral "validity" stops short of moral "reality." Moral reality is the concrete act and its living embodiment in the human person. Stopping short of moral reality, goodness remains in the realm of the subject's intention. In this understanding: "Man is not 'good' as a spiritual-corporeal reality."[76] The only place in which validity, the truth, and reality, being, exists, is the subject. Therefore, only values, the good which can be "evaluated," exist in the intention of the subject. Values which are valid in being real, such as virtues, disappear.

The sense that one can be good by becoming a certain kind of being, the concept of human perfection, is lost. This perfection Guardini describes as:

> Well-balanced being: just action and noble predisposition; right principles that have become part and parcel of a man's nature; a mode of life in full accord with the moral law, from which health

---

73. Ibid., 44.
74. Ibid.
75. Ibid., 45. Cf. "Church and Man's," 129.
76. Guardini, *The Conversion of Augustine*, 47.

and beauty of body and soul, rich achievement, and a full well-rounded existence can flower.[77]

In short, it is *arete* which leads to *eudaimonia*. Validity and reality coincide. In the virtuous person, moral validity flows into right being, and right being into right intention.

For Guardini, in the human person, value takes "flesh." He expresses this idea thus:

> [Man] is the basic figure of reality: not untrammeled spirit alone, not mere vitality, but the whole man, his body the expression of his intellectual soul and the intermediary between his soul and the world. The inner realm reveals itself in the outer; the outer is appropriated by the inner . . . Intention grows into act. Value assumes the "flesh" of actual being. The ideal does not merely soar above being; it becomes real, and its reality is valid.[78]

In Christ, this enfleshment takes on a new dimension. Christ has freed this embodied spirit from the fallenness of its nature. This is spiritual freedom, sustained by grace and faith. It extends into the psychological and the cultural realms. As Guardini explains:

> Thus the new inwardness and independence of the Western spirit came into being. Reaching maturity, that spirit was enabled at last to free itself, to a hitherto inconceivable degree, from nature's bonds, to stand on its own, to lead an existence of its own planning and accomplishment. A new image of man arose; man born into nature is now succeeded by man, the venturer into freedom.[79]

Paradoxically, this new freedom has enabled a new rebellion. Without faith, a new "emancipation" takes place—the domination of nature. Thus: "Thinking, planning, shaping, man grows more and more dependent on himself, utilizing the given materials in nature, life, and the psyche for the creation of a form of existence which he himself has designed and willed."[80]

There comes into being that which Guardini calls a "pure" spirituality, the precursor to a Kantian "pure" ethics. Abstract conceptualism leads to the isolated inwardness of the subject, an inwardness cut off from "the other,"

---

77. Ibid., 48.
78. Ibid., 49.
79. Ibid., 50.

80. Ibid. Here, Guardini's understanding of freedom could be integrated with Ratzinger's explanation of the distorted concepts of freedom arising from the Protestant Reformation and the Enlightenment.

from the universal, from being. The goodness and value of being is lost. Thus: "the old ethics of values and reality is replaced by the formal ethics of an abstract duty emptied of its world content and severed from reality."[81]

The alternative to this is what Guardini calls the conquest and assimilation of values. By this he means that the moral good becomes a metaphysical good, a goodness of one's own being. One does not merely have just intentions, one acts justly and becomes just. Furthermore, one's conscience is able to identify which values should be pursued at the right time and in the right way. As Guardini expresses it: "although every value is valid *per se*, it does not follow that it has the right to command. Only the given, right value incorporated into the right order of a specific existence, has this right." It is only possible to acquire a value by affirming its validity. The value "is realized and acquired in exact proportion to the reverence in which it is held by the mind."[82] The mind must do the value justice. Hence, the absolute value, the real value, the highest value, *the* value is the truth, which can only be grasped by love.

Guardini identifies the meaning of truth to Augustine as "ultimate significance and strictest obligation." Truth is not limited to the realm of knowledge— it is "a basic stipulation of being," it determines being.[83] The nature of truth is to be found in the relation between that which is to its "norm," the "idea" which one has of that which is. That which is has truth. It also has value. The coincidence of being and truth can be asserted also with regard to the moral imperative. This imperative is "simultaneously 'ethical' and 'actual': ethical as the subject of the moral act, 'actual' because 'virtue' is the norm of perfection for the really human being."[84]

Here we come to the importance of "value" for Guardini. For him:

> [Truth] and goodness are not merely "norms," but also "values." Taking the valid as our overall concept, "norm" is that aspect of the valid which relates it to the person, not by constraint . . . but by the majesty and significance of validity as such, which claim for themselves the freedom of self-determination. Freedom feels itself answerable to the norm, whether it obeys it or not. On the other hand, "value" is that aspect of the valid which renders it estimable in a man's eyes, again not by force, but by the intrinsic splendor of the value itself, which likewise turns to a corresponding faculty in man: let us call it the freedom of evaluation

---

81. Ibid., 52.
82. Ibid., 54.
83. Ibid., 57.
84. Ibid., 59.

or appraisal. In the broader sense of the word, "norm" has something static about it, something eternally right, immutable, lofty. Man's relation to it is a somewhat "distant" one; the sovereignty of the norm is meant to reign in the conscience. "Value" is dynamic. It has a certain spiritual vibrancy, the warm glow of costliness. That is why it stirs to action, desire, and a striving for unity. The norm calls to obedience; the value, to estimation and participation.[85]

A separation of norm from value, of obedience from esteem, leads first to the ethics of Kant, and then, in reaction, to those of Nietzsche—the reaction of warm amorality to cold duty. Herein lies the cause and nature of the modern misconception of freedom. As Guardini explains:

> Only from this standpoint is it possible to understand modern "amoralism" or aestheticism, namely, as an attempt to escape from the harness of duty frozen norms into the "freedom" of nature or of intellectual values—a "freedom" which appears to be guaranteed in that it is based on the biological or on the artistically beautiful.[86]

For Guardini, the correct name for "esteem" is *eros*. It is conscience and *eros* which correspond to the two forms of validity, "norm" and "value." In the human person, conscience and *eros* are one, though Guardini cannot find a precise name for this unity. For him:

> "Conscience" suggests that inwardness can and should respond to the just demands of the norm; "Eros," that the essential foundation of existence is value, the word implying readiness to respond to being's tremors of costliness with the excitement of striving to participate in them.[87]

Here we come finally to Guardini's definition of the heart. It is "[the] inwardness that responds to value." It is "both faculty and realm of human entirety." However, "[this] does not mean the life of the emotions as opposed to that of the mind; the heart itself is 'mind,' but it is evaluating mind, not merely mind obedient to the norm. It is mind warmed and moved by value toward value: mind as Eros-bearer."[88]

---

85. Ibid.
86. Ibid., 60 n. 1.
87. Ibid., 60.
88. Ibid. Can Guardini's understanding of *eros*, and the heart as Eros-bearer, further elucidate Ratzinger's account of the relationship between *eros* and *agape*?

As well as being essentially related to truth and goodness, the heart is also essentially related to beauty, be it in a person, in nature or a work of art. Thus Guardini writes:

> What is meant here becomes more intelligible when we note how the words "the beautiful" are used by Plato—or Dante. They proclaim validity, not as norm, but as value, worth. They are not used lightly or sensually, but exactingly, with the strict obligations of perfection. Strictness is the realm of the valuable—this is beauty. Outlet and bearer of the Eros as the appraising, beauty-experiencing movement of the spirit relevant to the body—realm of the living person in which Eros is condition, faculty, being—that is the heart.[89]

We should now be able to grasp Guardini's reading of Pascal's anthropology of the heart. He identifies *le coeur* as the central reality of Pascal's anthropology. He also identifies what his understanding is not. It is not the emotional in opposition to the logical, feeling to intellect, or "soul" to "mind." Rather "heart" *is* mind, that is to say, a manifestation of the mind. For Guardini's Pascal: "The act of the heart is an act productive of knowledge. Certain objects only become given in the act of the heart. But they do not remain there in a-rational intuition, but are accessible to intellectual and rational penetration."[90]

For Guardini, the "phenomenon" of the heart "depends on the interrelationship between knowledge and will, apprehension of truth and love—objectively expressed, between essence and value." This "value" is "the character of the preciousness of things: that which makes them worthy of being." When the mind comes in contact with the "value," it is "sensible" to it. This "mind" of which Guardini speaks is not the "theoretical" mind, the reason, but "the mind which appreciates and values, that is . . . the heart."[91] This "heart":

> is the mind, so far as it gets into proximity of the blood, into the feeling, living fiber of the body . . . Heart is the mind rendered ardent and sensitive by the blood, but which at the same time ascends into the clarity of contemplation, the distinctness of form, the precision of judgment. Heart is the organ of love . . . [a love which] implies . . . the relationship of the center of man's desires and feelings to the idea; the movement from the blood

---

89. Ibid., 60–61.
90. Guardini, *Pascal for Our Time*, 129.
91. Ibid., 130.

to the mind, from the presence of the body to the eternity of the mind. It is what is experienced in the heart.[92]

Guardini bases this position upon his understanding of Pascal's anthropology, especially as found in Pascal's brief *Discourse on the Passion of Love*. The "neat" or clear mind has "neat" passions. The great and neat mind loves with ardor and sees clearly what it loves. The more one has this kind of mind, the greater one's passions will be, since the passions are sentiments and ideas which, although occasioned by the body, belong exclusively to the mind. Rather than opposing reason to love, Pascal claims that they are one and the same thing.[93]

In Guardini's reading of Pascal, the heart grasps the value of being—of all being, but more so human being, and above all, the being which manifests itself through revelation, the holiness of God. Heart is the organ of the *esprit de finesse*. It has a flexibility of thought which penetrates to the heart of the other.[94] This is how Guardini reads Pascal's most famous axiom. To know truth not just by reason but by the heart, to know first principles, is a function of the heart. However, this function is not simply the intuition of what cannot be demonstrated. Rather, it is the work of the "appreciating mind" as opposed to the "theoretical mind." As Guardini expresses it: "Knowledge presupposes love. One will know the truth—really know it, in the most profound sense, with the passion of appropriation—to the extent that one is loving."[95]

For Guardini, love is active as well as passive. It takes the initiative and moves towards value. He identifies love as freedom. One loves a value, but one must choose between values. The choice of values leads either to freedom or slavery, depending upon the appropriateness of the value chosen. Furthermore, one's attitude to the value can be either one of submission or domination. So Guardini asks:

> [Whether] the will of the heart permits the value or the image of the value to develop purely out of itself, which at the same time means that this heart must rise above and beyond itself;

---

92. Ibid. Cf. "Church and Man's," 129.

93. Guardini, *Pascal for Our Time*, 130-31. Guardini refers the reader to Blaise Pascal, *Pensées et Opuscules*, 124-133. For an English translation, see "Discourse on the Passion of Love," 417-426. On the identity of love and reason, Guardini claims to find the same idea in Plato, Augustine and Dante.

94. Guardini, *Pascal for Our Time*, 131-32.

95. Ibid., 133.

or whether the heart subordinates what it encounters to its own volition, makes it subservient to itself.[96]

For Guardini, choosing the right value and submitting to it, allowing it to be itself rather than twist it to our own ends, is the definition of a pure heart. Sin renders the heart impure, since the sinner "endeavors to subordinate by force the freedom of what is valid to his own volition." Because sin exercises its influence above all in the mind, it also does so in the depths of the heart, and threatens to become: "An evil prior decision which precedes all individual decisions."[97] Rather than allowing the value to develop purely out of itself, Guardini holds that this *a priori* decision does the following.

> [It] strives to confer autonomy on values, and in this way to make them instruments of the revolt against God. It influences the force of the heart and seeks thus to falsify the true image of things. It troubles the view for value, misleads the value sentiment, diverts the judgment of value—and the danger is all the greater as the heart, in the characteristic immediacy of its acts, feels so sure of itself and is not willing to believe in the possibility of an error. In reality, nothing can err in a way as profound, as fateful, and as difficult to set right as the heart.[98]

Let us conclude with a brief summary of the essence of Guardini's anthropology of the heart. The truth is that in attempting such an anthropology he set himself an exceedingly difficult task. If we are to say anything about the human person we must distinguish between different elements and faculties in that personality—the body, the senses, the emotions, the intellect, the memory, the will. Yet making such distinctions can lead to the impression that the human person is simply a complicated mechanism, with various parts working together in order to function. The sense of the integrity of the person can be diminished or lost.

For Guardini, the heart is the place of reconciliation between the two halves of the human person, the sensual and the intellectual. It is the "heart" which makes us specifically human, since angels have spiritual intellect and animals have embodied senses. The heart is the place where spiritual mind becomes human soul, and animal corporeity becomes human body. The heart is also the place of reconciliation of the moral and the spiritual. The heart is evaluating mind, mind as eros-bearer. We might also say that it is "knowing passion." It is able to grasp not just truth, but also the

---

96. Ibid.
97. Ibid., 134.
98. Ibid.

transcendentals of goodness and beauty. It is the place of union of knowing and loving. The heart is the whole person participating in knowing, and the whole person participating in loving. Only when we love can we truly know. This is purity of heart. The heart is this organ of love. This love is both passive and active. Not only is it drawn to the good, true and beautiful, but it actively seeks them out. Love is freedom. It is only through participation in the life of God that heart truly becomes heart, truly integrated, truly human, truly knowing, truly loving, truly pure, truly free.

Von Hildebrand's Understanding

Dietrich von Hildebrand gives an alternative definition of "heart" to that given thus far. He holds that, for the most part, it is "characteristic of the heart in its true and most specific sense that it is chosen as representative of man's inner life, and that the heart, rather than the intellect or will, is identified with the soul as such."[99] He goes on to identify the "heart" as the center of human affectivity. Thus, "just as the intellect is the root of all acts of knowledge, the heart is the organ of all affectivity: all wishing, all desiring, all 'being *affected*.'"[100] Von Hildebrand gradually refines his definition of the heart. More precisely, it is the center of affectivity. It can be contrasted not just with the will and intellect, but with the less central strata of affectivity. These strata von Hildebrand characterizes as "non-spiritual," that is, the agreeable or disagreeable feelings which attend upon bodily pains and pleasures.[101] Distinguishing between bodily and psychic feelings, he holds that not all psychic feelings can be classified as "spiritual." There are psychic states such as "jolliness" and depression, and what he calls spiritual affective responses such as joy, sorrow, love or compassion. He distinguishes between them on the grounds that the former are not "intentional," that is to say, they do not have "a meaningful conscious relation to an object."[102] Thus:

> [Psychic] states are "caused" either by bodily processes or by psychic ones, whereas affective responses are "motivated." Never can an authentic affective response come into existence by mere causation, but only by motivation. Real joy necessarily implies not only the consciousness of an object about which we are

---

99. Von Hildebrand, *The Sacred Heart*, 47. Von Hildebrand sees the intellect, will and heart as the three fundamental "capacities" of the human person. It is to the heart that the "affective sphere" belongs (25–49).
100. Ibid., 48.
101. Ibid., 49–52.
102. Ibid., 54.

rejoicing, but also an awareness that it is this object which is the reason for this joy. In rejoicing over the recovery of a friend, we know that it is this event which engenders and motivates our joy. The recovery of our friend is thus connected with our joy by a meaningful and intelligible relation. [Von Hildebrand goes on to contrast this with the conviviality caused by drinking alcohol.][103]

Von Hildebrand further refines his definition of the "heart" by distinguishing between what he calls "energized" and "tender" affectivity. The former is "temperamental," for example, the pleasure experienced in sports or in displaying one's talents. According to him:

> [The latter] manifests itself in love in all its categories: filial and parental love, friendship, brotherly and sisterly love, conjugal love and love of neighbor. It displays itself in "being moved," in enthusiasm, in deep authentic sorrow, in gratitude, in tears of grateful joy, or in contrition. It is this type of affectivity which includes the capacity for a noble surrender, affectivity in which the heart is involved.[104]

For von Hildebrand, this is the "affectivity" spoken of in the Song of Songs.

> The more the lover wants to dwell in his love; the more he aspires to experience the full depth of his love; the more he wants to recollect himself and to allow his love to unfold itself in a deep contemplative rhythm; the more he longs for the interpenetration of his soul with the soul of his beloved—a longing expressed in the words *cor ad cor loquitur*, "heart speaks to heart," and displaying itself in the eyes of the lover seeking the eyes of his beloved—the more he will possess true affectivity.[105]

For von Hildebrand, if one truly has a "tender affectivity," the more one's experience of the object of this affectivity will be "awakened." And the more one's affectivity is awakened, the greater the joy that one will experience. Thus: "The more conscious a joy is, the more its object is seen and understood in its full meaning; the more awakened and outspoken the response, the more the joy is lived."[106] In other words, the deeper one's joy in the beloved, the deeper one's knowledge of the beloved, and the deeper that knowledge, the deeper the joy. Love, joy and knowledge mutually reinforce

---

103. Ibid, 54–55.
104. Ibid., 77.
105. Ibid., 79.
106. Ibid., 81.

each other. Thus: "It belongs to the very nature of affective experiences that a deep joy or a deep love, through each possesses a theme of its own, is penetrated by the awareness that our joy or our love is objectively justified and objectively valid."[107]

Although von Hildebrand gives a more limited definition of "heart," especially when compared with Guardini and Ratzinger, it would be premature to dismiss it too readily. The reason for this is that it is von Hildebrand's definition which most closely accords with the understanding of the heart which seems to pervade *Haurietis aquas*, and the description of Christ the new Adam given in *Gaudium et spes*.

Pius XII's Understanding

In *Haurietis aquas*, Pius XII quotes his immediate predecessor to the effect that: "[Devotion to the Sacred Heart] leads our minds more quickly than any other to an intimate knowledge of Christ the Lord and inclines our hearts more effectively to love him," making a distinction between the mind knowing and the heart loving.[108] According to Pius XII, the heart of Jesus, the "noblest part of his human nature,"[109] the body's noblest member, is *physically* the seat of the emotions.[110] Pius XII goes on to quote Sts. Justin Martyr, Basil, John Chrysostom, Ambrose, Jerome and Augustine as witnesses to the effect that Christ shared our human emotions.[111] Later, *Gaudium et spes* will describe the human nature of the new Adam in the following terms.

> Human nature, by the very fact that it was assumed, not absorbed, by him, has been raised in us also to a dignity beyond compare. For, by his incarnation, he, the son of God, has in a certain way united himself with each man. He worked with human hands, he thought with a human mind. He acted with a human will, and with *a human heart he loved*.[112]

---

107. Ibid., 83.
108. Pius XI, *Miserentissimus redemptor*, 167, quoted in *HA*, 216.
109. *HA*, 219.
110. Ibid., 227.
111. Ibid., 228–30.

112. *GS*, no. 22. Italics not in the original. This is by no means the only reference to the human heart in the conciliar document, which although mentioned constantly is never explicitly defined.

Common Ground in Understanding the Heart

What common ground is there between Ratzinger's accounts and these others on the nature of the human heart? First, most (Sacred Scripture, patristic theologians such as Origen and St. Augustine, medieval theologians such as St. Bernard and St. Bonaventure, Pascal, Bl. Newman, the brothers Rahner, and Guardini) acknowledge the heart as the place of encounter with God.[113] Furthermore, since St. Thomas equates "heart" in the biblical sense with spirit, one cannot rule out a Thomistic openness to it being the place of such an encounter. Second, almost all speak of the heart as the place of the passions.[114]

In common with Augustine, Pascal, Newman and Guardini, Ratzinger thinks of the heart as the place that "knows." Like Pascal and Guardini, he regards the heart as the center of one's inner life. However, Ratzinger does not say anything about the heart knowing first principles. Unlike Pascal and Newman he does not contrast the perception of the heart with Enlightenment reasoning. Not just "reasoning," but all reason has its limits. The "comprehension" spoken of in Ephesians 3:14–19 is that of a lover.[115] Ratzinger's understanding of the heart's perceptive power is in its ability to know "the other." By means of the heart God is perceived. The heart is "man's inner eye."[116] It is the heart that must inquire after God, must "seek his face."[117] Following Guardini, Newman, Augustine and ultimately the Beatitudes, it is the "pure of heart" who see God.

At first sight it may appear that Ratzinger's and von Hildebrand's definitions of the heart are contradictory. However, although von Hildebrand restricts his understanding of the heart to the place of affectivity, there is some common ground. Like Ratzinger, von Hildebrand regards the heart as "knowing." Spiritual affective responses are "intentional," they have a meaningful conscious relation to an object. One is "aware" that the object of affective responses such as joy, sorrow, love or compassion is the "reason" for these responses. The relationship between the response and the object

---

113. Cf. *Jesus I*, 92: "The organ for seeing God is the heart."

114. Cf. *Behold*, 56: "... the heart is the epitome of the passions..."

115. *Behold*, 55. As Ratzinger says: "As long ago as the Fathers, in particular in the pseudo-Dionysian tradition, this passage had led theologians to stress that reason had its limits." And: "For 'you only see properly with your heart,' as Saint-Exupéry's Little Prince says. (And the Little Prince can be taken as a symbol for that childlikeness which we must regain if we are to find our way back out of the clever foolishness of the adult world and into man's true nature, which is beyond mere reason)" (55).

116. *Jesus I*, 93.

117. Ibid., 94.

is "a meaningful and intelligible relation." Von Hildebrand characterizes the affective response of the heart, along with acts of willing and thinking, as a "conscious spiritual act."[118]

There seems to be a further similarity between Ratzinger and von Hildebrand. Ratzinger states that: "In order for man to become capable of perceiving God, the energies of his existence must work in harmony. His will must be pure and so too must the underlying affective dimension of his soul, which gives intelligence and will their direction."[119] For von Hildebrand, because "tender affectivity" is "aware," "intentional," and "conscious," it also has a "directive" role.

> The truly affective man, the man with an awakened heart, is precisely the one who grasps that what matters is the objective situation and whether there is reason to rejoice and to be happy. It is in taking the objective situation seriously, in being concerned with the question of whether the objective situation calls for happiness, for joy, or for sorrow, that the great, superabundant spiritual affective experiences are engendered.[120]

When someone perceives what is really good, true, and beautiful; when someone knows conceptually that it is really good, true, and beautiful; when someone's will is pure; he or she will desire and pursue that object. As Ratzinger says: "Speaking of the *heart* in this way means precisely that man's perceptive powers play in concert."[121]

Ratzinger does not regard the "heart" as exclusively spiritual. A "spirituality of the heart" is also a bodily spirituality, a spirituality of the senses. "[The] heart is the hub of the senses, the place where spirit and sense meet, interpenetrate and unite."[122] In order for the perceptive powers of the human person to "play in concert," there must be, according to Ratzinger:

> [a] proper interplay of body and soul, since this is essential for the totality of the creature we call "man." Man's fundamental affective disposition actually depends on just this unity of body and soul and on man's acceptance of being both body and spirit. This means he places his body under the discipline of the spirit, yet does not isolate intellect and will. Rather, he accepts himself as coming from God and thereby also acknowledges and lives out the bodiliness of his existence as an enrichment for the

118. Von Hildebrand, *The Sacred Heart*, 81.
119. *Jesus I*, 92–93.
120. Von Hildebrand, *The Sacred Heart*, 82–83.
121. *Jesus I*, 93. Italics in original.
122. *Behold*, 56.

spirit. The heart—the wholeness of man—must be pure, interiorly open and free, in order for man to be able to see God.[123]

Furthermore, Ratzinger states that:

> [because of human bodiliness] man needs to see, he needs this kind of silent beholding which becomes a touching, if he is to become aware of the mysteries of God. He must set his foot on the "ladder" of the body in order to climb it and so find the path along which faith invites him.[124]

How has Ratzinger come to his ultimate conclusion that the human "heart" is the "place" of the integration of the intellect, will, passions and senses, of the body and the soul? Amongst the major identifiable sources is the use of the term in Sacred Scripture and the Fathers, as well as the patristic investigations of Hugo Rahner, and the teaching of *Haurietis aquas*. Certainly, the *Theological Dictionary of the New Testament* is a favorite work of Ratzinger, and its definition of "heart," together with Ratzinger's own reflections on the biblical witness, would explain his understanding of the heart as the integrating center of the intellect, will and passions, whilst further anthropological reflections on the relationship between the emotions and the bodily senses would lead to his final, comprehensive understanding. The heart sees, thinks, ponders, chooses, feels, and beats. If it does all these things it cannot simply be any one of these things, but must be the union of all these things. Ultimately, Ratzinger's understanding of the heart enshrines the superiority of love over knowledge, or rather, that love engenders a certain kind of knowledge which is superior to understanding the meaning of an essence, affirming the truth of a proposition, or proving one truth from another. As he expressed it in his Apostolic Letter announcing the year of faith, speaking of the means by which people come to faith in Jesus:

> [Knowing] the content to be believed is not sufficient unless the heart, the authentic sacred space within the person, is opened by grace that allows the eyes to see below the surface and to understand that what has been proclaimed is the word of God.[125]

---

123. *Jesus I*, 93.

124. *Behold*, 54. Cf. Karl Rahner's understanding of the "heart" as inclusive of human bodiliness, and the physical heart as a "natural symbol" of the whole human person, in "Some Theses," 132–38.

125. Benedict XVI, *Porta fidei*, no. 10.

This is the lover's knowledge of the beloved. Nor is this love a "cold charity." It is a passionate love which desires and finds joy in the beloved. For Ratzinger, "love is the eye, and to love is to see."[126]

It is difficult to study Guardini's anthropology of the heart and not see there a major source for Ratzinger's.[127] It could be argued that both Augustine's and Pascal's understanding of the heart have been mediated to Ratzinger through Guardini. One might even say that Ratzinger's understanding is substantially "condensed" Guardini—substantially, but not entirely. There are two main differences. First, Ratzinger does not go into the same depth of detail as does Guardini, especially in comparison with Guardini's notion of "value." Second, Ratzinger's anthropology of the heart has a far greater biblical foundation.

Having said all this, it must also be said that, on occasion, Ratzinger does speak of the heart as a distinct human faculty apart from other human faculties. For example, in his final volume of *Jesus of Nazareth*, in recounting the Virgin Mary's response to Gabriel's message, he says that: "[Mary] stands before us as a woman of great interiority, who holds heart and mind in harmony and seeks to understand the context, the overall significance of God's message."[128] Indeed, Sacred Scripture itself, on occasion, also makes a distinction between such entities as "heart," "soul," and "mind." We need go no further than the greatest of the commandments to affirm this: "You

---

126. *Behold*, 55. In this the "Augustinian" nature of Ratzinger's anthropological understanding comes to the fore. Cf. Peters, *The Logic of the Heart*, 60: "Central to Augustine's theory of reason and faith is his conviction that our reasoning about how to live well as humans ought to be directed and molded by our needs and desires as feeling agents who are fundamentally, and above all else, lovers. The centrality of love in Augustine's thinking underlies his affirmation of the priority, at least in one sense, of belief over rational understanding." It would be interesting to contrast Ratzinger's anthropology with that of Wojtyla. As Rowland explains: "Since postmodern thought is very much rooted in the Romantic reaction against the philosophy of the eighteenth century and focused on topics like the uniqueness of each and every human being, it is impossible to deal with it unless one moves beyond the boundaries of Aristotelian categories. Both John Paul II and Benedict XVI understood this from their earliest pastoral years and while one worked on developing the Thomist tradition in a more personalist direction, the other worked on mining the Augustinian tradition with reference to the same pastoral ends. Wojtyla was working on the Aquinas-John of the Cross-Mounier-Scheler line, while Ratzinger was working on the Augustinian-Newman-Guardini-Buber-Wust line . . . Both however were concerned to re-establish relations between intellectual judgement and the movements of the human heart. Wojtyla spoke of the 'theatre of the inner self,' Ratzinger more often, simply of the heart" (Rowland, *Benedict XVI*, 155).

127. It may also be the case that Guardini's anthropology of freedom has influenced Ratzinger's. See Guardini, *The Conversion of Augustine*, 43–44, 50, and 59–60; and *Pascal for Our Time*, 133–34.

128. Ratzinger, *Jesus of Nazareth: The Infancy Narratives*, 33.

shall love the Lord your God with all your heart, and with all your soul, and with all your mind" (Matt 22:37). This simply shows us that the term is not univocal, and that whilst Ratzinger very often uses it in its "integral," "synthetic" sense, both he and others such as St. Thomas and von Hildebrand are not wrong when they use it in a more "discrete" and "analytic" sense. Yet, although Ratzinger does not do so, we can appeal to what we are told about Mary in Luke's Gospel on behalf of a synthetic understanding of the heart. After the visit of the shepherds, we are told that: "Mary kept all these things, pondering them in her heart" (Luke 2:19). The passage in Greek reads: ἡ δὲ Μαριὰμ πάντα συνετήρει τὰ ῥήματα ταυτα συμβάλλουσα ἐν τῃ καρδίᾳ αὐτης. We should note that the word which we translate as "pondering," συμβάλλουσα, is the present active participle of συμβάλειν, which means "to throw together," and is the word from which our term "symbol" is derived. So, we could say that Mary's heart is the place where all that has happened to her with regard to Jesus is brought together—her memory of all the events pertaining to Jesus, and all the thoughts and feelings attendant upon those events, are made present and grow together into one coherent whole, the whole that is the pure heart of Mary.

12

The Symbolic Theology of the Father's Heart

Symbol over Concept

Although the Old Testament speaks of God having a heart far less frequently than it speaks of the human heart, such occurrences are spread throughout it. As applied to God, "heart" is used in the same senses as it is used of human beings. Thus, God is grieved to the heart (cf. Gen 6:6). He ponders in his heart (cf. Gen 8:21), and the thoughts of his heart stand for all generations (cf. Ps 33:11). He accomplishes the intentions of his heart (cf. Jer 23:20 and 30:24). He will give his people shepherds after his own heart (cf. Jer 3:15), and he does not afflict and grieve his people from his heart (cf. Lam 3:33). His eyes and his heart will be in the temple forever (cf. 1 Kgs 9:3; 2 Chr 7:16). His heart recoils against handing his people over to destruction (cf. Hos 11:8). Are these occurrences to be dismissed simply as anthropomorphisms and no more?[1]

Does Ratzinger understand the term "heart," as applied to God, in a metaphorical or an analogical sense? For example, when Hosea speaks prophetically of God's heart recoiling within him, of his compassion growing warm and tender, is this to be placed in the same category as the Psalmist asking to be guarded as the apple of God's eye and hidden in the shadow of his wings (cf. Ps 17:8)? Furthermore, why does Ratzinger prefer the "image language of the body" to abstract concepts? Why does he think that such language gives us a deeper understanding of God's dispositions toward man

---

1. It is noteworthy that in *Haurietis aquas*, in his elucidation of the love of God as displayed in the Old Testament, Pius XII makes no mention of the heart of God. See HA, 220–23.

than conceptual language does?[2] At first glance he would seem to be saying that *images* enable us to understand God better than *concepts* do. If we think of understanding only in terms of the intellect, even the intellect informed through the senses, this seems to be nonsense. However, Ratzinger holds that it is the *heart* that *sees*. This means that knowing is not simply an intellectual activity, but an activity that involves the whole person. We know God, not as an object of study, but in a personal encounter. The heart is the organ of seeing, that is to say, we see through loving. It is the lover who truly sees, who truly knows, the beloved. It is in yearning for God, loving God, enjoying God, that we know God. Just as a woman's experience, with its sensation, emotion and self-giving, of relating to the helpless child within her, is summed up by the word "womb," so our experience of knowing and loving God in our sensual, emotional, intellectual and volitional life is summed up by the word "heart."

This is the burden of Ratzinger's commentary on Ephesians 3:18–19: "[that you] may have power to comprehend with all the saints what is the breadth and length and height and depth, and to know the love of Christ which surpasses knowledge, that you may be filled with all the fullness of God." Thus Ratzinger comments:

> As long ago as the Fathers, in particular of the pseudo-Dionysian tradition, this passage had led theologians to stress that reason had its limits. This is the origin, in the latter tradition, of the *ignote cognoscere*, knowing in unknowing, which leads to the concept of *docta ignorantia*, thus the mysticism of darkness comes about where love alone is able to see. Many texts could be quoted here, for instance, Gregory the Great's "*Amor ipse notitia est*"; Hugh of St. Victor's "*Intrat dilectio et appropinquat, ubi scientia foris est*"; or Richard of St. Victor's beautiful formulation: "*Amor occulus est et amare videre est*" ("love is the eye, and to love is to see").[3]

In *Jesus of Nazareth*, in the context of his discussion on maternal images of God in Sacred Scripture, Ratzinger states: "The image language of the body furnishes us . . . with a deeper understanding of God's disposition toward man than any conceptual language could."[4] In his use of images such as heart with reference to God, Ratzinger is one with the *ressourcement* theologians of the twentieth century in their adoption of the symbolic theology of the Fathers. Anthony Sciglitano gives an excellent introduction

2. *Jesus I*, 139.
3. *Behold*, 55.
4. *Jesus I*, 139.

to the *ressourcement* retrieval of this way of theologizing.⁵ He points out how theologians such as de Lubac, Congar, Balthasar and Chenu did the following.

> [They] systematically [elevate] symbol (*Vorstellung*) over concept (*Begriff*). This does not mean that they turn to an irrationalist form of theology, but rather that human reason needs to be regulated by the symbolic world of Scripture and Christian worship, within which a deeper reason is disclosed that can heal and perfect distorted or inadequate human reason. This divine reason, however, cannot be reduced to human propositions and univocal statements; rather, it presents itself in the paradoxical joinings of spirit and matter, meaning and expression that can disclose a reality that transcends human rationality, yet does not destroy it. Indeed, only insofar as these paradoxical forms guide reason, can reason itself find its true vocation. Put otherwise, symbolic paradox reveals divine mystery.⁶

---

5. Sciglitano, "Pope Benedict XVI," 174–78. For another example of Ratzinger's use of symbolic theology, see his account of Easter symbolism in *Behold*, 112–13.

6. Ibid, 175. For the thinking of various *ressourcement* theologians on the patristic symbolic theology that lasted into the twelfth century, see Chenu, *Nature, Man and Society*, xix and 102–3; Lubac, *Corpus Mysticum*, 231–33; and Congar, *The Word and the Spirit*, 4, where he says: "It is clear that we shall reach the eternal Trinity only by way of the economic Trinity. The theologian has to follow this way and follow it in faith, trying to interpret and construe the mystery by using concepts. That at least is the tradition of the great scholastic theologians. But it is possible to do theology in a different way, as, for example, St Bernard did. At the risk of remaining imprecise in certain respects, Luther wanted to keep the terminology of the Word of God, while rejecting metaphysics and scholasticism. The many paradoxical and dialectical expressions which he used also presumably correspond to the feeling which he experienced of non-homogeneity between the natural or rational order and the order of redemption. A symbol is the place where and the means by which we can apprehend realities which the concept fragments in its attempt to reproduce them exactly. It is also apt to indicate the transcendence of revealed spiritual realities. One may take a more rational expression as an adequate statement. Images do not allow such an illusion. Thomas Aquinas comes close to supposing that in this respect the coarsest are the most fitting. Perhaps I should say: the more material, but they can also be suggestive and beautiful." Congar's Thomistic reference is to be found in the *ST* I, q. 1, a. 9, ad 3: "As Dionysius says (Coel. Hier. i), it is more fitting that divine truths should be expounded under the figure of less noble than of nobler bodies, and this for three reasons. First, because thereby men's minds are the better preserved from error. For then it is clear that these things are not literal descriptions of divine truths, which might have been open to doubt had they been expressed under the figure of nobler bodies, especially for those who could think of nothing nobler than bodies. Secondly, because this is more befitting the knowledge of God that we have in this life. For what He is not is clearer to us than what He is. Therefore similitudes drawn from things farthest away from God form within us a truer estimate that God is above whatsoever we may say or think of Him. Thirdly, because

Here, we need to understand what is meant by "mystery." As Gabriel Marcel says, a mystery is not to be confused with a problem.

> A problem is something which I meet, which I find complete before me, but which I can therefore lay siege to and reduce. But a mystery is something in which I myself am involved, and it can therefore only be thought of as "a sphere where the distinction between what is in me and what is before me loses its meaning and its initial validity." A genuine problem is subject to an appropriate technique by the exercise of which it is defined; whereas a mystery by definition transcends every conceivable technique.[7]

We could add "and every conceivable thought." In the case of the mystery of God, we encounter this mystery in our personal relationship with him. We cannot know God as an object, only as a Thou in an I-Thou relationship.

So, what are these images of God's heart attempting to convey? Since God is spirit and not bodily, do we regulate the love of God to a level something *less* than human love, something anemic in comparison? As God is "God and not man" (Hos 11:9), is his love to be understood as *more than*, or *less than* human? Is spirit something more ephemeral, less substantial, than matter? There is the danger of regarding God as a kind of super angel, bodiless and therefore passionless. In fact, there may be danger in simply thinking of pure spirits as passionless. C. S. Lewis, in his novel *Perelandra*, describes such spirits in his account of how the assumed appearance of angel-like "eldila" affected his protagonist Ransom.

> The faces surprised him very much. Nothing less like the "angel" of popular art could well be imagined. The rich variety, the hint of undeveloped possibilities, which make the interest of human faces, were entirely absent. One single, changeless expression— so clear that it hurt and dazzled—was stamped on each and there was nothing else there at all ... What this one thing was he could not be certain. He concluded in the end that it was charity. But it was terrifyingly different from the expression of human charity, which we always see either blossoming out of, or hastening to descend into, natural affection. Here there was no affection at all ... Pure, spiritual, intellectual love shot from their faces like

---

thereby divine truths are the better hidden from the unworthy." For a recent discussion of the *ressourcement* reappropriation of patristic symbolical theology, see Komonchak, "Returning from Exile," 35–48.

7. Marcel, *The Mystery of Being*, 211–12.

barbed lightning. It was so unlike the love we experience that its expression could easily be mistaken for ferocity.[8]

Should we agree with Lewis, or do pure spirits undergo something which is analogous to human passion? Likewise, an unwary reading of *Haurietis aquas* can lead us to think of God as passionless. Therein, Pius XII states:

> [If] we are really to be able, as far as man can in this life, "to comprehend, with all the saints, what is the breadth and length and height and depth" of the hidden charity of the Incarnate Word towards his Heavenly Father and towards sin-stained man, then we must bear in mind that his love is not only a spiritual love, such as befits God (inasmuch as "God is a Spirit"). True the love which God bore our first parents and the Hebrew people was a purely spiritual love. And the language of human love, conjugal and parental, which we find in the Psalms, in the Prophetical writings and in the Canticle of Canticles, is simply a token and symbol of the utterly real yet purely spiritual charity with which God loves the human race. But the love which breathes in the Gospels, and the Epistles and in the pages of the Apocalypse, wherein the love of the Heart of Jesus is depicted, is not merely divine charity, but indicates also human sentiments of love.[9]

The use of expressions such as "only a spiritual love," and especially "merely divine charity" can give the impression that the love of God lacks something which human love possesses.

It seems axiomatic that since God has no body he can have no passions. Yet Ratzinger, after affirming that "suffering presupposes the ability to suffer, it presupposes the faculty of the emotions," goes on to affirm that the Father suffers.[10] He states that it was Origen "who grasped most profoundly the idea of the suffering God and made bold to say that it could not be restricted to the suffering humanity of Jesus but also affected the Christian picture of God."[11] According to Ratzinger, not only does the Father suffer in allowing the Son to suffer, but the Holy Spirit also shares in this suffering, groaning within us, as St. Paul says (cf. Rom 8:26).[12] Furthermore, he sees Origen as giving the normative definition for interpreting the theme of the suffering God: "When you hear someone speak of God's passions, always apply

---

8. Lewis, *Perelandra*, 168–69.
9. *HA*, 226.
10. *Behold*, 57–58.
11. Ibid., 58.
12. Ibid.

what is said to love."[13] He sees Origen's position being developed by St. Bernard's dictum: *"impassibilis est Deus, sed non incompassibilis."*[14] Yet, he thinks that St. Bernard's line of thought does not do full justice to the reality of God's suffering given in Scripture and tradition.[15] In spite of all this, Ratzinger thinks that this position does not lead to a new Patripassianism, such as that apparently proposed by Jürgen Moltmann.[16]

The Influence of Von Balthasar and Maritain

This is as far as Ratzinger, on his own account, explicitly takes the question of the suffering of God. However, we may be able to flesh out his understanding by investigating the thought on this matter of the various theologians to whom he refers approvingly. For Ratzinger, one of the key points of reference on this question is the work of von Balthasar.[17] It seems that Ratzinger has arrived at his understanding of Origen on the suffering of the Father via von Balthasar. According to von Balthasar, Origen's position is not patripassian. He is not advocating a physical interpretation of the suffering of God. Rather, it is the position that whatever perfections are to be found in creatures are to be found in a pre-eminent way in God. It is, according to von Balthasar, as the Psalmist says: "He who formed the eye, does he not see? (Ps 94:9)."[18] Von Balthasar sees validity in Origen's understanding of the *pathos* of God because it is not the same as the normal Greek understanding of *pathos* as an external misfortune which is contrary to one's will. The *passio* of the pity of the eternal Son for our fallen distress is freely chosen, and what is true of the Son is true of the Father.[19]

For Ratzinger, the key to understanding the suffering of God is the recognition that God is love. On this point he refers to the work of Jean Galot and Jacques Maritain.[20] Galot claims that, on the question of God's

---

13. Ibid.

14. *Behold*, 58, no. 10.

15. Ibid., 58–59, no. 11.

16. Ibid. Cf. Moltmann, *The Crucified God*, 267–78. Oakes describes Moltmann's Patripassianism as "a lazy attribution of human emotions to God." See Oakes, *Infinity Dwindling to Infancy*, 298.

17. For an analysis of von Balthasar's theology of God's pain, and its implications for the possibility of eternal damnation, God's relationship with the world, and the divine attributes, see O'Hanlon, *The Immutability of God*, 69–87.

18. Balthasar, *A Theological Anthropology*, 276.

19. Balthasar, *Theo-Drama*, 218–21.

20. See Galot, *Dieu souffre-t-il?*, and Maritain, "Quelques réflections," 5–27. For an analysis of the thought of Galot and Maritain on this question, see von Balthasar,

apatheia, scholastic and modern theologies do not do justice to the witness of the Old Testament, in particular, the implications of the new covenant.[21] For Galot, since the Incarnation is a work of the whole Trinity, the whole human life of the Son, especially his passion, is both a work of and revelation of the Father.[22] It is the Father who sacrifices his Son and accepts from himself and the church the Son thus surrendered as a sacrifice for sin.[23] For Galot, the Son is primarily the "revealer of the Father's suffering."[24] Only secondarily is he the offering of the world to the Father through the Son.[25] On the question of how far God is affected by sin and pain in the world, Galot goes on to distinguish between the impassible trinitarian life of God and the choice of the divine Persons to lovingly create a world which can involve them in pain.[26] This mysterious suffering is analogous to pain in the world. It pertains to the highest love in God and is a perfection of his nature. It is a real suffering, but it is also a joyful suffering.[27] Galot concludes

---

Theo-Drama, 239–42; and Emery, "The Immutability of the God," 52–59.

21. Galot, *Dieu souffre-t-il?*, 119–22.

22. Ibid., 38–118. Germane to this point is a reference by Oakes to "an intra-trinitarian kenosis." He maintains that Barth, Ratzinger, Kasper and von Balthasar all recognised the following point, expressed by Thomas Thompson: "If Jesus of Nazareth is identical in person with the eternally existent Son of God, one hypostasis of three in the Christian conception of God, that is, if God's presence in Christ is a 'substantial presence' of the Logos, then there must be *some* description of his transition in status from an exclusively divine mode of being to a human mode of being" (Thompson, "Nineteenth-Century Kenotic Christology," 108; quoted by Oakes in *Infinity Dwindling to Infancy*, 330). However, one should not assume that Ratzinger's position is identical to von Balthasar's.

23. Galot, *Dieu souffre-t-il?*, 95. The International Theological Commission asserted that God's impassibility is not to be understood as indicating an indifference to human suffering. It sought to reconcile the tension between God's impassibility and compassion by grounding the Incarnation in the prior being of God: "The eternal generation of the Son and his role as the immaculate Lamb who would pour out this precious blood are equally eternal and precede the free creation of the world (cf. 1 Peter 1:19ff; Eph 1:7). In this sense there is a very close correspondence between the gift of divinity that the Father gives to the Son and the gift by which the Father consigns his Son to the abandonment of the Cross. Since, however, the Resurrection is also present in the eternal plan of God, the suffering of 'separation' is always overcome by the joy of union; the compassion of the Trinitarian God for the suffering of the Word is properly understood as the work of most perfect love, which is normally a source of joy" (Sharkey, *International Theological Commission*, 222). Cf. Oakes, *Infinity Dwindling to Infancy*, 424.

24. Galot, *Dieu souffre-t-il?*, 189–90.

25. Ibid., 190.

26. Ibid., 167.

27. Ibid., 147–53 and 172–73. Galot goes on to point out that even in human life, suffering for a great object can bring satisfaction (181).

with a question which does not fit with the approach he has thus far taken, wondering if "the bond between pain and love" might, after all, be located in the inner life of the Trinity.[28] He wonders if this joyful suffering might have its foundation in the reciprocal "ecstatic love" of the Persons. He asks if this innermost self-renunciation be "the primal origin of those renunciations that are bounded up with love for humanity and that, as such, have a painful side."[29]

Von Balthasar questions the validity of Galot's distinction between the Trinity's relation to the world being touched while the divine inner life remains untouched as being at variance with the tradition.[30] Since Ratzinger, although he refers to Galot's book as "important," contents himself with referring his reader to von Balthasar's summary of Galot's position, we can infer that he agrees with von Balthasar's criticism of this position.[31]

Von Balthasar believes that Galot has seized imperfectly upon the essence of what Maritain has attempted to explain. Von Balthasar explains Maritain's insight thus.

> Noting that the pain that comes to us in the world "imparts to us an incomparably fruitful and precious nobility" and that it has its origin, by analogy, in God, as attested by Scripture (*viscera misericordiae*), Galot endeavors to identify this essential attribute in God. We have no name for it: in contrast to our suffering and grief, it implies no imperfection; we can perhaps speak of it as "the triumphant seizing, adopting and overcoming" of pain, even of death. "Sin does something to God that reaches his divine depths, not by causing him to suffer something caused by the creature, but by causing the creature in its relationship with God to migrate to the side of that unnamed divine perfection, that eternal prototype in him, which in us is pain." Maritain regards it as part of the incomprehensible paradox of the divine blessedness that "its flames are simultaneously the eternal glory of triumphant possession . . . and the eternal glory of triumphant acceptance," which latter has been made known to us in the suffering and death of the Crucified . . . So Maritain can say that "God 'suffers' with us; indeed, he suffers far more than we do"; he "suffers with us," has com-passion, as long as there is suffering in the world.[32]

28. Ibid., 174.
29. Ibid., 174–76.
30. Balthasar, *Theo-Drama*, 242.
31. *Behold*, 58–59, no. 11.
32. Balthasar, *Theo-Drama*, 242–43. The interior quotations are from a reprint

Since Ratzinger refers to Maritain's essay approvingly, calling it a "remarkable treatise," quotes Maritain's conclusion that God suffers with us and, indeed, more than we do, and draws our attention to von Balthasar's summary in which von Balthasar agrees with Maritain's argument, one can infer that Ratzinger agrees with both Maritain's position and von Balthasar's understanding of it.[33]

This being so, we should investigate more fully Maritain's position. Gilles Emery gives an admiring but ultimately critical assessment of Maritain's position.[34] According to Emery, Maritain's point of departure is the Thomistic teaching on the divine names. Thomas distinguishes between names attributed to God by metaphor and by analogy. The former imply limitation incompatible with divine perfection whereas the latter do not.[35] For example, when we call God "wise," we signify a perfection that really exists in God. However, the reality signified by this word "wise" surpasses our concept of wisdom. Furthermore, human wisdom is distinct from man's essence, but God's wisdom is not distinct from his essence. Wisdom, as signified in God, is beyond human comprehension.[36]

---

of Maritain's essay in *Approches sans entraves*, 307, 311, 312, and 316. Von Balthasar characterises Maritain as a Thomist who, on this particular point, adopts a position contrary to St. Thomas. However, whilst it is true that Thomas rejects the idea that the passions of the appetite can be found in God, he affirms that love and joy can be properly predicated of God, since they imply no imperfection. See *ST* I, q. 20, a. 1, ad 2: "In the passions of the sensitive appetite there may be distinguished a certain material element—namely, the bodily change—and a certain formal element, which is on the part of the appetite. Thus in anger, as the Philosopher says (De Anima iii, 15, 63, 64), the material element is the kindling of the blood about the heart; but the formal, the appetite for revenge. Again, as regards the formal element of certain passions a certain imperfection is implied, as in desire, which is of the good we have not, and in sorrow, which is about the evil we have. This applies also to anger, which supposes sorrow. Certain other passions, however, as love and joy, imply no imperfection. Since therefore none of these can be attributed to God on their material side, as has been said (ad 1); neither can those that even on their formal side imply imperfection be attributed to Him; except metaphorically, and from likeness of effects, as already shown (3, 2, ad 2; 19, 11). Whereas, those that do not imply imperfection, such as love and joy, can be properly predicated of God, though without attributing passion to Him, as said before (19, 11)." For a fuller treatment of the question, see Aquinas, *Summa contra Gentiles*, I, q. 89 and q. 90. Since Thomas acknowledges that love and joy, which are passions of the sensitive appetite in human beings, can be found in God, the idea of God having a "joyful suffering" would not necessarily contradict Thomas' position.

33. See *Behold*, 58–59, no. 11.

34. See Emery, "The Immutability of the God," 55–59. Emery asserts that notions of kenoticism do not appear in Maritain's writings. This raises the question as to whether or not Oakes is correct in attributing an intra-trinitarian kenosis to Ratzinger.

35. See ibid., 55, for a clear and lucid explanation of this point. Cf. *ST* I, q.13, a.3.

36. *ST* I, q. 13, a.5.

According to Emery, Maritain "pushes this doctrine of St. Thomas higher and to its furthest point when reflecting on mercy."[37] Maritain recognizes that, according to Thomas, whereas the human person who shows mercy to one in distress is affected by the distress of the other, God does not experience mercy as a passion tied to the sensible appetite. Since God is immaterial and immutable he is not afflicted in himself but is merciful in his effects. Thomas distinguishes the passion from its effects.[38] However, for Maritain, this position does not do justice to the Gospel's teaching on mercy. Maritain asks if it is not necessary to attribute mercy to God in just the same way as we attribute love to him. Should we not say that mercy, like love, exists in God not just according to what it does, but according to what it is?[39] Accordingly, Maritain proposes that we acknowledge mercy in God as a perfection of his being. However, we can have no name for, or conception of, this perfection.[40] The suffering intrinsic to the human experience of mercy would be our participation in this unnamable perfection of God. Since this human experience of the suffering of love is not only a privation, but also has a positive and noble element, it is a perfection, which, analogically, has a "mysterious exemplar" in God.[41]

Whilst Emery asserts that Maritain's position displays an exceptional depth, nonetheless, he questions whether or not it is necessary to distinguish this supposed mercy in God from the very charity of God. He states: "When we employ the word 'mercy,' does this not signify precisely *the incomprehensible love of God* in its bountiful activity (in its effects in creatures who suffer evil)?"[42] However, it seems to me that Emery, although he proposes an alternative to Maritain's position, has not thereby refuted it. Since we cannot completely comprehend God's love, might not this divine mercy be an aspect of it?[43]

It seems that something similar to Maritain's position is held by C. S. Lewis. Perhaps, in *The Great Divorce*, he can help us to understand the

---

37. Emery, "The Immutability of the God," 56.
38. *ST* I, q. 21, a.3; and II–II, q. 30, a.2.
39. Maritain, "Quelques réflexions," 16–17.
40. Ibid.
41. Ibid., 17 and 21–22. Essentially, this dispute concerns the *via negationis*—what is, or is not, an imperfection in the creature. If this "noble" suffering is a perfection, then it pertains to the *via eminentiae*.
42. Emery, "The Immutability of the God," 58.
43. Of course, the remaining dilemma is how God can be merciful if there is no one to whom he can show mercy, that is to say, before sin enters the world. This in turn raises the question of the relation between eternity and time. Is there any "before" for God?

nature of this divine compassion and our eternal "migration" to it in an answer he gives to the question of why the damnation of the lost does not dilute the joy of the saved, why the saved are not saddened by the plight of the damned: "The action of Pity will live forever: but the passion of Pity will not. The passion of pity, the pity we merely suffer . . . that will die." But the action "leaps quicker than light from the highest place to the lowest to bring healing and joy, whatever the cost to itself. It changes darkness into light and evil into good."[44] Applied to God, this characterization of pity expresses the paradox of a passion which is not passive, but active. In this sense it is a suffering which is a perfection rather than an imperfection. The mercy of God is neither passionate, nor sub-passionate, but super-passionate.

Ratzinger and John Paul II on the Mercy of God

Ratzinger concludes his comments on the God who is *impassibilis—sed non incompassibilis* by referring us to St. John Paul II's encyclical *Dives in misericordia*, which according to Ratzinger takes up this very point. In particular, he draws our attention to "its highly significant note 52."[45] Since John Paul II does not write with scholastic precision in his letter on the mercy of God, identifying his teaching on the question of a God who cannot suffer, but can be compassionate, is no easy task. There seems to be a certain ambiguity on his part regarding the nature of mercy as a divine attribute and the human experience of that mercy. One the one hand, he outlines a particular relationship between love, justice and mercy which defines mercy as the *revelation* of love which is greater than justice.[46] Believing in the love of the Father revealed in the Son means "*believing in mercy*. For mercy is an indispensable dimension of love; it is as it were love's second name."[47] Herein, John Paul II seems to be saying that we experience God's love as mercy. Furthermore, he states that:

> Some theologians affirm that mercy is the greatest of the attributes and perfections of God, and the Bible, Tradition and the whole faith life of the People of God provide particular proofs of this. It is not a question here of the perfection of the inscrutable essence of God in the mystery of divinity itself, but of the perfection and attribute whereby man, in the intimate truth of

---

44. Lewis, *The Great Divorce*, 111–12.
45. *Behold*, 58–59, no. 11.
46. John Paul II, *Dives in misericordia*, no. 4.
47. Ibid., no. 7.

his existence, encounters the living God particularly closely and particularly often.[48]

Thus far, for John Paul II, it seems that mercy is not a perfection of God in himself, but the way in which human persons experience that love in their fallen condition. However, when we look closely at the note that Ratzinger particularly refers to, we seem to find a different perspective. Note 52 is a long analysis of the Old Testament terminology used to define the mercy of God. In particular, it analyzes the meaning of two terms, *hesed* and *rahamim*. The first of these "indicates a profound attitude of 'goodness.'" It "also means 'grace' or 'love,'" as well as fidelity. It is a "love that gives, love more powerful than betrayal, grace stronger than sin."[49] The second of these is derived from the root *rehem*, meaning "womb." Hence, it denotes the love of a mother. According to John Paul II:

> [This love] is completely gratuitous, not merited, and . . . in this aspect it constitutes an inner necessity: an exigency of the heart . . . Against this psychological background, *rahamim* generates a whole range of feelings, including goodness and tenderness, patience and understanding, that is, readiness to forgive.[50]

One should immediately recognize the similarity of this understanding with Ratzinger's understanding of *rahamim* in his mediations on the Father's heart in *Jesus of Nazareth*.[51]

John Paul II claims that both the terms *hesed* and *rahamim*, as well as some other lesser used terms, present an image of God's "*anxious love, which in contact with evil, and in particular with the sin of the individual and of the people, is manifested as mercy.*"[52] He notes that these terms used to denote the mercy of God "clearly show their *original anthropomorphic aspect* . . . [an] obviously anthropomorphic 'psychology' of God."[53] However, while John Paul II indicates to us that these terms cannot be used univocally of the Creator and creatures, it should be noted that *hesed* is a conceptual term and *rahamim* is derived from a material image. *Hesed* is analogical and *rahamim* is metaphorical. Ratzinger's preference for *rahamim* in describing the mercy of God brings us back to his conviction that "symbolic,"

---

48. Ibid., no. 13.
49. Ibid., no. 4, fn. 52.
50. Ibid.
51. *Jesus I*, 139, 197, and 207.
52. John Paul II, *Dives in misericordia*, no. 4, fn. 52.
53. Ibid.

"metaphorical" language, at least in some instances, can give us a deeper understanding than conceptual language of God's dispositions towards us.

Before concluding this critique of Ratzinger's understanding of the Father's heart, let it be said that John Paul II's discussion of the meaning of the term *hesed* may have some relevance to the question of whether or not Maritain's, and hence Ratzinger's, understanding of the immanent suffering of God is valid. John Paul II states that when *hesed* is established between two individuals, "they do not just wish each other well; they are also faithful to each other by virtue of an interior commitment, and therefore also *by virtue of a faithfulness to themselves*." In the Old Testament, God's fidelity to his unfaithful people is "*on God's part, fidelity to himself* . . . 'It is not for your sake, O house of Israel, that I am about to act, but for the sake of my holy name' (Ezek 36:22) . . . the God of the covenant is really 'responsible for his love.'"[54] In his mediation upon the mercy of the Father as revealed in the parable of the prodigal son, John Paul II reiterates this point. Thus we read:

> The father of the prodigal son *is faithful to his fatherhood, faithful to the love* that he had always lavished on his son . . . The father's fidelity to himself—a trait already known by the Old Testament term *hesed*—is at the same time expressed in a manner particularly charged with affection . . . The father's fidelity to himself is totally concentrated upon the humanity of the lost son, upon his dignity . . . Going on, one can say that the love for the son, the love that springs from the very essence of Fatherhood, in a way obliges the father to be concerned about his son's dignity.[55]

What does it mean for God the Father to be faithful to himself? What does it mean to speak of a love which springs from the very essence of Fatherhood in a way that obliges? Furthermore, what does all this mean for the relationship between the Father and the Only-Begotten Son?

---

54. Ibid.
55. Ibid., no. 6.

13

The Heart of Jesus in Christ and the Church

The Heart of Jesus: Divine Love in a Human Heart?

In an Australian hymn by James Phillip McAuley and Richard Connolly entitled "The Sacred Heart of Jesus," the antiphon says: "Jesus, in your heart we find love of the Father and mankind; these two loves to us impart, divine love in a human heart."[1] The last phrase raises the question—what love *do* we find emanating from the heart of Jesus? If the heart is identical to the person, the ego, then it makes no sense to speak of Jesus as having a human heart, since he is a divine Person. Yet if, as Ratzinger holds, the heart is the place of integration of the intellect, will, passions and senses, of the body and the soul, the place of the personal integration of these elements of human nature, then one can speak of Jesus having a human heart. It will be the integrated humanity of a divine Person.

An attempt has been made to demonstrate that Ratzinger presents us with an anthropology of the human heart and a theology of the Father's heart. To what extent does he bring them together in a Christology of the heart of Jesus? Ratzinger does not directly address the question of the nature of this heart. Rather, he reveals his thoughts on its nature within the context of devotion to it. The first question we need to answer is whether he intends his anthropology of the heart to be applied to the heart of Jesus, or only to the human hearts of those who are devoted to Jesus. For the human heart of Jesus is unique amongst hearts. No other human heart is that of a divine Person. The second question pertains to the relationship between the heart of the Father and the heart of Jesus.

---

1. McAuley and Connolly, "The Sacred Heart of Jesus," no. 142.

In his paper on the substance and foundation of devotion to the Sacred Heart, Ratzinger states that he simply seeks to trace the answers of *Haurietis aquas* to the questions which had been raised regarding the continuing value of the devotion in the wake of Vatican II. He claims that his reflections, in the light of subsequent theological work, seek to clarify and draw out the teaching of the encyclical.[2] Turning to that encyclical, we find that its fundamental dogmatic position is as follows.

> In the first place . . . our worship rests on the acknowledged principle that his Heart, the noblest part of his human nature, is united hypostatically to the Person of the Word of God; and therefore we render to it the same worship of supreme adoration with which the Church honors the Person of the Incarnate Son of God himself.[3]

The heart of Jesus is a divinized human heart. According to Pius XII, the love which comes from the heart of Jesus is not only a spiritual love, as befits the God who is spirit (cf. John 4:24), not only divine charity, but is also the human emotion of love. Pius XII grounds the origin of this emotion in the physical heart of Jesus. For him:

> [The] Heart of Jesus Christ, hypostatically united to the Person of the Divine Word, beat with the pulsations of love and of all the other emotions. At the same time so perfect was the agreement and harmony between these emotions and both his human will, filled as it was with divine charity, and that infinite love itself, which the Father communicates with the Son and with the Holy Spirit, that there was never between these three loves in Jesus Christ any disharmony or disagreement.[4]

Here we see that, for Pius XII, the human love of Christ is to be found in the harmony between his emotions and his human will, that is to say, between the passion of love and the act of love. Furthermore, the human will of Jesus is infused with divine charity. Between this two-fold human love and the love of God there is complete harmony. Pius XII appeals to the writers such as Sts. Justin Martyr, Basil, John Chrysostom, Ambrose, Jerome, Augustine and John Damascene to support the position that Jesus Christ took upon himself a perfect human nature which included human emotions.[5]

---

2. *Behold*, 51.
3. *HA*, 219.
4. Ibid., 227.
5. Ibid., 228–30.

Even though neither Sacred Scripture nor the writings of the Fathers explicitly refer the emotions of Jesus to his physical heart, Pius XII maintains that the emotions and the physical heart are necessarily linked. It is not that the physical heart is the source of the emotions, but that the emotions impinge upon the physical heart. The physical heart responds to the emotions. These emotions are of the soul, and they "quiver" and "throb" with the love of Jesus' human and divine will. For these reasons, Pius XII regards the Sacred Heart of Jesus as "the principle token and sign of that threefold love wherewith the Divine Redeemer ceaselessly loves both his eternal Father and all mankind." The heart of Jesus is the sign of the love which the Word shares with the Father and the Holy Spirit, and also "the sign of that white-hot charity which was infused into Christ's human soul, and which enriches his human will."[6] Pius XII explains the relationship between this charity of Christ and his knowledge by appealing to St. Thomas: "The acts of this charity are illumined and guided by Christ's twofold most perfect knowledge and his bestowed or infused knowledge."[7] The heart of Jesus is also a sign of his emotional affection. Indeed, because his body was formed by the Holy Spirit in the womb of the Virgin Mary, it enjoyed more perfectly this power.[8] Pius XII maintains that Sacred Scripture and "the approved sources of Catholic belief" locate the harmonious threefold love of Jesus Christ in his "all-holy Soul."[9]

According to Pius XII, the heart of Jesus pulsates with a love that is both human and divine. The love which he wills is in perfect accord with "the emotions of his human will and with the Divine Love."[10] Furthermore, his manifold emotions are both "divine as well as human."[11] These statements raise two questions. First, is Pius XII saying that some of the emotions of Jesus were human emotions, and some of them are divine emotions, in which case, what can be meant by divine emotions, or is he trying to say that the emotions of Jesus, being the human emotions of a divine Person, are simultaneously human and divine? Second, what does he mean by attributing emotions to the will, since emotions arise from the senses? Certainly, Pius XII attributes to the heart of Jesus both human and divine love. He states that:

6. Ibid., 231.
7. Ibid. Cf. *ST* III, q. 9, aa. 1–3.
8. Ibid. Cf. *ST* III, q. 33, a. 2, ad 3; and q. 46, a. 6.
9. Ibid., 231–32.
10. Ibid., 233.
11. Ibid.

> When we worship the most Sacred Heart of Jesus Christ, in it and through it we are worshipping both the uncreated love of the Word of God, and at the same time his human love and his other emotions and virtues.[12]

According to Pius XII, the physical heart of Jesus is a natural symbol of the person of the Word because of the hypostatic union. Since both the human and divine natures are united in the person of Christ, he holds the following.

> [Our] minds can conceive how incredibly close is the union between the emotional love of the physical Heart of Christ and this twofold spiritual love, the human and the divine. For not only must we say that these loves co-exist in the adorable Person of the Divine Redeemer, but also that they are united one to another by a natural link, inasmuch as the human and emotional loves are subjected to the divine, and reflect it in an imperfect, or analogical, way. For there is not in the Heart of Jesus, nor do we adore therein, a formal image, that is a perfect, and completely adequate sign of his divine love. Nor do We contend that you should thus conceive of the Sacred Heart. For the essential nature of the divine love cannot possibly be adequately expressed by any created image.[13]

We can see that Pius XII's approach tends to leave the emotions somewhat stranded and not completely integrated within human nature. He speaks of human love as a "spiritual" love, whilst emotional love seems to be only physical, although there also seems to be some element of contradiction in his position, such that the emotions are variously located in the physical heart, in the will and in the soul. Furthermore, his apparent distinction between "human" and "emotional" loves is rather startling. Are not the emotions of a human being human?

Ratzinger sees in *Haurietis aquas* an anthropology and theology of bodily existence. According to him, the body is the self-expression of the spirit, its image. It is the visible form of the person, and since the human person is the image of God, the body is the place where the divine becomes visible. This is why the Bible is able to present the mystery of God in terms of the metaphors of the body. This presentation is a preparation for the Incarnation. In the Incarnation of the Logos, wherein the Word makes the "flesh" its own, we find the fulfillment of a process which has been taking place since creation—the drawing of all "flesh" to Spirit. For Ratzinger:

---

12. Ibid., 240.
13. Ibid., 248.

> [The] Incarnation can only take place because the flesh has always been the Spirit's outward expression and hence a possible dwelling place for the Word; on the other hand it is only the Son's Incarnation that imparts to man and the visible world their ultimate and innermost meaning.[14]

The Incarnation means that God transcends himself and enters into the passion of the human being. This self-transcendence brings to light the inner transcendence of the whole of creation, with "body" being the self-transcending movement towards spirit, and through spirit, towards God. In the human passions of Jesus, "the anthropomorphisms of the Old Testament are radicalized and attain their ultimate depth of meaning."[15] In Jesus, and especially in his pierced heart, the invisible God becomes visible. Doubting Thomas, in touching the Lord, "recognizes what is beyond touch and yet actually does touch it; he beholds the invisible and yet actually sees it."[16] Strikingly, Ratzinger quotes a passage of St. Bonaventure: "The wound of the body also reveals the spiritual wound . . . Let us look through the visible wound to the invisible wound of love!"[17] For Ratzinger, the corporality of Jesus, especially his pierced heart, reveals the love of the Father for us, a love which is an "invisible wound." This brings us back to the question of God's impassibility. For Ratzinger: "The passion of Jesus is the drama of the divine Heart [as portrayed in Hosea 11] . . . The pierced Heart of the crucified Son is the literal fulfillment of the prophecy of the Heart of God."[18]

We have gone some way towards answering our question about the relationship between the heart of Jesus and the Father's heart. But what of the humanity of the heart of Jesus? Ratzinger answers our question by citing *Haurietis aquas* to the effect that the love to be found in the incarnate Word is not only a spiritual love like that which is given expression in the Old Testament, but that the love of the heart of Jesus is also a fully human love, since the Word did not assume an imaginary body.[19] Indeed, the spirituality of the heart which we are invited to enter into is the spirituality of the place where "sense and spirit meet, interpenetrate and unite," and corresponds "to the bodily nature of the divine-human love of Jesus Christ."[20] The heart of Jesus must be a fully human heart, for this heart is not just an expression of

---

14. *Behold*, 52. Cf. *Introduction*, 319–22.
15. Ibid., 57.
16. Ibid., 53.
17. *Behold*, 53. Cf. *HA*, 241.
18. *Behold*, 64.
19. Ibid., 55–56. Citing *Haurietis aquas*, AAS 38 (1956) II, 322–23.
20. Ibid., 56.

the human passions, but also the "passion" of being human. The heart is the epitome of the passions, and without it there could have been no Passion on the part of the Son.

If the heart of Jesus is a truly human heart, wherein lies the difference between his heart and ours? Ratzinger puts it this way—the Stoics saw the heart as the guiding power of the human being, that which "held things together." For Cicero and Seneca, the heart was that which held a being together. The task of this heart is self-preservation, holding together all that belongs to it. But the heart of Jesus has "overturned" this definition (cf. Hos 11:8). It engages in self-surrender rather than self-preservation. This heart saves by opening itself, by giving itself away. Rather than being only the place of integration, it allows itself to "collapse."[21] In *Spe salvi*, Benedict XVI states that we can encounter the God who "in Christ has shown us his face and opened his heart [to us]."[22] It is in this heart that we encounter the heart of the Father. It is this heart which calls to our heart.

We can see that, although Pius XII appeals to Sacred Scripture and the Fathers in order to explain the nature of the heart of Jesus, he looks at this heart through a Thomistic lens. Ironically, although Ratzinger is sometimes accused of being Platonic (where Platonic seems to be equivalent to wrong), it is in fact St. Thomas who, in this instance, is Platonic. As Ratzinger says: "In Platonic anthropology it is possible to distinguish individual potencies of the soul, which are related to one another in a hierarchical order: intellect, will, sensibility."[23] This is the approach taken by Pius XII, who focuses upon two human loves, the emotional and volitional, with divine love making a third love in Jesus. For the Platonists, the intellect is the center of the human being. In contrast, Ratzinger's approach is Stoical. For the Stoics, the heart is the unifying center of the human being. The "primal fire" has its seat in the heart. As Ratzinger explains:

> This single, invigorating energy . . . transforms itself in accord with the various life functions which serve to preserve and benefit the living being and becomes now hearing, now sight, now thought, now imagination. It is always the same and yet operates in different modes, which implies that there is a kind of ladder of inwardness. The primal fire which sustains the cosmos is called logos; thus its spark in us is called "the logos in us."[24]

---

21. Ibid., 69.
22. *SS*, no. 4.
23. *Behold*, 66.
24. Ibid., 66–67.

Ratzinger maintains that it was Origen who took up this insight and gave it a Christian understanding. According to Ratzinger, Origen teaches that:

> It is the Logos which is at the center of us all—without our knowing—for the center of man is the heart, and in the heart this is... the guiding energy of the whole, which is the Logos. It is the Logos which enables us to be logic-al, to correspond to the Logos; he is the image of God after which we were created. Here the word "heart" has expanded beyond the reason and denotes "a deeper level of the spiritual/intellectual existence, where direct contact takes place with the divine." It is here, in the heart, that the birth of the divine Logos in man takes place, that man is united with the personal incarnate Word of God.[25]

If we wish to give a simple account of the essential difference between the approach of Pius XII and that of Ratzinger, it would be difficult to do better than to say that Pius XII's is essentially analytic, whilst Ratzinger's is essentially synthetic. Although one is tempted to call Ratzinger's approach Augustinian, it is in fact biblical, that is to say, it works from the biblical symbol of the heart, a symbol which was adopted independently by the Stoics, and taken up by Origen, Augustine, Pascal, Newman and Guardini.

The Importance of the Eucharist for a Spiritual Christology

We have seen how Ratzinger sees the pierced side of Jesus as the source of both the church and the sacraments. The water and the blood which issue from the self-sacrifice of Jesus symbolize Baptism and the Eucharist, the source of the church. This self-sacrifice of Jesus is essentially prayer. The mystery of Easter, the prayer event of Easter, is the source of the Eucharist. Jesus transforms the sacrificial prayer of Israel. As Ratzinger says: "Jesus Christ now gave this prayer a heart that opens the locked door; this heart is his love, in which God is victorious and conquers death." Our Eucharistic Prayer is the "continuation of this prayer of Jesus at the Last Supper and is thereby the heart of the Eucharist."[26] As a "memorial," the Eucharist makes present the sacrificial prayer of Jesus and enables us to participate in it. In the Eucharist, Jesus has given us a "new heart" whereby we can unite our entire selves with his sacrifice. His sacrifice becomes ours, and "our own life and suffering, our own hoping and loving, can also become fruitful, in the

---

25. Ibid., 67–68. The interior quotation is from Ivánka, *Plato christianus*, 326.
26. Ratzinger, *God is Near Us*, 49. Cf. *DCE*, no. 13; and *SC*, no. 11.

new heart he has given us . . . when the Eucharist is celebrated, the whole mystery of the Church, her living heart, the Lord, is present."[27]

We can see here that Ratzinger has extended his concept of the heart beyond that of the human heart, and even the human heart of Jesus. In the Eucharist, we not only contemplate the pierced heart of Jesus, we enter that heart. We are given a new heart, which, in a mysterious way, is the heart of Jesus himself. Not only that, but the Eucharist becomes the living heart of the church, and this heart is Jesus himself. Furthermore, in the Eucharist we find the church's "heart of hearts" in the Eucharistic Prayer.[28] We can see that, for Ratzinger, the Eucharist is the answer to the question: "How can *we* live as baptized people, to whom Paul's words must apply: 'I live, yet not I, but Christ liveth in me'" (Gal 2:20)?[29] Contemplating the pierced heart of Jesus, not just during the Eucharistic Celebration, but at other times, especially in adoration of the Blessed Sacrament, is our way into participation in the eucharistic mystery of Jesus' self-oblation.

However, this is not the whole answer provided by Ratzinger. In the ecclesiology of Acts 2:42, he sees two pairs of concepts, the linking of the teaching of the Apostles with fellowship with the Apostles, and the linking of the Eucharist with praying. The teaching of and fellowship with the Apostles is continued in the successors of the Apostles. Furthermore, the praying of the church finds its center of gravity in the Eucharist, which is revealed as

---

27. Ibid., 50 and 52.
28. Ibid., 49.
29. *Behold*, 91. Cf. Ratzinger, "The Presence of the Lord in the Sacrament," in *God is Near Us*, 77–78, where, commenting upon St. Paul's account of the Eucharist in the sixth chapter of 1 Corinthians, he says: "To help us understand the Eucharist, [St. Paul] refers us to the words in the creation story: 'The two [= man and wife] shall become one' (Gen 2:24). And he adds: 'He who is united to the Lord becomes one spirit [that is, shares a single new existence in the Holy Spirit] with him' (1 Cor 6:17). When we hear this, we at once have some notion of how the presence of Jesus Christ is to be understood. It is not something at rest but is a power that catches us up and works to draw us within itself. Augustine had a profound grasp of this in his teaching on Communion. In the period before his conversion, when he was struggling with the incarnational aspect of Christian belief, which he found impossible to approach from the point of view of Platonic idealism, he had a sort of vision, in which he heard a voice saying to him: 'I am the bread of the strong, eat me! But you will not transform me and make me part of you; rather, I will transform you and make you part of me' (Augustine, *Confessions*, bk. 7, 10:16). In the normal process of eating, the human is the stronger being. He takes things in, and they are assimilated into him, so that they become part of his own substance. They are transformed within him and go to build up his bodily life. But in the mutual relation with Christ it is the other way around; he is the heart, the truly existent being. When we communicate, this means that we are taken out of ourselves, that we are assimilated into him, that we become one with him and, through him, with the fellowship of our brethren."

the heart of church life. The one concept which unites all of these aspects is *koinonia*. It unites the two realities of Eucharist and community. This unity is achieved in two ways. There is an ecclesial unity brought about by the link between apostolic teaching and the celebration of the Eucharist. This link grounds the worship of the church in a "constantly maintained tradition and its ecclesial form."[30] This being with the Apostles, this continuing in the teaching of the Apostles, is essential for the continuing unity of the church.

The second way is a *koinonia* of charity, especially for the poor. Fellowship in the Body of Christ means fellowship with other believers. This means giving both spiritual and physical life to each other. If Christ is to live in us, it is necessary but insufficient for us to participate in the Eucharist. We cannot just live in a supposed communion with Christ alone. We must also live in true communion with our brothers and sisters *in* Christ. It is in this sense that Ratzinger's spiritual Christology is more than a contemplative Christology, a prayed Christology. It must also be a lived Christology. "It is no longer I who *live*, but Christ who *lives* in me."

However, for Ratzinger, the vertical dimension of *koinonia* is the ultimate foundation for its horizontal dimension. We can only be in communion with the brethren if we are in communion with the death and Resurrection of Jesus, "the incarnate Son, and hence communion with the eternal, triune Love of God."[31] Communion with him is communion with God since, in the person of Jesus Christ, divine and human nature interpenetrate.

As Ratzinger sees it, when we do enter into *koinonia* in the body and blood of Christ in the Eucharist, we become both members of Christ and members of each other. The goal of this eucharistic communion is to "break up" the old "I" and create a new "We." In a sense, we can say that we are "transubstantiated" into this new "we." Consequently, to be in communion with Christ, but not in communion with the brethren, introduces a schism into one's very being.

This brings us ultimately to the question of freedom. In order to love the brethren one needs to enter into the freedom of Jesus. In order to love the brethren, at an existential level, one must enter into the *koinonia* of Jesus' human will with that of his Father. In order to love the brethren one must participate in this *theosis*. Since it is in the Eucharist that Christ's redeeming sacrifice is made present, and in the Eucharist that Christ gives himself to us and builds up his Body, the Eucharist is the place wherein the ultimate communion between God and man, and hence the ultimate communion between the Christian brethren, take place.

30. *Behold*, 77.
31. Ibid., 86.

In keeping with his theology of the heart, this communion of love is not meant to be mere sentiment. It is born of a union of our wills with the will of God. However, it should also awaken within us "a feeling of deep joy born of the experience of being loved" by God. This encounter is meant to engage the whole person, will, intellect and emotions. "[The] 'yes' of our will to his will unites our intellect, will and sentiments in the all-embracing act of love ... [This] communion of will increases in a communion of thought and sentiment, and thus our will and God's will increasingly coincide."[32] This transformation through love also affects our relationships with others. Thus: "I can love even the person whom I do not like or even know. One begins to see with the eyes of Christ. His friend is my friend."[33]

Having addressed Ratzinger's theology of the eucharistic heart of the church, we can ask two decisive questions. The first is—can the church have a heart? In a passage already referred to, Ratzinger identifies the church as a "new subject" which is by nature greater than any individual person.[34] In commenting on this particular passage, Francis Martin says:

> "Subject" as the term is being used here may be defined as "the locus of agential receptivity and active engagement." Employed this way the primary reference must be to a person, predicated analogously of divine and human persons. There is also the use of the term to apply to collective entities as "subjects," the state, a family, a race, and so forth, which can be loci of receptivity and engagement but whose unity is found in a bond that is external to the persons who make it up. There is, however, a third way of being a subject, and this is the way of the Church, the Body of Christ that is neither a person, defined as "the incommunicably proper existence of spiritual nature," nor a collectivity. In Thomas Aquinas's opinion, the Church, which is the Mystical Body of Christ, may be considered as a "quasi-person" united to Christ, its Head. It is this mystical person that is the subject of Revelation and its interpreter.[35]

If the church is a "quasi-person," united to Christ, then analogously we can speak of it as having a heart. Yet, can the Eucharist be the heart of the church? Whereas on the former point we find congruence between the thought of

32. *DCE*, no. 17.
33. Ibid., no. 18.
34. Ratzinger, *The Nature and Mission of Theology*, 61.
35. Martin, "Joseph Ratzinger," 286–87. The interior quotation is from Richard of St. Victor, cited by Ratzinger in, "Concerning the Notion of Person in Theology," 449. Aquinas' opinion on the church as a quasi-person can be found in *ST* III, q. 49, c.; and III, q. 48, a. 2, ad 1.

St. Thomas and that of Ratzinger, with regard to this second question there appears to be incongruence. In response to the question of whether Christ is the head of the church, Thomas says that although Christ is the head, the Holy Spirit is the heart.[36] On the contrary, Ratzinger's thought seems to be more in keeping with that of St. Bonaventure. According to Yves Congar, St. Albert the Great, St. Thomas and St. Bonaventure all "referred to the *De motu cordis* of Aristotle, for whom the heart was the principle of life, on the basis of which a man was constructed and lived."[37] As Congar comments:

> Bonaventure arrived at the idea that Christ was the heart of the Church and so expressed his own fervent Christocentrism. Christ is for him the *medius*, the middle, and the sovereign *hierarcha* of the world, giving the Holy Spirit and all the *charismata*. Thomas Aquinas, on the other hand, relying on Aristotle and his Arabic commentators, makes the Holy Spirit the heart of the Church.[38]

It should be said that Benedict XVI is aware of the importance of the Holy Spirit for bringing about the transformation of the heart of the believer and the heart of the church. In words already quoted, he says:

> By dying on the Cross—as Saint John tells us—Jesus "gave up his Spirit" (John 19:30), anticipating the gift of the Holy Spirit that he would make after his Resurrection (cf. John 20:22). This was to fulfill the promise of "rivers of living water" that would flow out of the hearts of believers, through the outpouring of the Spirit (cf. John 7:38–39). The Spirit, in fact, is the interior power which harmonizes their hearts with Christ's heart and moves them to love their brethren as Christ loved them. The Spirit is also the energy which transforms the heart of the ecclesial

---

36. *ST* III, q. 8, a. 1, ad 3., where St. Thomas says: "The head has a manifest preeminence over the other exterior members; but the heart has a certain hidden influence. And hence the Holy Ghost is likened to the heart, since He invisibly quickens and unifies the Church; but Christ is likened to the Head in His visible nature in which man is set over man." See also *De Veritate* q. 29, a. 4, ad 7., where Thomas says: "By the heart, accordingly, the divinity of Christ or the Holy Spirit can be meant; but by the head, Christ Himself in His visible nature, which is under the influence of the nature of the invisible divinity."

37. Congar, *The Word and the Spirit*, 61.

38. Ibid. For Bonaventure's position, Congar refers to Bonaventure's *Collationes in Hexaemeron*. Immediately, one's thoughts fly to Ratzinger's *habilitation* thesis on this very work. However, although Ratzinger shows that he is aware of Bonaventure's characterization of Christ as the center of all things, including time and history, he makes no mention of Bonaventure identifying Christ as the heart of the Church. See Ratzinger, *The Theology of History in St. Bonaventure*, 110, 118 and 146.

community, so that it becomes a witness before the world to the love of the Father, who wishes to make humanity a single family in his Son.[39]

Can we bring together the thought of St. Thomas Aquinas and Joseph Ratzinger by saying that if the Eucharist is the heart of the quasi-person which is the mystical Body of Christ united to its head, then, just as the heart of Jesus is the source of the Holy Spirit for believers, so too that heart, present in the Eucharist, remains the source of the Holy Spirit for those who participate in it?

---

39. *DCE*, no. 19. Cf. *SC*, no. 8, where Benedict XVI writes: "Jesus Christ, who 'through the eternal Spirit offered himself without blemish to God' (Heb 9:14), makes us, in the gift of the Eucharist, sharers in God's own life."

Development

14

An Unfinished Symphony—Completing Ratzinger's Spiritual Christology

The Integration of Ratzinger's Spiritual Christology

In an interview with Peter Seewald, Ratzinger recounts that, before his call to be archbishop of Munich and Freising: "I felt that . . . at this period of my life . . . I had found my own theological vision and could now create an *oeuvre* with which I would contribute something to the whole of theology."[1] As we know, the subsequent course of his life meant that this hope has been only partially fulfilled. His spiritual Christology could be taken as a specific example of this unfinished work.

Hahn has characterized this work as symphonic rather than systematic. Ratzinger's style is more Patristic than Thomistic. As Hahn says: "In the Fathers we find the notion that truth consists of a unity of diverse elements, much as a symphony brings into a single, harmonious whole the music played on a variety of instruments."[2] Pursuing this metaphor, one could characterize Ratzinger's spiritual Christology as an unfinished symphony, though not in a Schubertian sense. Rather than missing whole movements, it could be said that the scoring is incomplete. Some sections are more thoroughly scored than others. The "christological theses section" is more or less finished. The "theology of the heart section" is substantially complete. But the "pneumatological section" and the "eucharistic section" are more lightly scored.

---

1. Ratzinger, *Salt of the Earth*, 81.
2. Hahn, *Covenant and Communion*, 16.

To vary the metaphor, Ratzinger's spiritual Christology could be likened to a tapestry rather than a treatise. Herein, an attempt has been made to analyze a synthesis, to identify the particular strands with which he has woven his Christology. The danger is that in unraveling the tapestry one loses sight of the overall scene. In this final chapter an attempt will be made to show how the various strands are woven together to form a scene, the extent to which this scene is incomplete, and offer some suggestions as to how the tapestry might be completed.

That the picture is incomplete is admitted by Ratzinger himself. In the Preface to *Behold the Pierced One* he states that he did not have time to make a study of the theme of a spiritual Christology suggested to him by his reflections on the Sacred Heart and found by him in the texts of Constantinople III. He claims that, in lieu of a systematic study of this theme, this spiritual Christology found its way into other works, which he then collected in *Behold the Pierced One*. It is here maintained that, since then, this spiritual Christology has found its way into more works, most notably *Jesus of Nazareth*, but also his letters on Christian love and the Eucharist.

An attempt has already been made to assess the internal integration of each of the three specific elements of Ratzinger's spiritual Christology. In order to complete the analysis we need to assess the integration of the three elements with each other. This assessment can be made by examining how well Ratzinger applies his "integrating principles." Earlier, it was said that prayer is *an* integrating principle of Ratzinger's spiritual Christology, not *the* integrating principle. There is another—the heart. Calling these Ratzinger's integrating principles should not be taken to mean that he explicitly identifies them as such, only that he employs them as such. Be that as it may, it is proposed that a third integrating principle is required, that of the Holy Spirit acting in the heart of Jesus and our hearts, and in the prayer of Jesus and our prayer. We must become Christologians in this sense also. A practical Christology requires a practical pneumatology.

We have seen that prayer is the integrating principle in six out of the seven christological theses—the prayer of Jesus in the filial, soteriological and volitional theses, and our participation in that prayer in the personal, ecclesial and hermeneutical theses. If we see the volitional thesis as the culmination of the dogmatic thesis, we can say that prayer is the integrating principle of all seven theses.

Also, we have seen that, concerning the integration of the heart with these theses, we find Ratzinger's anthropology of the heart especially associated with his personal thesis. In particular, let us recall Ratzinger's advocacy of a theology of the heart in the sense of a contemplative theology. Furthermore, we find his theology of the Father's heart associated with his filial thesis, and his Christology of the heart of Jesus with his soteriological thesis. When we come to the ecclesial thesis, although we do not find an ecclesiology of the heart in *Jesus of Nazareth*, the beginnings of such an ecclesiology can be found in works such as *God is Near Us*, *Deus caritas est*, and *Sacramentum caritatis*.

When we come to the remaining three theses—the hermeneutical, dogmatic and volitional—we do not find "heart" being used as an integrating principle. Hence, there is room for the development of a "hermeneutic of the heart," and for work on how the whole humanity of Jesus, not just his human will, but also his intellect, passions and body, are in harmony with the whole of the divine nature, not just the divine will. Perhaps we need a "Maximus of the Heart." Guardini, in particular, has provided a solid foundation for such a person.

Besides developing Ratzinger's theology of the heart as an integrating principle in his spiritual Christology, there are other ways in which it could be fleshed out further. One springs to mind immediately. Although the basis of this theology is biblical, we should recall that Ratzinger's scriptural sources for it are principally to be found in the Old Testament and the Gospel of John. Can an examination of the rest of the New Testament contribute to a more solid biblical foundation?

Since the heart is presented by Ratzinger, at least in its anthropological manifestation, as the integration of the person—and Jesus, the Father, and the church are presented by Ratzinger as "persons" each having a heart— it will be necessary also to investigate Ratzinger's understanding of "person."

Having more than one integrating principle means that they, in turn, need to be brought into harmony—the harmony of the prayer of the pure of heart. Furthermore, if a spiritual Christology requires a third integrating principle, the Holy Spirit, then we need to address the relationship between the Holy Spirit and the seven christological theses, as well as that between the Holy Spirit and the heart. These are immense tasks, and here only an incomplete outline can be given of what needs to be done.

The Heart and the Person

In Ratzinger's spiritual Christology we are presented with four hearts. One is that of Hosea 11—the heart of God—which in John 1 is referred to as the heart of the Father. Another is the human heart. A third is the heart of Jesus, and the last is the heart of the church. Ratzinger identifies the heart, at least in the anthropological sense, as the integration of the person. Used in these senses, the term "heart" is a metaphor, an image, whether it is used of human persons, God, Jesus Christ, or the church. Yet the term "person" is used, in the first instance, of God, only analogically of human persons, and in an even more derivative way of the church. Furthermore, Jesus is a divine person with a human heart, and the church is a quasi-person with a heart. All of this raises a number of questions. If the heart is the integration of the human person, what does it mean when used of a divine person, or an incarnate divine person, or a quasi-person? How can the term "heart" be used of God when God is three divine persons? How does the term "heart" affect our understanding of the nature of, and relationship between, five persons—the Father, Son and Holy Spirit, the human person, and the ecclesial quasi-person, as well as the relation between the human persons who make up the Body of Christ? In order to attempt answers to these questions we must investigate Ratzinger's understanding of "person." In doing so, we shall find that his concept of person has theological (in the sense of pertaining to God *per se*), christological, anthropological, trinitarian and ecclesiological implications.

Person as Relation

What, then, is Ratzinger's understanding of person? Fortunately, in a 1966 essay entitled *Zum Personverständnis in der Dogmatik* (On the Understanding of Person in Dogmatics), he gives us a clear and concise outline of his thought on this question. To begin with, Ratzinger holds that the Christian concept of person requires some development. In his estimation, patristic theologians were more successful in explaining what person is not, rather than what person is.[3]

After investigating how the use of the term *prosopon/persona* originated and developed in the early church, Ratzinger reaches the conclusion that it was developed in order to express "the idea of dialogue and of God as a dialogical Being."[4] In the doctrine that God is one being in three persons, the term person is to be understood as "relation." According to Augustine and late patristic theology, the three persons in God are, by their very nature, relations. Relatedness is not something added onto the person, but *is* the person. The person exists only as relation. The persons in God are nothing other than the act of relating to each other. Ratzinger concretely explains this as follows.

3. Ratzinger, "On the Understanding of 'Person' in Theology," 193. For Ratzinger, it was Maximus the Confessor who went the farthest in developing the patristic Christological concept of person.

4. Ibid., 185. Cf. *Introduction*, 182.

> [The] first Person begets, not as though the act of begetting a Son was something added on to the complete Person, but rather he *is* the act of begetting, of surrendering himself, or pouring himself out. The Person is identical with this act of self-giving. Therefore, one could define the first Person as self-giving in fruitful knowledge and love—not the self-giving one in whom there is an act of self-giving, but rather self-giving itself, pure act.[5]

With this concept of relation a new category is added to the two great categorical forms of antiquity, substance and accident. This new category is that of pure actuality, pure relativity, not lying on the level of substance, nor affecting or dividing substance as such.[6]

Ratzinger holds that the nature of person as pure relativity is expounded in Sacred Scripture, especially in Johannine theology. Thus, when Jesus says, "The Son can do nothing of his own accord" (John 5:19), and, "I and the Father are one" (John 10:30), this means the following.

> [They] are one precisely because he [the Son] has nothing of his own, because he does not set himself up alongside the Father as a separate substance but, rather, is oriented toward him in total relativity and represents nothing but relativity toward him, a relatedness that singles out and reserves for itself nothing of its own.[7]

Following from this:

> [The anthropological implications of this nature of person are that, in being a disciple of Jesus] man does not reserve what is merely his own, does not strive to develop the substance of his self-enclosed ego, but rather enters into pure relativity directed toward the other and toward God and precisely in this way truly comes to himself and comes into the fullness of what is his own, because he enters into union with that to which he is related.[8]

The decisive meaning of person is revealed in Sacred Scripture not as self-enclosed substance, but as total relatedness. Although the fullness of relatedness can only be entered into in God, Ratzinger sees divine personhood

---

5. Ibid., 186. Cf. *Introduction*, 183.
6. Ibid., 187. Cf. *Introduction*, 182–84.
7. Ibid. Cf. *Introduction*, 185–90.
8. Ibid.

as a signpost pointing the way for all personal being, both christological and anthropological.[9]

The Christological, Anthropological, Trinitarian and Ecclesiological Understanding of Person

When we come to the christological concept of person, Ratzinger addresses this issue by way of the difficulties experienced in answering the question: Who and what is this Christ? The answer of the patristic church he presents thus: He has two natures and one person, a divine and human nature, but only a divine person.[10] In describing the recurring misunderstandings of this formula, Ratzinger identifies the root problem being that the one divine personhood of Christ led to the conclusion that Jesus was not fully human, that there must have been a deficit, something lacking in his human nature. Arianism and Apollinarism denied that he had a human soul, Monophysitism that he had a human nature, Monotheletism that he had a human will, and Monenergism that he had the exercise of that will. Ratzinger identifies the source of these errors in the notion that since personhood "is the highest, most characteristic summit of humanity, [and] it is lacking in Jesus; therefore humanity is not present in him in its entirety."[11]

At this point, one must ask if Ratzinger's diagnosis is entirely correct. Given that, by his own account, the original Christian concept of person was used to explain how one God could be Father, Son and Holy Spirit, in patristic times *was* personhood regarded as the highest, most characteristic summit of humanity? Certainly, the antagonists in these debates would have thought of human beings as being bodily, passionate, intellectual, and volitional, but did they have a concept of human personhood?

Ratzinger goes on to recount the vicissitudes faced by the christological concept of person in achieving the integration of its philosophical and theological aspects. Here, the unintentional villain of the piece is Boethius, with his concept of the person as *naturae rationalis individua substantia* (the individual substance of a rational nature). Ratzinger sees this restriction of the concept of person to the level of substance rendering it useless for explaining anything about the Trinity or Christ. He attributes the beginnings of an existential understanding of person to Richard of St. Victor, with his definition of person as *spiritualis naturae incommunicabilis existentia* (a distinct and incommunicable existence of a spiritual nature). Unfortunately,

---

9. Ibid., 187–88.
10. Ibid., 189–90.
11. Ibid., 190.

claims Ratzinger, the category of existence developed by Scholastic theology was restricted to Christology and the doctrine of the Trinity. Thus, for Ratzinger, the Christology and Trinitarian theology of Aquinas rises to the existential level, whilst his philosophy of the human person remains at the pre-Christian level of essence. Since the Christian concept of person was not extended to the totality of human thought, the union of the divine and human in Christ remains an absolutely unique ontological exception.[12]

For Ratzinger, however, this is not the scriptural picture of Christ. The Christ presented there is certainly unique, but not a speculative exception. Rather, "in him is manifested for the first time what is meant by the riddle named 'man.'"[13] The Christ presented therein is the last Adam, the "second man." He is characterized as the genuine fulfillment of the idea "man." This means that the christological concept of person is the full anthropological concept. Yet, as Ratzinger sees it, the theology of the person has still to come to complete maturity.[14]

Very briefly, Ratzinger puts down some thoughts as to how this theology could be developed. He makes three points. The first is on the nature of "spirit" and the anthropological implications of that nature. He asserts that the essence of spirit is being-in-relation. Spirit has a double existence in that it "not only *is* but also *understands* itself and *possesses* itself."[15] Whereas matter is "thrown upon itself," spirit "designs itself." Openness, relatedness to the whole, is an essential element of spirit. In order to possess itself it must go beyond itself. It only becomes itself by being with the other. "Being with the other is its form of being with itself."[16] Furthermore, spirit is that which is not only able to think about itself and existence in general, but is also able to think about the wholly other—God. Anthropologically this means that if the human person is more with himself the more he reaches beyond himself to be with the other, to be most fully with oneself requires that one is with the wholly Other—God. Relatedness to the other constitutes the human person. Relatedness to the wholly Other constitutes the fullness of the human person.[17]

The second point develops the anthropological implications of the reality of Christ. Here the fact that the person of the Logos has two natures, the human and the divine, "means that being-with-the-other is radically

12. Ibid., 190–91.
13. Ibid., 192.
14. Ibid., 192–93.
15. Ibid., 193.
16. Ibid.
17. Ibid., 193–94.

present in him." At every moment relatedness towards the wholly Other is "the foundation of his consciousness and the basis of his existence." Yet this "being-totally-with-the-other . . . does not abolish his being-with-himself but . . . brings it to fulfillment."[18]

Ratzinger admits that the terminology *una persona-duae naturae* remains contingent, and that it is not without its problems.

> [Yet] the decisive result for the concept of person and for our understanding of man is . . . completely clear . . . In Christ, the man who is entirely with God, humanity is not abolished but, rather, arrives at its highest potential, which consists of self-surpassing that leads into the absolute and of having one's own relatedness caught up into the absolute character of divine love.[19]

As a part of this second point, Ratzinger reconciles history and ontology in Christ. Since, in Christ, mankind has arrived at its highest potential, the definition of man must be dynamic, at least temporally. As Ratzinger so strikingly puts it:

> Christ is like a signpost indicating where humanity is tending (since as long as history is under way humanity never completely catches up with itself). At the same time, it becomes evident that such a definition of humanity shows man and the person in their historicity. If person is relatedness toward the eternal, then the being-on-the-way of human history is implied at the same time along with the relatedness.[20]

Here we have, in both Christ and the human person, the reconciliation of ontology with history.

The third point develops the trinitarian and ecclesial/anthropological implications of this second point. Christology "adds to the idea of I and Thou the idea of We." Christ, the last Adam, the ultimate man, "appears in the testimonies of the faith as the comprehensive space in which the We of men is gathered in to the Father . . . in which the We of mankind is gathered into the Thou of God."[21] For Ratzinger, this point has not been sufficiently examined in modern philosophy, even Christian philosophy. Ratzinger goes beyond Buber's insight in asserting that:

> [In] Christianity there is not simply a dialogical principle in the modern sense of a purely I-Thou relationship—neither from the

---

18. Ibid., 194.
19. Ibid.
20. Ibid., 194–95.
21. Ibid., 195.

perspective of man, who is stationed in the historical continuity of the People of God, in the comprehensive historical We that supports him; nor from the perspective of God, who for his part is not a simple I but once again the We of Father, Son, and Spirit.[22]

For both God and man, there is no pure I or Thou; rather, the I is nestled in the larger We. That God is not simply an I is fundamental for the Christian theological concept of person. This concept denies the way in which ancient philosophy defined God in terms of unity, but has given to multiplicity, which the ancient world saw as a disintegration of unity, an equality with unity.[23] In the Trinitarian We: "the space of the human We is already and simultaneously prepared."[24] The Christian's relation with God is not simply I and Thou, but through Christ in the Holy Spirit to the Father. The Spirit who is Love gathers us into the We of the one Christ. In Christ, we are united "at the same time with one another and to the common Thou of the one Father."[25]

Ratzinger sees the theological understanding of the We-reality of God as being of great importance for Christian piety. For the exclusion of this We-reality from that piety in the Western Church he holds both Augustine and Thomas Aquinas responsible, although in apportioning blame he has, since penning *Zum Personverständnis in der Dogmatik*, shifted the bulk of the responsibility to St. Thomas. In Ratzinger's eyes, Augustine was correct in basing his anthropology on his theology of the Trinity, but took a "fateful shortcut."

> [Augustine reads] the Divine Persons into man's interior as corresponding to faculties within the soul [thus setting up] a correspondence between man as a whole and the Divine Substance, so that the trinitarian concept of person is not applied immediately and with its full import to the human condition.[26]

In explaining the mitigation of his sentence against Augustine, Ratzinger says that he came to see Augustine's psychological analogy of the Trinity as being "kept in balance by factors in the tradition." He came to regard as more radical Aquinas' separation of "the philosophical doctrine of the one

22. Ibid.
23. Ibid. Cf. *Introduction*, 178–79.
24. Ibid.
25. Ibid., 196.
26. Ibid., 189. By specifically identifying the exclusion of the We-reality of God from the piety of the Western Church, is Ratzinger implying that he does not think it to be excluded from that of the Eastern Church?

God and the theological doctrine of the Trinity" which, in Ratzinger's view "led Thomas to regard as legitimate the formula 'God is *una persona*,' which in the early Church was considered heretical."[27]

Relation for Integration and Integration for Relation

What follows is a brief and admittedly incomplete attempt to draw out some implications of Ratzinger's understanding of "heart" and "person." The divine persons do not need to be integrated within themselves. They are each pure relation. So to what does the heart of God refer? It cannot be just the heart of the Father. Although John 1:18 speaks of the Son being close to the Father's heart, it cannot mean that the Father has a heart, but the Son does not. Or that the Father has a heart, and, but implication, so has the Son. There is no instance in Sacred Scripture of the Word *asarkos* being spoken of as having a heart, nor is the Holy Spirit spoken of as having a heart. Therefore, the Father's heart must be the heart of God *per se*. The only two alternatives would be that the Father possesses something which the Son does not, or a tri-theism which attributes a heart to each of the divine persons.

What is meant be the heart of God, the heart of the Father? Should it be equated with the will of God, or the love of God? If we equate it with the will of God, then, it would only express something of God's relationship with creatures. Yet we are told that it expresses something in the relation between the Father and the divine Son, who then in his Incarnation makes the Father known (cf. John 1:18). Therefore, we must equate the heart of God with the love of God, the mutual self-gift of the Father and the Son in the Holy Spirit. In its relation with a fallen creation, this heart is experienced as the mercy of God.

According to Ratzinger, divine personhood points the way for all personal being, both christological and anthropological. When we come to the heart of Jesus Christ, we come to the human heart of a divine person. The human heart of Christ is the integration of his humanity—of body, intellect, will and emotions. Is it also the integration of his humanity with the divinity of his Person? Since the human heart of Christ reveals the divine heart of God, it must conform to the divine heart. While Maximus and Constantinople III focused on the union of humanity and divinity in Christ as the conforming of his human will, as the highest expression of his humanity, to the divine will, such a focus can allow a subtle angelism to creep in if it is not balanced with an integral view of the union of humanity and divinity

---

27. Ratzinger, "On the Understanding of 'Person' in Theology," 196, no. 12. Cf. *ST* III, q. 3, a. 3, ad. 1.

in Christ. The whole of Christ's integrated humanity, his heart, conforms to the divine heart. Though Christ learned to obey through suffering, this was a bodily and psychic suffering which he experienced—a suffering feared, understood, accepted and endured. It is the further investigation of this conformity that is the province of a hoped for Maximus of the Heart.

Although divine personhood points the way to both christological and anthropological personhood, of the two, the christological concept of person is the full anthropological concept. Because Christ is a divine person with both a human and divine nature, being-with-the-other is radically present in him, in his human as well as his divine nature. In Christ, self-surpassing humanity has come into existence.

Moving on to the human person, this person is a person only by analogy. The human person is not pure relation, but is able to enter into relation. Because the human person is not pure relation, that person requires integration. That which can refuse relation must be oriented to relation. Furthermore, if the archetype of the human person is Christ, a divine person with a human nature, then the goal for this human person must be an ever deeper entry into pure relativity with God and with others. It is in this way that the human person will become truly himself. Human integration, the heart, can only become a truly human heart within the relation of the incarnate only begotten Son with the Father. This integration for relation must take place through communion with and transformation by the "kenotic" heart of Christ, a heart that is integrated for relation.

This transformation of human persons by the divinized humanity of Christ takes place within the We of the Father, Son and Holy Spirit. It takes place within Christ, wherein the We of human persons is gathered to the Father through the Holy Spirit. It takes place within the quasi-person of the church. It combines the integration of human persons within themselves, and with God and other human persons. It is the integration of the human "Body of Christ" in itself and with the divine Head, so that the Head becomes corporately human as well as being divine, and the Body becomes divine as well as corporately human. This integration takes place most profoundly in the Eucharist.

For Christ, the human person, and the church, integration cannot be treated separately from relation. Integration takes place within relation, and integration enables relation. Yet relation comes first. Human integration is not self-generated. It can only take place within relation, with God and other human persons in the Body of Christ.

As has been said, for God *per se*, the divine persons, being pure relations, do not require integration. Nor does the one God require integration. Yet something akin to integration takes place within God, the begetting of the Son by the Father, and the giving of the Son to the Father in the Holy Spirit. Following this pattern, we need to account for the role of the Holy Spirit in the integration within relation of the incarnate Son and the Father, as well as the Spirit's role within the integration of human persons, within themselves and with each other, which takes place within the integration within relation of the incarnate Son and the Father—that is to say, within the reality which we call the church.

A Meditation on Three Hearts in the New Testament

The Meaning of "Heart" in the New Testament

In the previous chapter it was noted that two questions need to be answered about Ratzinger's theology of the heart. The first was whether he intends his anthropology of the heart to be applied to the heart of Jesus, or only to the human hearts of those who are devoted to Jesus. The second was about the nature of the relationship between the heart of the Father and the heart of Jesus. It was also noted that Ratzinger had made some progress in answering these two questions. First, through his portrayal of the heart of the Father as one which is full of *rahamim* (mercy).[28] Second, by identifying the pierced heart of Jesus, as portrayed in the Gospel of John, as the fulfillment of the Hosea's prophecy of the heart of God.[29] Third, by indicating that this pierced heart is the source of the Holy Spirit, who harmonizes the hearts of believers with the heart of Jesus.[30] Yet, in his mediations upon the hearts of God, Jesus, and the believer, Ratzinger does not draw much upon the synoptic Gospels, nor upon the rest of the New Testament. In the hope of expanding his insights into these hearts, there follows a brief mediation on the meaning of the heart in the New Testament, in order to further the identification of our own hearts with the hearts of Jesus and his *Abba*.

In the New Testament the term *kardia* is used over 150 times. In all bar one of these instances it is used to refer to the human heart exclusively. The one exception is Jesus' self-reference to his own heart as meek and humble (cf. Matt 11:29). It is never used with reference to God the Father. It is used to refer to the dwelling place of human desires and passions, thinking and willing, and the center of the human person to which God turns, where the religious life is rooted, and wherein moral conduct is determined.[31] On

---

28. *Jesus I*, 139, 197, and 207.
29. *Behold*, 64.
30. See *DCE*, no. 19; and *SC*, no. 8.
31. Baumgärtel and Behm, "καρδια," 611–12.

occasion it is used in contradistinction to the mind (2 Cor 3:14-15; Phil 4:7; Heb 8:10 and 10:16; Rev 2:23), to the soul (cf. 1 Pet 1:22), to the soul and mind (cf. Matt 22:37) and to the conscience (1 Tim 1:5). Very occasionally, it is used to indicate the self (Col 2:2: "that their hearts [they themselves] may be encouraged"; Jas 5:5: "fattened your hearts [yourselves]"; 1 John 3:19: "reassure our hearts [ourselves]; and most famously in 1 Pet 3:4: "the hidden person of the heart"). However, it is more often used in the following senses. As the affective center of the human person it is the locus of joy (cf. John 16:22; Acts 2:26 and 14:17), sadness (cf. John 14:1; 14:27 and 16:6; Acts 21:13; Rom 9:2; 2 Cor 2:4), fear (cf. John 14:27), anger (cf. Acts 7:54), desire (cf. Matt 6:21; Rom 10:1), lust (cf. Matt 5:28; Rom 1:24), avarice (cf. 2 Pet 2:14) and hatred (cf. Jas 3:14). As the intellectual center of the human person it is the locus of thought (cf. Matt 9:4 and 24:48; Mark 7:21 and 11:23; Luke 2:35 and 9:47; Rom 10:6; Rev 18:7), understanding (cf. Matt 13:15 and 24:48; John 12:40; Acts 28:27; Rom 1:21; 1 Cor 2:9; Heb 4:12), doubt and questioning (cf. Mark 11:23; Luke 24:38; Rom 10:6), deception (cf. Jas 1:26) and belief (cf. Luke 24:25; Heb 3:12). As the volitional center of the human person it is the locus of intention (cf. Acts 8:22; 1 Cor 4:5), and decision (cf. Luke 6:45 and 21:14; Acts 5:3-4; 7:39 and 11:23; 1 Cor 7:37 and 14:25; 2 Cor 9:7). The heart is also the locus of imagination (cf. Luke 1:51), and memory (cf. Luke 1:66; 2:19 and 2:51). As the moral center of the human person it is the locus of virtue, including theological virtue (cf. Luke 8:15; Acts 2:46 and 15:9; Rom 6:17 and 10:9; 2 Thess 3:5). It is the locus of conscience (cf. 1 John 3:20). It is the locus of that holiness which is normally called singleness or purity of heart (cf. Matt 5:8; Acts 15:9; Eph 6:5; Col 3:22; 1 Thess 3:13; 2 Tim 2:22; Heb 10:22).

The heart is also the locus of relation with God. It is the place which God searches and knows (cf. Luke 16:15; Rom 8:27; 1 Thess 2:4). It is the place of revelation (Luke 24:32; Acts 2:37; Rom 2:15; 2 Cor 3:3 and 4:6; Eph 1:18), as well as that refusal of revelation which is often called "hardness of heart" (cf. Mark 3:5; 6:52 and 8:17; Matt 13:19; John 12:40; Acts 8:21; Rom 2:5; Eph 4:18). It is the locus of God's indwelling, in Christ (cf. Gal 4:6; Eph 3:17; 2 Pet 1:19), and in the Holy Spirit (cf. Rom 5:5; 2 Cor 1:22). The heart is also the locus of relation with other human persons (cf. Matt 18:35; Acts 16:14; 2 Cor 7:2), captured most movingly in St. Paul's plea to the brethren in Corinth: "Our mouth is open to you, Corinthians; our heart is wide. You are not restricted by us, but you are restricted in your own affections. In return—I speak to you as children—widen your hearts also" (2 Cor 6:11-13). In a way which is analogous to the indwelling of God in the human heart, St. Paul even identifies it as the place wherein other human persons dwell: "I have said before that you are in our hearts, to die together and to live together" (2 Cor 7:3; cf. Phil 1:7).

We know from experience that the human activities of feeling, thinking, deciding, imagining, and remembering never happen in isolation from each other. For example, when Jesus says in Matthew 15:19: "For out of the heart come evil thoughts, murder, adultery, fornication, theft, false witness, slander," we know that such thoughts must be accompanied by various passions, chosen by the will, visualized in the imagination, and perhaps recalled in the memory. This use is in contrast to its occasional use in contradistinction to the external aspect of the human person (cf. Acts 7:51; Rom 2:28–29), either their physical presence (cf. 1 Thess 2:17), how they are perceived by others (cf. 2 Cor 5:12), or how they represent themselves to others (cf. Mark 7:6). Ultimately, as we have seen, the heart is the place of relation to God and other human persons, an activity which also involves the passions, knowledge, will, imagination and memory.

The above meditation is helpful with regard to the human heart, but what of the heart of Jesus (one reference), the heart of God (no reference), and the relationship between these three hearts? Both Joachim Becker and Hugo Rahner have drawn our attention to the use of *splagchna* (bowels) as a biblical synonym for heart. To this avenue of investigation we now turn.

Splagchna as a Synonym for *Kardia*

Jesus Christ is the servant-king, the king with the heart of a shepherd. In the synoptic Gospels there are a number of accounts of the compassion shown by this king. In Matthew's Gospel we are told that it was the compassion of Jesus which led him to express his desire for workers who can participate in his mission.

> And Jesus went about all the cities and villages, teaching in their synagogues and preaching the gospel of the kingdom, and healing every disease and every infirmity. When he saw the crowds, he had compassion for them, because they were harassed and helpless, like sheep without a shepherd. Then he said to his disciples, "The harvest is plentiful, but the laborers are few; pray therefore the Lord of the harvest to send out laborers into his harvest" (Matt 9:35–38).

Also in Matthew we have the account of Jesus withdrawing with his apostles to a lonely place (cf. Matt 14:13). However, his plan to allow his disciples to rest is upset by circumstances (cf. Mark 6:30). "But when the crowds heard of it, they followed him on foot from the towns. As he went ashore he saw a great throng; and he had compassion on them, and he healed their sick" (Matt 14:13–14, cf. Mark 6:34). After doing this, Jesus then feeds a large crowd with five loaves and two fish (cf. Matt 14:15–21, and Mark 6:35–44). Subsequently, the motive for his doing so is revealed, when he feeds another large crowd with seven loaves and a few small fish. "Then Jesus called his disciples to him and said, 'I have compassion on the crowd, because they have been with me now three days, and have nothing to eat; and I am unwilling to send them away hungry, lest they faint on the way'" (Matt 15:32; cf. Mark 8:1–9). Jesus has compassion on the crowd, so he feeds them. This compassion of Jesus is explicitly revealed in four other Gospel episodes. In Matthew: "They [two blind men] said to him [Jesus], 'Lord, let our eyes be opened.' And Jesus in pity [compassion] touched their eyes, and immediately they received their sight and followed him" (Matt 20:32–33). In Luke: "And when the Lord saw her [the widow of Nain], he had compassion on her and said to her, 'Do not weep'" (Luke 7:13). In Mark: "Moved with pity [compassion], he [Jesus] stretched out his hand and touched him [a leper], and said to him 'I will; be clean'" (Mark 1:41). Again, the father of a boy possessed by a deaf and dumb spirit begs Jesus to show compassion for them with the words: "[If] you can do anything, have pity [compassion] on us and help us" (Mark 9:22).

The word used for compassion in each of these instances is derived from the Greek *splagchna*—the bowels. Only once, in Proverbs 12:10, is the term used in the LXX to translate the Hebrew *rahamim*. Later in Proverbs, where is there is no Hebrew original (cf. Prov 17:5), it is used in the sense "to be merciful." Instead, the normal LXX equivalent for *rahamim* is not *splagchna* but *oiktirmoi*. We should also note that the verb derived from *splagchna* is occasionally used in the LXX to denote a sacrificial action. Sometimes, the noun is used to denote the bowels, in both the literal sense and as the "seat of feeling."[32]

This raises the question of why a term so rarely associated in the LXX with the concept of compassion becomes so prominent when a speaking of the compassion of Jesus. For an answer we must begin with the pre-Christian pagan Greek usage of the term. In early Greek literature the noun denotes the inward parts of a sacrifice, especially the nobler parts, the heart, liver, lungs, and kidneys, "which are separated in the sacrifice and consumed by the participants at the beginning of the sacrificial meal."[33] From here, the word could be applied to the sacrifice itself. Later, it is used to denote the

---

32. Köster, "σπλάγχνον," 550–51.
33. Ibid., 548.

"inward parts" of man, both generally, and to refer specifically to organs like the liver, lungs, or spleen. Finally, it comes to be used as a particularly forceful term for the lower parts of the body, especially the womb and the loins. The *splagchna* are also seen as the seat of impulsive passions such as anger, anxious desire, and love, and finally come to mean the heart in the sense of the center of personal feeling and sensibility. However, in this sense, the *splagchna* are distinct from the *kardia*, which is seen as the seat of the nobler affections, such as love and hate, courage and fear, joy and sorrow. Nor are the *splagchna* seen as the seat of heart-felt mercy, or used to denote mercy itself.[34]

Why, then, do the synoptic evangelists choose this particular Greek word to denote the compassion of Jesus, rather than the usual *oiktirmoi*? Contemporaneous with the time of Christ we find that, twice in Philo's writings, *splagchna* refers to the "inward being," "heart," or "soul."[35] More contentious is the use of the term in *The Testaments of the Twelve Patriarchs*, since a debate continues over the exact status of this work. Is it a pre-Christian Jewish work with Christian interpolations, or a post-Gospel Christian work?[36] If it is the former, then it could be a possible source for the synoptic use of *splagchna* in its nominal, verbal and adjectival forms. In *The Testaments*, *splagchna* can be a portion of man's inward parts as the seat of feelings, and the center of human feeling and sensibility generally, that is, the whole person in respect of the depth and force of feeling. It can also refer to man's nobler feelings and higher will. But above all, the *splagchna* are presented as the seat of mercy, such that *splagchna eleous* is used to mean "loving mercy." In *The Testaments*, the originally crude term *splagchna* is even used to denote the mercy of God himself. In *The Testaments* as a whole, *splagchna* has completely replaced the LXX use of *oiktiro*, and become the Greek term used to denote *rahamim*.[37]

A definite answer to the question of whether or not the synoptic use of *splagchna* has been derived from or influenced by the use of the term in *The Testaments* cannot be given. We can only note the change from the LXX to the synoptic Gospels in favor of a preference for referring to the compassion of Jesus in a strikingly visceral way. How, then, does this change relate to the portrayal of the heart of Jesus in the synoptic Gospels, since the synoptic evangelists, with the exception of Matthew 11:29 ("for I am gentle and lowly

---

34. Ibid., 549.

35. Ibid., 553.

36. For the former position, see Kee, "Testaments of the Twelve Patriarchs," 775–828. For the latter, see Jonge, "The Main Issues," 147–63.

37. Köster, "σπλάγχνον," 551–52.

in heart") make no direct reference to that heart. Since with God there is no coincidence, only providence, this change, coupled with the fact that the Greek term *splagchna* was used of the inward parts of a sacrifice, including the heart, and came to mean the heart in the sense of the center of personal feeling and sensibility, can be viewed typologically. The compassion of Jesus in the synoptic Gospels is not just a "suffering with" others, but can be seen as springing from a sacrificial heart, a kenotic heart.

This compassion of Jesus shows us the compassion of our heavenly Father—the same term is used in the parable of the Prodigal Son to describe the compassion of the father. "And he arose and came to his father. But while he was yet at a distance, his father saw him and had compassion [*esplagchnisthe*], and ran and embraced him and kissed him" (Luke 15:20).[38] Zechariah too portrays the mercy of God as issuing from his *splagchna* (cf. Luke 1:78). Stepping outside the synoptic Gospels for a moment, we find in the Letter of James the compassion and mercy of the Lord Jesus being referred to in the same terms as are used in the Old Testament to refer to the compassion and mercy of God, terms which are reminiscent of the Hebrew formula "the LORD is compassionate [gracious, kind] and merciful" (cf. Jas 5:11, Ps 103:8 and 111:4, Exod 34:6, and Joel 2:13).[39]

What is more, the term is used of the Good Samaritan, indicating that we are called by Jesus to exercise the same compassion for our neighbor as that shown by the Father and the incarnate Son. "But a Samaritan, as he journeyed, came to where he was; and when he saw him, he had compassion [*esplagchnisthe*]" (Luke 10:33). Nor is this call to compassion limited to Luke's Gospel, since we find the same term used in the Matthean parable of the unforgiving servant, where the king, "out of pity [*splagchnistheis*]" (Matt 18:27), forgives the servant who owed him ten thousand talents his debt. Interestingly, when the king condemns this same servant for failing to show like mercy to his fellow servant, the term he uses for mercy is *eleos*. "[And] should not you have had mercy [*eleesai*] on your fellow servant, as I had mercy [*eleesa*] on you" (Matt 18:33), thereby indicating the equivalence of the two terms. At this point we should recall how Ratzinger, aware that this Greek term is equivalent to the Hebrew *rahamim*, sees its connection with the "womb/heart."[40]

---

38. At this point we should recall what Ratzinger says about the compassion of God's heart: "Because God is God, the Holy One, he acts as no man could act. God has a heart, and this heart turns, so to speak, against God himself: Here in Hosea, as in the Gospel, we encounter once again the word *compassion*, which is expressed by means of the image of the maternal womb" (*Jesus I*, 207).

39. Köster, "σπλάγχνον," 557.

40. *Jesus I*, 197.

In his exposition of how Paul uses the term *splagchna*, Helmut Köster maintains that it has lost completely the sense of creaturely or natural emotions, or the sense of "mercy" as found in *The Testaments of the Twelve Patriarchs*, and, with other anthropological terms such as *kardia* and *nous*, come to be used for the whole man, especially in the Christian's capacity, *qua* Christian, to give and experience interpersonal love. According to Köster, for Paul, *splagchna* "concerns and expresses the total personality at the deepest level."[41] For example, in 2 Cor 6:11b–12, *splagchna* is parallel to *kardia*. "Corinthians; our heart [*kardia*] is wide. You are not restricted by us, but you are restricted in your own affections [*splagchnois*]." Again, in 2 Cor 7:13b and 15a, *splagchna*, used as a synonym for heart, is parallel to *pneuma*, "because his [Titus'] spirit [*pneuma*] has been set at rest by you all . . . And his heart [*splagchna*] goes out all the more to you." In Philemon, *splagchna* "is again used for the whole person which in the depths of its emotional life has experienced refreshment through consolation and love."[42] Thus: "For I have derived much joy and comfort from your love [*agape*], my brother, because the hearts [*splagchna*] of the saints have been refreshed through you" (Phlm 7). Also: "I am sending him back to you, sending my very heart [*splagchna*]" (Phlm 12). And again: "Refresh my heart [*splagchna*] in Christ" (Phlm 20). According to Köster, in Phil 1:8, "For God is my witness, how I yearn for you all with the affection [*splagchnois*] of Christ Jesus," the term is used as a synonym of *agape*.[43] Here:

> [For] Paul emotions which might be regarded as personal inclinations are an expression of this being ἐν Χριστῷ, and they have their origin here. Only in the light of this basic relation of the believer to Christ . . . can one understand the addition of Χριστοῦ Ἰησοῦ (gen. auctoris) to ἐν σπλάγχνοις. This love and affection which grip and profoundly move the whole man are possible only in Christ.[44]

For Köster, the other instance in Philippians of the use of *splagchna* is also a synonym of *agape*. Thus:

> εἴ τις σπλάγχνα καὶ οἰκτιρμοί (Phil 2:1) is to be taken as a summary of the three preceding clauses in which Paul appeals with an oath to the distinctive marks of the life of the Christian community. If elsewhere in Paul σπλάγχνα means the capacity of

---

41. Köster, "σπλάγχνον," 555.
42. Ibid.
43. Ibid., 556.
44. Ibid.

man for love or man as one who loves, in this context the word can only mean "love" itself. The word is used in a transferred sense and as a synonym of ἀγάπη, though it is distinct from this inasmuch as it is not a virtue, but love as the mutual experience and gift among Christians. In this sense σπλάγχνα is to be differentiated somewhat from the parallel οἰκτιρμοί. σπλάγχνα καὶ οἰκτιρμοί is thus a pregnant phrase in which "love from the heart" and "personal sympathy" comprehensively describe the essential elements in Christian dealings.[45]

Does the above investigation of development in the use of the term *splagchna* in pre-Christian Greek literature, the LXX, the *The Testaments of the Twelve Patriarchs* and the New Testament support Ratzinger's understanding of the term "heart"? As regards the heart of Jesus, the use of the term corresponds with Ratzinger's conviction that the heart of Jesus is kenotic. Also, Köster's conviction that, for St. Paul, *splagchna* comes to be used for the whole man, the total personality at its deepest level, harmonizes with Ratzinger's position that the *kardia* is the integration of the human person. Furthermore, Köster's identification of *splagchna* as the Christian's capacity to give and experience interpersonal love is in keeping with the position that the human heart is not self-generating, but is human integration within relation.

Developing a Pneumatological Method

The Testimony of the Apostolic Church

Without the Holy Spirit there can be no Christology as such, let alone a spiritual Christology, because without the Holy Spirit there is no Christ, nor Christians. Without the Holy Spirit we cannot pray to the Father (cf. Rom 8:15 and Gal 4:6). Without the Holy Spirit we cannot evangelize (cf. Acts 1:8). Without the Holy Spirit there is no church (cf. Eph 2:21–22). Without the Holy Spirit there are no Apostles, nor do they have any successors (cf. Acts 2:4; 2 Tim 1:13–14). Without the Holy Spirit there are no Holy

---

45. Ibid., 555–56. Since Köster does not regard Colossians as authentically Pauline, he treats the use of *splagchna* in Col 3:12 as dependent on Phil 2:1. Thus: "σπλάγχνα οἰκτιρμοῦ is one of several Christian virtues in Col. 3:12 . . . The phase can hardly have been coined without literary dependence on σπλάγχνα καὶ οἰκτιρμοί in Phil 2:1 (556)." See also Eph 4:32 for the use of *splagchna* to denote the compassion or tenderheartedness that Christians are meant to display towards each other. Köster sees the term being used in the same way in 1 Pet 3:8. In fact, he sees a hortatory use of the term, corresponding to its theological use, in the Pauline, Petrine and Johannine literature (cf. 1 John 3:17) (557).

Scriptures (cf. 2 Pet 1:21). Without the Holy Spirit there is no freedom, no *theosis* (cf. 2 Cor 3:16–17).

As with the analysis of the christological theses, before proceeding to the "content" of belief about the Holy Spirit, the "method" of the Spirit will be addressed. Concerning the Holy Spirit, what strikes me in reading the New Testament from the Acts of the Apostles onwards is the experiential and demonstrable presence and activity of the Holy Spirit in Christians. This is so omnipresent, especially in the Acts of the Apostles, that to give an exhaustive account of it would require a book in itself. In short, those who have received the Holy Spirit, and who are empowered to act by the Spirit, *know* it. It is not only at Pentecost that the reception and action of the Holy Spirit is tangible (cf. Acts 1:8 and 2:1–38). The New Testament from Acts onward testifies to an ongoing Pentecost. The tangible outpouring of the Spirit continues (cf. Acts 4:31; 8:15–19; 10:44–47; 11:15–16 and 19:2–16). Christians are filled with the Holy Spirit, speak in the Spirit, are addressed by the Spirit, are caught up by the Spirit, are comforted by the Spirit, are sent by the Spirit, and are filled with joy by the Spirit.

In many of the letters in the New Testament an appeal is made to a shared experience which Christians have of the Holy Spirit. God's love has been poured into their hearts through the gift of the Holy Spirit (cf. Rom 5:5). The Spirit is the spirit of sonship, enabling them to cry out, "Abba, Father" (cf. Rom 8:15; Gal 4:6), and it is only through the Spirit that they can confess that "Jesus is Lord" (cf. 1 Cor 12:3). They are able to worship God in the Spirit (cf. Eph 6:18; Phil 3:3; Jude 1:20). Without the Spirit they cannot pray as they ought to (cf. Rom 8:26–27). The Spirit bears witness to them that they are children of God (cf. Rom 8:16). The Spirit is a guarantee in their hearts who convinces them of the truth of the Gospel and enables them to know that God is dwelling in them (cf. 2 Cor 1:22 and 5:5; 1 Thess 1:5; 1 John 3:24, 4:13 and 5:7–8). The Spirit grants spiritual gifts to them in order to build up the Body of Christ (cf. 1 Cor 12:1–13). The Spirit works miracles among them (cf. 1 Cor 2:4; Gal 3:5; Heb 2:4). They are able to "live in the Spirit," being led by the Spirit and walking in the Spirit (cf. Gal 5:5–25). In the power of the Holy Spirit they are able to put to death the deeds of the flesh (cf. Rom 8:2–15; Gal 5:5–25). If they do so they experience the fruit of the Spirit—love, joy, peace, patience, kindness, goodness, faithfulness, gentleness and self-control (cf. Gal 5:22–23; Rom 12:11 and 15:13; 1 Thess 1:6; 2 Tim 1:7). Their minds are renewed by the Spirit (cf. Rom 8:5 and 12:2; Eph 4:23). They are able to understand "spiritual truths" and the gifts that God has bestowed upon them (cf. 1 Cor 2:12–15; Eph 1:17; Heb 6:4).

There are five possibilities concerning this testimony—either the presence and activity of the Holy Spirit described in the New Testament is a fiction, a kind of Christian propaganda; or it is an ideal, a Christianity only to be realized in the kingdom; or it is an exaggeration, expressing a desire for an unattained Christianity; or it is an exception, an experience of super-Christianity; or it is the rule, the experience of normal Christianity. If the last is the case, then, the experience of many contemporary Christians must be called sub-Christian. How can we discover which is the case? The phenomenal growth of Pentecostal ecclesial communities and the charismatic movement in the twentieth and twenty-first centuries gives reason to think that something akin to the experience of the Holy Spirit described in the New Testament can be the experience of contemporary Christians, but, in the end, the only way for one to be certain is practical—to ask the Father for the gift of the Holy Spirit (cf. Luke 11:13). If the presence and activity of the Holy Spirit as described in the New Testament is the norm, then it behooves anyone who wishes to practice a spiritual Christology to strive to live in the Spirit—to put to death the deeds of the flesh, and to pray, think and act in the Spirit. We must make our own the belief of someone like St. Seraphim of Sarov—the goal of the Christian life is the acquisition of the Holy Spirit.[46] This includes those who are academic theologians.

Although prayer is an integrating principle of Ratzinger's spiritual Christology, we have seen that it is a lived as well as a contemplated Christology. With regard to the personal thesis, we find that prayer and life are interrelated. They mutually determine each other. So, it is insufficient to attempt to pray in the Spirit if the rest of one's life is lived in the flesh. Indeed, one will be unable to do so. Here, the action of the Holy Spirit in the human heart should be addressed, if we take the heart to be the place of personal integration. How does the Holy Spirit purify our hearts? Furthermore, how can we have a prayerful hermeneutic of the Spirit, which is also a hermeneutic of the heart? How can we put into practice the exhortation of *Dei Verbum* that since the books of Sacred Scripture "were written through the inspiration of the Holy Spirit" they must be "read and interpreted with the help of the same Spirit by means of whom [they were] written"?[47]

The Acts of the Apostles consistently speaks of Christians being "filled with the Holy Spirit," or being "full of the Spirit" (cf. Acts 2:4, 6:3, 7:55, 9:17, 11:24, 13:9 and 13:52). Christians become the dwelling place of the Spirit (cf. Rom 8:9; 1 Cor 3:16 and 6:19; Eph 2:22; 2 Tim 1:14). Yet, wherein dwells the Spirit who Christians are given and with whom they are filled? Although the Holy Spirit is presented as enlightening and renewing the minds of Christians (cf. Rom 8:5–6; 1 Cor 2:13; Eph 4:23), and inspiring

---

46. Boosalis, *The Joy of the Holy*, 4, 20–21, 28, 35–36, and *passim*
47. DV, nos. 11 and 12. Cf. VD, no. 15.

peace and joy in the passions of Christians (cf. Rom 12:11 and 14:17; 1 Thess 1:6), neither the mind nor the passions are presented as the dwelling place of the Spirit. The place which is thus presented is the heart. "God has sent the Spirit of his Son into our hearts, crying, 'Abba! Father!'" (Gal 4:6). It is by searching the hearts of Christians when they pray in the Spirit that God "knows what is the mind of the Spirit" (Rom 8:27). Furthermore: "God has set his seal upon us and given us his Spirit in our hearts as a guarantee" (2 Cor 1:22). This guarantee is the love of God which "has been poured into our hearts through the Holy Spirit which has been given to us" (Rom 5:5). The only alternative dwelling place of the Spirit which is given is the body of the Christian, and that is in the particular context of sexual immorality (cf. 1 Cor 6:12–19).[48]

The harmonization of the personal and hermeneutical theses with the work of the Holy Spirit certainly presents us with a great deal of work. However, the main challenge to developing a pneumatological method arises in relation to the ecclesial thesis. For we must not only account for the action of the Holy Spirit in individual believers but also his action in the Body of Christ which is composed of those believers.

Intimations of an Augustinian Pneumatological Method

Although Ratzinger does not employ an explicitly pneumatological method in his spiritual Christology, as it happens, there is evidence that he has an awareness of the relationship between pneumatology and spirituality, an awareness that draws upon both Western theology and Eastern liturgy. Regarding the former, in a 1974 work, Ratzinger looks at the nature of this relationship, basing his thoughts on St. Augustine's doctrine of the Holy Spirit. Before doing so, however, Ratzinger outlines three conditions for speaking validly about the Holy Spirit. First, such talk cannot be based on pure theory, but "must touch an experienced reality that has been interpreted and communicated in thought." Second, this experience must be tested, so that "one's own spirit" does not replace the Holy Spirit. Third, one's speech about the Holy Spirit must be after the Holy Spirit's own mode of being, which is characterized "by not speaking on his own" (John 16:13). Hence, one can only trust that one is speaking of a genuine experience of the Spirit when it has been tested "in front of and standing in the context of the whole, i.e. when one submits the experience of 'spirit' to the entirety of the Church."

---

48. On this point, we must not fall into a Greek body-soul dualism, but maintain the Hebrew understanding of the psychosomatic unity of the human person.

The presupposition for this submission is "faith that the Church herself—when she truly exists as Church—is a creation of the Spirit."[49]

In attempting to grasp the unique character of the Holy Spirit via an investigation of the name "Holy Spirit," Augustine comes to the conclusion that the Spirit can be defined as *communio*. Since, according to Ratzinger, Augustine's understanding of Spirit has moved from a universal and a metaphysical one to one which is the dynamic self-giving of the Father and the Son to each other, *communio* "thereby becomes an essential element of the notion of the Spirit, thus truly giving it content and thoroughly personalizing it."[50] Ratzinger goes so far as to claim that, for Augustine:

> Only one who knows what "Holy Spirit" is, can know what spirit means. And only one who begins to know what God is, can know what Holy Spirit is. Furthermore, only one who begins to have an idea of what Holy Spirit is, can begin to know who God is.[51]

Since the term *communio* already has a fundamentally ecclesial meaning for Augustine, according to Ratzinger:

> [This] opens pneumatology up into ecclesiology, and the reverse connection of ecclesiology into theology. Becoming a Christian means becoming *communio* and thereby entering into the mode of being of the Holy Spirit. But it can also only happen through the Holy Spirit, who is the power of communication, mediating it, making it possible and is himself a person.[52]

Besides analyzing the name of the Holy Spirit, on the basis of biblical pneumatology, Augustine also sees the terms "love" and "gift" as names of the Holy Spirit. Concerning "love," and basing his thought especially on the Johannine definition of God as love (cf. 1 John 4:15–17), Augustine identifies the Holy Spirit as the God who is love. God communicates himself in the Holy Spirit as love. The presence of the Holy Spirit is proclaimed in the manner of love. Therefore, Ratzinger reads Augustine as holding that: "The basic and central meaning of what the Holy Spirit is and what he effects is ultimately not 'knowledge' but love." For Augustine, this leads to a practical

---

49. Ratzinger, "The Holy Spirit as Communio," 325.

50. Ibid., 328.

51. Ibid. Note the mutual reinforcement of knowing God, the Holy Spirit, and spirit.

52. Ibid., 327.

question: "What does love mean as a criterion of the Holy Spirit and therefore also a criterion of being a Christian and of the Church?"[53]

However, for Ratzinger, "knowledge" is also caused by the love of the Holy Spirit, since love creates "abiding."

> Love proves itself in constancy. Love is not recognizable right at any given moment, or in just one moment; instead, love abides, overcomes vacillation, and bears eternity within itself, which also shows, in my opinion, the connection between love and truth.[54]

From these reflections upon Augustine's doctrine of the Holy Spirit, Ratzinger derives a "doctrine of the discernment of spirits and a directive for the spiritual life." The basic activity of the Holy Spirit is "unifying love entering into abiding." The Spirit is not present in speaking in one's own name or seeking one's own fame, that is to say, in factions. Rather: "*Pneuma* is present precisely in remembering (John 14:26) and unifying."[55]

When we come to Ratzinger's reflections upon Augustine's understanding of the Holy Spirit as "gift," we do find an implicit connection with his later spiritual Christology. Augustine develops his understanding on the basis of Jesus' conversation with the Samaritan woman (cf. John 4:7–14), and its connection with his promise of living water to those who believe in him (cf. John 7:37–39), and with the drinking of the one Spirit in 1 Corinthians 12:13. Herein lies the connection between Christology and pneumatology for Augustine. According to Ratzinger, for Augustine: "The well of the Spirit is the crucified Christ. From him each Christian becomes the well of the Spirit."[56]

According to Ratzinger, for Augustine, the Holy Spirit is "in his essence the gift of God, God as self-donating, God as self-distributing, as gift."[57] The gift of God is God himself. Thus Ratzinger states:

> [God] is the content of Christian prayer. He is the only gift adequate to the divinity. God gives as God nothing other than God, giving himself and with himself everything. Proper Christian prayer does not plead for something or other but for the gift of God which God is, for him. Augustine expresses this beautifully by interpreting as a matter of course the plea of the "Our Father,"

53. Ibid., 329.
54. Ibid.
55. Ibid., 330.
56. Ibid., 331.
57. Ibid., 332.

> "*Give* us our daily bread," in terms of the Holy Spirit. *He* is "our bread," ours as one who is not ours, as something completely given. "Our" spirit is not our spirit.[58]

In Ratzinger's estimation, Augustine develops the eschatological significance of *pneuma* as love and gift in such a way that it forms the basis of his entire sacramental theology and ecclesiology. For Augustine, *caritas* is not opposed to justice but is itself the judgment of God. Those on the right hand are those who love, while those on the left hand are those who do not (cf. Matt 25). Appealing to both St. Paul and St. James, Augustine identifies saving faith as pneumatologically inspired faith—faith working through love (cf. Gal 5:6; 1 Cor 13:1–3; Jas 2:19).[59] This, for Augustine, is why the Donatists stand under the judgment of God. Despite the fact that they have valid sacraments, they have broken the bonds of love. In placing their own idea of perfection above the unity of the church, they have departed from the true faith. In Augustine's language, the church is love. Ratzinger holds that this is a dogmatic thesis for Augustine. As he explains:

> As a creation of the Spirit, the Church is the body of the Lord built up by the *pneuma*, and thus also becomes the body of Christ when the *pneuma* forms men and women for "communio." This creation, this Church, is God's "gift" in the world, and this "gift" is love.[60]

Augustine's dogmatic thesis is also a practical one. Unless we accept our brothers and sisters in humility and love, bearing with each one's faults, the Holy Spirit will be missing. To remain in the church is not automatically to have *caritas*, but whoever does not "willingly" remain in the church leaves *caritas* behind. Therefore, "one possesses the Holy Spirit to the degree that one loves the Church."[61] By this we should understand the church in its members, not the church as a monolith. Ratzinger concedes that the identification of the church with love also has its dangers. One can see "love" as "the self-evident content of the institution" instead of seeing the need for the Spirit to bring about the church's transformation into love.[62] On the other

---

58. Ibid.
59. Ibid., 333.
60. Ibid., 334.

61. Ibid. I think that the adverb *willingly* is important. One can remain in the Church, but *unwillingly*, that is, without a whole-hearted acceptance of its faith and life. We should also note that to "love the Church" does not mean to love it as an "institution," but to "love the brethren." Every Christian belongs to the institutional Church, that is, to the Church which Christ instituted.

62. Ibid., 335.

hand, one can contrast a "church of the Spirit" with an "official church" or an "empirical Catholic Church."[63] However, this is to mistake Augustine's axiological understanding of the Spirit for an ontological one. Rather, the opposite of the Spirit is not matter, but "the world." "Spirit" can be worldly, and also may be unable to go beyond the inner-worldly.[64] The church cannot be divided up into "spirit" and "institution." The church is visible and "empirical" in the sacraments and the word. However, one cannot look for the Spirit only in external signs. One sees the Spirit at work in a "unifying love entering into abiding."[65]

Finally, Ratzinger concludes with a reflection upon the ecclesial significance of the connection between Christ and the Spirit. The gifts of the Holy Spirit, in which the ultimate gift is the Spirit himself, are the gift of the glorious risen and ascended Christ. According to Ratzinger, in two apparently contradictory ways of reading the Vulgate version of Psalm 67—"You receive gifts in men," and "He gave gifts to men," Augustine sees the ambiguity of the christological mystery itself. As Ratzinger says:

> Christ, the one who ascended, also remains the one who descended. He stands both on the side of the God who gives and the men and women who receive. He is head and body, giving from the side of God and receiving from the side of humanity ... this is what joins ecclesiology and christology. In the Church he remains the one who descends. The Church is Christ as the one who descended, a continuation of the humanity of Christ.[66]

Since the gift of Jesus Christ is the Holy Spirit, and the church is Jesus receiving the Holy Spirit to form a divinized humanity in which human persons can participate, then it is the Spirit who makes us the church, the Body of Christ. To use what Ratzinger calls Augustine's favorite ecclesiological and pneumatological idea, it is the Lord who builds the House of the Spirit which is the church. In doing so, the Lord "imprisons" captivity and gives us the gift of the Spirit (cf. Ps 67; Eph 4). In imprisoning captivity, Christ imprisons "the devil ... man's bondage, exile, a luring away from self."[67] He replaces our apparent freedom with the freedom of the Spirit, the freedom of belonging to the house of God, the freedom of the truth, the freedom of one's true self.[68]

63. Ibid., 336.
64. Ibid., 328.
65. Ibid., 336.
66. Ibid., 337.
67. Ibid., 338.
68. Ibid., 338–39.

In these thoughts one can hear many of the *leitmotifs* of Ratzinger's spiritual Christology—*communio*, the unity of knowledge and love, the crucified Christ as the font of the Spirit, God as the content of Christian prayer, faith working through love, our descending and ascending with Jesus, the church as the presence of Christ in the world, and the spiritual terminus of freedom. The significance of these thoughts for a pneumatological method is that they contain the foundation for an ecclesially based pneumatological method—only those who live in the ecclesial *communio* of love can truly say that they are "led by the Spirit."

Intimations of a Pneumatological Method Inspired by the Eastern Liturgy

The role of the Holy Spirit in Christology is essential—as Congar says of his Christology, "no Christology without pneumatology and no pneumatology without Christology."[69] Yet, Ratzinger gives an essential counter balance to this insight—in speaking of the Holy Spirit, one must not simply impose a symmetry between Christ and the Holy Spirit, in as much as whatever is said about Christ must correspond to what is said about the Holy Spirit. Both Christ and the Spirit belong to the Trinity, which is not to be understood as a symmetrical coexistence. The danger in following such a path lies in coming to believe in three divinities, rather than one God in three Persons.[70]

---

69. Congar, *The Word and the Spirit*, 1. See also Congar, *I Believe in the Holy Spirit*, 1:15–64; and 3:165–73. For a brief exposition of Congar's understanding of the relationship between Jesus Christ and the Holy Spirit, see Groppe, *Yves Congar's Theology of the Holy Spirit*, 69–75. Besides the work of Congar, the question of the essential connection between pneumatology and Christology, also called "Spirit Christology," has been addressed by such theologians as Bobrinskoy, "The Indwelling of the Spirit in Christ," 49–65; Coffey, "The Gift of the Holy Spirit," 202–23; "The 'Incarnation' of the Holy Spirit in Christ," 466–80; *Grace: The Gift of the Holy Spirit*; *Deus Trinitas: The Doctrine of the Triune God*; "The Spirit of Christ as Entelechy," 363–98; "Spirit Christology and the Trinity," 315–38; and *Did You Receive the Holy Spirit When You Believed?*; De la Potterie, "The Anointing of Christ," 155–84; Del Colle, *Christ and the Spirit*; Dunn, *Jesus and the Spirit*; Habets, "Spirit Christology," 199–34; and *The Anointed Son*; Haight, "The Case for Spirit Christology," 257–87; Lampe, "The Holy Spirit and the Person of Christ," 111–30; and *God as Spirit*; McDonnell, "The Determinative Doctrine of the Holy Spirit," 142–59; and "A Trinitarian Theology of the Holy Spirit?," 191–227; Newman, *A Spirit Christology*; Nissiotos, "Pneumatological Christology as a Presupposition of Ecclesiology," 235–52; O'Byrne, *Spirit Christology and Trinity in the Theology of David Coffey*; O'Donnell, "In Him and Over Him," 25–45; Pinnock, *Flame of Love*; Rosato, "Spirit Christology," 423–49; and Schoonenberg, "Spirit Christology and Logos Christology," 350–75.

70. Ratzinger, "The Holy Spirit and the Church," 63.

According to Ratzinger, one cannot speak of the Holy Spirit without speaking of the Trinity of God, and the church. This reality is presented to us in the liturgy of the Eastern Church which, on Pentecost Sunday, celebrates the feast of the Most Holy Trinity, on Monday, the outpouring of the Holy Spirit, and on the following Sunday, the feast of All Saints. Presented here for our participation is the reality that it is the essence of the Holy Spirit to direct us into the unity of the triune God. The Holy Spirit teaches us "to see Christ entirely in the mystery of the trinitarian God as our way to the Father in perpetual conversation of love with him."[71]

Ratzinger holds that, in pointing to the Trinity, the Holy Spirit also points to us. The trinitarian God is the archetype of the church. In the Trinity, mankind once more becomes the one Adam. In a passage which unites human history and ontology in the triune God, Ratzinger states:

> Church does not mean another idea in addition to man, but rather man on the way to himself. If the Holy Spirit expresses and is the unity of God, then he is the real vital element of the Church in which distinction is reconciled in togetherness and the dispersed pieces of Adam are fit together again.[72]

That the Eastern liturgical representation of the Holy Spirit begins with the celebration of the Holy Trinity emphasizes Ratzinger's point that the Holy Spirit can never be thought of in isolation from the "other." The paradox of the Spirit is that he is simultaneously the mystery of the unity and community of God, the oneness of God and exchange within God. For us, it is the Spirit who tells us God's ideal for us—we can only be truly one when we find ourselves in a higher unity. It is the Holy Spirit who enables oneself to remain oneself and yet "touch the other from inside."[73] It is the Spirit who enables one to reconcile the I with the Thou. At this point, Ratzinger says something that is germane to a question raised earlier about the connection between integration and relation. "I and Thou, however, cannot reconcile if man remains unreconciled with his own I."[74]

For Ratzinger, this "theory," that in the Trinity the unity between the I and the Thou is brought about in the Holy Spirit, is being put into practice, as it were, in the concrete historical reality of the church. As in the Eastern liturgy, the founding of the church at Pentecost follows the day after the Feast of the Trinity on Pentecost Sunday, so on the following Sunday

71. Ibid., 65.
72. Ibid.
73. Ibid., 67.
74. Ibid.

is celebrated the feast of All Saints. As Ratzinger sees it, the church of the present moment is suspended between the "ever-growing" church of the end, and the earthly church which began in the Cenacle.[75]

At this point, Ratzinger does something unusual—he proposes a reciprocal iconography—the church as an icon of the Holy Spirit, and the Holy Spirit as an icon of the church. Regarding the first, if Christ is both the icon of the Father and the icon of man, the church is the icon of the Holy Spirit, inasmuch as the deepest part of her nature is to overcome the boundary between I and Thou. Indeed, the "Church is mankind being brought into the way of life of the trinitarian God."[76]

If the church is the icon of the Holy Spirit, in that the Spirit is the Spirit of unity, Ratzinger does not overlook an equally important aspect of the iconography of the first Pentecost. Just as the tongues of fire separated and came to rest on each person gathered in the Cenacle, so too is the Holy Spirit given to each one personally and uniquely. Whilst Christ has assumed human *nature*, the Holy Spirit is given to each *person*. The unity of the church does not come about through the loss of personality, but through its completion as "infinite openness." The catholicity of the church does not consist in each one acting "from his own will and his own genius. Everyone must act, speak, think, from the communion of the new We of the Church that stands in intercommunion with the We of the triune God."[77]

As one of this new We, each one is called to live through a conscience formed by faith, a "conscience that creates not from [its] own but rather from the faith received in common."[78] Here, the Holy Spirit becomes the icon of the church, inasmuch as he guides believers into all truth, not on the basis for his own authority, but from what he hears within the We of the Trinity (cf. John 16:13). So, too, the members of the church are meant to speak what they hear within the We of the church. With profound insight, Ratzinger states:

> Becoming Christian means receiving the whole Church into oneself, or, rather, allowing oneself to be taken up into her. When I speak, think, act, I do so as a Christian always in the whole and from the whole. Thus the Spirit comes to the Word, and thus men come together. They come outwardly to one another only if they came to one other inwardly: if I have become

---

75. Ibid., 68. The use of this term "ever-growing" seems to indicate that Ratzinger's idea of our ultimate communion with the Trinity and each other is anything but static.
76. Ibid., 68–69.
77. Ibid., 70.
78. Ibid.

inwardly broad, open, and large; if I have received the others through my co-believing and co-loving so that I am no longer ever alone but rather my whole essence is characterized by this "co-."[79]

Once again, Ratzinger uses the words of St. Paul in an attempt to summarize the nature of this "co"—"It is no longer I who live, but Christ who lives in me" (Gal 2:20). To be "in Christ" and to have Christ in one is a process of death that breaks the limits of the I. "The I loses itself in order to find itself anew in a larger subject that spans heaven and earth, past, present, and future, and therein touches truth itself."[80]

This second embryonic pneumatological method could be seen as complementing the first. It has a greater trinitarian emphasis, and stresses the relationship between trinitarian theology and ecclesiology. It too lays a foundation for an ecclesially based pneumatological method, one which emphasizes co-believing and co-loving. In it we can also find some of the *leitmotifs* of Ratzinger's spiritual Christology—the church as man on the way to himself, the reconciliation of the I and the Thou in the We, and the most fundamental of them all: "It is no longer I who live, but Christ we lives in me." Indeed, in light of this method, this last theme could be recast in the form: "It is no longer I who live, but the *Church* who lives in me." Amongst other possible questions, this recasting raises that of what implications Ratzinger's pneumatological method may have for our understanding of the *sensus fidei* and the *sensus fidelium*.

Expanding the Pneumatological Content

As Congar says, the role of the Holy Spirit in Christology is essential. Without the action of the Holy Spirit there would have been no Incarnation, no Jesus the Christ (cf. Matt 1:18 and 20; Luke 1:35). Through the Holy Spirit the power of the Most High overshadows Mary, and she conceives the Son of God in her womb. According John Paul II, the "entire activity of Jesus of Nazareth is carried out in the active presence of the Holy Spirit."[81] The Gospels proclaim the presence of the Holy Spirit in Jesus and the action of the Holy Spirit through Jesus. The Spirit descends upon him at his Baptism (cf. Matt 3:16; Luke 3:22; John 1:13). This anointing of the Holy Spirit comes from the Father (cf. Matt 12:18; Luke 4:18; John 3:34). The Spirit leads Jesus

79. Ibid., 71.
80. Ibid.
81. John Paul II, *Dominum et vivificantem*, no. 20. Here activity is taken to mean definite conscious and willed acts.

into the desert where he faces his temptations (cf. Matt 4:1; Luke 4:1). It is in the power of the same Spirit that Jesus carries out his ministry (cf. Luke 4:14). Without the Holy Spirit there is no proclamation of the Kingdom, nor are there any healings, exorcisms or miracles (cf. Matt 12:28; Luke 4:18–19; Acts 10:38). Without the Holy Spirit there is no Atoning Sacrifice (cf. Heb 9:13–14). Without the Holy Spirit there is no Resurrection (cf. Rom 8:11). Without the Holy Spirit there would be no risen Christ to pour out the self-same Spirit upon us (cf. Acts 2:33). Therefore, it will be necessary to establish the role of the Holy Spirit in the prayer of Jesus to the Father, his communion with the Father, which includes his sacrificial offering of himself to the Father, and the outpouring of the Holy Spirit upon believers by the Father and the Son—that is to say, an integration of the Holy Spirit with the filial and soteriological theses.

We have already touched upon this communion, and seen that prayer to the Father was a constant accompaniment to the mission of Jesus. However, when it comes to the activity of the Holy Spirit in that prayer, there are only three explicit occurrences where the veil of intimacy is drawn aside and others are allowed the privilege of witnessing this communion—the Baptism of Jesus, his Transfiguration, and that episode peculiar to Luke's Gospel, where, in the presence of the seventy, Jesus "rejoiced in the Holy Spirit and said: 'I thank you, Father, Lord of heaven and earth, that you have hidden these things from the wise and understanding and revealed them to babes; yes, Father, for such was your gracious will'" (Luke 10:21). In a beautiful commentary upon this passage, John Paul II writes:

> Jesus rejoices at the fatherhood of God: he rejoices because it has been given to him to reveal this fatherhood; he rejoices, finally, as at the particular outpouring of this divine fatherhood on the "little ones." And the evangelist describes all this as "rejoicing in the Holy Spirit."[82]

Furthermore:

> That which during the theophany at the Jordan came so to speak "from outside," from on high, here comes "from within," that is to say *from the depths of who Jesus is*. It is another revelation of the Father and the Son, united in the Holy Spirit. Jesus speaks only of the fatherhood of God and of his own sonship—he does not speak directly of the Spirit who is Love and thereby the union of the Father and the Son. Nonetheless, *what he says of the Father and himself—the Son flows* from that *fullness of the Spirit* which is in him, which fills his heart, pervades his own

---

82. Ibid.

"I," inspires and enlivens his action from the depths. Hence that "rejoicing in the Holy Spirit," a union of which he is perfectly aware, is expressed in that "rejoicing" which in a certain way renders "perceptible" its hidden source.[83]

However, we must not only address the question of Jesus' rejoicing in the Spirit. In the soteriological thesis in particular, along with the "suffering" of the Father, we must also face the question of the "passion" of the Holy Spirit, the Spirit who sighs within us (cf. Rom 8:26), the Spirit who we can grieve (cf. Eph 4: 30). Just as Jesus rejoiced in the Spirit, did he also suffer grief "in the Spirit?" Was his heart pierced "in the Spirit?"

Turning to the dogmatic and volitional theses, Ratzinger states that: "The core of the dogma defined in the councils of the early church consists in the statement that Jesus is the true Son of God, of the same essence as the Father and, through the Incarnation, equally of the same essence as us."[84] Yet the christological dogma of Chalcedon does not address the question of the role of the Holy Spirit in bringing about the integration of the two natures of the Son of God "without confusion, without change, without division, without separation," nor is the question of the role of the Holy Spirit in integrating the divine and human wills of the Word made flesh addressed by Constantinople III.[85] If we are to develop the dogmatic and volitional theses along pneumatological lines, thereby making them truly trinitarian theses, there is a need to address the role of the Holy Spirit in the integration of Christ's humanity with his divinity. As they stand, these theses are binitarian rather than trinitarian.

The Eucharist as the Ultimate Symbolon of a Spiritual Christology

Because Christians do not participate in the prayer of Jesus to the Father in the Holy Spirit as isolated individuals, but as members of the Body of Christ, in order to have a spiritual Christology one needs to harmonize all three

---

83. Ibid., 21. The question of whether or not John Paul II goes beyond the biblical data is one which could be settled through praxis, that is, by one asking the Father for the gift of the Holy Spirit in his or her own heart.

84. *Behold*, 32.

85. The only ecumenical council which has addressed a pneumatological issue is the First Council of Constantinople, which affirmed the divinity of the Holy Spirit and added to the Nicene Creed the clauses which refer to the Spirit, the Church, Baptism, the Resurrection and eternal life. Apart from this, the only other "intervention" in the Creed regarding the Spirit is the addition of the *filioque* in the West.

integrating principles—prayer, heart and Holy Spirit—corporately. That is to say, the harmonization must be ecclesial. In Ratzinger's spiritual Christology we have identified prayer as the ultimate source of theology, indeed, that prayer *is* theology. However, it must, in the end, be ecclesial prayer. As Congar has said, the highest mode of theology is doxology.[86] Therefore, the "place" of this complete integration must be the celebration of the Eucharist.

The celebration of the Eucharist is the *symbolon* of the personal, ecclesial and hermeneutical theses, and of the believer's heart, the Father's heart and the heart of Jesus in the heart of the church. In this celebration the sacrificial prayer of Jesus to the Father is made present, and we are able to individually and corporately participate in this offering. Through this participation, our "hermeneutic" of that in which we participate grows. The celebration of the Eucharist, not the study, the library or the lecture hall, is the origin of our understanding of the Apostolic Tradition handed on by apostolic celebrants, the Canon of Sacred Scripture, and the Symbol of Faith. The Eucharist is the place where everything in our Christian life is brought together—God and man, Heaven and earth, yesterday, today and forever.

Ultimately, the celebration of the Eucharist is the *symbolon* of the prayer of the believer from the heart of the believer participating in the prayer of Jesus from the heart of Jesus addressed to the heart of the Father in the *koinonia* of the Holy Spirit. We all share in the *koinonia* of this Spirit (cf. 2 Cor 13:14). By this one Spirit we have all been baptized into one body and all made to drink of this same Spirit (cf. 1 Cor 12:13). Not only the bodies of individual Christians, but the whole church is the Temple of God in the Spirit (cf. Eph 2:21–22). We are one Body in the unity of the Spirit (cf. Eph 4:3–4). We have this *koinonia* in our eucharistic participation in the body and blood of Christ. We are one body because we all partake of the one bread (cf. 1 Cor 10:16–17).[87] The worship of the church identifies the source

---

86. Congar, *The Word and the Spirit*, 5. On the question of liturgical worship as theology *par excellence*, see Schmemann, *Introduction to Liturgical Theology*, and *Liturgy and Tradition*; Kavanagh, *On Liturgical Theology*; and especially Fagerberg, *Theologia Prima*. Of particular interest is how Fagerberg links *askesis* with liturgy as theology.

87. St. Augustine comments on this passage in a manner which draws out, in a profound way, the relationship between being the Body of Christ and receiving the Body of Christ, and the consequences of not truly "receiving what we are": "So now, if you want to understand the body of Christ, listen to the Apostle Paul speaking to the faithful: 'You are the body of Christ, member for member.' [1 Cor 12:27] If you, therefore, are Christ's body and members, it is your own mystery that is placed on the Lord's table! It is your own mystery that you are receiving! You are saying 'Amen' to what you are: your response is a personal signature, affirming your faith. When you hear 'The body of Christ,' you reply 'Amen.' Be a member of Christ's body, then, so that your 'Amen' may ring true! But what role does the bread play? We have no theory of our own to propose here; listen, instead, to what Paul says about this sacrament: 'The

of this *koinonia* as the Holy Spirit.[88] The ultimate result of this *koinonia* is the *theosis* which is also called freedom. "Now the Lord is the Spirit, and where the Spirit of the Lord is, there is freedom. And we all, with unveiled face, beholding the glory of the Lord, are being changed into his likeness from one decree of glory to another; for this comes from the Lord who is the Spirit" (2 Cor 3:17–18). To participate in this freedom means to participate in the mercy of the Father, especially to the poor and to those who have offended us. Those who participate in this eucharistic freedom will leave their gifts at the altar, and go and be reconciled with their brethren, before they return to offer their gifts (cf. Matt 5:23–24).

Spiritual Christology must become eucharistic theology, not in the sense of a theology of the Eucharist, but in the sense that all theology must be eucharistic. Or, to put it another way, we must theologize eucharistically. There is only one who theologizes eucharistically, Jesus the Christ, and we must participate in his pneumatic theologizing. Then we shall be on the way to freedom, on the way to *koinonia*, on the way to *theosis*, on the way to our *Abba*.

---

bread is one, and we, though many, are one body.' [1 Cor 10:17] Understand and rejoice: unity, truth, faithfulness, love. 'One bread,' he says. What is this one bread? Is it not the 'one body,' formed from many? Remember: bread doesn't come from a single grain, but from many. When you received exorcism, you were 'ground.' When you were baptized, you were 'leavened.' When you received the fire of the Holy Spirit, you were 'baked.' Be what you see; receive what you are . . . In the visible object of bread, many grains are gathered into one just as the faithful (so Scripture says) form 'a single heart and mind in God.' [Acts 4:32] . . . This is the image chosen by Christ our Lord to show how, at his own table, the mystery of our unity and peace is solemnly consecrated. All who fail to keep the bond of peace after entering this mystery receive not a sacrament that benefits them, but an indictment that condemns them" (Augustine, *Sermon 272*).

88. From the earliest times the worshipping Church has called upon the Holy Spirit to transform the bread and wine into the Body and Blood of Christ, and to transform all who share in that Body and Blood into the one Body of Christ. Besides the second, third and fourth Eucharistic Prayers of the Roman Liturgy, for other examples see Jasper and Cuming, *Prayers of the Eucharist*. Therein we find references to the Holy Spirit being called down upon the gifts in *The Apostolic Tradition* of Hippolytus (23), the Anaphora of Saints Addai and Mari (28), the Third Anaphora of the Apostle Peter (33), the Liturgy of Saint Mark (53 and 54), the *Lectures* of Cyril of Jerusalem (58 and 59), *The Apostolic Constitutions*, Book 8 (77), the Anaphora of *Testamentum Domini* (82), the Anaphora of the Twelve Apostles (95); and consequently filling those who partake of the gifts in *The Apostolic Tradition* of Hippolytus (23), *The Apostolic Constitutions*, Book 8 (77); or being poured out upon both the gifts and the worshippers in the Anaphora of Basil of Caesarea (36), the Liturgy of St. James (63–64), the *Lectures* of Theodore of Mopsuestia (86), the Liturgy of St. John Chrysostom (90), and the Liturgy of St. Basil (101).

The Last Homily

After analyzing Ratzinger's earlier Christology, it was suggested that a suitable title for him could be Doctor of Reconciliation. Now, having investigated his spiritual Christology, an alternative title can be proposed—Doctor of Freedom. For those who have a de-spiritualized notion of freedom, this title may be seen as ironic, but for those who understand true freedom to be that of the children of God, no whiff of irony will be detected.

As the first draft of the final chapter of this work, in its dissertational incarnation, was being completed, it so happened that Benedict XVI was completing his papacy. For me there was a touch of divine providence in his last public homily, given on Ash Wednesday. The first reading, from the prophet Joel, gave Benedict an opportunity to reiterate the core of his spiritual Christology. I can think of no better conclusion to this study than to listen in our hearts to his words.

> The readings that have been proclaimed provide us with ideas that, with the grace of God, we are called to make concrete attitudes and behaviors during this Lent. The Church proposes to us, first, the strong appeal that the prophet Joel addressed to the people of Israel: "Thus says the Lord, return to me with all your heart, with fasting, with weeping, and with mourning" (2:12). Please note the phrase "with all my heart," which means from the center of our thoughts and feelings, from the roots of our decisions, choices and actions, with a gesture of total and radical freedom. But is this return to God possible? Yes, because there is a force that does not reside in our hearts, but that emanates from the heart of God. It is the power of his mercy. The prophet says, further: "Return to the Lord your God, for he is gracious and merciful, slow to anger, rich in faithful love, ready to repent of evil" (v. 13). The return to the Lord is possible as a "grace," because it is the work of God and the fruit of that faith that we place in His mercy. But this return to God becomes a reality in

our lives only when the grace of God penetrates to our inmost being and shakes it, giving us the power to "rend our hearts." The same prophet causes these words from God to resonate: "Rend your hearts and not your garments" (v. 13). In fact, even today, many are ready to "rend their garments" before scandals and injustices—of course, made by others—but few seem willing to act on their own "heart," on their own conscience and their own intentions, letting the Lord transform, renew and convert. That "return to me with all your heart," then, is a reminder that involves not only the individual, but the community. We have heard, also in the first reading: "Play the horn in Zion, proclaim a solemn fast, call a sacred assembly. Gather the people, convoke a solemn assembly, call the old, gather the children and the infants at the breast; let the bridegroom leave his room and the bride her bridal chamber" (vv.15-16). The community dimension is an essential element in faith and Christian life. Christ came "to gather into one the children of God who are scattered abroad" (cf. John 11:52). The "we" of the Church is the community in which Jesus brings us together (cf. John 12:32): faith is necessarily ecclesial. And this is important to remember and to live in this time of Lent: each person is aware that he or she does not face the penitential journey alone, but together with many brothers and sisters in the Church . . .Behold, now is the acceptable time, now is the day of salvation" (2 Cor 6:2). The words of the Apostle Paul to the Christians of Corinth resonate for us, too, with an urgency that does not allow omission or inaction. The word "now" repeated several times says that we cannot let this time pass us by, it is offered to us as a unique opportunity. And the Apostle's gaze focuses on the sharing that Christ chose to characterize his life, taking on everything human to the point of bearing the very burden of men's sins. The phrase St. Paul uses is very strong: "God made him sin for our sake." Jesus, the innocent one, the Holy One, "He who knew no sin" (2 Cor 5:21), bears the burden of sin, sharing with humanity its outcome of death, and death on the cross. The reconciliation offered to us has cost a high price, that of the cross raised on Golgotha, on which was hung the Son of God made man. In this immersion of God in human suffering and in the abyss of evil lies the root of our justification. The "return to God with all your heart" in our Lenten journey passes through the cross, following Christ on the road to Calvary, the total gift of self. It is a way on which to learn every day to come out more and more from our selfishness and our closures, to make room for God who opens and transforms the heart. And St. Paul recalls how the announcement of the Cross resounds to us through the preaching of the Word, of which the Apostle himself is an ambassador; it is a call for us to make this Lenten journey characterized by a more careful and assiduous listening to the Word of God, the light that illuminates our steps.[1]

---

1. Benedict XVI, "Ash Wednesday Homily."

Bibliography

Ambrose. *Expositio Evangelii secundum Lucam*. In *Patrologia Latina* 15, edited by Jacques Paul Migne. Paris: Apud Garnier Fratres, 1845.
Aristotle. *Nicomachean Ethics*. In *Aristotle II*, edited by Mortimer J. Adler et al., 339–444. Translated by W. D. Ross. Great Books of the Western World 8. 2nd ed. Chicago: Encyclopaedia Britannica, 1990.
Augustine. *Civitas Dei*. Cited by Romano Guardini in *The Conversion of Augustine*. No bibliographical details given as to the particular edition.
———. *Confessions*. Edited by Gillian Clark. Cambridge: Cambridge University Press, 1995.
———. *Expositions on the Book of Psalms*. In *St. Augustine*, edited by Philip Schaff, 409–19. The Nicene and Post-Nicene Fathers of the Christian Church, first series 8. Grand Rapids, MI: Eerdmans, 1984.
———. *Sermon 272*. http://www.earlychurchtexts.com/public/Augustine_sermon_272 _eucharist. htm.
Bacon, Francis. *Novum Organum*. Cited by Benedict XVI in *Spe salvi*. No bibliographical details given as to the particular edition.
Baier, Walter. "Key Issues in Medieval Sacred Heart Piety." In *Faith in Christ and the Worship of Christ: New Approaches to Devotion to Christ*, edited by Leo Scheffczyk, 81–99. San Francisco: Ignatius, 1986.
Balthasar, Hans Urs von. *Mysterium Paschale: The Mystery of Easter*. Translated and with an introduction by Aidan Nichols. Edinburgh: T. & T. Clark, 1990.
———. *Theo-Drama: Theological Dramatic Theory*. Vol. 5. Translated by Graham Harrison. San Francisco: Ignatius, 1998.
———. *A Theological Anthropology*. Translated by William Glen-Doepel. London: Sheed & Ward, 1967.
———. *Theologie der Drei Tage*. Einsiedeln: Benzinger, 1970.
Barton, Stephen C. "New Testament Interpretation as Performance." *Scottish Journal of Theology* 52 (1999) 179–208.
Bathrellos, Demetrios. *The Byzantine Christ: Person, Nature, and Will in the Christology of Saint Maximus the Confessor*. Oxford: Oxford University Press, 2004.
Baumgärtel, Friedrich, and Johannes Behm. "καρδια." In *Theological Dictionary of the New Testament*, edited by Gerhard Kittel. Translated and edited by Geoffrey W. Bromiley, 3:605–14. Grand Rapids: Eerdmans, 1965.
Beck, Hans-Georg. "Die Frühbyzantinische Kirche." In *Handbuch der Kirchengeschichte*, edited by Hubert Jedin, 2:3–92. Freiburg: Herder, 1975.

Becker, Joachim. "The Heart in the Language of the Bible." In *Faith in Christ and the Worship of Christ: New Approaches to Devotion to Christ*, edited by Leo Scheffczyk, 23–31. San Francisco: Ignatius, 1986.

Behr, John. *The Case Against Diodore and Theodore: Texts and their Contexts*. Oxford: Oxford University Press, 2011.

Benedict XVI. "Address of his holiness Benedict XVI to the participants in the international congress organized to commemorate the 40th anniversary of the Dogmatic Constitution on Divine Revelation '*Dei Verbum*.'" September 16, 2005. http://www.vatican.va/holy_father/benedict_xvi/speeches/2005/september/documents/.

———. "Ash Wednesday Homily." March 13, 2013. http://www.zenit.org/en/articles/benedict-xvi-s-homily-at-ash-wednesday-mass?utm_campaign=dailyhtml&utm_medium=email&utm_ source=dispatch.

———. *Deus caritas est*. Australian ed. Strathfield, NSW: St Pauls, 2006.

———. "Homily, Mass of Possession of the Chair of the Bishop of Rome." *L'Osservatore Romano*. Weekly edition in English (May 11, 2005) 3.

———. "Homily of His Holiness Benedict XVI." 2010. http://w2.vatican.va/content/benedict-xvi/en/homilies/2010/documents/hf_ben-xvi_hom_20100523_pentecoste.html.

———. "Monastic Theology and Scholastic Theology." General Audience. October 28, 2009. http.www.vatican.va/holy_father/benedict_xvi/audiences/2009/documents/hf_ben-xvi_aud_20091028_en.html.

———. *Porta fidei*. Australian ed. Strathfield, NSW: St Pauls, 2012.

———. *Sacramentum caritatis*. Australian ed. Strathfield, NSW: St Pauls, 2007.

———. *Spe salvi*. Australian ed. Strathfield, NSW: St Pauls, 2007.

———. "Two Theological Models in Comparison: Bernard and Abelard." General Audience. November 4, 2009. http.www.vatican.va/holy_father/benedict_xvi/audiences/2009/documents /hf_ben-xvi_aud _ 20091104_en.html.

———. *Verbum Domini*. Australian ed. Strathfield, NSW: St Pauls, 2010.

Berthold, George C., ed. *Maximus the Confessor: Selected Writings*. New York: Paulist, 1985.

Bloomfield, S. T. *The Greek New Testament with English Notes*. Vol. 1. First American edition from the second London edition. Boston: Perkins and Marvin, 1837.

Blowers, Paul M. "The Passion of Jesus Christ in Maximus the Confessor: A Reconsideration." In *Studia Patristica*, edited by M. F. Wiles and E. J. Yarnold, 37:361–77. Leuven: Peeters, 2001.

Blowers, Paul M., and Robert Louis Wilken. *On the Cosmic Mystery of Jesus Christ: St. Maximus the Confessor*. Crestwood, NY: St. Vladimir's Seminary, 2003.

Bobrinskoy, Boris. "The Indwelling of the Spirit in Christ: 'Pneumatic Christology' in the Cappadocian Fathers." *St. Vladimir's Theological Quarterly* 28 (1984) 49–65.

Bockmuehl, Markus. "Saints' Lives as Exegesis." In *The Pope and Jesus of Nazareth*, edited by Adrian Pabst and Angus Paddison, 119–33. London: SCM, 2009.

Boersma, Hans. "History and Faith in Pope Benedict's *Jesus of Nazareth*." *Nova et Vetera*, English edition 10 (2012) 985–91.

Bonagura, David G. "*Logos* to Son in the Christology of Joseph Ratzinger/Benedict XVI." *New Blackfriars* 93 (2012) 475–88.

Boosalis, Harry M. *The Joy of the Holy: St. Seraphim of Sarov and Orthodox Spiritual Life*. With translations of the *Conversation with Motovilov* and *Spiritual Instructions* by Sergei D. Arhipov. South Canaan, PA: St. Tikhon's Seminary, 1993.

Butler, Sara. "Benedict XVI: Apostle of the 'Pierced Heart of Jesus.'" In *The Pontificate of Benedict XVI: Its Premises and Promises*, edited by William G. Rusch, 144–67. Grand Rapids, MI: Eerdmans, 2009.

Casarella, Peter J. "Searching for the Face of the Lord in Ratzinger's *Jesus of Nazareth*." In *The Pope and Jesus of Nazareth*, edited by Adrian Pabst and Angus Paddison, 83–93. London: SCM, 2009.

Catechism of the Catholic Church. 2nd ed. Homebush, NSW: St. Pauls, 1997.

Chadwick, Henry. *Origen: Contra Celsum*. Cambridge: Cambridge University Press, 1965.

Chenu, Marie-Dominique. *Nature, Man and Society in the Twelfth Century*. Translated by Jerome Taylor and Lester K. Little. Toronto: University of Toronto Press, 1997.

Coffey, David. *Deus Trinitas: The Doctrine of the Triune God*. Oxford: Oxford University Press, 1999.

———. *Did You Receive the Holy Spirit When You Believed? Some Basic Questions for Pneumatology*. Milwaukee, WI: Marquette University Press, 2005.

———. "The Gift of the Holy Spirit." *Irish Theological Quarterly* 38 (1971) 202–23.

———. *Grace: The Gift of the Holy Spirit*. Sydney: Catholic Institute of Sydney, 1979.

———. "The 'Incarnation' of the Holy Spirit in Christ." *Theological Studies* 45 (1984) 466–80.

———. "Spirit Christology and the Trinity." In *Advents of the Spirit: An Introduction to the Current Study of Pneumatology*, edited by E. Hinze Bradford and D. Lyle Dabney, 315–38. Milwaukee, WI: Marquette University Press, 2001.

———. "The Spirit of Christ as Entelechy." *Philosophy and Theology* 13 (2001) 363–98.

Collins, Christopher S. *The Word Made Love: The Dialogical Theology of Joseph Ratzinger/Benedict XVI*. Collegeville, MN: Liturgical, 2013.

Congar, Yves. *I Believe in the Holy Spirit*. Vols. 1 and 3. Translated by David Smith. New York: Seabury, 1983.

———. *The Mystery of the Church*. 2nd rev. ed. Translated by A. V. Littledale. London: Geoffrey Chapman, 1965.

———. *The Word and the Spirit*. Translated by David Smith. London: Geoffrey Chapman, 1986.

Corkery, James. *Joseph Ratzinger's Theological Ideas: Wise Cautions and Legitimate Hopes*. Mahwah, NJ: Paulist, 2009.

Cortez, Marc. *Theological Anthropology: A Guide for the Perplexed*. London: T. & T. Clark, 2010.

Cyril of Alexandria. *Contra Julianum*. In *Patrologia Graeca*, edited by Jacques Paul Migne, 76:503–1058. Paris: Apud Garnier Fratres, 1863.

Daniélou, Jean. *Essai sur le mystère de l'histoire*. Paris: Éditions du Seuil, 1953.

Davis, Ellen F., and Richard B. Hays. "Nine Theses on the Interpretation of Scripture." In *The Art of Reading Scripture*, edited by Ellen F. Davis and Richard B. Hays, 1–5. Grand Rapids: Eerdmans, 2003.

Deines, Roland. "Can the 'Real' Jesus be Identified with the Historical Jesus? A Review of the Pope's Challenge to Biblical Scholarship and the Ongoing Debate." In *The Pope and Jesus of Nazareth*, edited by Adrian Pabst and Angus Paddison, 199–232. London: SCM, 2009.

Del Colle, Ralph. *Christ and the Spirit: Spirit Christology in Trinitarian Perspective.* Oxford: Oxford University Press, 1994.

Denzinger, Heinrich. *Enchiridion symbolorum definitionum et declarationum de rebus fidei et morum: Compendium of Creeds, Definitions and Declarations on Matters of Faith and Morals.* Edited by Robert Fastiggi et al. 43rd rev. ed. San Francisco: Ignatius, 2012.

Descartes, René. *Discourse on the Method of Rightly Conducting the Reason and Seeking for Truth in the Sciences.* In *Bacon, Descartes, Spinoza,* edited by Mortimer J. Adler et al., 265–91. Translated by Elizabeth S. Haldane and G. R. T. Ross. Great Books of the Western World 28. 2nd ed. Chicago: Encyclopaedia Britannica, 1990.

The Documents of Vatican II with Notes and Index: Vatican Translation. Australian ed. Strathfield, NSW: St Pauls, 2009.

Dunn, James D. G. *Jesus and the Holy Spirit: A Study of the Religious and Charismatic Experience of Jesus and the First Christians as Reflected in the New Testament.* London: SCM, 1978.

Elders, Leo. "The Inner Life of Jesus in the Theology and Devotion of Saint Thomas Aquinas." In *Faith in Christ and the Worship of Christ: New Approaches to Devotion to Christ,* edited by Leo Scheffczyk, 65–79. San Francisco: Ignatius, 1986.

Emery, Giles. "The Immutability of the God of Love and the Problem of Language Concerning the 'Suffering of God.'" In *Divine Impassibility and the Mystery of Human Suffering,* edited by James F. Keating and Thomas Joseph White, 27–76. Grand Rapids: Eerdmans, 2009.

"Encyclical Letter (*Haurietis Aquas*) of Pope Pius XII on Devotion to the Sacred Heart of Jesus." In *Heart of the Saviour,* edited by Joseph Stierli, 211–59. Translated by Geoffrey Crawfurd. New York: Herder & Herder, 1957.

Evagrius Ponticus. *De oratione.* In *The Praktikos and Chapters on Prayer,* translated by John Eudes Bamberger, 52–80. Spencer, MA: Cistercian, 1970.

Fagerberg, David W. *Theologia Prima: What is Liturgical Theology?* 2nd ed. Chicago: Hillenbrand, 2004.

Fairbairn, Donald. *Grace and Christology in the Early Church.* Oxford: Oxford University Press, 2003.

Farkasfalvy, Denis. "*Jesus of Nazareth* and the Renewal of New Testament Theology." *International Catholic Review: Communio* 34 (2007) 438–53.

Ferreira, M. Jamie. "The Grammar of the Heart: Newman on Faith and Imagination." In *Discourse and Context: An Interdisciplinary Study of John Henry Newman,* edited by Gerard Magill, 129–43. Carbondale, IL: Southern Illinois University Press, 1993.

Flannery, Austin, ed. *Vatican Council II: The Conciliar and Post Conciliar Documents.* New rev. ed. Dublin: Dominican, 1992.

Fowl, Stephen E., and L. Gregory Jones. *Reading in Communion: Scripture and Ethics in Christian Life.* Grand Rapids, MI: Eerdmans, 1991.

Gaál, Emery de. *The Theology of Pope Benedict XVI: The Christocentric Shift.* New York: Palgrave Macmillan, 2010.

Gadenz, Pablo T. "Jesus the New Temple in the Thought of Pope Benedict XVI." *Nova et Vetera,* English edition 11 (2013) 211–30.

Gagey, Henri-Jérôme. "Once There Was No Historical Jesus." In *The Pope and Jesus of Nazareth,* edited by Adrian Pabst and Angus Paddison, 13–20. London: SCM, 2009.

Galot, Jean. *Dieu souffre-t-il?* Paris: Lethielleux, 1976.
Gavrilyuk, Paul. *The Suffering of the Impassible God: The Dialectics of Patristic Thought*. Oxford: Oxford University Press, 2004.
Gregory of Nyssa. *De hominis opificio*. In *Patrologia Graeca*, edited by Jacques Paul Migne, 44:123-256. Paris: Apud Garnier Fratres, 1863.
Groppe, Elizabeth Teresa. *Yves Congar's Theology of the Holy Spirit*. Oxford: Oxford University Press, 2004.
Gross, Heinrich. "Das Hohelied der Liebe Gottes." In *Mysterium der Gnade (Festschrift J. Auer)*, edited by H. Roßmann and J. Ratzinger, 83-91. Regensburg: Pustet, 1975.
Guardini, Romano. *The Conversion of Augustine*. Translated by Elinor Briefs. London: Sands, 1960.
———. *Pascal for Our Time*. Translated by Brian Thompson. New York: Herder & Herder, 1966.
———. *The Word of God: On Faith, Hope and Charity*. Translated by Stella Lange. Chicago: Henry Regnery, 1963.
Guillou, Marie-Joseph le. "Quelques Réflexions sur Constantinople III et la Sotéreriologie de Maxime." In *Maximus Confessor: Actes du Symposium sur Maxime le Confesseur, Fribourg, 2-5 Septembre 1980*, edited by Felix Heinzer and Christoph Schönborn, 235-37. Fribourg: Éditions Universitaires, 1982.
Habets, Myk. *The Anointed Son: A Trinitarian Spirit Christology*. Eugene, OR: Pickwick, 2010.
———. "Spirit Christology: Seeing in Stereo." *Journal of Pentecostal Theology* 11 (2003) 199-234.
Hahn, Scott W. *Covenant and Communion: The Biblical Theology of Pope Benedict XVI*. San Francisco: Ignatius, 2009.
Haight, Roger. "The Case for Spirit Christology." *Theological Studies* 53 (1992) 257-87.
———. *The Future of Christology*. New York: Continuum, 2005.
Hanson, R. P. C., ed. *Selections from Justin Martyr's Dialogue with Trypho, a Jew*. London: Lutterworth, 1963.
Harnack, Adolf von. *Das Wesen des Christentums*. Stuttgart: Ehrenfried Klotz, 1950.
Harrington, Daniel J. "Benedict's Passion." *America* 204 (2011) 28-29.
Hays, Richard B. "Ratzinger's Johannine Jesus: A Challenge to Enlightenment Historiography." In *The Pope and Jesus of Nazareth*, edited by Adrian Pabst and Angus Paddison, 109-18. London: SCM, 2009.
Heer, Joseph. "The Soteriological Significance of the Johannine Image of the Pierced Savior." In *Faith in Christ and the Worship of Christ: New Approaches to Devotion to Christ*, edited by Leo Scheffczyk, 33-46. San Francisco: Ignatius, 1986.
Hengel, Martin. *The Johannine Question*. Translated by John Bowden. London: SCM, 1989.
Hildebrand, Dietrich von. *The Sacred Heart: Source of Christian Affectivity*. Baltimore: Helicon, 1965.
Hoping, Helmut. "Gemeinschaft mit Christus: Christologie und Liturgie bei Joseph Ratzinger." *Internationale katholische Zeitschrift Communio* 35 (2006) 558-72.
Hughes, Brian W. "*Une Source Cachée*: Blaise Pascal's Influence upon John Henry Newman." *Newman Studies Journal* 7 (2010) 29-44.
Huovinen, Eero. "The Pope and Jesus." *Pro Ecclesia* 17 (2008) 139-51.
Ivánka, Endre von. *Plato christianus*. Einsiedeln: Johannes, 1964.

Jasper, R. C. D., and G. J. Cuming, eds. *Prayers of the Eucharist: Early and Reformed.* 2nd ed. New York: Oxford University Press, 1980.
Jerome. *Epistolae 64.* In *Corpus Scriptorum Ecclesiasticorum Latinorum* 54.
John Chrysostom. *Catechesis.* In *Sources Chrétiennes* 50. Reprint of the first edition, revised and corrected. Paris: Cerf, 2005.
John Paul II. *Dives in misericordia.* Homebush, NSW: St Pauls, 1980.
———. *Dominicae cenae.* Boston: Pauline, 2003.
———. *Dominum et vivificantem.* Homebush, NSW: St Pauls, 1986.
———. *Fides et ratio.* Australian ed. Strathfield, NSW: St Pauls, 1998.
———. *Redemptor hominis.* Melbourne: ACTS, 1979.
Johnson, Luke Timothy. "Jesus of Nazareth: From the Baptism in the Jordan to the Transfiguration." *Modern Theology* 24 (2008) 318–20.
Jonge, Marinus de. "The Main Issues in the Study of the Testaments of the Twelve Patriarchs." In *Jewish Eschatology, Early Christian Christology and the Testaments of the Twelve Patriarchs: Collected Essays of Marinus de Jonge,* 147–63. Leiden: Brill, 1991.
Josephus. *Antiquities of the Jews.* In *The Works of Josephus.* Translated by William Whiston. Peabody, MA: Hendrickson, 1987.
Kant, Immanuel. *Werke.* Vols. 4 and 6. Edited by W. Weischedel. Wiesbaden: Insel, 1956.
Kasper, Walter. "Das Wesen des Christlichen. B.'" *Theologische Revue* 65 (1969) 182–88.
———. *Jesus the Christ.* London: Burns & Oates, 1976.
———. "Theorie und Praxis innerhalb einer *theologia crucis*: Antwort auf Joseph Ratzingers Glaube, Geschichte und Philosophie. Zum Echo auf *Einfürhung in das Christentum.*" *Hochland* 62 (1970) 152–57.
Kavanagh, Aidan. *On Liturgical Theology: The Hale Memorial Lectures of Seabury-Western Theological Seminary, 1981.* New York: Pueblo, 1984.
Kee, Howard C. "Testaments of the Twelve Patriarchs." In *The Old Testament Pseudepigrapha,* edited by James H. Charlesworth, 1:775–828. Garden City, NY: Doubleday, 1983.
Kereszty, Roch. "The Challenge of *Jesus of Nazareth* for Theologians." *International Catholic Review: Communio* 34 (2007) 454–74.
Kerr, Fergus. "If Jesus Knew He Was God, How Did It Work?" In *The Pope and Jesus of Nazareth,* edited by Adrian Pabst and Angus Paddison, 50–67. London: SCM, 2009.
Komonchak, Joseph. "Returning from Exile: Catholic Theology in the 1930s." In *The Twentieth Century: A Theological Overview,* edited by Gregory Baum, 35–48. Maryknoll, NY: Orbis, 1999.
Köster, Helmut. "σπλάγχνον." In *Theological Dictionary of the New Testament,* edited by Gerhard Kittel et al., 7:548–59. Translated by Geoffrey W. Bromiley. Grand Rapids, MI: Eerdmans, 1965.
Kreeft, Peter. *Christianity for Modern Pagans; Pascal's Pensées Outlined, Edited and Explained.* San Francisco: Ignatius, 1993.
———. *Socratic Logic: A Logic Text using Socratic Method, Platonic Questions, and Aristotelian Principles.* 2nd ed. South Bend, IN: St Augustine's, 2005.
Krieg, Robert. "Cardinal Ratzinger, Max Scheler and Christology." *Irish Theological Quarterly* 47 (1980) 205–19.

---. "Who do you say I am? Christology: What It Is and Why It Matters." *Commonweal* 129 (March 22, 2002) 12–16.
Lactantius. *De opificio Dei*. In *Corpus Scriptorum Ecclesiasticorum Latinorum* 27.
Lam, Cong Quy Joseph. *Joseph Ratzinger's Theological Retractations*. Bern: Peter Lang, 2013.
Lampe, Geoffrey. *God as Spirit*. London: SCM, 1977.
---. "The Holy Spirit and the Person of Christ." In *Christ, Faith and History*, edited by S. W. Sykes and J. P. Clayton, 111–30. Cambridge: Cambridge University Press, 1972.
Lash, Nicholas. *Theology on the Way to Emmaus*. London: SCM, 1986.
Lewis, C. S. *The Four Loves*. Glasgow: Collins, 1977.
---. *The Great Divorce: A Dream*. Glasgow: Collins, 1972.
---. *Perelandra*. London: Pan, 1953.
Lincicum, David. "Benedict's Jesus and the Rehabilitation of Christian Figural Reading." *Journal of Theological Interpretation* 2 (2008) 285–91.
Louth, Andrew. *Maximus the Confessor*. London: Routledge, 1996.
---. "Why Did the Syrians Reject the Council of Chalcedon?" In *Chalcedon in Context: Church Councils 400–700*, edited by Richard Price and Mary Whitby, 107–16. Liverpool: Liverpool University Press, 2009.
Lubac, Henri de. *Corpus Mysticum: The Eucharist and the Church in the Middle Ages*. Edited by Lawrence Paul Hemming and Susan Frank Parsons. Translated by Gemma Simmonds et al. Notre Dame, IN: University of Notre Dame Press, 2006.
Macquarrie, John. *Jesus Christ in Modern Thought*. London: SCM, 1990.
Marcel, Gabriel. *The Mystery of Being: Reflection and Mystery*. Translated by G. S. Fraser. South Bend, IN: St. Augustine's, 2001.
Maritain, Jacques. "Quelques réflexions sur le savoir théologique." *Revue Thomiste* 77 (1969) 5–27.
Martin, Francis. "Joseph Ratzinger, Benedict XVI, on Biblical Interpretation: Two Leading Principles." *Nova et Vetera*, English edition 5 (2007) 285–314.
Martínez, Francisco Javier. "Christ of History, Jesus of Faith." In *The Pope and Jesus of Nazareth*, edited by Adrian Pabst and Angus Paddison, 21–49. London: SCM, 2009.
Marx, Karl, and Friedrich Engels. *Werke* 3. Berlin: Dietz, 1961–71.
Maximus the Confessor. *Ambiguum*. In *Patrologia Graeca*, edited by Jacques Paul Migne, 91:1031–1418. Paris: Apud Garnier Fratres, 1865.
---. *Disputio cum Pyrrho* (*Disputation with Pyrrhus*). In *Patrologia Graeca*, edited by Jacques Paul Migne, 91:287–354. Paris: Apud Garnier Fratres, 1865.
---. *Mystagogia* (*The Church's Mystagogy*). In *Patrologia Graeca*, edited by Jacques Paul Migne, 91:657–718. Paris: Apud Garnier Fratres, 1865.
---. *Opuscula Theologica et Polemica*. In *Patrologia Graeca*, edited by Jacques Paul Migne, 91:9–286. Paris: Apud Garnier Fratres, 1865.
---. *Orationis Dominicae Expositio* (*Commentary on the Our Father*). In *Patrologia Graeca*, edited by Jacques Paul Migne, 90:871–910. Paris: Apud Garnier Fratres, 1865.
---. *Quaestiones ad Thalassium de Scriptura sacra LXI* (*61st Question to Thalassius*). In *Patrologia Graeca*, edited by Jacques Paul Migne, 90:625–46. Paris: Apud Garnier Fratres, 1865.

McAuley, James Phillip, and Richard Connolly. "The Sacred Heart of Jesus." In *The Living Parish Hymn Book*, edited by Anthony Newman, no. 142. Sydney: Halstead, 1969.

McDonnell, Kilian. "The Determinative Doctrine of the Holy Spirit." *Theology Today* 39 (1982) 142–59.

———. "A Trinitarian Theology of the Holy Spirit?" *Theological Studies* 46 (1985) 191–227.

McFarland, Ian A. "'Willing Is Not Choosing': Some Anthropological Implications of Dyothelite Christology." *International Journal of Systematic Theology* 9 (2007) 3–23.

Miles, Jack. "Between Theology and Exegesis." *Commonweal* 134 (July 13, 2007) 20–24.

Moberly, R. W. L. "The Use of the Old Testament in *Jesus of Nazareth*." In *The Pope and Jesus of Nazareth*, edited by Adrian Pabst and Angus Paddison, 97–108. London: SCM, 2009.

Moltmann, Jürgen. *The Crucified God*. Translated by R. A. Wilson and John Bowden. London: SCM, 1974.

Monk Vartholomaeos. "The Heart in the Hesychastic Treatises of St Gregory of Palamas." http://www.oldenglishchurch.org.uk/the_heart_in_the_hesychastic_treatises _of_st_gregory_palamas.pdf.

Montague, S. M., George T. *The Holy Spirit: Growth of a Biblical Tradition*. New York: Paulist, 1976.

Moreland, J. P., and William Lane Craig. *Philosophical Foundations for a Christian Worldview*. Downers Grove, IL: InterVarsity, 2003.

Murphy, Joseph. *Christ Our Joy: The Theological Vision of Pope Benedict XVI*. San Francisco: Ignatius, 2008.

Neusner, Jacob. *A Rabbi Talks with Jesus*. Montreal: McGill-Queen's University Press, 2000.

Newman, John Henry. *An Essay in Aid of a Grammar of Assent*. Westminster, MD: Christian Classics, 1973.

———. *Newman's University Sermons: Fifteen Sermons Preached before the University of Oxford 1826–43*. Introduction by D. M. MacKinnon and J. D. Holmes. London: SPCK, 1970.

Newman, Paul. *A Spirit Christology: Recovering the Biblical Paradigm*. Lanham, MD: University Press of America, 1987.

Nichols, Aidan. "Walter Kasper and His Theological Programme." *New Blackfriars* 67 (1986) 16–24.

Nissiotos, Nikos. "Pneumatological Christology as a Presupposition of Ecclesiology." In *Oecumenica 1967*, edited by Friedrich Wilhelm Kantzenbach and Vilmos Vajta, 235–52. Minneapolis, MN: Augsburg, 1967.

Oakes, Edward T. *Infinity Dwindled to Infancy: A Catholic and Evangelical Christology*. Grand Rapids, MI: Eerdmans, 2011.

O'Brien, George Dennis. "Who's Listening?" In *The Pope and Jesus of Nazareth*, edited by Adrian Pabst and Angus Paddison, 262–77. London: SCM, 2009.

O'Byrne, Declan. *Spirit Christology and Trinity in the Theology of David Coffey*. New York: Peter Lang, 2010.

O'Donnell, John. "In Him and Over Him: The Holy Spirit in the Life of Jesus." *Gregorianum* 70 (1989) 25–45.

O'Hanlon, Gerard F. *The Immutability of God in the Theology of Hans Urs von Balthasar.* Cambridge: Cambridge University Press, 1990.
Oliver, Simon. "Christ, Descent and Participation." In *The Pope and Jesus of Nazareth*, edited by Adrian Pabst and Angus Paddison, 68–82. London: SCM, 2009.
Origen. In Joa. In *Griechischen Christlichen Schriftsteller, Origenes Werke* 4. Leipzig: Hinrichs, 1903.
Paddison, Angus. "Following Jesus with Pope Benedict." In *The Pope and Jesus of Nazareth*, edited by Adrian Pabst and Angus Paddison, 176–95. London: SCM, 2009.
Pannenberg, Wolfhart. *Jesus: God and Man.* Translated by Lewis L. Wilkins and Duane A. Priebe. London: SCM, 1968.
Pascal, Blaise. "Discourse on the Passion of Love." In *Thoughts, Letters and Minor Works*, 417–26. Harvard Classics 48. New York: Collier, 1909–1917.
———. *Pensées.* Edited by Léon Brunschvicg. Paris: Hachette, 1897.
———. *Pensées,* Translated by A. J. Krailsheimer. London: Penguin Classics, 1966.
———. *Pensées et Opuscules.* Edited by Léon Brunschvicg. 6th ed. Paris: Hachette, 1912.
Peter Lombard. *Sententiarum Quatuor Libri, Liber Secundus Sententiarum, Distinctio XXIV.* In *Opera Omnia S. Bonaventurae, Ad Claras Aquas* 2, 549–53. 1885.
Peters, James R. *The Logic of the Heart: Augustine, Pascal and the Rationality of Faith.* Grand Rapids, MI: Baker Academic, 2009.
Pinnock, Clark H. *Flame of Love: A Theology of the Holy Spirit.* Dowers Grove, IL: InterVarsity, 1996.
Pius XI. *Miserentissimus redemptor. Acta Apostolicae Sedis.* (A.A.S.) 20 (1928) 165–78.
Pius XII. *Haurietis aquas. Acta Apostolicae Sedis.* (A.A.S.) 48 (1956) 309–53.
Potterie, Ignace de la. "The Anointing of Christ." In *Word and Mystery: Biblical Essays on the Person and Mission of Christ*, edited by Leo J. O'Donovan, 155–84. New York: Newman, 1968.
Rahner, Hugo. "The Beginnings of the Devotion in Patristic Times." In *Heart of the Saviour*, edited by Joseph Stierli, 37–57. Translated by Paul Andrews. New York: Herder & Herder, 1957.
———. "On the Biblical Basis of the Devotion." In *Heart of the Saviour*, edited by Joseph Stierli, 15–35. Translated by Paul Andrews. New York: Herder & Herder, 1957.
———. *Symbole der Kirche: Die Ekklesiologie der Väter.* Salzburg: Müller, 1964.
Rahner, Karl. *Hearers of the Word: Laying the Foundation for a Philosophy of Religion.* Translated by Joseph Donceel. New York: Continuum, 1994.
———. "Some Theses on the Theology of the Devotion." In *Heart of the Saviour*, edited by Joseph Stierli, 131–55. Translated by Paul Andrews. New York: Herder & Herder, 1957.
———. "The Theology of Symbol." In *Theological Investigations*, 4:221–52. Translated by Kevin Smyth. New York: Seabury, 1975.
———. "Two Basic Types of Christology." In *Theological Investigations*, 13:213–23. Translated by David Bourke. New York: Seabury, 1975.
Rahner, Karl, and Herbert Vorgrimler. "Man." In *Concise Theological Dictionary*, edited by Cornelius Ernst, 270–71. Translated by Richard Strachan. London: Burns & Oates, 1965.

Bibliography

Ratzinger, Joseph. *Behold the Pierced One: An Approach to a Spiritual Christology.* Translated by Graham Harrison. San Francisco: Ignatius, 1986. German original: *Schauen auf den Durchbohrten.* Einsiedeln: Johannes, 1984.

———. "Bilan et perspectives." *Actes des journées liturgiques de Fontgombault* (July 2001) 22–24.

———. "The Church and Man's Calling—Introductory Article and Chapter One—The Dignity of the Human Person—Pastoral Constitution on the Church in the Modern World." In *Commentary on the Documents of Vatican II*, edited by Herbert Vorgrimler, 5:115–63. Translated by J. W. O'Hara. London: Burns & Oates, 1969.

———. "Concerning the Notion of Person in Theology." Translated by Michael Waldstein. *International Catholic Review: Communio* 17 (1990) 439–54. German original: "Zum Personenverständnis in der Theologie." In *Dogma und Verkündigung*, 205–23. München: Erich Wewel, 1973.

———. *Daughter Zion: Meditations on the Church's Marian Belief.* Translated by John M. McDermott. San Francisco: Ignatius, 1983. German original: *Die Tochter Zion.* Einsiedeln: Johannes, 1977.

———. "The End of Time." In *The End of Time? The Provocation of Talking about God: Proceedings of a Meeting of Joseph Cardinal Ratzinger, Johann Baptist Metz, Jürgen Moltmann, and Eveline Goodman-Thau in Ahaus*, edited by Tiemo Rainer Peters and Claus Urban, 4–25. Translated by J. Matthew Ashley. Mahwah, NJ: Paulist, 2004. German original to be found in: *Ende der Zeit?* Mainz: Matthias-Grünewald, 1999.

———. *Eucharistie: Mitte der Kirche.* München: Erich Wewel, 1978. Published in English in *God is Near Us: The Eucharist, The Heart of Life*, 27–93.

———. *Feast of Faith: Approaches to a Theology of the Liturgy.* Translated by Graham Harrison. San Francisco: Ignatius, 1986. German original: *Das Fest des Glaubens.* Einsiedeln: Johannes, 1981.

———. "Freedom and Constraint in the Church." In *Church, Ecumenism, and Politics: New Endeavours in Ecclesiology*, 175–92. Translated by Michael J. Miller et al. San Francisco: Ignatius, 2008. German original: *Kirche, Ökumene und Politik.* Cinisello Balsamo, Italy: Edizioni Paoline, 1987.

———. "Geist und Freiheit—Freiheit und Bindung." In *Über den Heiligen Geist*, 59–64. Augsburg: Sankt Ulrich, 2012.

———. *God is Near Us: The Eucharist, The Heart of Life.* Translated by Henry Taylor. San Francisco: Ignatius, 2003. German original: *Gott ist uns nah. Eucharistie: Mitte des Lebens.* Edited by Stephan Otto Horn and Vinzennz Pfnür. Augsburg: Sankt Ulrich, 2001.

———. *The God of Jesus Christ: Meditations on the Triune God.* Translated by Brian McNeil. San Francisco: Ignatius, 2006. German original: *Der Gott Jesu Christi: Betrachtungen über den Dreieinigen Gott.* München: Kösel, 1976.

———. *Gospel, Catechesis, Catechism: Sidelights in the Catechism of the Catholic Church.* San Francisco: Ignatius, 1997. Original German: *Evangelium—Katechese—Katechismus: Streiflichter auf den Katechismus der katholischen Kirche.* München: Neue Stadt, 1995.

———. "The Holy Spirit and the Church." In *Images of Hope: Meditations on Major Feasts*, 63–73. Translated by John Rock and Graham Harrison. San Francisco: Ignatius, 2006. German original: *Bilder der Hoffnung.* Freiburg im Breisgau: Herder, 1997.

———. "The Holy Spirit as Communio: Concerning the Relationship of Pneumatology and Spirituality in Augustine." Translated by Peter Casarella. *International Catholic Review: Communio* 25 (1998) 324–39. German original: "Der Heilige Geist als communion: Zum Verhältnis von Pneumatologie und Spiritualität bei Augustinus." In *Erfahrung und Theologie des Heiligen Geistes*, edited by C. Heitmann and H. Mühlen, 223–39. München: Agentur des Rauhen Hauses Hamburg, 1974.

———. *Introduction to Christianity*. Translated by J. R. Foster and Michael J. Miller. San Francisco: Ignatius, 2004. German original: *Einführung in das Christenum*. München: Kösel, 1968.

———. *Jesus of Nazareth: From the Baptism in the Jordan to the Transfiguration*. Translated by Adrian J. Walker. New York: Doubleday, 2007. Simultaneously published in German as *Jesus von Nazareth. Erster Teil. Von der Taufe im Jordan bis zur Verklärung*. Freiburg im Breisgau: Herder, 2007.

———. *Jesus of Nazareth: Holy Week: From the Entrance into Jerusalem to the Resurrection*. Translated by Philip J. Whitmore. San Francisco: Ignatius, 2011. German original: *Jesus von Nazareth. Zweiter Teil. Vom Einzug in Jerusalem bis zur Auferstehung*. Città del Vaticano: Libreria Editrice Vaticana, 2011.

———. *Jesus of Nazareth: The Infancy Narratives*. Translated by Philip J. Whitmore. New York: Image, 2012. German original: *Jesus von Nazareth. Prolog. Der Kindheitgeschichten*. Città del Vaticano: Libreria Editrice Vaticana, 2012.

———. "L'eucaristia al centro della comunità e della sua mission." Special offprint. Collevalenza, 1983.

———. "Loi de l'Eglise et liberté du chrétie." Service culturel de l'Ambassade de France près la Saint-Siège, November 24, 1983.

———. *Many Religions—One Covenant: Israel, the Church, and the World*. Translated by Graham Harrison. San Francisco: Ignatius, 1999. German original: *Die Vielfalt der Religionen und der Eine Bund*. Hagen: Urfeld, 1998.

———. "Mind, Spirit and Love: A Meditation on Pentecost." In *Dogma and Preaching: Applying Christian Doctrine to Daily Life*, edited by Michael J. Miller, 316–20. Translated by Michael J. Miller and Matthew J. Connell. San Francisco: Ignatius, 2011. German original: "Der Verstand, der Geist und die Liebe." In *Dogma und Verkündigung*, 367–72. München: Erich Wewel, 1973.

———. *The Nature and Mission of Theology: Essays to Orient Theology in Today's Debates*. Translated by Adrian Walker. San Francisco: Ignatius, 1995. German original: *Wesen und Auftrag der Theologie: Versuche zu ihrer Ortsbestimmung im Disput der Gegenwart*. Einsiedeln: Johannes, 1993.

———. *A New Song for the Lord: Faith in Christ and Liturgy Today*. Translated by Martha M. Matesich. New York: Crossroad, 1996. German original: *Ein Neues Lied für den Herrn: Christusglaube und Liturgie in der Gegenwart*. Freiburg im Breisgau: Herder, 1995.

———. *Pilgrim Fellowship of Faith: The Church as Communion*. Translated by Henry Taylor. San Francisco: Ignatius, 2005. German original: *Weg Gemeinschaft des Glaubens: Kirche als Communio*. Augsburg: Sankt Ulrich, 2002.

———. *Principles of Catholic Theology: Building Stones for a Fundamental Theology*. Translated by Mary Frances McCarthy. San Francisco: Ignatius, 1987. German original: *Theologische Prinzipienlehre*. München: Erich Wewel, 1982.

———. *Salt of the Earth: Christianity and the Catholic Church at the End of Millennium: An Interview with Peter Seewald*. Translated by Adrian Walker. San Francisco: Ignatius, 1997. German original: *Salz der Erde: Christentum und katholische Kirche an der Jahrtausendwende*. München: Deutsche Anstalt, 1996.

———. "Schlußwort zu der Diskussion mit W. Kasper." *Hochland* 62 (1970) 157–59.

———. "Schriftauslegung im Widerstreit: Zur Frage nach Grundlagen und Weg der Exegese heute." In *Schriftauslegung im Widerstreit, Quaestiones Disputatae*, edited by Joseph Ratzinger, 117:15–44. Freiburg im Breisgau: Herder, 1989. A partial translation can be found in *Biblical Interpretation in Crisis: The Ratzinger Conference on Bible and Church*, edited by Richard John Neuhaus, 1–23. Grand Rapids, MI: Eerdmans, 1989.

———. *The Spirit of the Liturgy*. Translated by John Saward. San Francisco: Ignatius, 2000. German original: *Einführung in den Geist der Liturgie*. Freiburg im Breisgau: Herder, 2000.

———. *The Theology of History in St. Bonaventure*. Translated by Zachary Hayes. Chicago: Franciscan Herald, 1989. German original: *Die Geschichtstheologie des heiligen Bonaventura*. München: Schnell & Steiner, 1959.

———. "Thesen zur Christologie." In *Dogma und Verkündigung*, 133–36. München: Erich Wewel, 1973. An English translation can be found in Joseph Ratzinger, *Dogma and Preaching: Applying Christian Doctrine to Daily Life*, edited by Michael J. Miller, 117–20. Translated by Michael J. Miller and Matthew J. Connell. San Francisco: Ignatius, 2011.

———. "Truth and Freedom." Translated by Adrian Walker. *International Catholic Review: Communio* 23 (1996) 16–35. German original: "Freiheit und Wahrheit." *Internationale katholische Zeitschift Communio* 24 (1995) 526–42.

———. "Was ist Theologie?" *Internationale katholische Zeitschift Communio* 8 (1979) 121–28. Published in English in Joseph Ratzinger, *Principles of Catholic Theology: Building Stones for a Fundamental Theology*, 315–22. Translated by Mary Frances McCarthy. San Francisco: Ignatius, 1987.

Rausch, Thomas P. *Pope Benedict XVI: An Introduction to His Theological Vision*. Mahwah, NJ: Paulist, 2009.

Revelations of the Sacred Heart to Blessed Margaret Mary and the History of Her Life: from the French of Monseigneur Bougaud, Bishop of Laval. 2nd ed. Translated by a Visitandine of Baltimore. New York: Benziger, 1890. The original French account can be found in St. Margaret Mary Alacoque. "Mémorie." In *Life and Works of Blessed Margaret Mary Alacoque*. 2 vols. Paris: Poussielgue, 1867.

Richard of St. Victor. *De Gradibus Charitatis*. In *Patrologia Latina*, edited by Jacques Paul Migne, 196:1195–1208. Paris: Apud Garnier Fratres, 1855.

Riches, Aaron. "After Chalcedon: The Oneness of Christ and the Dyothelite Mediation of his Theandric Unity." *Modern Theology* 24 (2008) 199–224.

———. *Ecce Homo: On the Divine Unity of Christ*. Grand Rapids, MI: Eerdmans, 2016.

Rist, John M. *Augustine: Ancient Thought Baptized*. Cambridge: Cambridge University Press, 1994.

Root, Michael. "Jesus and the Pope: Ecumenical Reflections on Benedict XVI's *Jesus of Nazareth*." *Pro Ecclesia* 17 (2008) 152–58.

Rosato, Philip J. "Spirit Christology: Ambiguity and Promise." *Theological Studies* 38 (1977) 423–49.

Rowland, Tracey. *Benedict XVI: A Guide for the Perplexed*. London: T. & T. Clark, 2010.

———. *Ratzinger's Faith: The Theology of Pope Benedict XVI*. Oxford: Oxford University Press, 2008.

———. "The Rôle of Natural Law and Natural Right in the Search for a Universal Ethics." In *Searching for a Universal Ethic: Multidisciplinary, Ecumenical, and Interfaith Responses to the Catholic Natural Law Tradition*, edited by John Berkman and William C. Mattison III, 156–66. Grand Rapids, MI: Eerdmans, 2014.

Sands, Paul Francis. *The Justification of Religious Faith in Søren Kierkegaard, John Henry Newman, and William James*. Piscatway, NJ: Gorgias, 2004.

Schlier, Heinrich. *Der Römerbrief*. Freiburg: Herder, 1977.

Schmemann, Alexander, *Introduction to Liturgical Theology*. Translated by Asheleigh E. Moorhouse. Crestwood, NY: St. Vladimir's Seminary, 1966.

———. *Liturgy and Tradition: Theological Reflections of Alexander Schmemann*. Edited by Thomas Fisch. Crestwood, NY: St. Vladimir's Seminary, 1990.

Schoonenberg, Piet. "Spirit Christology and Logos Christology." *Bijdragen* 38 (1977) 350–75.

Schwager, Raymund. *Der wunderbare Tausch: zur Geschichte und Deutung der Erlösungslehre*. München: Kösel, 1986.

Sciglitano, Anthony. "Pope Benedict XVI's *Jesus of Nazareth*: Agape and Logos." *Pro Ecclesia* 17 (2008) 159–85.

Sharkey, Michael, ed. *International Theological Commission: Texts and Documents, 1969–1985*. San Francisco: Ignatius, 1989.

Shute, Graham J. "Newman's Logic of the Heart." *Expository Times* 78 (May 1967) 232–35.

Staudt, R. Jared. "Reality and Sign: Thomas Aquinas and the Christological Exegesis of Pope Benedict XVI." *Nova et Vetera*, English edition 12 (2014) 331–63.

Suetonius. "Claudius." In *The Twelve Caesars*, edited by James Rives, 181–207. Translated by Robert Graves. Hammondsworth: Penguin, 1957.

Tacitus. *Annals*. In *Tacitus*, edited by Mortimer J. Adler et al., 1–184. Translated by Alfred John Church and William Jackson Brodribb. Great Books of the Western World 14. 2nd ed. Chicago: Encyclopaedia Britannica, 1990.

Thomas Aquinas. *De Veritate*. Translated by Robert W. Schmidt. Chicago: Henry Regnery, 1954.

———. *On the Truth of the Catholic Faith (Summa contra Gentiles), Book One: God*. Translated by Anton G. Pegis. Garden City, NY: Doubleday, 1955.

———. "Prayer for a Priestly Heart." http://www.catholicity.com/prayer/prayer-for-a-priestly-heart.html.

———. *The Summa Theologica of St. Thomas Aquinas*. Translated by Fathers of the English Dominican Province. New York: Benziger, 1948.

Thompson, Thomas R. "Nineteenth-Century Kenotic Christology: The Waxing, Waning, and Weighing of a Quest for a Coherent Orthodoxy." In *Exploring Kenotic Christology: The Self-Emptying of God*, edited by C. Stephan Evans, 74–111. Oxford: Oxford University Press, 2006.

Wallace-Hadrill, D. S. *Christian Antioch: A Study of Early Christian Thought in the East*. Cambridge: Cambridge University Press, 1982.

Wainwright, Geoffrey. "The 'New Worship' in Joseph Ratzinger's *Jesus of Nazareth*." *Nova et Vetera*, English edition 10 (2012) 993–1013.

Warnach, Viktor. *Agape: Die Liebe als Grundmotive der neutestamentlichen Theologie*. Düsseldorf: Patmos, 1951.

Watts, Thomas A. "Two Wills in Christ? Contemporary Objections Considered in the Light of a Critical Examination of Maximus the Confessor's *Disputation with Pyrrhus*." *Westminster Theological Journal* 71 (2009) 445–87.

Weinandy, Thomas G. *Jesus the Christ*. Huntington, IN: Our Sunday Visitor, 2003.

———. "Pope Benedict XVI: A Biblical Portrait of Jesus." *Nova et Vetera*, English edition 7 (2009) 19–34.

———. "The Son's Filial Relationship to the Father: Jesus as the New Moses." *Nova et Vetera*, English edition 11 (2013) 253–64.

Wostyn, Lode L. "Pope Benedict XVI and Joseph Ratzinger: Jesus of Nazareth." *East Asian Pastoral Review* 45 (2008) 91–104.

Wright, William M., IV. "A 'New Synthesis': Joseph Ratzinger's *Jesus of Nazareth*." *Nova et Vetera*, English edition 7 (2009) 35–66.

Index

Abba/Son dialogue, 11–13, 36, 43,
  53–55, 63, 70, 82, 112, 169, 182,
  220–21, 229
  Christians' participation in, 12, 53,
    202, 205n13, 221, 358, 360
Abelard
  "scholastic" theology and, 207–8
Adam, Karl
  on "factual monophysitism," 25
agape
  eros and, 190, 265–66, 268, 269,
    299n88
  "hour" of Jesus and, 163–64
  logos and, 31, 222
  philia and, 41
  splagchna and, 356
  Trinitarian, 32
Alacoque, St. Margaret Mary, 290n49
  revelation of the Sacred Heart to,
    176n121
Albert the Great, St.
  on the heart as the principle of life,
    334
Alexandria
  "school" of, 29, 181n149
Ambrose, St.
  on the blood and water flowing
    from Jesus' side, 194n27
  on Christ sharing our human emo-
    tions, 305, 325
Anselm, St.
  his theology of atonement, 14–15,
    39
anthropology
  Augustine's, 91–93, 291, 347

  biblical, 59, 91–92, 279
  of bodily existence, 86, 327
  cosmos and, 32–33, 50, 269–70
  dissociated, 64
  ecclesial, 201n2, 346
  exemplary man and, 12
  freedom and, 243, 256–59, 275–76,
    279
  heart and, xii, xiv, xviii, 58–61,
    90–93, 98, 279–310, 324, 340,
    341, 350, 356
  "high" Christology and, 18
  human sciences and, 72
  person and, 341–50
  Platonic, 91–92, 329
  politics and, 50
  Stoic, xii, 91–94
  theological, 29–30, 92n108, 108
  theology and, xvi, 9, 81, 82
Antioch
  "school" of, 29, 181n149
Apollinarism/Apollinarianism, 29,
    344
Arianism, 29, 344
  danger of a new version, 25, 52,
    102n6, 274–75
Aristotle
  on the heart as the principle of life,
    334
  on theology and the study of theol-
    ogy, 204
  on *theoria*, 201
Arnold, F. X.
  on "factual monophysitism," 25

ascending/descending
  eros/agape and, 190, 265–66
  exitus/reditus and, 222, 277
  of Jesus, 36–37, 114, 132, 154, 156, 162–63, 167, 203–4, 364
  with Jesus, 37, 132, 179, 202–4, 365
Ascension, 177–79
  descending of Jesus and, 222
  Descent into Hell and, 268
  empirical misconception of, 48
  eschatology and, 49
  freedom and, 265
  as Heaven, 48–49, 269
  in the Holy Spirit, 197n37
  mountain of, 154
  new form of the presence of Jesus, 178–79, 269
  Second Coming and, 50
  transformation of *bios* into *zoe* and, 269
Athanasius, St.
  Alexandrian Christology and, 181n149
  hermeneutics of the saints and, 113
Augustine, St.
  his anthropology of the heart, xii, 283–84, 306, 309
  on the centrality of love, 309n126
  on Christ sharing our human emotions, 305, 325
  on the common good, 258
  common ground with Ratzinger, 306
  on corporate personality, 134, 201n2
  on the divine persons, 342, 347
  his epistemology, 61, 283–84
  his exegetical principles, 118n82
  on the heart according to Guardini, 290–94
  on the heart according to Ratzinger, 59–61, 91, 280, 282–84, 306, 309, 330
  hermeneutics of the saints and, 113
  on the Holy Spirit, 360–64
  on the identity of love and reason, 301n93
  his influence of Ratzinger's theology, 63, 115, 280, 309n126, 330
  interiority and, 59–60, 291–93
  koinonia/communio and, 96, 331n29, 361, 363, 371n87
  on living in Christ, 201n2
  on the meaning of truth, 298
  on "natural reason" and "purified reason," 61, 285–86
  on *non posse non peccare*, 234n29
  on *non posse peccare*, 238n43
  his *philosophia cordis*, 60, 91
  his *philosophia* and *theologia cordis*, 279, 290
  "reason of faith" and, 109
  on true sacrifice, 276–77

Bacon, Francis.
  on the scientific method, 246
Baier, Walter
  on medieval devotion to the heart of Jesus, 284n20
Balthasar, Hans Urs von
  on Christ's descent into Hell, 103n12, 263n76, 264n78
  his influence on Ratzinger regarding the suffering of God, 316–19
  ressourcement theology and, 111, 313
  self-knowledge of Christ and, 112n53
  his theological anthropology, 29–30
Baptism
  our "ascension" and, 179
  into Christ, 269
  in the Nicene Creed, 370n85
  rule of faith and, 215
  as a sacramental event, 209
  symbolism of the water and the blood and, 56, 135, 173, 194, 330
Baptism of Jesus, 157–58
  Abba/Son dialogue and, 112
  Cross and, 156, 157, 162
  descent of the Holy Spirit and, 158–59, 368–69
  desire of Jesus and, 230–31
  Dyothelitism and, 167, 196, 223

Epiphany of Jesus as the Christ and, 198
filial thesis and, 221
Gethsemane and, 199
Jesus' descent into death and, 157, 222
Jesus' Descent into Hell and, 263n76
as a "prayer event," 121, 153, 154
Resurrection and, 157
solidarity with sinners and, 159, 240
soteriological thesis and, 156, 157–58
synoptic Gospels and, 184
temptations of Jesus and, 159, 240
Transfiguration and, 162, 197
Barton, Stephen C.
on biblical interpretation, 113n56
Basil the Great, St.
on Christ sharing our human emotions, 305, 325
Bathrellos, Demetrios
on Dyothelitism, 229n15, 233n23, 234n26
Baumgärtel, Friedrich
on the meaning of *kardia*, 281n6, 281n7, 350n31
Beatitudes, 127–32
discipleship and, 125, 126, 161, 188
hidden Christology of, 112, 126, 129, 132, 153, 161–62, 174
mountain of, 154
participation in the knowledge and will of the Son and, 175
purity of heart and, 306
Beck, Hans-Georg
on the gnomic will, 226n6
Becker, Joachim
on the human heart, 281n6, 281n7, 352
Behm, Johannes
on the meaning of *kardia*, 281, 350n31
Behr, John
on the "school" of Antioch, 181n149

Bernard of Clairvaux, St.
common ground with Ratzinger, 306
on devotion to the Sacred Heart, 91, 284
on the heart as the place of encounter with God, 306
"monastic" theology and, 207–8
patristic symbolic theology and, 313n6
his *philosophia* and *theologia cordis*, 290
on the suffering of God, 128–29, 153, 316
Berthold, George
on Maximus' treatment of *thelema* and *gnome*, 233n23
Bérulle, Pierre de, 290
bios
zoe and, 32, 44–46, 49, 267–68, 269
Bloomfield, S. T.
on the Alexandrian reading of John 7:37–39, 196n31
Blowers, Paul M.
on the Dyothelitism of Maximus, 232n21, 236n38
Bobrinskoy, Boris, 365n69
Bockmuehl, Markus
on Ratzinger's hermeneutics of the saints, 112–14, 118, 212
on Ratzinger and recent biblical scholarship, 105n18, 106n21
on Ratzinger's theological hermeneutic, 104n16
on the theological vocation, 115n69
Boersma, Hans
on Ratzinger's theological exegesis, 107n28
Bonagura, David G.
on Ratzinger's Johannine Christology, 27n95
Bonaventure, St.
on Christ as the heart of the church, 334
common ground with Ratzinger, 306
on devotion to the Sacred Heart, 87, 284, 328

Bonaventure, St. *(continued)*
  on the heart as the place of encounter with God, 306
  his influence on Ratzinger's theology, 63
  his *philosophia* and *theologia cordis*, 290
Boosalis, Harry M.
  on Seraphim of Sarov, 359n46
Buber, Martin
  Ratzinger's personalism and, 309n126
Bultmann, Rudolf
  his hermeneutical approach, 4–5, 7, 13, 24, 220
  idealization of faith and, 28
  on Jesus' abandonment by God, 172
  on Jesus' self-consecration as a sacrifice, 140
  on John's Gospel as rooted in Gnosticism, 148, 218
Butler, Sara
  on Ratzinger's spiritual Christology, 65–68, 242–43

Casarella, Peter J.
  on the ecclesial vocation of theologians, 115n69
  on Ratzinger's search for the face of God, 103, 112, 117n76
  on the "thickening of the Word," 108n38
Catherine of Siena, St., 290
Celsus, 216
Chalcedon, Council of
  Abba/Son dialogue and, 221, 223
  communicatio idiomatum and, 231n18
  Constantinople III and, xi, 64, 76, 96, 223, 226
  dogma of, 10, 13, 27, 39, 52, 55, 56, 68n23, 76, 102n6, 181, 183, 219, 221, 223–24, 231, 233
  dogmatic thesis and, 225
  Holy Spirit and, 370
  John's Gospel and, 27, 55, 68n23, 183
  Maximus and, 225

  personal and ecclesial theses and, 219
  volitional thesis and, xii, 223–24
Chenu, Marie-Dominique
  ressourcement theology and, 111, 313
Christology
  Aquinas', 345
  Alexandrian, 181n149
  Antiochene, 181n149
  ascending, 22
  biblical, xii, xv, 75, 82, 118
  Chalcedonian, 64
  Christ as his office/teaching/word/work, 5–6, 8, 12, 15, 29, 33, 55, 220–21
  of *communio*, vii, xiii, 185, 365
  cruciform, vii, 14, 30–31, 185
  dialogic, 36n2
  dogmatic, 75, 82
  dualism in, xv–xvi, 25, 29–30, 64
  dyothelite, 64
  ecclesiology and, 85, 102, 219, 364, 368
  Eucharist and, xiii, 56–58, 62, 94–98, 197–98, 330–35, 372
  freedom and, 228, 252, 262, 279
  heart of Jesus and, xii, 65, 85, 279, 324, 341
  hellenization and, 27, 102
  hidden, 126, 153, 161, 172, 174,
  high/from above, vii, xiii, xv, 18n64, 21–23, 26–27, 31, 75, 101–2, 106, 185–87
  historical Jesus and, 22, 24, 101–2, 185
  incarnational, vii, 14, 30–31, 55–56, 106, 185, 204
  Johannine, xiv, 7, 12–13, 26–27, 31, 32, 53, 54–55, 101–2, 104n16, 110, 115, 148, 183–85
  koinonia and, 94
  of the Letter to the Hebrews, 54, 183, 204
  liturgy and, 64, 65
  lived, 118, 121, 126–27, 142, 185, 201, 205, 213, 219, 332, 359

Index   395

low/from below, vii, xiii, xv, 21–23, 25, 75, 102–3, 185
Lukan, 54, 56, 183
Matthean, 101, 183
Maximian, 64, 275
Pauline, 16, 32, 115, 183
pneumatology and, 33–34, 85, 98, 192–97, 340, 341, 357, 359, 360, 362, 365, 368
prayer and, xi, xii, 55–56, 62, 63n2, 66n18, 70–71, 81, 126, 142, 188, 201, 204–5, 219, 332, 359, 371
Resurrection and, 68n23
synoptic, 27, 101, 115, 183
theology of revelation and, 63, 67
Trinity and, 97
Coffey, David, 365n69
Collins, Christopher S.
  on Ratzinger's Christology, 3n1, 12n38, 28n102, 30n107, 31n111, 36n2, 67n22
Colombiere, St. Claude de la, 290n49
Condren, Charles de, 290
Congar, Yves
  on Christology and pneumatology, 365, 368
  on doxology and theology, 371
  on the Holy Spirit and the church, 334
  on the piercing of Christ's side, 194n27
  Ratzinger's exegesis and, 108
  ressourcement theology and, 111, 313
Constantinople, First Council of
  on the Holy Spirit, 370n85
Constantinople, Third Council of
  Chalcedon and, xi, 76, 86, 98, 99
  Dyothelitism and, xv, 62–64, 224, 225, 233, 241, 348
  Holy Spirit and, 370
  human freedom and, 242–43
  neo-Chalcedonian theology and, 76, 84, 98, 220
  Ratzinger's spiritual Christology and, xi, 65–67, 96–97, 225–26, 233, 241, 242–43, 340

volitional thesis and, xii, 76–77, 83, 84, 180, 223–24
Corkery, James
  on Ratzinger's theology versus Kasper's, 18, 26
corporate personality
  biblical idea of, 16, 136
  church as, 134–36
  creation of Hell and, 268n101
  Cross and, 171, 203, 264–65
  heart and, 138
  Heaven and, 269
  Mary and, 139
  memory and, 136–37
  Paul and, 32
  Teilhard de Chardin and, 16, 32–33
  theoria and, xii, 201
  volitional thesis and, 182
Cortez, Marc
  on theological anthropology, 29n103
cosmology
  Ascension and, 48
  Christ and, 269–70
  covenant and, 164
  "descent" of God and, 36
  Descent into Hell and, 48
  Eucharist and, 277
  as history, 50, 270, 275
  liturgy and, 275
  person and, 33, 51, 53–54, 270
  reconciliation with anthropology, 32, 50
  responsibility and, 52
  Second Coming and, 50
  spirit and freedom and, 51, 242
  Stoics and, 92, 329
covenant
  creation and, 164, 275–76
  cosmos and, 164
  koinonia/communio and, 95
  new covenant
    heart of Jesus and, 93
    Jesus as the new ark, 163
    new presence of Jesus and, 177–78
    suffering of God and, 317
    words of institution and, 167

covenant *(continued)*
  old covenant
    fulfilment of the covenants and, 47
    freedom and, 250, 272
    mercy of God and, 323
    Psalms and, 134
    righteousness and, 129, 161
    Sabbath and, 276
Craig, William Lane
  on Dyothelitism, 224n68
creation
  anglo-saxon concept of freedom and, 247
  Baptism of Jesus and, 158
  church and, 361, 363
  of corporate man, 33
  covenant and, 164, 275–76
  drawing of all flesh to spirit and, 327–28
  economic view of freedom and, 254
  Eucharist and, 331n29
  exitus and, 279
  God's freedom and, 275
  God's impassibility and compassion and, 317n23
  heart of God and, 348
  of Heaven, 269
  of Hell, 268n101
  history and, 276
  Holy Spirit and, 193
  human nature and, 258
  human will and, 181, 232
  Incarnation and, 36–37, 55–56, 87
  participation in Christ and, 120, 203
  potential to dominate it, 246
  reditus and, 277
  Resurrection and, 48, 177
  Sabbath and, 275–76
  sacrifice of Christ and, 278
  Tabernacle and, 276
  theosis and, 276–77
  truth and freedom and, 274
  worship and, 164, 276–77
Creed, xiii, 13, 19, 22, 24, 28–30, 33, 35, 36, 51–52, 53, 68n23, 83, 185, 202, 215, 218, 220, 262
  Apostles', 3, 5–6, 22–23, 35, 39, 43–44, 48, 240
  Nicene, 35, 37, 46, 52, 370n85
Cross. *See also* theology, of the Cross
  Abba/Son dialogue and, 53, 54
  for all who suffer, 43, 134, 172, 222
  Ascension and, 178–79
  Baptism of Jesus and, 157–58
  Beatitudes and, 126, 128, 132, 161
  bios to *zoe* and, 267–68
  Christian faith and, 6–7, 31, 187, 202, 218, 220
  Christian negative theology and, 20
  church and, 135, 203, 209
  corporate personality and, 171, 203, 209, 222, 264
  as a cosmic liturgy, 41, 54, 173, 222
  creation and, 278
  eros to *agape* and, 266
  Eucharist and, 57, 190, 192
  as "exodus," 126, 161, 162, 274
  freedom and, 250, 261, 278
  glorification of God and, 170–71, 173, 176, 229
  God's impassibility and, 317n23
  heart of Jesus and, 65–66
  Holy Spirit and, 140, 191, 194n27, 261, 334
  hominization and, 31
  Israel and, 11, 43, 172, 222
  Jesus' prayer on, 43, 75, 172, 222
  Kingdom of God and, 125
  Last Supper and, 165–66
  mountain of, 154
  as movement from above to below, 36, 40, 132, 162, 203, 222
  as movement from below to above, 40, 162–63, 222
  new presence of Jesus and, 140, 178
  "passionate" love of God and, 190
  as prayer, 43, 163, 165, 170–72, 203, 222
  as present in Jesus' whole life, 162
  Psalm 22 and, 135, 147, 172
  as radical loneliness, 43
  Resurrection and, 14, 16, 126, 140, 157–58, 161, 165, 176, 178, 204, 266–68

as sacrifice, xii, 41–42, 54, 57, 163, 261–63, 278
Sermon on the Mount and, 166
temptations of Jesus and, 160, 172, 231, 239
theology of atonement and, 39–40
Transfiguration and, 162
transitional nature of Christ and, 16–17
as worship, 41, 54, 163, 165, 173, 221, 261–64, 278
Cuming, G. J.
on Eucharistic Prayers, 372n88
Cyprian, St.
on the gift of the Holy Spirit, 123
Cyril of Alexandria, St., 216n53
Alexandrian Christology and, 181n149
as a "type" of Ratzinger, 102n6

Daniélou, Jean
on the nature of Christ's sacrifice, 42, 58, 262–63
Ratzinger's exegesis and, 107n28, 108
on the Transfiguration, 155
Dante Alighieri, 290
on beauty, 300
on the Descent into Hell, 263n76
on the identity of love and reason, 301n93
Davis, Ellen F.
on biblical interpretation, 113n57
deification. *See theosis*
Deines, Roland
on *Jesus of Nazareth*, 106n21
on Ratzinger's approach to the historical Jesus, 110–11, 184
on Ratzinger's circular reasoning, 186
on Ratzinger's historical-critical methodology, 106n25
Del Colle, Ralph, 365n69
Denzinger, Heinrich
on the Christological dogma of Chalcedon, 181n148, 224n65, 233n22

on the Dyothelitism of Constantinople III, xvn11, 67n19, 96n126, 180n145, 223n64, 224n65, 224n67
on the natural knowledge of God at Vatican I, 61n112
Descartes, René
Cartesian reasoning and, 285n26
separation of heart and head by, 92n108
Descent into Hell
in the Apostles' Creed, 24, 43–44, 240
Ascension and, 268
Balthasar and, 103n12, 263n76, 264n78
Baptism of Jesus and, 157, 263n76
creation of Hell and, 268n101
death and, 264
descending of Jesus and, 222, 240, 262–64
empirical view of the cosmos and, 48
Gethsemane and, 263
Second Coming and, 50
temptations of Jesus and, 159
Diadochus of Photiki, 290n49
Diodore of Tarsus
his Antiochene Christology, 181n149
divinization. *See theosis*
Docetism, 29
Ratzinger as a Docetist, 102n6
Stoicism and, 89
doxology
metanoia and, 64
as theology, 371
dualism
anthropology/cosmology, 32–33, 50, 269–70
anthropology/theology, xvi, 9, 29–30, 81–82, 279n2
being/act, xvi, 13–14, 28–31, 81
Bible/Creed, 28
biblical/dogmatic Christology, 10, 76, 82, 220
body/soul, 59–60, 360n48

Index

dualism *(continued)*
  Christology/soteriology, xii, xv–xvi, 14–15, 30, 63, 70, 75, 81–82
  contemplative/systematic, xvi
  eternity/time, 49
  faith/history, 4, 28–30, 81–82, 218
  faith/reason, 79, 82, 89
  high/low Christology, xv, 21–22, 63, 75
  human/divine nature of Christ, xv, 64, 77, 185, 224, 226, 228
  individual/ecclesial faith, 82
  Jesus of history/Christ of faith, xv, 18n64, 22, 24, 28, 79, 82–83, 143, 224
  liturgical/devotional spirituality, 85
  monastic/scholastic theology, 206–8
  ontology/history, xvi, 14, 28–29, 254n44, 346, 366
  spirituality/theology, xv–xvi, 82, 117n79
  theologian/non-theologian, xvi–xvii, 82–83, 142, 205, 210–11
  theology of the heart/of reason, xvi, 206
  theology of the Incarnation/of the Cross, xvi, 13–14, 30–32, 75, 81–82, 204
Dunn, James D. G., 365n69
Dyothelitism,
  Christological dualism and, xv,
  of Constantinople III, xv, 63–64, 77–79, 97–98, 180–81, 223–24, 225–26, 233, 241, 242–43, 348–49, 370
  of Maximus, xviii, 64, 79, 181, 225–27, 232, 233–39, 241, 271, 348–49
  Ratzinger's use of, xviii, 62–63, 64, 67, 77–79, 97–98, 180–82, 223, 225–32, 239–41, 242–43, 271, 370

Ebionism, 29
ecclesiology
  anima ecclesiastica and, 201n2
  apostolic teaching and, 332
  Augustine's, 361–64
  Christology and, 85, 219, 364, 368
  communio and, 361, 365
  ecclesial communities, 359
  ecclesial dogma, 219
  ecclesial faith, 28, 83, 246, 374
  ecclesial symbolism, 38
  ecclesial thesis. *See* theses, ecclesial
  Eucharist and, 330–32, 371
  freedom and, 260
  freedom of Jesus and, 243
  harmonization with spiritual Christology, 370–71
  of the heart, 138–39, 192, 208–9, 334–35
  of the heart of Jesus, xii, xiv, xviii, 279, 341
  hermeneutics and, 107, 108n38, 117, 211, 219
  Kant and, 246–47
  Kingdom of God and, 124
  koinonia and, 94, 331–32
  Lukan, 94
  person and, 342, 346–47
  pneumatology and, 85, 98, 334–35, 361, 364–65, 368
  Psalm 22 and, 264
  "quasi-person" and, 342
  spirituality and, xiii, 96
  theological vocation and, 115
  theology and, 74, 361
  Trinitarian theology and, 368
  worship and, 332
Elders, Leo
  on Aquinas' anthropology of the heart, 284
Elijah
  Abba/Son dialogue and, 73
  "exodus" of Jesus and, 162, 272
  mount of the Beatitudes and, 126
Elizabeth of Thuringia, St., 290
Emery, Giles
  on Galot and the suffering of God, 316n20
  on Maritain and the suffering of God, 316n20, 319–20
Enlightenment, the
  concept of freedom and, 247, 257

Guardini's concept of freedom and, 297n80
historical correction of dogma and, 79
nature of reasoning and, 93n112, 306
epistemology
Aquinas', 61
Augustine's, 61, 283
first principle of, 83
Ratzinger's, 72, 74, 110, 141–42, 145, 211, 215n52, 218–19
scholastic, 215n52
theological, 72, 141–42, 145, 211, 218–19
eros
agape and, 190, 265–70
Guardini's understanding of, 299–300, 302
as "stronger than death," 44, 265
eschatology
freedom and, 268–71
gnomic will and, 235
of imminence, 49
Jesus and, 9
Kingdom of God and, 124
pneuma and, 363
realized, 102, 183
Resurrection and Ascension and, 49, 269
Transfiguration and, 155
Eucharist
adoration of the Blessed Sacrament and, 331
church and, 192, 198
corporate personality and, 135
cosmos and, 277
devotion to the Sacred Heart and, 66
eucharistia, 40, 166
eucharistic hermeneutic, 219
Eucharistic Prayer, 57–58, 179, 331
feeding of the 5,000 and, 189
freedom and, 332
gift of a new heart in, 58, 330–31
heart of, 57–58, 330
as the heart of the church, 58, 98, 193, 331, 333–35

heart of Jesus and, xvii, 65, 98, 173, 195, 198, 331
Holy Spirit and, 193–95, 219, 335
integration for relation and, 349
koinonia and, 94–96, 98, 191, 331–32
Last Supper and, 190
memory and, 139, 330
prayer of Jesus and, 62
presence of Jesus and, 179, 193–95
Psalm 22 and, 147–48
Resurrection and, 177–78
as a sacrifice, 57, 65, 190, 192, 330, 332
salvation history and, 190–91
spiritual Christology and, vii, xiv–xv, 67, 94–98, 121, 197–98, 330–35, 339–40
spirituality of, xi, xiii, xiv, xviii, 56–58, 62, 121, 197–98
as *symbolon* of a spiritual Christology, 370–72
theosis and, 277, 332
Eudes, St. John, 290n49
Eusebius of Caesarea, 216n53
Evagrius Ponticus, 290n49
on the vocation of the theologian, 82, 205
exegesis, 77, 106, 113, 143, 145, 150, 188
Augustine's, 118n82
canonical, 104, 107, 144–45, 186
historical-critical, 72, 79, 116, 122, 142
of Jesus, 259
modern, 68, 83, 104, 105, 146
patristic, 105, 214
Ratzinger's, xvi, 103–10, 115–16, 186, 212
spiritual, 211n36
theological, 103, 107, 109, 212

Fagerberg, David W.
on liturgy as theology, 371n86
Fairbairn, Donald
on the "school" of Antioch, 181n149

Farkasfalvy, Denis
  on Ratzinger's exegesis, 108
  on Ratzinger's historical-critical methodology, 107–8
  on Ratzinger's theology of inspiration, 108n37, 213–14
Feast of Tabernacles
  Holy Spirit and, 174, 197
  Transfiguration and, 155, 197
Ferreira, M. Jamie
  on Newman's anthropology of the heart, 287n40
Flannery, Austin,
  his translation of Vatican II documents, 59n104, 213n42
Florensky, Pavel, 290
Fowl, Stephen E.
  on biblical interpretation, 113n56
Francis de Sales, St., 290
Francis of Assisi, St., 290
  hermeneutics of the saints and, 113
  lived Christology and, 127
freedom
  Abba/Son dialogue and, 62, 63n2, 67, 76, 79, 225, 227, 242, 252
  anthropology of, 256–59, 279, 309n127
  Ascension and, 265
  Beatitudes and, 127–28
  biblical meaning of, 259–261
  of choice, 234n25, 237, 251
  church and, 210, 243, 260
  concept of person and, 249
  of conscience, 245–46
  consciousness and, 254
  cosmology and, 51, 242, 254
  Chalcedon and, 76–77
  Constantinople III and, 77
  covenant and, 250, 272, 276
  creation and, 247, 254, 274–76, 278
  creative, 253
  Cross and, 250, 261, 278
  Dyothetitism and, 77–79, 97, 225–27, 232, 236–39, 242–43
  Enlightenment and, 247, 257, 297n80
  eros and, 265–66, 268
  eschatology and, 268–71
  Eucharist and, 191n17, 332, 372
  false ideas of, 243–45, 257
  in *Gaudium et spes*, 249–51
  Gethsemane and, 251–52
  gnomic willing and, 238–39, 271
  grace and, 51, 270–71
  heart and, 295–96, 302–3, 373
  Hell and, 249, 257
  history and, 259, 272
  Holy Spirit and, 133, 196, 261, 358, 364, 372
  human, 45n52, 51, 53, 62, 63n2, 67, 75–79, 127–28, 133, 181, 196, 225–28, 232, 236–39, 241, 242–78, 332, 364, 372
  human freedom of Jesus, 67, 77–79, 225–28, 232, 236–39, 241, 243, 250–52, 261–68, 271–78, 279, 332, 364, 372
  individualization of, 245–46
  interiority and, 258n56
  koinonia and, 332, 372
  liberation theology and, 244, 271–72
  as *liberum arbitrium*, 78, 226
  as license, 243–45
  liturgy and, 271–78
  logos and, 252, 254
  love and, 45, 51, 54, 242, 252, 254, 265–68, 270–71, 277, 301, 303
  natural theology and, 250
  natural will and, 238–39, 262, 271
  necessity and, 18, 21, 252, 254–55
  negation of, 243–44, 245, 271, 274, 297, 299
  participation in that of Jesus, 79, 225, 227, 241, 242, 250–52, 261–62, 271–78, 364, 372
  Paul and, 133, 260, 262
  philosophy of, 247–49, 250–51, 253, 254n44, 257
  political, 245–48, 251, 258, 260
  reason and, 246–47
  responsibility and, 51, 243–44, 258–59, 260, 270
  Resurrection and, 259, 265–68, 272–73
  Sabbath and, 275–76

spirit and, 45, 51, 54, 242, 270
theologians and, 81, 142
theology of, 243, 250–56, 260, 262, 265, 268, 275, 277–78, 279, 372
theosis and, 239, 242–43, 257, 259, 260, 273, 277–78, 332, 358, 372
Torah of the Messiah and, 133, 196
Trinity and, 77, 260–61
truth and, 51, 54, 75–76, 242, 245, 258, 260, 270, 274–75, 364
value and, 297–99, 301
worship and, 261, 265, 277–78

Gaál, Emery de
 on Ratzinger's understanding of the "Jesus of history" and the "Christ of faith," 18n64
 on Ratzinger's preferential option for John's Gospel, 26–27, 183
 on Ratzinger's understanding of revelation, 63
 on Ratzinger's spiritual Christology, 62–63, 67, 117n78, 242
Gadamer, Hans-Georg
 Ratzinger's hermeneutical method and, 113
Gagey, Henri-Jérôme
 on Ratzinger's circular reasoning, 110, 186
Galatians 2:20, viii, xiii, 97, 113, 127, 132, 201, 208, 211, 331, 332, 368
Galot, Jean
 his influence on Ratzinger regarding the suffering of God, 316–18
Gavrilyuk, Paul
 on the "school" of Antioch, 181n149
Gertrude the Great, St., 290
Gethsemane
 Baptism of Jesus and, 157, 197
 Descent into Hell and, 263
 dogma of Chalcedon and, 225
 freedom and, 251–52
 gnomic will and, 239
 identity of Jesus and, 231
 logos/tropos of Christ's human will and, 237
 Maximus and, 225, 227, 238n44

natural will of Jesus and, 232
 as a "prayer event," 121
 prayer of Jesus and, 63, 78, 157, 167–71, 180–82, 225, 227, 228–31, 236, 251–52
 psychological passion of Jesus in, 43
 Resurrection and, 176
 soteriological thesis and, 167–71
 temptations of Jesus and, 159, 223, 239
 theosis and, 238n44
 Transfiguration and, 162, 197
 volitional thesis and, 63, 156, 167, 180–82, 222
Gnosticism
 John's Gospel and, 148, 218
 Ratzinger and, 102–3
 Stoicism and Docetism and, 89
Gratry, Auguste-Joseph-Alphonse, 290
Gregory of Nyssa, St.
 his anthropology of the heart, 282n10
Gregory Palamas, St., 290n49
Groppe, Elizabeth Teresa
 on Congar's Christology and pneumatology, 365n69
Gross, Heinrich
 on the heart of God, 91
Guardini, Romano
 his anthropology of freedom, 309n127
 his anthropology of the heart, xii, 60n110, 280, 289–303, 305, 306, 309, 330, 341
 common ground with Ratzinger, 306, 309
 on the heart of Jesus, 149n129
Guillou, Marie-Joseph le
 on Maximus and Constantinople III, 225

Habets, Myk, 365n69
Hahn, Scott W.
 on Benedict XVI's biblical theology, 211n36

Hahn, Scott W. *(continued)*
  on the nature of Ratzinger's theology, 339
  on Ratzinger's spiritual Christology, 66n18
Haight, Roger, 102n6, 365n69
  on Rahner's Christology, 22, 185
Harnack, Adolf von
  his hermeneutical approach, 4, 7, 24, 120, 220
  idealization of history and, 28
Harrington, Daniel J.
  on Ratzinger's theological hermeneutic, 103–4, 117n77
Hays, Richard B.
  on biblical interpretation, 113n57
  on *Jesus of Nazareth*, 103n12, 106n21, 112n53, 116
  on Ratzinger's "high" Christology, 104n6
  on Ratzinger's historical-critical methodology, 104–5, 218n56
  on Ratzinger's Johannine Jesus, 102, 183–84
  on Ratzinger's theological hermeneutic, 117n77, 212
heart
  anthropology of, xii, xiv, xvii, xviii, 58–61, 66, 88, 90–93, 98, 122–23, 130, 279–310, 324, 329–30, 340, 341, 350, 352, 356
  Aquinas' understanding of, 284, 306, 310, 334
  Augustine's understanding of, xii, 59–61, 91, 280, 282–84, 290–94, 306, 309, 330
  biblical understanding of, 90–93, 280–82
  church and, xii, xiv, xviii, 58, 98, 138–39, 192–93, 208–9, 279, 331, 333–35, 341
  common ground on, 306–10
  corporate personality and, 138
  covenant and, 93
  creation and, 348
  Cross and, 334

Eucharist and, xvii, 57–58, 65–66, 98, 173, 193, 195, 198, 330–31, 333–35
  of the Father, xii, 149, 175–76, 311–23
  freedom and, 295–96, 302–3, 373
  of God, xvii, 91, 311n1, 348
  Guardini's understanding of, 289–303
  hermeneutics and, 341
  Hildebrand's understanding of, 303–5
  Holy Spirit and, 174, 334
  interiority and, 59–60, 131, 292, 307–8
  of Jesus, xin1, xii, xiv, xvii, xviii, 58, 65–66, 85–86, 88, 93, 98, 149, 173–74, 175–76, 194n27, 195, 198, 279, 282, 305, 315, 324, 325–30, 331, 334, 341, 349, 355, 357
  Kingdom of God and, 123
  koinonia and, 281
  Last Supper and, 149, 175–76
  liturgy and, 88, 282
  of Mary, 139, 309–10
  Maximus and, 341, 349
  medieval devotion to the Sacred Heart, 87, 91, 284, 328
  medieval understanding of, 284
  memory and, 351, 352
  Newman's understanding of, 286–88
  Pascal's understanding of, 285–86, 289–301, 309
  patristic understanding of, 90–93, 282–84
  Paul and, 351–52, 356–57
  person and, 341–42, 348–49
  philosophy and, xii, 91–93, 282n11, 286, 329
  Pius XII's understanding of, 305
  as the place of encounter with God, 283, 306
  Platonic understanding of, xii, 91
  as the principle of life, 334
  purity of, xiii, 126, 132, 174–75, 296, 303, 306, 341, 351

Rahner's understanding of, 288–89
reason and, 92n108, 285n26
revelation and, 281–82, 303, 351
Sacred Heart of Jesus, xi, xiii, xiv,
    53, 65–67, 85–88, 91–93, 98,
    176n121, 284, 305, 324–27, 340
Stoic understanding of, xii, 91–93,
    329
symbolic theology and, xii, 311–23
theologizing and, xvii
theology of, xi, xii, xiv–xvii, 56,
    58–61, 85–93, 98, 121, 197, 206,
    289, 333, 339, 340–41, 350
theosis and, 325
worship and, 66, 325, 327
Heaven, 136
    Ascension and, 24, 48–49, 179, 222,
        268, 269
    "ascent" of Jesus and, 163
    Baptism of Jesus and, 154, 157–58
    corporate person and, 49, 269, 368
    creation of, 49, 269
    "descent" of Jesus and, 36, 77, 222,
        226
    Eucharist and, 371
    as a gift, 268–69
    human nature and, 266
    Jesus as the "heavenly" man,
        135–36
    nature of, 48–49
    prayer of Jesus and, 189, 194n27
    theosis and, 79n69
Heer, Joseph
    on Jesus' handing over his spirit,
        195n30
    on the water and the blood flowing
        from Jesus' side, 194n27
Hell. *See also* Descent into Hell
    creation of, 268n101
    death and, 44, 264
    freedom and, 249, 257
    Jesus' hellish experience, 42,
        262–64
    meaning of the term, 43
    nature of, 43–44, 49, 249, 268–69
    "second death" and, 44
hellenization, 148
    Christianity and, 27

divine man and, 10, 24, 102
Hengel, Martin
    Ratzinger's use of him, 136–37, 148
hermeneutics
    of the Antichrist, 142–43
    Christological, 106–7, 117, 145, 211
    of communion, 117
    Day of Atonement and, 40
    of discipleship, 114, 118, 212–13
    eccesial, 107, 117, 211, 213–14
    ecclesial thesis and, 214, 216
    Eucharistic, 219
    of faith, xii, 80–81, 103, 114, 117,
        145, 211, 214–16, 219
    of *Gaudium et spes*, 249n24
    of the heart, 341
    Heaven and, 49
    "hermeneutical circle," 187, 218–19
    hermeneutical thesis. See theses,
        hermeneutical
    historical, 103, 114, 145, 214
    of *Jesus of Nazareth*, 67, 103–12,
        117–18
    Johannine, 183
    medieval, 111, 148
    memory of the church and, 74
    method of, 142–50, 219
    modern, 72
    of participation, 371
    patristic, 111, 148
    personal thesis and, 212, 216
    pneumatological, 219, 359
    positivistic, 145
    prayer and, 359
    presuppositions of, 216
    Resurrection and, 45
    rule of faith and, 187
    of the saints, 113–14, 118, 212–13
    theological, 103, 104, 110, 117, 186,
        211–12, 213
    of typology/figuration, 104n16
Hildebrand, Dietrich von
    his anthropology of the heart, 280,
        303–5, 310
    on Augustine's anthropology of the
        heart, 282
    common ground with Ratzinger,
        306–7

Hildebrand, Dietrich von *(continued)*
  on the neglect of the heart in philosophical enquiry, 92n108
historical-critical method
  canonical exegesis and, 145
  exclusive use of, 143
  faith/history dualism and, 4–5, 28
  hermeneutical thesis and, 79, 83, 84, 141
  "high" Christology and, 185
  "low" Christology and, 23
  positivism and, 4
  prayer of Jesus and, 65
  premises of, 24
  Ratzinger's use of, 23–24, 101–8, 110, 115–16, 144–45, 185–88, 211, 216–18
historical Jesus
  beginning with, 22–23, 24, 185
  biblical Christology and, xv
  Christ of faith and, xv, 18n64, 24, 28, 79–80, 83, 143, 224
  Creed and, 24, 28, 83, 185
  false, 9–10
  historical-critical method and, 23, 24, 64, 81, 102, 106, 185, 216–17
  Johannine Christology and, 110, 148, 184, 218
  "low" Christology and, 22, 25
  quests for, xv, 5
  Ratzinger and, 22–23, 24, 28, 63, 66, 102, 103n13, 104, 110, 116, 143, 148, 184, 185, 186, 218
  Son of God and, 3
  synoptic Gospels and, 12
history
  cosmology and, 50, 270, 275
  creation and, 276
  Eucharist and, 190–91
  faith and, 4–5, 28–31, 81–83, 218
  freedom and, 259, 272
  idealization of, 28
  Jesus of, xv, 18n64, 25n90, 64–65, 29, 83, 84, 145, 226
  liberation and, 259
  liturgy and, 275
  ontology and, xvi, 14, 28–29, 254n44, 346, 366
  of religions, 73
  revelation and, 108
  salvation and, 190–91
  worship and, 275–76
hominization
  animal to logos, 15
  corporate personality and, 16, 32–33
  divinization as the goal of, 15, 31
  full when God becomes man, 15, 32
  as the unification of the cosmos with the personal, 33
Hoping, Helmut
  on Ratzinger's spiritual Christology, 64n10, 117n78
Hughes, Brian W.
  on Newman's anthropology of the heart, 287n38
Huovinen, Eero
  on *Jesus of Nazareth*, 106n24
  on Ratzinger's biblical authors, 109
  on Ratzinger's historical-critical methodology, 109
  on how Ratzinger reads the Gospels, 106n23, 112n53, 116, 213–14
  on Ratzinger's theology of inspiration, 109
  on "reason of faith" (*Vernunft des Glaubens*), 109
  on "sleeping texts" (*Schläfertexte*), 109

Ignatius of Antioch, St., 290
interiority
  Augustine and, 59–60, 291–93, 347
  Dyothelitism and, 77, 226
  of the emotions, 292
  of freedom, 258n56
  Gaudium et spes and, 58–59
  Guardini and, 289–93
  heart and, 59–60, 131, 292, 307–8
  hesed and, 323
  of the Holy Spirit, 191–92, 334
  of Jesus, 126, 132, 159, 162, 175, 189
  listening and, 122

Mary and, 139, 309
Origen and, 124
possession of eternal life and, 273
poverty and, 127
presence of God and, 292
sacramental structure of, 209
Teilhard de Chardin and, 59
of theology, 206
theology of the body and, 60, 289–90
thirst for righteousness and, 129
of the Trinity, 175, 347
Ivánka, Endre von
    on Origen's anthropology of the heart, 93, 282n10, 330n25

James, St., 272, 355, 363
Jasper, R. C. D.
    on Eucharistic Prayers, 372n88
Jerome, St., 216n53
    his anthropology of the heart, 282n10
    on Christ sharing our human emotions, 305, 325
John 7:37–39
    Alexandrian and Ephesian reading of, 65–66, 194–96
John the Baptist, St., 157
John Chrysostom, St.
    on Christ sharing our human emotions, 305, 325
    on the gift of the Holy Spirit, 194n27
John of the Cross, St.
    Wojtyla's personalism and, 309n126
John Damascene, St.
    on Christ sharing our human emotions, 325
John the Evangelist, St., 272
    Abba/Son dialogue in, 12–13
    Baptism and Eucharist, 17
    "beloved disciple" and, 149–50
    fear of Jesus in, 169
    feeding of the 5,000 in, 189
    final prayer of Jesus in, 173
    "Gethsemane prayer" in, 168
    glorification in, 71, 126, 161
    "hour" of Jesus in, 126, 161, 163–64
    in *Jesus of Nazareth*, 184
    Johannine Question and, 218
    link between person and word, 7
    memory of, 137–39
    new Adam in, 56
    new Eve in, 136
    ontology of, 12–13, 55
    synoptic Gospels and, 188
John of Fécamp
    on devotion to the Sacred Heart, 284
John Paul II, St.
    on Christ and the Holy Spirit, 368
    on the Eucharist and the church, 192n21
    on faith and reason, 207
    on the mercy of God, 321–23
    his theological anthropology, 30n106
    his Thomistic personalism, 309n126
Johnson, Luke Timothy
    on *Jesus of Nazareth*, 105–6, 116, 187–88
    on Ratzinger's "high" Christology, 106
    on Ratzinger's historical-critical methodology, 105–6, 185n1
Jones, L. Gregory
    on biblical interpretation, 113n56
Jonge, Marinus de
    on the *Testaments of the Twelve Patriarchs*, 354n36
Josephus, 216n53
Julian the Apostate, 216n53
Jungmann, Josef
    on "factual monophysitism," 25
Justin Martyr, St., 216n53
    on Christ sharing our human emotions, 305, 325

Kant, Immanuel
    on faith in reason, 246–47
    his separation of metaphysics from morality, 296–98, 299
Kasper, Walter
    on Christology and soteriology, 14n48

Kasper, Walter *(continued)*
  on cosmology and anthropology, 50n76
  his critique of Ratzinger's theology, 17–18, 20–21, 26, 45n52, 87
  on Easter kerygma and stories, 46n56
  on Heaven and the Ascension of Jesus, 59n69
  his historical-critical methodology, 218n56
  intra-trinitarian kenosis and, 317n22
  nature of his Christology, 23
  on pneumatology and Christology, 33n122
Kavanagh, Aidan
  on liturgy as theology, 371n86
Kee, Howard C.
  on the *Testaments of the Twelve Patriarchs*, 354n36
kenosis
  of Christ, 103n12, 117
  of God, 52
  of the heart of Jesus, 349, 355, 357
  intra-trinitarian, 317n22, 319n34
  of the Son, 27, 55, 184
Kereszty, Roch
  on *Jesus of Nazareth*, 115–17, 183
  on Ratzinger's neo-patristic theology, 115–16
Kerr, Fergus
  on the self-knowledge of Christ, 112n53
Khomyakov, Aleksey, 290
Kierkegaard, Søren, 290
Kingdom of God
  as active, 124
  communion with Jesus and, 125
  "divine Lordship" and, 125
  as extra worldly, 183
  heart and, 123
  Holy Spirit and, 359, 369
  identification with Jesus, 125
  Jesus as eschatological prophet of, 9
  Jesus as preacher of, 110
  Jesus as servant of, 27, 101, 188
  kingdom of man and, 246

kingdom of reason and, 246
liberation theology and, 244
nature of, 124
pure religious faith and, 246
righteousness and, 157
Second Coming and, 179
synoptic Gospels and, 184
theologian's vocation and, 81, 142
theology of the Cross and, 166
koinonia/communio,
  Augustine on, 361
  of charity, 332
  Christology and, vii, 95, 365
  Dyothelitism and, 97, 332
  ecclesiology and, 361, 363, 365
  of the Eucharist, xiii, 94–96, 191, 332, 371
  freedom and, 372
  heart and, 281
  of the Holy Spirit, 361, 363, 371–72
  with Jesus, 332
  Ratzinger and, vii
  theosis and, xiii, 372
Komonchak, Joseph
  on *ressourcement* theology, 313n6
Köster, Helmut
  on *splagchna*, 353n32, 354n37, 355n39, 356–57
Kreeft, Peter
  on Pascal's understanding of "reason" and "heart," 285n26
Krieg, Robert
  on Ratzinger's "high" Christology, 23, 25, 185n1
  on Ratzinger's historical-critical methodology, 24
  on Ratzinger's idealism, 18n64

Lactantius
  his anthropology of the heart, 282n10
Lam, Cong Quy Joseph
  on Ratzinger's spiritual Christology, 63, 67
Lampe, Geoffrey, 365n69
Lash, Nicholas
  on biblical interpretation, 113n56
Last Supper

dating of, 188, 217–18
Eucharist and, 56–57, 190–91
eucharistia and *eulogia* and, 166
Eucharistic Prayer and, 57, 330
heart of Jesus and the Father and, 149, 175–76
Holy Spirit and, 194n27
memory and, 139
as a new Passover, 165–66
as a "prayer event," 121
Resurrection and, 177–78
Second Coming and, 179
soteriological thesis and, 70–71, 156, 165–67
theology of the Cross and, 166
Lewis, C. S.
"angelism" and, 314–15
on *eros* and *agape*, 266n91
on human freedom, 254n44
on the suffering of God, 320–21
Liberalism
freedom and, 245
liberation
eros and, 266
history of, 259
human nature and, 257
impossibility of, 245
individualization of, 245–46
Jesus' human freedom and, 76
Jesus' relationship with his Father and, 242
liberation theology and, 244, 271
as life, 275
nature of human freedom and, 75
as participation in Jesus' freedom, 225, 252
prayer of Jesus and, 62, 76
Rahner's concept of freedom and, 254n44
salvation and, xvi
self-liberation and, 256
truth and, 249, 274
two natures of Christ and, 77
Lincicum, David
on Ratzinger's circular reasoning, 185–86
on Ratzinger's figural reading of Sacred Scripture, 107, 214

on Ratzinger's hermeneutics, 211n37
liturgy
Baptism of Jesus and, 157
Bible and, 114
contemporary, 64
cosmic, 41, 54, 173, 222, 261, 275
Creed and, 215, 219
dualism in, 64, 86
Eastern, 157, 360, 365–68
eschatology and, 125
heart and, 88, 282
history and, 275
liturgical movement and, 65, 85–86
as participation in the freedom of Jesus, 271–78
pneumatological method and, 365–68
Ratzinger's liturgical theology, 165n68
reform of, 86
Resurrection and, 46
spiritual Christology and, 65, 67
as theology, 371n86
theology of, 46
logos
act and, 138,
as *agape*, 8, 31, 190, 222, 252, 254
as being, 252, 254
being-with-the-other and, 345–46
as consciousness, 254
as creative, 20, 254–55
dogma as *logos*-like
Dyothelitism and, 77–78, 97, 226–33
as freedom, 252, 254
heart of Jesus and, 88
"high" Christology and, 23n82, 27, 101
hominization and, 15, 31
human action/thought/willing/loving and, 268n101
human heart and, 92–93, 282, 329–30
as the "idea," 252
as the image of God, 26, 93, 330
incarnation of, 87–88, 190, 215, 241, 327

logos (continued)
  intra-trinitarian kenosis and, 317n22
  logike latreia and, 165
  memory and, 137–38
  Origen on, 92–93, 330
  as person, word and work, 7, 33
  as personal, 253–54
  primacy of, 17, 252–53
  as a property of the will, 235–37
  quasi-Nestorianism and, 25n90, 65
  Ratzinger and Aquinas on, 118n82
  sarx and, 3
  in Stoicism, 92
  wisdom and, 190
  worship and, 165n68
Lord's Prayer
  Dyothelitism and, 167–68
  Eucharist and, 148
  human heart and, 122–23, 130
  Jesus' inner disclosure and, 63
  Matthean use of, 184
  as a "prayer event," 121
  prayer of Jesus and, 153
Louth, Andrew
  on the "school" of Antioch, 181n149
  on *theosis*, 79n69
Lubac, Henri de
  on the Eucharist and the church, 192n21
  Ratzinger's exegesis and, 107n28, 108
  ressourcement theology and, 111, 313

Macarius the Egyptian, 216n53, 290n49
Macquarrie, John
  on Dyothelitism, 224n68
Marcel, Gabriel
  on the nature of mystery, 263, 314
  his *philosophia cordis*, 60
Maritain, Jacques
  his influence on Ratzinger, 316–20, 323
Martin, Francis
  on the church as a "quasi-person," 333
Martinez, Francisco Javier
  on Ratzinger's circular reasoning, 110n44
  on Ratzinger's neo-patristic theology, 115n68
Marx, Karl,
  on the future communist society, 245
Marxism
  anthropology and, 248
  its critique of democracy, 248
  as a future orientated ideology, 17
  nature of freedom and, 247, 251
  reason for its failure, 245
Mary, the Blessed Virgin
  heart of, 139, 309–10
  Holy Spirit and, 178, 197, 326, 368
  Jesus as born of, 24, 35–36, 326
  as the new Eve, 136
  remembering and, 139
  as a type of the church, 136
Maximus the Confessor, St.
  his anthropology, 79n69, 242
  his Christology, 64, 275
  Chalcedon and, 225
  Constantinople III and, 63n2, 64, 83, 225–26, 233, 241, 348
  his Dyothelitism, 225–41, 348–49
  on the gnomic will, 228, 234–41
  heart and, 341, 349
  on the natural and gnomic wills, 78, 226, 233–41, 271
  on *non posse non peccare*, 234n29
  on the person, 228n10, 342n3
  Ratzinger's use of his Dyothelitism, xviii, 63n2, 64, 78, 181, 225–32
  theosis and, 238n44, 242
  "thickening of the Word" and, 108n38
  on volitional movements, 229n15
  volitional thesis and, 83
McDonnell, Kilian, 365n69
McFarland, Ian A.
  on Maximus' Dyothelitism, 233–39
memory
  anthropology and, 302

Augustine and, 293
of the church, 67, 72, 74, 134,
    136–39, 141–142, 210, 214
ecclesial thesis and, 214
Eucharist and, 139
heart and, 351, 352
hermeneutics and, 214
Israel's worship and, 57
of Mary, 139, 310
pneumatic, 74, 138, 141, 210, 362
revelation and, 108, 214, 259
metanoia
    liturgy and, 64
    Ratzinger's theology and, 26
Miles, Jack
    on Ratzinger's "high" Christology, 102n6
    on Ratzinger's historical-critical methodology, 104n16
Moberly, R. W. L.
    on Ratzinger's exegesis, 104n16
    on Ratzinger's use of the Old Testament, 103n12, 117n76
Moltmann, Jürgen
    his Patripassianism, 316
    his phenomenology of hope for justice, 45n52
"monastic" theology
    versus "scholastic" theology, 206–8
Monenergism
    Chalcedon and, 224
    nature of, 344
Monk Vartholomaeos
    on the Eastern understanding of the heart, 290n49
Monophysitism
    Chalcedon and, 181, 231
    "factual," 25
    nature of, 344
    versus Nestorianism, 29
    Ratzinger's spiritual Christology and, 63
Monothelitism
    Chalcedon and, 181, 224
    Dyothelitism of Maximus and, 233
    nature of, 231, 344
Montague, George T.

on the gift of the Holy Spirit, 194n27, 195n30
Moreland, J. P.
    on Dyothelitism, 224n68
Moses, 276
    Abba/Son dialogue and, 73
    Christ's spiritualization of the law and, 133
    "exodus" of Jesus and, 162, 272
    interpretation of John 7:37–39 and, 197
    Jesus and, 103n12, 104n16, 117, 119, 126, 127, 146, 153–54, 271
    liberation theology and, 244, 271
    mount of the Beatitudes and, 126
    pierced side of Jesus and, 194n27
    Transfiguration and, 158, 162, 272
Mounier, Emmanuel
    Wojtyla's personalism and, 309n126
Murphy, Joseph
    on Ratzinger's spiritual Christology, 63n2, 242

National Socialism
    its concept of freedom, 247
neoscholasticism,
    Christology of, 116
    as "quasi-Nestorianism," 25n90, 64–65
    its rationalism, 61
Nestorianism
    danger of a new version, 25
    versus Monophysitism, 29, 181, 231
    "quasi-Nestorianism," 25n90, 64–65
    Ratzinger's spiritual Christology and, 63, 228
Nestorius
    Antiochene Christology and, 181n149
Neusner, Jacob
    on the Sermon on the Mount, 133–34, 223
Newman, Bl. John Henry
    his anthropology of the heart, xii, 88, 93, 280, 286–88, 290, 306, 330
    common ground with Ratzinger, 88, 93, 280, 306, 309n126

Newman, Bl. John Henry *(continued)*
  on conscience, 60
  his *philosophia* and *theologia cordis*, 290
Newman, Paul, 365n69
Nicaea, First Council of
  dogma of, 13, 27, 52, 55, 102n6, 183, 221, 223
  personal and ecclesial theses and, 219
Nichols, Aidan, 256n47
  on the neglect of the heart in philosophical enquiry, 92n108
Nietzsche, Friedrich, 290
  his concept of freedom, 247
Nissiotos, Nikos, 365n69

Oakes, Edward T.
  on God's impassibility, 317n23
  on intra-trinitarian kenosis, 317n22, 319n34
  on Moltmann's Patripassianism, 316n16
  on Pascal's understanding of reason, 285n26
O'Brien, George Dennis
  on Ratzinger's "high" Christology, 102–3, 185n1
O'Byrne, Declan, 365n69
O'Donnell, John, 365n69
O'Hanlon, Gerard F.
  on Balthasar's theology of God's pain, 316n17
O'Leary, Joseph S.
  on Ratzinger's historical-critical methodology, 103n13
Oliver, Simon
  on *Jesus of Nazareth*, 103n12, 117n76
omega point
  mind as the true ground of reality and, 50
  Second Coming and, 270
Origen, 216n53
  his anthropology of the heart, xii, 66, 92, 280, 282, 306, 330
  common ground with Ratzinger, 306

on the Kingdom of God, 124–25
on the suffering of God, 89, 315–16
Paddison, Angus
  on *Jesus of Nazareth*, 117n78
  on Ratzinger's circular reasoning, 186
  on Ratzinger's figural reading of Sacred Scripture, 216
  on Ratzinger's hermeneutic of discipleship, 114, 118, 213
  on Ratzinger's historical-critical methodology, 106, 214
Pannenberg, Wolfhart
  on Dyothelitism, 224n68
  on the "historical Jesus," 4
  his phenomenology of hope, 45n52
Pascal, Blaise
  his anthropology of the heart, xii, 59–60, 93, 280, 282n9, 285–86, 289–301, 306, 309, 330
  common ground with Ratzinger, 306
  on the heart according to Guardini, 289–301, 309
  his *philosophia* and *theologia cordis*, 290
Patripassianism
  Jürgen Moltmann and, 316
Paul, St., 94, 97, 113, 147, 166, 174, 208, 331, 363, 368, 374–75
  on the Body of Christ, 72, 95, 134, 209, 371n87
  on Christ as the new Adam, 32, 136
  his Christology, 16, 32, 115, 183
  corporate personality and, 16, 32
  on the Cross and Resurrection, 126, 161
  on freedom, 133, 260
  heart and, 351–52, 356–57
  Holy Spirit and, 84, 315
  image of God and, 73
  his use of *kardia*, 92n108
  nature of theology and, 208
  Pascal's understanding of the heart and, 286
  his *philosophia* and *theologia cordis*, 290

Index   411

Ratzinger's reading of 1 Cor 6:17, 331n29
on the Resurrection, 267–68
rhetoric for freedom and, 262
his use of *splagchna*, 356–57
Teilhard de Chardin and, 16, 32
theological epistemology and, 72
theology of the Cross and, 14
Torah of the Messiah and, 133
on worship, 165
Pentecost, 130, 194, 358, 366–67
person
 anthropological concept of, 349
 Christological concept of, 344–46, 349
 heart and, 341–42, 348–49
 "quasi-person" of the church, 333, 335, 342, 349
 as relation, 342
 theological concept of, 346–47
Peter Lombard
 on *liberum arbitrium*, 226n6
Peter, St., 149, 272
 his profession of faith, 39, 54, 69, 121, 122, 140, 154–55, 160, 162, 184, 221, 272
 his Pentecost proclamation, 47, 130
 second Beatitude and, 128
 his use of *splagchna*, 357n45
Peters, James R.
 on Augustine's anthropology, 309n126
philosophy
 ancient, 347
 Christian, 346
 common good and, 258
 Enlightenment, 309n126
 faith reduced to, 52
 of freedom, 248, 253, 254n44
 Greek, 26, 88–89, 92n108
 heart and, 282n11, 286
 of the human person, 345
 of interpersonal love, 249n25
 modern, 346
 principles of interpretation and, 208
philosophia cordis, 60, 91

philosophia and *theologia cordis*, 91, 279, 290
Pilate, 6, 24, 184, 187, 220
Pinnock, Clark H., 365n69
Pius XI
 on devotion to the Sacred Heart, 305
Pius XII
 common ground with Ratzinger, 65, 308
 Ephesian reading and, 195n28
 on God as passionless, 315
 on the heart, 305
 heart of God and, 311n1
 heart of Jesus and, xin1, 65, 86, 194n27, 282, 305, 315, 325–30
 Hildebrand on the heart and, 305
 Ratzinger on the heart and, xin1, 65, 86–87, 280, 308, 327–30
Plato
 his allegory of the cave, 18, 26
 identity of love and reason and, 301n93
 his *philosophia* and *theologia cordis*, 290
Platonism
 anthropology of, 91–92, 282n10, 329
 Aquinas and, 329
 Augustine and, 283, 333n29
 beauty and, 300
 biblical faith and, 92
 Christian faith and, 17
 on the heart, xii, 91
 Ratzinger's theology and, 17–18, 26, 87, 102–3, 329
pneumatology
 Augustine's, 360–65
 biblical, 361
 Christology and, 33n122, 85, 340, 362, 365
 content of, 368–70
 Constantinople I and, 370n85
 dogmatic/volitional theses and, 370
 Eastern, 365–68
 ecclesial thesis and, 360
 ecclesiology and 85, 94, 98, 361, 363, 364, 365, 368

pneumatology *(continued)*
  eschatology and, 363
  faith and, 363
  heart of Jesus and, 174
  lacuna in Ratzinger's, 98, 192–97, 339
  memory and, 138, 141, 362
  method of, 357–68
  sacramental theology and, 363
  sensus fidei/sensus fidelium and, 368
  theologizing and, 372
  Trinity and, 368
Porphyry, 216
positivism
  metaphysics and, 4
Potterie, Ignace de la, 365n69
"prayer events," 121, 122, 153, 162, 330
  as defining events of Jesus' life, 122, 153–54
Pseudo-Dionysius
  ignote cognoscere and, 88, 306n115, 312
  on the nature of theology, 204–5

Rahner, Hugo
  his anthropology of the heart, 281–82, 308
  common ground with Ratzinger, 308
  on devotion to the Sacred Heart, 85–87
  his Ephesian reading of John 7:37–39, 65–66
  on *splagchna* as a synonym for *kardia*, 352
Rahner, Karl
  his anthropology of the heart, 60, 280, 288–89, 306, 310
  common ground with Ratzinger, 280, 306
  his concept of freedom, 254n44
  on "factual monophysitism," 25
  on "high" versus "low" Christology, 22
  on nature and grace, 277n136
  his phenomenology of human freedom, 45n52
  Ratzinger's exegesis and, 108
  on the self-knowledge of Christ, 112n53
  his theological anthropology, 29–30
  his theology of inspiration, 108n37
Rausch, Thomas P.
  on the hellenization of Jesus, 102
  on Ratzinger's hermeneutics, 211n37
  on Ratzinger's "high" Christology, 102n6, 185n1
  on Ratzinger's "historical Jesus," 22–23
  on Ratzinger's historical-critical methodology, 104
  on Ratzinger's Johannine Jesus, 27, 101, 183
  on Ratzinger's understanding of the ministry of Jesus, 188
responsibility
  being-for others and, 257
  for creation, 48
  Ratzinger's definition of, 258–59
  determinism and, 243
  ethics and, 258
  freedom and, 51, 243–44, 259, 260, 270
  grace and, 51, 270
  interiority and, 59
  Rahner's understanding of, 254n44
  spirit and, 51, 270
ressourcement theology
  Ratzinger's theology and, 107n28, 111, 312–13
Resurrection
  Abba/Son dialogue and, 34, 42–43, 54, 56, 70, 171, 176–77, 202
  Baptism of Jesus and, 157–58
  Beatitudes and, 161
  as *bios* into *zoe*, 45–46, 177, 267–69
  confessional and narrative traditions of, 46–48, 223
  covenant and, 177–78
  creation and, 48, 177
  Constantinople I and, 370n85
  Cross and, 14, 16, 126, 140, 157–58, 161, 165, 176, 178, 204, 266–68
  discipleship and, 126

in earlier Christological theses, 68n23
eros and, 44
as *eros* into *agape*, 266–68
eschatology and, 49, 269
Eucharist and, 98, 139, 177–78, 190–91
freedom and, 259, 265–68, 272–73
Gethsemane and, 176
God's impassibility and, 317n23
hermeneutics and, 45
Holy Spirit and, 33, 140, 191, 215, 334, 369
Incarnation and, 43, 204
King of the Jews and, 40
koinonia and, 95, 332
Last Supper and, 166, 177–78
Last Supper, Crucifixion and, 56–57
liturgy and, 46
memory of the church and, 136, 138
new presence of Jesus and, 269
Paul and, 126, 161, 267–68
Psalm 2 and, 11, 147
Psalm 22 and, 147, 172
Ratzinger's historical-critical methodology and, 105, 187
Transfiguration and, 38
revelation
biblical, 106–7
Bonaventure's concept of, 63
of Christ, 61
church and, 333
contemplative theology and, 208
Eucharist and, 135
of the Father, 112, 317
of God, 154, 160, 263, 301
heart and, 281–82, 303, 351
as history, 108
history of religions and, 73
of the identity of *logos* and *agape*, 222
of love, 92n108, 190, 321
prayer of Jesus and, 69, 220
Resurrection and, 158
of the Sacred Heart, 176n121
scholastic method and, 207
theology of, 63, 67

of the Trinity, 158, 196, 369–70
Richard of St. Victor
on loving and seeing, 72, 312
on the nature of person, 333n35, 344
Riches, Aaron
on contemporary neo-Nestorianism, 25n90, 64
on the "Jesus of history" and the "Christ of faith," xv
on Ratzinger's spiritual Christology, 64–65, 67, 225n1
on the "school" of Antioch, 181n149
Rist, John M.
on Augustine's anthropology of the heart, 283
Root, Michael
on *Jesus of Nazareth*, 112n53
on a mistranslation in *Jesus of Nazareth*, 145n112
on participation in the prayer of Jesus, 117n78
on Ratzinger's use of the term "faith," 215n52
on Ratzinger's hermeneutic, 107, 117n77, 213
on Ratzinger's historical-critical methodology, 211
Rosato, Philip J., 365n69
Rosmini-Serbati, Bl. Antonio, 290
Rousseau, Jean-Jacques
his concept of nature, 247
Rowland, Tracey
on Augustine's concepts of "natural reason" and "purified reason," 61n115
on contemporary theological anthropology, 92n108
on the neglect of the heart in philosophical enquiry, 93n108
on Rahner's and Ratzinger's understanding of nature and grace, 277n136
on Ratzinger's interpretation of *Gaudium et spes*, 249n24
on comparing Ratzinger's and Wojtyla's anthropologies, 309n126

Rowland, Tracey *(continued)*
  on Wojtyla's personalism in *Gaudium et spes*, 249n25

Sabbath
  creation and, 275–76
  freedom and, 275–76
  Jesus as the Lord of, 184
  Jesus as the new, 133
  as a sign of the Covenant, 276
sacramental theology
  Augustine's, 363
sacrifice of Jesus
  Abba/Son dialogue and, 13, 55
  Baptism and, 56, 330
  Bultmann on, 140
  Christian hope and, 17
  church and, 192, 330
  consecration/sanctification and, 139–40, 171
  creation and, 278
  Cross as, xii, 41–42, 54, 57, 163, 261–63, 278
  Daniélou on, 42, 58, 262–63
  as *eros* becoming *agape*, 266
  estrangement from God and, 53
  Eucharist as, 40, 56–57, 65, 190, 191n15, 192, 330, 332
  identity of *logos* and *agape* and, 8
  heart and, 58, 330
  Holy Spirit and, 369
  hominization and, 8–9
  Incarnation and, 204
  intra-trinitarian kenosis and, 317n22
  as love, 262
  his natural will and, 262
  as obedience, 36, 40, 182, 222, 261
  old sacrifices and, 163
  as prayer, 57, 330
  priest and, 140, 164, 171, 261
  sacrificial prayer of Israel and, 330
  as spiritual, 165
  suffering and, 41–42, 171, 262
  theosis and, 276–78
  true sacrifice and, 276–77
  as word, 57–58, 165

  worship and, 40–42, 54, 139–40, 221–22, 261–62, 265, 276–78
Sands, Paul Francis
  on Newman on faith and reason, 287n36
Sartre, Jean-Paul
  on freedom, 248–49, 257
Scheler, Max
  Wojtyla's personalism and, 309n126
Schillebeeckx, Edward, 102n6
Schlier, Heinrich
  on the "passion" of the Holy Spirit, 89n96
Schmemann, Alexander
  on liturgy as theology, 371n86
"scholastic" theology
  versus "monastic theology," 206–8
scholasticism
  category of existence and, 344–45
  conceptual theology and, 313n6
  God's *apatheia* and, 316–17
  John Paul II's theology and, 321
  Luther's rejection of, 315n6
  Newman's approach to theology and, 286
  neo-scholasticism, 25n90, 61, 64–65, 116
  Pascal's anthropology of the heart and, 285
  Ratzinger's use of the term "faith" and, 215n52
  theology of, 206–8
Schoonenberg, Piet, 365n69
Schwager, Raymund
  on the gnomic will of Christ, 236n37
Sciglitano, Anthony
  on Ratzinger's hermeneutics, 111, 148n126
  on Ratzinger's neo-patristic theology, 111–12
  on Ratzinger's respiritualizaton of theology, 117n79
  on the *ressourcement* retrieval of patristic theology, 111–12, 312–13.
Second Coming
  cosmology and, 50

new presence of Jesus and, 38
omega point and, 270
responsibility and, 51, 270
Seraphim of Sarov, St.
　on the Holy Spirit, 359
Sermon on the Mount
　dogmatic thesis and, 223
　filial thesis and, 221
　hermeneutics of the saints and, 113–14, 212–13
　hidden Christology and, 126, 153, 172
　Jesus of Nazareth and, 184
　mount Sinai and, 126
　personal thesis and, 126–34
　as a "prayer event," 121
　soteriological thesis and, 161–62
　theology of the Cross and, 166
　Torah of the Messiah and, 167, 172
Sharkey, Michael
　on God's impassibility, 317n23
Shute, Graham J.
　on Newman's anthropology of the heart, 286, 288n41
"sleeping texts" (*Schläfertexte*)
　Ratzinger's theology of inspiration and, 109
Sobrino, Jon, 102n6
Sokolowski, Robert
　on the neglect of the heart in philosophical enquiry, 92n108
Soloviev (Solovyov), Vladimir, 290n49
soteriology
　Christology and, xii, xv–xvi, 14–15, 30, 63, 70, 75, 81–82
　worship and, 63
Spaemann, Robert
　on the neglect of the heart in philosophical enquiry, 92n108
Spirit Christology, 365n69
splagchna
　as a synonym for *kardia*, 352–57
Staudt, R. Jared
　on Aquinas' and Ratzinger's exegetical principles, 118n82
Stoic philosophy
　anthropology of the heart in, xii, 91–93, 329
　common ground with Ratzinger, 329–30
　Docetism and, 89
　"passionate" God and, 88–89
Suetonius, 216
symbolic theology
　of the Father's heart, xii, 311–23
　neo-patristic, 111–12
　patristic, 312–13
　rahamim and, 322–323
　ressourcement theology and, 111–12, 312–13

Tacitus, 216
Teilhard de Chardin, Pierre
　anthropological/cosmological dualism and, 32, 50
　taking up of *bios* into *zoe* and, 32, 45
　his complexification thesis, 32–33, 270, 277
　corporate personality and, 16, 32–33
　hominization and, 16, 33
　intériorité and, 59
　"omega" point and, 50
temple, 139, 195, 275
　church as, 371
　Jesus as the new, 101, 133, 135, 163
　liturgical performance and, 41, 222
　prayer of Jesus in Gethsemane and, 168
　presence of God in, 131n55, 311
　remembering of the disciples and, 137–38
　temptations of Jesus and, 160
Temptations of Jesus
　Baptism of Jesus and, 159
　Descent into Hell and, 159
　Holy Spirit and, 159, 196–97, 368–69
　Kingdom of God and, 124
　non posse peccare and, 238n43, 240–41
　passion of Jesus and, 172, 231
　personal thesis and, 121–22

Temptations of Jesus *(continued)*
  prayer of Jesus and, 154, 184
  presence in the whole life of Jesus, 159, 160, 163, 222–23, 239–40
  soteriological thesis and, 158–164
Teresa of Avila, St., 290
thaumaturgic
  acts, 197
  lacuna, 188–89
Theodore of Mopsuestia
  his Antiochene Christology, 181n149
theologians
  acquisition of the Holy Spirit and, 359
  Christ as "the Theologian," 211
  as "Christologians," 205, 340
  contemporary marginalization of, 115
  ecclesial hermeneutic and, 213
  on the "Jesus of history" versus the "Christ of faith," xv, 25n90, 64–65
  "low" Christology and, 102n6
  medieval, 115, 306
  "non-theologians" and, xvi–xvii, 142, 205, 210
  Orthodox, 290n49
  as pastors, 63, 115
  patristic, 306, 342
  personal and ecclesial theses and, 202, 204–5, 208, 212–13
  prayer and, 81, 82, 83, 142, 202, 205
  as preachers, 115
  Ratzinger as, xviii, 28, 228
  relationship with the church, 210, 213
  ressourcement, 107n28, 108, 312–13
  saints as, 142
  vocation of, 28, 81, 83, 115, 142, 204–5, 208, 211, 359
theologians, non, xvi–xvii, 142, 205, 210
theological anthropology
  Balthasar's, 29–30
  dualism and, xvi
  Hildebrand's, 92n108
  John Paul II's, 30n106
  Rahner's, 29–30
  Ratzinger's, 108
theologizing
  in Christ, 211
  eucharistically, 372
  as Guardini, 291
  heart and, xvii
  patristic, 312–13
  pneumatic, 372
  ressourcement, 312–13
theology
  contemplative, xvi, 208, 340
  of the Cross, vii, xvi, 13–14, 20, 22, 26, 30–31, 32, 39, 55, 75, 81–82, 156, 158, 166, 204
  of the heart, xi, xii, xiv–xvii, 56, 58–61, 85–93, 98, 121, 197, 206, 289, 333, 339, 340–41, 350
  of the Incarnation, vii, xvi, 13–14, 20, 22, 30–31, 32, 36–37, 55–56, 75, 81–82, 86–88, 204
  Johannine, 16, 26, 183, 343
  liberal, 124
  of liberation, 244, 271
  medieval, 306
  nature of, 82, 204–211
  neo-Chalcedonian, 78, 86, 99, 222
  neo-patristic, 111–12
  patristic, 82, 103n12, 111, 306, 313, 342
  of reason, xvi, 206
  ressourcement, 107n28, 111–12, 312–13
  study of, 204
  symbolic, xii, 111–12, 311–323
  systematic, xvi, 207
  Western, 96, 360
theoria
  Aristotle's, 201
  Jesus of Nazareth and, 201
  Ratzinger's spiritual Christology and, vii, xii–xiii, xiv–xv
  seven theses and, 202
theosis
  creation and, 276–77
  eros and, 265
  Eucharist and, 277, 332
  God's transcendence and, 274–75

Index

freedom and, 242–43, 260, 277–78, 358, 372
freedom of prosperity and power and, 160
freedom of radical autonomy and, 257
heart of Jesus and, 325
hellenization and, 102
Holy Spirit and, 193, 358, 364, 371–72
hominization and, 15, 31, 204
Jesus' exercise of human freedom and, 261
Jesus' humanity and, 77, 120, 177, 193, 202, 237, 242, 349
koinonia and, 372
love and, 277–78
matter and, 277
Maximus and, 79n69, 238, 239
participation in God's love and, 241
participation in the freedom of Jesus and, 67, 242, 332
participation in the prayer of Jesus and, 37, 54, 67, 120, 177, 202, 205, 242–43
participation in Trinitarian life and, 260
Ratzinger's spiritual Christology and, viii, xiii, 67, 242
sacrifice and, 276–78
self-divinization and, 277
theology of the Incarnation and, 13–14, 30, 32
worship and, 276–78
theses
content, xii, xvii–xviii, 85, 219–24, 340
dogmatic, xii, 68, 75–76, 82–85, 121, 180, 219–20, 223, 243, 340, 341, 370
earlier Christological, 68n23
ecclesial, xii, 68, 72–74, 82–85, 121, 134–40, 141, 142, 145, 155, 173, 185, 187, 194, 198, 202–11, 214, 216, 218–20, 225, 227, 340–41, 360, 369

filial, xi–xii, 68–72, 75, 81, 82–85, 120, 121, 143–44, 151–56, 196, 198, 219–21, 244, 340–41, 369
hermeneutical, xii, 68, 89–85, 141–50, 185, 198, 202, 211–20, 340–41, 360, 371
methodological, xii, xvii–xviii, 145, 185, 202–20, 340, 360
personal, xii, 68, 71–72, 82–85, 120–34, 137, 141, 142, 145, 155, 185, 187, 193, 202–11, 216, 218–19, 227, 340, 359–60, 371
soteriological, xii, 68, 70–71, 75, 81–85, 121, 156–79, 196, 198, 219–23, 340–41, 369–70
volitional, xii, 68, 76–79, 82–85, 120, 121, 156, 167, 180–82, 185, 219–20, 222, 223–24, 242–43, 278, 340–41, 370
Thomas Aquinas, St.
on analogy and metaphor as predicated of God, 319
his anthropology of the heart, 284, 306, 310
his Christology compared with that of *Jesus of Nazareth*, 118
on Christ's charity and knowledge, 326
on the church as a "quasi-person," 333–35
common ground with Ratzinger, 306, 335
his epistemology, 61
on faith as a *habitus*, 273
on the heart as the principle of life, 334
on the Holy Spirit as the heart of the church, 334
on love and joy being properly predicated of God, 318n32
on mercy as predicated of God, 320
as Platonic, 329
on the self-knowledge of Christ, 112n53
symbolic theology and, 313n6
his theology and philosophy of person, 345, 347–48
Wojtyla's personalism and, 319n126

Thompson, Thomas R.
  on intra-trinitarian kenosis, 317n22
Torah
  as being fulfilled in Jesus, 40, 157, 172
  caustic law and, 146–47
  consecration and, 173
  Jesus' re-lecturing of, 146
  Jesus as the Torah in person, 101, 133, 184, 223, 272
  John's Gospel and, 148, 218
  "of the Messiah," 133, 167, 196
  righteousness as fidelity to, 129, 157, 161
Transfiguration of Jesus
  Abba/Son dialogue and, 54, 115
  Baptism of Jesus and, 158
  Feast of Tabernacles and, 155, 197
  history of freedom and, 272
  Holy Spirit and, 34, 197, 369
  mountain in the life of Jesus, 154
  as a new kind of presence of Jesus, 178
  as a new Sinai, 272
  Peter's confession and, 155
  as a "prayer event," 121, 122, 162
  as a "Resurrection" appearance, 38–39, 221
  revelation and, 69–70
  synoptic Gospels and, 184
Trinity
  agape and, 32
  Aquinas on, 345
  Augustine on, 282n11, 347
  Balthasar's Christocentrism and, 30n106
  Baptism of Jesus and, 158
  church and, 38, 366–67, 368
  dialogue within, 34, 36, 42–43, 55, 58, 263
  dogmatic and volitional theses and, 370
  Dyothelitism and, 97, 226, 228, 233
  eternal and economic, 313n6
  freedom and, 77, 260–61
  Holy Spirit and, 196, 365–66
  impassibility and, 317–18
  Incarnation and, 317
  Jesus of Nazareth and, 116
  kenosis and, 317n22, 319n34
  person and, 342, 344–48
  pneumatological content and, 370
  pneumatological method and, 368
  prayer of Jesus and, 123, 180, 182, 229
  revelation of, 275
Trypho, 216

Vorgrimler, Herbert
  on theological anthropology, 29

Wainwright, Geoffrey
  on Ratzinger's understanding of worship, 131n55
Wallace-Hadrill, D. S.
  on the "school" of Antioch, 181n149
Warnach, Viktor
  on the heart as a spiritual reality, 282
Watts, Thomas A.
  on objections to Dyothelitism, 224
Weinandy, Thomas G.
  on Jesus as the model exegete, 145
  on the nature of Christian prayer, 117–18
  on the nature of *Jesus of Nazareth*, 116
  on Ratzinger's hermeneutics, 106–7, 211n37
  on the self-knowledge of Christ, 112n53
Wilken, Robert Louis
  on Maximus' Dyothelitism, 232n21
will
  deified, 237–39
  divine, 61, 63–64, 67, 77, 81, 97, 142, 167, 181, 226–30, 232, 236–38, 277, 326, 341, 348, 370
  divine, of the Logos, 77–78, 97, 226, 228–30
  of the Father, 38, 56, 63, 77–78, 97, 114, 133, 160, 168, 170–72, 175, 180–81, 196, 203, 226, 228–31, 238, 261, 332
  filial, 170

of God, 36, 77, 110, 123, 133, 157–58, 160, 168–69, 180, 191, 203, 222–23, 226, 232, 234–35, 238, 333, 348
gnomic, 78, 226, 228, 233–41, 271
human, of Christ, xii, 63–64, 67, 77–78, 97, 156, 167, 170, 175, 181–82, 196, 198, 202, 222, 226–39, 262, 305, 325–26, 332, 341, 344, 348, 370
human, of human persons, 142, 181, 232–33, 247
human, of the Logos, 77, 226, 227–31, 233, 268n101
natural, 78, 170, 181–82, 226, 229, 232, 233–35, 238–39, 262, 271
personal, 181, 232
of the Son, 38, 56, 78, 175, 182, 227, 229
synergy of, 63, 181–82, 232
worship
in and with Christ, 54, 135, 163, 262
knowing Christ and, 46
Christology/soteriology and, 63
complexification thesis and, 277
consecration/sanctification and, 139–40, 173
cosmos and, 277
covenant and, 276
creation and, 164, 275–77
Cross and, 40–42, 54, 70–71, 147, 163–65, 171–73, 221–22, 261–262, 264, 278
as *ein neuer Kult*, 131n55
Eucharist and, 277
freedom and, 261, 265, 277–78
history and, 275–76

Holy Spirit and, 193, 358, 371–72
of Israel, 57
koinonia and, 94, 332, 371–72
as *logike latreia*, 165
love and, 41, 164, 265, 277–78
memory of the church and, 74
as a movement from above to below, 40
of the nations, 147, 163
obedience and, 128, 261
Old Testament theology of, 163
of power, 160–61
Sacred Heart and, 66, 325, 327
as sacrifice, 40–42, 54, 139–40, 221–22, 261–62, 265, 276–78
suffering and, 41
symbolic theology and, 111–12, 313
theosis and, 276–77
Trinity and, 123
as a twofold movement, 261
Wostyn, Lode L.
on *Jesus of Nazareth*, 101n1
on Ratzinger's "high" Christology from above, 102n6, 185n1
Wright, William M.
on *Jesus of Nazareth*, 117n79
on Ratzinger's exegesis, 107n33
on Ratzinger's hermeneutics, 117n77, 214n44
on Ratzinger's neo-patristic theology, 111n49
Wust, Peter
Ratzinger's personalism and, 309n126

zoe
as eternal life, 139

www.ingramcontent.com/pod-product-compliance
Lightning Source LLC
Chambersburg PA
CBHW071225290426
44108CB00013B/1296